THE NATIONAL INSTITUTE OF
ECONOMIC AND SOCIAL RESEARCH

Economic and Social Studies
XXV

EXPORTS AND ECONOMIC GROWTH
OF DEVELOPING COUNTRIES

The National Institute of Economic and Social Research is an independent, non-profit-making body, founded in 1938. It has as its aim the promotion of realistic research, particularly in the field of economics. It conducts research by its own research staff and in co-operation with the universities and other academic bodies. The results of the work done under the Institute's auspices are published in several series, and a list of its publications up to the present time will be found at the end of this volume.

EXPORTS AND ECONOMIC GROWTH OF DEVELOPING COUNTRIES

A theoretical and empirical study of the
relationships between exports and economic growth,
with illustrative projections for 1975 for
the main overseas Sterling countries

ALFRED MAIZELS

ASSISTED BY

L. F. CAMPBELL-BOROSS

AND

P. B. W. RAYMENT

CAMBRIDGE
AT THE UNIVERSITY PRESS
1968

Published by the Syndics of the Cambridge University Press
Bentley House, 200 Euston Road, London, N.W.1
American Branch: 32 East 57th Street, New York, N.Y.10022

Library of Congress Catalogue Card Number: 68:26987
Standard Book Number: 521 06959 9

Printed in Great Britain
at the University Printing House, Cambridge
(Brooke Crutchley, University Printer)

CONTENTS

LIST OF TABLES

LIST OF FIGURES

PREFACE

This book is an empirical study of the exports and economic growth of a particular selection of developing countries. Its main purpose is to analyse past trends and relationships, and to use these as a basis for projecting exports and gross domestic product over the decade to 1975.

Analytically, the book falls into two parts. First, the past trend and future prospects of exports of individual countries had to be related to the movement of world trade in their particular export specialities. This part of the study necessitated an examination of some depth into trends in world demand and supply and the international trade of a considerable number of individual commodities; it also meant an assessment of probable future changes in the share of world exports held by each country concerned. Second, the country export projections were used as a basis for projecting the probable future growth rates of gross domestic product. This was done by using a simple macro-economic model of growth, designed for an under-developed economy where limited import availabilities constitute the effective constraint on the rate of economic growth.

In order to confine the statistical analysis to manageable proportions within the resources available, the range of countries covered was limited to the members of the Overseas Sterling Area. The background studies of individual commodities were correspondingly limited to the principal exports of these member countries. Although the book thus relates to a particular set of countries and commodities, the general approach, and the methods of analysis and projection used, would be applicable also to other developing countries.

The study was made possible by a grant from the Rockefeller Foundation, which financed the greater part of the work on individual commodity markets. Studies of particular commodities were also supported by the Colonial Economic Research Committee and by the Food and Agriculture Organization of the United Nations (F.A.O.). During the final stages, when the economic development plans of individual Sterling countries were being analysed, the research team was able to draw on a grant from the Ministry of Overseas Development for this and other work on the trade and growth prospects of countries in the Overseas Sterling Area.

Some results of the research have already been published. During the course of the commodity studies a close working relationship was established with the F.A.O. and two papers on jute were published in the F.A.O. *Monthly Bulletin of Agricultural Economics and Statistics* ('Trends in

World Demand for Jute Manufactures', in the issues for December 1960 and January 1961; and 'The Competitive Position of Jute Manufactures in Western Europe and the Far East', in the issue for March 1962). A study of the impact of synthetic materials on the hides and skins market was also contributed to an F.A.O. report (*Synthetics and their Effects on Agricultural Trade*), which was presented to the first United Nations Conference on Trade and Development in 1964. A detailed assessment of the factors affecting the trend in imports of food, beverages and tobacco into the industrial countries was published in the *National Institute Economic Review* for May 1962 (no. 20). A more general analysis of trends in exports from developing countries ('Trade and Development Problems of the Under-developed Countries: the Background to the United Nations Conference') was published in the May 1964 issue (no. 28) of the *Review*, and a summary of the principal results of the entire study in the issue for November 1966 (no. 38).

Mr C. T. Saunders, at that time the Director of the National Institute, took an active part in planning the early stages of the commodity studies, which greatly benefited from his able guidance. I am also indebted to Mr G. D. N. Worswick, the present Director of the Institute, both for his critical questioning of many sections of the draft and for his help in co-ordinating the final stages of the research, and to Mrs A. K. Jackson, the Executive Secretary of the Institute, for her constant and helpful support throughout. Thanks are also due to Miss M. J. Harington, the former Librarian of the Institute, for unfailingly providing the wide range of publications required for the research.

I was fortunate in having the assistance of Mr L. F. Campbell-Boross and Mr P. B. W. Rayment. Mr Campbell-Boross was responsible for a large part of the statistical analysis for the various commodity projections, as well as the preparation of a number of Appendix chapter drafts, and the presentation of the overall assessment of commodity prospects in Chapter 5. Mr Rayment prepared the analysis of the country development plans, and gave invaluable assistance in the country projections of exports and economic growth. Both Mr Campbell-Boross and Mr Rayment made many helpful suggestions for improvements in the argument and presentation at various places in the book. Special thanks are due to Mrs A. Morgan, who was alone responsible for the Appendix on manufactures, and to Mr J. A. Rowlatt and Mr C. Freeman, who collaborated with me in the studies on jute mentioned earlier. Mr Rowlatt also prepared the basic material on rubber. Others who assisted, at one time or another, in the analysis of material for the commodity projections were Mrs K. Jones, Mrs H. V. Stamler (part-time), Dr F. J. Glover, Mr S. F. Frowen, Mr I. A. Parker, Mr E. B. Riordan and Mr S. M. Taylor, and to all these I express my appreciation. Valuable statistical assistance was provided, in particular, by Miss R. Sturman and Mr P. Caines, Mr P. O'Brien, Mr R. Liebenthal and Mr J. Whittaker. Extensive computational work was carried out by the Institute's staff, especially by Miss B. M. A. Leighton and Miss M. R. Bickel, while Mrs P. Elliott, Miss C. M. Watkins and Miss B. Fedor all helped at various times to type drafts, the final draft of the book being typed by Miss B. Griffin.

My gratitude is also due to Mrs A. A. Rowlatt, a former librarian of the Institute, and to Mrs G. I. Barlow, who edited the manuscript and also prepared the index.

Finally, I must also thank Professor H. W. Arndt for helpful comments on the regressions for Australia, Professor J. Spraos and Mr E. Bennathan, both of whom provided a number of theoretical criticisms of the growth model as presented in an earlier draft, Mr P. O'Brien for theoretical comments and suggestions on improvements in presentation, and, once again, Mr C. T. Saunders for a large number of critical comments as a result of which the text has been considerably improved at many points.

A. M.

GENEVA
July 1967

CONVENTIONS AND SYMBOLS

Countries

'Overseas Sterling Area' (O.S.A.) includes all Sterling countries, other than the United Kingdom, which were in the Area in 1960 and 1961 (i.e. the 'Scheduled Territories' as defined by the Exchange Control Act, 1947 and subsequent amendments). 'Industrial countries' denotes the United States, Canada, Western Europe (including Turkey and Yugoslavia) and Japan. 'Centrally planned countries' denotes the socialist countries of Eastern Europe (including the Soviet Union but excluding Yugoslavia) and China. 'Primary-producing countries' includes all countries other than 'industrial' and 'centrally planned' countries.

The names and, in come cases, the frontiers of a number of countries included in the analysis have changed since the study began; in general, their present names are used. For Malawi, Rhodesia and Zambia some data can be given only for the former Federation of Rhodesia and Nyasaland as a whole (sometimes referred to as 'Rhodesia/Nyasaland'). Throughout, Malaya refers to the former states of Malaya, now known as West Malaysia. The figures shown for Tanzania refer to the former territory of Tanganyika only.

Units

Conversions of sterling values were made at rates in force before the 1967 devaluation.

Quantities are in metric units, unless otherwise stated.

'$ billion' denotes one thousand million dollars.

Details in tables may not add to totals because of rounding.

Years

Crop years, or fiscal years, are indicated by a stroke between two dates, e.g. 1960/1. Where a hyphen between two dates is used, this indicates an average over the calendar years concerned e.g. 1960–1.

Symbols

.. not available or not applicable.

o less than half the unit stated.

— nil.

INTRODUCTION AND SUMMARY OF FINDINGS

I. AIMS

The research study on which this book is based was developed with two main objects in view. The first was to make a quantitative assessment of the future export prospects of the Overseas Sterling Area taken as a whole, distinguishing separately the prospects for the main commodities concerned. This part of the study consists, in effect, of a series of detailed commodity analyses, with projections of world consumption and world trade for 1975 and, within this framework, an assessment of the probable level of exports from the Overseas Sterling Area in that year. Since export earnings constitute the main fund for the purchase of imports and since, moreover, the economic development of the area depends heavily on supplies of imported capital goods and intermediate products, such an assessment of export prospects is an essential ingredient of any more general projection of capital requirements (including aid for the less developed Sterling countries), and of the future economic growth of the area as a whole.

The second objective was rather more ambitious, namely, to utilize the results of the commodity projections in order to derive a consistent set of export projections for each of the main overseas Sterling countries; and to assess the implications of these projections for the future economic growth of the less developed member countries. The transition from a set of commodity projections to projections of exports from individual countries involves implicit or explicit assumptions concerning supply factors, not only in the countries to which the projections relate, but also in all competitive exporting countries. Since a detailed analysis of supply factors for individual countries inevitably falls outside the scope of the present study, the country projections of probable future export growth rates must be taken as indicative of broad orders of magnitude only. The problem is essentially the same as that faced by economic planners in less developed countries—though economic planners should be able to take the most important supply factors into account—and a comparison of the present country projections with those in the official Development Plans of the various Sterling countries has yielded some interesting conclusions.

The final part of the analysis, which attempts to relate these country export projections to economic growth in the less developed countries, is based on the use of a simple macro-economic model, linking exports and net capital flows with economic growth, via a capital–output relationship. The aim here was to present alternative sets of results implying alternative policy choices for governments. These choices include the rate of economic growth aimed for, as well as policies more specifically related to the stimulation of exports, the rate of import substitution, the pattern of investment and the rate of domestic saving. Although a consideration of the process of economic growth inevitably involves the problems of import substitution, savings and investment, the nature of the present inquiry invites a more detailed discussion of the problems of export policy than of policies affecting imports, saving and investment.

The study is confined to those countries which were members of the Overseas Sterling Area in the years 1960–1, the period chosen as the 'base' for the projection exercise.[1] Although limited to this group of countries, the method of analysis adopted could be considered as of more general application. To have widened the coverage to include all the non-Sterling developing countries would, however, have multiplied the research effort to an extent greater than the resources available. The projections for the individual countries are essentially illustrative of their potential for economic growth, on the basis of the various assumptions made. They do not attempt in any way to predict what each country will, in fact, achieve. Thus, although there have been a number of major political and other changes in some of the Sterling countries since the study was begun, these do not, in themselves, invalidate the general results of the analysis or their implications for economic policy.

2. PLAN OF THE BOOK

Part I is concerned essentially with setting the empirical and theoretical background to the projection exercise. The empirical background, describing the main post-war trends in exports, capital inflows and economic growth of the various overseas Sterling countries, is presented briefly in Chapter 1. Then, in Chapter 2, a simple macro-economic model is presented, while the following chapter sets out statistical estimates of the parameters of the model for those Sterling countries for which this type of analysis, based on time-series regression equations, can be supported by the available data.

Part II presents the various projections for 1975. After a discussion of the underlying assumptions made (Chapter 4), a summary is given, in Chapter 5, of the detailed projections of commodity exports from the Overseas Sterling Area. The next chapter attempts to convert these commodity projections into projections of the volume of exports from individual Sterling countries. A comparison is also made here between the resulting country export projections and those published in the Eco-

---

[1] Since the study began, Burma has left the Sterling Area.

nomic Development Plans of the countries concerned. In Chapter 7, the country export projections are combined with corresponding projections for exports of services and with alternative assumed levels of net capital inflows to arrive at projections of total foreign exchange availabilities of each Sterling country. Next, in Chapter 8, these latter projections are used, in the growth model already described, to project the probable rates of economic growth of each of the less developed Sterling countries, on the basis of the alternative assumptions made earlier. The growth model is also used 'in reverse'; starting with alternative target rates of growth, it shows the level of exports and, as an alternative, the level of net capital inflows that would be required in 1975 to meet the balance of payments deficit on current account in that year.

Finally, in Chapter 9, some of the major policy issues arising out of the previous analysis are discussed in the context of promoting economic growth in the Overseas Sterling Area, though with particular emphasis on the need to expand and diversify exports.

The detailed commodity studies which underpin the projections are summarized in the appendices.

3. THE ANALYTICAL BACKGROUND

Foreign trade projections

A considerable literature already exists on the problems involved in making projections of world trade by commodity groups and by individual commodities. Two main alternative approaches have been used. One involves the elaboration of econometric models relating world trade, or specific flows of trade, to the growth of income or industrial production in the various areas of the world. Projections using this approach would normally assume that the structural relationships emerging from the model as applied to past data will also hold good for the future; to this extent, they might well increase the margin of uncertainty which inevitably surrounds any economic projection. On the other hand, projections based on econometric models have the big advantage of yielding internally consistent results, if the model is correctly specified.[1] The other approach, more frequently encountered,

---

[1] For detailed elaboration of such global models see, for example, H. Neisser and F. Modigliani, *National Incomes and International Trade*, University of Illinois Press, 1953; and *Studies in Long-term Economic Projections for the World Economy: Aggregative Models*, United Nations, New York, 1964. The latter contains an essay by Professor E. S. Kirschen ('A Projection Model for the Developed Market Economies') which elaborates an econometric approach to the projection of trade flows for large groups of countries. This approach has been further developed in a number of studies published in *Cahiers Économiques de Bruxelles* (see, in particular, articles by Colette Duprez, Paul Kestens and Zivan Popovic in issue no. 28, 4ᵉ trimestre, 1965, and by Christian Tacquenier in issue no. 33, 1ᵉʳ trimestre, 1967).

involves separate consideration of trends in world production and demand (trade being taken as a residual balancing element) for individual
commodities. This is a 'partial' approach, in the sense that it makes
implicit assumptions about the interrelationships between different
commodity markets, so that one can never be certain that the projections for all the various commodities are mutually consistent. However, this approach has the advantage of allowing for a more flexible
adjustment of the implied parameters of a growth model by the use of
argument and informed judgement based on past trends and economic
relationships. The most important studies so far published using this
second method of approach have been projections for agricultural commodities in 1970 made by the United Nations Food and Agriculture
Organization (F.A.O.),[1] and those for all exports by developing countries
made by Professor Bela Balassa.[2]

The present study is also based on this latter approach so far as the
projections of commodity trade are concerned. Indeed, at several points
in the projections, use was made of the results—particularly of income
elasticities—presented in the studies by F.A.O. or Professor Balassa. A
major problem which all such projection studies face is whether or not
to assume that prices will change over the projection period and, if so,
how to make reasonably valid assumptions concerning such changes.
The F.A.O. study was based essentially on the general assumption that
no change would occur in relative prices of agricultural commodities,
but Professor Balassa faced the problem more directly and projected
price changes for some fifteen major primary commodities.[3] The
analytical problems involved in making price projections are, however,
far greater than those arising in demand projections alone, since the
former imply a knowledge of the structural relationships between price
and supply as well as between price and demand. The derivation of
valid supply functions, even for the major primary commodities, is a
field still largely unexplored, so that price projections for individual
commodities inevitably contain a very substantial margin of uncertainty.
In the present study, specific price assumptions have been made for only
a relatively few commodities.[4]

A second problem arising from the 'partial' approach adopted is that,
in the absence of a complete model of the world market for any product,
it is necessary to base the projections on what is considered the effective
constraint. For primary products, the present study assumes that the
volume of world trade is effectively determined by the movement of

[1] *Agricultural Commodities—Projections for 1970, Special Supplement* to *F.A.O. Commodity Review
1962*, F.A.O., Rome.
[2] B. Balassa, *Trade Prospects for Developing Countries*, Homewood, Illinois, 1964.
[3] *Ibid.* pp. 352–5 and table A15.1.
[4] See Chapter 5 for further discussion of the problems involved.

demand, and of production, in the industrial areas; exports from primary-producing countries, on this view, react to changes in the relevant economic magnitudes in the former group of countries. For manufactured goods, however, exports from primary-producing countries—and from the Overseas Sterling Area—form such a relatively small fraction of world trade that the effective constraint on their growth must be assumed to lie essentially on the supply side (apart from textiles and clothing, imports of which into the industrial countries are subject to quantitative controls).

A third problem arises in the present study when the commodity trade projections are used as a basis for projecting exports from individual countries. Here again, supply factors peculiar to particular countries become of major importance. This is a projection problem which has to be faced each time an Economic Development Plan is prepared by any developing country. The analytical problem is to devise a method of ensuring consistency between the supply assumptions made for competing exporting countries in the light of a given projection of the future growth in world demand and in world trade of the commodities concerned. The method used in the present study to ensure such consistency[1] is little more than a rough approximation, but in the absence of a detailed analysis of supply factors in each exporting country, it would seem to yield reasonably useful results. The alternative approach, of extrapolating past rates of export growth of individual countries, could not provide justifiable projections in terms of the underlying assumptions of the exercise; nor would there be any reason to suppose that such country projections would be mutually consistent, given the changing patterns of world trade and of exportable supplies of the countries concerned.

Economic growth projections

In recent years, a number of independent projections have been made of the balance of payments 'gap' of the developing countries which would arise in a future period if these countries were to achieve certain target rates of economic growth. Projections of this gap by the United Nations,[2] by Professor Balassa[3] and by the present author[4] were all based essentially on a comparison of export projections for the developing countries with projections of the level of imports they would require in the target year in order to sustain the rate of economic growth assumed. These various projections all implicitly assumed that foreign

---

[1] See Chapter 6.
[2] *World Economic Survey, 1963*, vol. i, United Nations, New York, 1964.
[3] *Op. cit.* ch. 4.
[4] A. Maizels, *Industrial Growth and World Trade*, Cambridge, 1963, ch. 15.

exchange availabilities constituted the effective limitation on the economic growth rate of an under-developed economy. Another approach to the projection problem was adopted by Professor Rosenstein-Rodan, who projected the foreign assistance requirements of individual developing countries by applying a model in which savings constituted the effective growth constraint.[1]

A major analytical difficulty arising in several of the earlier projections based on the relationship of economic growth to foreign trade was that they related to large groupings of developing countries. Apart from the fact that this global approach inevitably increases the margin of error of any projection, a more important limitation was that it prevented the use of an economic model of growth in an under-developed country heavily dependent on imports for supplies of capital goods. There was, moreover, the further analytical problem of whether to base such a model on the assumption that economic growth in under-developed countries is essentially limited by the volume of domestic savings plus the amount they can borrow from abroad, as in Professor Rosenstein-Rodan's model; or whether to use the assumption that the growth of such countries is essentially limited by their foreign exchange availabilities, as in the other studies mentioned earlier.

An elegant solution to this latter problem was provided by a major theoretical 'breakthrough' in a series of pioneering studies associated with the name of Professor Hollis B. Chenery.[2] The macro-economic version of the model, set out in considerable detail by Professor Chenery and Alan M. Strout,[3] and discussed in some detail in Chapter 2 below, has been the effective inspiration of the empirical results of the present study. The model used here differs, however, in some important respects from the Chenery–Strout model, particularly insofar as it assumes, to begin with, that foreign exchange availability remains the effective constraint on economic growth of the less developed countries of the Overseas Sterling Area. An innovation in the present study is the use of the model, not only to project export or foreign aid 'requirements' for alternative target rates of economic growth for individual countries but, by reversing the sequence of events in the model, to project probable economic growth rates on the basis of the export projections and of alternative assumed capital inflow levels.

[1] P. N. Rosenstein-Rodan, 'International Aid for Underdeveloped Countries', *Review of Economics and Statistics*, vol. 43, May 1961.

[2] H. B. Chenery and M. Bruno, 'Development Alternatives in an Open Economy: the Case of Israel', *Economic Journal*, vol. 72, March 1962; H. B. Chenery and A. MacEwen, 'Optimal Patterns of Growth and Aid: the Case of Pakistan', *Pakistan Development Review*, Summer 1966; H. B. Chenery and A. M. Strout, 'Foreign Assistance and Economic Development', *American Economic Review*, vol. 56, September 1966.

[3] *Loc. cit.*

4. SUMMARY OF FINDINGS

The post-war trends

A distinction is made, at the outset, between two main groups of overseas Sterling countries: the 'more developed' and the 'less developed'. The countries in the former group are considerably more industrialized, have a far more adequate economic infrastructure, enjoy in general a higher income per head, while their domestic saving finances a higher proportion of domestic investment, than is the case for the less developed countries. Because of these and other differences, including differences in the relative importance of exports in the economy, a given rate of export growth is likely to be associated with very different rates of economic growth in the various Sterling countries.

Several major changes have occurred in the relative position of the Overseas Sterling Area in the world economy over the post-war period. First, there has been a marked decline in the Area's share of total world exports, reflecting the relatively rapid growth of trade among the industrial countries, rather than any loss of trade to other primary-exporting regions. Second, the Area has suffered an appreciable worsening in its terms of trade; this, too, is a feature common to both Sterling and non-Sterling primary-exporters. Third, a substantial decline has occurred in the relative importance of the United Kingdom as a market for the Area's exports, this being a continuation of a long-term structural change in the economic relationships between the Overseas Sterling Area, Britain and the rest of the world.

The export experience of the different Sterling countries has varied widely over the post-war period. One reason is that exports of most Sterling countries are concentrated on a limited number of commodities, so that total exports tend to reflect world market conditions for particular groups of commodities. Another reason is that any country can influence its share of world trade in particular commodities by its own policies, and changes in economic and fiscal policies have influenced both 'real' and monetary conditions to varying degrees in the different Sterling countries over the post-war period.

Equally, there is great diversity among Sterling countries in the relative importance of merchandise trade in their balances of payments. Exports in 1964–5 from Burma and Zambia, for example, exceeded current debits (imports plus net invisible payments abroad) while, at the other extreme, exports from Ghana, India and Pakistan all fell far short of covering their current debit payments. The payments gap, where it exists, was filled in those years mainly by government transactions and official donations (Ceylon, Pakistan and East Africa), by official loans, including capital from international financial institutions

(India, Malawi and Jamaica), or by private foreign investment (Malaysia, Nigeria and the West Indian Territories). For the Overseas Sterling Area as a whole, by far the largest part of private foreign investment goes to Australia, while India gets the greater part of the total inflow of official funds. This wide variation in the relative importance of exports on the credit side of the balance of payments—which applies over time for individual countries, as well as between countries in any year—emphasizes the tenuous character of the relationship between exports and the process of economic growth.

This conclusion would seem to hold on *a priori* grounds, even though regressions of gross domestic product (GDP) on export volume for nine Sterling countries for the period 1950–62 gave good statistical results for all but one country.

Ex ante and ex post models of growth and trade

A simple aggregative macro-economic model of the interrelationships between the foreign trade and domestic sectors of a less developed country can be derived from the main national accounting identities. The basic model used is closely related to the *ex ante* model developed by Professor Hollis B. Chenery and Alan M. Strout.[1] This model distinguishes two *ex ante* gaps in the process of economic growth, namely, the trade gap (the difference between imports and exports of goods and services) and the savings gap (the difference between investment and domestic savings). Since the decisions to save, to invest, to import and to export are made by different—though overlapping- -groups of people, the two *ex ante* gaps cannot be expected to be identical. However, the two gaps are necessarily equal *ex post*, so that the *ex ante* inequality implies an adjustment in the four main variables— savings, investment, imports and exports—towards some equilibrium position.

Chenery and Strout distinguish three major constraints on economic growth in less developed countries. The first consists of the limitation imposed by the availability of human skills and organizational ability; the second of the limit set on investment by the supply of domestic savings, supplemented by the available net capital borrowing from abroad; while the third constraint consists of the limit set on imports by exports and net borrowing from abroad. For any given target rate of growth, two *ex ante* gaps are generated (ignoring the skill limit for this purpose, as one that would come into operation at relatively high rates of growth). The savings gap is generated by the relationship between investment and the target growth in gross domestic product via an incremental capital–output ratio (ICOR), on the one

---

[1] Detailed references are given in Chapter 2.

hand, and an *ex ante* savings function, on the other. The trade gap is generated, given the rate of export growth as determined exogenously, by a relationship between income growth and growth in the minimum level of imports consistent with that rate of income growth. The larger of the two *ex ante* gaps can be regarded as the effective constraint on the rate of economic growth.

A major limitation to the Chenery–Strout model in its simplified form is that it does not allow for interrelationships between the variables involved in the two *ex ante* gaps. In particular, there is likely to be a relationship between variations in exports and variations in domestic savings, either because the propensity to save is higher in the export sector of an under-developed country than that in other sectors or because government savings rely heavily on the income from taxes on foreign trade. Given such a relationship, a rise in the projected rate of export growth would reduce both the *ex ante* gaps.

The Chenery–Strout model can also be improved by making a distinction between gross domestic product and gross national product (the difference representing net factor payments abroad, including interest and dividends on foreign investments); and by making some allowance for possible future changes in the terms of trade of the various under-developed countries being considered.

The main difficulty in applying the two-gap *ex ante* approach in practice (as is argued in Chapter 2) is, however, the lack, or unreliability, of the basic statistical data relating to domestic saving and investment for most under-developed countries. For this reason, estimates of past *ex ante* savings propensities are inevitably subject to considerable error in most cases. It also implies that projections of the *ex ante* savings gap corresponding to any target rate of economic growth are likely to be appreciably less reliable than corresponding projections for the foreign trade gap. An alternative approach suggested in Chapter 2 is to project the prospective trade gap for a given rate of economic growth; and by deducting this from the projected investment required to support the output target, to derive domestic savings as a residual. This approach implies essentially an *ex post* model of growth, in which domestic savings adjust to changes in the trade gap. The implicit assumption that the economy is in a phase of trade-constrained growth can then be tested by comparing the savings derived residually with the level of savings which would result if the past relationship between savings and income is projected up to the target year.

This model of trade-constrained growth can be used for two purposes. Given a projection of exports and of capital inflows, the model can be used to determine the probable rate of economic growth, on the basis of specific values for the various parameters. The model can also be used, in reverse, to determine the amount of net capital inflow required to support a given target rate of economic growth, on the basis of a projected growth rate of exports.

The structural parameters of economic growth

The *ex post* model described above is assumed to work through two major relationships. The first postulates a relationship between the volume of capital goods imports and the capacity to import (defined as the value of exports of goods and services plus the net inflow of long-term capital). The second relationship is between the volume of capital goods imports and the level of investment in fixed capital assets. In Chapter 3, these two relationships are investigated statistically for two countries, while the combined relationship—investment in fixed capital as a function of the capacity to import—is investigated for a sample of eight other countries in the Overseas Sterling Area.

From regression equations, covering generally the period from 1951 to 1961, it was found that the long-term elasticity of investment with respect to unit changes in the capacity to import ranged between 0·7 and 1·0 for six of the ten countries in the sample. Special factors appeared to be at work in the other countries to produce relatively low, or relatively high, investment elasticities during the 1950s.

The relation between domestic savings and exports was also investigated by the use of regression equations for eleven countries, covering differing periods between 1950 and 1963. For nine of these countries, the use of exports as an independent variable improved the statistical 'explanation' of the movement in domestic savings, compared with the usual form of function relating savings to gross domestic product. Although the results are essentially illustrative, they support the view that there is likely to be a positive association between exports and savings in many primary-exporting countries.

The relationship between investment in fixed capital and the associated increase in real output can conveniently be expressed in terms of an incremental capital–output ratio. These ratios are computed for twelve overseas Sterling countries for the decade or so up to the early 1960s. There are large inter-country differences, the incremental capital–output ratio being highest, over the period, for Australia and Ireland and lowest for Jamaica and Trinidad.

Computed rates of growth in gross domestic product are also presented in Chapter 3 for each of nine Sterling countries, on the assumption that the investment elasticity for each country reflected solely the long-term relationship, as revealed by the relevant regressions. These computed growth rates are then subdivided to show the respective 'contributions' of three structural factors, namely, the incremental capital–output ratio, the investment elasticity, and the proportion of GDP invested in fixed capital in the initial year of the period covered. This analysis shows, for example, that had the capacity to import remained stationary for all countries, the GDP would have grown fastest in Jamaica, South Africa and Trinidad, and slowest in India, Ceylon and Ireland. The capacity to import did not, of course, remain constant over the period covered (roughly 1950–62), while the rate at which increases in import capacity were transformed into new fixed capital assets varied substantially from one country to another. Trinidad, for example, started off the period at a slight disadvantage compared with Jamaica in terms of the initial proportion of GDP invested, enjoyed a somewhat more rapid growth in its capacity to import, and was much more successful in transforming its increase in foreign exchange resources into fixed capital investment.

The model is also used to indicate the probable impact of changes in the terms of trade on the growth rate of GDP over the period covered by the regressions. Assuming that the structural parameters would have remained unchanged had there been no changes in the terms of trade, it would appear that the adverse movement in Australia's terms of trade reduced that country's rate of growth in GDP by about $1\frac{1}{2}$ per cent a year (over the period 1950–62). For Burma and Trinidad, the loss was roughly $\frac{1}{2}$ per cent a year, and somewhat less than this for Jamaica. For the other countries in the sample, the terms-of-trade loss was negligible.

Basic assumptions made for the projections

In Part II, the *ex post* model expounded in Chapter 2 is used as the theoretical framework for projecting the probable economic growth rates of the less developed Sterling countries. First of all (Chapter 4), the underlying assumptions of the projections are set out. One basic hypothesis is that the tempo of world economic activity, and the rate of growth in world trade, is largely determined by the rate of growth in real income in the industrial countries (North America, Western Europe and Japan). Separate assumptions are made, for each main industrial country, relating to the future rate of growth in population and in real income per head. The population estimates used for 1975 are based mainly on the 'medium' projections made by the United Nations.

Since projections of the future rate of growth in real income per head are necessarily uncertain, two alternatives were taken for each industrial area: a low assumption, expressing a 'reasonable minimum' judged in the light of recent experience; and a 'relatively high' rate, implying a greater strain on resources and a conscious policy of achieving a fast rate of economic growth. For the industrial countries as a whole, the assumptions made imply that their total gross domestic product will rise by some 4 to 4½ per cent a year, on average, from 1960–1 (the base period used) to 1975, compared with rather more than 5 per cent a year during the first half of the 1960s and just over 3½ per cent a year in the later 1950s.

These assumptions relating to the future growth of gross domestic product in turn imply corresponding assumptions for manufacturing production. The relationships between the past rates of growth in manufacturing production and in gross domestic product—for each of the main industrial countries—have been used to derive a consistent set of future growth rates for manufacturing output in the industrial areas.

The commodity projections

These assumptions about growth rates of population, gross domestic product and manufacturing production are the starting point for projections of industrial countries' demand for the principal primary products exported by Sterling Area countries (Chapter 5). The world economic and political background throughout the period is assumed to be one where there is no major war; where the degree of protection maintained by industrial countries against primary products remains much as it is now; and where, although the substitution of synthetic for natural materials proceeds at much the same rate as in previous years, there are no major new technical developments such as to produce dramatic and irreversible changes in the demand for the raw material exports of Overseas Sterling Area countries. Some relative price assumptions are necessarily implicit in these commodity projections. For most commodities, it is assumed that relative prices remain unchanged from the 1960–1 base, though for a few commodities certain changes have been assumed.

For the principal foods and beverages, the projections of the probable levels of demand in the main industrial countries were based mainly on the assumed rates of growth in income per head, on estimates of income elasticities and on the estimated growth of population. The income elasticities were generally derived from time series for the past decade—or some portion of the decade, supported, where appropriate, by evidence from family budgets or cross-country regressions. In total, consumption of food, beverages and tobacco is expected to rise by 2·3 to 2·7 per cent a year between 1960–1 and 1975, according to which income-growth assumption is used. This compares with a growth rate of 2·7 per cent between 1952–4 and 1960–1 for the same items: so the growth rate is projected to slow down unless economic growth follows the higher of the two courses assumed.

For the industrial materials, a detailed analysis of end-uses was made where possible. Probable future trends in the consumption of each end-product were assessed, and allowance was also made for trends in substitution by other materials. Because of the complexities of the market, a rather different method was used for apparel fibres and the non-ferrous metals. The rate of growth of consumption of the selected materials, taken as a group, is projected at some 3 to $3\frac{1}{2}$ per cent a year for the industrial countries as a group. For Japan, a much higher rate (6 per cent) is projected, while—at the other extreme—the growth in consumption is projected at only about $2\frac{1}{2}$ per cent a year in the United Kingdom. For all countries, these figures are much lower than the expected rate of increase in manufacturing production: the input of natural materials per unit of manufacturing output is expected to decline everywhere over the fifteen years or so of the projection period—by two-fifths in Japan, one-third in the European Economic Community (E.E.C.) and 'other Western Europe', one-quarter in Britain, and one-sixth in North America. These declines are, quite largely, the consequence of the continued displacement of natural materials by synthetic ones; it is mainly because this process had gone further by the early 1960s in Britain and North America that the expected decline in the input–output ratio is lower in these countries.

For tropical products, the projection of imports into industrial countries in 1975 can be taken to be the same as the consumption projections, though allowance has been made for tea production in Japan. For temperate-zone agricultural products, however, the proportion of consumption likely to be met from imports will depend heavily on the protectionist policies of the industrial countries. On present policies the import proportion for sugar seems likely to decline further; indeed, this decline has been kept moderate only on the assumption that an international agreement will be reached at some stage in the near future which will include some kind of production limitation in the developed sugar-importing countries. European countries are also likely to become more self-sufficient in the production of meat and dairy products. For fruit, on the other hand, there may be some modest rise in the import content of consumption, particularly as overseas fruit-processing industries develop.

In total, net imports of food, beverages and tobacco seem likely to rise slightly faster than consumption. But this conclusion is complicated by the fact that this group includes two items—wheat and wheat flour and rice—of which the industrial countries are net exporters; and their net exports of these products are also expected to rise rather more slowly than their consumption. If wheat and wheat flour and rice are excluded, the import content of the remaining products is expected to decline somewhat.

For some natural materials, it is assumed that the import content—imports from non-industrial countries as a proportion of consumption in the industrial countries—will rise. This may be true for cotton, though here the outlook is heavily dependent on the effect of the United States Agriculture Act of November 1965. It may also be true for non-ferrous metals, as more primary-producing countries shift towards further processing of their ores. On the other hand, the import content of vegetable oils and oilseeds and of hides and skins is expected to drop substantially. On balance, even taking natural materials alone, imports seem likely to rise rather more slowly than consumption—mainly because demand for non-ferrous metals, with a relatively low import content, is expected to increase much faster than demand for rubber, wool, or jute, with much higher import contents. Taking natural materials and synthetics together, the discrepancy between industrial countries' consumption and imports is much greater. The rise in consumption becomes 4·3 per cent a year on the low income-growth assumption, and 5·4 per cent on the high; and the increase in the volume of imports becomes less than half as great—1·6 per cent and 2·0 per cent a year, respectively. For synthetic materials not only take the place of natural materials in the industrial countries; they do so as well to some extent in the primary-producing countries themselves, which, by and large, import them from the industrial countries.

These synthetic materials, of course, displace other materials which are not included in the figures here—timber, paper and steel, for example. This must be allowed for in any attempt to quantify the extent to which the development of synthetic materials has reduced imports of the particular collection of natural materials considered here. Roughly, one can say that the further inroads of synthetics between 1960–1 and 1975 seem likely to reduce net imports of natural materials into the industrial countries by between one-fifth and one-tenth, according to the income-growth assumption made.

These consumption and net import figures for the industrial countries formed the basis of the projections of Overseas Sterling Area exports. An attempt was made to assess how the Sterling Area share of industrial countries' imports would change for each of the main commodities. This included assessments of the different supply prospects of Sterling and non-Sterling primary-producing countries, and allowances for likely changes in preferential systems. Assumptions also had to be made about the likely expansion in the market for Sterling products in other areas of the world.

The projections suggest that, even on optimistic assumptions about economic growth in the industrial countries, Overseas Sterling Area exports of food, beverages and tobacco are likely to rise a good deal more slowly than in the past decade. It is true that the 1953–4 to 1960–1 trend was helped by high Australian wheat exports to China at the end of the period; but the probable slowing-down is still quite marked even if wheat is excluded from the figures. Sterling Area exports of natural materials, on the other hand, are projected to rise at much the same rate as over the past decade, if one takes the mid point of the high and low assumptions about economic growth in the industrial countries.

The problems of projecting the Sterling Area countries' exports of manufactures are somewhat different from those of projecting their exports of primary products. For manufactures, the growth of total demand for manufactures in the industrial areas is clearly not the dominant element: their share in the total market is far too small. Separate projections were made for exports of cotton textiles and clothing from Asian Sterling countries and for the steel, machinery and metal manufactures group. For both these groups, the future level of export earnings from manufactures depends significantly on the action of the exporting countries. It would seem possible for total overseas Sterling exports of manufactures to be two and a half to three times as large in 1975 as in 1960–1, but the very tentative nature of such figures should be emphasized. The influences that in practice determine the growth of exports of manufactures from developing countries are not susceptible to precise measurement. It is reasonable to expect, for instance, that further industrialization will be accompanied not only by a broadening of the export base but also, at least in some countries, by appreciable shifts in costs relative to those of established exporting countries. Since there is little evidence on the nature and extent of these changes, any projections of the probable export volume of manufactured goods must necessarily remain tentative.

The country export projections

The projections of world import demand for the export products of the Overseas Sterling Area provide a basis for assessing the export prospects of individual Sterling countries (Chapter 6).

Calculations of export potential were made by constructing for each country an index (weighted by the importance of each product in the country's exports in 1960–1) which shows the likely growth in the world market for its products. These projections of specific 'world export market' indices for each country for the period 1960–1 to 1975 can be compared with the past movement of the same indices for the period 1953–5 to 1960–1. There are four main conclusions which emerge from this comparison. First, for all Sterling countries together, the movement of world demand may be about as favourable in the future as in the past—the relevant volume index of world exports rose by 3·5 per cent a year from 1953–5 to 1960–1, and is projected to rise by 3 per cent a year, over the projection period, on the low income assumption, and by 3·7 per cent a year on the high assumption. Second, whereas the world export demand prospect is less favourable in the future than in the past for the more developed Sterling countries, it is more favourable for the less developed countries. Third, there would seem to be a tendency for those countries which have in the past enjoyed a relatively fast growing market to continue to do so in the future, and vice versa. Finally, the inter-country differences in projected rates of export growth arising from the two income-growth assumptions are in general much less important than the differences arising solely out of differing commodity patterns of exports.

These world export demand indices, specific for each country, merely indicate the rate at which its effective foreign market has expanded, or is projected to expand. A country's exports are unlikely to move exactly in line with this index, with no change in share at all; in most countries the movement of national exports has deviated in one direction or the other from the world market index. This could be because of a conscious effort at diversification, or because the country has improved its share in world exports of its traditional primary commodities.

For the more developed Sterling countries the projection problem is, perhaps, less difficult than for the rest, since apart from South Africa they all account for fairly substantial shares of world exports. It would seem unlikely that their overall shares in world exports will show any appreciable change in the period up to 1975. For the less developed Sterling countries, however, separate assumptions about changes in shares of world exports have been made, based partly on past performance and partly on an assessment of the realism of each country's own export plans.

One major conclusion from the projection calculation for the twenty countries covered is that, with only a few exceptions, the mean rate of export growth over the coming decade will generally be lower than that achieved over the period from 1953–5 to 1960–1. This is true for all countries except Nigeria, India, Pakistan and Ceylon (and Iceland, on the higher income assumption). The deceleration in export growth rates is only marginal for Australia and Malaya; but for Trinidad and Kenya, it is quite marked. Even on the more optimistic assumption about incomes in the industrial countries, fifteen of the twenty countries are still projected to have slower export growth rates in the future than in the period from 1953–5 to 1960–1.

Exports, capital flows, and import capacity

Before these export projections can be used in an assessment of the probable future import capacity of the less developed Sterling countries, other elements of the balance of payments have to be projected or assumed. Alternative assumptions are made (in Chapter 7) about the net inflow of long-term capital from abroad in 1975, and the remaining elements (exports of services and net factor payments abroad) are projected on the basis of these assumptions and of the export projections.

The level of the net official capital inflow into the less developed countries in 1975 depends very largely on the aid policies of the donor countries. After a rapid expansion from the mid 1950s to 1961, there has been virtually no further increase; the 1965 figure was less than 3 per cent above that in 1961. For the projections, two alternative assumptions regarding total aid outflows to the less developed areas of the world are made: the low aid assumption takes the 1975 total at $6½ billion, the same as the 1962-3 average, while the high aid assumption takes it at $12 billion, the upper limit derived by assuming an increase in the same proportion as total real income in the developed countries. There seems no strong reason for assuming that the Overseas Sterling Area's share of this aid will change considerably: so basically the same two assumptions are made for the less developed Sterling Area countries—either that aid might be £565 million in 1975 (the same as in 1962-3), or that it might be £1,000 million. These alternative totals have been divided among the various less developed Sterling countries on the arbitrary assumption that aid should be inversely related to the level of GDP per head in the recipient countries. The use of this criterion attempts to introduce the principle of progressive redistribution of income, by allowing relatively more aid to poorer countries than to richer ones.

Exports of services were projected on the assumption that the fairly close relationship between earnings from goods and from services over the past decade will continue, unless some specific change was suggested by planned developments in shipping income (as for India) or in tourism (as for Jamaica and several other countries). Net factor payments abroad consist essentially of interest, profit and dividends on foreign capital investment; in the present projections, it has been assumed that by 1975 the mean rate of interest on official loans will be 3 per cent—which is also the assumption made in the Indian draft Perspective Plan. For private capital investments, the mean interest rate is taken at 5½ per cent for India, while for all other less developed countries a rate of 7½ per cent has been assumed.

All the elements are now available for projections of total foreign exchange income at current prices; to turn these into 'capacity to import', they must be deflated by the movement in import prices. Over the past decade or so, import prices of the members of the Overseas Sterling Area have generally shown relatively little fluctuation. One of the main reasons for this relative stability is probably that a slight downward trend in import prices of primary products and fuel in general has been counterbalanced by an upward trend in the prices of imports of manufactured goods. It seems not unreasonable to suppose that this relative stability will continue—and certainly, given the margins of error in the rest of the projection, there would be no great point in projecting a small movement of import prices in either direction. It was therefore assumed that import unit values in 1975 would generally be the same as in the base period 1960–1, and growth rates were thus derived for the capacity to import. With two alternative assumptions about growth rates in the industrial countries, and two alternative assumptions about aid, there are four alternative projections of import capacity; and these can be compared, in some cases, with figures for the past, and also with figures in the less developed countries' Plans.

Investment and economic growth

The growth model used (in Chapter 8) makes use of the concept of 'investment elasticity', which measures, for a particular country, the degree of reaction of investment in fixed capital assets to changes in its capacity to import. This relationship is assumed to work through two sub-relationships: changes in the capacity to import influence the volume of imported capital goods that become available, and changes in these in turn influence the level of investment in fixed capital assets. For nine Sterling Area countries, investment elasticities were computed from past figures; additional evidence was derived from the Economic Development Plans of the overseas Sterling countries. The application of the assumed investment elasticities to the projected rates of growth in the capacity to import yields projections of the growth rate in each country of gross domestic fixed capital formation. For most countries, even on the high assumptions, the projected rate of growth of capital investment is a great deal lower than the rate incorporated in the various countries' Plans.

The growth model used postulates a definite relationship between investment in fixed capital assets and the rate of growth in gross domestic product—a relationship usually expressed as the increase in capital which is needed to produce a given increase in output: the incremental capital–output ratio. For some countries, this relationship can be calculated for the 1950s, while for most of them, some incremental capital–output ratio is incorporated into the Plan, either implicitly or explicitly. Where there are both computed figures for the 1950s and Plan figures for the 1960s, it appears in general that the Plan ICORs do not differ a great deal from the calculated figures. In the present projections, it has been generally asssumed that the attempts to reduce the incremental capital–output ratio through economic planning will only be partially successful, and that the actual value of the ICOR for the projection period will be somewhere between the planned value and the value calculated for the 1950s.

From these assumed incremental capital–output ratios, rates of growth in gross domestic product can be projected for the period 1960–1 to 1975 which are compatible with the assumptions made about the rate of expansion in the industrial areas and the total foreign exchange receipts of the various less developed Sterling countries. These projected growth rates can be compared with those incorporated in the Plans of the twelve countries which have published them. In seven instances, the present projections are lower than the figures given in the Plans. In three instances—Jamaica, Trinidad and Malaya—the projected and planned growth rates are about the same, while in the case of Nigeria and Zambia the projected rates exceed the planned figures.

The major reason for the differences between these two sets of figures lies in the different assumptions made about the likely increase in exports and the likely inflow of foreign capital. To some extent, that is, the Plans rest on incompatible assumptions about gaining shares in world markets and also increasing shares of the foreign aid available. To this extent, the projections given here, since they embody an internally consistent set of assumptions about the commodity pattern of world trade, are likely to be more realistic in aggregate. It seems probable that, to achieve their planned rates of growth, most Sterling countries would require a much bigger increase in their total foreign exchange receipts than they are likely to obtain on present prospects.

The projections given here assumed, with some exceptions, that commodity prices would not be significantly different in 1975 from those in the base period 1960–1; also, no change was assumed in the Overseas Sterling Area countries' import prices. It is possible to give some sort of indication of the changes which might follow from different assumptions: for example, a 10 per cent rise in import prices, or a 10 per cent fall in export earnings, could lower the projected growth rates of GDP by anything from 0·1 to 0·4 per cent a year; and if the two were combined, the effect in reducing growth rates would range from 0·2 to 0·9 per cent annually; it would be 0·5 per cent a year, or rather more, for India, Malaya, Kenya, Rhodesia, Tanzania and Zambia, which would represent a substantial loss in real income when cumulated over the whole period up to 1975.

The less developed countries of the Sterling Area all have a fairly rapid increase in population in prospect between now and 1975. There are only three of these thirteen countries for which even the highest of the four projected annual growth rates shows an increase in gross domestic product per head of over $2\frac{1}{2}$ per cent: Tanzania, Zambia and Jamaica. Since the present average level of real product per head in the majority of the less developed overseas Sterling countries is relatively low, these projected rates of growth are hardly likely to result in a dramatic rise in living standards during the period up to 1975. If one takes the six poorest of the thirteen overseas Sterling countries in this analysis, Burma, India, Pakistan, Kenya, Nigeria and Tanzania, in all of which income per head in 1960–1 was under £30, and which between them comprise well over 90 per cent of the population of the Overseas Sterling Area, the most optimistic growth rate predicted here would still leave them with an income per head of under £50 (at 1960–1 prices) in 1975. If these optimistic growth rates continued indefinitely, none of these six countries would reach an income of £100 a year this century.

The approach so far has been to attempt to calculate what growth rates are likely in the Overseas Sterling Area, assuming certain rates of expansion in the industrial world, and on two different assumptions about aid. Another approach—using the same growth model—is to set a target rate of growth, in terms of either gross domestic product or gross domestic product per head, and calculate what (in terms of the model) this might imply, either for the level of aid or for export earnings.

Briefly, to raise the growth rate of gross domestic product in each of the thirteen countries to 5 per cent a year would require roughly four times the capital inflow achieved in 1962–3 (or double the amount of capital inflow which was projected for 1975 on the more optimistic assumption), if no increase in exports of goods and services above the level projected is assumed. To raise the annual growth rate of gross domestic product per head in these countries to a rate of $2\frac{1}{2}$ per cent a year would need as much as two and a half times the 1975 'optimistic' quantity of aid (on the same assumption of no further growth in exports).

Some rough quantification, too, can be made for the effects of possible new policies designed to limit the interest burden which the less developed countries have to bear. One possibility would be to limit the proportion which interest and dividend payments bear to total export earnings; another would be to reduce the average rate on the loans they receive below the usual market rate. In either case, presumably, some new international financial agency would be required to cover the loss.

An alternative approach to financing the foreign trade gaps projected for 1975 is to assume that they are entirely bridged by an expansion of exports over and above the levels projected. Taking the thirteen less developed Sterling Area countries together, their total exports—on the more optimistic of the projections—would rise by 4·5 per cent a year on average. To bring their import capacity up to a figure which would enable each country to achieve a 5 per cent growth rate of GDP would require an overall 5·3 per cent export growth rate; and, to take as the target a 2½ per cent growth rate of GDP per head in all countries would need a 5·9 per cent export growth rate. These 'required' export growth rates assume no increase in aid above the more optimistic assumption made earlier.

A general conclusion which can be drawn from these calculations is that no single line of policy can be expected by itself to support a reasonable minimum rate of economic growth in most of these less developed Sterling countries. What is required is a series of interrelated policy changes which would result in increased foreign exchange availabilities both from merchandise exports and on invisible and capital accounts.

Policy issues

There appear to be four main policy issues for the Overseas Sterling Area countries: the need to increase the competitiveness in world export markets of their traditional exports; the need to diversify their export structure away from a 'stagnant' to a 'dynamic' commodity pattern; the need for co-operation among the less developed countries in order to expand the volume of their intra-trade; and the need to expand their exports to the group of centrally planned countries. These are discussed in some detail in Chapter 9.

Increasing export competitiveness in commodities such as tropical beverages, in which competition in the world market is essentially among the less developed countries alone, may improve the position of one less developed country, but is likely to do so at the expense of another; so this is in no way a general solution. But there are also products, such as natural rubber and vegetable oils and oilseeds, where the main competition is with producers in the main importing countries; for such products, increased investment in quality improvements and the introduction of standard grades, where appropriate, would considerably improve the competitive position of overseas Sterling countries.

The second policy issue for the less developed countries—the problem of export diversification—is perhaps the most important. Development planning in these countries needs to allow for structural change in the export sector. The planners need to make careful and objective assessments of the probable future trends in world demand for both present and potential export commodities, so that a rationally based programme of diversification into relatively expanding export lines can be drawn up. To the extent that the more 'dynamic' commodities would normally consist of manufactured goods (including semi-manufactures), export diversification also implies industrialization. Although the early stages of industrialization normally consist of the development of import-saving industries, thought also needs to be given to the possibilities of inaugurating new industries specifically orientated to export markets; if import-saving industries can be expanded in scale at diminishing unit costs, it is possible that they may become viable exporting industries.

Third, intra-trade between primary-producing countries could be more vigorously expanded; it is at the moment small in relation to their populations and national incomes. There is scope for a good deal more trade in food, as well as in semi-processed and manufactured goods; for manufactured goods, this would help to provide the size of market which would make new manufactures economically viable. Finally, there is still undoubtedly scope in expanding trade with centrally planned countries, whose consumption of tropical beverages and several other primary commodities is still very low in relation to population and the level of economic activity.

There are two areas in particular where the trade policies of *industrial countries* impinge on the growth prospects of less developed countries. First, there is the protection of domestic producers; second, there are the policies of the industrial countries with regard to international commodity arrangements.

Direct competition between imports from overseas Sterling countries and home produce is particularly important for sugar and vegetable oils and oilseeds. Any agreement to limit the production of sugar in the industrial countries themselves could be of considerable value to Sterling Area exports. Protection of domestic manufacturing industries is also general practice in the industrial countries. In all these countries, the rates of import duty tend to be generally higher, the greater the degree of fabrication of the product, the crude material often being imported free of duty. Under such conditions, the effective rate of protection for domestic industries, measured in relation to value added in production, is usually considerably higher than the nominal tariff rate on imports of the finished product. A change in the tariff structure of the industrial countries so as to reduce the effective tariffs on such manufactures or, alternatively, the introduction of a general system of tariff preferences on imports from all less developed countries, whether Sterling or not, would be likely to stimulate the expansion of manufactured exports from such countries on a substantial scale.

The case for a drastic relaxation in the network of import restrictions and of the protectionist systems now prevalent in the main industrial countries rests not simply on the beneficial impact of such relaxation on the export prospects of the less developed countries; more generally, by promoting a new and expanded level of specialization in both economically advanced and less developed countries, it would allow both groups of countries to achieve a more efficient allocation of economic resources, and thus a higher level of real income than they would otherwise enjoy.

In addition, any increase in foreign exchange earnings by the less developed countries which would accrue from the relaxation of protectionism would very largely be spent on purchases of capital equipment and other manufactures required for development purposes from the industrial countries. This 'feed-back' effect would support the trend within the latter countries towards a relative concentration of activity on capital goods and other technically more sophisticated products while, at the same time, providing a substantial balance of payments offset to the increased cost of imports from the less developed countries.

The other area in which the trade policies of the industrial countries impinge heavily on the export prospects of the less developed countries is the field of international commodity arrangements. An examination of possible alternative institutional arrangements designed to promote the export earnings of the less developed countries from primary products obviously falls outside the scope of the present study. One point which is perhaps worth making is that it is important to change the traditional view of intergovernmental commodity arrangements, including formal commodity agreements, as devices designed primarily to stabilize the world price to one in which such arrangements are regarded as a means of phasing out excess capacity (and of preventing the emergence of excess capacity in the future) by providing producing countries with resources adequate for financing appropriate diversification programmes. To the extent that international commodity arrangements are not able, in practice, to achieve this objective, there is a case for appropriate financial transfers to the producing countries in need of such diversification.

The main policy question about aid for the less developed countries is whether a substantial increase above the current level is likely to be forthcoming. From 1961 to 1964, the total hardly rose; and throughout that period it was some 30 per cent below the target figure of 1 per cent of the national incomes of the developed industrial countries. Even if it now begins to rise in line with national incomes, so that it roughly doubles between 1962–3 and 1975, it might still be insufficient to bring about adequate economic growth rates in the poorer Sterling Area countries. The problem here is hardly an economic problem, since an increase in aid even to a level of 2 per cent of national income would not be a major economic sacrifice for the principal industrial countries; it is more a question of political will. What appears to be required on the part of the developed donor countries is the provision of a co-ordinated long-term programme of aid commitments on a substantially higher level than at present. For their part, the poorer Sterling countries must endeavour to find less capital-intensive ways of promoting economic growth than they have done in the past.

PART 1

PAST TRENDS
AND RELATIONSHIPS

CHAPTER I

THE POST-WAR TRENDS

I. MORE DEVELOPED AND LESS DEVELOPED COUNTRIES

This book is concerned essentially with the relationship between exports, capital inflows and economic growth in under-developed countries. This relationship is neither simple nor unique; nor is it necessarily unchanging over time. Moreover, it cannot be expected that a given export expansion will have similar effects on the economies of countries differing in size, in stage of industrial development, in income levels or in the relative importance of exports in the whole economy.

In later chapters, a theoretical model is developed and applied to the actual post-war experience of a particular group of under-developed countries, namely, those which are members of the Sterling Area. On the basis of the results, and of their own development plans, alternative projections of economic growth rates are made for each of these countries for the period up to 1975. The projections for exports, and for total foreign exchange inflows, however, have been extended to cover the more economically advanced countries of the Overseas Sterling Area such as Australia and New Zealand, as well as those generally recognized as under-developed.

It is therefore useful, at the outset, to define these two groups of Sterling countries more precisely, and to indicate some of their principal economic characteristics which appear, prima facie, relevant to the relationship between their export trade and their economic growth rates. Table 1.1 shows some of the relevant data for a recent year (1964) for size of population, gross domestic product and exports of five more developed and eighteen less developed Sterling countries. The former group are considerably more industrialized, have a far more adequate economic infrastructure, and enjoy in general a higher level of income per head, while their domestic saving tends to account for a significantly higher proportion of domestic investment than is the case for the less developed countries. All these various aspects of economic development cannot be summarized in any simple index, such as gross domestic product (GDP) per head. The relatively high level of GDP per head in Libya and Trinidad, for example, reflects essentially the operations of the large international oil corporations, rather than an advanced stage of economic development.

The five more developed countries accounted in 1964 for less than 5 per cent of the total population of the Overseas Sterling Area (excluding the

Table 1.1. *Population, gross domestic product and exports of overseas Sterling countries, 1964*

	Popula-tion	GDP^a	GDP^a per head	Exports^b	Exports as proportion of GDP
	(*Million*)	(*£ million*)	(*£*)	(*£ million*)	(%)
MORE DEVELOPED COUNTRIES					
Australia	11·1	6,715	605	1,084	16
New Zealand	2·6	1,620	625	386	24
South Africa^c	18·0	3,550	180	476	13
Iceland	0·2	125	660	40	32
Ireland	2·9	790	275	222	28
Total	35	12,800	365	2,207	17
LESS DEVELOPED COUNTRIES					
Large					
Burma	24	515	20	85	17
India	472	14,900	30	621	4
Nigeria	56	1,115	20	215	19
Pakistan	101	3,170	30	140	4
Total	653	19,700	30	1,062	5
Small					
Ceylon	11·0	520	50	140	27
Hong Kong^d	3·6	390	110	312	80
Malaysia^d	8·9	775	85	301	39
Singapore	1·8	300	165	198	66
Ghana	7·5	625	85	104	17
Kenya	9·1	280	30	51	18
Libya	1·6	335	210	253	76
Malawi	3·8	60	15	13	21
Rhodesia	4·1	320	80	138	43
Tanzania	10·0	225	20	70	31
Uganda	7·4	205	25	66	33
Zambia	3·6	240	65	168	70
Jamaica	1·7	270	160	78	29
Trinidad and Tobago	1·0	225	235	134	60
Other Sterling countries^e	10·6	710	65	245	35
Total^e	86	5,480	65	2,271	41
TOTAL^e	773	37,980	50	5,540	15

SOURCES: *Yearbook of National Accounts Statistics, 1965,* United Nations, New York, 1966; *Monthly Bulletin of Statistics,* United Nations, New York; *The Commonwealth and the Sterling Area: Statistical Abstract no. 86, 1965,* H.M. Stationery Office, London, 1966.

^a Gross domestic product at factor cost; national statistics converted to Sterling, where appropriate, at official exchange rates. Figures—which include some estimates—have been rounded to nearest £5 million (for GDP) or nearest £5 (for GDP per head).
^b Merchandise exports, valued f.o.b.
^c Including South-West Africa.
^d Data for 1963, covering Malaya, North Borneo (now Sabah) and Sarawak.
^e Excluding some countries (mainly Sterling countries in the Middle East) for which GDP data not available.

Middle East oil countries), but for a third of the Area's gross product, and as much as two-fifths of its total exports. The less developed countries, with which the later analysis is mainly concerned, thus in aggregate account for the overwhelming proportion of the Area's population but are, on average, much poorer and have very much lower export earnings per head.

Among the less developed countries, a distinction is made between 'large' and 'small', in terms of size of population (the dividing line being taken at 20 million people). The four large countries—Burma, India, Nigeria and Pakistan—all have considerable peasant populations and their average gross product per head is only about half that of the small less developed countries (£30 as against £65 per head in 1964); moreover, their relative dependence on exports is considerably smaller (only 5 per cent, as against about 40 per cent of exports in total GDP for the small countries). These two relationships imply a third; namely, that the value of exports per head from the small less developed countries is, on average, 16 times as great as for the large ones (£260 as against £16 per head in 1964).

Because of these differences in size, and the associated differences in the relative importance of the export sector in the economy, any given rate of growth in exports is likely to be associated with very different rates of growth in the gross products of the various Sterling countries. There are, moreover, two further reasons why this could be so. First, insofar as the relative importance of the subsistence (or non-monetary) sector varies from one country to another,[1] the multiplier effect of a given export expansion on the rest of the economy is likely to differ, since the subsistence producers may not react to any substantial extent, in terms of either output or demand, to changes in the (monetary) export sector. Indeed, insofar as a growth in exports is likely to attract a proportion of the subsistence producers into the monetary sector, the probability is that the aggregate of subsistence production would decline. Second, because there is a wide divergence, among the overseas Sterling countries, in the balance between the government and private sectors of the economy, the effects of a given expansion in exports could be different, in different countries, to the extent that the role played by government in economic development differs from that of private enterprise. In particular, the financing of public investment projects by

---

[1] Much caution is needed in comparing imputed values of subsistence production in different countries. Nonetheless, some approximate orders of magnitude can be established. In Tanzania, for example, the imputed value of subsistence farm output appears to have represented about 30 per cent of that country's gross domestic product in 1964; in both Kenya and Uganda, the corresponding proportion appears to have been about one-quarter in that year (see *Yearbook of National Accounts Statistics, 1965*, United Nations, New York, 1966).

taxes on exports[1] would almost certainly result in a higher level of investment (and, presumably, a higher rate of growth in the economy as a whole), as a result of an increase in exports, than would a *laissez-faire* system enjoying the same export expansion.

It is equally true, of course, that even if a definite relationship can be established over a past period between the movement of exports and the rate of growth of the economy as a whole, this relationship may not hold to quite the same extent in the future. Structural relationships between the different economic sectors change with economic growth, the role played by government may change, and changes in production techniques or in the pattern of demand are also likely to influence the outcome.

Before turning to an examination of such structural relationships, it is necessary to review the principal changes over the past decade or so in the external sector and in the rate of economic growth of the main overseas Sterling countries.

2. EXPORTS AND THE BALANCE OF PAYMENTS

It is useful, to begin with, to place the post-war export experience of the Overseas Sterling Area in the wider context of changes in the world economy. Over the period since the late 1940s, several major changes have occurred in the Area's relative trading position. First, there has been a marked decline in the Area's share of the total value of world exports. In this, the overseas Sterling countries have not been unique; rather, they have shared the general experience of all the primary-exporting regions of the world.

The outstanding feature of the development of world trade over the entire post-war period has, in fact, been the rapid and sustained growth of trade among the industrial countries of the world. The declining share of world trade accounted for by the primary-producing areas thus reflects to a large extent the more intensive interchange of goods among the industrial countries; though, as will be seen later, it is also a result, in part, of the continued application of restrictions on trade in primary commodities, whereas trade in manufactured goods has benefited substantially from successive relaxations of import restrictions in the main industrial areas.

Within the total trade of the primary-producing countries, the export experience of the Overseas Sterling Area has, in total, been slightly more favourable than that of the non-Sterling primary-producing countries. Over the period from 1952–4 to 1960–1, for example, exports from over-

---

[1] Ceylon, India and Malaysia are among the Sterling countries which derive an appreciable proportion of total government revenue from export taxes.

seas Sterling countries rose on average by 3·8 per cent a year in value; those from non-Sterling primary producers by 3·3 per cent a year. From 1960–1 to 1964–5, exports from both groups of countries rose at a relatively fast rate in value terms, though once again the rise for Sterling countries, 7·3 per cent a year, somewhat exceeded that for non-Sterling primary-producers, 6·2 per cent a year.

If the comparison is made with the immediate pre-war position, the difference in export experience of the two groups of countries is much bigger. By 1964–5, the exports of the Sterling group were not far short of two and a half times the volume before the war, whereas for the non-Sterling primary producers the rise over pre-war volume was only some two-thirds. The lower rate of growth in the non-Sterling group is due to a number of factors, which include the economic and political difficulties of a small group of South-East Asian countries, particularly Indonesia and South Vietnam, and the high rates of domestic inflation which have characterized several economies in Latin America.[1]

The second main feature of the post-war development has been an appreciable deterioration in the terms of trade, which, again, has affected both Sterling and non-Sterling primary-producing countries. To take the same two periods as before, the ratio of export to import unit values fell by about 8 per cent between 1952–4 and 1960–1 for both the Sterling and non-Sterling primary-producers. For the countries of the O.S.A. taken as a group, this deterioration was equivalent to a loss of some £1400 million in export earnings during 1960–1. Over the first half of the 1960s there was little change, one way or another, in the terms of trade of either Sterling or non-Sterling primary-producing countries. Within each of the two groups, however, the terms of trade of individual countries continued to show marked changes.

Third, there has been a marked decline over the post-war period in the relative importance of the United Kingdom as a market for overseas Sterling countries' exports. This is one aspect of the diminished interdependence between Britain and the rest of the Sterling Area, compared with the total trade and payments relationships of each. By the end of the 1940s, Britain was taking one-third of all exports from the Overseas Sterling Area; the proportion remained at one-third up to the mid 1950s, and then declined to one-quarter by 1963–5. The main gainers have been the non-Sterling countries other than Western Europe and North America, reflecting, in the main, a relatively large growth in Sterling exports to Japan and to the centrally planned countries, and also a rise in items such as textile manufactures to other (non-Sterling) developing countries.

[1] Gertrud Lovasy, 'Inflation and Exports in Primary Producing Countries', *Staff Papers*, vol. 9, no. 1, March 1962 (International Monetary Fund, Washington).

The decline over the past decade in Britain's importance as a market has been a widespread phenomenon throughout the Sterling Area. Comparing the position in 1964 with that a decade earlier, for example, Britain's share of total exports declined from 72 to 38 per cent for Nigeria, 36 to 18 per cent for Australia and 67 to 49 per cent for New Zealand. This decline is even more marked if the comparison is made with the pre-war period[1] rather than the early 1950s, hence the evidence points to a continuation of an underlying structural change in the economic relationships between the O.S.A., Britain and the rest of the world.

One possible reason for the relative decline of Britain as a market for overseas Sterling countries' exports may have been that the British economy was growing more slowly than the other main import markets for primary produce. It is true that imports of food and industrial materials into the United Kingdom—the largest single market for Sterling primary commodities—grew at a much slower rate than did imports into other countries. But it is also true that for both these commodity groups, the Sterling Area's share of Britain's imports fell off substantially over the period, while the share held by other industrial countries rose markedly.

A fourth aspect—which would indeed apply to any large grouping of countries—is that the export experience of the different Sterling countries has shown a wide range of variation over the post-war period. This variation reflects two distinct elements in the trading position of each country, and both are discussed at some length in later chapters.[2] The first is that exports of the great majority of the overseas Sterling countries tend to be heavily concentrated on a limited number of commodities, so that the movement in their total exports tends to reflect world market conditions for their particular commodity specializations. The second element is that an individual country can influence its share of world trade in its specialist commodities by its own policies, whether these relate to 'real' factors, such as physical productivity, export promotion, improvements in quality and so on, or to monetary factors, such as movements in internal costs—including export subsidies and taxes—or in its foreign exchange rate. Because both elements are liable to substantial and, at times, rapid changes, the relative position and prospects of individual Sterling countries are also liable to appreciable shifts over time.

There is equally great diversity among the countries of the O.S.A. in the role played by merchandise trade in their balance of payments positions. This can be seen from Table 1.2, which shows the relative

---

[1] In 1938, almost two-fifths of all overseas Sterling countries' exports went to the United Kingdom.

[2] See, in particular, Chapter 6.

importance of the main items in the total debits and credits of a selection of Sterling countries for a recent period (1964–5 averages). These totals are, in fact, a mixture of gross and net items, since the official accounts for some countries show the gross transactions only for merchandise trade, gold production and intergovernment transactions. On this basis, the relative importance of merchandise trade in total debits or total credits is exaggerated; moreover, the figures for different countries are not strictly comparable, because of a number of differences in definition, particularly in the treatment of undistributed profits of foreign enterprises. These differences do not, however, prevent some comparisons being made.

There is wide variation between the different countries in the relative importance of imports and net invisibles in total debits. After deducting approximate estimates of freight and insurance on imports from those import figures recorded on a c.i.f. basis,[1] it would seem that imports (valued on an approximate f.o.b. basis) generally represent over 75 per cent of total debits, as defined here. Of all the countries shown in Table 1.2, only Zambia had a proportion of imports to total debits much below this. On the other hand, for Ireland, Malawi, Hong Kong, the West Indian and other British Territories, imports exceeded total credits, since the net invisible balance for these countries was a credit item[2] mainly because they are tourist centres or because of remittances home by emigrant workers.

For all the other Sterling countries, the balance on invisible account has been negative. For these, the major debit items are interest on foreign investment and freight and insurance charges on imports. Interest, profit and dividends accruing to foreign companies are particularly important in Zambia (mainly the profits of the copper companies), and such interest payments accounted in 1964 for nearly two-thirds of the total adverse balance on invisible account for Zambia (or over 40 per cent of the value of merchandise imports). Invisible payments abroad are also relatively heavy for the three East African countries, Ghana and Nigeria, again mainly as a result of freight and insurance charges and payments in respect of foreign investment (though the net balance for foreign travel is also substantially adverse for Nigeria).

Among the more developed Sterling countries, imports (valued f.o.b.) represented about 80 per cent of total debits in 1964–5 for Australia, New Zealand and South Africa, and over 90 per cent for Iceland (but Ireland, as already mentioned, has a favourable net invisible balance).

There is, equally, a large variation from country to country in the

---

[1] See Table 1.2, footnote *h*.

[2] For Jamaica, the recorded net credit for invisibles is estimated to be offset by freight and insurance on imports.

Table 1.2. *The balance of payments for Overseas Sterling Area countries, 1964–5*[a]

| | Debits | | | Credits | | | | | |
	Imports f.o.b.	In-visibles (net)[b]	Total	Exports f.o.b.	Government transac-tions[c]	Gold[d]	Long-term capital[e] Private	Official	Total
	(Percentage of total)		*(£ million)*	*(Percentage of total)*					*(£ million)*
MORE DEVELOPED COUNTRIES									
Australia[f]	84	16	1,265	87	−3	1	15[k]	−1	1,208
New Zealand[gk]	79	21	389	93	−2	—	8	1	398
South Africa	85	15	999	58	—	40	1	1	937
Iceland	96	4	46	88	4	—	8	—	49
Ireland	125[h]	−25	252	85	—	—	13	2	251
Total	87	13	2,951	78	−1	14	9	0	2,843
LESS DEVELOPED COUNTRIES									
Burma	80[h]	20	86	99	−4	—	—	5	84
Ceylon	86[h]	14	148	95	3	—	—	1	145
Hong Kong	114	−14	447	98	—	—	2	—	399
India	82[h]	18	1,080	54	13	—	0[m]	33	1,131
Malaysia[i]	81	19	450	85	7	—	7	1	485
Pakistan	90	10	374	52	24[l]	—	3	21	357
East Africa[j]	76[h]	24	181	92	8	1	−7	6	196
Ghana	80	20	170	78	−2	7	5	12	135
Malawi	129	−29	14	93	−7	—	7	7	14
Nigeria	67[h]	33	322	78	3	—	19	—	304
Zambia	58	42	137	114	—	—	−6	−8	153
Jamaica	88[h]	12	92	94	—	—	1[k]	5	84
Trinidad and Tobago	84	16	166	83	1	—	9	7	161
West Indian Territories	235	−135	49	61	—	—	36	3	75
Other British Colonial Territories	128	−28	122	96	—	—	2	2	107
Total	88	12	3,838	76	7	0	4	13	3,830
Other O.S.A.[n]	70	30	1,718	86	9	1	2	2	1,796
Total O.S.A.	84	16	8,507	79	5	5	5	6	8,469

SOURCES: *The Commonwealth and the Sterling Area: Statistical Abstract no. 86, 1965*, H.M.S.O., London 1966; *United Kingdom Balance of Payments 1966*, H.M.S.O., London, 1966.

[a] The difference between total credits and total debits represents the net balance of monetary movements, private short-term capital and 'errors and omissions'.

[b] Excludes Government transactions and official donations on current account.

[c] Government transactions and official donations on current account.

[d] Production less domestic consumption.

[e] Short-term capital, banking and other monetary movements have been excluded as far as possible, though a small amount of private short-term capital is probably included. The

relative importance of exports in financing the debit side of the accounts. At one extreme, was Zambia which had a surplus of merchandise exports over total debits in 1964–5, while at the other extreme were Ghana, India and Pakistan, whose exports fell far short of covering their current debits; in 1964–5, exports represented about three-quarters of the debit total for Ghana, and only about 60 per cent for India and Pakistan (see Fig. 1.1).

The payments gap between total debits and merchandise exports, where it exists, is filled by different combinations of private and official capital, government transactions and grants and gold production. Gold is of major importance only to South Africa; in 1964–5, gold production in that country represented more than two-thirds of the value of merchandise exports, gold output having substantially increased over the past decade. Government transactions and official donations are the major credit items, apart from exports, only in Ceylon, Pakistan and East Africa. Of the private long-term capital, by far the largest proportion goes to Australia, while India gets the greater part of the total inflow of official funds.

There is, therefore, a marked difference in the relative importance of the non-merchandise credit items between the more developed and the less developed Sterling countries. In the former, the main credits— apart from gold, which is clearly a special case—come from private capital inflows; these provided one-tenth of total credits in 1964–5 for the more developed Sterling countries other than South Africa. In the less developed group, however, official long-term aid and official donations on current account were the mainstay, together representing about one-fifth of total credits for these countries. However, for both groups of countries, the relative importance of merchandise exports in total credits was the same (just under 80 per cent) in 1964–5.

---

figures are not strictly comparable between countries because of differences in coverage, particularly with regard to the undistributed profits of foreign enterprises, which are excluded for South Africa, India, Pakistan and Ceylon. For Ireland, Malawi and Zambia, the undistributed profits of branches are included, but not those of subsidiaries.

[f] Adjusted to calendar year basis from financial years ending 30 June.

[g] Adjusted to calendar year basis from financial years ending 31 March.

[h] Imports were converted to f.o.b. basis by making the following deductions from the recorded c.i.f. figures: 10 per cent for Ireland and Jamaica; 12 per cent for Burma and Ceylon; and 15 per cent for India, East Africa and Nigeria.

[i] Malaya, Sabah and Sarawak.

[j] Kenya, Tanzania and Uganda.

[k] 1964 only.

[l] From July 1964 includes transactions of the Indus Basin Development Fund.

[m] From April 1964 includes lending to private sector by I.B.R.D. and foreign governments.

[n] This is a residual and contains various 'errors and omissions' and adjustments to national statistics. It includes, inter alia, Guyana, Rhodesia and the Persian Gulf sheikhdoms.

Apart from official aid in the form of grants and loans, the more-developed countries play a major role in the total Overseas Sterling Area inflow of foreign exchange; in 1964–5, for instance, they accounted for one-third of merchandise exports, virtually all the gold production and nearly two-thirds of the net inflow of private long-term capital. Within the less developed group, moreover, the distribution by country of private long-term capital inflows is very uneven, Malaysia, Nigeria and the West Indies together accounting for the greater part of the total.

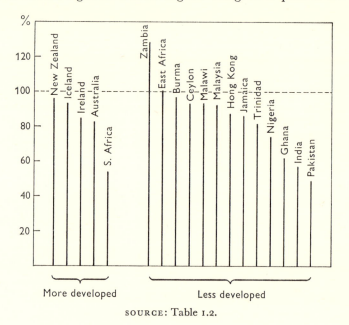

SOURCE: Table 1.2.

Fig. 1.1. Exports as a proportion of total debits, 1964–5.

As already mentioned, India receives the bulk (about 70 per cent) of the total inflow of official long-term capital, while Pakistan, India and Malaysia were the main recipients of government grants.

Differences in the relative magnitudes of the various debit and credit items have also been important over time. Comparing 1964–5 with 1952–4, changes in merchandise imports accounted for over 75 per cent of the increase in total debits in six out of the ten countries for which the relevant data are available (see Table 1.3). For Burma, Uganda and New Zealand the increase in invisibles was nearly one-half of that for imports. Among the more developed countries, invisibles accounted for substantial proportions of the increase in total debits over this period. On the other hand, net invisible payments were reduced in Ceylon and in Ireland net invisible receipts increased.

Table 1.3. *Contribution of main items to change in total debits and credits in the balance of payments of selected Sterling countries, 1952–4 to 1964–5*

| | Change in debits | | | Change in credits | | | | | |
	Imports f.o.b.	In-visibles (net)	Total	Exports f.o.b.	Govern-ment transac-tions	Gold[d]	Long-term capital Private	Official	Total
	(Percentage of total)		*(£ million)*	*(Percentage of total)*					*(£ million)*
Australia	83	17	624	79	−2	—	28[a]	−4	639
New Zealand[a]	62	38	143	75	2	−1	19	5	129
South Africa	86	14	495	57	—	51	−6	−2	430
Ireland	125	−25	125	86	−3	—	15	2	120
Burma	60	40	10	−38	35	—	11	92	10
Ceylon	111	−11	22	99	13	—	7	−19	22
India[a]	73	27	633	27	19	—	—	54	667
Pakistan	92	8	242[b]	14	58	—	4	24	242[b]
Uganda[c]	69	31	8	103	..	..	−3		6
Trinidad and Tobago[c]	77	23	104	82	1	—	12	5	101

SOURCES: *Balance of Payments Yearbook, vol. 8, 1952–54,* International Monetary Fund, Washington 1957; Table 1.2 above.

[a] 1952–4 to 1964.
[b] Based on Sterling values; in terms of Pakistani rupees the percentages would be different from those shown here (the contribution of exports to the increase in total credits, for example, would be considerably higher).
[c] 1952–4 to 1962–3.   [d] Production less domestic consumption.

Similarly, there have been marked variations in the contribution made by the various credit items to the change in total credits over the past decade. Of the ten countries, exports accounted for 75 per cent or more of the increase in total credits in six countries; in Pakistan and India, at the other extreme, exports contributed only one-seventh or one-quarter of the total credit increase, reflecting the expansion in official aid to these countries, while for Burma exports actually declined. Of the more developed Sterling countries, the expansion in private long-term capital investments contributed 20 to 30 per cent of the rise in total credits in Australia and New Zealand. South Africa has been somewhat exceptional—in 1952–4 there was a net inflow of private long-term capital of £40 million a year, but from 1959 to 1964 there was an annual average net outflow of approximately the same amount; in 1965 there was a net inflow of £39 million, the first net inflow since 1958.

The wide variation in the relative importance of merchandise exports in the total credit position, both as between the different Sterling countries in any one year, and over time for many individual countries, emphasizes the tenuous character of the relationship between exports and the process of economic growth. As will be seen in later chapters, an assessment of probable future economic growth rates necessarily involves projections or assumptions relating to both the credit and debit sides of the balance of payments.

3. THE CONCEPT AND MEASUREMENT OF ECONOMIC GROWTH

By 'economic growth' is usually meant a secular improvement in material well-being of the population of a given country or region. In the welfare sense, 'material well-being' would include leisure as well as the availability of marketable goods and services, and would also make allowance for the human effort involved in economic activities. No one has yet attempted to construct measures of the growth in welfare in this comprehensive sense. The conventional approach is to measure the value at constant prices of the total national output of goods and services including, where appropriate, an imputed value for goods and services produced in the non-monetary sectors of the under-developed countries. Such output indicators, however defined, are essentially measures of gross output, and can be applied in welfare terms only on the assumption that the ratios of leisure to work and of input of effort to output of goods and services remain constant.

There are two other general conceptual difficulties which need to be considered at the outset. First, one difficulty in comparing growth rates of different countries (or of one country over different periods), is that the growth rate—however calculated—will be affected by the community's collective choice between consumption and savings. A country which saved a high proportion of its income would tend to have a higher rate of economic growth, but a lower level of personal consumption, than another country at the same stage of economic development which preferred to save relatively little. The interpretation of differences in growth rates thus needs to be somewhat cautious if the welfare aspects of economic growth are under consideration.

Second, while it is possible to measure actual rates of economic growth, it is very much more difficult to measure the corresponding *potential* rates, i.e. the rates at which different economies would grow if, with the given pattern of demand, all their resources were used in optimal combinations. It might well be that countries which were growing relatively slowly were also operating near their potential (or maximum) growth rates, while the fast-growers were not. If so, it would not be without significance to compare the ratio of actual to potential growth rates for each country. Such a ratio would indicate the relative efficiency with which the various countries were making use of their available resources. It might also be relevant when considering the suitability of existing economic and social institutions for the promotion of economic growth in under-developed countries.

Given that measurement is essentially confined to actual growth rates, there is a distinction to be made between several concepts of the national product which can be measured. The two most important for present purposes are the *gross domestic product* (GDP)[1] and the *gross national product* (GNP), the difference between the two being the inclusion in the latter, but not in the former, of net factor payments abroad. Since factor payments abroad—essentially interest on loans, and profits and dividends on invested capital—may represent a substantial debit item for many countries, it is important in such cases to distinguish the two concepts and to have separate measures for each.

Changes over time in GDP or GNP at constant prices can be derived by deflating each main component by its appropriate price index and aggregating. There is, however, a choice of deflation method for the foreign trade sector which yields an important conceptual difference. If imports and exports are deflated separately, the net trade figures represent, in principle, changes in volume terms in the trade balance. If, however, the deflator (either import prices or export prices) is applied to the net balance, the effect is to adjust the GDP or GNP total for changes in the terms of trade. The latter thus approximates to an *income* concept, whereas the former (unadjusted for changes in the terms of trade) more closely resembles a *product* concept.

In the following discussion, the unadjusted concept is generally used as the indicator of economic growth, not because the terms-of-trade effect is unimportant, but because it is less difficult, in principle, to assess the probable future rate of growth in the unadjusted totals than it would be to make any reasonable allowance for likely changes in the terms of trade.

Measurement difficulties

Even if GDP and GNP (before adjustment for changes in the terms of trade) are accepted as reasonable indicators, in principle, of economic growth, there remain considerable difficulties in practice in making reliable and consistent estimates of them. In the first place, such estimates imply accurate knowledge of economic activity in quantitative terms in all sectors of an economy. Such knowledge is not available even

[1] The gross domestic product is the value attributable to factor services rendered to resident producers of a given country before deduction of provision for the consumption of fixed capital. It is also equal to the sum of consumption expenditures, gross domestic capital formation and net exports of goods and services.

in most highly developed economies; in under-developed countries, large gaps generally exist in the availability of statistical data, though systematic sampling is being more widely used to fill some of the more important gaps.

Another major measurement problem in under-developed countries concerns the value of output of the non-monetary sector. Errors in imputing such value could easily distort the recorded overall rate of growth of the economy. Since the non-monetary sector tends to decline in relative importance with economic growth, any under-estimate of the value of non-monetary output will result in an over-estimate of the rate of growth in GDP. If, however, with improvement in methods of collecting statistical data, the imputed value of non-monetary output is increased, this would tend to overstate the rate of economic growth unless the estimates of non-monetary output for past periods were increased correspondingly.

The difficulties of statistical measurement are considerably increased when the estimates of GDP or GNP are converted from current to 'constant' prices. The difficulties are, once again, most acute in less developed economies, which generally have less adequate price information. The published official figures of many countries for GDP or GNP at constant prices contain numerous assumptions about the movement of prices in various sectors of their economies.

Because of these various conceptual and statistical difficulties,[1] the available figures of economic growth rates must be accepted with some reservation. Small differences between countries should be taken as within the margin of error inherent in such estimates. However, in practice, very wide differences are found in estimated growth rates in 'real' terms, and these must be assumed to reflect significant differences in the rate of growth of output of goods and services.

The pattern of economic growth

Any overall economic measurement, such as GDP or GNP, necessarily obscures structural changes within an expanding economy. Economic growth is not simply an increase in the availability of all goods and services in the same proportions; it implies important structural changes in the patterns of demand and production, and may be associated also with changes in the distribution of wealth and income.

---

[1] Only some of the more important difficulties and qualifications have been mentioned here. For a fuller survey of the problem, see *The Meaning and Measurement of Economic Growth*, *Supplement* to the *Treasury Information Bulletin*, November 1964, Commonwealth Treasury, Canberra. The Australian Treasury argument has been criticized in some detail by B. D. Haig in *Australian Economic Papers*, vol. 4, June–December 1965. See also Oscar Morgenstern, *On the Accuracy of Economic Observations*, Princeton University Press, 1963.

A given increase in national income would clearly have different welfare implications in two countries, in one of which income was highly concentrated in the hands of relatively few people, while in the second income was fairly evenly distributed. Changes in income distribution, however, fall outside the scope of the present study.

Structural changes in demand and production patterns associated with economic growth[1] are also, strictly, outside our present scope, though it is of interest at this stage to note some of the changes that have occurred in the main overseas Sterling countries. Table 1.4 shows the relative contribution of agriculture, mining, manufacturing and other economic sectors to GDP in a recent period (1960–2), and the changes since 1953–5. The relative contribution of manufacturing is considerably higher in the more developed countries (25–30 per cent of GDP) than in the less developed, where the proportion ranges from 5 or 6 per cent for Ceylon and Uganda up to 18 per cent for India.

In most countries, the relative importance of manufacturing increased from the early 1950s though in some (Jamaica, for example) mining was the main dynamic sector; in all countries, the relative importance of agriculture declined. At the same time, there was a large variation in the relative contribution made by 'other sectors', which consist largely of services—including internal trade, transport and communications and government operations. These services generally tend to expand with economic growth, at a faster rate than GDP in total, though the reverse was true of the period after 1953–5 in a few countries, for special reasons.

Structural changes such as these must be expected to continue in the future. Although in the rest of this book economic growth is assumed to be measured by changes in the total product of each country, the various structural changes are implied in the overall totals, and should be borne in mind in the later discussion.

4. EXPORTS, CAPITAL INFLOWS AND ECONOMIC GROWTH:
SOME GENERAL RELATIONSHIPS

The relationship between changes in exports and changes in the gross product can be traced for most of the larger trading countries of the Overseas Sterling Area over the period since the early 1950s. Table 1.5 summarizes the available data for rates of growth in exports and gross

---

[1] For a fuller treatment of such structural changes, see H. B. Chenery, 'Patterns of Industrial Growth', *American Economic Review*, vol. 50, no. 4, September 1960; A. Maizels, *Industrial Growth and World Trade*, Cambridge, 1963, ch. 2; and *A Study of Industrial Growth*, United Nations, New York, 1963.

Table 1.4. *Contribution of major economic sectors to gross domestic product[a] in selected Sterling countries: 1960–2 and change from 1953–5 (percentage of GDP)*

	1960–2[b]				Change from 1953–5[c]			
	Agri-culture	Mining	Manu-facturing	Other sectors	Agri-culture	Mining	Manu-facturing	Other sectors
MORE DEVELOPED COUNTRIES								
Australia	12	2	29	57	−3	−1	+1	+3
Ireland	24		31	45	−6		+4	+2
South Africa[d]	11	13	25	51	−3	+1	+1	+1
LESS DEVELOPED COUNTRIES								
Malta	7	7	17	69	0	−2	+9	−8
Cyprus	23	9	11	57	−6	−3	0	+9
Burma[e]	43	2	14	41	0	0	+4	−4
Ceylon	47	0	5	48	−7	0	0	+7
Malaya	38	6	9	47	..	..	..	..
India[d]	47	1	18	34	−1	0	+1	−1
Pakistan[d]	54	0	13	33	−4	0	+3	+1
Rhodesia/Nyasa-land[f]	21	22	10	47	0	−6	+2	+3
Kenya	40	0	10	50	−4	0	0	+4
Mauritius	26	0	17	57	−6	0	−4	+10
Tanzania	58	4	7	32	−5	0	+1	+4
Uganda	61	2	6	31	−5	+1	−2	+6
Guyana	26	13	14	47	−3	+2	0	0
Jamaica	13	9	13	66	−8	+5	0	+3
Trinidad and Tobago	11	30	13	46	−7	−1	0	+8

SOURCE: *Yearbook of National Accounts Statistics, 1963*, United Nations, New York, 1964.

[a] Valued at factor cost.
[b] 1960–1 for Malaya, Pakistan and Jamaica; 1960 for Guyana.
[c] 1954–5 for Kenya and the former Federation of Rhodesia and Nyasaland; 1955 for South Africa and Malta.
[d] Net domestic product at factor cost.
[e] Valued at market prices.
[f] Malawi, Rhodesia and Zambia.

product in eighteen countries, and also shows the comparable changes in total population, the terms of trade and the capacity to import.[1]

Over this period—generally almost a decade—in every country listed the gross product in real terms has risen faster than total population. Apart from Ireland and Jamaica, both of them countries with appreciable emigration rates, total population has increased about 2 to 3 per cent a year in almost all the countries. The variation in rates of growth

[1] The capacity to import indicates the purchasing power of exports in terms of a unit of imports. Thus it is equivalent to the value of exports divided by the price of imports (or the volume of exports multiplied by the terms of trade).

Table 1.5. *Relation between growth rates of population, gross product and exports, 1953–62 (annual percentage rates of growth, compound)*

	Period	Popula-tion	Values at constant prices GDP	GNP	Merchan-dise exports	Terms of trade[a]	Capacity to import[b]
MORE DEVELOPED COUNTRIES							
Australia	1954–60[c]	2·2	3·7	3·7	4·9	−5·6	−1·0
Iceland	1953–61	2·3	5·3	4·8	5·9	2·4	8·5
Ireland	1953–61	−0·6	1·8	1·3	5·2	−0·3	4·9
New Zealand	1955–60[c]	2·1	4·1	..	3·9	−2·5	1·3
LESS DEVELOPED COUNTRIES							
Burma	1953–61	1·8	4·7	4·7	3·7	..	..
Ceylon	1953–61	2·6	3·4	3·7	1·7	1·1	2·9
Malaya	1956–60	3·2	4·1	..	4·3	0·5	4·8
India	1953–60	1·8	3·5[d]	3·4[d]	1·5	1·1	2·6
Pakistan	1953–61	1·9	2·9[d]	2·9[d]	−2·3	−2·8	−5·0
Kenya	1954–62	2·9	5·4	..	10·1	−1·9	8·0
Nigeria	1953–6	1·9	3·0	..	4·0	−1·8	2·2
Rhodesia/Nyasa-land	1955–61	2·8	5·6	6·3	7·4	−5·0	2·0
Malawi	1955–61	2·1	3·9[e]	..	5·1	..	..
Rhodesia	1955–61	3·3	6·2[e]	..	7·2	..	..
Zambia	1955–61	2·8	7·4[e]	..	7·1	..	..
Tanzania	1954–61	1·8	3·5	..	7·3	−1·1	6·1
Jamaica	1954–9	0·8	8·0	7·5	8·1	−2·0	6·1
Trinidad and Tobago	1953–60	3·1	10·1	..	10·2	−0·8	9·3

SOURCES: *Yearbook of National Accounts Statistics; Yearbook of International Trade Statistics;* and *Monthly Bulletin of Statistics,* United Nations, New York; and National Economic Development Plans.

  [a] Ratio of export unit value to import unit value.
  [b] Export volume multiplied by terms of trade.
  [c] Years beginning July (Australia) or April (New Zealand).
  [d] Net domestic (or national) product.
  [e] Excluding output of subsistence sector.
NOTE: Rates of growth have been calculated for changes between three-year periods centred in the years stated. For example, for Australia, the percentages relate to changes from the average for 1953–5 to the average for 1959–61.

in real product has been very much greater than in population. At one extreme, real product has increased by less than 2 per cent a year (Ireland), while at the other extreme, rates as high as 8 to 10 per cent a year have been achieved (Jamaica and Trinidad). Thus, the variation between countries in the rate of improvement in real product per head is attributable mainly to differences in the rate at which the total product has increased.

Although differences between growth rates in GDP and GNP are significant for some countries, these are nonetheless small compared with the inter-country variation. For Ceylon and Rhodesia/Nyasaland, GNP rose faster than GDP, reflecting a slower growth in interest and dividend payments to foreigners than in domestic output; in Iceland, Ireland, and Jamaica, the reverse process occurred.

There was a wide dispersion in rates of export growth. Pakistan was exceptional, however, in suffering a decline in export volume over the period, resulting, in the main, from the development of the domestic cotton textile industry and the consequent home use of raw cotton that would otherwise have been available for export. For both India and Ceylon, the rate of export growth (under 2 per cent a year) was substantially lower than that achieved by other Sterling countries. Kenya and Trinidad both achieved a high average rate of 10 per cent a year, though the majority of the countries' export growth rates fell within a range of 5 to 7 per cent.

At first sight there appears to be a rough correspondence between the rates of growth of exports and GDP, taking the eighteen countries as a group (see Fig. 1.2). Pakistan is, admittedly, exceptional for the reason already given, while Kenya's experience was also somewhat abnormal inasmuch as the relatively high rate of export growth achieved was not reflected in a relatively high growth rate of GDP. The main reason for this was a decline in private net capital formation (particularly sharp in large-scale farming) during the period of political uncertainty up to the attainment of Kenyan independence in 1963.[1] Excluding Pakistan, there does seem to have been a general positive correlation between the export and GDP growth rates of the countries depicted in Fig. 1.2. However, the relationship is clearly not a close one:[2] while it is true that the four countries with the highest growth rates of GDP were also in the top export growth group, it is likewise true that India and Ceylon, with low export growth rates, achieved much the same rate of GDP growth as Malaya, Malawi, Australia and Tanzania, all with very much higher rates of export growth.

The relationship is not improved—indeed it is weakened—if the export rate is corrected for changes in the terms of trade. The resultant growth rate (for the capacity to import) can be computed for only fourteen countries, but this is sufficient to show that no significant cross-country relationship exists between the growth rates of GDP and the

[1] See *The Growth of the Economy, 1954–1962*, Government of Kenya, 1963.
[2] A linear regression of GDP growth rates on export growth rates for sixteen countries (i.e. excluding Pakistan) yielded a regression coefficient 0.55 (± 0.15), with $R^2 = 0.474$.

capacity to import (see Fig. 1.3). If exports (either adjusted or un-adjusted for changes in the terms of trade) are in fact causally related to the growth of GDP they can be only one element in the causal process.

In so far as exports contribute to growth because they finance imports, the other credit elements in the balance of payments must also be considered as contributing to growth via the capacity to import. Of these other credit items, the most important for the overseas Sterling

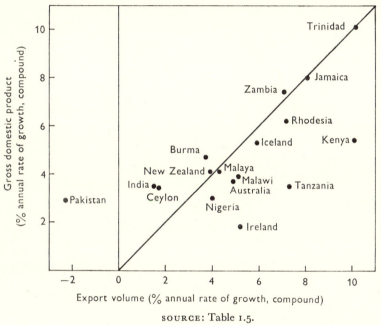

SOURCE: Table 1.5.

Fig. 1.2. Relation between annual rates of growth in export volume and real gross domestic product, 1953–62.

countries consists of long-term capital inflows, whether on private account or on governmental account in the form of aid (grants or loans). The importance of capital inflows in relation to exports varies widely from country to country. India is, perhaps, exceptional inasmuch as net long-term capital inflows in a recent period (1960–2) represented virtually one-half the total value of exports (see Table 1.6). The corresponding proportion for Ghana, one-third, was also exceptionally high, reflecting, in part, foreign investment in connection with the Volta River development scheme. For Australia, Pakistan and the countries of former British East Africa, capital inflows in 1960–2 represented about a fifth of export earnings, while in Ireland, Malaya and Jamaica the proportion was about a tenth. Capital inflows represented only a marginal proportion of export earnings for Ceylon and Nigeria (though there has been a substantial increase in foreign investment in the new petroleum fields in Nigeria since 1960–2), while there was a net outflow of funds on capital account from South Africa in this period.

With the increase in total foreign investments, an increase in debt service charges must be expected. In the majority of countries, the net capital inflow exceeds the net payment of interest and dividends on

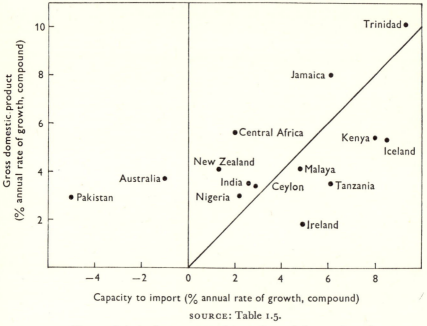

SOURCE: Table 1.5.

Fig. 1.3. Relation between annual rates of growth in capacity to import and real gross domestic product, 1953–62.

foreign investment. In four countries (Ceylon, Malaya, Jamaica and Trinidad), however, net factor payments abroad in 1960–2 exceeded the net capital inflow in that period, while in another three countries (Australia, Iceland and New Zealand), factor payments abroad represented over half the net amount of capital inflows.

Comparisons of net capital inflows in 1960–2 with those of 1953–5 can be made for ten of the countries listed in Table 1.6. The results generally show a substantial rise for some countries (India and Pakistan, for example) and modest increases for others. If these capital inflows are added to exports, and the total deflated by the movement in import unit values, an index of the capacity to import (adjusted for capital inflows) is obtained. Fig. 1.4 depicts the relationship between the rate of growth in this index and that in GDP.[1] There are some dramatic changes, compared with the position shown in Fig. 1.3, for India and Pakistan and, to a lesser extent, for Australia, reflecting the substantial increase in net capital inflows into these countries over the period. However, the inter-country correlation between changes in the capacity to import and changes in GDP is not improved by this adjustment for capital flows.[2]

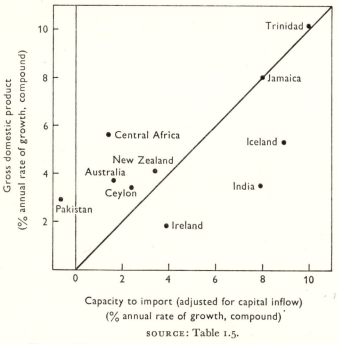

Capacity to import (adjusted for capital inflow)
(% annual rate of growth, compound)

SOURCE: Table 1.5.

Fig. 1.4. Relation between annual rates of growth in capacity to import (adjusted for capital inflow) and real gross domestic product, 1953–62.

If, instead of comparing rates of growth between countries, comparisons are made over time for each country separately, much closer correlations can be derived. There appears, for example, to have been a close relationship over the past decade between the volume of exports and real GDP in most overseas Sterling countries for which the relevant series can be assembled. Table 1.7 summarizes the results of linear

[1] GDP rates are as in Table 1.5. For Burma, India and Pakistan, net government transfer receipts on current account (which include grants under the Colombo Plan) were also included in the calculation.

[2] Excluding Pakistan, a linear regression of GDP growth rates on growth rates in the capacity to import (adjusted for capital inflow) showed a regression coefficient of 0·46 ($\pm$0·23), with $R^2 = 0·372$. The corresponding regression for the same nine countries before allowing for capital inflow showed a regression coefficient of 0·46 ($\pm$0·22), with $R^2 = 0·382$.

Table 1.6. *Finance of current deficit and net factor payments abroad in relation to exports, 1960–2*

	Finance of current deficit				
	Long-term capital inflow (net)[a]	Short-term capital and monetary movements (net)[b]	Total	Net factor payments abroad	Value of exports[c]
	(*Percentage of export value*)				(*$ million*)
MORE DEVELOPED COUNTRIES					
Australia	19	0	19	12	2,290
Iceland	5	−9	−4	4	75
Ireland	9	−2	7	−14	448
New Zealand	13	3	16	7	822
South Africa	−6	−6	−12	13	2,120
LESS DEVELOPED COUNTRIES					
Burma	7	−4	3	1	242
Ceylon	1	7	8	2	370
Malaya	8	−10	−2	9	805
India	47	5	52	11	1,390
Pakistan	19	0	19	2	402
East Africa	19	−17	2	8	375
Ghana	36	0	36	6	296
Nigeria	3	1	4	..	470
Jamaica	11	0	11	14	176
Trinidad and Tobago[d]	14	3	17	21	291

SOURCES: *Yearbook of National Accounts Statistics, 1963*, United Nations, New York, 1964; *Balance of Payments Yearbook, vol. 15, 1958–62*, I.M.F., Washington; *The Commonwealth and the Sterling Area: Statistical Abstract no. 84, 1963*, H.M.S.O., London, 1964.

[a] Private and public, including aid.   [b] Including errors and omissions.
[c] Excluding gold.   [d] 1960–1.

regressions of GDP on export volume for nine Sterling countries, generally covering the period 1950–2 to 1960–2. For all except India, the closeness of fit of the regression equations to the data is high. Over this period, the results indicate that, India apart, a 10 per cent increase in export volume was associated with an increase in GDP of 5 or 6 per cent for Australia, Ireland and South Africa, of 7 or 8 per cent for Iceland, the former Federation of Rhodesia and Nyasaland, Jamaica and Trinidad, and of as much as 15 per cent for Ceylon.[1]

[1] These percentages represent the 'growth elasticity' of GDP in relation to export volume and were derived by multiplying the value for *b* in Table 1.7 by the mean ratios of exports to GDP for the period covered.

Table 1.7. *Summary of results of regressions of GDP on the volume of exports, 1951–62[a]*

	Period	*b*	R^2
MORE DEVELOPED COUNTRIES			
Australia	1950–62	4·39 (0·34)	0·939
Iceland	1950–61	3·53 (0·37)	0·899
Ireland	1950–62	2·05 (0·28)	0·826
South Africa	1950–60	4·08 (0·23)	0·971
LESS DEVELOPED COUNTRIES			
Ceylon	1952–62	5·78 (0·98)	0·794
India	1952–62	10·78 (10·61)	0·103
Rhodesia/Nyasaland	1954–62	1·72 (0·19)	0·917
Jamaica	1950–60	3·48 (0·04)	0·970
Trinidad and Tobago	1951–61	1·52 (0·11)	0·957

SOURCES: As for Table 1.1.

[a] Based on linear regression of the form $Q_t = a + bX_t$, where Q = GDP and X = export volume.

However, it seems unlikely on *a priori* grounds that the relationship between export volume and GDP could, in fact, have been as high as is suggested by these regression results, for the various reasons already given. Moreover, time-series regressions of GDP on the capacity to import (adjusted for net capital inflows) for the same nine countries gave significantly worse fits to the data for five countries, about the same for three others, while for India the fit was quite good.[1] The generally better results for export volume than for the capacity to import are the opposite of what one would expect, which suggests that other factors may have been operating to influence both exports and GDP.

It is not, of course, surprising that there is no simple or universal relationship between exports and GDP, since exports are only one element in the process of economic growth. To trace the causal connexions involved, it is necessary to elaborate a model of a developing economy in which foreign trade plays a significant role. A simple model of this kind is set out in the following chapter, while Chapter 3 summarizes some quantitative results based on this model.

[1] For India, using the form $Q_t = a + b^* Z_t$, where Z represents the capacity to import, adjusted for net capital inflow, $b^* = 8·34$ ($\pm 1·08$), with $R^2 = 0·868$. This implies a growth elasticity of GDP with respect to Z of 0·63 ($\pm 0·08$).

CHAPTER 2

EX ANTE AND *EX POST* MODELS
OF GROWTH AND TRADE

I. AGGREGATIVE VERSUS SECTORAL MODELS

In the following sections, a simple macro-economic model of the re-lationship between economic growth and foreign trade is presented, making use of changes in the relevant national aggregates of real product, exports, imports, saving and investment. The aggregative approach, apart from its simplicity in both exposition and application, has the further advantage that it can be applied uniformly to a fairly wide range of countries, including several which still do not possess a full range of national accounts statistics.

It should, however, be recognized that the use of an aggregative model can have quite severe limitations if economic growth involves a bias in growth in terms of relative supply or demand for goods normally entering international trade; in other words, if the process of growth increases or decreases a country's relative dependence on international trade.[1] The reasons for these biases in the patterns of demand and out-put must be sought in terms of changing resource availabilities, the asymmetric growth of factor supplies, the varying economies of scale in different activities, and the different incidence of 'technical progress' in different industries, on the side of output; and consumer preference patterns and technical input–output relations, on the side of demand. But whatever the reasons for biased growth, the implication is that the macro-relation between trade and the gross product is not necessarily a stable one. The qualification is less important in the simpler economies, such as those less developed countries which are small and also heavily dependent on a few export crops, but it can be vital in a more complex economy where the process of import substitution can appreciably affect the import content of consumption or the proportion of produc-tion exported.

For purposes of national economic planning, it would of course be essential to consider the development of individual sectors separately,[2] including the changing interrelationships between the sectors. The

---

[1] See H. G. Johnson, *International Trade and Economic Growth*, London, 1958. Professor Johnson classifies the effects of economic growth on consumption and production (abstracting from changes in prices) into three types, viz. pro-trade bias, neutral and anti-trade bias (*ibid.* pp. 76–8).

[2] Indeed, in the planning of investment, it would also be necessary to consider individual projects.

object here, however, is not to formulate the outlines of an economic development plan; nor is it to evaluate the effectiveness of those development plans at present in force. The aim is, rather, to indicate in broad terms how changes in the export sector react back on the rate of growth of a developing economy and, where possible, to assess the relative orders of magnitude of the various reaction effects involved. For these less ambitious aims, an aggregative model should provide the broad picture required of the relevant interrelationships over the past. For projecting into the future, however, some allowance has to be made for the probable trade biases of economic growth; further discussion of this aspect is left until the projection analysis of Part II.

While the approach taken here is essentially aggregative as regards the economic development of individual overseas Sterling countries, the analysis of the export sector is based, as already indicated, on a series of detailed commodity studies. In this particular respect, the model can be considered a disaggregated one.

2. THE CHENERY–STROUT *EX ANTE* GROWTH MODEL

An aggregative economic model can readily be built on the main national accounting identities. These can be set out in accounting terms in the following matrix form, where Y = gross national product, C = consumption, S = gross domestic savings, I = gross domestic investment, X = exports of goods and services, M = import of goods and services, and F = net inflow of foreign capital.

Table 2.1. *A simple national accounting matrix*

	Production account	Appropriation account	Accumulation account	External account	Total
Production account	—	C	I	X	$C+I+X$
Appropriation account	Y	—	—	—	Y
Accumulation account	—	S	—	F	$S+F$
External account	M	—	—	—	M
Total	$Y+M$	$C+S$	I	$X+F$	

Since the national accounts are built up on the double-entry system, the totals in the final column of Table 2.1 must be identically equal to the corresponding totals in the final row. Thus we have the following four basic identities:

$$Y + M \equiv C + I + X, \qquad (2\cdot1)$$

$$C + S \equiv Y, \qquad (2\cdot2)$$

$$I \equiv S + F, \tag{2.3}$$

$$X + F \equiv M. \tag{2.4}$$

Only three of these four basic identities are independent; given any three of the equations, the fourth can immediately be derived. Thus, the seven variables in Table 2.1 are linked by three independent identities, so that a further four equations are required to make the system determinate.

Before considering the nature of such a determinate system, it is important to derive a further identity from the basic identities. By combining (2.1) and (2.2), we have:

$$I - S \equiv M - X. \tag{2.4a}$$

This states that the difference between investment and domestic savings (henceforth termed the 'savings gap') is equal to the difference between imports and exports of goods and services (the 'trade gap'). This is an identity which is also implied in (2.3) and (2.4), since both gaps are there defined as equalling the net inflow of foreign capital, F. Thus, the foreign capital inflow into a capital-importing country plays a dual role: it fills the gap between the imports the country requires for its development and the earnings it derives from its exports and at the same time it supplements the supply of domestic savings in financing the required level of investment.

This equality between the savings gap and the trade gap is purely an *ex post* equality, since the national accounts describe the relationships between the variables after the event, that is, after they have had time to adjust from an *ex ante* position. Since the decisions to save, to invest, to import and to export are made by different—though overlapping—groups of people, they are not normally mutually consistent. Thus, the usual situation would be where the *ex ante* savings gap differs from the *ex ante* trade gap, being either greater or smaller.

However, the two gaps as defined here are necessarily equal *ex post*, so that the *ex ante* inequality implies that the four variables in equation (2.4a) adjust towards some equilibrium position. In this process of adjustment, intended savings may, for example, exceed the opportunities of profitable investment, so that some *ex ante* savings will, in the event, be frustrated. In similar fashion, some intended imports may not in the event be realized or, on the other hand, an excess of realized over anticipated exports or capital inflow may allow for a level of imports above that planned or anticipated.

This distinction between the *ex ante* and *ex post* situations is useful not only from an expository viewpoint, insofar as it illuminates the process of mutual adjustment of the main economic variables in the growth process. It is also useful as revealing some of the main policy problems before the government of a developing country which is aiming at maximizing its rate of economic growth for a given anticipated level of export earnings and foreign capital inflow.

There are, of course, a large number of ways in which a given number of macro-economic variables can be combined into an economic model. A model specifically designed to throw up the policy issues implied in the divergence between the two *ex ante* financing gaps has been worked out in great detail by Professor Hollis B. Chenery and M. Bruno and applied to the economic development of Israel.[1] The Chenery–Bruno model was applied to a detailed sectoral analysis of the Israeli economy, using an input–output approach, while a further development of the basic model has recently been made by Professor Chenery and Alan Strout in terms of the usual macro-variables.[2]

Chenery and Strout distinguish three major constraints on economic growth in less developed countries. The first consists of a limitation on the availability of human skills (both labour skills and the managerial skills of government and productive enterprise). Whether or not the available supply of skills becomes an effective bottleneck depends in part on the planned rate of growth, since the skill limitation comes into operation only above a certain 'critical' rate of growth. The critical level is that rate of growth at which the national product can be increased if investment resources (domestic and foreign) and imported commodities are freely available at constant prices.[3]

In some less developed countries, the present rate of growth could not be accelerated appreciably without immediate strains appearing in the available supply of people with sufficient training or skills to operate an increased stock of machinery and plant, or to manage efficiently a more complex economy. At the same time, it is probably true to say that for most less developed countries the skill limitation is not likely to be the most critical bottleneck in the medium-term future, taking into account even the limited scale of existing education and training and existing possibilities of importing foreign technicians and managerial personnel where this is necessary for achieving their development targets.

The second constraint consists of the limit set on investment by the supply of domestic savings, supplemented by the available net capital borrowing from abroad; while the third constraint consists of the limit

---

[1] Hollis B. Chenery and M. Bruno, 'Development Alternatives in an Open Economy: the Case of Israel', *Economic Journal*, March 1962.

[2] Hollis B. Chenery and Alan M. Strout, 'Foreign Assistance and Economic Development', *American Economic Review*, vol. 56, September 1966. A similar approach can also be found in a recent article by R. McKinnon ('Foreign Exchange Constraints in Economic Development and Efficient Aid Allocation', *Economic Journal*, June 1964).

[3] Chenery and Strout, *loc. cit.* p. 10.

set on imports and net borrowing. For any given target rate of growth in real output set by the national planning authorities, two *ex ante* financing gaps are then generated. The savings gap is generated by the relationship between investment and the target growth in real output, via an incremental capital–output ratio, on the one hand, and an *ex ante* savings function on the other. The trade gap is generated, given the rate of export growth as being determined outside the system, by a relationship between income growth and growth in the minimum level of imports which is consistent with that growth.[1] This 'minimum' level of imports is an essential concept in the Chenery–Strout model. It represents the value of those foreign goods which the country could not do without—to achieve a given rate of economic growth—even though it had as much domestic resources as it could use, given the structure of its output and its demand, and the existing technical possibilities of production. What constitutes such a minimum level of imports for a particular country in a given period would depend on the relationships between the structure of output and of demand in the widest sense (including, for example, luxury imports by entrepreneurs if, without them, economic growth would be adversely affected). Though the concept can be defined in principle in this way, any quantitative estimate of the minimum level of imports consistent with a given target rate of growth of GNP for a particular country must inevitably be subject to an appreciable margin of error.

The working of the model can be depicted on a chart relating the target rate of growth in gross national product (GNP) to the required level of net capital imports (as in Fig. 2.1). Variations in the planned rate of growth, r, are shown along the horizontal axis, and the required net capital inflow consistent with each growth rate along the vertical axis. If the anticipated growth rate in exports is given, then as r increases, the net capital inflow required also increases. The straight line F^T denotes how the trade gap to be financed by the net capital inflow would move as r varied, while the curved line F^S shows the corresponding movement in the savings gap.[2]

At point R_1, both *ex ante* gaps are equal and if the planned growth is r_0, the required net foreign financing will be OF_0, and the system can grow at the planned rate without any further adjustments, assuming that the foreign finance is forthcoming. At any other planned rate of growth, however, the two *ex ante* gaps will diverge; at rates less than r_0, the trade gap will be the larger, while the savings gap is the larger at

---

[1] The formal Chenery–Strout model is set out in the annexe to this chapter. What constitutes a 'minimum' level of imports is, of course, open to some argument.

[2] The linear relationship between F and r for the trade gap and the curvilinear relationship for the savings gap arise out of the assumptions of the model (see annexe to this chapter).

higher rates of growth. If the planned growth rate is r_1 $(r_1 < r_0)$, the trade gap $= r_1 P_1$ $(= OF_1)$, though the savings gap is only $r_1 P_3$. To achieve this rate of growth, r_1, it is necessary to borrow abroad a net amount of $P_1 P_3$ in excess of the difference between *ex ante* savings and the anticipated volume of investment. In these circumstances, a proportion of intended

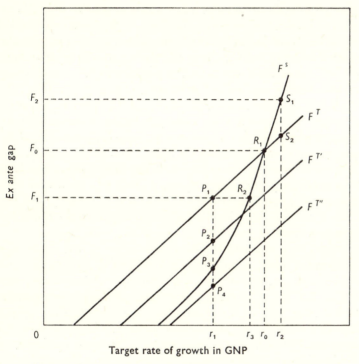

Fig. 2.1. The two *ex ante* gaps in relation to different target growth rates.

savings becomes, in the event, frustrated. This is brought about by consumers spending more and saving less (because of the reduced attractiveness of investment relative to consumption, so that the savings potential is not fully exploited) and/or by less government saving (implying some cut in taxation).

If, on the other hand, the planned growth rate is r_2 $(r_2 > r_0)$, then the required level of net foreign borrowing, determined by the *ex ante* savings gap, would be $r_2 S_1$ $(= OF_2)$. This is $S_1 S_2$ in excess of the *ex ante* trade gap, so that sufficient additional foreign exchange would be available in the target year to increase imports above the minimum level consistent with a growth rate of r_2 (e.g. by increasing the volume of imports of consumer goods and/or the monetary reserves). Since the economy is assumed to be in a phase of savings-constrained growth, any imports exceeding the 'minimum' level consistent with the target rate of growth in GNP would not result in a higher rate of growth being achieved. The essential reason for this is that the economy no longer has available the requisite amounts and kinds of domestic resources which would need to be combined with imports—for example, of additional capital goods—in order to achieve a faster rate of growth than planned.

How is this model affected by variations in the anticipated growth rate of exports? If the growth rate of exports is expected to rise above the rate implied in the line F^T, the *ex ante* trade gap will be described by a new line, $F^{T'}$, which is lower than, but parallel to,[1] F^T. At this higher export growth rate, r_1 can be achieved with a net capital inflow of only $r_1 P_2$, or $P_1 P_2$ less than previously. However, on the assumptions of this model, changes in exports do not influence either domestic savings or domestic investment, so that variations in exports do not affect the *ex ante* savings gap. It could happen, therefore, that an increase in anticipated exports could reduce the *ex ante* trade gap below the *ex ante* savings gap. If, for example, the trade gap line falls to $F^{T''}$, then r_1 would be achieved by a net capital inflow of $r_1 P_3$, which would be $P_3 P_4$ in excess of the *ex ante* trade gap, with implied adjustments in planned imports or in the monetary reserves.

As the target rate of growth is increased above r_0, the required net foreign borrowing would tend to increase further so long as the *ex ante* marginal propensity to save is less than double the required investment proportion of the gross product.[2] Moreover, as was shown earlier, a higher growth rate than r_0, if it is financed by foreign capital, will tend to be associated with import relaxations which are likely to lead to reduced foreign aid in subsequent periods (though this might, to some extent, be offset by a higher level of private investment from abroad). For both these reasons, the planning authority might find it expedient not to plan for an overall rate of growth in excess of r_0. On the other hand, a planned rate of growth much below r_0 might lead to an appreciable volume of frustrated savings, and, to this extent, an incentive would exist for the planning authority not to plan for a growth rate much below r_0.

In practice, any country planning its overall growth rate in this way could well pass from a period of trade-constrained growth to one of savings-constrained growth, and back again, as export prospects changed, or if it were planned to change some of the basic relationships

---

[1] It is assumed here, for simplicity of exposition, that the marginal propensity to import remains constant though the growth rate of exports changes. If, however, the marginal propensity to import changes, then $F^{T'}$ will no longer be parallel to F^T (see also equation (2·14) in the annexe to this chapter).

[2] This is demonstrated in the annexe (equation (2·13)).

(for instance, to raise the community's savings propensity by taxation or higher interest rates). Where, however, the foreign exchange constraint has dominated the economic planning process for some time, the planned rate of growth could well be set below r_0 for a number of successive plan periods; for such countries, the savings constraint would not come into effect at all.

The simplified Chenery–Strout model set out above defines the required amount of net capital inflow (including aid) consistent with any planned growth rate of a less developed economy. This is a useful approach because it reveals the order of magnitude of capital flows consistent with specified rates of economic growth in the less developed countries. However, since the volume of private capital and inter-government aid cannot necessarily be assumed to be highly elastic, it is also worth asking a further question which is not envisaged in the Chenery–Strout formulation, namely, what is the rate of economic growth implied by a given projected rate of export growth and an assumed ceiling level of net borrowing or aid from abroad?

In terms of the simplified Chenery–Strout model, the answer can be derived by reversing the direction of causality. Thus, in Fig. 2.1, if F^T denotes the *ex ante* trade gap, a volume of net borrowing or aid from abroad equal to OF_1 would imply a rate of growth of r_1. As the projected export growth rate is increased, the same amount of foreign borrowing or aid would imply higher rates of economic growth, as determined by the trade-gap relationship, until the savings-constrained phase is reached. For example, if the increase in the export growth rate is represented by a movement from F^T to $F^{T'}$, the net inflow of capital of OF_1 would imply a rate of growth of r_3, which is determined by the intersection of the F_1 line with the F^S curve. This is a somewhat lower growth rate than would have been attained had the savings gap not exceeded the trade gap at that point. Thus, on this model, any expansion in the rate of export growth has no effect, one way or the other, on the overall growth rate of GDP during the savings-constrained phase. As Fig. 2.1 shows, this phase is likely to come into operation at relatively high planned rates of growth.

3. SOME ADAPTATIONS OF THE CHENERY–STROUT MODEL

A major limitation of the simplified Chenery–Strout model outlined above is the assumption that the two *ex ante* gaps are generated quite independently of each other. This is an over-simplification which could result in misleading conclusions in some cases. There are, in fact, a number of interrelationships between the internal and external variables of a developing economy, any of which could assume major importance in particular situations. Of these, three seem of fairly general importance for less developed exporting countries.

The first is that variations in exports might well result in associated variations in domestic savings. This could occur either because the propensity to save is higher in the export sector than elsewhere or because government savings rely heavily on taxes on foreign trade.[1] In Malaya, for example, the ratio of savings to income of the tin and rubber companies is no doubt considerably higher than that of companies producing for the home market (and certainly much higher than for peasants), while in 1963 Customs duties were estimated to bring in over 40 per cent of total tax revenue. It seems probable that in countries like Malaya a close relationship exists between changes in exports (and thus in the net income of the export sector) and changes in gross domestic savings. Equally, in other countries, in which relatively little revenue is derived from duties on foreign trade and in which the savings ratio does not differ markedly from one sector to another, a close relationship between exports and savings would not be expected to exist.

However, where such a relationship does exist, then a rise in the projected rate of export growth would reduce the *ex ante* savings gap as well as reducing the *ex ante* trade gap. While, however, the trade gap would be reduced by an amount equal to the increase in exports, the savings gap would decline by an amount dependent not only on the increase in the net income of the export sector, but also on that sector's marginal propensity to save. In any event, it would seem that the Chenery–Strout model would overstate the *ex ante* savings gap for countries having a significant savings response to export changes.

Another possible effect of variations in exports would be on the incremental capital–output ratio, which has so far been assumed constant. If, for example, exports were mainly of agricultural produce, and if an increase in exports could be derived with little or no increase in new investment in capital assets, the growth would reduce the *ex ante* trade gap for a given growth rate in GDP, while the *ex ante* savings gap would be reduced as a result of a fall in the incremental capital–output ratio. There is, however, no necessary connexion between exports and the incremental capital–output ratio; the relationship depends very much on which sector provides the expansion in exports, on the capital–output ratios of the various sectors, and on the indirect effects in other sectors of the initial export expansion.

The second adaptation of the Chenery–Strout model that seems necessary is to make a distinction between the gross *domestic* product and the

---

[1] Furthermore, over a period of time a sustained growth in exports could result in a rise in the marginal savings propensities in other sectors also.

gross *national* product. The difference represents net factor payments including interest and dividends on foreign investments. For some countries, net factor payments abroad are already a considerable burden on the balance of payments, while for some they represent an appreciable proportion even of GNP. The advantages of treating these interest and other payments separately are, first, that investment can then be related to output (rather than to income), which is evidently a more appropriate relationship, and, second, that it reveals the interest rate on foreign capital as a possible policy instrument. Moreover, a given target rate of growth in GDP can then be shown to imply alternative growth rates in GNP according to the average rate of interest assumed on new foreign borrowing. The average interest rate will be influenced by the relative proportions of private and public capital inflows and possibly also by the relative importance of the different foreign investing countries.

A third desirable adaptation, relatively simple in theory but extremely difficult in practice, is to make a specific allowance for the effect of probable future changes in the terms of trade on net capital inflow requirements or on the rate of economic growth.

4. A COMPUTABLE *EX POST* GROWTH MODEL

The Chenery–Strout model as described above, particularly if some or all of the suggested adaptations are made, is eminently suitable in selecting optimum planned growth rates and the associated levels of foreign capital requirements. It is also especially useful in assessing the realism and consistency of published development plans. For such purposes, it is appropriate to consider the structural parameters— especially the marginal propensities to import and to save—as policy variables which should reflect the general aims of economic development. Thus it is not essential, for the use of this model, to estimate statistically the past marginal propensities, since the planned future propensities may have little or no relationship to them. It is not, however, possible to judge the realism of such 'planned' propensities without at the same time having made estimates of the corresponding *ex ante* relationships for a past period. Since the historical evidence is necessarily *ex post*, the estimation of *ex ante* relationships requires careful specification of a rather complex model in which the variable under consideration adjusts to some desired *ex ante* level. The statistical estimation of, for example, savings propensities based on a model of this type would be possible for a number of the economically developed countries with fairly reliable statistical series on savings. However, for the great majority of under-developed countries it would not be practicable to estimate such relationships because of the lack, or unreliability, of the basic statistical data.

By contrast, the foreign trade statistics of under-developed countries are generally of a good standard of reliability,[1] while the balance of payments accounts are in most cases reliable within a reasonable margin of error. Moreover, most under-developed countries regularly publish series of the volume and unit value of imports and exports, and for those that do not, such series can be compiled from the detailed published trade returns. For this reason, it would seem that projections of foreign trade, and thus of the prospective trade gap, consistent with any given rate of economic growth, are likely to be more reliable than projections of the *ex ante* savings gap.

An alternative approach to the estimation of the two *ex ante* gaps would therefore be to project the magnitude of the prospective trade gap for a given rate of economic growth, using (*a*) an independent projection of exports based, *inter alia*, on the probable future movements in the world market and (*b*) the *ex post* relationship between imports and income derived from past figures. This would yield a projection of the actual 'gap' in the balance of payments in the target year, on the assumption that the past marginal propensity to import would also hold in the future. By deducting this projected trade gap from the projected investment required to support the output target, one can derive domestic savings as a residual. This is an *ex post* model, in which domestic savings adjust to changes in the trade gap. In terms of the Chenery–Strout model, the underlying assumption is that the economy has been, and will remain, in a phase of trade-constrained growth.[2]

This assumption can, however, be tested by comparing the savings derived residually with the level of savings which would result if the past relationship between savings and income (or savings, exports and non-export incomes), were to be projected up to the target year. If this projection gave much the same total for domestic savings as was found by the residual assumption, then it would seem that, in that particular country, savings could be assumed to react in a residual fashion. In that case, no further government policy measures would appear to be necessary to influence the level of savings. For other countries, though,

[1] The main exception relates to overland trade between adjacent under-developed countries, most or all of which might go on without being recorded by Customs offices.

[2] Strictly speaking, the approach suggested here cannot be used for economies which have, in the past, been in a phase of savings-constrained growth, because for such economies past imports are likely to have been inflated as part of the adjustment of the system towards equality of the (smaller) *ex ante* trade gap with the *ex ante* savings gap. However, some appropriate downward adjustments can be made, in practice, for marginal import propensities which are clearly inflated (particularly if the inflation is mainly in consumer goods categories).

the two projections might well be very different, thus implying the need for appropriate changes in government fiscal policies.

This type of *ex post* model thus has certain policy implications, though these arise incidentally. However, the objective of the present study is not to propound a policy model for economic planning, nor to examine methods of appraising the efficiency of a given plan or its execution. Rather, it is to make a broad assessment, in quantitative terms, of the rates of economic growth implied in alternative export projections for given countries. For this more modest purpose, an *ex post* model of the type outlined here appears to be an appropriate one. It should provide reasonably reliable orders of magnitude on the basis of specified assumptions about net capital inflows, including alternative assumptions about the magnitudes of the various parameters to allow for probable future changes in the economic structures of the developing countries. Moreover, by the 'residual test' the financing gap between savings and investment can also be examined for the need for possible policy changes.

The import propensity

It was suggested above that the trade gap can be projected by an independent estimate of future exports and by an *ex post* relationship between imports and income. However, since imports consist of a wide variety of goods with different end-uses, a more reliable projection of imports can usually be made by disaggregating them into a number of sub-groups: for example, capital goods, intermediate products and consumer goods.

Thus, a given target rate of income growth would imply a given level of investment and given rates of growth of home production of capital goods and consumer goods. Imports of capital goods in the target year would thus depend on investment and on the planned home output of capital goods; imports of intermediate products would depend on the planned level of home output in sectors using such products; while imports of consumer goods would depend on the marginal propensity to consume and the degree of planned import substitution in this field. By deducting projected exports from the total of projected imports, after allowing for net invisible payments, the amount of net capital borrowing from abroad required to support the target rate of growth is derived.

The position is, however, somewhat different if the net capital inflow is assumed as given. In that case, given also the export projection, the total of imports which can be financed in the target year is already determined. Thus, if any two of the major sub-groups of imports are projected on the basis of relationships between demand and home output, the third can be derived as a residual. To simplify the model, it can be assumed that imports fall into two main sub-groups: capital goods, including intermediate products for the capital goods industries, and consumer goods, including intermediate products for the consumer goods industries. The first, capital goods, group is assumed to have import priority, in the sense that any shortfall in the capacity to import, compared with the expected or planned level, will fall wholly or mainly on consumer goods imports; while any excess above that level will benefit capital goods in the main, but might still leave room for some relaxation in restrictions on imports of consumer goods. On this model, then, imports of capital goods depend essentially on the capacity to import; they do not vary residually after the country's requirements for consumer goods imports have been met.[1]

Exports and gross product

The level of investment in an under-developed economy will depend heavily on the availability of imported capital goods, though the relationship cannot be assumed necessarily to remain constant. The degree of dependence is likely to be higher the less developed the industrial sector of the economy. To the extent that investment is associated with the level of capital goods imports, it is thereby also associated with the capacity to import. Since it can be assumed, as previously, that the level of investment is associated with a corresponding rate of growth of GDP via an incremental capital–output ratio, it follows that a given rate of growth in exports can be linked to a corresponding rate of growth in output, on specific assumptions regarding the net capital inflow and the magnitude of the various parameters.

The relationship between the growth rates in exports and GDP, on the assumptions underlying this model, are depicted in Fig. 2.2. The curve F indicates how the growth rate of GDP (r) will vary for given variations in the rate of export growth (ϵ), assuming fixed values of the parameters involved in the various functional relationships already described and a fixed amount of net capital inflow from abroad. Because of the shape of the F curve,[2] successive increases of equal amounts in ϵ will result in smaller and smaller increases in r.

As net capital inflow changes, the position of the F curve also changes. The curve F', for example, represents the relation between ϵ and r on the assumption that the net capital inflow is fixed at a correspondingly higher level implied in curve F. At this higher level of borrowing from abroad, a higher level of investment becomes possible and, assuming a

---

[1] The alternative assumption, that consumer goods imports are determined by a constant marginal propensity to import, while capital goods imports vary according to the difference between the capacity to import and the value of consumer goods imports, is often made (see, for example, *Studies in Long-term Economic Projections for the World Economy: Aggregate Models*, United Nations, New York, 1964, p. 53), but seems generally less realistic than the assumption made here.   [2] The formulae for the curves in Fig. 2.2 are given in the annexe to this chapter.

constant incremental capital–output ratio, a higher growth rate in GDP. Thus, if exports grow at rate ϵ_1, r_1 can now rise to r_2, the equivalent result to an increase in exports—at the initial level of borrowing from abroad—to a growth rate of ϵ_2.

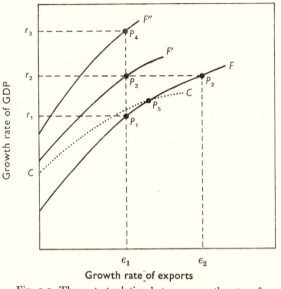

Fig. 2.2. The *ex post* relation between growth rates of exports and of gross domestic product.

Curves F and F' are both based on the assumption, already mentioned, that the values of the various parameters remain unchanged. If this assumption does not hold, then of course the relationship depicted in the F curves of Fig. 2.2 will not provide a valid projection of future growth rates. One possibility which is worth further examination here is that the incremental capital–output ratio during the period of projection is significantly different from that of the recent past. In the first place, this ratio is likely to be higher, the higher the proportion of GDP invested and the lower the rate of increase in the labour force or in the rate of technical progress.[1] The incremental capital–output ratio will

---

[1] If variations in gross domestic product (Q) can be expressed in terms of a Cobb–Douglas type of function, such that:
$$Q = a K^{\alpha} L^{\beta} e^{\rho t},$$
where K is a measure of productive capital assets, L represents the active labour force, and ρ a constant rate of technical progress. The incremental capital–output ratio, σ, can then be written:
$$\sigma = \frac{1}{\alpha/\bar{\sigma} + (\beta l + \rho)/c},$$
where $\bar{\sigma}$ is the average capital–output ratio in the base period ($= K_0/Q_0$), l is the proportionate rate of change in the labour force, and c is the ratio of new investment to total output ($= \Delta K/Q_0$).

also be influenced by the pattern of new investment between the different economic sectors, since the sectoral incremental capital–output ratios are likely to differ widely among the various sectors.

If it is assumed, for illustrative purposes, that the overall incremental capital–output ratio will decline, then the rate of growth in GDP consistent with any given rate of export growth will be increased. The new relationship is shown in the curve F'' in Fig. 2.2. This curve assumes the same net capital inflow as for curve F, but a lower incremental capital–output ratio (which not only shifts the curve upwards, but also results in a steeper rate of climb). Thus, a rate of export growth of ϵ_1 would now be consistent with a growth rate of GDP of r_3, which—for the particular set of curves shown in Fig. 2.2—appreciably exceeds the rate, r_2, consistent with the assumed increase in net borrowing from abroad with an unchanged capital–output ratio. Other combinations of assumptions about the capital–output ratio and the net capital inflow can also be shown in Fig. 2.2. For example, the curve CC assumes the same net capital inflow as for F', but a higher incremental capital–output ratio. For this situation, a rate of export growth of ϵ_1 would be associated with a slightly higher growth rate of GDP than for the original F curve (which assumed a lower net capital inflow as well as a lower capital–output ratio); but at relatively high rates of export growth (to the right of P_5), curve CC would be associated with lower growth rates of GDP than would the original F curve.

Each curve shown in Fig. 2.2 is essentially a 'schedule' of relationships between ϵ and r on the basis of a constant incremental capital–output ratio. The actual time path of growth of a given economy would depend also on whether, and to what extent, the capital–output ratio changed during the growth process. It seems likely that at higher rates of growth, further increases in output would become progressively more difficult to achieve per unit of investment; in other words, the capital–output ratio is likely to rise as the growth rate itself rises above a critical level, irrespective of whether the growth is financed mainly by increased exports or by increased borrowing from abroad. If this were so, then the dynamic relationship between ϵ and r would be more correctly depicted by, for example, curve F up to point P_5, then CC thereafter.

Savings as a residual

As already mentioned, the residual variation in this *ex post* model is supplied by domestic savings. As a check on the applicability of the model to growth in a particular country, the residual savings requirement in the target year can be compared with the savings that would have accrued if the past relationship between savings, exports and non-export incomes were to hold for the future.

The relative magnitudes of domestic savings as derived residually and as derived from past functional relationships are depicted in Fig. 2.3 for varying rates of growth of GDP. The straight line S_t'' assumes a linear relationship between savings and the rate of growth of GDP, while the curve S_t' assumes that savings are a function of exports as well as of non-export incomes. Savings as derived residually from the model are represented by the curve S_t. At rate of growth of r_1, savings would be either r_1P_1 (on the linear relationship) or r_1P_2 (on the curvilinear relationship), whereas the required *ex post* volume of domestic savings would be only r_1P_3. Thus, at this growth rate, P_1P_3 (or P_2P_3) of savings

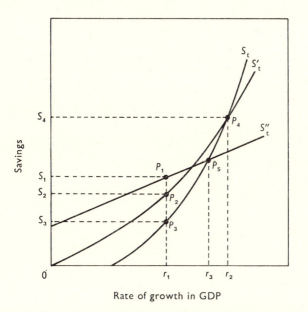

Fig. 2.3. *Ex post* savings in relation to the rate of growth in GDP.

would be frustrated. Required savings would be less than expected savings at growth rates lower than r_2 on the curvilinear savings function, or r_3 on the linear function. Since S_t'' and S_t intersect at P_5, and S_t' and S_t at P_4, these represent growth rates at which required savings would exactly equal the savings that would have been forthcoming on the basis of the relevant historical savings functions. At growth rates higher than these, the savings constraint comes into operation, and growth will be limited unless savings rates are increased by government tax policies or otherwise. If the required increase in savings rates is a relatively modest one, then it can reasonably be assumed that the increase can be achieved by appropriate changes in monetary or fiscal policies; if not, then the lower level of savings that seems probable would reduce the rate of economic growth which would otherwise be attained.

Capital inflows and aid

Assuming that domestic savings do, in fact, react in the residual way described above, the *ex post* model can be used, in reverse, to determine the amount of net capital inflow required to support a target of growth of GDP, on the basis of a given growth rate of exports. This can readily be seen from Fig. 2.2; assuming that the export growth rate is given as e_1, and the target rate of growth in GDP as r_2, then the net capital inflow would be that taken in the calculation of the F' curve.

In the next chapter, this *ex post* model is tested on the experience of a number of overseas Sterling countries since the early 1950s.

ANNEXE. MATHEMATICAL FORMULATION OF THE MODELS

I. THE *EX ANTE* CHENERY–STROUT GROWTH MODEL

The four accounting identities have already been described in Chapter 2; these are repeated below for convenience:

$$Y + M \equiv C + I + X, \qquad (2\cdot1)$$

$$C + S \equiv Y, \qquad (2\cdot2)$$

$$I \equiv S + F, \qquad (2\cdot3)$$

$$X + F \equiv M, \qquad (2\cdot4)$$

the symbols having the following meaning:

Y = gross national product,

C = consumption,

S = gross domestic savings,

I = gross investment,

X = exports of goods and services,

M = imports of goods and services,

F = balance of payments on current account,

all variables being measured in real terms.

Of the four identities, three are independent, the fourth being determinate given the others. Thus, for seven variables and three independent identities, the system is determinate on the addition of a further four equations.

The model sets out five structural equations, however, though only four are operative in any given growth phase. These are:

$$Y_t^* = Y_0(1 + r^*)^t, \qquad (2\cdot5)$$

where r^* is the target rate of growth, and t the target year of the plan, starting from year 0. (The asterisk is used to distinguish target or planned values from *ex post* values of parameters or variables.)

$$I_t^* = \sigma r^* Y_t^*; \qquad (2\cdot6)$$

where σ represents an incremental capital–output ratio.

$$X_t = X_0(1 + \epsilon)^t, \qquad (2\cdot7)$$

where ϵ represents the rate of growth of exports, which is assumed to be exogenously determined by the development of the world market.

$$S_t^* = s_0 + s_1^* Y_t^* \qquad (2\cdot8)$$

describes a savings function, s_1^* being the *ex ante* marginal propensity to save.

$$M_t^* = m_0 + m_1^* Y_t^* \qquad (2\cdot9)$$

describes the *minimum* level of imports necessary to sustain the planned level of real national product; m_1^* can then be regarded as the marginal 'necessity' to import.

The *ex ante* savings gap $(I^* - S^*)$ will be equal to the *ex ante* trade gap $(M^* - X)$ only in special circumstances. Normally, one can expect one *ex ante* gap to exceed the other. If the savings gap is the larger, equation (2.8) is operative, while (2.9) is not; if, on the other hand, the trade gap is the larger, the reverse position holds.

Chenery and Strout distinguish a phase of growth in which an upper limit to r^* is in effective operation, as a result of limitations on the supply of skill. During this phase, two sub-phases can be distinguished according to which of the two *ex ante* gaps is the larger. The major difficulty in applying this part of the model statistically is the ambiguity surrounding the concept of skill limitation. In any event, it seems probable that for the majority of overseas Sterling countries which form the specific subject of the present book, the effective limitation to growth, in the form of a trade or a savings constraint, comes into operation before the skill limit imposes a ceiling on the possible rate of growth. For both these reasons, the solutions to the Chenery–Strout model for the two sub-phases of skill-limited growth are not given here.[1] The solutions

[1] See Chenery and Strout, *loc. cit.*, for the full description of this sub-model.

to the model for the other two phases of growth (the savings constraint
and the trade constraint) are found by combining the relevant equations given earlier, as shown in Table 2.2.

Table 2.2. *Solution of the simplified Chenery–Strout model
with no effective skill limitation*

	Savings-constrained growth[a]	Trade-constrained growth[b]
(1) Y_t^*	$Y_0 (1+r^*)^t$	$Y_0 (1+r^*)^t$
(2) I_t^*	$\sigma r^* Y_t^*$	$\sigma r^* Y_t^*$
(3) S_t^*	$s_0 + s_1^* Y_t^*$	$(\sigma r^* - m_1^*) Y_t^* + X_t - m_0$
(4) X_t	$X_0 (1+\epsilon)^t$	$X_0 (1+\epsilon)^t$
(5) M_t or M_t^*	$(\sigma r^* - s_1^*) Y_t^* + X_t - s_0$	$m_0 + m_1^* Y_t$
(6) F_t	$(\sigma r^* - s_1^*) Y_t^* - s_0$	$m_1^* Y_t^* + m_0 - X_t$
(7) C_t	$(1 - s_1^*) Y_t^* - s_0$	$(1 - \sigma r^* + m_1^*) Y_t^* - X_t + m_0$

[a] Combining equations (2.1) to (2.4) with (2.5) to (2.8).
[b] Combining equations (2.1) to (2.4) with (2.5) to (2.7) and (2.9).

The interesting feature of the solutions is that while an increase in
exports reduces the requirement for net capital inflow for any target
rate of growth when the trade gap is the larger of the two *ex ante* gaps,
variations in exports have no effect on the capital inflow requirement
in the savings-constrained phase of growth.

The relationship between F and r^* can be conveniently illustrated if
the following approximations are used:

$$(1+r^*)^t = 1+r^*t; \tag{2.10}$$

$$(1+\epsilon)^t = 1+\epsilon t. \tag{2.11}$$

These approximations can reasonably be used if r^* and ϵ are not large
and t is also relatively small (e.g., for the projection period used here,
$t = 10\text{--}15$ years); for $r^* = 0.03$, $(1+r^*)^t = 1.34$ for $t = 10$, whereas
$1+r^*t = 1.30$, for example. The 'simple interest' approximation is
used here purely for algebraic convenience; the demonstration of the
relationships between the variables in the system would not be essentially changed had the 'compound interest' formulae been used, but
the results would have been considerably more complicated.

The solutions for F can now be written as:

$$F_t^s = (\sigma t Y_0) r^{*2} + Y_0(\sigma - s_1^* t) r^* - (s_1^* Y_0 + s_0), \tag{2.12}$$

where F_t^s represents the net capital inflow requirement in a phase of
savings-constrained growth. In this phase, the gradient of F_t^s is:

$$\frac{dF_t^s}{dr^*} = Y_0\{\sigma + t (2h - s_1^*)\}, \tag{2.13}$$

where $h(= \sigma r^*)$ represents the required investment ratio of GNP. Thus, F_t^s will rise even if the *ex ante* savings propensity equals the required investment ratio, so long as $s_1^* < 2h + \sigma/t$.

The net capital inflow in a phase of trade-constrained growth would be:

$$F_t^T = (m_1^* t Y_0) r^* + \{m_0 + m_1^* Y_0 - X_0(1 + \epsilon t)\}, \qquad (2.14)$$

representing the corresponding net capital inflow when growth is subject to a trade constraint. Since (2.12) is a quadratic in r^*, F_t^s will rise at an increasing rate as r^* rises, whereas F_t^T will increase at a constant rate for a given value of ϵ (and of the other parameters). These relationships are depicted in Fig. 2.1 (p. 55).

If, however, F_t^T is fixed, then r^* depends on the rate of export growth:

$$r^* = \left(\frac{X_0}{m_1^* Y_0}\right) \epsilon + \frac{1}{t}\left(\frac{X_0 + F_t - m_0}{m_1^* Y_0} - 1\right). \qquad (2.15)$$

The corresponding r^* for a fixed F_t^s can be found by solving the quadratic equation (2.12).

2. SOME ADAPTATIONS OF THE CHENERY–STROUT MODEL

(a) Savings related to exports

The hypothesis that domestic savings are a function of exports can be expressed in simple form as follows, where S_t denotes *ex post* savings:

$$S_t = s_0 + s_1(Y_t - X_t) + s_2 X_t. \qquad (2.16)$$

This states that the degree of dependence of savings on exports is different in magnitude from the corresponding dependence on income arising in the rest of the economy. Equation (2.16) can be rewritten as:

$$S_t = s_0 + s_1 Y_t + (s_2 - s_1) X_t. \qquad (2.16a)$$

The net foreign capital borrowing required for any planned rate of growth will then be, in the savings-constrained phase:

$$F_t^s = (Y_0 \, \sigma t) r^{*2} + \{Y_0(\sigma - s_1 t)\} r^* - \{(s_2 - s_1) t X_0\}\epsilon$$
$$- \{s_0 + (s_2 - s_1) X_0 + s_1 Y_0\}. \qquad (2.17)$$

Thus, as ϵ rises, F^s falls by an amount equal to a proportion, $(s_2 - s_1) t$, of the rise in exports.

(b) The distinction between GDP and GNP

GNP can be defined as:

$$Y = Q - iD, \qquad (2.18)$$

where Q represents *GDP*, D the net total of foreign debt and i the mean rate of interest or dividend payable thereon. The relationship between investment and growth is now more appropriately stated in terms of Q, thus:

$$I_t = \sigma \bar{r}^* Q_t^*, \qquad (2.6a)$$

where $\bar{r}^*$ represents the planned growth rate in GDP, as distinct from r^*, the planned growth rate in GNP.

Imports and exports have now to be redefined so as to exclude net factor payments abroad. Thus, if

$$X_t' = X_0'(1+\epsilon)^t \qquad (2.7a)$$

and

$$M_t' = m_0' + m_1' Y_t^* \qquad (2.9a)$$

represent the redefined variables, the required net capital inflow in the trade-constrained phase of growth would be:

$$
\begin{aligned}
F_t^T &= M_t' - X_t' + iD_{t-1} \\
&= (m_1' t Q_0)\bar{r}^* - X_t' + i(1 - m_1') D_{t-1} + (m_0' + m_1' Q_0). \qquad (2.19)
\end{aligned}
$$

It is assumed that net factor payments abroad are related to the total debt outstanding at the end of the previous period. Equation (2.19) states that the higher these payments abroad, the lower will be the required net capital inflow for a given planned growth rate in GDP (assuming also a given level of exports). This is because higher net factor payments imply a lower level of GNP (to which imports are related) for a given planned level of GDP.

If the net capital inflow is fixed, the growth rate in GDP will be:

$$\bar{r}^* = \frac{1}{t Q_0}\left(\frac{F_t + X_t - (m_0' + m_1' Q_0)}{m_1'} + iD_{t-1}\right), \qquad (2.20)$$

which is derived directly from (2.19). Combining (2.18) and (2.19), we have:

$$r^* = \frac{1}{t Y_0}\left(\frac{F_t + X_t - (m_0' + m_1' Q_0)}{m_1'} + i\left[D_0 - \sum_0^{t-1} F(t-1)\right]\right). \qquad (2.21)$$

The corresponding rates of growth during the savings-constrained phase can be derived in a similar way, by combining (2.6a) and (2.18) with the previous set of equations.

(c) Changes in the terms of trade

In the final year of a plan, the balance of payments must be projected as balancing in the estimated prices of that year, rather than in the prices of the year in which the plan is being made. In other words, balance must be sought in terms of current prices, not at constant prices (or 'real' terms). To allow for this the export variable X' can be re-written pX' in (2.19), (2.20) and (2.21), where p represents export prices in terms of import prices as *numéraire*. In this way, it would be possible to estimate net capital inflow requirements on alternative assumptions about rates of export growth and terms of trade.

3. A COMPUTABLE *EX POST* GROWTH MODEL

Assume, as before, that investment and GDP are related via an incremental capital–output ratio; but that Q can be regarded as the dependent variable:

$$Q_t = I_t/\sigma r. \tag{2.22}$$

Since these are *ex post* values, not planned or expected values, no asterisks are used here. Assume, too, that both exports and the net capital inflow are exogenously determined, and that these together determine the level of imports.

$$M_t = X_t + F_t, \tag{2.23}$$

abstracting, for the moment, from changes in the terms of trade, and including net factor payments and receipts in the import and export totals, respectively. Imports of capital goods (including intermediate products for the capital goods industries), M^I, are assumed to vary with the capacity to import:

$$M_t^I = a_1 + b_1(X_{t-1} + F_{t-1}), \tag{2.24}$$

given a year's lag between the two. Imports of consumer goods (including intermediate products for consumer goods industries) are then determined as a residual:

$$
\begin{aligned}
M_t^c &= M_t - M_t^I \\
&= (X_t + F_t) - b_1(X_{t-1} + F_{t-1}) - a_1.
\end{aligned}
\tag{2.25}
$$

Domestic investment is assumed to be determined by the volume of imports of capital goods, as follows:

$$
\begin{aligned}
I_t &= a_2 + b_2 M_t^I \\
&= (a_2 + a_1 b_2) + b_1 b_2(X_{t-1} + F_{t-1}),
\end{aligned}
\tag{2.26}
$$

so that

$$Q_t = \frac{1}{\sigma r}\left((a_2 + a_1 b_2) + b_1 b_2(X_{t-1} + F_{t-1})\right). \tag{2.27}$$

From (2.27), the relationship between the growth rate of GDP (r) and that of exports (ϵ) can be derived:

$$r(1 + rt) = \left(\frac{b_1 b_2(t-1)}{\sigma} \cdot \frac{X_0}{Q_0}\right)\epsilon + \left(\frac{a_2 + a_1 b_2 + b_1 b_2(X_0 + F_{t-1})}{\sigma Q_0}\right), \tag{2.28}$$

assuming the approximation (2.10) is valid.

This quadratic equation implies a diminishing rate of growth in GDP for given percentage increases in exports, assuming a fixed level of F.

Ex post savings are assumed to adjust to the difference between investment and the net capital inflow:

$$S_t = (\sigma t Q_0) r^2 + (\sigma Q_0) r - F_t. \tag{2.29}$$

On the other hand, had the past observed relationship between domestic savings, exports and income in the non-export sector been assumed to hold for the future also, the expected level of savings in year t would be:

$$S'_t = s'_0 + s'_1(Q_t - X_t) + s'_2 X_t$$
$$= s'_0 + s'_1 Q_t + (s'_2 - s'_1) X_t. \tag{2.16b}$$

Combining this with (2.10), (2.11) and (2.26), (2.16b) can be written:

$$S'_t = \left(Q_0(s'_2 - s'_1) \frac{\sigma t}{b_1 b_2} \right) r^2 + \left(Q_0 \left[s'_1 t + (s'_2 - s'_1) \frac{\sigma}{b_1 b_2} \right] \right) r$$
$$- \left\{ (s'_2 - s'_1) \left(F_t + \frac{a_2 + a_1 b_2}{b_1 b_2} \right) - (s'_1 Q_0 + s'_0) \right\}. \tag{2.30}$$

This again is a quadratic, implying that savings rise at an increasing rate as r increases. Whether S'_t will rise at a faster rate than S_t depends mainly on whether $(s'_2 - s'_1)$ is greater than $b_1 b_2$; if not, the coefficient of r^2 will be lower in S'_t, which would then rise at a slower rate than S_t, especially at relatively high values of r. In the latter case, the required level of savings, S_t, would exceed the savings level that would emerge from the continuation of past relationships, and growth would enter the 'savings-constrained' phase described in the Chenery *ex ante* model. If S'_t exceeds S_t, then there will be some frustrated savings.

If the rate of export growth is given, the *ex post* model can also be used to determine the amount of net capital inflow that would be consistent with any target rate of growth of GDP. If the target growth rate is $\bar{r}^*$, then the required net capital inflow, F_t, can be derived from equation (2.27) as:[1]

$$F_t = \left(\frac{\sigma Q_0 . t + 1}{b_1 b_2} \right) \bar{r}^{*2} + \left(\frac{\sigma Q_0}{b_1 b_2} \right) \bar{r}^* - \left(X_t + \frac{a_2 + a_1 b_2}{b_1 b_2} \right). \tag{2.31}$$

Appropriate adjustments can be made to this equation, if required, to allow for net factor payments abroad and for possible changes in the terms of trade.

---

[1] Cf. equation (2.14) which defines the required net capital inflow in the trade-constrained phase of growth on the Chenery–Strout model.

CHAPTER 3

THE STRUCTURAL PARAMETERS OF ECONOMIC GROWTH

I. SOME STATISTICAL LIMITATIONS

In this chapter the statistical evidence of economic growth in the period from 1950 to the early 1960s is analysed, on the basis of the simple *ex post* model outlined towards the end of Chapter 2, for as many of the overseas Sterling countries as possible. Though the model as described strictly applies only to under-developed countries, mainly because these are heavily dependent on imports for their supplies of capital goods, it seemed useful to derive corresponding parameters for the more developed Sterling countries, so that the results of the statistical analyses for the less developed countries can be interpreted against a wider background. For all the Sterling countries covered by the analysis, the statistical material used consists of the annual national accounts of the different countries, supplemented as necessary from their official balance of payments statistics.

One major gap in the availability of continuous statistical series arises from changes in national (or statistical) boundaries over this period. Such boundary changes make regression analyses of time series virtually impossible for Malaysia (previously the Federation of Malaya, Sarawak and Sabah, and, earlier still, Malaya, Sarawak and North Borneo), and for the former member countries of the Federation of Rhodesia and of British East Africa. For Malawi, Rhodesia and Zambia (the former members of the Rhodesian Federation), however, separate national accounts, but not separate balance of payments statistics, are now available annually back to 1954, so that some separate analyses for these three countries are possible.

A second major gap arises purely from the lack of adequate statistics. The difficulties of compiling reliable statistics of the national accounts, or even of the main economic sectors separately, particularly in the less developed countries, have already been touched upon in Chapter 1. This, in itself, would not explain the relatively sophisticated set of national accounts available for some of the less developed Sterling countries, such as Malawi, Jamaica and Zambia, while for others— notably Hong Kong and the Persian Gulf sheikhdoms—no statistics on these lines are available at all. Moreover, between the two extremes are a number of important countries, particularly Nigeria, for which the available national accounts data are too scrappy or unreliable to be of any use for the type of analyses envisaged here.[1]

Finally, of those countries which do publish regular and adequate national accounts statistics, some do, and others do not, provide the main component series both at current and at constant prices. The conversion of current- to constant-price series is inevitably a somewhat involved and difficult process, as was pointed out earlier.[2] Yet the availability of constant-price data is an essential pre-requisite for a meaningful statistical analysis, since the inclusion of price changes in the variables must be expected to give spuriously high correlations as well as to distort the magnitudes of the 'real' parameters.

Of the twenty-two countries of the Overseas Sterling Area for which some detailed national accounts data are given in the United Nations *Yearbook of National Accounts Statistics*, which is the major source used here, only eleven give the main components of national product or national expenditure both at current prices and revalued at the prices of a single year.[3] However, a number of the remainder are relatively very small countries, including Barbados, Cyprus, Malta and Mauritius, and these are in any case excluded from the country projections presented in Part II. For South Africa and Trinidad, independent estimates of changes in national product or national expenditure are, fortunately, available from academic sources.[4] This still leaves a number of important overseas Sterling countries for which adequate constant-price series are not yet available, and which have perforce to be omitted from the present analyses: these countries include Guyana, Ghana, Kenya, New Zealand, Tanzania and Uganda.

As a result of these various inadequacies, lacunae or discontinuities in the basic statistical material, the derivation of the structural parameters of the model can be attempted only for about ten or twelve Sterling countries; moreover, the countries included vary somewhat according to the parameter being estimated.[5] Nonetheless, the coverage is wide enough for some useful results to be derived for use in the projections of gross product in Chapter 8. The simple *ex post* model set out

---

[1] There seems little doubt that the efficiency of the official statistical collection, analysis and presentation of economic data needs drastic improvement in a number of the less developed Sterling countries.

[2] See p. 40.

[3] This relates to the 1963 issue of the *Yearbook*.

[4] G. J. Hupkes and M. van den Berg, *A Survey of Contemporary Economic Conditions and Prospects for 1962*, Bureau for Economic Research, University of Stellenbosch, 1961; Frank Rampersad, *Growth and Structural Change in the Economy of Trinidad and Tobago, 1951–1961*, Institute of Social and Economic Research, University of the West Indies, Jamaica, 1964.

[5] The implication of this is that the economic development plans of those countries which do not yet possess adequate statistical data on a national accounts basis necessarily contain a wide margin of error as regards the underlying structural relationships, whether these are explicitly stated or only implied.

in Chapter 2 was based on the hypothesis that fixed capital investment is the dynamic element in economic growth and that, in primary-exporting countries, the level of investment is largely determined by the capacity to import. In the following sections, the relationships between investment and gross product and between investment and the capacity to import are examined in more detail for individual overseas Sterling countries.

2. THE RELATIONSHIP BETWEEN INVESTMENT AND GROSS PRODUCT

There is considerable variation among the different Sterling countries in the proportion of their gross product devoted to capital formation. Gross investment in fixed capital during the early 1960s ranged from only 10 per cent of gross domestic product in Uganda to over 20 per cent in Australia, New Zealand, Iceland and Trinidad (see Table 3.1). For the majority of the less developed Sterling countries, the proportion was between 14 and 20 per cent, which is not very different from the corresponding proportions for many European countries. This is essentially a new situation, since before the inauguration of economic planning in most of these countries during the 1950s, the investment proportion in the less developed Sterling countries was generally appreciably lower than now.

On the other hand, the attainment of an investment proportion as high as 15–20 per cent of gross product in a low-income country does not have the same meaning as it would have in a developed country of Western Europe. For one thing, the proportion of investment which has to be devoted to building up the economic infrastructure of roads, harbours, hospitals, schools and so on is inevitably far higher in countries at a relatively early stage of economic development. The major difference, however, is that the lower real income in these countries means that the absolute volume of investment resources available per head of the population is much smaller than in the developed countries, even though the investment proportion is similar. As Table 3.1 shows, gross fixed capital formation per head in 1960–2 was under £5 per annum in almost all the less developed Sterling countries in Asia and Africa, compared with over £100 per head per annum in Australia, New Zealand and Iceland. Jamaica and Trinidad, among the less developed countries, are in an intermediate position as a result of large investments from abroad in bauxite mining (Jamaica) and in the petroleum industry (Trinidad). The intermediate position of South Africa is largely a reflection of the peculiar dual economy, with relatively large and depressed African communities, in that country;

Table 3.1. *Gross capital formation in selected overseas Sterling countries, 1960–2*

	As proportion of GDP			Fixed capital formation	
	Fixed capital formation	Stocks	Total	Total	Per head
	(%)	(%)	(%)	(£ million)	(£)
MORE DEVELOPED COUNTRIES					
Australia	24·2	1·3	25·5	1,356	129
New Zealand	22·4	1·2	23·6	311	128
South Africa	18·8	0·6	19·4	549	34
Iceland	25·9	0·1	26·0	21	116
Ireland	15·1	1·2	16·3	104	37
LESS DEVELOPED COUNTRIES					
Burma	15·3	1·4	16·7	72	3
Ceylon	14·2	−0·1	14·1	71	7
Malaya	13·6	1·7	15·3	97	14
India[a]	17·3	1·7	19·0	1,966	5
Ghana	19·7	−0·6	19·1	99	14
Kenya	15·4	··	15·4	36	4
Rhodesia/Nyasaland	19·6	2·2	21·8	104	10
Malawi	15·2	2·1	17·3	7	2
Rhodesia	19·4	1·4	20·8	59	16
Zambia	18·2	4·7	22·9	38	12
Tanganyika	15·1	··	15·1	31	3
Uganda	10·4	··	10·4	16	2
Jamaica	19·3	1·3	20·6	50	30
Trinidad and Tobago	27·6	0·6	28·2	57	66

SOURCES: *Yearbook of National Accounts Statistics, 1963*, United Nations, New York, 1964; *Economic Survey of Asia and the Far East, 1963*, Economic Commission for Asia and the Far East, Bangkok, 1964; national statistics.

[a] 1960–1.

that of Ireland reflects the relatively low investment proportion for a developed country, as well as the relatively high contribution of agriculture in the Irish economy.[1] Fig. 3.1, which gives the relationship between the proportion of gross fixed capital formation in GDP and the value of fixed capital investment per head of population, clearly shows the great differences between the various groups of countries in this respect.

Investment in stocks generally represents only 1 or 2 per cent of gross domestic product (GDP) in these countries though, of course, there is considerable year-to-year fluctuation. Zambia is exceptional in having

[1] See Table 1.4.

a stock accumulation representing almost 5 per cent of gross domestic product in 1960–2, as a result of the expanding operations of the copper refineries.

To some considerable extent, the variation in fixed capital formation per head reflects the different sectoral patterns of growth in the different countries. Statistical information on the distribution of capital formation

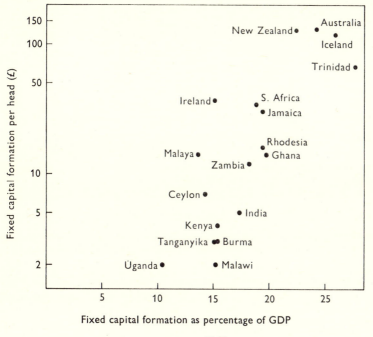

SOURCE: Table 3.1.

Fig. 3.1. Relationship between investment ratio and investment per head, 1960–2 (semi-logarithmic scale).

by sector is available in comparable form for only seven countries, four of which are in the less developed group (see Table 3.2). Within the latter group, there is considerable diversity of experience, since capital investment tends to be fairly closely related to natural resource endowments. In Trinidad, for example, over one-third of all gross fixed capital formation in 1960–2 was in the mining and quarrying sector (petroleum and asphalt), while the same sector (copper) took almost one-fifth of the total in the former Federation of Rhodesia and Nyasaland. The full sectoral detail is not available for Jamaica, but it would seem that fixed investment in that country was relatively heavy in the services sector

Table 3.2. *Distribution of fixed capital formation by sector in selected overseas Sterling countries, 1960–2 (percentages)*

	More developed			Less developed			
	Australia[a]	Iceland	Ireland[b]	Rhodesia/ Nyasaland	Tanzania	Jamaica	Trinidad
Agriculture, forestry, fishing	12	20	20	11	10	10	2
Mining and quarrying	1 }	12	{ 3	18	3	3	36
Manufacturing	16 }		{ 19	8	7	11	
Construction	2	2	2	1	5	..[c]	
Electricity, gas and water	11	8	6	12	3	4	
Transportation, storage and communication	18	23	17	15	18	..[c]	62
Dwellings	19	23	13	12	27	16	
Other services	21	13	22	22	28	56	
TOTAL	100	100	100	100	100	100	100

SOURCE: *Yearbook of National Accounts Statistics, 1963*, United Nations, New York, 1964.

[a] 1960–1. [b] 1960. [c] Included in 'other services'.

(which includes an important tourist industry) and in manufacturing.[1] In the more developed countries, the proportion of total fixed capital formation devoted to the manufacturing sector is generally higher than in the less developed areas, but otherwise the sectoral patterns are not substantially different after allowance is made for investments in resource-based industries.

The distribution of investment by sector is, however, only an indistinct guide to the pattern of economic growth of the different economies because the relationship between investment and the increment in output (i.e. the incremental capital–output ratio, or ICOR) is likely to differ considerably from one sector to another. This is not only because the effectiveness with which new capital is used varies from one use to another, but also because new investment is not necessarily an essential element in any given expansion in output. Output can also be increased by taking up existing unused capacity, or by improving the productivity of the existing capital already being utilized by applying better techniques or by improving the supply of complementary skills.[2]

Thus the relationship between investment and the growth of output

[1] In the mid 1950s, there was heavy capital investment in the Jamaican bauxite industry.
[2] Consideration of the more fundamental social and institutional barriers to the widespread adoption of better techniques, or the improved supply of skills, falls outside the scope of the present discussion.

is, to some extent, a tenuous one, as was pointed out in Chapter 2. Nonetheless, the concept of the ICOR is a useful one, both by sectors and for the economy as a whole, provided its limitations are kept in mind, or assumed to be a constant of economic growth. The overall ICOR, for the economy as a whole, can be measured for twelve overseas Sterling countries over the past decade or so; Table 3.3 summarizes the results of the relevant regression equations.[1] This method of calculation gives the average ICOR over the period as a whole; for every country, though, there have been large year-to-year fluctuations in the value of the ICOR.

The results show a large inter-country variation in ICORs. Among the four more developed countries, the highest ICOR, for Australia, exceeds the lowest (for South Africa) by about 60 per cent; among the less developed countries, the ICOR achieved for Rhodesia, the highest, was virtually double that for Jamaica, the lowest; but six of the eight countries had ICORs between 3·0 and 5·0.

Since the ICOR is the resultant expression of the relationship between investment and economic growth, it is also possible to express the rate of economic growth as the ratio of the investment ratio (i.e. the proportion of fixed investment to GDP) to the ICOR. The relationship is algebraically precise, though subject to the qualifications of interpretation already mentioned. In this sense, it is possible to increase the rate of economic growth either by raising the investment ratio or by reducing the ICOR. The average relationship between the two over the decade up to the early 1960s is depicted in Fig. 3.2 for the countries for which the ICOR can be computed. Of the twelve countries included, eight had rates of growth averaging between 3 and 5 per cent per annum and, of these, the countries investing relatively high proportions of GDP in fixed capital assets generally found that this was offset by higher ICORs. Thus, Ceylon achieved much the same average growth rate as Australia as a result of combining a lower ICOR with a lower investment ratio. Ireland had a relatively high ICOR for its investment ratio of 15 per cent, whereas the ICORs achieved by both Jamaica and Trinidad were exceptionally low, especially in view of their high investment ratios.

For a single country, with a fairly settled pattern of investment, continued increases in the investment ratio are likely, after a certain point

---

[1] The equations were of the form:

$$Q_t = A + \frac{1}{\sigma} \cdot \sum_{0}^{t-1} I_t,$$

where Q = gross domestic product and I = gross domestic fixed capital formation, both measured at the constant prices of the same year, A = a constant and σ = the incremental gross capital–output ratio. The equation assumes an average one-year time lag between new investment and the associated increase in output.

Table 3.3. *Estimates of the gross incremental capital–output ratio for selected overseas Sterling countries, 1950–62[a]*

	Period	Gross incremental capital–output ratio	R^2
MORE DEVELOPED COUNTRIES			
Australia	1953–62	6·49 (0·31)	0·980
South Africa	1951–60	4·05 (0·16)	0·985
Iceland	1950–61	4·69 (0·36)	0·929
Ireland	1950–61	5·80 (0·66)	0·861
LESS DEVELOPED COUNTRIES			
Burma	1950–60	3·83 (0·28)	0·948
Ceylon	1951–61	3·39 (0·26)	0·940
India	1950–60	4·69 (0.24)	0·977
Rhodesia/Nyasaland	1954–61	4·82 (0·34)	0·964
Malawi	1954–62	4·97 (0·54)	0·907
Rhodesia	1954–62	5·30 (0·35)	0·966
Zambia	1954–62	4·25 (0·49)	0·894
Jamaica	1953–60	3·01 (0·66)	0·955
Trinidad and Tobago	1951–60	2·93 (0·15)	0·978

SOURCES: *Yearbook of National Accounts Statistics*, United Nations, New York; national statistics.

[a] Based on regressions of annual data (see text).

is reached, to yield diminishing increments of output, either because limitations of absorptive capacity of the economy come into play, or because it becomes progressively more difficult to find relatively profitable outlets for new investment. To some extent, too, this factor may be operating between countries, the relatively high ICOR for Australia, compared with Ceylon, for example, being associated in part with the relatively much higher Australian investment ratio. However, the different ICORs of the different countries also reflect a number of other factors, among which differences in the sectoral pattern of growth are of some importance. The overall ICOR for an economy can be defined as the weighted average of the ICORs for the individual sectors, the weights being the increments in sector outputs over the period concerned. Thus, assuming that the sector ICORs were the same in all countries, the overall ICORs would reflect the country differences in the pattern of output expansion. This assumption is not, however, generally valid and quite large differences appear to exist in the ICORs for the same sector as between different countries; the same is no doubt true for individual countries, where the sectoral ICORs could also show appreciable variations over a period of time.

Nonetheless, some broad generalizations can be made. For most countries, the ICOR is generally relatively small for some sectors, notably for agriculture (unless large irrigation schemes or other land works are in progress); this is mainly because an increased yield of crops or increased output of animal products is as likely to result from improved farm practices as from the increased use of farm implements and

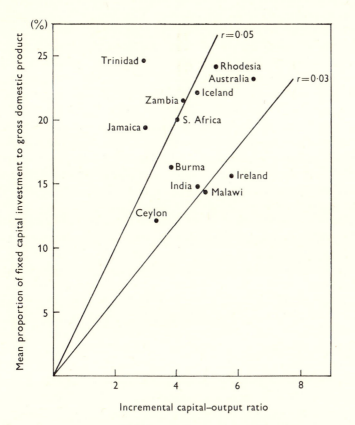

SOURCES: Table 3.3, and regression working sheets.

Fig. 3.2. Relation between investment proportion of GDP and the ICOR, 1950–4 to 1959–62 (r=rate of growth in GDP).

machinery. At the other extreme are housing, transportation, electricity, gas and water supply, and petroleum, all of which are relatively capital-intensive.

Statistical information on the sectoral pattern of the expansion in the volume of GDP since the mid 1950s is available in reasonably comparable form for only a limited number of Sterling countries (see

Table 3.4).[1] Two features appear to emerge from these data. First, for several countries the expansion in output was concentrated in only two or three sectors which, together, effectively determined the overall ICOR; in Burma, for example, these sectors were agriculture and miscellaneous services (which include government and the armed forces, as well as industry), while in Nigeria they were agriculture, construction and transportation. The second feature, more generally applicable, is the great diversity of experience in the pattern of sectoral growth. Jamaica and Trinidad are, to a large extent, exceptional in that the agricultural sector played a very minor role in the expansion of their gross products over the period shown. The relatively low ICOR achieved by Jamaica appears to have been partly due to the productivity of investment in bauxite mining, and partly to that of the tourist industry. For Trinidad, a recent analysis gave the sectoral ICORs as 1·25 for agriculture, 2·1 for manufacturing (other than sugar), 3·6 for sugar, 4·2 for oil and asphalt and 2·6 for the rest of the private sector,[2] the weighted mean, 3·1, being mainly a reflection of developments in petroleum and miscellaneous services.[3] Nigeria is probably more typical of many tropical under-developed countries, almost half the total increase estimated in Nigerian GDP from 1951–2 to 1956–7 (the last period for which this series is available) being contributed by agriculture. This would imply that over this period the overall ICOR for Nigeria was relatively low; however, the more recent developments in the petroleum industry have almost certainly increased the overall ICOR appreciably.

In the South-East Asian countries the rate of growth has been very uneven from year to year, reflecting either climatic variations affecting crop output or physical bottlenecks in transport or materials (in turn the result of inadequate planning or lack of external finance for needed imports), or other inappropriate policy measures. In addition, a substantial proportion of investment, particularly in the public sector, has perforce been devoted to building up the basic social services—particularly health and education—and the economic infrastructure, such as transport, all of which inevitably have long gestation periods. These various factors have tended to raise the overall ICORs of these countries over the past decade, but should allow them to grow at a faster rate in some future period. Apart from these general factors, there have been

---

[1] A number of other Sterling countries publish sectoral output figures in terms of current prices, but these could be misleading in the present context because it cannot be assumed that sector output prices have moved in a uniform way. This is another area in which more detailed and reliable statistical information is urgently needed.

[2] Rampersad, *op. cit.*

[3] The difference between this result and the overall ICOR of 2·93 shown in Table 3.3 for Trinidad arises from differences in the method of calculation.

Table 3.4. *Distribution of the increase in gross domestic product by sector in certain less developed Sterling countries, 1953–5 to 1960–2 (percentages[a])*

	Burma	India	Pakistan	Nigeria[b]	Jamaica[c]	Trinidad and Tobago
Agriculture, forestry, fishing	27	30	26	48	4	7
Mining and quarrying	5		2	1	16	34
Manufacturing	..[d]	} 18	34	7	15	12
Construction	..[d]		..[d]	14	15	7
Electricity, gas and water	3		..[e]	..[e]	1	} 40
Transportation, storage and communication	1		7	28	6	
Dwellings	3	} 52	4	1	0	
Other services	62		29	1	43	
TOTAL	100	100[f]	100[f]	100	100	100

SOURCES: *Yearbook of National Accounts Statistics*, United Nations, New York; Rampersad, *op. cit.*

[a] In terms of constant prices.   [b] 1951–2 to 1956–7.
[c] 1953–5 to 1960.   [d] Included in 'other services'.
[e] Included in 'manufacturing'.   [f] Net domestic product.

features peculiar to particular countries, such as the economic dislocation in Burma in the early 1950s caused by a virtual civil war, with its prolonged aftermath of shortages and bottlenecks in communications, and the difficulties encountered in both India and Pakistan in increasing food production to meet the expansion in home requirements, which have themselves held back the development in other sectors also.

In the face of such diversities, the surprising thing is, perhaps, that the overall ICORs for the less developed Sterling countries of South-East Asia and Africa are as close to each other as appears from Fig. 3.2. This presumably reflects the operation of a number of offsetting factors within each country. To the extent that such offsetting is likely to operate in the future also, some stability in the overall ICORs may be assumed; but, in view of the many structural and other factors involved, all of which are likely to be in process of change, it would be unwise to assume that the various ICORs will, in fact, remain constant. The problem of making reasonable assumptions for the future relation between investment and economic growth is discussed further in Chapter 8.

3. THE RELATIONSHIP BETWEEN INVESTMENT
AND THE CAPACITY TO IMPORT

The simple *ex post* model presented in Chapter 2 postulated a relationship between the level of fixed capital formation and the capacity to import.[1] This relationship is assumed to operate through two separate sub-relationships: imports of capital goods are assumed to depend on the capacity to import, while the level of investment in fixed capital is taken as dependent on the volume of capital goods imported. Before investigating these relationships over time, it is useful to consider the inter-country variation. Table 3.5 shows imports of capital goods, and materials for capital goods,[2] as a proportion of total imports and of gross domestic fixed capital formation in 1960–2. Since, in the long run, the capacity to import can be expected to approximate to total imports, the use of the latter should be some indication of the inter-country variation in the relationship between capital goods imports and the capacity to import.

Though virtually all the Sterling countries have instituted measures at one time or another over the past decade to increase the share of 'development goods' in total imports, there is nevertheless a wide range in the country percentages. However, of the nineteen countries shown, nine had proportions of capital goods and materials to total imports within the range of 25 to 35 per cent, while the proportions for a further six countries were between 35 and 50 per cent. For four countries— India, Pakistan, Guyana and Jamaica—the capital goods proportion exceeded 50 per cent. These differences are partly a reflection of the different economic structures of the various countries; some countries are much more heavily dependent on imports of food or fuel than others, for example. The import proportions also reflect, to some extent, the differing impact of government policies in restricting imports of consumer goods and of other 'less essential' imports.

Comparable figures for the 1950s are not very readily available, mainly because of classification changes in the published statistics.[3] However, reasonably comparable data can be derived for the period 1953–5 for sixteen of the nineteen countries listed in Table 3.5. Of these, nine showed changes of less than five percentage points in the

---

[1] See also annexe to Chapter 2, Section 3, p. 71.

[2] For this purpose, 'capital goods' were defined as machinery and transport equipment (less passenger road vehicles), metal manufactures and scientific instruments; 'materials for capital goods' were defined as timber, stone, metalliferous ores, metals and non-metallic mineral manufactures.

[3] This applies particularly to the statistics published by the United Nations. Separate series for imports of capital goods could, no doubt, be constructed from the detailed national trade returns.

Table 3.5. *Imports of capital goods and materials for capital goods in relation to total imports and gross domestic fixed capital formation, 1960–2 (percentages)*

	As proportion of total imports			As proportion of GDFCF[a]		
	Capital goods	Materials	Total	Capital goods	Materials	Total
MORE DEVELOPED COUNTRIES						
Australia	26	8	34	16	5	21
New Zealand	31	14	45	30	14	44
South Africa	29	8	37	31	8	39
Iceland	34	12	46	44	15	59
Ireland	20	8	28	50	19	69
LESS DEVELOPED COUNTRIES						
Burma	31	10	41	36	11	47
Ceylon	20	9	29	38	17	55
Malaya	18	13	31	47[b]	30[b]	77[b]
India	43	9	52	17[c]	4[c]	21[c]
Pakistan	44	16	60	..	..	..
Ghana	24	8	32	32	11	43
Kenya[d]	25	8	33	65[e]	17	82
Nigeria	24	9	33	..	..	..
Rhodesia/Nyasaland	33	9	42	45	12	57
Tanzania[d]	24	9	33	30	11	41
Uganda[d]	22	7	29	38	11	49
Guyana	28[b]	7[b]	35[b]	49[c]	11[c]	60[c]
Jamaica	25	9	34	40[b]	14[b]	57[b]
Trinidad and Tobago	15	6	21	32	13	45

SOURCES: *Yearbook of International Trade Statistics, 1963* and *Yearbook of National Accounts Statistics, 1963*, United Nations, New York, 1964; *Economic Survey of Asia and the Far East, 1963*, E.C.A.F.E., Bangkok, 1964.

[a] Gross domestic fixed capital formation.   [b] 1960–1.   [c] 1960.   [d] 1961–2.
[e] Including imports of passenger road vehicles (which are included in the figures for gross fixed capital formation).

proportion of capital goods, including materials, in total imports, comparing 1953–5 with 1960–2;[1] the remaining seven countries showed changes of between five and ten percentage points.[2] The majority of the changes in the proportions of capital goods in total imports were upwards over the period in these fourteen countries, indicating a generally increasing dependence on capital goods imports for their investment programmes.

[1] Australia, Iceland, Ireland, New Zealand, Ceylon, Pakistan, Nigeria, former Federation of Rhodesia and Nyasaland, and Jamaica.
[2] Kenya, Tanzania, Uganda, Ghana, Burma, India and Guyana.

The import content of fixed capital investment also varies widely from one country to another (right-hand side of Table 3.5). To some extent, the variation may be due to statistical reasons (since imports of capital goods or materials in any period are not necessarily incorporated in investment during the same period), or to government policies, such as discriminatory import restrictions, which may result in higher relative prices for capital goods in some countries than in others. Nonetheless, the range in the import-content percentages is far too large to be accounted for in this way; for Malaya and Kenya, for example, the import content was in the region of 80 per cent in 1960–2, compared with only some 20 per cent for Australia and India. The latter are the only 'large' countries in the Overseas Sterling Area in terms of the quantum of fixed capital investment,[1] and both have developed their domestic capital goods industries. Insofar as the import content of investment reflects the stage of industrial development reached, as well as size,[2] it cannot be expected to change very rapidly, or by any appreciable extent within a relatively short period such as a decade. Indeed, for the majority (seven out of eleven) of the countries for which reasonably comparable data are available for 1953–5, the import content proportions in that period differed by less than five percentage points from those shown in Table 3.5 for 1960–2.[3]

Analysis of time series

A more rigorous examination of the interrelations between the capacity to import, imports of capital goods and the level of investment in fixed capital assets can be made by a regression analysis of the relevant annual data for the various overseas Sterling countries. As was pointed out earlier, the available data are limited in scope, as well as in reliability, and reasonably valid results can be expected for only a limited number of countries. Since it was essential to use values in constant prices, for some countries these were obtained on an approximate basis by applying the most relevant price series available.[4] Such estimates add a further element of error to the basic data, and thus to the regression results, but it is not thought that the latter have been unduly distorted for this reason.

[1] Together they accounted for probably about 60 per cent of all gross fixed capital investment in the Overseas Sterling Area (excluding the Persian Gulf sheikhdoms) in 1960–2 (see Table 3.1).

[2] For a statistical demonstration of this relationship, see A. Maizels, *Industrial Growth and World Trade*, Cambridge, 1963, p. 268. The relationship is also revealed in the statistical analysis by Professor H. B. Chenery ('Patterns of Industrial Growth', cited on p. 41 above).

[3] These comparisons inevitably contain a fair margin of error, for the reasons mentioned in the text.

[4] If no relevant price series were available in published sources, estimates at constant prices were not attempted.

The two sub-relationships—imports of capital goods as a function of the capacity to import, and investment in fixed capital as a function of imports of capital goods—have been tested for only two countries, Australia and India. The difficulty here was the construction of a reliable and consistent annual series for the volume of imports of capital goods, including materials for incorporation in capital goods. The Australian statistical authorities publish a monthly analysis of Australian imports by end-use,[1] distinguishing, *inter alia*, capital equipment (essentially machinery and plant, and transport equipment) and producers' materials. These two groups were added together, after deducting an allowance for producers' materials used in consumer goods industries,[2] and the total value was then deflated by the implicit price index for fixed capital formation in the Australian national accounts. For India, an annual analysis of imports by end-use is published by the Economic Commission for Asia and the Far East (E.C.A.F.E.) in their *Annual Survey*. The totals for Indian imports of 'capital goods' and 'materials chiefly for capital goods' were then deflated by the implicit price index for Indian net domestic product; the lack of a more appropriate price deflator for fixed capital investment in India undoubtedly adds to the margin of error in the calculation.

For these regressions, the 'capacity to import' was defined as the total value of exports of goods and services, net factor payments abroad and net inflow of long-term capital on private and official account, deflated by the import price index. On this definition, the capacity to import excludes all the short-term capital flows and short-term monetary movements, whether private or official (including changes in the monetary reserves). The rationale of this procedure is that we are concerned essentially with the longer-term trends in exports and capital flows as influences on the trend rate of economic growth; the short-term fluctuations can reasonably be expected to cancel themselves out over a period of years, so would not be a significant influence on the longer-term relationship.

However, the short-term capital and monetary movements do influence the changes in the volume of imports, if only because any gap between the cost of imports and the export of goods and services plus the long-term capital inflow is necessarily met by an increase in short-term credits from abroad. To make some allowance for the influence of such short-term factors, the regressions were extended to include the

[1] See *Monthly Review of Business Statistics*, Commonwealth Bureau of Census and Statistics, Canberra.

[2] A more detailed analysis of Australian imports in 1960–2 showed that about two-thirds of the imports classified as "producers' materials for use in manufacturing (other than in motor vehicle assembly)" consisted of materials normally used by the consumer goods industries, and this proportion was deducted from the total for this category for each year.

level of monetary reserves at the beginning of the year. To the extent that short-term import policy in many countries is based on the maintenance of the monetary reserves above some minimum level, any decline in the reserves would result in a more restrictive import policy in the immediate period ahead. On the other hand, such a decline could be offset by short-term borrowing abroad, thus obviating the need for policy changes. In either case, changes in the reserves should be a good indicator of part, at least, of the short-term influences on actual imports.

The regression results for Australia and India are given in Tables 3.6 and 3.7. Taking first the relationship between the volume of capital goods imports (M_c) and the capacity to import (Z), the simple regression of M_{ct} on Z_{t-1} explained only about one-half the variance in M_c over the decade or so covered for both countries. The introduction of changes in the monetary reserves (R) improved the regression significantly for Australia, but not for India; for the latter country, neither coefficient in the second regression differed significantly from zero. The addition of the capacity to import without a time lag (Z_t) did not add much to the explanation of changes in capital goods imports; for India, once again, none of the regression coefficients differed significantly from zero, so that only the first regression for that country could be regarded as acceptable (and even that, as already mentioned, explained only half the variance in M_c). For both countries, the coefficient of Z_{t-1} was reasonably stable, showing little or no change, comparing the first with the second regression; over the period covered by the calculations, imports of capital goods rose on average by about one-third (Australia) or one-half (India) of a given expansion in the capacity to import. The relatively poor regression results for India, compared with those for Australia, would seem to be largely due to the recurrent food shortages suffered by India and the need for heavy imports of grain in certain years.

Turning now to the second sub-relationship, that between gross domestic fixed capital formation (I) and imports of capital goods and materials (M_c), Table 3.7 shows the results of three alternative regression equations for the two illustrative countries.

The unlagged regression of I on M_c produced a satisfactory fit to the data for India, the equation explaining almost 90 per cent of the variance in I. Though the value of R^2 rose slightly on the addition of a one-year lag in M_c, the coefficient of the lagged variable was not significantly different from zero. The introduction of an exponential distributed lag (regression 3)[1] also increased the goodness of fit of the

---

[1] The assumptions here are, first, that for each level of imports of capital goods there is some equilibrium level of fixed capital investment, I^*, such that:

$$I_t^* = \alpha + \beta M_t; \tag{3.1}$$

Table 3.6. *Results of regressions[a] of imports of capital goods on the capacity to import and the level of monetary reserves: Australia and India, 1951–62*

| | Regression | Coefficient of | | | R^2 |
		Z_t	Z_{t-1}	R_{t-1}	
Australia (1953–62)	1	—	0·37 (0·12)	—	0·493
	2	—	0·34 (0·10)	0·44 (0·13)	0·736
	3	0·14 (0·10)	0·22 (0·13)	0·44 (0·12)	0·804
India (1951–61)	1	—	0·50 (0.22)	—	0·462
	2	—	0·51 (0·35)	0·01 (0·18)	0·463
	3	−0·43 (0·62)	0·65 (0·42)	−0·10 (0·25)	0·519

SOURCES: *Yearbook of National Accounts Statistics, 1963*, United Nations, New York, 1964; *Balance of Payments Yearbook, vol. 15, 1958–62*, I.M.F., Washington, 1964.

[a] Linear regressions of the form: $M_{c_t} = a + b_1 Z_t + b_2 Z_{t-1} + cR_{t-1}$ were used, where $M_c =$ imports of capital goods (including materials for capital goods), $Z =$ capacity to import, and $R =$ level of monetary reserves at the end of the year, all values expressed in constant prices of the same year.

regression, but only to a small extent compared with the first, unlagged, regression. The distributed lag regression would indicate that there was no significant short-term reaction of gross fixed investment in India to variations in capital goods imports, the effects of such variations being essentially spread over a number of years.[1]

For Australia, by contrast, the unlagged regression of I on M_c explained under 60 per cent of the variance in I, while the addition of a one-year lag made the fit marginally worse. The use of the distributed lag equation, however, resulted in a dramatic improvement in the fit,

and, second, that actual investment adjusts towards this equilibrium level in the following way:

$$I_t - I_{t-1} = \lambda(I_t^* - I_{t-1}). \tag{3.2}$$

Substituting (3.1) in (3.2) and re-arranging:

$$I_t = \lambda\alpha + \lambda\beta M_t + (1 - \lambda)I_{t-1}. \tag{3.3}$$

The long-term adjustment of I to M is given by β in (3.1), which can be found from the parameters of a linear regression equation of the form:

$$I_t = a + bM_t + cI_{t-1}, \tag{3.4}$$

since

$$\beta = b/(1 - c).$$

[1] The import content of gross fixed capital investment in India in 1960 was about one-fifth, and the long-term investment elasticity (with respect to imports of capital goods) over the 1950s was 0·73.

Table 3.7. *Results of regressions[a] of gross domestic fixed capital formation on imports of capital goods: Australia and India, 1951–62*

	Regression	M_{ct}	M_{ct-1}	I_{t-1}	R^2
			Coefficient of		
Australia (1953–62)	1	2·11 (0·60)	—		0·582
	2	1·76 (0·23)	1·03 (0·21)	—	0·575
	3	1·03 (0·25)	—	0·82 (0·10)	0·953
India (1951–60)	1	3·34 (0·44)	—	—	0·879
	2	2·78 (0·77)	0·44 (0·78)	—	0·898
	3	1·17 (0·79)	—	0·68 (0·23)	0·947

SOURCES: As for Table 3.6 and *Economic Survey of Asia and the Far East*, E.C.A.F.E.

[a] Linear regressions of the form: $I_t = a + b_1 M_{ct} + b_2 M_{ct-1} + c I_{t-1}$ were used, where I = gross domestic fixed capital formation at constant prices and M_c = imports of capital goods (including materials for capital goods) at constant prices.

and both the coefficients of the independent variables were statistically significant. Allowing for the fact that the import content of gross domestic fixed capital formation in Australia in 1960–2 was one-fifth, the long-term investment elasticity (with respect to capital goods imports) can be estimated at 1·1 for the period covered by the regression: that is, a rate of growth of 10 per cent in capital goods imports would be associated in the long term with a rate of growth of 11 per cent in the volume of gross domestic fixed capital formation.[1]

By combining the equations for the two sub-relationships, estimates of the short- and long-term elasticities of investment in fixed capital with respect to the capacity to import can be obtained. For Australia, the combination of equation (2) in Table 3.6 and equation (3) in Table 3.7 yields marginal propensities to invest of 0·35 (short-term) and 1·95 (long-term); at the 1960–2 ratio of the capacity to import to investment in fixed capital (0·74), these represent elasticities of 0·26 and 1·4 respectively. For India, the short-term elasticity of investment with respect to changes in the capacity to import would appear from the regressions to

---

[1] Though the regression results for Australia appear statistically satisfactory, the magnitude of the long-term investment elasticity would seem unduly large for a developed country. Moreover, although domestic investment may lag behind imports of materials used in domestic production of capital goods, in a country like Australia it seems more likely that imports of capital goods will lag behind domestic fixed capital formation.

be not significantly different from zero. For an estimate of the magnitude of the long-term investment elasticity, the first regression for India in Table 3.6 can be combined with the third regression in Table 3.7. This yields an estimate of 0·82, the ratio of the capacity to import to investment in fixed capital being 0·44 (in 1960).[1]

Though similar calculations for the two sub-relationships cannot readily be made for other overseas Sterling countries, comparable results can be achieved by eliminating the common variable in the sub-relationships, namely, imports of capital goods, and relating investment in fixed capital directly to the capacity to import.[2] Regression equations on this basis can be computed for eight overseas Sterling countries for slightly varying periods of from seven to ten years, and the results of three alternative regression equations for each country—one including a distributed lag—are given in Table 3.8.

For most countries, the inclusion of a distributed lag improved the goodness of fit of the regressions; Jamaica was an exception to the rule, however, and for both Iceland and Trinidad and Tobago, also, the results excluding the distributed lag were the preferable ones. The magnitude of the marginal propensity to invest, as defined here, depends to some extent on the relative size of fixed capital investment in relation to the capacity to import. Since this relationship varies considerably from one country to another, it is perhaps more useful to consider the elasticity of fixed investment, rather than the marginal propensity. The short- and long-term elasticities, as well as the corresponding marginal propensities, are shown separately in Table 3.9 for those countries (including Australia and India) for which they can be distinguished on the basis of the distributed lag regressions. For Iceland, Jamaica and Trinidad, the elasticities have been derived from regression (1) in Table 3.8.

Of the ten countries, seven have long-term investment elasticities under 1·0, and of these, six have elasticities ranging between 0·7 and 1·0. South Africa has the lowest long-term elasticity, 0·46 and Australia the highest, 1·44, except for the former Federation of Rhodesia and Nyasaland, the result for which is partly a reflection of the assumption that the period covered by the calculation, 1955–62, can be divided into two

---

[1] Had the first regressions in Tables 3.6 and 3.7 been combined, the investment elasticity for India would be 0·74.

[2] Combining the two sub-relationships:

$$Mc_t = a_1 + b_1 Z_{t-1} + c_1 R_{t-1} \qquad (3.5)$$

and

$$I_t = a_2 + b_2 Mc_t + c_2 I_{t-1}, \qquad (3.6)$$

we have

$$I_t = (a_1 b_2 + a_2) + b_1 b_2 Z_{t-1} + b_2 c_1 R_{t-1} + c_2 I_{t-1}, \qquad (3.7)$$

so that the long-term marginal propensity to invest (with respect to the capacity to import) is $b_1 b_2 / (1 - c_2)$, on the assumption that changes in R have only short-period effects.

Table 3.8. *Results of regressions[a] of gross domestic fixed capital formation on the capacity to import and the level of reserves*

		Coefficient of			
	Regression	Z_{t-1}	R_{t-1}	I_{t-1}	R^2
MORE DEVELOPED COUNTRIES					
South Africa (1951–60)	1	0·49 (0·23)	—	—	0·353
	2	0.49 (0·12)	−1·22 (0·25)	—	0·838
	3	0·16 (0·04)	0·96 (0·06)	0·54 (0·05)	0·993
Iceland (1951–60)	1	0·69 (0·06)	—	—	0·952
	2	0·71 (0·08)	−0·82 (2·98)	—	0·952
	3	−0·04 (0·31)	5·88 (3·56)	0·88 (0·36)	0·976
Ireland (1951–62)	1	0·22 (0·08)	—	—	0·405
	2	0·21 (0·08)	0·11 (0·12)	—	0·452
	3	0·18 (0·04)	0·43 (0·13)	0·39 (0·19)	0·883
LESS DEVELOPED COUNTRIES					
Burma (1951–61)	1	0·63 (0·23)	—	—	0·454
	2	0·60 (0·18)	−0·61 (0·22)	—	0·719
	3	0·39 (0·15)	−0·18 (0·19)	0·51 (0·15)	0·892
Ceylon (1951–62)	1	0·27 (0·10)	—	—	0·418
	2	0·27 (0·10)	−0·19 (0·12)	—	0·554
	3	0·08 (0·09)	−0·01 (0·09)	0·77 (0·22)	0·822
Rhodesia/Nyasaland[b] (1955–62)	1	1·93 (0·57)	—	—	0·871
	2	1·88 (0·59)	−0·38 (0·43)	—	0·892
	3	1·25 (0·14)	−1·15 (0·12)	0·58 (0·06)	0·997
Jamaica (1953–60)	1	0·62 (0·12)	—	—	0·824
	3	1·44 (0·76)	—	−0·81 (0·80)	0·792
Trinidad and Tobago (1952–61)	1	0·66 (0·06)	—	—	0·932
	3	0·56 (0·35)	—	0·15 (0·53)	0·935

SOURCES: As for Table 3.6.

[a] Linear regressions of the form: $I_t = a + bZ_{t-1} + cR_{t-1} + dI_{t-1}$ (see Table 3.6, footnote a for definitions).

[b] The regressions included a dummy variable to distinguish the period 1955–8 from 1959–62.

sub-periods, 1955–8 and 1959–62—effected in the regression by the use of a dummy variable—within each of which the relationship between investment and the capacity to import was essentially similar, but between which a major discontinuity in investment (there was a fall of nearly 10 per cent from 1958 to 1959 in the volume of investment in fixed capital, though the capacity to import rose by nearly 20 per cent) resulted mainly from the political uncertainties in the period before independence was attained by Malawi and Zambia. Moreover, the investment total was expanding with unusual rapidity in the first sub-period, partly as a result of the construction of the Kariba Dam. It would seem, therefore, that the result obtained for Rhodesia/Nyasaland would be of dubious value for projecting the investment-capacity–import relationship for any of the three constituent countries of the former Federation.

Some further guidance on the probable future relationship between investment in fixed capital and the capacity to import can be gained from the Economic Development Plans of a number of the less developed Sterling countries. The relevant data are discussed in Chapter 8, in relation to the long-term elasticities shown in Table 3.9. As far as the past development is concerned, the evidence analysed here shows that there has been a fairly definite relationship—closer in the long term than in the short—between the movement in the capacity to import and that in investment in fixed capital for a number of overseas Sterling Area countries. Though similar calculations cannot at present be made for other countries in the Area, it seems reasonable to assume that such a relationship exists in the majority of those countries also.

4. THE RELATIONSHIP BETWEEN SAVINGS, GROSS PRODUCT AND EXPORTS

It was suggested in Chapter 2 that there were *a priori* reasons for believing that domestic savings in many primary-exporting countries would be likely to fluctuate with changes in the volume of exports.[1] The two reasons advanced there were, first, that the propensity to save might be higher in the export sector than in other sectors and, second, that movements in exports would cause significant movements in government revenues (where taxes on foreign trade contributed a substantial proportion of the total government revenues) and these movements would, in turn, influence the level of government investment.

One way of testing this hypothesis is to see whether the volume of domestic savings is, in fact, more closely related to the volume of exports

[1] See p. 58.

Table 3.9. *Marginal propensities and elasticities of investment in fixed capital with respect to the capacity to import*

	Marginal propensity to invest			Elasticity of investment[a]	
	Short-term	Long-term	Z_{t-1}/I_t	Short-term	Long-term
MORE DEVELOPED COUNTRIES					
Australia	0·35	1·95	0·74	0·26	1·45
South Africa	0·16	0·35	1·31[b]	0·21	0·46
Iceland		0·69	1·26[b]		0·87
Ireland	0·18	0·30	2·50	0·45	0·75
LESS DEVELOPED COUNTRIES					
Burma	0·30	0·60	1·17	0·35	0·70
Ceylon	..	0·34	2·70	..	0·92
India		1·67	0·44[b]		0·74
Rhodesia/Nyasaland	1·25	3·01	2·29	2·86	6·89
Jamaica		0·62	1·32[b]		0·82
Trinidad and Tobago		0·66	2·04[c]		1·34

SOURCES: Tables 3.6, 3.7, 3.8.

[a] For 1960–2, to which period the ratios shown for Z_{t-1}/I_t relate (unless otherwise stated).
[b] 1960.   [c] 1960–1.

than it is to the gross domestic product as a whole, or to the product of the non-export sectors. This can be done for eleven countries, for each of which two regression equations (based on annual data for periods of seven to twelve years) were calculated, one relating savings[1] to GDP, the other to exports and to GDP minus exports (see Table 3.10). From the first regression for each country, estimates of the marginal propensity to save—in the usual sense—can be obtained. Over the periods covered, which generally correspond to the decade of the 1950s, the marginal propensity to save was as high as 0·20 or above for every country in the table, except Jamaica (0·15) and Malawi (for which the savings propensity appears to have been negative). The result for Malawi reflects an upward trend in the current balance of payments deficit (and thus in net borrowing from abroad) over the period from 1954, whereas the volume of capital formation showed no uptrend from 1957 to 1961 and, indeed, fell off between 1961 and 1963.

[1] The volume of domestic savings was derived as a residual after deducting the balance of payments on current account, valued at constant prices, from gross domestic capital formation, also valued at constant prices.

Table 3.10. *Summary of results of regressions of gross domestic savings on GDP and exports*

| | Period | Coefficient of[a] | | | R^2 |
		Q	X	$Q–X$	
MORE DEVELOPED COUNTRIES					
Australia	1950–62	0·28 (0·07)	—	—	0·588
		—	2·85 (0·68)	−0·42 (0·19)	0·831
South Africa	1950–60	0·32 (0·02)	—	—	0·974
		—	0·57 (0·36)	0·24 (0·12)	0·966
Iceland	1950–61	0·24 (0·03)	—	—	0·896
		—	0·26 (0·23)	0·23 (0·08)	0·896
Ireland	1950–62	0·20 (0·05)	—	—	0·625
		—	0·49 (0·13)	0·00 (0·09)	0·756
LESS DEVELOPED COUNTRIES					
Burma	1950–61	0·20 (0·03)	—	—	0·789
		—	0·59 (0·19)	0·12 (0·05)	0·858
India	1950–60	0·32 (0·05)	—	—	0·809
		—	2·23 (0·99)	0·30 (0·05)	0·874
Rhodesia/Nyasaland	1952–62	0·47 (0·02)	—	—	0·982
		—	0·51 (0·08)	0·42 (0·09)	0·983
Malawi	1954–63	−0·27 (0·07)	—	—	0·660
		—	−0·62 (0·25)	−0·13 (0·12)	0·741
Rhodesia	1954–63	0·34 (0·04)	—	—	0·892
		—	0·57 (0·23)	0·21 (0·13)	0·906
Zambia	1954–63	0·57 (0·07)	—	—	0·895
		—	0·75 (0·34)	−0·15 (0·37)	0·932
Jamaica	1953–60	0·15 (0·03)	—	—	0·840
		—	0·24 (0·31)	0·11 (0·12)	0·843
Trinidad and Tobago	1951–61	0·22 (0·03)	—	—	0·888
		—	0·38 (0·05)	−0·05 (0·09)	0·951

SOURCES: *Yearbook of National Accounts Statistics*, various issues, United Nations, New York; *Monthly Bulletin of Statistics*, United Nations, New York; national trade statistics.

[a] Based on regressions of annual data at constant prices. The equations used were:

$$S_t = a + bQ_t \quad \text{and} \quad S_t = a' + b'X_t + c(Q_t - X_t),$$

where S = gross domestic saving, Q = gross domestic product and X = merchandise exports.

Relating the volume of savings to exports and the remainder of the gross domestic product, as in the second regression for each country, resulted in a marked improvement in the goodness of fit of the regressions for Australia and Ireland, and moderate improvements for Burma, India, Rhodesia, Zambia and Trinidad. Indeed, for Australia, Ireland, Rhodesia, Zambia and Trinidad, the relationship between domestic savings and output other than exports was not significant (or meaningful); in all three countries the movement of exports provided a good 'explanation' of the movement of domestic savings. For South Africa and Jamaica, by contrast, the 'explanation' was worsened by the introduction of exports as a separate variable.

These regression results must be taken purely as illustrative of the probable relationships existing between exports and savings. In the present state of lack of reliable statistics of domestic savings in the majority of the countries concerned, the estimation of the volume of savings by the residual method used here inevitably involves an appreciable margin of error and possible biases in the regression results. Nonetheless, the regression results can reasonably be taken as supporting the view, expressed in Chapter 2, that there is likely to be a positive association in many primary-exporting countries between exports and saving. To this extent, any reduction in the *ex ante* 'trade gap' due to a rise in exports would make an indirect contribution to reducing the *ex ante* 'savings gap' also.

5. COMPUTED AND ACTUAL GROWTH RATES

It is convenient, at this stage, to summarize briefly the statistical findings set out above. It should perhaps be emphasized that the underlying hypothesis has been that in primary-exporting countries, such as those in the Overseas Sterling Area, the essential constraint on economic growth lies in the difficulty of increasing the capacity to import, defined as the sum total of export earnings and net long-term capital inflow. Domestic savings are assumed to act as a residual, adjusting to the difference between domestic investment to be financed, and the net inflow of capital, both long-term and short-term.

On this hypothesis, it can be assumed that the mechanism through which the 'trade constraint' operates is via the supply of imported capital goods which, in turn, determines, or at least heavily influences, the volume of investment in fixed capital assets. The rate of growth of an economy in which this mechanism operates can thus be assumed to reflect two fundamental ratios or relationships: first, the degree to which foreign exchange can be transformed into capital assets and, second, the degree to which the increase in capital assets can be transformed into additional output. The latter transformation can be expressed in terms of an incremental capital–output ratio, the former in terms of an incremental propensity to invest—with respect to the capacity to import—or in terms of the corresponding investment elasticity. Countries differ substantially among themselves not only as regards their capital–output ratios, but also, as Table 3.9 shows, as regards their investment propensities or elasticities.

For the decade of the 1950s, with which the various regressions have been essentially concerned, a comparison can usefully be made between the actual rates of growth of GDP in the various Sterling countries and the rates of growth that would have been achieved if the relationship between investment and the capacity to import reflected solely the long-term adjustment, as indicated in Table 3.9. The computed growth rate for each country can then be expressed as the result of the interaction of three structural factors, combined with the rate of growth of the capacity to import. The three structural factors, according to the simple *ex post* model elaborated in Chapter 2, are the incremental capital–output ratio; the investment elasticity (with respect to the capacity to import); and the initial proportion of the GDP which is invested in fixed capital assets. Thus, if there is no increase in the capacity to import, the model assumes that investment will remain at the initial level, and the rate of growth in GDP will then be determined by the relationship between that initial level and the incremental capital–output ratio. To the extent that the capacity to import rises, there will be an associated rise in the level of investment (its extent depending on the investment elasticity) and consequently in the growth rate of GDP.[1]

The results of computing the rate of growth in GDP by combining the structural parameters with the mean rates of growth in the capacity to import are summarized in Table 3.11, which also compares the computed rates with the actual rates of growth achieved. The computed rates for the four more developed countries were either identical or slightly higher than the actuals, while for the less developed countries, they were all lower than the actuals. It is unlikely, however, that this difference for the two groups of countries is more than a coincidence, though it does suggest that, over the periods covered, the rate of investment in the less developed countries was positively associated with the short-term influences in the balance of payments situation, which were excluded from the estimates of the investment elasticities.

Taking all nine countries as a group, the computed rates give a good

---

[1] Using the notation on p. 67, the rate of growth in GDP can be written:

$$r = I_t^{\cdot}/\sigma Q_t. \tag{3.8}$$

The level of I and Q in period t can also be expressed in terms of their respective levels in an initial period, o, and their mean rates of growth (i and r, respectively) in the interim:

$$r = \frac{I_0(1+i)^t}{\sigma Q_0(1+r)^t}. \tag{3.9}$$

Using the long-term relationship between I and Z (the capacity to import) implied in (3.1) and (3.7), and substituting the investment elasticity, β^*, for the investment propensity, $\beta(= \beta^* I_t/Z_{t-1})$, we have:

$$r_c(1+r_c)^t = \frac{I_0}{\sigma Q_0}(1+\beta^* z)^t, \tag{3.10}$$

where z represents the mean rate of growth in Z. Once the right-hand side of (3.10) is evaluated, the equation can be solved for r_c (the computed rate of growth in GDP).

M E E

Table 3.11. *Computed and actual growth rates of GDP*[a]

					Growth rates of GDP		
	$I_0/\sigma Q_0$	β^*	z	$(1+\beta^* z)^t$	r_c	r	$r_c - r$
	(%)		(% p.a.)		(% per annum)		
MORE DEVELOPED COUNTRIES							
Australia	3·5	1·45	3·7	1·60	3·9	3·6	0·3
South Africa	6·1	0·46	3·2	1·14	4·6	4·4	0·2
Iceland	4·1	0·87[b]	8·7	1·93	5·1	5·1	—
Ireland	3·0	0·75	3·9	1·37	3·0	2·6	0·4
LESS DEVELOPED COUNTRIES							
Burma	4·1	0·70	2·3	1·17	3·4	4·6	−1·2
Ceylon	2·9	0·92	2·3	1·26	2·7	3·5	−0·8
India	2·4	0·82	3·4	1·32	2·5	3·8	−1·3
Jamaica	6·8	0·82[b]	8·2	1·58	6·8	7·4	−0·6
Trinidad and Tobago	6·1	1·34[b]	9·1	2·82	8·3	10·0	−1·7

SOURCES: Tables 3.3, 3.9. See p. 97, n. 1, for explanation of the symbols at the head of columns.

[a] Generally, for the decade of the 1950s (for precise periods, see Tables 3.3, 3.6, 3.7, 3.8). The actual growth rates of GDP ($= r$) relate to the periods covered by the regressions; for this reason, and also because of the different method of calculation, they differ somewhat from those shown in Table 1.5 for some countries. The values for I_0 and Q_0 are trend values for the first year of the relevant regression period.

[b] These elasticities are not based on exponential lag regressions (see Table 3.9).

representation of the range of growth rates actually achieved (see Fig. 3.3). A regression of the actual on the computed rates shows that 89 per cent of the variance in the former is accounted for by the computation in Table 3.11.[1]

The computation also helps to explain the differences in growth rates of the various countries in terms of the *ex post* growth model. Thus, the first column of Table 3.11 indicates that, had the capacity to import been stationary for all countries, the GDP would have grown fastest in Jamaica, South Africa and Trinidad and slowest in India, Ceylon and Ireland. This would arise because in the former three countries the combination of the initial proportion of GDP invested in fixed capital with the incremental capital–output ratio was highest, while for the latter three countries it was lowest.

However, the capacity to import did not remain constant; on the contrary, it increased at very different rates for the different countries, as shown in the third column (z) of Table 3.11. Moreover, the rate at

[1] The equation was: $r = 0·04 + 1·11 r_c$; $R^2 = 0·895$.
(0·14)

which these increases in import capacity were transformed into new capital investments (β^* in Table 3.11) also varied substantially. Thus Trinidad, which started off the period at a slight disadvantage compared with Jamaica in terms of the initial proportion of GDP invested, enjoyed a somewhat more rapid growth in its capacity to import but above all was much more successful in transforming its increase in foreign exchange resources into investment in fixed capital. On the other hand, Iceland achieved a much higher growth rate than Burma,

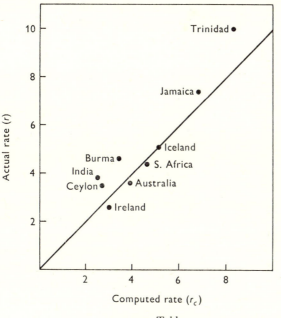

SOURCE: Table 3.11.

Fig. 3.3. Relationship between computed and actual growth rates of GDP (% per annum, compound).

mainly because of a higher rate of growth in the capacity to import; the initial positions of the two countries were identical, and there was only a relatively small difference in their investment elasticities.

The net effect of the various parameters on the growth rates of GDP at different rates of growth in the capacity to import can more clearly be shown in chart form (Fig. 3.4). If the structural parameters remain constant, then each country will move along its own curve as its capacity to import rises or falls. The point of intersection of each curve with the vertical axis indicates the GDP growth rate that would be achieved with no change in the initial level of the capacity to import; while the gradient of the curve reflects essentially the magnitude of the investment elasticity.[1] Because each country starts from a different initial position in terms of the proportion of GDP devoted to fixed capital investment (because each is operating with different incremental capital–output ratios and different investment elasticities), there is no necessary cross-country relationship between the growth rate of GDP and that of the capacity to import.[2] Indeed, it could easily happen that a country with a relatively low rate of increase in its capacity to import could achieve a higher growth rate of GDP than another country with a higher rate of increase in the capacity to import but with a lower investment elasticity and/or a lower initial 'growth rate position'.

The terms-of-trade effect

Part of the change in a country's capacity to import over any given period can be attributed to movements in its terms of trade.[3] Over the past decade, the terms of trade have generally worsened for primary-producing countries, and to this extent their capacity to import has been depressed. Individual countries have attempted to offset this deterioration—with greater or lesser success—by increased borrowing from wealthier countries and from the international financial agencies. Had the terms of trade of these countries not deteriorated, they may, or may not, have attempted to borrow increased amounts of capital from abroad. What they would have done in such hypothetical circumstances cannot be known and so cannot be assessed quantitatively. It is therefore not possible to measure the *net* effect of a deterioration in a country's terms of trade on its overall balance of payments position, though it seems very probable that a substantial proportion of the capital inflow into many less developed countries over the last decade arose because of payments difficulties caused by falling export prices.

However, the effect of a change in a country's terms of trade on its capacity to import, and on its rate of growth in GDP, can be calculated on the basis of some specific assumption about the net capital inflow. There are, in fact, three possible hypothetical combinations of assumptions: first, that the terms of trade had remained unchanged over the period considered, but that the net capital inflow had increased (or decreased) by the amount that it actually had; second—the reverse of the first—that the net capital inflow had remained unchanged, but that the terms of trade had moved as they actually had; and, third, that both had remained unchanged. Which of the three assumptions would yield

---

[1] See equation (3.10) on p. 97.

[2] This confirms the conclusion reached in Chapter 1.

[3] In this section, the 'terms of trade' relate to the ratio of export prices to import prices (the 'net barter' terms of trade).

the highest rate of increase in the capacity to import would depend on the initial relationship between exports and the net capital inflow and on the direction and relative rates of change in each.

Of these three possible alternatives, the first would seem the most appropriate in the present context to an assessment of the effects of changes in the terms of trade, and it is the one adopted here. For each

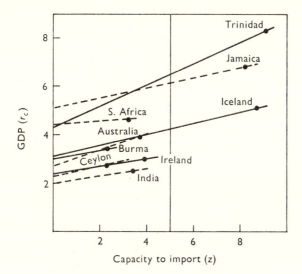

Fig. 3.4. Relationship between rates of growth in the capacity to import and in GDP (% per annum, compound).

of the nine countries in Table 3.11, a new series for the capacity to import was calculated, differing from the earlier one only in that merchandise exports were deflated by the country's export price index instead of its import price index.[1] The difference between this recalculated series and the series for the capacity to import as usually calculated indicates the effect on the latter of changes in the terms of trade.[2]

The mean rate of change in the capacity to import, adjusted for changes in the terms of merchandise trade, is shown for each of the nine

[1] A more sophisticated alternative would have been to deflate exports of both goods and services by appropriate export price indices, but reliable price indices for exports of services are not available for most countries.

[2] The capacity to import in the present context was defined earlier (see p. 87) as the purchasing power over imports of the foreign exchange derived from exports of goods and services, net factor payments abroad and net capital inflows. Thus:

$$Z = 1/P_m(X + X_s + N + F), \qquad (3.11)$$

where Z represents the capacity to import; X and X_s the value of exports of goods and services, respectively; N the net factor payments abroad; F the net capital inflow; and P_m import countries in the first column (z^*) of Table 3.12.[1] For most of these countries, the recalculated series rose at a faster rate than did the original series (z in Table 3.11), reflecting the deterioration in their terms of trade over the period covered. The terms-of-trade effect, as defined here, was particularly large for Australia and Burma, though of some importance also for South Africa, India and Trinidad. For Ireland and Ceylon, there was no change, on balance, in their terms of trade over the periods covered by the previous regressions, while for Iceland, exceptionally, there was a moderate improvement.[2]

The rate at which the gross product of each country would have grown had it experienced no changes in its terms of trade can also be calculated, provided it is assumed that, over the period considered, the structural relationships of the *ex post* model (particularly, the values of σ and β^*) would have remained unchanged for each country, in spite of the different movement now assumed for the terms of trade. On this basis, growth rates of GDP corresponding to the recalculated (or hypothetical) growth rates of the capacity to import can be computed; these are shown in the second column (r_c^*) of Table 3.12, the differences between these and the GDP growth rates previously computed being shown in the next column $(r_c^* - r_c)$.

The terms-of-trade effect on the growth rate of GDP appears to have been quite substantial for Australia, which, on the various assumptions made, would have achieved a growth rate almost $1\frac{1}{2}$ per cent per annum greater than the actual had there been no deterioration in the terms of trade. Burma and Trinidad would each have increased their rate of economic growth by roughly $\frac{1}{2}$ per cent per annum, and Jamaica by somewhat less. For the other countries, the terms-of-trade effect would have been negligible.

It will, however, be recalled that the growth rates originally computed differed, for most countries, from the growth rates actually achieved (see Table 3.11). The residuals can be assumed to reflect factors, particularly the short-period elements in the balance of payments, arising outside the long-period relationship assumed in the model. In order to

prices. The capacity to import, adjusted for changes in the terms of trade, can then be defined as:

$$Z^* = 1/P_m(X_s + N + F) + X/P_x, \tag{3.12}$$

where P_x is the export price index. The difference between the two series depends entirely on the movement in the terms of merchandise trade:

$$Z - Z^* = Q_x(P_x/P_m - 1), \tag{3.13}$$

where Q_x represents the volume of exports.

[1] z^* represents the rate of change in Z^*, as derived from regression equations.

[2] Precise calculations cannot be made for the Overseas Sterling Area as a whole, but the approximate effect of assuming no change in the terms of trade would have been to increase the rate of growth in the Area's capacity to import from 4·5 to 5·2 per cent per annum over the period from 1952–4 to 1962–3.

Table 3.12. *Estimated effect on GDP of changes in the terms of trade*[a]

	z^*	r_c^*	$r_c^*-r_c$	$r+r_c^*-r_c$	GDP per head, 1960–2 Hypo-thetical[b]	Actual	Ratio
	(% *per annum, compound*)				$(\pounds)$	$(\pounds)$	(%)
MORE DEVELOPED COUNTRIES							
Australia	7·6	5·2	1·3	4·9	610	535	114
South Africa	4·5	4·7	0·1	4·5	182	180	101
Iceland	7·1	4·7	−0·4	4·7	435	450	96
Ireland	3·9	3·0	0	2·6	245	245	100
LESS DEVELOPED COUNTRIES							
Burma	5·9	4·0	0·6	5·2	21	20	106
Ceylon	2·3	2·7	0	3·5	50	50	100
India	4·0	2·6	0·1	3·9	26	26	101
Jamaica	9·8	7·1	0·3	7·7	165	160	103
Trinidad and Tobago	10·0	8·7	0·4	10·4	250	240	104

SOURCES: As for Tables 3.1, 3.6. See footnotes on pp. 101, 102, for explanation of the symbols at the head of columns.

[a] The terms-of-trade effect on the growth rate of GDP ($r_c^*-r_c$) relates to the period covered by the regressions for each country (see Tables 3.3, 3.6, 3.7, 3.8).

[b] Actual GDP per head in 1960–2, adjusted for the terms-of-trade effect over a notional ten-year period.

estimate the (hypothetical) growth rates of GDP which each country would have achieved had there been no changes in its terms of trade, a further assumption needs to be made, namely, that the residual element shown in Table 3.11 would also be unaffected had foreign trade prices not moved as in fact they did. On this assumption, the growth rates adjusted for changes in the terms of trade, and allowing also for the residuals in the computation, can be computed, and these are shown in the fourth column ($r+r_c^*-r_c$) in Table 3.12.

Finally, it is of some interest to assess the probable effect on the level of GDP per head which would have resulted had there been no change in the terms of trade. Taking a notional period of ten years for this purpose for all nine countries,[1] the cumulative effect on the growth rate of there having been no change in the terms of trade can be derived, on the various assumptions mentioned earlier. Thus, for Australia, the growth rate of GDP would have been higher than it actually was by 1·3 per cent per annum, so that at the end of the decade, i.e. by 1960–2, GDP (and GDP per head) would have been higher by 14 per cent. This and the corresponding percentage differences for the other countries are shown

[1] Most of the regressions on which Table 3.12 is based related to periods of nine or ten years.

in the final column of Table 3.12. For most of these countries, the terms-of-trade effect on the level of GDP per head in 1960–2 would have been marginal, on the assumptions made.

In projecting future levels of GDP, however, it cannot be assumed that the structural parameters of the *ex post* model will remain constant. The inherent instability of the incremental capital–output ratio has already been discussed. The investment elasticity is subject to similar limitations, since it, too, is an *ex post* description of the relationship between two variables, the capacity to import and investment in fixed capital, which are, moreover, linked indirectly by an intermediate variable, imports of capital goods, with a time lag interposed. The investment elasticity can be increased, either by increasing the ratio of capital goods in total imports (which, in the longer run, is financed by the capacity to import, as defined here); or by reducing the import content of fixed capital investments, or both. The appreciable variation that still exists between countries in the magnitude of the investment elasticity indicates that there is ample scope for further improvement here. The probable future magnitudes of the structural parameters for the main overseas Sterling countries are discussed further in Chapter 8, as a basis for the projections of the rates of growth in their gross products in the period up to 1975.

PART II

PROJECTIONS FOR 1975

CHAPTER 4

A BASIS FOR PROJECTION

I. FORECASTS, TARGETS AND PROJECTIONS

The projections of future exports from the Overseas Sterling Area and of the implications of these projections for economic growth in the various Sterling countries are necessarily based on a working hypothesis about the interdependence of the Overseas Sterling Area with the industrial countries, and on a series of assumptions relating, in particular, to economic growth in the latter group of countries. Before examining these assumptions in any detail, it is worth emphasizing at the outset an important distinction between three alternative ways of considering future developments, each of which is useful for a particular purpose.

The first alternative is an economic *forecast* or *prediction*, taking account as far as possible of likely future changes that might influence the trade or economic growth of the countries concerned. Economic forecasting of this type is a regular activity of government in many countries, but it is inevitably confined to the short-run future; predicting medium- or long-term changes is subject to so large an error as to be of little value in practice. A second alternative is the establishment of a *target* rate of growth (or future level) of trade or national product at which to aim. The target may be a single rate of growth for the national product, or it may consist of multiple objectives (not all of which may, in the event, prove to be mutually consistent). This is essentially a policy-oriented approach, since the target will imply policy changes in many directions in order to achieve it.

The third alternative is a *projection* of the future rate of growth, the future pattern of trade, or any other economic magnitude, on the basis of specific assumptions concerning the variables—both structural and governmental policies—which are likely to influence the outcome. The explicit statement of assumptions is an essential part of the concept of a 'projection', since it allows for an evaluation of the probable impact of any given variation in the assumptions on the projected levels of consumption, production or trade. Thus, projections are essentially neutral as between alternative policies; their function is rather to present the contrast between the probable results of each alternative. In so far as projections reveal unfavourable tendencies which are likely to develop in the future (for example, a decline in prices or in demand), they clearly have policy implications. Indeed, the adoption of appropriate new policies designed to prevent such unfavourable results from arising would in itself be a justification for making the projection, though such policy changes would be expected to 'invalidate' the projection, in the sense that the basic assumptions relating to government policies would themselves be changed.

Although projections can be made without postulating targets, the reverse does not hold. Every economic development plan is based, explicitly or implicitly, on a target or a set of interrelated targets; but the implications of such targets for different sectors of the economy, or for government policies, can be rationally set out only on the basis of 'projections' as defined above. The main assumptions on which the projections in later chapters are based are set out below. In addition to making projections of trade and economic growth of the less developed countries of the Overseas Sterling Area, the implications for capital inflow of a set of target rates of growth are also worked out.

The projection period

When the research for this study was being planned, statistical data for world production and trade in the main Sterling commodities were generally available up to 1960 or 1961, and the intention was to arrive at projections for about fifteen years ahead, that is for the year 1975 or thereabouts. Although, in the course of research, data for the years 1962–5 became available, the 'projection year' has been kept at 1975. The rationale of this is that a period of ten to fifteen years is long enough for temporary and cyclical factors to be evened out, thus allowing the study to focus attention on the underlying trends; at the same time, it is short enough to minimize the risk of some completely new factors emerging which might seriously invalidate the projections. Moreover, if the projections are made on the basis of alternative policies, it can reasonably be assumed that a decade or so is sufficient time for changes in policies to have taken effect.

2. THE GENERAL ASSUMPTIONS

The working hypothesis on which this book is based is that the economies of the main industrial countries constitute the essential dynamic element in the world economy. They represent, in a sense, the 'leading sector', while the primary-producing countries are essentially reacting, in one form or another, to the economic developments in the industrial countries.

Put in this rather bald form, the hypothesis is probably much less true of how the world economy works today than it was for, say, the world before 1914. The more developed among the primary-producing countries have by now established themselves on a path of self-sustaining growth, aided by a substantial degree of industrial development. Yet even Australia, the most industrialized of the primary-producing countries, is powerfully influenced in her economic development by the fortunes of her major exports to the industrial countries, and by the inflow of new capital and the pace of immigration from them.

It follows from this hypothesis that the underlying assumptions of any projection of the exports of the Overseas Sterling Area must necessarily relate to the demand for such products in the main industrial areas. Demand itself can be taken as mainly a reflection of total real incomes and of relative prices. As regards total incomes, the assumptions must relate to the rates of growth of population and of real income per head, the two components of total income; these are discussed below. The problem of how to treat relative price changes in the projections is then explored.

The population assumptions

Over the past decade, from 1954 to 1964–5, the total population of the industrial countries has been increasing at an average rate of 1·2 per cent per annum, the growth rate being the same both in the late 1950s and during the first half of the 1960s (see Table 4.1). Within this total, Canada has been exceptional in having an average rate of population growth in excess of 2 per cent a year, though there was a marked decline in the rate of growth from the first part of the period to the second. Canada's crude birth rate is relatively high compared with other industrial countries, her death rate is lower, and during the 1950s she absorbed at least a million immigrants. The rate of population growth in the United States averaged 1·6 per cent a year over the decade; this rate, though considerably below Canada's, was still higher than in the other industrial areas. Both the E.E.C. and Japan had population growth rates of 1·0 per cent a year, while in other countries of continental Western Europe population rose in aggregate by 1·3 per cent a year. In Britain, by contrast, the rate of population growth was well below 1 per cent a year, though in the first half of the 1960s the rate of growth (0·8 per cent a year) was significantly higher than in the latter part of the 1950s (only 0·5 per cent a year).

Population has been growing in the primary-exporting countries of the world at double the rate of the industrial countries; as can be seen from Table 4.1, the rate of population growth in both Sterling and non-Sterling primary-exporting countries continued to rise in the first half of the 1960s, compared with the later 1950s.

For 1975, Table 4.1 shows the population as given in the 'medium projection' recently published by the United Nations,[1] except that for

[1] *Provisional Report on World Population Prospects, as assessed in 1963,* United Nations, New York, 1964.

Table 4.1. *Population of the main industrial and primary-exporting countries, 1954–65 and projections for 1975*

		Total population			Rates of growth		
					1954 to 1960–1	1960–1 to 1964–5	1960–1 to 1975
	1954	1960–1	1964–5	1975			
	(Millions)				*(% per annum)*		
INDUSTRIAL COUNTRIES							
United Kingdom	51·0	52·7	54·4	58·5	0·5	0·8	0·7
E.E.C.	162·6	172·7	180·6	191·7	0·9	1·1	0·7
Other Western Europe[a]	120·2	130·0	136·8	154·1	1·2	1·3	1·2
United States	163·1	182·3	193·4	223·0	1·7	1·5	1·4
Canada	15·3	18·1	19·5	23·8	2·6	1·9	1·9
Japan	88·0	93·7	97·4	106·2	1·0	1·0	0·9
Total	600	650	682	757	1·2	1·2	1·1
PRIMARY-EXPORTING COUNTRIES							
Overseas Sterling Area[b]	621	710	782	1,009	2·1	2·4	2·5
Non-Sterling countries	546	649	724	948	2·7	2·8	2·7
Total	1,167	1,359	1,506	1,957	2·4	2·6	2·6

SOURCES: *Monthly Bulletin of Statistics*, United Nations, New York; *Provisional Report on World Population Prospects, as assessed in 1963*, United Nations, New York, 1964; *Annual Abstract of Statistics*, no. 100, 1963, Central Statistical Office, London.

[a] Austria, Denmark, Finland, Greece, Iceland, Ireland, Norway, Portugal, Spain, Sweden, Switzerland, Turkey and Yugoslavia.

[b] Excluding Iceland and Ireland. Also excluding the Middle East oil countries with a population of about two million in recent years.

the United Kingdom the official British projection has been used.[1] For the period 1960–1 to 1975, the projected rate of population growth is generally lower than the average rate for the past decade for the industrial countries, but somewhat higher than the past rate for the Overseas Sterling Area; for other primary-producing countries, no change in the rate of population growth is expected on the basis of the United Nations medium projections.

The income assumptions

Over the past decade, real income per head increased at very different rates in the different industrial countries. Japan has consistently maintained the fastest growth rate, average real income per head in that country having increased by nearly 9 per cent a year over the decade to

[1] The United Nations 'medium' projection for the total population of the United Kingdom in 1975 (56·2 million) was based on an earlier official estimate.

1964–5. Among the other industrial countries, the pattern of growth changed dramatically between the later 1950s and the first half of the 1960s. In the earlier period, the fastest growth (nearly 5 per cent a year) was achieved by the E.E.C. countries, whereas both the United States and Canada achieved only a marginal rate of growth in real income per head (under 1 per cent a year). Britain and other Western Europe (2 and $3\frac{1}{2}$ per cent a year, respectively) were in intermediate positions. By the early 1960s, however, the rate of economic growth in North America had accelerated sharply, the high growth rate being maintained for a relatively prolonged period. In the E.E.C. countries, by contrast, there was a series of restraints on growth, resulting from government measures to correct balance of payments deficits, or to counteract internal inflationary pressures, in certain of these countries in particular years. As a result of these divergent tendencies, the spread between countries in the rate of growth in real income per head was considerably diminished in the first half of the 1960s (see Table 4.2).

The underlying assumption made here is that this more recent convergence in country rates of income growth will set the pattern for the coming decade, but that generally the high growth rates achieved in the early 1960s will not be maintained over the whole period up to 1975. In view of the inevitable uncertainty surrounding any projection of growth rates, two assumptions have been made for each industrial area. The low income-growth rate (assumption A) expresses a 'reasonable minimum' which national economic policy, if sensibly used, should be able to achieve; the higher growth basis (assumption B) implies a greater strain on resources and a conscious policy aimed at achieving a relatively fast rate of economic growth.

For Britain, the higher growth assumption is almost double the average for the past decade, and is slightly higher than the rate (3·1 per cent per annum) implied in the official target for the period 1964–70.[1] The lower growth assumption for Britain, 2·5 per cent a year, although some 40 per cent above the average growth rate for the previous decade, can be regarded as a reasonable minimum provided the balance of payments constraint is not too severe.[2] For the E.E.C. area, the past rate of growth over the whole decade up to 1964–5 is taken, in effect, as the future maximum rate; the lower rate is taken as equal to the maximum for the United Kingdom. The future rates of growth in 'other Western Europe' are assumed to lie intermediate between the rates achieved in

[1] The government target rate of growth in GDP, embodied in the National Plan for 1964–70, was 3·8 per cent a year. (*The National Plan*, Cmnd. 2764, H.M.S.O., 1965.)

[2] For Britain, the rate of growth assumed would now appear to be on the high side if the forecast of 3 to $3\frac{1}{2}$ per cent a year growth made by the National Institute of Economic and Social Research for the period 1967–70 is justified (see *National Institute Economic Review*, no. 39, February 1967).

Table 4.2. *Real product[a] per head in the main industrial countries, 1953–5 to 1964–5 and projections for 1975*

	Rates of growth							
			1960–1 to 1975		Actual		Projected 1975	
	1953–5 to 1960–1	1960–1 to 1964–5	A	B	1960–1	1964–5	A	B
	(% *per annum*)				($ *at 1960–1 prices*)			
United Kingdom	2·0	2·3	2·5	3·5	1,400	1,530	2,000	2,300
E.E.C.	4·8	3·8	3·5	4·5	1,170	1,355	1,930	2,210
Other Western Europe	3·4[b]	5·1	3·5	4·0	590	720	970	1,040
United States	0·8	3·4	2·0	2·5	2,585	2,955	3,450	3,700
Canada	0·8	3·4	2·0	2·5	1,780	2,035	2,370	2,540
Japan	8·9	8·6	6·0	7·0	470	650	1,090	1,250
TOTAL	2·4	3·9	2·9	3·5	1,385	1,615	2,080	2,300

SOURCES: *Yearbook of National Accounts Statistics, 1965; Monthly Bulletin of Statistics*, United Nations, New York.

[a] Gross domestic product at factor cost at 1960–1 prices. Converted into U.S. dollars by using estimated purchasing-power parity rates.
[b] Excluding Spain.

the later 1950s and in the early 1960s. For both Canada and the United States a reduction in the high growth rates of the early 1960s has been assumed (to 2 per cent per annum on the lower growth assumption and to 2½ per cent per annum on the higher). These assumed reductions are consistent with the basic hypothesis—discussed later—of no major war, to the extent that the high and sustained rate of economic growth in the United States in the mid 1960s was associated with the demands created by the war in Vietnam. There is also, probably, some implied assumption that from 1965 to 1975, the average growth rate will be adversely affected by one or more short recessions. For Japan, a somewhat reduced growth rate compared with that achieved over the past decade is assumed.

These various assumptions imply that for the industrial countries as a whole, the rate of growth in GDP per head will decline from almost 4 per cent a year over the first half of the 1960s, to some 3 and 3½ per cent a year respectively, on assumptions A and B, over the decade up to 1975. This decline results very largely from the assumption made about the reduced rate of growth in the United States.

By combining the assumptions about rates of growth in GDP per head with the United Nations population estimates, a set of projections of total GDP, in terms of base period (1960–1) prices, can be obtained.

These are shown in Table 4.3. The figures indicate the extent to which the totals for the industrial areas are dominated by the United States and the E.E.C. countries; together, these two accounted for about three-quarters of the aggregate GDP of all the industrial countries in both 1960–1 and 1964–5.

Because the populations of the United States and Canada are growing considerably more rapidly than is that of Western Europe, the rates of growth in the total GDP of the two continental areas do not diverge as much as do the growth rates for GDP per head. For the United States, the total GDP is assumed to increase at much the same rate as for Britain,[1] though still at a significantly lower rate than for continental Western Europe. For the industrial areas as a whole, aggregate GDP is assumed to rise by some 4 to $4\frac{1}{2}$ per cent a year, on average, from 1960–1 to 1975, compared with rather more than 5 per cent a year during the first half of the 1960s.[2]

[1] See p. 111, n. 2.

[2] For convenience of comparison with Table 4.3, the assumptions about future growth rates of GNP made in two recent comprehensive studies, by F.A.O. and by Professor Bela Balassa, are summarized below:

	F.A.O.[a] 1957–9 to 1969–71		Balassa[b] 1960–70		1970–5	
	A	B	I	II	I	II
			(% per annum)			
Western Europe	4·2	5·2	3·9	4·4	3·7	4·3
United Kingdom	2·4	3·4	2·9	3·4	2·6	3·1
E.E.C.	4·7[c]	5·5[c]	4·1	4·6	4·0	4·5
E.F.T.A.[d]	2·7	3·7	3·2	3·7	2·8	3·3
Southern Europe[e]	4·9	6·2	4·9	6·0	4·8	5·8
United States	3·0	4·3	3·9	4·4	3·6	4·1
Canada	3·4	4·8	4·5	5·0	4·0	4·4
Japan	6·0	7·0	5·4	6·4	5·0	6·0

SOURCES: *Agricultural Commodities—Projections for 1970, Special Supplement* to *F.A.O. Commodity Review, 1962*, F.A.O., Rome, 1962; Bela A. Balassa, *Trade Prospects for Developing Countries*, Homewood, Illinois, 1964.

[a] Assumption A is broadly in line with the trends of the 1950s; assumption B with announced targets or published national plans, and generally corresponds with the progress considered feasible under favourable conditions.

[b] Assumption I represents the 'most likely' estimate on the basis of past experience and information on prospective changes; assumption II is a high or optimistic estimate which is still within the range of possibilities, provided that appropriate economic policies are followed.

[c] Real consumption expenditure.

[d] The F.A.O. figures include the United Kingdom; Professor Balassa's figures relate to 'Northern Europe', which is equivalent to continental E.F.T.A. *minus* Portugal *plus* Finland, Iceland and Ireland.

[e] The F.A.O. figures relate to 'Mediterranean' countries (Greece, Portugal, Spain and Yugoslavia); Professor Balassa also includes Turkey in 'Southern Europe'.

Table 4.3. *Total real product^a in the main industrial countries, 1953–5 to 1964–5 and projections for 1975*

	Rates of growth				Actual		Projected 1975	
	1953–5 to 1960–1	1960–1 to 1964–5	1960–1 to 1975 A	B	1960–1	1964–5	A	B
	(% *per annum*)				($ *billion at 1960–1 prices*)			
United Kingdom	2·6	3·1	3·2	4·3	74	83	117	135
E.E.C.	5·8	4·9	4·3	5·3	202	245	369	425
Other Western Europe	4·8^b	6·4	4·7	5·2	77	99	150	161
United States	2·5	4·9	3·4	3·9	471	571	768	824
Canada	3·4	5·4	4·0	4·5	32	40	56	61
Japan	10·0	9·7	6·9	7·9	44	63	116	133
TOTAL	3·7	5·2	4·0	4·6	900	1,101	1,577	1,738

SOURCES: As for Tables 4.1 and 4.2.

^a GDP at factor cost at 1960–1 prices. Converted into U.S. dollars by using estimated purchasing-power parity rates.
^b Excluding Spain.

Manufacturing production

In most countries, both developed and under-developed, manufacturing production tends to grow at a faster rate than does the total gross product, either because productivity in manufacturing grows faster than in agriculture or in service industries or because workers are moving out of agriculture into industry. The relationship between the rates of growth of manufacturing and of GDP can be conveniently expressed in terms of a 'production elasticity', which measures the ratio of the two rates of growth. Table 4.4 shows the magnitudes of these production elasticities, derived from regression equations, for the main industrial countries for the period 1953–63. Japan has the highest elasticity, a 10 per cent rise in real GDP in that country being associated, on average, with a 16 per cent rise in manufacturing output over this period. The lowest elasticities are found for the United States and Canada, the latter being the only industrial country shown having an elasticity below unity.[1]

Projections of the rates of growth in manufacturing production for the period up to 1975 can be made on the basis of the alternative income-growth assumptions and of a production elasticity for each country. It is possible that this elasticity may change somewhat, over the coming decade, from its value in the recent past; but, generally

[1] This reflects the unusually rapid expansion of the mineral industries in Canada over the past decade.

Table 4.4. *Manufacturing production in the main industrial countries, 1953–5 to 1964–5 and projections for 1975*

	Production elasticity[a]	Rates of growth			
		1953–5 to 1960–1	1960–1 to 1964–5	1960–1 to 1975	
				A	B
		(% *per annum*)			
United Kingdom	1·26 (0·06)	2·7	3·5	3·9	5·1
E.E.C.	1·38 (0·04)	7·9	5·9	5·4	6·6
Other Western Europe	1·43 (0·03)	6·3	7·7	6·1	6·7
United States	1·13 (0·09)	2·8	6·1	3·8	4·3
Canada	0·93 (0·06)	3·1	7·6	3·7	4·2
Japan	1·59 (0·05)	16·1	11·9	9·3	10·4
Total	··	4·5	6·4	4·6	5·4

SOURCES: *Industrial Statistics, 1900–1962*, O.E.C.D., Paris; *Monthly Bulletin of Statistics*, and *Yearbook of National Accounts Statistics, 1965*, United Nations, New York.

[a] Regression coefficients derived from regression of manufacturing production index (M) on gross domestic product (Q) in the form:

$$\log M = \log a + b \log Q$$

using annual figures for the period 1953–63, inclusive. The standard errors of the coefficient (b) are given in parentheses; R^2 varied from 0·958 for the United States to 0·996 for 'other Western Europe'.

speaking, no appreciable changes seem likely (the standard errors of the elasticities are all very small) and the elasticities as calculated have been used here for the projections of manufacturing production.

On the lower income-growth assumption, the calculations show that manufacturing production would rise by nearly 4 per cent per annum in Britain and North America, by 5½ per cent per annum in E.E.C. countries, and by 6 and 9½ per cent per annum respectively in 'other Western Europe' and Japan. The growth rates are all ½ or 1 per cent higher on the more optimistic income-growth assumption.

These projections for manufacturing output are consistent with the basic population and income assumptions, and are generally more appropriate reference points for projecting consumption of industrial materials than are the total GDP estimates.

The world background

Any projection of the future course of world trade, or of economic growth in countries heavily dependent on foreign trade, necessarily makes assumptions concerning world economic and political conditions. Such assumptions are often not made explicitly, but they are worth explicit consideration here since they are fundamental to the whole of the later exercise. The concept of 'world conditions' is all-embracing and includes any factor which, if changed, would significantly alter any of the quantitative projections. Of the many such factors, four appear to be of particular importance in the present context.

First, an underlying assumption is that over the period of projection there will be neither a major war nor a major economic recession. This *caveat* is obvious enough in relation to a world war, for example, but a 'major' war must here be interpreted to include (for example) the war in Vietnam which, if prolonged over a period of years, could well result in sharp price rises in 'sensitive' commodities such as natural rubber and tin, and thus in a distortion of the more 'normal' workings of the world commodity markets. If this should occur, it would probably invalidate the greater part of the projections presented in later chapters.

A second general assumption is that economic growth in the industrial countries can be achieved without any serious balance of payments difficulties or, at least, without a shortage of liquid reserves giving rise to import restrictions. To some extent, the possibility of the balance of payments situation being an effective constraint on the rate of economic growth has been allowed for in the low income-growth assumption A.

Third, no allowance can reasonably be made for quite new technological developments in the industrial countries. It is conceivable that during the projection period there will be a number of new scientific or technological developments resulting in a dramatic and irreversible change in the demand for certain of the raw material exports of the overseas Sterling countries. Such possible future developments cannot be foreseen, and certainly no quantitative allowance can be made—in either direction—for their possible effect on the trading position of the countries affected. In so far as the detailed commodity projections assume the continuance of past trends, including past rates of substitution of natural materials by synthetics, the projections make allowance for further technological progress at much the same rate of development as in the past. But they do not allow for future new processes which, by themselves, would result in significant changes in recent trends. While such new developments could conceivably result for a few countries in quite different export prospects from those projected here, it is most improbable that, in the relatively short span of ten to fifteen years, new technologies would be developed to influence substantially the export prospects of the majority of Sterling countries.

Fourth, a basic assumption in all the commodity projections is that government policies in the industrial countries affecting the degree of protection against imports continue in much the same form, and to much the same extent, as they are at present. This assumption is necessary, not only because otherwise there would be a large range of possible policies from which it would be difficult, if not impossible, to choose the most 'realistic'; but also because it allows some quantitative assessment to be made of the likely effect of specific changes in present policies on the economic position of particular Sterling countries or of the Overseas Sterling Area as a whole.

3. THE COMMODITY AND COUNTRY PROJECTIONS

Within the framework set by the various assumptions relating to the growth of real incomes in the industrial countries and to the world economic and political background, further, more specific, assumptions need to be made for the detailed projections of world trade in particular commodities and for the share of each Sterling country in the projected world trade totals. These more detailed assumptions are discussed again in Chapter 5, summarizing the results of the commodity projections, and in Chapter 6, which sets out the country projections. Here, it suffices to focus attention on what is, perhaps, the central issue, namely, what should be assumed about the future course of commodity prices.

The uncertainty about future price trends imparts an inevitable margin of error to any projection in this field and, in our present state of knowledge about the determinants of price changes, there is no really satisfactory way of meeting this problem. The usual method of approach in making a commodity projection is to assume that relative prices remain unchanged throughout the period covered. On this assumption, projections of world consumption and trade can be made in terms of 'constant' prices, and then compared with projections, made independently, of world production and exportable supplies. The projections of production would, of course, have to take account of trends in yields or productivity, as well as the assumption of constant relative prices. Any significant discrepancy between the consumption and production projections would imply either an appropriate change in prices, or changes in government policies to ensure that relative prices did, in fact, remain substantially unchanged.[1]

An alternative approach would be to arrive at estimates of probable future price changes by a method of successive approximation. The confrontation of consumption and production projections might indicate that prices were likely to change, in the absence of policy changes. If so, a more appropriate price could then be assumed and new consumption and production projections arrived at. The process could be repeated until the two projections were more or less in balance.[2]

[1] This was the approach used—apart from a few exceptions—in the recent F.A.O. projections of production, consumption and trade in agricultural commodities (see *Agricultural Commodities—Projections for 1970*, cited on p. 113).

[2] This was essentially the approach adopted by Professor Balassa, *op. cit.*

Though the second approach is clearly preferable in principle, it does to some extent lend an air of spurious precision to the projection exercise, mainly because so little is at present known about the elasticity of production of most primary commodities with respect to price changes. The price elasticity of production may vary considerably from one country to another and from peasant cultivators to estates, while equally there may be significant differences in the time lags between price changes and the resulting changes in output. On the other hand, there may be some primary commodities for which it is known that the price elasticity of production is normally low and where the main determinants are technical in character.

In the present study, emphasis has been laid on the first approach in the detailed commodity projections. For a few commodities, however, additional projections have been made on alternative assumptions about future relative prices, based on assessments of probable future levels of world output. This has been done for a limited number of commodities —including non-ferrous metals, cocoa and natural rubber which, together, account for a substantial proportion of total exports of primary commodities from overseas Sterling countries.

The problem of the probable future trend in prices must also be faced in the country projections. For a country exporting only one commodity, the problem is no different from that already discussed. For countries with more diversified exports, however, the change in export unit value will be a weighted average of the corresponding changes for the constituent export commodities. Since price movements of different primary commodities can be expected to be offsetting to a greater or lesser extent, the range of price variation is likely to be smaller for countries—apart from one-commodity specialists—than for commodities. For the country projections, then, the problem can be met by making alternative assumptions for export unit values as a whole, based as far as possible on the commodity analyses. This is discussed further in later chapters.

In a complete world model, the effects of assumed rates of growth in the industrial areas on the exports of the primary-producing countries would not be considered as the end of the exercise, since the latter's export experience would itself influence their demand for imports from the industrial areas and, to this extent, the rates of growth initially assumed would be affected. This 'feed-back' effect is necessarily ignored in the present study, to the extent that it differs significantly from its magnitude over the past decade, for to have allowed for it and to have worked it through the various projections by successive approximations, would have involved an investment of resources outside the scope of the study. However, it is not likely that projections adjusted for the 'feed-back' effect would be significantly different from those presented in this study,[1] especially in view of the margin of error inevitably associated with any projections of the future.

[1] Exports from industrial to primary-producing countries in 1964–5 represented only 3 per cent of the aggregate GDP of the industrial countries in that period.

CHAPTER 5

SUMMARY OF THE COMMODITY PROJECTIONS[1]

I. METHOD OF APPROACH

Since by far the greater proportion of the exports of the Overseas Sterling Area are directed to the markets of the main industrial countries, the first step in projecting the probable level of these exports in 1975 was to make alternative projections for that year of the consumption of each main commodity in the industrial countries. Next, estimates were made of the proportion of consumption which was likely to be met by imports in 1975, based on past trends and on assumptions about the future growth of domestic production in the industrial countries. These import proportions, when combined with the consumption projections, yielded projections of the probable level of imports of each commodity into each of the main industrial countries, or country groups, in 1975. The share of the overseas Sterling countries in the industrial countries' imports of each commodity was then projected to 1975, thus allowing consistent projections to be made of the volume of exports from the Overseas Sterling Area to the industrial countries. Finally, specific assumptions were made, for each commodity separately, of the likely level (or alternative levels) of overseas Sterling exports to other primary-producing countries and to the centrally planned countries.

The consumption projections

For the principal foods and beverages, the projections of the probable levels of consumption in the main industrial countries were based mainly on estimates of income elasticities and of the likely growth in population. The income elasticities were generally derived from time series for the past decade, or some portion of the decade, supported, where appropriate, by evidence from family budget surveys or cross-country regressions. Where there appeared to be a definite tendency for the income elasticity to decline as the level of *per caput* consumption rose (as with tropical beverages and sugar), allowances for further declines were made, where appropriate, in the elasticities assumed in the projections for the different industrial countries. For meat and dairy produce, separate calculations involving different income elasticities were necessary for the main varieties included; the prospects for meat consumption, for example, show a much sharper rise in beef and veal and in poultry meat than in other types. Among dairy products, too, an allow-

---

[1] For further detail by individual commodities, see Appendices A–C.

ance was made for a probable modest shift in consumer tastes away from fatty foods, including butter. For fruit, demand is relatively more income-elastic for the more processed forms—fruit juices and canned fruit—than for fresh fruit.

Among the industrial materials, a detailed analysis of end-uses was made for jute, natural rubber, vegetable oils and oilseeds and hides and skins. This revealed the impact on the demand for the primary commodity of different rates of change in consumption of the various end-products, and of substitution by other materials within each end-use. For jute, separate analyses were made, as far as possible, for consumption in packaging, floor coverings and other uses; for rubber, consumption in vehicle tyres and other uses; for vegetable oils, consumption in soap, margarine and other uses; and for hides and skins, consumption in footwear and other uses. Probable future trends in the consumption of each end-product were assessed, generally on the basis of estimated income elasticities for the projection period, allowing, as appropriate, for relevant differences within the end-product (for example, the income elasticities for men's, women's and children's shoes differ greatly among themselves for all the industrial countries).

Allowance was also necessary, within each end-use, for the probable trends in substitution by other materials. Apart from natural rubber, it was assumed that relative prices of the various natural materials would be much the same in 1975 as in the early 1960s. However, recent rates of substitution arising essentially from technological changes were assumed to continue—usually at reduced rates—in the future. Thus, for jute, the substitution of paper sacks and, more recently, of polyethylene packaging, was taken to continue, as was also the mechanization of port and internal distribution centres in the main industrial countries (thus further reducing the need for the packaging of bulk foods or materials); however, it was also assumed that bulk-handling techniques of this type would not make any appreciable impact on the demand for jute packaging in the less-developed countries in the period up to 1975.

For vegetable oils, the main substitution—also assumed to continue —has been in the growing use of inedible animal fats in the manufacture of soap, and of lard and marine oils in the manufacture of margarine. The demand for margarine changes significantly when butter prices change, and in the projections a fall in the ratio of butter to margarine prices in the E.E.C. area has been assumed over the coming decade, as a result of the common agricultural policy. For hides and skins, the growing use of synthetic rubber soling for footwear has already made substantial inroads into a major end-use of leather, particularly in the United States and the United Kingdom, and the substitution process has been assumed to spread increasingly during the next decade to the other industrial countries. A more recent development has been the introduction of synthetic leather for use in footwear uppers; if prices of this new synthetic can be substantially reduced, it would probably result in a serious reduction in world demand for natural leather.

Substitution against natural rubber has been intensified with the introduction in recent years of new synthetic stereo rubbers, which have the same chemical properties as natural rubber. Though much of the new capacity for synthetic rubbers now on stream, or planned, competes with other synthetic rubbers rather than with natural, there seems little doubt that the growth of the synthetic industry will continue, and will exert a downward pressure on the price of natural rubber. For the projection, it has been assumed that the natural rubber price in 1975 will be some 35 to 40 per cent below the 1960–1 average.[1]

A similar approach, in terms of end-uses, could have been adopted for apparel fibres and non-ferrous metals. However, the complexities of the markets for these commodities—particularly the intricate network of price substitution as between different fibres and as between different metals in the various end-uses—put this more detailed approach beyond the resources available for this study. Instead, the consumption projections in these cases were made in two stages. First, total consumption of all apparel fibres,[2] and of all the main non-ferrous metals,[3] was projected. For the fibres, this was done by valuing the quantity of each consumed at the average prices of 1960–1, and relating the value of consumption per head of population to the level of gross domestic product per head, also valued at constant prices. This was done by use of a semi-logarithmic relationship for each of the industrial areas; this function implies a declining elasticity of demand for textile products as real income per head rises. The results were then applied to the assumed rise of real income per head in each industrial area between 1960–1 and 1975. A similar procedure was followed for the non-ferrous metals, except that the correlation in this case was with the relevant indices of manufacturing production in each industrial area.

The second stage of the projection was to divide the 1975 totals into their component commodities. The division of the apparel fibres projection into cotton, wool, rayon and synthetic fibres for each country was based partly on past trends in the share of each in the total, and partly on a judgement that the future decline in the share held by cotton and wool would be much slower than over the past decade, mainly because new technologies are being applied to the natural fibres—such as the

---

[1] This corresponds to a 1975 price of 17 to 20 pence per lb.
[2] Cotton, wool and man-made fibres (cellulosic and synthetic).
[3] Aluminium, copper, lead, tin and zinc.

use of synthetic finishes—and they appear likely to improve their relative competitive position.

For the non-ferrous metals, the division of the total projection for 1975 into the various metals was based, in part, on the assumption that aluminium will continue to displace other metals—particularly copper —for technological reasons, at much the same rate as over the past decade; and, in part, on the assumption that the prices of copper and tin would be significantly higher, in relation to other non-ferrous metals prices, than they were in 1960–1. More specifically, it was assumed that the ratio of copper to aluminium prices would rise by 25 per cent over the projection period, while the tin/aluminium price ratio would rise by 35 per cent.[1]

Import content of consumption

For tropical products, such as coffee, cocoa, tea and raw jute, which are not produced in the industrial countries (Japan's tea production being an exception), the consumption projection can be taken as indicating the import requirements of the industrial countries in 1975. For temperate-zone agricultural products, however, the movement in the proportion of consumption likely to be met from imports will depend heavily on the protectionist policies of the industrial countries. The import proportion is virtually certain to decline further for sugar if recent trends in production continue in the industrial countries; a moderate decline in this proportion has, in fact, been taken on the assumption that, at some stage in the near future, an international agreement will be reached, one of the features of which will be some form of production limitation in the developed sugar-importing countries.

The likely trend in the import content of meat consumption is to some extent problematical in view of the uncertainty about the impact of the common agricultural policy in the E.E.C. countries on the output of livestock products. The probability seems to be, however, that the E.E.C. area as a whole will become either a marginal net importer, or a marginal net exporter, by the early 1970s, the expansion envisaged in French meat production being roughly sufficient to meet the likely import requirements of the other Common Market countries at that period. Production in North America and the United Kingdom is likely to rise further, especially if a rise occurs in the ratio of livestock-product prices to feedingstuff prices, which seems a reasonable anticipation. On balance, however, the import content of meat consumption seems unlikely to change very much from the position of the early 1960s; the projections indicate a decline in E.E.C. net imports, offset by higher imports into the United States and, to a lesser degree, into Britain.

[1] See Appendix B6 for further discussion.

For fruit, however, some modest rise in the import content of consumption has been assumed, reflecting the probable extension of fruit-processing for export in the primary-producing countries. Since fruit juices, canned and other processed fruit enjoy higher income elasticities of demand than do most fresh fruits, the development of overseas fruit-processing industries is likely to be associated with some shift in consumer expenditures in the industrial countries towards imports.

Among the industrial materials, increases are anticipated in the import content of consumption of raw cotton and raw wool in the industrial countries, though for cotton the outlook is heavily dependent on the effect of the United States Agriculture Act of November 1965, the objectives of which are to reduce output and expand exports in order to bring down the current excessive level of stocks. By a reduction in the support price for cotton, some decline in United States export prices will be achieved. It could result in a decline in marginal production in primary-producing countries, but this could be offset by improved yields and by the improved competitive position of cotton in relation to other fibres. The import content of elastomer consumption is assumed to continue to decline with the further expansion now envisaged in synthetic rubber production; the projection takes into account the probable future expansion in the consumption of the synthetic stereo rubbers mentioned above. For vegetable oils and oilseeds, too, it seems reasonable to assume a fall in the import proportion as a result of the probable future growth in soya production in the United States, the increase in substitution of animal fats for vegetable oils in both soap and margarine production, and the continued protection of rapeseed production in continental Western Europe. However, in this analysis attention was focused on the main 'Sterling' oils and, for these, net imports can reasonably be expected to rise at the same rate as consumption (see Appendix B4).

For non-ferrous metals, on the other hand, the import content of consumption has been assumed to rise, a shift towards more processed metals (particularly aluminium) in the imports from primary-producing countries more than offsetting a further expansion of mine production and secondary-metal output in the industrial countries.

The share of the Overseas Sterling Area in imports by the industrial countries

Projections of the proportion of the industrial countries' imports likely to come from Sterling sources were based, in part, on simple extrapolation of recent trends. Wherever possible, however, the extrapolations were adjusted to allow for the different production potentials of Sterling and non-Sterling primary-producing countries and for changes in preferential systems now in train in the main industrial countries.

The Sterling share of industrial countries' imports of coffee has been assumed to rise moderately between the early 1960s and 1975. Much will depend, in the case of coffee, on the operation of the production control provisions of the International Coffee Agreement and whether, in practice, these make adequate allowance for shifts in consumer preferences (for example, towards the African *robusta* variety most used in the production of soluble coffee). For cocoa, no further increase has been assumed in the Sterling share from the level reached in 1964–5, though some further gains in yields seem likely in the period up to 1970 in Ghana and Nigeria. However, here too the net result will depend heavily on the provisions for control of production embodied in any international agreement that might be negotiated. For tea, the Sterling share of world trade declined between 1953–7 and 1960–1, but has since regained this loss. It has been assumed that the Sterling share will remain at much the same level as in the mid-1960s, although a major uncertainty here is the extent to which Indonesia can expand her production for export.

The Sterling share of sugar imports into the industrial countries appears likely to rise over the projection period in view of the expansion of output in Australia and other Sterling countries since the break between the United States and Cuba in 1961. For vegetable oils and oilseeds, too, the Sterling producers' share in the markets of continental Western Europe is assumed to grow as a result of reduced tariff preferences in the French market enjoyed by the former French African countries. Moreover, the Sterling producers are more likely to achieve a substantial increase in exportable output than are the African countries now associated with the E.E.C. under the Yaoundé Convention; and, furthermore, the association of Nigeria with the E.E.C. as from mid 1966 will strengthen this trend. The Sterling share of meat imports into the British market is unlikely to change substantially from that of the base period, but the recent gains in the Sterling share of meat imports into the United States—mainly in manufacturing grades of beef—are assumed to continue in the future.

Britain should probably remain the preponderant market for the Sterling Area's exports of butter and cheese. Commonwealth supplies of cheese in the British market are protected by a tariff preference, but imports of butter are duty-free, though since 1961 butter imports have been subject to quota arrangements. If the quotas are continued, they are likely to stabilize the share of British imports coming from overseas Sterling countries. For cheese, little change in the Sterling share of British imports is envisaged, for Continental cheeses have only a limited market in Britain.

Sterling raw cotton exports account for under one-tenth of world cotton exports, but they represent some two-fifths, by value, of total exports from Uganda. The Sterling share of the world total will probably show a moderate rise over the projection period, although—as already indicated—the outlook is particularly uncertain in view of recent United States legislation which will result in reduced export prices. The projection assumes the continuation of exports from Sterling producers to China. The Sterling share of raw wool imports into the industrial countries (about three-quarters of the total, by value, in 1960–1) is assumed to remain much the same or, at best, to show only a marginal improvement, in 1975, compared with the early 1960s.

Natural rubber production has increased more rapidly in Sterling than in non-Sterling countries over the past decade. This differential has been assumed to continue, taking into account recent trends in new plantings and productivity in the main producing areas. By 1975, the Overseas Sterling Area could account for about 55 per cent of world natural rubber output, as against 47 per cent in 1964–5 and 44 per cent in the mid 1950s. However, this assumes little recovery in Indonesian production, though good potential exists in that country. For the non-ferrous metals as a group, a moderate increase in the Sterling share of industrial countries' imports is assumed to occur, with loss of share in aluminium (including bauxite) and in copper being offset by a fairly large rise in tin and a smaller one in lead.

Volume and value projections

As was explained in Chapter 4, the present set of projections is based essentially on the general assumption that relative prices of the main primary commodities will be much the same in 1975 as they were in 1960–1.[1] A more sophisticated approach, if systematically applied, would involve making projections of production, as well as of consumption, at alternative levels of relative prices, before arriving at the most likely price level at which the world market would be in approximate balance. Apart from the fact that the resources required for such an analysis would put it well beyond the scope of this book, it is doubtful whether, in our present state of knowledge of the variables involved, reliable supply functions could be computed for all, or even the majority, of the main primary commodities.

Moreover, it would not have been sensible to assume small changes in market prices, one way or the other, over the projection period, since these would have had no significance in view of the margins of error which are inevitably involved in projections of the type presented here. Substantial price changes, on the other hand, can legitimately be assumed only when the available trends appear very definite and prob-

[1] See the discussion on pages 117 and 118.

ably enduring. Several distinct cases can be distinguished. The first is where supply appears to be very inelastic (as, for example, where production is subject to technological limitations), or where output can be increased only at substantially higher unit costs. Where output is technologically limited, the rise in demand would be accompanied by a corresponding rise in price. Of the various primary commodities considered in the appendices, tin comes perhaps closer to this category than any other though, even for tin, world output is likely to rise somewhat if tin prices increase, as production in sub-marginal mines or mining areas becomes profitable. Though copper production is likely to be substantially expanded in the decade up to 1975, it seems probable that this expansion will be achieved only at appreciably higher unit costs than those of the early 1960s. For both tin and copper, the buoyancy of world demand seems likely to continue, so it is reasonable to assume that by 1975 their prices will have risen significantly compared with the price of aluminium—their major competitor—which, if anything, could well decline in 'real' terms.[1] In making the detailed projections, the rise in the tin/aluminium price ratio over the period up to 1975 has been taken at 35 per cent, the corresponding increase for copper/aluminium prices being assumed to be 25 per cent.

A second case is where a natural raw material is subject to displacement by synthetic materials, which effectively determine the price of the natural product. For natural rubber, which falls in this category, it has been assumed—as mentioned above—that the price in 1975 will have declined by some 35 to 40 per cent from the 1960–1 average level.

The years 1963–5 witnessed a dramatic price reversal in the free market for sugar, reflecting sharp variations in supplies available for sale on residual markets outside the main preferential trading channels.[2] Apart from this extreme short-run price instability, the world sugar market is characterized by a large structural surplus of production. Unless some form of international agreement is arrived at in the near future, the prospects are for a period of extremely low free-market prices, combined with burdensome surplus stocks. Again, the negotiation of an international agreement has been assumed, for purposes of the projections, which would embody some form of production control so as to maintain the free market price at reasonably remunerative levels for the producing countries. For this purpose, a 'reasonably remunerative level' has been taken as not being significantly different from the

---

[1] Since electric power represents the major single cost element in aluminium production, the price of aluminium in relation to all other prices (i.e. its price in 'real' terms) should decline as the efficiency of electric power generation increases.

[2] That is, United States imports, imports under the Commonwealth Sugar Agreement, imports by France and Portugal from their associated overseas territories, and imports by the Soviet Union from Cuba.

average price for 1960–1 (3·0 U.S. cents per lb.), while it has also been assumed that prices ruling in the preferential channels of trade would be maintained over the projection period.

For the other primary commodities covered by the projections, it does not seem possible to attempt an assessment of the probable direction or magnitude of future price changes. Since the projection period is a decade or longer, this would seem sufficiently long for world production to adjust to the growth in world demand—even, in some cases, to over-adjust so as to reverse the previous price trend. For such commodities, a general assumption has perforce been made that their relative prices will remain the same in 1975 as they were in 1960–1. This 'blanket' assumption does not imply a belief that no relative price changes are likely to occur, merely that no reliable assessment of their probable magnitudes has been possible within the scope of the present study.

2. CONSUMPTION AND NET IMPORTS OF THE INDUSTRIAL COUNTRIES

On the basis of the various assumptions outlined above—and which are discussed in more detail in the appendices—projections of consumption and net imports of the major primary products have been made for the industrial countries in 1975, and these are briefly summarized in Table 5.1. The products covered by the projections accounted for some three-quarters, by value, of all primary commodities exported by the Overseas Sterling Area in 1960–1.

Consumption of the selected *foods*, *beverages* and *tobacco* included in the calculation[1] is projected to rise between 1960–1 and 1975 by 2·3 to 2·7 per cent a year in volume terms, according to which income-growth assumption is used; this compares with an average growth rate of 2·7 per cent a year between 1952–4 and 1960–1 for the same items, so that the growth rate in consumption is projected to slow down unless the higher income-growth level is attained. The volume of net imports of food, beverages and tobacco is projected to rise in total at much the same rate as consumption.

Consumption of selected *natural materials*[2] shown in Table 5.1 has been confined to products prominent in the export trade of overseas Sterling countries. These, taken together, are projected to rise by 3·1 to 3·7 per cent a year, by volume, over the period to 1975, compared with 3·1 per cent a year between 1952–4 and 1960–1. The spread between the growth rates on the two income assumptions (0·6 per cent a year)

[1] Tropical beverages, sugar, meat, dairy products, fruit, cereals and tobacco.
[2] Apparel fibres, jute, rubber, vegetable oils and oilseeds, hides and skins and non-ferrous metals.

Table 5.1. *Consumption and net imports of selected foods and industrial materials in the industrial countries, 1960–3, and projections for 1975*

| | 1960–1 | 1962–3 | 1975 | | Average rate of growth 1960–1 to 1975 | |
			A	B	A	B
	(£000 m. at 1960–1 prices)				*(% p.a. compound)*	
Food, beverages and tobacco:						
Consumption	18·9	19·9	26·3	28·0	2·3	2·7
Net imports	1·6	1·8	2·2	2·3	2·4	2·7
Industrial materials[a]:						
Natural: Consumption	5·2	5·5	8·0	8·8	3·1	3·7
Net imports	1·9	2·0	2·8	3·1	2·9	3·6
Natural *plus* synthetic:						
Consumption	8·8	10·4	16·7	19·4	4·6	5·7
Net imports	1·5	1·6	2·0	2·1	2·1	2·4

SOURCES: Appendices A and B.
[a] Excluding iron and steel, and forest products.

is greater than that for food, beverages and tobacco, reflecting the higher income elasticity for industrial materials than for most foods and beverages. The rise in the projected growth rate for natural materials, compared with the actual rate achieved over the recent past, is due in large part to the assumption that the rate of economic growth in the United States in the 1960s and the first half of the 1970s will be appreciably higher than the low rate attained in the 1950s.

Unlike the projections for food, beverages and tobacco, those for natural materials show a decline in the import content of consumption in the period up to 1975. The volume of net imports of natural materials by the industrial countries is projected to rise by only 2·9 to 3·6 per cent a year (according to the income-growth assumption chosen), the import content of consumption for this collection of materials showing a corresponding decline. The projected rise in consumption of synthetic materials, however (about 6 per cent a year on the lower and 8 per cent a year on the higher income-growth assumption), is about double the growth rates projected for consumption of natural materials. This asymmetry is essentially a continuation of the trends which were so notable a feature of economic growth in the industrial countries during the 1950s.[1] However, the projections indicate a probable slowing down of

[1] See A. Maizels, L. F. Campbell-Boross and P. B. W. Rayment, 'Trade and Development Problems of the Under-developed Countries: the Background to the United Nations' Conference', *National Institute Economic Review*, no. 28, May 1964.

MEE

the unusually rapid rate of growth in consumption of synthetic materials in the earlier period (about 12½ per cent a year, on average, from 1952–4 to 1960–1); whereas, as already indicated, the growth rate of consumption of natural materials—though remaining considerably lower than for the synthetics—is likely to rise somewhat on the basis of the higher income-growth assumption.

For all the industrial materials—both natural and synthetic—included in the projections, consumption is estimated to grow by 4·6 to 5·7 per cent a year, according to the income-growth assumption adopted, while net imports would grow by only 2·1 to 2·4 per cent a year. The latter growth rates are significantly below those for the natural materials alone, since they assume that net exports of synthetic materials from the industrial countries grow at the same (fast) rate as does their consumption.

The impact of substitution of domestic production against imports of natural materials can be approximately assessed from these overall results. If net imports of natural materials were to rise, over the projection period, in the same proportion as consumption of such materials, net imports into the industrial countries in 1975 would amount to £2·9 billion and £3·2 billion,[1] on assumptions A and B respectively, or some £93 million higher than the corresponding projections. If, however, net imports of natural materials are assumed to rise in proportion to consumption of both natural and synthetic materials, net imports of natural materials in 1975 would become £3·5 billion on assumption A and £4·1 billion on assumption B. Thus, the loss to net imports resulting from the displacement of synthetic for natural materials would be £0·7 billion and £0·3 billion, respectively, on the lower (A) and higher (B) income-growth assumptions. The projections indicate that a much sharper adverse impact in the imports of natural materials is likely to result from their continued displacement by synthetics than from the substitution of domestic for imported natural materials.

Food and beverages

For the industrial countries, the projected growth rates in consumption of the main foods and beverages exported by the Overseas Sterling Area are summarized in Table 5.2. For simplicity of presentation, this shows only the arithmetic averages of the growth rates based on assumptions A and B; further details can be found in the relevant commodity chapters of Appendix A.

For the industrial countries as a whole, consumption of all the selected foods and beverages is projected to rise by rather less than 3 per cent a year, in volume, over the period 1960–1 to 1975. Somewhat faster rates

---

[1] Values quoted in this paragraph are at 1960–1 prices.

Table 5.2. *Projected annual rates of growth of the consumption of selected foods in the industrial areas, 1960–1 to 1975[a] (percentage per annum, compound)*

	United Kingdom	E.E.C.	Other Western Europe	United States	Canada	Japan	Total
Coffee	3·1	2·7	..[b]	1·4	..[b]	..[b]	2·6
Tea	0·7	..[b]	..[b]	2·3	..[b]	3·6	1·6
Cocoa	2·5	2·5	4·0	2·5	..[b]	..[b]	2·8
Tropical beverages	1·4	2·6	4·3	1·6	3·4	4·4	2·4
Sugar	0·7	2·4	2·1	1·0	2·5	4·4	1·8
Meat	1·6	3·1	5·0	2·3	3·0	8·3	2·9
Butter	1·6	1·9	1·2	−0·3	0·2	10·9	1·3
Cheese	2·0	2·3	3·5	2·4	3·3	2·8	2·5
Apples and pears	3·0	3·2	3·2	2·2	2·8	6·1	3·2
Citrus fruit	3·2	3·8	3·9	2·4	3·3	6·2	3·4
Bananas	2·4	2·8	3·1	1·8	2·4	7·2	2·5
Canned fruit	2·6	5·3	5·8	2·0	2·7	8·0	3·1
Total fruit	2·9	3·4	3·4	2·2	2·9	6·4	3·2
TOTAL	1·7	2·9	4·0	2·1	2·8	6·5	2·7
Per caput consumption	*0·9*	*2·2*	*2·9*	*0·7*	*0·8*	*5·6*	*1·6*

SOURCE: Appendix A.

[a] Mid-points of projections A and B.　　[b] No separate projections were made.

of growth in consumption are projected for fruit, while, at the other extreme, the projections show average annual growth rates of only 1 to 1½ per cent a year for tea and butter. These differences in projected growth rates are, in effect, a continuation of corresponding differences over the past decade,[1] though the projections indicate that the dispersion will probably be smaller in future than hitherto.

Of the main industrial countries, the fastest growth in food consumption is projected for Japan and 'other Western Europe'; the Japanese growth rate projected for these selected foods and beverages (6½ per cent a year) is more than double the average for all the industrial countries combined. This asymmetrical pattern of consumption growth, with a few exceptions, is generally repeated in the projections for individual foods and beverages. Among the high-income countries of North America and Western Europe, an appreciably slower growth rate for consumption of the selected foods and beverages is projected in the United States and Britain than in the E.E.C. countries.

In the United States, the absolute level of butter consumption is projected to decline somewhat, the effect of population growth being assumed to be more than offset by a change in consumer tastes away

[1] See note on p. 129.

from fatty foods, including butter. Sugar, banana, and coffee consumption are all projected to rise by 1 to 2 per cent a year, on average, reflecting essentially the increasing demands of a growing population. In the United Kingdom, a further shift in preferences from tea to coffee has been projected, while consumption of meat, cheese and fruit can be expected to rise faster than of foods such as sugar for which *per caput* consumption is already at a relatively high level. A similar pattern of change is implied in the projections for continental Western Europe, the variations between the E.E.C. countries and the rest reflecting very largely the differences in income elasticities at different *per caput* levels of consumption. For Japan, relatively high consumption-growth rates are projected for all the selected foods and beverages.

Taking into account the estimated growth in population up to 1975, the projections indicate a relatively slow rate of growth in the volume of *per caput* consumption of these foods and beverages in Britain, the United States and Canada (under 1 per cent a year), a rather faster increase in continental Western Europe (2 to 3 per cent a year), and relatively fast growth in Japan (about $5\frac{1}{2}$ per cent a year).

These differences imply that the various industrial areas will make very different contributions to the total growth in food consumption over the projection period. The United States, for example, accounted for some two-fifths of the total value of consumption of all the selected foods and beverages in the industrial areas in 1960–1, but would—on the basis of the projections—account for under one-third of the value of the increment in consumption over the period to 1975. The United Kingdom, likewise, would account for a smaller proportion of the increment in consumption of the selected foods and beverages in the period up to 1975 (6 per cent) than the corresponding proportion in 1960–1 (11 per cent). The E.E.C. countries would, however, increase their relative contributions on the basis of the projections; these countries accounted for almost one-third of the industrial countries' total consumption of the selected items in 1960–1 and are projected to account for a slightly larger proportion of the increment up to 1975. Both Japan and 'other Western Europe' are projected to become considerably more important in the total consumption of the selected foods and beverages (Table 5.3).

The commodity pattern of consumption of foods and beverages in the industrial countries is, however, markedly different from that of their imports, as can be seen from Table 5.4. In 1960–1, for example, meat and cereals together represented some two-thirds of the value of consumption of the selected items in the industrial countries, compared with only one-sixth of their net imports (excluding wheat and rice). However, the projections indicate a faster than average growth in meat

Table 5.3. *Distribution of consumption of selected foods in the industrial areas, 1960–1, and changes from 1960–1 to 1975*[a]

	United Kingdom	E.E.C.	Other Western Europe	United States	Canada	Japan	Total (=100%)
	(%)	(%)	(%)	(%)	(%)	(%)	(£000 m. at 1960–1 prices)
DISTRIBUTION IN 1960–1							
Coffee	2	27	12	56	3	1	0·59
Tea	56	5	4	12	5	18	0·18
Cocoa	11	43	10	32	2	2	0·14
Total	14	25	10	44	3	4	0·90
Sugar	13	25	14	38	4	6	0·77
Meat	11	29	8	47	4	1	7·21
Dairy products[b]	13	41	15	28	3	0	1·53
Fruit	7	36	13	34	4	6	1·91
TOTAL	11	30	10	43	4	2	12·32
PROJECTED CHANGES FROM 1960–1 TO 1975							
Coffee	3	31	..	30	..	..	+0·26
Tea	29	..	..	20	..	48	+0·05
Cocoa	10	37	15	28	..	..	+0·07
Total	8	28	22	28	5	9	+0·37
Sugar	5	34	15	21	5	20	+0·23
Meat	6	32	17	35	4	5	+3·65
Dairy products[b]	10	45	21	20	2	2	+0·48
Fruit	6	39	14	22	3	16	+1·12
TOTAL	6	35	17	30	4	8	+5·85

SOURCE: Appendix A.

[a] Mid-points of projections A and B.   [b] Butter and cheese only.

consumption but a slower than average growth in consumption of coarse grains. Similarly, among the major net imports, consumption trends are also offsetting to a large extent; the relatively fast growth in consumption projected for coffee, cocoa and fruit, for example, is largely offset by a relatively slow consumption growth projected for tea, butter and sugar. On balance, the net effect of the projected changes in the pattern of food consumption in the industrial countries on the volume of net imports is likely to be purely marginal.

On the assumption that no appreciable change will occur in the domestic policies of the industrial countries as to protection of domestic agriculture, the projections indicate the probability of a decline in the import content of consumption, if wheat and rice (which are net exports

Table 5.4. *Consumption and net imports of selected foods, beverages and tobacco in the industrial countries, 1960–3, and projections for 1975*

	Consumption			Net imports		
	1960–1	Volume index[a]		1960–1	Volume index[a]	
		1962–3	1975		1962–3	1975
			A B			A B
	(£000 m.)	(1960–1 = 100)		(£000 m.)	(1960–1 = 100)	
Coffee	0·59	110	140 150	0·59	110	140 150
Tea	0·18	104	125 130	0·14	106	120 120
Cocoa	0·14	108	145 150	0·14	108	145 150
Tropical beverages	0·90	109	140 145	0·87	109	140 145
Sugar	0·77	103	125 130	0·31	112	115 120
Meat	7·21	107	145 155	0·24	135[b]	145 145
Butter	0·73	109	115 120	0·06	110	120 125
Cheese	0·80	111	140 145	0·01	148	180 200
Fruit[c]	1·91	100	150 165	0·25	107	155 165
Wheat and wheat flour	1·63	103	125 130	−0·33	115[e]	130[e] 140[e]
Rice[d]	0·45	113	120 125	−0·03	132[e]	100[e] 120[e]
Coarse grains[d]	3·84	102	135 145	0·09	132	160 170
Tobacco[d]	0·71	107	135 140	0·09	135	140 160
TOTAL	18·94	105	140 150	1·56	116	140 145
TOTAL excluding wheat and rice	16·86	105	140 150	1·91	116	140 145

SOURCE: Appendix A.

[a] Indices for 1975 have been rounded to nearest 5.

[b] The volume of meat imports into industrial countries from Latin America declined in 1964 and 1965.

[c] Apples and pears, citrus fruit, bananas and canned fruit.

[d] For these items, the projections relate to industrial countries taken as a group.

[e] Indices of net exports from the industrial countries.

for the industrial countries) are excluded. This would reflect increasing self-sufficiency in the industrial countries for sugar, meat and fruit. The major influence, however, on the volume of net imports of food, beverages and tobacco would be the stimulus to consumption resulting from higher population and from the growth in real income per head as assumed in the projections.[1]

[1] The change in the volume of net imports between 1960–1 and 1975 can be written as:

$$\Delta M = \Sigma s_1 C_1 - \Sigma s_0 C_0,$$

where s represents the share of net imports in consumption, C, and o and 1 indicate the periods 1960–1 and 1975, respectively. ΔM can also be written as:

$$\Delta M = \Sigma s_0 C_0 \left\{ \frac{\Sigma C_1}{\Sigma C_0} - 1 \right\} + \left\{ \Sigma s_0 C_1 - \Sigma s_0 C_0 \frac{\Sigma C_1}{\Sigma C_0} \right\} + \{ \Sigma s_1 C_1 - \Sigma s_0 C_1 \},$$

where the first term represents the change in the volume of net imports that can be attributable to the change in the total volume of food consumption of the items considered; the

Industrial materials

As indicated earlier, the projections show a considerably faster growth rate in consumption of industrial materials than of foods, beverages and tobacco over the period up to 1975 (see Table 5.1). However, among the industrial materials, large differences are projected for the growth rates of consumption of the various items, as can be seen from Table 5.5, which, for convenience of presentation, shows only the averages of the growth rates on assumptions A and B.

Consumption of raw cotton and 'Sterling' vegetable oils and oilseeds, at one extreme, is estimated to rise by only about 1 per cent a year, on average, whereas for non-ferrous metals, at the other extreme, the average growth rate projected is not far short of 5 per cent a year. In intermediate positions are jute, natural rubber, raw wool, and hides and skins, although the mean of the projected growth rates on assumptions A and B exceeds $2\frac{1}{2}$ per cent a year only in the case of natural rubber. The non-ferrous metals, taken as a group, are thus quite exceptional among the 'traditional' industrial materials in having such a relatively rapid consumption growth projected for the period covered.

The rate of growth of consumption of the selected materials, taken as a group, is projected at some $2\frac{1}{2}$ to 4 per cent a year for all the industrial countries, or country groups, except Japan, for which a higher rate (over 6 per cent) is projected.[1] The latter reflects, in part, the assumption made earlier that Japanese manufacturing production will rise faster than that of the other industrial countries. However, the rate of growth projected for the consumption of these industrial materials is considerably lower than the assumed rate of increase in industrial output in Japan. Consequently, the projections imply a substantial decline, by two-fifths, comparing 1975 with 1960–1, in the consumption of these materials per unit of manufacturing production in that country. Corresponding declines in the input–output ratios in manufacturing industry are implied in the projections for E.E.C. (one-third) and 'other Western Europe' (also one-third), though these are both appreciably less than that projected for Japan. For Britain and the

---

second term indicates the corresponding change attributable to the change in the pattern of consumption (at 1960–1 weights); and the third term represents the change attributable to the change in the share of net imports in the consumption of the various items. Using this formula, the value of net imports of the selected items of food, beverages and tobacco would rise from £1·95 billion in 1960–1 to £2·86 billion (at 1960–1 prices) in 1975, on assumption B —an increase of £0·91 billion. This latter figure is composed of an increase of £0·94 billion attributable to the rise projected in total consumption, an increase of £0·02 billion due to the shift in commodity pattern of consumption, and a decrease of £0·05 billion due to a loss of share of net imports in consumption.

[1] As already explained, these rates are the averages of the two projections based respectively on assumptions A and B.

Table 5.5. *Projected annual rates of growth of the consumption of selected industrial materials in the industrial areas, 1960–1 to 1975[a]* (*percentage per annum, compound*)

	United Kingdom	E.E.C.	Other Western Europe	United States	Canada	Japan	Total
Raw cotton	−0·8	0·9	2·2	0·4	3·6	−0·1	0·7
Raw wool	1·0	1·8	1·8	0·6	3·9	2·8	1·6
Raw jute and jute goods	1·2	0·8	2·0	2·5	2·0	5·2	2·0
Natural rubber	1·6	3·1	5·5	1·1	2·0	4·6	2·7
Vegetable oils and oilseeds[b]	0·7	0·7	1·7	1·5		6·3	1·2
Hides and skins	0·3	2·4	4·2	−0·3	1·0	5·8	2·0
Non-ferrous metals	3·5	4·6	5·7	3·8	5·0	9·2	4·8
TOTAL	2·4	3·3	4·0	2·7	3·9	6·4	3·4
Projected growth rates in manufacturing production[c]	4·5	6·0	6·4	4·1	4·0	9·9	5·0
Consumption of above natural materials per unit of manufacturing production in 1975 (1960–1 = 100)	74	69	72	83	99	63	80

SOURCE: Appendix B.

[a] Mid-points of projections A and B.
[b] 'Sterling' oils and oilseeds only (see Appendix B4).
[c] Based on projections in Table 4.4.

United States, the input–output ratios are projected to decline by about one-quarter and one-fifth, respectively, over the projection period (Table 5.5).

These projected declines in the ratio of consumption of the selected 'traditional' materials to the volume of manufacturing production must very largely be considered a continuation of the underlying structural changes that were mentioned earlier,[1] particularly the continued displacement of natural by synthetic raw materials. A major reason for the more rapid decline in the ratio of natural materials input to manufacturing output in continental Western Europe and Japan over the period up to 1975 is that in both areas the substitution of synthetics for natural materials is anticipated to proceed at a faster rate in the late 1960s and early 1970s than in the United States (or even Britain), where relatively greater inroads by synthetics had been made by the early 1960s.

[1] See A. Maizels, L. F. Campbell-Boross and P. B. W. Rayment, 'Trade and Development Problems of the Under-developed Countries' (cited on p. 129).

This general pattern of projected faster growth rates for the consumption of natural industrial materials in continental Western Europe and
Japan than in Britain and the United States can also be seen in the projections for the individual materials, as summarized in Table 5.5—
though there are a few exceptions. One is the relatively fast growth in
consumption of jute and jute goods projected for the United States,
reflecting in part the likely growth in demand for jute packaging and
carpet backing in that country. For natural rubber, the projected rates
of growth in consumption are very low for Britain and North America
(less than 2 per cent a year), compared with over 3 per cent a year in
continental Western Europe and nearly 5 per cent a year in Japan; this
large difference results mainly from the assumption that the elasticity
of rubber consumption (with respect to real income) is much higher in
the latter countries than in the former.

Taking the selected industrial materials as a whole, the projections
indicate little change in the relative importance of the different industrial areas in total consumption. The major exception to this generaliza-
tion is Japan, which accounted for one-tenth of the value of consumption
of all these materials in the industrial countries in 1960–1, but is projected to consume almost a quarter of the increase up to 1975. The
United States share is projected to fall from just under two-fifths to
about a quarter of the total, and the E.E.C. share to remain just over
a quarter. Britain's share, however, is projected to decline marginally
from the one-eighth held in 1960–1 (Table 5.6).

The relative contribution of each industrial country to the projected
increment in consumption is likely to vary considerably from one commodity to another. Japan, for example, is projected to account for as
much as one-quarter of the increment in consumption of raw wool,
natural rubber, vegetable oils, hides and skins and non-ferrous metals.
On the other hand, Japan's contribution to the growth of consumption
of cotton is projected as negative. The United States is projected to
contribute about half the total expansion in jute consumption in the
industrial areas, but with an absolute decline in the consumption of
hides and skins. Britain's contribution is projected to be relatively
greatest (about one-tenth of the total increment in consumption) for
jute, oils and oilseeds, non-ferrous metals and raw wool, while an absolute decline in Britain's cotton consumption is projected.

As to the E.E.C. countries, their contribution to the total increase in
consumption not only differs widely from one commodity to another
but is in some cases very large. For wool, natural rubber, vegetable oils
and oilseeds, and hides and skins, the E.E.C.'s contribution to the growth
in consumption is larger than that of any of the other countries or country
groups, while for cotton and non-ferrous metals the E.E.C. still accounts

Table 5.6. *Distribution of consumption of selected industrial materials in the industrial areas, 1960–1, and changes from 1960–1 to 1975[a]*

	United Kingdom	E.E.C.	Other Western Europe	United States	Canada	Japan	Total (=100%)
	(%)	(%)	(%)	(%)	(%)	(%)	(£000 m. at 1960–1 prices)
DISTRIBUTION IN 1960–1							
Raw cotton	7	21	12	44	3	13	0·96
Raw wool	14	31	16	24	2	13	0·53
Raw jute and jute goods	17	26	9	38	5	5	0·12
Total	10	25	13	37	3	12	1·61
Natural rubber	13	30	8	34	2	13	0·31
Vegetable oils and oilseeds[b]	19	48	11	19		3	0·24
Hides and skins	11	32	15	34	2	6	0·30
Non-ferrous metals	13	27	7	41	3	9	2·73
TOTAL	12	27	10	38	3	10	5·19
PROJECTED CHANGES FROM 1960–1 TO 1975							
Raw cotton	−7	27	40	25	16	−1	+0·11
Raw wool	8	33	19	8	6	25	+0·13
Raw jute and jute goods	10	10	9	49	4	18	+0·04
Total	2	28	26	20	10	14	+0·28
Natural rubber	7	34	20	13	2	24	+0·15
Vegetable oils and oilseeds[b]	10	26	16	23		25	+0·04
Hides and skins	2	39	38	−5	1	25	+0·10
Non-ferrous metals	9	25	9	31	3	23	+2·64
TOTAL	8	26	12	28	3	23	+3·21

SOURCE: Appendix B.

[a] Mid-points of projections A and B.
[b] 'Sterling' oils and oilseeds only (see Appendix B4).

for a quarter or more of the total increase. For 'other Western Europe', the greatest relative contribution to the increment in consumption is projected for raw cotton (two-fifths of the total); the least for jute and non-ferrous metals (less than one-tenth).

The projections of consumption summarized in Tables 5.5 and 5.6 relate to the main natural materials exported by the Overseas Sterling Area. The outstanding feature of the projections for industrial materials, however, is the continued displacement of natural by synthetic materials. The bases of the projections for consumption of synthetic fibres and synthetic rubber have already been noted, and more detailed explanations are given in the relevant chapters of Appendix B. For plastic materials and synthetic detergents, a still rapid growth in consumption has been assumed, though in each case the projected growth rate is somewhat below the fast growth rates achieved over the past decade. If synthetics are included, the total consumption of the materials included in Table 5.7 is projected to rise in the period up to 1975 by 4.5 and 5.6 per cent a year on assumptions A and B respectively. Within this total, consumption of synthetics is projected to grow at 6 per cent a year (assumption A) or 8 per cent a year (assumption B).

This further switch into synthetic materials—the consumption of which is likely to be met entirely by domestic production in the industrial areas—will have an adverse effect on the demand for imported natural materials. Net imports of the main natural materials (as listed in Table 5.7) amounted to £1·87 billion in the period 1960–1, and are projected to rise, on the more optimistic assumption B, to about £3.09 billion (at 1960–1 prices) by 1975. The increase of £1·22 billion over the period can be attributed almost entirely to the assumed expansion in industrial output in the industrial countries; this factor alone would have been responsible for an increase of some £2·8 billion in net imports of natural materials over the projection period. These hypothetical gains would, however, be partially offset by a loss of £1·2 billion in net imports which can be attributed to the effects of the substitution of domestically produced for imported materials. Of this import-substitution effect, about £0·8 billion would result from the further substitution of natural by synthetic materials implied in the projections, the remaining £0·4 billion reflecting the projected shift in the pattern of consumption of natural materials away from materials (particularly the textiles and natural rubber) with a relatively high import content.[1]

The hypothetical loss of £0·8 billion a year in net imports of natural materials into the industrial countries by 1975 (on the more optimistic income-growth assumption) may, however, be somewhat overstated, to the extent that the growth in synthetics consumption results in a displacement of materials not included in the calculation. Of the latter, timber, paper and steel are probably the most important potential losers to new synthetic developments; since the impact of their displacement by synthetics on net imports into the industrial countries is likely to be relatively small in value terms, some allowance for this factor needs to be made. Though no precise calculation can be attempted in view of the complex patterns of substitution when the various end-uses of

[1] The figures quoted were derived by applying the formula on p. 134, n. 1, to the data in Table 5.7.

Table 5.7. *Consumption and net imports of selected industrial materials in the industrial countries, 1960–3, and projections for 1975*

	Consumption				Net imports			
	1960–1	Volume index[a]			1960–1	Volume index[a]		
		1962–3	1975			1962–3	1975	
			A	B			A	B
	(£000 m.)	(1960–1 = 100)			(£000 m.)	(1960–1 = 100)		
NATURAL MATERIALS								
Raw cotton	0·96	98	110	115	0·19	134	155	170
Raw wool	0·53	102	120	130	0·42	100	130	140
Raw jute and jute goods	0·12	111	125	140	0·11	110	125	140
Total	1·61	100	115	120	0·71	110	135	150
Natural rubber	0·31	104	140	155	0·30	104	140	155
Vegetable oils and oilseeds[b]	0·24	101	115	125	0·24	101	115	125
Hides and skins	0·30	108	130	140	0·07	107	120	130
Non-ferrous metals	2·73	110	190	205	0·55	101	200	220
Total, natural	5·19	107	155	170	1·87	105	150	165
of which: *agricultural*	*2·46*	*102*	*120*	*130*	*1·32*	*107*	*130*	*145*
SYNTHETIC MATERIALS								
Man-made fibres:								
Cellulosic	0·54	122	140	145	−0·12	75[c]	..	
Non-cellulosic	0·86	155	215	230	−0·05	158[c]	..	
Synthetic rubber	0·34	121	280	315	−0·04	109[c]	..	
Plastic materials	1·45	135	300	400	−0·14	120[c]	..	
Synthetic detergents	0·41	117	200	250	−0·01	..	..	
Total, synthetic	3·60	134	245	300	−0·36	108[c]	225[c]	280[c]
TOTAL industrial materials	8·79	118	190	220	1·51	105	135	140

SOURCE: Appendix B.

[a] Indices for 1975 have been rounded to nearest 5.
[b] 'Sterling' oils and oilseeds only (see Appendix B4).
[c] Indices of net exports from the industrial countries. The projections for 1975 assume the same proportionate increase in net exports of each synthetic material as for the corresponding projection of consumption.

different materials are considered, it would seem that the adverse effect of the projected growth rates in the consumption of synthetics on the net imports of natural materials into the industrial countries might be of the order of £0·7 billion on the more optimistic income-growth assumption, and £0·4 to £0·5 billion on the less. These are notional 'losses' to the value of net imports of natural materials, based on comparing projected levels of net imports in 1975 with what these levels would be if the proportionate usage of natural and synthetic materials remained unchanged between 1960–1 and 1975. They are, nonetheless, interesting as indicating the broad orders of magnitude of the problem: that is, that the continued encroachment of synthetics would be likely to reduce net imports of natural materials into the industrial countries by 1975 by between one-tenth and one-fifth, according to the income-growth assumption made.

3. EXPORTS FROM THE OVERSEAS STERLING AREA

As indicated earlier, the projections of exports of the main primary commodities from overseas Sterling countries were very largely based on the corresponding projections of net imports into the industrial countries. In addition, separate projections, or assumptions, were made concerning the future trend of exports from Sterling countries to other primary-producing areas and to the centrally planned countries. As can be seen from Table 5.8, exports from the Overseas Sterling Area to primary-producing countries have accounted for one-half or more of total exports in recent years for rice and jute manufactures, for about one-third in the case of tea and cotton, about one-quarter for wheat, and one-sixth for coffee and natural rubber. Sterling Area exports to the centrally planned countries have, in recent years, represented one-tenth or more of total exports for cotton, rubber, wheat, rice, cocoa and, more recently, jute and jute manufactures.

Exports to primary-producing countries

Net imports of both coffee and tea into primary-producing countries are projected to rise faster between 1960–1 and 1975 than imports into industrial countries. This difference is especially notable in the case of *tea*. The primary-producing countries' imports are projected to rise by about $1\frac{1}{2}$ to 2 per cent annually, as against an annual increase of under $1\frac{1}{2}$ per cent for the industrial countries. It is estimated that some shift will take place in the distribution of O.S.A. tea exports in favour of the primary-producing markets. Helped by this expanding market, the annual growth rate of Sterling tea exports could reach nearly 2 per cent.

About 15 per cent of O.S.A. *coffee* exports is marketed in primary-producing countries, but the O.S.A.'s share in total world trade of coffee is under 10 per cent. The slightly faster growth of demand from primary-producing countries is thus not likely to affect the O.S.A.'s prospects of coffee exports in 1975.

Wheat exports from Australia, the main wheat exporter of the Overseas Sterling Area, to other primary-producers take up between one-quarter and one-third of her total wheat exports. There are great

Table 5.8. *Exports of selected commodities from the Overseas Sterling Area by area of destination, 1960–5 (percentage of total exports in each commodity)*[a]

	Industrial countries			Primary-producing countries			Centrally planned countries		
	1960–1	1962–3	1964–5	1960–1	1962–3	1964–5	1960–1	1962–3	1964–5
Coffee	77	81	76	20	15	15	3	4	9
Tea	66	65	62	31	32	34	3	3	4
Cocoa	89	86	84	6	4	5	5	10	11
Wheat and wheat flour	38	23	21	33	25	22	29	52	57
Rice	8	5	8	81	84	81	11	11	11
Raw cotton	55	51	42[b]	35	30	33[b]	10	19	25[b]
Rubber	67	63	61	14	15	17	19	22	22
Jute	61	72	64[c]	32	20	23[c]	7	8	13[c]
Jute manufactures	42	43	41[c]	54	53	49[c]	4	4	10[c]

SOURCES: *Tropical Products Quarterly, Plantation Crops, Grain Crops* and *Industrial Fibres*, Commonwealth Economic Committee, London; *Quarterly Bulletin*, International Cotton Advisory Committee, Washington; *Rubber Statistical Bulletin*, International Rubber Study Group, London.

[a] Percentages based on quantities exported.   [b] 1964/5 crop year only.   [c] 1964 only.

fluctuations in the purchases of wheat by the major importing countries, and it is difficult to make reasonable assumptions about the future size of this trade. It has been assumed here that Overseas Sterling Area wheat exports to primary-producing countries will rise at the same rate as exports to all areas, i.e. by 25 to 35 per cent from 1960–1 to 1975.

More than four-fifths of *rice* exports from the Overseas Sterling Area (mostly from Burma) goes to primary-producing countries. This proportion would be even higher if the quantities purchased by China, but actually shipped mainly to Ceylon and Cuba, were included. There is a general trend in the main rice-importing countries to strive towards self-sufficiency; the possibility, on assumption A, of a 10 per cent decline in O.S.A. exports of rice between 1960–1 and 1975 reflects this trend.

About one-third of the O.S.A. *raw cotton* exports go to primary-producing countries and these rose rapidly in the first half of the 1960s (on average, by about 9 per cent a year). Future prospects depend very much on the growing requirements of the textile industries of countries such as Hong Kong, and an annual rate of growth of 6 per cent has been assumed here. However, one factor which may hamper the growth of exports from the Area to other developing countries is the likely continuation of cotton shipments from the United States under foreign aid programmes.

The primary-producers' share in O.S.A. exports of *natural rubber* has been increasing slowly, from 14 to 17 per cent between 1960–1 and 1964–5. The projections imply a fairly rapid growth of natural rubber consumption in the primary-producing countries, and assume that in these areas natural rubber will probably hold between 35 to 45 per cent of the total rubber market. Total rubber consumption in these areas is, however, likely to remain below 1 kg. per head on average. O.S.A. exports to primary-producing countries are projected to increase at a rate of about 5 per cent per annum up to 1975.

Jute consumption in both the industrial and the primary-producing areas is estimated to grow at a lower rate over the decade up to 1975 than in the preceding decade. The projected increase in world demand for jute (outside the centrally planned countries and the jute-producing countries) is roughly 1½ to 2 per cent a year on the low income-growth assumption and 2 to 2½ per cent a year on the higher income basis. Although packaging remains the major application of jute in the industrial countries, these show an increase over the last ten years in the relative importance of floor coverings and a corresponding decline in the relative importance of packaging uses. In the primary-producing countries, virtually all jute consumed is for packaging. Although it cannot be ruled out that a large-scale substitution by synthetic materials could significantly change the prospect for jute consumption in its traditional outlets, it has been assumed that no major 'breakthrough' by synthetics will have made a drastic adverse impact on jute requirements by 1975.

Exports to centrally planned countries

The share of exports to centrally planned countries in total O.S.A. *cocoa* exports more than doubled between 1960–1 and 1964–5, and about trebled in the case of *coffee* exports during the same period. This was the continuation of a trend which started in the mid 1950s. The rise in the centrally planned countries' imports between 1953–7 and 1960–1 accounted for almost 20 per cent of the world total increase of cocoa exports and 9 per cent of coffee exports.

Bearing in mind that the Eastern European countries' coffee and cocoa consumption is still well below the level reached in Western Europe, there is still considerable room for significant expansion in their imports of these beverages. In the projections, a generally favourable development of official trade relations was assumed for the coming decade between Eastern European countries and the Overseas Sterling Area producers, and a continuation of the recent upward trend in imports of tropical beverages was assumed. However, the projected O.S.A. coffee exports are only marginally affected by including this growing demand for coffee from Eastern Europe. The effect of increasing demand from centrally planned countries is more significant for the projections of cocoa exports. This inclusion resulted in about a 10 to 15 per cent increase in total O.S.A. exports of cocoa by 1975, compared with 1964–5, above the growth projected for the demand in industrial countries.

In 1962–3, the centrally planned countries became the main market for Australian *wheat*, this country being virtually the only Overseas Sterling Area wheat exporter. China imported in this period nearly $2\frac{1}{2}$ million tons of wheat a year, as against $1\frac{1}{2}$ million tons in 1960–1; the Soviet Union also purchased about $1\frac{1}{2}$ million tons of wheat from Australia in 1963. It is impossible to foresee the development of these exports, but it is perhaps reasonable to assume that China's substantial wheat imports will continue into the 1970s, but not those of the Soviet Union.

Among industrial materials, both *cotton* and *natural rubber* exports to centrally planned countries accounted in 1964–5 for about one-quarter of total O.S.A. exports in each of these commodities. While for rubber the share of the centrally planned countries increased only slightly during the past five years, for cotton it has risen from 10 per cent in 1960–1 to 25 per cent in 1964–5. Most of these cotton exports went from Pakistan and Uganda to China. Though it is unlikely that the increase will continue on this scale, it can be assumed that this new market— together with the increasing importance of primary-producers in total Overseas Sterling Area exports of cotton—will allow for a modest increase of O.S.A. cotton exports during the period up to 1975.

It is assumed that the centrally planned countries will require in 1975 about double the quantity of natural rubber imported in 1960–1 ($c.\frac{1}{2}$ million tons annually) despite plans to increase rapidly their synthetic rubber production. The projections in Appendix B 3 show that the output of natural rubber in the Sterling Area will increase by about three-quarters, and that world output will be in the region of $\frac{3}{4}$ million tons more than world demand. However, a higher rate of growth than assumed here for imports into the centrally planned countries could well absorb a large part of the excess output of natural rubber in the O.S.A. producing countries.

Exports from the Overseas Sterling Area

Table 5.9 summarizes the projections of Sterling countries' exports of the main primary commodities on the basis of the projections of net imports into the industrial countries, of exports from the Sterling Area to other primary-producing countries, and of the assumptions made about future exports to the centrally planned area. For all the foods and beverages included, the projections indicate an average annual growth

Table 5.9. *Exports from the Overseas Sterling Area of selected foods and industrial materials, 1960–5, and projections for 1975*

				Volume index		Rates of growth, 1960–1 to 1975	
	1960–1	1962–3	1964–5	1975 A	1975 B	A	B
	(£ million)			(1960–1 = 100)		(% per annum, compound)	
FOOD, BEVERAGES AND TOBACCO							
Coffee	42	116	132	235	250	6·1	6·5
Tea	186	109	109	130	130	1·8	1·8
Cocoa	108	115	132	165	175	3·6	3·9
Sugar	101	134	151	140	145	2·5	2·6
Meat	180	116	126	135	140	2·1	2·5
Butter	71	107	119	130	135	1·8	2·1
Cheese	24	115	120	130	135	1·8	2·1
Fruit[a]	78	112	128	160	180	3·3	4·1
Wheat and wheat flour	96	116[b]	147[b]	125	135	1·6	2·1
Rice	65	106	87	90	110	−0·7	0·7
Coarse grains	36	182[c]	86	160	180	3·3	4·1
Tobacco	54	120	147	130	140	1·8	2·5
Total	1,041	117	124	140	150	2·5	2·8
INDUSTRIAL MATERIALS							
Raw cotton	57	119[d]	136[d]	145	165	2·6	3·5
Raw wool	442	102	103	130	140	1·8	2·5
Raw jute and jute goods	188	110	115	130	145	1·8	2·5
Natural rubber	248	104	93	180	195	4·1	4·7
Vegetable oils and oilseeds	147	108	100	115	125	1·0	1·6
Hides and skins	86	109	110	125	135	1·6	2·1
Non-ferrous metals	325	105	115	210	235	5·3	6·1
Total	1,494	106	112	155	170	3·1	3·7
TOTAL	2,535	111	117	150	160	2·8	3·3

SOURCES: Appendices A and B.

[a] Apples and pears, citrus fruit, bananas and canned fruit.
[b] The increases were entirely due to large purchases of Australian wheat by China.
[c] There were exceptionally large exports of maize from South Africa in these years.
[d] Inflated by abnormally high exports from Pakistan in 1963–5.

rate in export volume of 2½ to 3 per cent, according to the income-growth assumption adopted. For the industrial materials, the projected growth rates are about 3 per cent a year on the lower income-growth assumption, and over 3½ per cent a year on the higher. Within both groups there are large variations in the projected export growth rates among the different commodities, reflecting in the main a similar variation in the projections for exports from the O.S.A. to the industrial countries, which were discussed above.

The selected primary commodities for which detailed projections of exports from Sterling countries have been made accounted for over 85 per cent of the value of all primary-commodity exports from these countries in 1960–1. Though no corresponding detailed projections have been made in the present study for the varied collection of relatively small primary-commodity exports from the overseas Sterling countries, approximate estimates were made for most of these smaller items on the basis of the results of other studies.[1] These indicated that, on balance, the rate of export growth of these miscellaneous items was likely to exceed that of the major commodities discussed previously. This would appear to be so, particularly, for timber, iron ore and the minor non-ferrous metals, exports of which are estimated to increase at a considerably faster rate than the average for the major materials for which detailed projections have been made.

The allowance for these minor primary commodities increased the projected export growth rate for food, beverages and tobacco only marginally, but for industrial materials the projected growth rates were increased to over $3\frac{1}{2}$ per cent a year on assumption A, and over 4 per cent a year on assumption B (Table 5.10).

Manufactures

The O.S.A. export trade in manufactures is fundamentally different in character from its trade in primary products. It has been argued that, in the former case, the most important single factor in the development of trade is the growth of import demand in the industrial areas. For manufactures this is manifestly not the case, as the nature and evolution of trade over the past decade clearly illustrate.

Since the latter years of the 1950s, the half-dozen countries that contribute over 90 per cent of O.S.A. domestic exports of manufactures[2] have raised the value of trade, measured at current prices, by about 10 per cent per year on average. Growth has generally been concentrated in a limited range of products sold either to industrial countries or to nearby Sterling Area markets. There is, however, no consistent pattern discernible as between countries. Hong Kong and Ireland have advanced on a fairly broad front, though both, and Hong Kong in particular, concentrate on textiles, clothing and a range of simple finished goods.

---

[1] The other studies used were Bela Balassa, *Trade Prospects for Developing Countries* (ref. p. 113 above) and *Agricultural Commodities–Projections for 1970, Special Supplement* to *F.A.O. Commodity Review, 1962*, F.A.O., Rome. In a few cases, later projections by the F.A.O. were used as given in *Agricultural Commodities—Projections for 1975 and 1985*, F.A.O., Rome, 1967.

[2] SITC 5, 6, 7 and 8 excluding leather, diamonds and precious stones, non-ferrous metals and jute textiles. The discussion in this section relates only to goods produced in the exporting countries, excluding re-exports of manufactures from Hong Kong and (so far as possible) other countries covered. Exports of manufactures from Aden, Malaya and Singapore have been wholly excluded, since re-exports cannot be distinguished from domestic exports.

Table 5.10. *Total exports from the Overseas Sterling Area,*
1960–5, and projections for 1975

	1960–1	1964–5	Projections for 1975[a]		Rates of growth 1960–1 to 1975[a]	
			A	B	A	B
	(£000 m. at 1960–1 prices)				*(% per annum, compound)*	
FOOD, BEVERAGES AND TOBACCO						
Selected items	1·04	1·29	1·5	1·6	2·5	2·8
Other[b]	0·30	0·32	0·4	0·5	2·7	3·3
Total	1·34	1·61	1·9	2·1	2·5	2·9
INDUSTRIAL MATERIALS[c]						
Selected items	1·49	1·67	2·3	2·5	3·1	3·7
Other[d]	0·47	0·57	0·9	1·0	4·8	5·0
Total	1·96	2·24	3·2	3·5	3·6	4·1
MANUFACTURES[e]	0·49	0·70	1·4	1·4	7·5	7·5
TOTAL	3·80	4·55	6·5	6·9	3·8	4·2

SOURCES: Appendices A and B; see also discussion in accompanying text.

[a] For simplicity of presentation, the projections are shown as single figures: strictly, they must be considered as having fairly wide margins of probability. For manufactures, for example, the projections show average rates of growth of 6·8 to 8·2 per cent per annum for both A and B assumptions.

[b] Including, *inter alia*, fish and fish preparations, live animals, dried fruit, fresh fruit other than selected, feeding-stuffs, spices and animal fats.

[c] Including base metals, jute manufactures and rough-tanned leather.

[d] Including, *inter alia*, minor non-ferrous metals, ores and scrap, diamonds, timber, iron ore and vegetable fibres other than cotton and jute.

[e] Excluding non-ferrous metals, jute manufactures, leather and precious stones. Figures relate to domestic exports only and exclude all exports of manufactures from Aden, Malaya and Singapore.

Pakistan has rapidly built up an export trade in cotton textiles, and Australia in steel, machinery and metal manufactures; growth rates in other commodity groups have been high but the absolute value of exports has so far been relatively small. India, with trade again heavily concentrated on textiles, has lagged behind; while South Africa, with a commodity pattern of trade similar to Australia's, has suffered a decline in sales.

This diversity of experience reflects essentially the supply conditions in the exporting countries themselves. Since O.S.A. exporters are marginal suppliers of goods other than textiles and clothing, world import demand for manufactures neither serves to explain past performances nor gives much guidance as to future potential. Outside

Hong Kong, the growth of O.S.A. exports of manufactures up to 1975 will be principally determined by producers' ability to achieve a surplus of supply over demand from their own protected domestic markets, by the movement of costs and prices, which are as much a function of general economic conditions as of industrial policy or expansion, and by commercial policies in both exporting and importing areas. Already a number of overseas Sterling countries deploy a variety of export incentives, while in respect of 'low-labour-cost' Asian goods the importing countries significantly limit the level of trade by means of tariffs and quota restrictions.

A detailed examination of the influence of all these factors on actual or potential exports of the whole range of manufactures[1] from overseas Sterling countries would fall outside the scope of the present study. Separate estimates have, however, been made for two broad groups of particular concern to major O.S.A. exporters of manufactures—cotton textiles and clothing from Asian Sterling countries, and the steel, machinery and metal manufactures group. In the first case, future world import demand for yarn and cloth was estimated on the basis of alternative assumptions about cotton consumption, commercial policies in the industrial areas and import replacement in developing countries that are currently net importers of cotton textiles; the exports of the three main O.S.A. exporters in 1975 were estimated by reference to this total. Hong Kong's clothing exports were projected in the light of what appeared most likely to be the trend of import demand in the industrial areas, allowing for some further increase in Hong Kong's share of continental European markets. For steel, machinery and metal manufactures, on the other hand, the trend in world demand is unlikely to be the major influence on exports from overseas Sterling countries, which would still be marginal suppliers to world markets even by 1975; the future trend in exports was, instead, estimated in the light of the producing countries' recent performance, indications of their present ability to compete in world markets, and their plans to raise exports over the next five to ten years. A similar procedure was followed—but in much less detail—in respect of all other manufactures exported by overseas Sterling countries.

The projections quoted in Appendix C for exports of manufactures in 1975 are thus unrelated to the assumed growth of incomes in industrial areas, which appears likely to have only a marginal influence on the development of this trade. In general they refer to the range of values within which exports are most probably expected to fall. For textiles and

---

[1] Official plans to develop exports of manufactures imply not only a big increase in their importance relative to total exports but also considerable diversification by the introduction of new products. This aspect is discussed further in Chapter 6.

clothing the limits of this range reflect alternative assumptions about the movement of world import demand; for all other major products the range is determined by alternative views as to the ability of the exporting countries to supply manufactures at competitive prices.

The increase in the volume of world import demand for cotton textiles, excluding the intra-trade of the industrial areas and imports into the centrally planned countries, is estimated at just over 25 per cent between 1960–1 and 1975 on the low projection but nearly 55 per cent on the high, the greater part of the difference between the two arising from alternative assumptions on rates of consumption growth in Asian and African markets, to which the main Sterling Area exporters make well over half their sales. It has been assumed that the O.S.A. share in the total will remain constant, changes in one country's share balancing out against others; but in estimating 1975 earnings (at 1960–1 prices) the likelihood of a switch to a higher proportion of finished goods in exports has been taken into account. Allowing for this, the rise in earnings from cotton textiles is projected at about 10 per cent more than would otherwise be the case, and these figures may well be under-estimates, since they do not take into account the effect on export prices of a possible simultaneous rise in quality. Hong Kong's clothing exports appear likely to grow very much faster, reaching three to four times the 1960–1 level, that is, roughly twice the level recorded in 1964. Though India and Pakistan should also achieve high rates of growth, the actual volume of their clothing exports is not likely to be large by 1975.

For the steel, machinery and metal manufactures group, the exports of the major existing suppliers were separately projected. Three of the countries concerned—Australia, South Africa and India—should have a comparative advantage in this class, by virtue of their possession of abundant raw material supplies for the production of cheap steel. But whereas Australia has reached the point, in terms of capacity and production costs, where this advantage can be exploited in overseas markets, neither South Africa nor India yet appears to have done so. Although, therefore, a straightforward projection of past trends in Australian exports (modified only to allow for a probably inevitable slackening in the rate of growth as the absolute volume of exports increases) agrees closely with official export projections, the fulfilment of South African export targets implies a sharp reduction in costs which is likely to be inhibited by import-replacement policies; and the targets set by Indian planners imply nothing less than a revolution in India's industrial efficiency combined with an apparently unattainable increase in production capacity if home as well as export demand is to be satisfied. Thus the rates of export increase allowed for South Africa and India, though high, are considerably lower than these two countries hope to achieve. Ireland and Hong Kong are exporters of a different kind, relying on a labour-cost rather than a material-cost advantage. Ireland had by 1965 almost surpassed the planned target for exports in 1970, and a projection of current trends has again been preferred to reliance on official plans. For Hong Kong, the projection has been modified to take account of the typical growth pattern of a major export-orientated industry, in this case typified by transistor radios where the value of exports has grown from nothing to about one-fifth of the group total in the space of four years.

The combined projection for these countries gives a level of exports in 1975 roughly three to three and a half times as high as in 1960–1, the annual average rate of increase ranging from just under 8 to over 9 per cent. From 1960–1 to 1964, the annual average rate of increase was 8 per cent, despite a fall in South African exports over the period.

The projections for the two big commodity classes underline the point that the future level of export earnings from manufactures depends significantly on the action of exporting countries. It would seem possible for total O.S.A. exports of manufactures to be two and a half to three times as large in 1975 as in 1960–1, but the very tentative nature of these figures should be emphasized. The influences which in practice determine the growth of exports of manufactures from 'new' industrial countries are not susceptible to precise measurement. It is reasonable to expect, for instance, that further industrialization in the O.S.A. will be accompanied not only by a broadening of the export base but also, at least in some countries, by big shifts in costs relative to those of established exporters. Since there is little evidence about the nature and extent of these changes, any projections of probable export volume must necessarily remain tentative.

For simplicity of presentation, however, the summary shown in Table 5.10 gives only the mid-points of the projection ranges for both manufactures and primary products. For all exports from the O.S.A., the projections indicate an average annual growth rate of 3·8 per cent on the low income-growth assumption, and 4·2 per cent on the high; these growth rates must be interpreted as orders of magnitude only, subject to fairly wide margins of probable error.

CHAPTER 6

THE COUNTRY PROJECTIONS

I. IMPLICATIONS OF THE COMMODITY PROJECTIONS

The projections of the growth in international trade, and of the exports of the Overseas Sterling Area, by main commodity, as summarized in the previous chapter, form the background against which a consistent set of export projections can be made for each of the main Sterling countries.

Projections of world exports[1] by commodity cannot, however, be directly related to the exports of an individual country, partly because each country can, to a greater or lesser extent, diversify its economic structure in favour of commodities for which the world market is relatively expansive, and away from those for which it is relatively stagnant. Such diversification has tended to be confined in the past very largely to countries at a relatively high stage of economic development, though more diversification of exports is now being planned by many of the less developed countries. The other reason why projections of world exports of individual commodities cannot be applied as they stand to individual countries is that they ignore changes in the conditions of supply of particular commodities in the various exporting countries, which could lead to changes in their shares of the total world export market.

Nonetheless, the commodity trade projections are basic for an assessment of export prospects for any primary-producing country, since they represent the world market framework within which it has to operate. In the next section, the implications of the commodity trade projections for each main Sterling country are examined, on the assumption that each maintains a constant share of the world trade total. This assumption is then dropped and alternative export projections for each country are presented. Finally, these projections are compared with the rates of export growth used in the Economic Development Plans of the various Sterling countries.

[1] The projections of world exports of individual commodities are based essentially on the projections of net imports into the industrial countries, but they also include various assumptions regarding total net imports into the centrally planned countries and into the developing countries themselves. Also, there are a few commodities which have been excluded from the projections in Chapter 5 on the grounds of their relative unimportance in total O.S.A. exports but which, nevertheless, may be very important to individual countries—one example is sisal. In these latter cases the projections made by F.A.O. or by Professor Bela Balassa are usually drawn upon.

The projections of world trade summarized in Chapter 5 cover a wide range of prospective rates of growth for the different commodities. Since the overseas Sterling countries differ greatly in their commodity specializations, the range in the commodity projections implies very different rates of growth in the world market facing the export sectors of the different countries.

For convenience, the commodities for which detailed trade projections have been made have been grouped into five categories in Table 6.1, according to the projected increase in the volume of world trade between 1960–1 and 1975. The table also separates the individual commodities according to the magnitude of total exports from the Overseas Sterling Area in 1960–1. The projected growth rates used for the analysis are the arithmetic means of the A and B projections; this seemed to be a simple way of demonstrating the general relationships between the commodity projections. This type of analysis depends, to some extent, on the detail with which the commodities are subdivided. Had tea, coffee and cocoa, for example, been considered as one item, tropical beverages, this would then have been classified in group II. However, it is unlikely that the general picture revealed would have been significantly changed by a less detailed, or even by a much more detailed, commodity classification.

There is, indeed, a general picture which emerges for agricultural primary products, namely, that the majority of the main export commodities in value terms (wool, tea, cocoa, sugar, and vegetable oils and oilseeds) show relatively low projected export growth rates, the agricultural products with the brightest export prospects being now relatively small in terms of value (fishmeal and fruit juice). There are, of course, exceptions to the general rule; hardwood—not strictly an agricultural product—has good growth prospects and is already of some importance in Sterling Area exports, while meat, though much larger in value terms, has somewhat better growth prospects than the other large agricultural export commodities. Natural rubber, however, is not really an exception to the 'inverse rule' if account is taken of the probable decline in its price.

This tendency for an inverse association to exist between the present magnitude of exports of agricultural produce and the prospective rate of growth in the world market constitutes a major retarding factor in the growth prospects of a considerable number of Sterling countries. There is, however, a mitigating factor of some importance which should be mentioned at the outset, namely, that for a number of agricultural products, world market prospects seem rather better for the more processed forms than for the crude forms in which such products have been traditionally found in world trade. The point does not emerge very clearly from Table 6.1, which is designed mainly to compare the

Table 6.1. *Commodity export projections[a] in relation to exports from the Overseas Sterling Area in 1960–1*

Projected rate of growth in world exports,[b] 1960–1 to 1975	Overseas Sterling Area exports in 1960–1				
	Under £25 million	£25–50 million	£50–100 million	£100–250 million	Over £250 million
(% *per annum, compound*)					
Group I Under 1·5	—	Live animals	Butter Rice Hides and skins	Tea Sugar	—
Group II 1·5–2·5	Bananas Spices Sisal	Fish	Wheat Raw jute *Tin* *Cotton goods*	Vegetable oils and oilseeds *Jute goods*	Raw wool
Group III 2·5–5·0	Cheese Apples and pears Citrus fruit *Lead* *Zinc*	Coffee Canned fruit	Tobacco Raw cotton	Cocoa Meat Natural rubber	—
Group IV 5·0–7·5	Fishmeal Fruit juice	*Iron ore*	Hardwood *Diamonds*	*Copper* *Clothing*	*Miscellaneous manufactures*
Group V Over 7·5	—	*Aluminium[c]*	*Machinery and transport equipment Chemicals*	—	*Petroleum[d]*

SOURCES: Tables 5.4 and 5.5.

[a] Minerals and manufactures shown in italics.
[b] Mean of projections A and B.
[c] Including bauxite and alumina.
[d] Crude and refined.

variation in growth rates for the main commodities without distinguishing degrees of processing; but it is apparent in the fruit group (e.g. fruit juice in relation to fresh fruit) and it also tends to operate in the case of some other foods (e.g. instant coffee and chocolate).

In this respect, processed foods are more akin to manufactures; for these and minerals—both petroleum and metals—the 'inverse rule' does not appear to apply. The export prospect for petroleum is one of continued rapid expansion, in spite of its present large value in world trade. Export prospects are also relatively good for the non-ferrous metals (especially for aluminium and its ores) and for iron ore, though the volume of trade in tin seems likely to be limited by supply constraints. For manufactures, world trade prospects are likely to remain extremely favourable, particularly for chemicals and for machinery and transport equipment. For textiles and clothing, much depends on the import policies of the main industrial countries. The present projections assume a modest degree of relaxation of the present restrictions on 'low-cost' imports into these countries.

An indication of how the different world trade prospects for the various commodities are likely to impinge on the export prospects for individual Sterling countries is given in Table 6.2, which shows the distribution of a large sample of the exports of a selection of overseas Sterling countries in 1960–1 by the five commodity categories previously distinguished. Although the proportion of exports covered by the sample varies appreciably (as much as one-third of the exports from Ireland and South Africa being too heterogeneous for classification here), several conclusions appear to emerge. First, there is an enormous variation in the export growth potentials facing the various countries, ranging from Burma at one extreme (with two-thirds of her exports in the lowest growth-rate group) to Jamaica at the other (with half her exports in the top group). Second, there is no necessary relation between export growth prospects and the stage of economic development; both the more developed and the less developed groups contain countries specializing in products with low growth prospects. Third, while no 'average' can be very meaningful in view of the wide dispersion in market prospects, it is of some interest to note that the distribution of exports in 1960–1 was somewhat more favourable for the less developed than for the more developed countries.

Among the more developed countries, Australian export prospects are, to a large extent, dominated by the relatively low projected growth rate in world demand for wool, while wool and butter dominate the export potential for New Zealand; by contrast, South Africa has one-third of her classified exports in group IV (mainly manufactures). South Africa's export pattern in the early 1960s was thus much more 'industrialized' than either Australia's or New Zealand's and, in this sense, was more favourably placed to benefit from future expansion in world trade.

Of the sixteen less developed Sterling countries for which this commodity classification is shown in Table 6.2, five countries had more than half their exports falling in groups I and II, while nine had three-quarters or more falling in the first three groups. Only four countries (Hong Kong, Zambia, Jamaica and Trinidad) were fortunate in having over half their 1960–1 exports in the two highest growth-rate groups (minerals or manufactures).

A first approximation to a set of country export projections can now

Table 6.2. *Export patterns in relation to commodity export projections*

	\multicolumn{7}{c}{Commodity export projection group}						
	I	II	III	IV	V	Unclassi-fied	Total exports
	\multicolumn{6}{c}{(% of total exports in 1960–1)}						*(£ million)*
MORE DEVELOPED COUNTRIES							
Australia	8	52	10	7	1	22	756
New Zealand	20	35	30	2	—	13	288
South Africa	1	17	10	33	—	36	413
Iceland	3	80	2	11	—	3	28
Ireland	5	—	43	18	—	34	161
Total	9	36	16	14	0	25	1,646
LESS DEVELOPED COUNTRIES							
Burma	67	5	3	10	—	16	79
Ceylon	64	15	19	—	—	2	130
Malaya	—	24	59	7	—	10	324
Hong Kong	4	18	1	62	10	5	246
India	22	38	2	15	—	24	483
Pakistan	12	78	—	—	—	10	142
Ghana	—	—	71	23	1	5	104
Kenya	20	14	45	6	—	15	37
Malawi	45	1	37	—	—	11	9
Nigeria	2	44	34	4	5	9	164
Rhodesia	1	1	57	17	—	25	67
Tanzania	7	40	34	12	—	9	49
Uganda	7	8	73	8	—	5	43
Zambia	—	—	4	93	—	4	125
Jamaica	23	12	1	5	50	10	58
Trinidad and Tobago	8	1	0	79	5	7	110
Total	14	25	22	24	3	12	2,170
TOTAL	12	30	19	19	2	18	3,816

SOURCES: Table 6.1 and *Yearbook of International Trade Statistics*, United Nations, New York.

be made on two assumptions. The first is that the sample of classified commodities is representative of all exports, from each country, as regards the average rate of growth in the volume of world trade. This assumption is a reasonable one for countries where the sample covers a high proportion of export trade, but it is not necessarily valid for the others. The second assumption is that each country's share of world trade in its own specialized 'basket' of exports will be the same in 1975 as it was in 1960–1. On these assumptions an index of the volume of world exports of each country's particular 'basket' of exports can be computed as an indicator of the change over the period in its foreign market potential.[1] The results of this calculation are summarized in Table 6.3.

For all the Sterling countries taken together, the projected rate of export growth, on the two assumptions mentioned, would not be very different over the period from 1960–1 to 1975 from that for the past period from 1953–5. Excluding Hong Kong, the mean projected growth rate would be somewhat lower than the past rate (3·2 as against 3·5 per cent per annum) on the lower income-growth assumption (A), and somewhat higher (3·8 per cent) on the higher income-growth basis (B). However, there appears to be a striking difference between the results for the more developed and the less developed groups. For the former, the projected export growth rates are smaller, on *either* income-growth assumption, than the rate actually achieved between 1953–5 and 1960–1, whereas for the latter group of countries, both the projected export growth rates exceed the average for the past period. In other words, the commodity projections imply that the change in the pattern of world trade over the next decade or so is likely to be more favourable for the exports of the less developed Sterling countries than the actual change in pattern was over the past decade; whereas, for the more developed countries, the trading pattern is likely to become, on balance, significantly less favourable. As a result, the mean rate of growth in world trade is projected to be virtually the same for both groups of countries[2] for the period up to 1975, whereas from 1953–5 to 1960–1 the world market for the export products of the more developed countries was growing at an appreciably higher rate than that for the exports of the less developed countries.

The relative importance of individual countries in the total export earnings of the Overseas Sterling Area would also change considerably, on the basis of the assumptions made above. Australia and New Zealand

---

[1] This index is simply a weighted mean of indices of the volume of world trade in each commodity, using the 1960–1 pattern of country exports as weights. Thus, if $p_{i1}q_{i1}$ is the value of exports of commodity i in 1960–1 from any given country, and $P_{i1}Q_{i2}/P_{i1}Q_{i1}$ the corresponding volume index for world trade in 1975 compared with 1960–1, the projected 'world' export index for that country would be:

$$W_2 = \frac{\sum_{1}^{n}(p_{i1}q_{i1})\,(P_{i1}Q_{i2}/P_{i1}Q_{i1})}{\sum_{1}^{n}(p_{i1}q_{i1})}.$$

The world export index for 1960–1 compared with 1953–5, W_1, would be similar to W_2, except that the term $P_{i1}Q_{i2}/P_{i1}Q_{i1}$ would be changed to $P_{i1}Q_{i1}/P_{i1}Q_{i0}$, where $P_{i1}Q_{i0}$ refers to the volume of world exports in 1953–5 valued at 1960–1 prices.

[2] Excluding Hong Kong from the comparison, because of the lack of a volume index of exports from that country. If Hong Kong is included, the mean projected growth rate of exports up to 1975 is somewhat higher for the less developed than for the more developed countries, on the assumptions made.

Table 6.3. *Projection of exports from selected overseas Sterling countries on the basis of constant shares of world trade*

	Rate of growth in volume of world exports[a]			Exports on a constant share basis[b]		
	1953–5 to 1960–1	1960–1 to 1975		1960–1	1975	
		A	B		A	B
	(% per annum, compound)			(£ million at 1960–1 prices)		
MORE DEVELOPED COUNTRIES						
Australia	3·9	2·5	3·1	756	1,080	1,175
New Zealand	3·6	2·3	2·7	288	400	425
South Africa	5·7	5·0	5·6	413	835	905
Iceland	4·9	4·7	5·4	28	55	60
Ireland	6·9	3·6	4·2	161	270	290
Total	4·5	3·3	3·8	1,646	2,640	2,855
LESS DEVELOPED COUNTRIES						
Burma	4·8	1·7	2·3	79	100	110
Ceylon	1·1	1·4	1·8	130	160	170
Malaya	0·9	2·6	3·2	324	470	510
Hong Kong	··	5·4	6·1	246	530	580
India	2·0	2·7	3·2	483	710	765
Pakistan	−0·8	1·5	2·0	142	175	190
Ghana	5·1	4·9	5·3	104	205	220
Kenya	3·9	2·7	3·2	37	55	60
Malawi	2·2	2·0	2·2	9	10	15
Nigeria	2·0	2·7	3·6	164	240	270
Rhodesia	4·1	3·5	4·3	67	110	125
Tanzania	3·1	2·7	3·4	49	70	80
Uganda	3·5	2·8	3·3	43	65	70
Zambia	8·5	5·2	5·9	125	260	285
Jamaica	6·4	6·8	7·6	58	150	170
Trinidad and Tobago	5·2	4·4	5·1	110	205	230
Total	··	3·4	4·0	2,170	3,515	3,850
Total excluding Hong Kong	2·6	3·1	3·8	1,924	2,485	3,270
TOTAL	··	3·3	3·9	3,816	6,155	6,705
TOTAL excluding Hong Kong	3·5	3·2	3·8	3,570	5,625	6,125

SOURCES: As for Table 6.2.

[a] For the sample of commodities classified in groups I-V in Table 6.2. The 'world' export index for each country is derived by weighting the indices for world trade in individual commodities by the country's relative value of exports of each commodity in 1960–1.

[b] Total exports; the projections have been arrived at by applying the projected growth rates for the sample to the totals for 1960–1.

together, for example, accounted for 27½ per cent of total exports of the twenty-one countries included in Table 6.3 in 1960–1, but by 1975 the corresponding proportion would have declined to about 24 per cent on the basis of these projections. On the other hand, Hong Kong, Ghana and Zambia, which together accounted for 12½ per cent of the total in 1960–1, would by 1975 account for over 16 per cent.

It is also of interest to compare the projections of the 'world' export indices for each country with the corresponding indices for the past period, from 1953–5 to 1960–1 (see also Fig. 6.1). Of the twenty

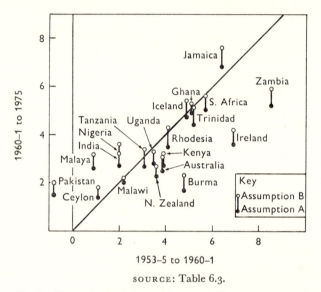

SOURCE: Table 6.3.

Fig. 6.1. Rates of growth in world export indices: 1953–5 to 1960–1 and 1960–1 to 1975 (percentage per annum, compound).

countries for which this comparison can be made, the mean of the A and B projections exceeded the past world export index for only eight countries; for almost all of these, the projected improvement in world market prospects was fairly marginal. For Malaya particularly, it should be borne in mind that the improvement shown is in terms of constant prices; further discussion of the probable value change in Malayan exports is provided later in this chapter.

For the majority of the countries for which the world export projections were lower than the past rates of growth, the shortfall was also fairly marginal. There were, however, a number of countries—Ireland, Burma and Zambia—for which a considerable decline is projected in the rate of growth in the volume of world trade in their particular 'baskets' of export products.

Nonetheless, although the relation between past and projected future growth rates in world trade is a very varied one, two general conclusions appear to emerge. First, those countries which in the recent past have enjoyed a relatively fast-growing world market are, by and large, the same countries which are projected to continue to do so; vice versa, countries which in the past have faced a relatively stagnant or slowly growing world market are projected—though with a number of notable exceptions—to continue to be in much the same position in the coming decade. Second, the difference in projected rates of export growth arising from the two income-growth assumptions (which is generally of the order of about 0·5 per cent per annum) is of a second order of significance in comparison with the much larger inter-country differences in export prospects arising solely out of their differing commodity patterns of export.

It should be emphasized that these projections are based on the underlying assumption that the protectionist policies of the industrial countries will not be substantially different in 1975 from the position in the early 1960s. Any appreciable relaxation would benefit, in the main, temperate-zone agricultural produce (particularly sugar, vegetable oils and oilseeds and raw cotton), processed foods and manufactured goods, and such relaxations would thus tend to fall unevenly among the various overseas Sterling countries.

2. CHANGING SHARES OF WORLD EXPORTS

The movement in the volume of world trade in the 'basket' of goods exported by a given country indicates the rate at which its effective foreign market is expanding. It does not necessarily indicate, however, the rate at which its exports will, in fact, expand for the reasons given earlier, namely, that it can succeed in increasing (or suffer a decrease in) its share of the world export market for individual commodities, and can diversify its export pattern towards (or away from) commodities which are relatively the most dynamic in world trade.

Changes in the commodity pattern of exports reflect changes in demand and supply, both in the primary-producing countries and in the outside world. Externally, changes in the pattern of world demand, the development of synthetic substitutes, changes in relative costs of production in competing countries and changes in government protectionist policies may all influence the pattern of exports from individual primary-producing countries. Internally, changes in export patterns can originate from changes in resource availabilities, particularly from the discovery of new mineral resources, or more intensive exploitation of already known resources, or they may reflect a conscious attempt at diversification through selective industrialization or selective changes in agricultural production.

The need to diversify the export pattern towards commodities in which world demand is relatively dynamic is now generally accepted by the less developed countries. Apart from expanding mineral exports—which can be done by relatively few countries—such diversification can, in general, successfully be achieved only by developing a processing and manufacturing sector. A deliberate attempt to do this is being made by a number of the less developed Sterling countries. Ghana, for example, plans to diversify into alumina, cocoa butter and paste, and plywood, while Ceylon, Jamaica, Trinidad and Zambia all include in their current economic plans the development of an export trade in manufactures. Countries which are at a lower stage of economic development than these are, however, unlikely to have the resources for some considerable time to invest in manufacturing plants which could compete effectively in export markets. Kenya, for example, recognizes that few of her manufacturing industries are currently competitive in world markets, so their growth in the future must depend on the growth of domestic demand and import substitution. In the longer run, increases in productivity and the creation and development of efficient industries based on Kenya's primary production should permit an expansion of manufacturing exports and the more rapid creation of employment opportunities in manufacturing.[1]

Any substantial movement towards the diversification of the export structure lies in the future for the majority of the less developed Sterling countries. Over the past decade, therefore, the predominant factor explaining changes in these countries' overall share of world trade in their own 'baskets' of export commodities has tended to be changes in their market share of their traditional exports, rather than a structural change in their export patterns.

The relationship between the growth in the world market, as measured by the world export index for each country, and the growth in national exports has, indeed, varied greatly over the past decade (see Table 6.4). Kenya is exceptional, in so far as her exports increased by some 115 per cent in volume from 1953–5 to 1960–1, whereas world exports of the Kenyan 'basket' of export commodities rose by only 33 per cent. This difference reflects in the main a sharp rise in Kenya's share of the world coffee market over the period. At the other extreme, India's exports in 1960–1 were marginally lower, in volume terms, than the 1953–5 average, though her world export index was higher by almost 15 per cent. However, for nearly half the countries (eight out of twenty), their national export indices were within 10 percentage points, either

---

[1] *Development Plan, 1964–1970*, Government of Kenya, Nairobi, 1964, p. 33.

Table 6.4. *Rates of growth in exports[a] in relation to shares of world trade, 1953–5 to 1960–1*

	Volume of exports in 1960–1[b]		Ratio of national to world indices	Shares of world trade[c]	
	World exports[d]	National exports		1953–5	1960–1
	(*1953–5 = 100*)		(%)	(%)	(%)
MORE DEVELOPED COUNTRIES					
Australia	128	132	103	30·7	30·4
New Zealand	126	125	100	26·2	28·5
South Africa	143	140	98	3·4	3·3
Iceland	136	132	108	5·0	5·0
Ireland	154	148	96	15·6	10·5
LESS DEVELOPED COUNTRIES					
Burma	136	121	89	21·8	18·5
Ceylon	108	110	102	23·1	37·3
Malaya	106	142	134	26·1	31·7
India	114	97	86	45·4	39·1
Pakistan	95	85	90	64·3	50·3
Ghana	139	155	112	23·6	28·1
Kenya	133	217	163	9·9	13·1
Malawi	114	140	124	1·1	1·4
Nigeria	116	133	115	13·2	11·3
Rhodesia	127	163	128	6·5	8·3
Tanzania	126	147	118	17·4	13·7
Uganda	130	153	118	2·1	2·1
Zambia	163	151	93	20·7	19·3
Jamaica	149	187	125	3·4	8·8
Trinidad and Tobago	139	184	133	3·7	5·3

SOURCES: *Yearbook of International Trade Statistics*, United Nations, New York; national trade statistics.

[a] Based on the sample of commodities classified in groups I–V in Table 6.2.

[b] Both the 'world' and 'national' export indices were weighted by the 1960–1 pattern of exports.

[c] Mean share of world exports for the sample, weighted by the relative importance of each commodity, by value, in total exports from each country. The value weights for both periods were in terms of 1960–1 prices.   [d] See footnote a to Table 6.3.

way, of their world export indices, while for another seven countries, the differences were between 10 and 20 percentage points.

Largely associated with these differences in the movements of national exports and of world exports have been changes in each country's overall share of world trade in its own 'basket' of exports (Table 6.4). The shares of world trade for this purpose have been computed by weighting the share for each commodity in each of the two periods by the country's export pattern, in terms of value, during 1960–1. Pakistan suffered a large decline in her overall share of world trade (from 64 to 50 per cent), while smaller, though still important, declines were shown for India and Tanzania. Ceylon showed a major rise in share, Ghana a more modest one.

As already indicated, these changes in overall market shares were generally attributable, in the main, to changes in shares of world trade in the traditional exports of the overseas Sterling countries. The relative importance of such changes in shares, compared with changes in the commodity pattern of exports, can be seen from the first section of Table 6.5.[1] The increases in overall share achieved by both Ceylon and Ghana reflected essentially their increased shares of world trade in tea and cocoa, respectively. Similarly for India the decline in overall share was caused by decreases in her share of world trade in tea and jute manufactures. For Pakistan and Tanzania, however, the decreases in overall shares reflected, in the main, shifts in export patterns. For Pakistan, the development of the home textile industry made possible an increase in exports of jute manufactures at the expense of raw jute, and of cotton manufactures at the expense of raw cotton. This switch into manufactured goods automatically reduces Pakistan's overall share of world trade in her export items taken as a whole.

These changes in world trade shares have been computed on the basis of the actual pattern of exports from each country. An alternative system of weighting would be to use the relative value of world exports as weights.[2] The results of this alternative approach (see the second section of Table 6.5), however, measure different factors from those already discussed. For example, on the country weighting, Ceylon showed an increase in her share of world trade, after eliminating the pattern effect, whereas on the world trade weighting, no share effect

---

[1] The change in the overall share held by a country in world trade is defined as:

$$\Delta s = \frac{\sum\limits_{1}^{n} s_1 v_1}{\sum\limits_{1}^{n} v_1} - \frac{\sum\limits_{1}^{n} s_0 v_0}{\sum\limits_{1}^{n} v_0},$$

where s denotes the share of exports in world trade in an individual commodity and v the value of the country's exports at constant (1960–1) prices. This expression can be divided into 'share' and 'pattern' changes in various ways. The method used here is as follows:

$$\Delta s = \left\{ \frac{\sum\limits_{1}^{n} s_1 v_1}{\sum\limits_{1}^{n} v_1} - \frac{\sum\limits_{1}^{n} s_0 v_1}{\sum\limits_{1}^{n} v_1} \right\} + \left\{ \frac{\sum\limits_{1}^{n} s_0 v_1}{\sum\limits_{1}^{n} v_1} - \frac{\sum\limits_{1}^{n} s_0 v_0}{\sum\limits_{1}^{n} v_0} \right\},$$

where the first element represents the change attributable to changes in export shares of the individual commodities (using current weights), and the second the change attributable to changes in the country's export pattern (using base weights).

[2] The formula used was the same as that shown in the footnote above, except that v (country exports) is replaced by V (world exports).

Table 6.5. *Changes in shares of world trade, 1953 to 1960–1 (percentages)*

	Weighted by country exports[a]				Weighted by world exports[a]			
		Change from 1953–5				Change from 1953–5		
	1960–1	Total	Shares	Pattern	1960–1	Total	Shares	Pattern
MORE DEVELOPED COUNTRIES								
Australia	30·4	−0·3	+0·7	−1·0	13·9	−0·4	+0·2	−0·6
New Zealand	28·5	+2·3	+1·8	+0·5	19·9	−0·6	−0·3	−0·3
South Africa	3·3	−0·1	—	−0·1	1·1	−0·1	—	−0·1
Iceland	5·0	—	+0·2	−0·2	1·7	+0·1	+0·2	−0·1
Ireland	10·5	−5·1	−4·7	−0·4	0·5	−0·2	−0·2	—
LESS DEVELOPED COUNTRIES								
Burma	18·5	−3·3	−2·9	−0·4	3·1	+0·1	−0·3	+0·4
Ceylon	37·3	+14·2	+12·7	+1·5	8·0	−0·5	—	−0·5
Malaya	31·7	+5·6	+7·7	−2·1	15·1	+8·0	+3·4	+4·6
India	39·1	−6·3	−5·6	−0·7	8·2	−2·5	−1·6	−0·9
Pakistan	50·3	−14·0	−3·9	−10·1	4·6	−1·9	−0·6	−1·3
Ghana	28·1	+4·5	+4·2	+0·3	18·0	+0·8	+1·7	−0·9
Kenya	13·1	+3·2	+2·7	+0·5	0·7	+0·2	+0·3	−0·1
Malawi	1·4	+0·3	+0·3	—	0·8	+0·1	+0·2	−0·1
Nigeria	11·3	−1·9	−0·5	−1·4	3·2	−0·2	+0·1	−0·3
Rhodesia	8·3	+1·8	+2·1	−0·3	2·0	+0·4	+0·4	—
Tanzania	13·7	−3·7	−0·6	−3·1	1·3	+0·1	+0·1	—
Uganda	2·1	—	+0·4	−0·4	1·7	+0·2	+0·3	−0·1
Zambia	19·3	−1·4	−1·6	+0·2	10·9	+0·8	−0·9	+1·7
Jamaica	8·8	+5·4	+3·1	+2·3	2·6	+0·8	+0·6	+0·2
Trinidad and Tobago	5·3	+1·6	−0·5	+2·1	2·1	+0·4	+0·6	−0·2

SOURCES: As for Table 6.4.

[a] Using values of exports in 1960–1 as weights.

remains. This is because, on the latter basis, the rise in Ceylon's share of world tea exports is exactly offset by declines in her share of exports of vegetable oils and oilseeds, natural rubber and desiccated coconut. However, on the country weighting, tea is of such dominating importance in Ceylon's exports that the gain here far outweighs the losses in the other items.

Equally, the pattern effect has a different meaning from that on the country weighting. A positive change in the final column of Table 6.5 indicates a shift in the pattern of world trade in favour of the particular 'basket' of exports of the country listed. Only Malaya, Zambia and Jamaica fall in this category. For Malaya, this reflects a faster rate of growth in world trade in rubber and iron ore than in tin (in which world trade actually declined over the period). For Zambia, it indicates a faster growth in world copper exports than in other exports from that country; for Jamaica, similarly, it indicates a relatively rapid expansion of world trade in bauxite and sugar. Adverse shifts in world trading patterns have generally been small; only for Pakistan did the shift in the world trade pattern result in a loss of more than 1 per cent of the overall share of world trade.[1]

One hypothesis which can be tested statistically is that the relative export performance of a given country (that is, the movement in its exports in relation to the corresponding movement in the relevant world export index) is inversely associated with its share of world trade. The argument here would be that countries which are marginal suppliers can, with a relatively small economic effort, readily increase their share of world trade, while a similar economic effort by the large trading countries would not have much impact on their own (large) share of the world export total.

There might be several economic reasons for this asymmetry. First, it could happen that world demand rises faster than capacity in the principal producing countries, so that output would tend to expand in the marginal supplying countries to fill the gap. Second, if the world price of the commodity was rising, this would tend to stimulate production more in the small producing countries than in the large ones for a number of primary commodities (though coffee is a clear case of high prices stimulating a big expansion in the largest producing country); on the other hand, a falling trend in world prices would be likely to result in marginal producers going out of production, and such producers are probably more important, relatively, in the marginal exporting countries. Third, where production was initially on a fairly small scale, in a marginal exporting country, substantial economies of scale may be reaped in some cases by an expansion in output, thus allowing exports to become more competitive in price and so gain a larger share of world trade. Finally, it may be government policy in a number of importing countries to diversify the sources of supply of a range of 'strategic' commodities; to the extent that this is so, discriminatory trade or purchasing policies would tend to encourage exports from the small producing countries.

The role played by countries which are marginal suppliers will, in practice, depend heavily on the way their producers react to changes in world prices and on the way the world market for the particular commodity is organized. A marginal exporting country is in much the same position as a small firm producing for a relatively large market. The small firm cannot itself influence the ruling price and its output depends

---

[1] This result is, however, somewhat spurious since the shift in the pattern of world trade in Pakistan's export 'basket' essentially reflected Pakistan's own policy of expanding exports of jute goods at the expense of raw jute.

heavily on its level of profitability at the current price and on its anticipation of future price movements. Similarly, the marginal exporting
country can raise its share of the world market, for one or more of the
reasons mentioned earlier; but if the process threatens the established
share of the large traditional exporters, the latter may then take defensive action. However, this defensive action is unlikely to take the form
of price-cutting for those commodities where the price elasticity of
demand is less than unity.

With the development of national economic planning, most governments of the less developed countries now keep a close watch on the
changing share of the world market held by their major export products.
Where this share is falling, remedial policy changes may be made to
restore the former share. In the last resort, this may involve devaluation
of the currency; but before that point is reached, a wide variety of policy
measures are available in order to improve the competitive position of
its exporters. Remedial action of this kind will depend, to some extent,
on the contribution to the country's total export earnings; where that
contribution is small, remedial action may be of marginal importance if,
indeed, any such action is taken. Moreover, even a falling market share
may be tolerable if the general balance of payments situation and
prospects look reasonably healthy. Consequently, countries with large
shares of the world export market may not, in some situations, take
defensive policy measures to offset encroachments on their traditional
export markets by other, smaller, exporting countries.[1]

A suitable test for this hypothesis is to compare the ratio of the indices
of national exports to world exports for each country, as shown in
Table 6.4 (which compares 1960–1 with 1953–5), with the shares of
each country in world trade in the initial period, after eliminating the
effect of the changing country pattern of exports on each country's
share.[2] The general relationship (see Fig. 6.2) does, indeed, support the
hypothesis, though the inverse relationship is evidently a fairly loose
one.[3] For the seventeen countries covered, a least-squares regression of

---

[1] For a detailed study of India's export performance in terms of oligopoly theory, see
Manmohan Singh, *India's Export Trends and the Prospects for Self-sustained Growth*, Oxford,
Clarendon Press, 1964.

[2] In other words, the 'share' represents what the 1953–5 share would have been had each
country's commodity pattern in that period been the same as it was in 1960–1. In terms of
the previous notation, the adjusted share is:

$$s_0 = \sum_1^n s_0 v_1 \Big/ \sum_1^n v_1.$$

[3] Support for this hypothesis is also to be found in Barend A. de Vries, *The Export Experience of Developing Countries*, Baltimore, Johns Hopkins Press, 1967, who attempts a
systematic analysis of the relationship between variations in export performance and characteristics of countries' economic situations and policies, using linear regression techniques. This
analysis, covering twenty-nine developing countries, confirms that, over the period 1953 to

the ratio of national to world export indices on the adjusted world export share in 1953–5 (and on the square of that share) 'explained' about two-thirds of the variance in the dependent variable.[1] At one extreme, there are six countries (other than South Africa) each accounting for less than 10 per cent on average of world exports in their 1960–1

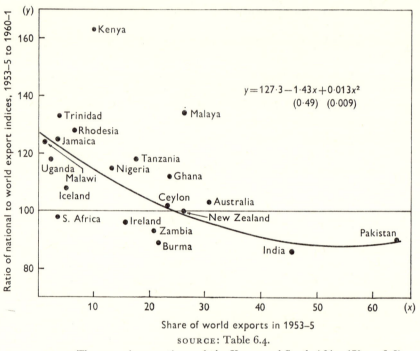

SOURCE: Table 6.4.

NOTE: The regression equation excludes Kenya and South Africa ($R^2 = 0.648$).

Fig. 6.2. Ratio of national to world export indices in relation to share of world trade.

'basket' of commodities, and all of these increased their exports more rapidly than world trade in the corresponding commodity 'baskets'. At the other extreme, however, of the eight countries each accounting for over 20 per cent of world trade, four increased their exports more slowly than their world export indices, three increased them faster, and for

1963, countries with a relatively small overall share in world commodity markets at the beginning of the period showed better export performance over the period than those with larger market shares. In addition, he also found that performance tended to be better for countries with higher growth rates in agriculture; this would lend support to the hypothesis below (p. 167) that differences in supply conditions are likely to be the principal explanation of different export performance among those countries with only small overall shares in world trade.

[1] The first derivative ($dy/dx = 0.026x - 1.43$) falls from -1.3 for $x = 5$ per cent to -0.4 for $x = 40$ per cent.

the remaining country—New Zealand—exports rose at the same rate as world trade.

For the marginal exporting countries—those accounting for under 10 per cent, on average, of world exports—there was a considerable variation in their relative export performance over the period. For Trinidad and Rhodesia, for example, the volume indices of national exports in 1960–1 were some 30 per cent higher than the corresponding world trade indices, whereas for Iceland the excess was only about 10 per cent. The majority of this group, however, had national indices in the range 15 to 30 per cent above their respective world trade indices.

This variation reflects essentially the different impact of supply factors in the marginal exporting countries. The relatively fast increase in exports from Trinidad is entirely explained by a substantial expansion of petroleum refineries in that country by the international oil companies, associated with the development of marine oilfields since 1955. Kenya—which was excluded from the regression as being unrepresentative in this respect—is another example of sharp domestic expansion, this time in agricultural production; the growth in output of coffee and tea for export was particularly rapid in relation to the development of world trade in these beverages. The relatively low ratio of national to world exports for Iceland (108 per cent) is, however, spurious to some extent, since world trade in fish, Iceland's major export, tends to be concentrated within continents. The rapid expansion of the Japanese fish catch since the early 1950s was a principal reason for the increase in world trade in fish, though an appreciable proportion of Japanese exports goes to markets in South East Asia, in which Iceland cannot, in fact, compete.

Of the countries with a substantial initial share in world exports, both Australia and New Zealand increased their exports over the period at much the same rate as world trade in their particular commodity 'baskets'. Ghana, however, achieved a considerably faster rate of growth of exports than that indicated by the corresponding world trade index. One possible reason for this is that the falling trend in world cocoa prices over the period concerned led to some marginal producing countries being squeezed out of production; another, more likely, reason is that inflation in several Latin American countries led to a reduction in their exports of cocoa.[1]

The shortfalls in exports from India and Pakistan relative to world trade in their respective export commodities are interrelated. The Pakistani industrialization programme, which began with the first

---

[1] See Gertrud Lovasy, 'Inflation and Exports in Primary Producing Countries', *Staff Papers*, vol. 9, no. 1. March 1962, International Monetary Fund, Washington.

Five-Year Plan in 1955, resulted in a sharp switch in the commodity pattern of exports away from textile fibres (raw jute and raw cotton) in favour of textile manufactures (jute and cotton goods). In view of Pakistan's lower costs of production, compared with India's,[1] Pakistan was able to gain appreciably at India's expense in the world market for textiles. At the same time, however, Pakistan's internal requirements for textile fibres grew so rapidly that, in spite of the switch in composition, there was an absolute decline in the volume of textile exports, taking fibres and manufactures together. The offset in the balance of payments, Pakistan's imports of cotton goods having been virtually eliminated by 1960–1, must of course be kept in mind in interpreting this development.

Broadly, the distribution of countries in Fig. 6.2 reflects the varying significance of world import demand as a determinant of a country's level of exports. More specifically, the *relative* importance of domestic supply and world demand in determining the rate of growth of a country's exports will vary according to its share in world trade. The greater a country's share in world trade the more probable that its exports will grow more or less in line with the growth in world import demand for the product it exports. The smaller its share, the more important is its ability to produce for export at prevailing world prices, and, as might be expected, there is a tendency for a greater dispersion of export ratios among those countries with the smallest shares in world trade, that is, countries where supply is the main determinant of exports.

The export projections

In order to allow for probable future changes in the share of world exports held by each country, some general assumption needs to be made. On the basis of the experience of the past decade, as analysed above, it seems reasonable to assume that the inverse association between initial shares of world trade, on the one hand, and the relative performance of exports (in relation to the growth of world trade in a comparable 'basket' of goods) will generally continue to hold over the next decade or so. The only exception would be for countries for which there is fairly firm evidence of supply limitations in relation to the projected growth of world trade.

Even so, any projection of relative export performance is necessarily subject to a considerable margin of error, not only because the inverse rule is only loosely applicable, but also because an appropriate allowance needs to be made for the probable shift in the commodity pattern

---

[1] Pakistan's lower production costs in jute goods are due partly to her export duty on raw jute, which raises costs, relatively, in Indian jute mills.

of exports towards, or away from, the more dynamic commodities in world trade.

For the more developed Sterling countries, the projection problem is, perhaps, less difficult than for the rest, since—apart from South Africa —they all account for fairly substantial shares of world exports, so that it is unlikely that their overall shares will show any appreciable change, one way or the other, in the period up to 1975. In Table 6.6, it has been assumed that the volume of exports of the commodities covered by Table 6.3, footnote a, from each of these more developed countries rises in much the same proportion as their respective projected world export indices.[1] For Australia and Iceland, a marginal rise in the ratio of national to world exports is projected; for Australia, this assumes arbitrarily some further expansion in wheat sales to China,[2] while for Iceland the assumption is simply that relative export performance in the coming decade will not be significally different from that of the past one. For the other more developed countries, however, no significant change in their relative export performance is projected, though it is necessary to allow for some margin of error, as shown in Table 6.6.

There remains the problem of projecting the future course of exports of items not included in the sample of commodities for which past relative export performance was calculated. Here, the projections must depend largely on the present and prospective commodity composition of the exports concerned. For example, the main items omitted from the Australian sample are coarse grains and miscellaneous foodstuffs, miscellaneous raw materials, coal and refined petroleum. Allowing for a sizeable growth in exportable supplies of the non-food items, particularly coal and iron ore, and for increases for foods in line with the world export projections for these categories, it would appear probable that the non-sample group of exports is likely to grow at a considerably faster rate than the items, mostly traditional primary products (though also including manufactures), which were included in the sample analysis.[3]

For Ireland and South Africa, however, the future rate of export growth in the items omitted from the sample seems likely to increase at a slower pace than the sample as a whole. The items omitted from the Irish sample consist mainly of beer, chocolate, miscellaneous materials,

---

[1] Corresponding to the projected export growth rates shown in Table 6.3.

[2] If there were no wheat sales to China, the projected volume indices for total Australian exports in 1975 would be 165 (A) and 185 (B).

[3] The discovery of large mineral resources in the last few years should provide a favourable element in the growth of exports. The *Report of the Committee of Economic Enquiry*, vol. I, Canberra, May 1965 (the 'Vernon Report') projected the growth of mineral exports between 1962–3 and 1975 at between 6·1 and 6·9 per cent per annum, in contrast to 2·7 and 3·0 per cent for rural exports.

parcel post and special transactions, while most of the sample is accounted for by meat and manufactured goods, exports of which are likely to expand considerably faster than those of the omitted items.

For South Africa, nearly half the value of the omitted items consists of uranium and other fissionable materials, and most of the rest is made up of maize, other foods and asbestos. Exports of uranium from South Africa have been falling since 1960–1, but in the longer run it seems unlikely that the decline will continue in view of the atomic energy expansion plans of a number of industrial countries. Any projection of uranium exports is necessarily surrounded by a very large error; here, it is assumed, arbitrarily, that the recent decline is reversed and that by about 1975 the 1960–1 level will have been regained. Consequently, the mean projected rate of growth of exports for the omitted items as a whole is relatively quite small.

Among the less developed Sterling countries by contrast, some appreciable deviations between the course of national exports and of world trade in their specialist export 'baskets' must be expected. The specific assumptions for the different countries are shown in Table 6.7. Of the sixteen countries listed, the majority (eleven countries) are projected to gain in their share of world trade over the next decade or so; four countries are projected to lose some of their present share, while the remaining country—Ghana—is assumed to keep her 1960–1 share unchanged.

Kenya, Tanzania and Pakistan are projected as having the highest ratios of national to world exports (115–130 per cent) in 1975 compared with 1960–1. For Kenya, this is a considerable reduction from the high ratio of 163 per cent for the period 1953–5 to 1960–1; but for Tanzania, the projected range implies no significant change from that for the past period. Though Kenya cannot expect to increase her share of world coffee exports very substantially in the future, as she did over the past decade, particularly if the present International Coffee Agreement (or a similar agreement based on export quotas, or even on production controls) can be assumed to be in operation in the 1970s, she seems likely to gain in market share for a number of manufactures, tea, and perhaps sisal. For Tanzania, the relatively fast-growing exports, compared with world trade, seem likely to be cotton, tea and diamonds.

For Pakistan, it is assumed that the industrialization programme, though likely to result in reduced export surplus of some materials, such as raw jute, will also expand exports of jute and cotton manufactures (both of which are included in the sample used in the projections) by a substantial amount. On balance, Pakistan's overall market share seems likely to increase significantly.

Table 6.6. *Projection of exports from the more developed overseas Sterling countries in 1975 on the basis of changing shares of world trade*

	Exports in 1960–1	Assumed ratio of national to world export indices in 1975	Projection of exports in 1975[a]			
			Volume		Value	
			A	B	A	B
	(£ million)	(%)	(1960–1 = 100)		(£ million at 1960–1 prices)	
Australia						
Sample	590	100–110	150	165	880	960
Other[b]	166	..	250	300	415	495
Total	756	..	170	195	1,295	1,455
New Zealand						
Sample	251	95–105	140	145	350	370
Other[c]	38	..	140	150	55	60
Total	289	..	140	150	405	430
South Africa						
Sample	264	95–105	205	225	540	590
Other[d]	149	..	110	120	165	180
Total	413	..	170	185	705	770
Iceland	28	100–110	200	220	55	60
Ireland						
Sample	106	95–105	170	180	180	190
Other[e]	55	..	120	135	65	75
Total	161	..	150	165	245	265
TOTAL	1,646	..	165	180	2,705	2,980

SOURCES: *Yearbook of International Trade Statistics*, United Nations, New York; Table 6.3.

[a] Taking the mid points of the assumed ratios shown in the second column for each projection for convenience of presentation. All the projections have been rounded to the nearest five.

[b] Mainly miscellaneous foods and raw materials, coal and refined petroleum.

[c] Mainly miscellaneous foods and raw materials.

[d] Mainly uranium and other fissionable materials, asbestos, and miscellaneous foods.

[e] Mainly chocolate, beer, parcel post and temporary exports.

In the next group, in terms of the projected ratio of national to world exports, are Hong Kong, India, Malawi, Rhodesia and Uganda, for each of which the 1975 ratio is assumed to fall in the range 110–120 per cent of 1960–1. The assumption implies, for Hong Kong, some modest relaxations in the present degree of restrictions on her textile and clothing exports to the industrial countries, but Hong Kong is also likely to increase her share of world trade in other consumer manufactures.

Table 6.7. *Projection of exports from the less developed overseas Sterling countries in 1975 on the basis of changing shares of world trade*

	Exports in 1960–1	Assumed ratio of national to world export indices in 1975	Projection of exports in 1975[a]			
			Volume		Value	
			A	B	A	B
	(£ million)	(%)	(1960–1 = 100)		(£ million at 1960–1 prices)	
Burma						
Sample	67	85–95	115	125	75	85
Other[b]	12	..	125	125	15	15
Total	79	..	115	125	90	100
Ceylon	130	100–110	130	135	170	175
Malaya						
Sample	291	105–115	170	180	500	535
Other[c]	33	..	145	160	50	55
Total	324	..	170	180	550	590
Hong Kong	246	110–120	235	260	575	640
India						
Sample	368	110–120	170	180	625	660
Other[d]	115	..	115	125	130	145
Total	483	..	155	165	755	805
Pakistan						
Sample	128[f]	120–130	155	165	225	245
Other[e]	14[f]	..	300	350	45	55
Total	142[f]	..	165	185	270	300
Ghana						
Aluminium	$\frac{1}{2}$	..	..	..	20	25
Other	103$\frac{1}{2}$	95–105	200	210	205	220
Total	104	..	215	230	225	245
Kenya						
Sample	34	115–125	195	210	65	70
Other[g]	3	..	125	135	5	5
Total	37	..	190	200	70	75
Malawi	9	110–120	150	160	15	15
Nigeria						
Sample						
Petroleum	8	..	3,250	3,250	260	260
Other sample	137	105–115	150	175	205	240
Other[h]	19	..	165	190	35	40
Total	164	..	305	330	500	**540**

Table 6.7 (cont.)

	Exports in 1960-1	Assumed ratio of national to world export indices in 1975	Projection of exports in 1975[a] Volume		Value	
			A	B	A	B
	(£ million)	(%)	(1960-1 = 100)		(£ million at 1960-1 prices)	
Rhodesia						
Sample	51	110-120	190	210	95	105
Other[i]	16	..	190	220	30	35
Total	67	..	190	210	125	140
Tanzania	49	115-125	190	205	90	100
Uganda	43	110-120	210	225	90	95
Zambia	125	90-100	200	220	250	275
Jamaica						
Sample	53	85-95	230	260	120	140
Other[j]	5	..	130	150	5	5
Total	58	..	215	250	125	145
Trinidad and Tobago	110	70-80	140	155	155	170
TOTAL	2,170	..	185	205	4,055	4,410

SOURCES: As for Table 6.6.

[a] Taking the mid points of the assumed ratios shown in the second column for each projection for convenience of presentation. All the projections have been rounded to the nearest five.

[b] Mainly food and feeding-stuffs.

[c] Mainly food, miscellaneous raw materials and re-exported manufactures.

[d] Mainly miscellaneous foods and raw materials.

[e] Mainly miscellaneous raw materials and manufactures.

[f] Exports from Pakistan were abnormally low in 1961, the average for 1960 and 1962 being 15 per cent higher, in volume, than that for 1960 and 1961. The projected indices for 1975 have been applied to the average of 1960 and 1962 (£162 million at 1960-1 prices).

[g] Mainly miscellaneous foods.

[h] Mainly miscellaneous minerals and other raw materials.

[i] Mainly asbestos and other raw materials.

[j] Mainly miscellaneous foods.

India is assumed to achieve a modest increase in market share in the period up to 1975. India's share of world tea exports is, however, likely to decline further, losing not only to Ceylon but also to the lower-cost producing countries in Africa, where production costs are generally lower than in India. A further decline in market shares for jute manufactures is also probable as a result of expanding export supplies in Pakistan. The prospects for cotton goods are more complex. A number of India's present markets are in the under-developed countries, many of which have plans to develop their own textile industries. To the extent that they are successful, the import market for cheap cotton goods is likely to contract. On the other hand, a more liberal import policy by the industrial countries could result in an increase in Indian cotton textile exports, but a rapid growth in domestic consumption in India herself might well hold back the required growth in export supplies. It also seems likely that India's market share of world trade in other manufactures (particularly in light engineering goods) will rise, on the general assumptions of the present projections, and these could, in the event, make a fairly substantial contribution to the growth in Indian exports over the coming decade, though the expansion in exports of manufactures is likely to be considerably smaller than that envisaged in the third and fourth Five-Year Plans. This conclusion would seem to be reinforced by the decision to re-shape the fourth Plan (1965/6 to 1970/1) in favour of the defence industries, following the clash with Pakistan in 1965.

For the other countries in this group, the projected ratios are either marginally lower (Malawi and Rhodesia), or about the same (Uganda) as those for the past decade, implying that, in the absence of definite supply limitations, it seems probable that their previous more rapid export growth will continue, in relation to the growth in their world export indices.

The third group consists of three countries—Ceylon, Malaya and Nigeria—for each of which a modest increase is assumed to occur by 1975 in the ratio of national to world exports, the ratio being projected at either 100–110 or 105–115 per cent of 1960–1. For Ceylon, some further gain in market share is assumed for tea, while Malaya seems likely to continue to displace Indonesia in the export trade in rubber and tin, though the rate of displacement is assumed to have fallen off appreciably compared with the period since the mid 1950s.

Nigeria's share of world cocoa exports is assumed to remain essentially unchanged and there may well be a decline in her market share for oils and oilseeds, in view of the probable further expansion in competing exportable supplies of soya beans from the United States. The major dynamic element in the export prospect is, however, petroleum. Production in the Eastern Region of the country was under 1 million tons in 1960, but rose rapidly to 4·7 million tons in 1964. In 1965, new oilfields were discovered in the Mid-West Region, and in 1966 production of crude oil was over 20 million tons. It seems probable that the rapid growth in output will continue into the 1970s. In view of the inevitable uncertainties surrounding the early stages of development, no reliable estimates of petroleum exports in 1975 can be made. It is assumed here that they will be equivalent to 50 million tons of crude petroleum.

For Ghana, the ratio of national to world exports is assumed to remain unchanged for her traditional exports. Ghana's share of world cocoa exports has increased since the mid 1950s, reflecting the substantially higher crops of the early 1960s, but it seems unlikely, with the development of cocoa production in a number of other tropical countries, that Ghana's share can be significantly higher in 1975 than in 1960–1. The principal change in prospect arises from the development of an aluminium smelting industry based on cheap electric power from the Volta river. The companies concerned are planning a smelting capacity of some 100,000 tons by 1969/70, almost all of which is likely to be available for export. On the general assumptions about economic growth in the industrial countries—which underlie the present projections— world demand for aluminium is likely to continue to rise rapidly in the 1970s. Consequently, it seems probable that Ghanaian aluminium capacity will be further extended after 1969/70. It is assumed here that Ghana's development plans for aluminium will not be adversely affected by foreign exchange difficulties resulting from low cocoa prices, since the required foreign capital investment for the aluminium industry appears to be securely committed. By 1975, aluminium exports are assumed to have risen to between 135 and 165 thousand tons; on this basis, aluminium would then provide about 10 per cent of all Ghana's export earnings (see Table 6.7).[1]

Zambia is assumed to lose marginally in her share of world copper exports as a result of more rapid expansion in other producing countries (particularly Chile). The decline assumed in Burma's ratio of national to world exports essentially implies a continuation of her previous loss of share of world trade in rice; this would reflect, in part, the assumption that exportable supplies would grow faster in some other Far East countries (such as Thailand), and also that exports from the United States are likely to grow in relative importance as the traditional net-importing countries of South-East Asia turn to growing more of their own rice requirements. For Jamaica, a fall in market share of world trade in bauxite has been assumed in view of the developments, in progress or planned, in a number of other countries with large bauxite deposits (particularly in West Africa). The projected substantial decline in market share for Trinidad is based on the assumption that

---

[1] This is the effect on gross export earnings. However, since the Volta Aluminium Company will be operating only an aluminium smelter until about 1977, when an alumina processing plant will be built, Ghana will be importing alumina (mainly from Jamaica) while continuing to export her own high-grade bauxite as crushed ore. Aluminium is therefore unlikely to have a major impact on Ghana's net *payments* position until after the mid 1970s.

new low-cost sources of petroleum (in North Africa and Nigeria), as well as the possibility of an appreciable oil surplus for export emerging in the Soviet Union, would tend to make Trinidadian output less competitive. Thus, in the event of no new major marine oilfields being discovered, the rapid growth of Trinidad's petroleum output in recent years is not likely to be maintained in the future.

These various assumptions about the future course of national exports from the less developed countries, in relation to world exports, relate to the sample of commodities for which separate projections have been made. For countries such as Ceylon, Malawi and Zambia, the sample covers such a high percentage of total exports that the proportionate increase in exports projected for the sample has been assumed to apply to the total. For nine of the sixteen countries in Table 6.7, however, separate consideration of the probable future trend of exports omitted from the sample calculations was necessary. The projections for these other exports, shown in Table 6.7, are based on their commodity composition in relation to the projections already made.[1]

By far the largest group of exports omitted from the sample was that for India, the most important items here being a variety of industrial materials (natural gums and resins, manganese ore, mica, etc.) and miscellaneous foods and feeding-stuffs. A substantial expansion in exports seems unlikely, partly because of India's recurrent food shortage problems, though exports of coffee and spices should grow appreciably, and partly because of substitution for Indian exports of manganese ore (by, for example, Brazilian supplies) and for mica (by synthetic substitutes).[2]

For Malaya, the main items omitted from the sample were fish, fruit and other foods, and a variety of miscellaneous materials and manufactures (including considerable re-exports). A good deal of uncertainty inevitably surrounds the export prospects for this heterogenous group, particularly the future of the re-export trade through Singapore. It has been assumed here that, on average, exports in the omitted items will grow at a somewhat lower rate than those included in the sample. For Pakistan, a relatively high growth rate in exports of the omitted items (which include 'new' types of manufactures) has been assumed; but for Burma, the omitted items (mainly vegetables and oilcake) are not likely to show any great expansion.

The projected growth rates in the volume of exports from the different

---

[1] In several cases, commodities which were minor exports omitted from the sample for a particular country were also major exports from other countries, so that world trade projections for these were available. In other cases, approximate projections were made, based in part on recent export trends from the particular country.

[2] See Manmohan Singh, *op. cit.*, for a more detailed discussion of India's export prospects in these items.

overseas Sterling countries on the basis of the various assumptions made about changing shares of world trade are substantially different for some countries from those shown earlier (see Table 6.3) on the assumption of constant shares. The differences between the two projections depend also, for certain countries, on the inclusion in the 'changing shares' projection of a separate assessment of export prospects for minor items excluded from the sample.

The projections on the 'changing shares' basis are significantly higher than those based on constant shares for all the African Sterling countries, and particularly for Nigeria, Kenya, Tanzania and Uganda (see Table 6.8). For Jamaica and Trinidad, however, the projected loss of share of world exports reduces the rate of export growth by some $1\frac{1}{2}$ and 2 percentage points a year, respectively. Among the Sterling countries in Asia, the 'changing shares' projection is lower than that based on constant shares for Burma, but is higher for the rest. For the more developed countries, the more sophisticated projection, assuming changing shares and allowing separately for non-sample exports, resulted in significantly lower growth rates of exports for Australia, Ireland and South Africa, and marginally higher growth rates for Iceland and New Zealand.

One major conclusion from the projection calculation is that, with only a few exceptions, the mean rate of export growth over the coming decade will generally be lower than that achieved over the past period from 1953–5 (see also Fig. 6.3). The major shortfalls, compared with past growth rates, are projected for Trinidad and Kenya, for reasons explained earlier. At the other extreme are Nigeria, India, Pakistan and Ceylon, for all of which the projected growth rates are significantly above the past ones. The projected rate for Iceland is higher than the past rate on assumption B, but marginally lower on assumption A. For all the other Sterling countries shown in Fig. 6.3, the projected rates are below the past ones, though for some—notably Australia and Malaya—the differences are fairly marginal.

A second conclusion is that the improvement in export prospects which results from changing the assumptions about the future rate of growth of real income in the industrial countries from a less optimistic view (assumption A), to a more optimistic one (assumption B), is very much smaller than the decline compared with past rates of growth in exports. For most countries, moving from the low to the high income-growth assumption is associated with a rise of about 0·6 to 0·8 per cent per annum in the rate of export growth; the decline in the projected export growth rates compared with those for 1953–5 to 1960–1, however, is considerably greater than this for many of the Sterling countries (for nine of the nineteen countries for which the comparison could be made, the shortfall compared with the past export growth rate exceeded 2 per cent per annum).

This general retardation projected in the rate of export growth of the majority of overseas Sterling countries essentially reflects the implications of the underlying assumptions made earlier. Of these, perhaps the most important are that, in the industrial countries, the relatively low income elasticities of demand for the major foods and beverages will remain much the same in the future as in the recent past; that the

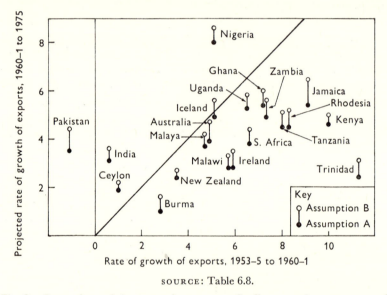

SOURCE: Table 6.8.

Fig. 6.3. Rates of growth in exports from overseas Sterling countries: 1953–5 to 1960–1 in relation to projections for 1960–1 to 1975 (percentage per annum, compound).

inroads of synthetic materials in the markets of natural industrial materials will continue to spread; and that only relatively modest relaxations can be anticipated in the present degree of restriction imposed on imports of temperate-zone agricultural foods and of 'low-cost' manufactures. As regards the less developed Sterling countries, the further assumption implicit in the projections is that there is likely to be relatively little diversification of exports by most countries, even by the early 1970s. A growing export trade in processed foods and materials and in manufactures would, however, be possible for a number of the less developed countries, but this would require some important changes in policy, both in the industrial countries where the elimination of import restrictions is particularly urgent and in the various less developed countries themselves. These policy issues are discussed further in Chapter 9.

The export projections for individual countries must therefore be interpreted carefully in the light of the assumptions on which they are based. Different assumptions concerning, say, the future rate of substitution of synthetic fibres for cotton and wool, or the degree to which beet sugar continues to be subsidized, would result in very different export projections for some Sterling countries from the ones given here; so, of course, would the adoption of different assumptions about the future course of commodity prices. Moreover, the projected export growth rates are necessarily subject to a considerable margin of error, whatever the specific assumptions made. They must therefore be taken purely as probable orders of magnitude; the projections in Table 6.8 are given as single rates solely for simplicity of presentation.

Finally, there is one assumption which has so far remained implicit, but which is worthy of explicit mention here. Since the prices of the majority of commodities have been assumed not to be significantly different in 1975 from what they were in 1960–1, the problem of the influence of inflationary pressures in the various Sterling countries on their shares of world exports does not arise. In effect, it has been assumed that internal price and cost inflation is kept within reasonable limits in all the overseas Sterling countries. To the extent that governments do not succeed in doing so, this could adversely affect their countries' export shares by an appreciable amount.[1]

Country and commodity projections

As a result of allowing for probable changes in country shares of world trade, the export projections for both the more developed Sterling countries and the sample of less developed countries are rather more optimistic than those shown in Table 6.3 based on the assumption of constant shares. For the more developed group as a whole, the constant-share projection showed annual rates of increase of exports of 3·3 and 3·8 per cent, on assumptions A and B respectively; allowing for changing shares of trade, the figures rise to 3·5 and 4·2 per cent. For the sample of less developed countries, the rise was from 3·4 and 4·0 per cent to 4·4 and 5·0 per cent, on the alternative income-growth assumptions.

Although the projections for individual countries are largely based on the commodity projections presented in Chapter 5, the adjustments to allow for probable changes in shares of world trade were made independently of the assumptions made in Chapter 5, which considered

[1] Miss Gertrud Lovasy has shown that there was a marked inverse relationship between the rise in internal prices (measured by cost-of-living indices) and changes in the volume of exports, for over thirty primary-exporting countries, taking the period from 1948 to 1958 (Lovasy, *loc. cit.*).

Table 6.8. *Summary of country export projections on basis of constant, and of changing, shares of world trade (percentage per annum, compound)*

	Actual growth rate of exports 1953–5 to 1960–1[a]	Projected growth rate of exports, 1960–1 to 1975			
		Assuming constant shares[b]		Assuming changing shares	
		A	B	A	B
MORE DEVELOPED COUNTRIES					
Australia	4·9	2·5	3·1	3·9	4·7
New Zealand	3·5	2·3	2·7	2·4	2·7
South Africa	6·6	5·1	5·7	3·8	4·4
Iceland	5·1	4·7	5·4	4·9	5·6
Ireland	5·9	3·6	4·2	2·8	3·5
LESS DEVELOPED COUNTRIES					
Burma	2·8	1·7	2·3	1·0	1·6
Ceylon	1·0	1·5	1·8	1·9	2·2
Malaya	4·7	2·6	3·2	3·7	4·2
Hong Kong	..	5·4	6·1	6·1	6·8
India	0·6	2·7	3·2	3·1	3·6
Pakistan	− 1·1[c]	1·5	2·0	3·5	4·4
Ghana	7·2	4·9	5·3	5·4	6·0
Kenya	10·0	2·6	3·0	4·6	5·0
Malawi	5·7[d]	2·0	2·4	2·8	3·3
Nigeria	5·1	2·7	3·6	8·0	8·6
Rhodesia	8·3[d]	3·5	4·3	4·5	5·2
Tanzania	8·0	2·7	3·4	4·5	5·1
Uganda	6·5	2·8	3·3	5·3	5·8
Zambia	7·3	5·2	5·9	4·9	5·6
Jamaica	9·1	6·8	7·6	5·4	6·5
Trinidad and Tobago	11·3	4·4	5·1	2·4	3·1

SOURCES: Tables 6.3, 6.6 and 6.7; *Yearbook of International Trade Statistics*, 1963, United Nations, New York, 1965.

[a] Based on official indices of export volume. These indices differ from those shown in Table 6.4, partly because the latter relate only to the sample of commodities for each country, while the official indices relate to all exports; and partly because the official indices are generally base-weighted (though the base period differs considerably from one country to another), while the sample index is weighted by 1960–1 values.

[b] These projected rates relate only to the sample of commodities for each country (see Table 6.2 for the percentage of total exports covered).

[c] Based on a linear regression using estimated volume indices for the years 1954–62. Had the unusually good exports of 1953 been included, however, the average rate of decline would have been greater (− 2·4 per cent per annum, compound, for both 1953–60 and 1953–62).

[d] Excluding intra-trade between the countries of the former Federation of Rhodesia and Nyasaland.

changes in shares of world trade in various commodities of the whole Overseas Sterling Area. There could, therefore, be some divergence between the country and commodity projections for the Area taken as a whole. To compare the two sets of projections, however, it is necessary to make export projections for the less developed countries not included in Table 6.7. The comparison can, however, be considerably simplified if it explicitly excludes mineral fuels, since on this basis the Persian Gulf sheikhdoms are automatically excluded (and it would be exceedingly difficult to make reasoned projections for these), as are also the coal and petroleum exports of a considerable number of other less developed Sterling countries.[1] Petroleum exports from Nigeria and Trinidad have already been projected to 1975 for Table 6.7, while similar projections of coal and petroleum exports from Australia have been made for Table 6.6.

Excluding mineral fuels, exports from countries excluded from the sample of less developed countries amounted to some £400 million in 1960–1, or about 10 per cent of total overseas Sterling Area exports (excluding fuels). Of this, well over half (£240 million in 1960–1) was accounted for by Singapore, while another quarter came from Guyana, Sierra Leone, Cyprus and Mauritius. The rest came from a considerable number of small exporting countries. The projection for this group thus depends heavily on the probable future trend in exports from Singapore. It is not possible to make an export projection for Singapore with any pretence of reasonable accuracy, mainly because the export totals include a considerable volume of re-export trade, much of it originating in Indonesia and China as well as in Britain and the United States.[2] The future of economic relations with Indonesia and China will undoubtedly have an important influence on the trend of Singapore's exports, and clearly no reliable forecast can be made here. One important post-war trend which seems very relevant in this context is the general decline of the world's entrepôt trade not only in Singapore but in other large entrepôt centres also, including the United Kingdom. The decline reflects, in the main, the desire of primary-producing countries to sell direct to importing countries, rather than via intermediaries in merchanting centres. If this trend continues, which seems likely, then Singapore's total export trade, including re-exports, is likely to grow relatively slowly. For present purposes, it is arbitrarily assumed to grow at an annual rate of 1·3 and 1·6 per cent on assumptions A and B respectively.

Projections for the other main exporting countries excluded from the

---

[1] The most important of these being Libya, Singapore, Aden, Brunei and Sabah.

[2] Re-exports of Malayan produce have already been deducted, so far as possible, to arrive at the Singapore export total used here.

sample were made on the basis of their export specializations, and on available information concerning their probable expansion in exportable supplies. Guyana[1] and Cyprus seem, on this basis, to have more optimistic export prospects than Sierra Leone and Mauritius.

Allowing for the countries excluded from the sample, the rate of growth in the value of exports (other than mineral fuels) from the Overseas Sterling Area is projected to rise by 3·6 per cent a year between 1960–1 and 1975 on assumption A, and by 4·3 per cent a year on assumption B. These results are derived by adding the projections for the individual Sterling countries. The corresponding projections arrived at from the commodity side are very close to these and the two sets of projections are placed together in Table 6.9. There is a small difference in coverage which amounts to about 7 per cent in the base year; this is due to the inclusion in the country totals of several items excluded from the commodity projections (sisal, for example) and the further inclusion of estimates for various residual items in the country totals. Nevertheless, these differences are not very large and the differences in the two sets of projected growth rates are certainly well within the margin of error associated with this type of projection. For this reason, it does not seem appropriate to alter either, or both, of the projections to make them show exactly the same totals; to do so would result merely in a spurious accuracy. In the later discussion of probable future trends in exports and gross domestic product, the country projections given in Tables 6.6 and 6.7 are used as the relevant orders of magnitude for export growth on the various assumptions made.

3. THE COUNTRY EXPORT PROJECTIONS IN RELATION TO OFFICIAL EXPORT PLANS

All the less developed countries included in the sample for which detailed export projections have been presented in the previous section have published Economic Development Plans; so, too, have Iceland and Ireland among the more developed Sterling countries. Before making use of the projections on the lines of the *ex post* model discussed in Chapter 2, it is of interest to compare them with the planned rates of growth of exports which governments have published as their working targets.

Unfortunately, direct comparisons of the projections with the published Development Plans are subject to a number of major qualifications. First, the plans of most countries apply to a relatively short period, usually five years, and most of the current plans are due to end in the

---

[1] For Guyana, the projection was based on a detailed assessment of export prospects by A. Kundu, 'The Economy of British Guiana, 1960–1975', *Social and Economic Studies*, vol. 12, no. 3, September 1963.

Table 6.9. *Comparison of export projections for the Overseas Sterling Area by country and commodity*

	Exports 1960–1	Projections for 1975		Rate of growth, 1960–1 to 1975	
		A	B	A	B
		(£ million at 1960–1 prices)		(% per annum compound)	
COUNTRY PROJECTIONS					
More developed countries	1,646	2,705	2,980	3·5	4·2
Less developed countries					
(i) Sample[a]	2,170	4,055	4,410	4·4	5·0
(ii) Others[b] (excluding mineral fuels)	399	495	535	1·5	2·0
Total	4,215	7,255	7,925	3·9	4·5
Minus mineral fuels from Australia, Nigeria and Trinidad	125	460	480	9·5	9·8
TOTAL	4,090	6,795	7,445	3·6	4·3
COMMODITY PROJECTIONS					
Principal commodities (exported by O.S.A.)	3,797	6,520	6,885	3·8	4·2
Miscellaneous exports	293	..	..	..	..
TOTAL	4,090	..	..	..	..

SOURCES: Tables 5.10, 6.6 and 6.7.

[a] Countries for which detailed projections have been made (see Table 6.7).
[b] See text pp. 181–2.

late 1960s. Only one[1] covers virtually the same period (1960–1 to 1975) used for the projections made here. The great diversity of the actual periods covered by the various Development Plans can be seen from Table 6.10; hardly any two countries are planning over identical periods. This diversity is, perhaps, not unexpected since economic development planning began in some countries, such as India and Pakistan, in the mid 1950s, whereas in the newly independent countries of Africa, for example, economic planning is in its infancy. Moreover, since the major limitations on economic growth vary so much from country to country, each must judge for itself the most appropriate period to take for the successful operation of a plan. However, after the experience of operating at least one or two plans has been gained by all these countries—say, by 1970—it would seem sensible to aim for uniformity in the planning periods. This would allow much more easily for the development

[1] The 'Perspective Plan' for India covers the period from 1960/1 to 1975/6.

of international co-ordination of the details of the various plans, particularly within the less developed regions of the world.[1]

A second limitation is that not all the Development Plans are very explicit about their assumptions and projections for the export sector. As can be seen from Table 6.10, Malawi does not include any export projection, while about half the countries show only overall export totals to be aimed at. Only Ceylon, India, Pakistan, Ghana, Kenya, Zambia and Trinidad include detailed export projections by main commodity in their current Plans.

There are, in principle, two alternative ways of arriving at an export target. One approach is to assess the probable trends in world demand for the exportable goods available and the possibilities of increasing the country's share of world trade in its traditional export lines, as well as of economic adaptation to diversify into the more dynamic commodities in world trade. An effective export target would be based on this assessment, but would also take into account the probable impact of alternative fiscal and other policies designed to improve export performance. The alternative approach is to set a target for economic growth from which a required level of imports can be derived. If a total of net capital inflow, including aid, is known or can be assumed, the difference between this total and the required level of imports must be met by exports. Thus, on this approach, a 'required' export target is derived and policy can then be directed to achieve it. Of the various Sterling countries which operate Development Plans, only Ireland uses this residual export target approach (see Table 6.10), so that for Ireland no valid comparison can be made between the official export target and the export projection made earlier.[2]

Though the official export targets of the other Sterling countries are comparable in kind with the projections in Tables 6.6 and 6.7, any comparisons between the two must be related to the general assumptions made. In the present study, the export projections for each Sterling country are based on the same alternative assumptions about the growth of real income in the industrial countries, the protectionist policies of these countries, the rate of displacement of natural by synthetic materials and, where appropriate, the probable change in relative commodity prices. Because of this standard basis, the present set of country export projections is internally consistent. If, however, the

---

[1] Regional co-ordination in development planning would, of course, involve co-operation between Sterling and non-Sterling countries.

[2] *Second Programme for Economic Expansion*, Stationery Office, Dublin, 1963. It might be argued that this 'required export target' approach is more suitable for those countries whose share in world trade is very small, i.e. where domestic supply factors are more important than world demand as a determinant of exports (see the argument on p. 168). Indeed, the Irish Plan justifies the 'residual target' in terms of Ireland's marginal supplier situation.

Table 6.10. *Export Plans of certain overseas Sterling countries during the 1960s*

	Economic Development Plan		No export target or projection	Residual export target only	Export projection	
	No. of years	Period			Total only	Detailed commodity projections
MORE DEVELOPED COUNTRIES						
Iceland	4	1963–6			*	
Ireland	{5	1959/60–63/4	*			
	7	1964–70		*		
LESS DEVELOPED COUNTRIES						
Burma	4	1961/2–64/5				*
Ceylon	{10	1959–68				*
	5	1966–71				*
Malaya	5	1961–5			*	.. ᵃ
India	{5	1960/1–65/6				*
	5	1966/7–70/1				*
Pakistan	{5	1960/1–64/5				*
	5	1965/6–69/70				*
Ghana	7	1963/4–69/70				*
Kenya	6	1964–70				*
Malawi	5	1965–9	*			
Nigeria	6	1962–8			*	
Tanzania	5	1964–9			*	.. ᵃ
Uganda	5	1966–71			*	
Zambia	4	1966–70				*
Jamaica	5	1963–8			*	
Trinidad and Tobago	5	1964–8				*

SOURCES: Economic Development Plans of the various countries listed.

ᵃ Includes production targets for the main export commodities.

planning authorities of the various Sterling countries have made different assumptions from these, their export projections, or export targets, will not be comparable with the projections of the present study. Moreover, the targets could well be non-comparable among themselves, if the underlying assumptions are mutually inconsistent.

Very few of the plans, however, contain any discussion of the probable growth in world demand for their main export commodities or of the relevance of the rate of growth in real income in the main industrial countries to changes in world demand. The Ghanaian Plan is exceptional in its relatively sophisticated discussion of probable changes in the world economic situation, and their likely effect on Ghana's own merchandise trade.[1] Those plans which do discuss the probable future

[1] See *Seven-Year Development Plan, 1963/4–1969/70*, Accra, 1964, pp. 224–8. A detailed analysis of world demand trends was also given in the *Report of the UN/ECA/FAO Economic Survey Mission on the Economic Development of Zambia*, Ndola, 1964.

trends in the world market for their exports (for example, the Indian and Pakistani Plans), assume either implicitly or explicitly the continuance of recent rates of growth, or do not relate the discussion to any particular assumptions about the rate of growth in the main industrial areas.

The problem of increasing the share of world exports is given much more attention in the published Plans than that of the rate of growth in world demand. This is generally a sensible approach for most Sterling countries which at present enjoy a relatively small percentage share of world trade in their main export items: a small increase in that share—even with a constant volume of world trade—could lead to a sizeable rise in their export receipts. Several countries have proceeded on the assumption that they can sell abroad the whole of their exportable surplus of particular crops; this is so for Kenya (sisal, tea, coffee and cotton) and Tanzania (sisal and coffee). Others make explicit assumptions concerning their shares of the export market: Ghana, for example, assumes no change in her share of world cocoa exports,[1] the UN/ECA/FAO Report for Zambia made a similar assumption for Zambian copper,[2] while Pakistan assumes that she will achieve an increased share of exports of jute manufactures.[3]

In many cases, however, the change in share of world trade implied in the Plan figures for future exports cannot be deduced because no indication is given of the probable development of world trade. In other cases, apparently conflicting assumptions are implied in the export plans of different countries. Tea is an example: India's share of world tea exports fell off during the 1950s (from 44 per cent in 1953–5 to 39 per cent in 1960–1), though there has been a recovery in share in more recent years, mainly as a result of reductions in the export duty on tea and the suspension of export controls towards the end of 1961. The Perspective Plan asssumes that India's tea exports will rise by 3·0 per cent a year, on average, from 1961/2 to 1975/6. Ceylon, on the other hand, had gained appreciably in market share since the early 1950s, and her Plan (published in 1958) argued that rising consumption within India would put pressure on India's exportable tea surplus, and thus allow Ceylon further to increase her share of the world export total. The low-cost African tea producers—such as Kenya and Tanzania—

[1] *Seven-Year Development Plan*, p. 233.

[2] UN/ECA/FAO Report, p. 39. Since independence in 1964, Zambia has operated a number of short-term transitional plans while the long-term plan was being prepared. The *Report of the UN/ECA/FAO Economic Survey Mission* was accepted by the Zambian Government as a basis for planning and was used for comparison with the projections made here. The *First National Development Plan* was published in July 1966.

[3] *Outline of the Third Five-Year Plan (1965–70)*, Government of Pakistan, Karachi, August 1964, p. 69.

are also projecting increases in their share of the world market, with some justification given the cost disparity between East African and Indian teas.[1] These various assumptions can be mutually consistent only if the volume of world trade in tea rises at a substantially higher rate than that projected in Chapter 5, or if tea prices fall off sufficiently to induce a very considerable expansion in world demand. In the latter event, however, because the price elasticity of demand for tea is less than unity, export receipts from tea would decline for all the tea-exporting countries.

This sort of mutual inconsistency in export planning can arise haphazardly, either as a result of not relating the export forecast to probable trends in world trade, or as a result of a country's decision to expand its share of trade in particular items. The first case, that of haphazard planning, can be overcome if the appropriate international agencies were accepted by governments as responsible for the estimates of future trends in world trade in individual commodities. Such estimates could also be prepared on the basis of alternative assumptions regarding relevant government policies, assumptions which could be subject to prior agreement by governments themselves. The second case, that of inconsistent planning, would lead to a waste of resources (given that the estimate of the trend in world trade turns out to be reasonably correct) if all the output cannot be sold at the anticipated price, or to a price fall and consequent loss in earnings if the total output is cleared on the world market. A detailed comparison of export targets, comparing one country with another, could also be made the responsibility of an appropriate international agency, and this might well require adjustments in particular export plans where alternative investment and output targets would seem to be more profitable.

These various qualifications attaching to the published export plans of the different overseas Sterling countries generally imply that they are not strictly comparable with the projections made here. It is, nonetheless, of interest to make the comparisons, if only to attempt to explain any major differences between the two. The relevant figures, comparing published plans with the present set of export projections, are set out in Table 6.11 for all the Sterling countries (fifteen in all) for which this is possible. The table also shows the value of exports which would be attained by 1975 if the plan rates of growth were achieved, on average, for the whole period from 1960–1; these hypothetical exports are then compared, in the final column of the table, with the mean of the A and B projections shown in Tables 6.6 and 6.7. Ireland is included for completeness although, as already mentioned, the official export target for

---

[1] Although for a commodity like tea, with numerous qualities and varieties, cost alone is not decisive.

Table 6.11. *Comparison of planned growth rates of exports with actual and projected growth rates*

	Actual growth rate, 1953–5 to 1960–1	Projected growth 1960–1 to 1975		Planned growth rate	Planned 'hypothetical' exports in 1975[a]	
		A	B		Value	As proportion of projected value[b]
	(% per annum, compound)				(£ million)	(%)
MORE DEVELOPED COUNTRIES						
Iceland	5·1	4·9	5·6	4·5	53	90
Ireland	5·9	2·8	3·5	6·9[e]	425	167
LESS DEVELOPED COUNTRIES						
Burma	2·8	1·0	1·6	7·5	225	236
Ceylon	1·0	1·9	2·2	2·7	191	110
Malaya	4·7	3·7	4·2	4·1[d]	578	101
India	0·6	3·1	3·6	3·5[e]	795	102
Pakistan	−1·1[h]	3·5	4·4	3·0[f]	250[g]	94
Ghana	7·2	5·4	6·0	5·9	239	102
Kenya	10·0	4·6	5·0	4·8	72	100
Nigeria	5·1	8·0	8·6	5·5[i]	360[i]	69
Tanzania	8·0	4·5	5·1	6·7	123	130
Uganda	6·5	5·8	5·8	4·4	180	86
Zambia	7·3	4·9	5·6	4·3	230	87
Jamaica	9·1	5·4	6·5	4·0	103	76
Trinidad and Tobago	11·3	2·4	3·1	2·2	151	93

SOURCES: Tables 6.6, 6.7 and 6.8; national Economic Development Plans.

[a] Value of exports which would be attained in 1975 if the planned growth rate were achieved, on average, over the whole period 1960–1 to 1975.

[b] Taking the mean of the A and B projections in Tables 6.6 and 6.7.

[c] 'Required' export growth rate.

[d] Approximate rate, based on target export values adjusted for assumed price decline in exports of natural rubber.

[e] Target for third Five-Year Plan (1960/1–65/6). For the fourth Plan (1966/7–1970/1) the target has been increased to 7·9 per cent growth per annum (see *Notes on Perspective of Development, India: 1960–61 to 1975–76*, New Delhi, 1964, pp. 168–9). For the period 1961/2 to 1975/6, the average growth rate of exports envisaged is 6·5 per cent per annum.

[f] Target for second Five-Year Plan (1960/1–64/5). For the third Plan (1965/6–69/70), the target has been increased to 9·4 per cent per annum.

[g] Based on average exports in 1960 and 1962.

[h] See footnote c to Table 6.8.

[i] The Nigerian export target for 1968 was in terms of 'current prices', though the price assumptions made were not stated.

that country is a residual 'requirement' and is thus different in kind, and therefore not comparable with, the export projection.

For the majority of the other Sterling countries the projected growth rate of exports fell short of the export plan rates, while, with the exception of Kenya, they exceeded the plan rates in the remaining countries. The substantial shortfalls compared with the plan rates were for Burma, India and Pakistan (if the Plans for the period subsequent to 1965 are taken), and Tanzania. The comparison for Burma is really rather artificial, since the second Four-Year Plan became inoperative when the government which produced it (in 1961) was overthrown.[1]

For India, the projected growth rate for exports on the higher income-growth assumption was virtually the same ($3\frac{1}{2}$ per cent per annum) as that in the third Five-Year Plan (1960/1 to 1965/6), but the Perspective Plan, published in 1964, envisages a sharp increase in the rate of growth in exports, to 6·5 per cent per annum, on the average for the period 1961/2 to 1975/6.[2] Over half the expansion in the value of exports over this period is envisaged as coming from 'new' manufactures, such as electrical machinery, engineering goods, metals, chemicals and rubber manufactures; together, exports of these manufactures are expected to rise by as much as 16 per cent per annum, which, on past performance and in view of the inevitable impact of increased defence expenditure on the civilian sector of India's manufacturing industries, appears much too optimistic. The prospects for exports of traditional agricultural produce (the case of tea has already been mentioned) also appear to be somewhat on the optimistic side.

For Pakistan, too, the latest Five-Year Plan (for 1965/6 to 1969/70) puts the export growth rate at 9·4 per cent per annum—a very substantial increase compared with that in the previous Plan (3·0 per cent per annum), or with the present projections (3·1 to 3·9 per cent per annum). The largest export increases envisaged in the latest Plan are for the 'newer' types of manufactures, including cotton manufactures, processed fish and paper, which are expected to rise in volume by over 20 per cent per annum. In addition, a substantial expansion (by 13 per cent per annum) is planned for exports of jute goods; the Plan assumes that Pakistan can double her share of world jute goods exports over the quinquennium, from 10 per cent to 20 per cent, and that the import requirements of the less developed areas and of the centrally planned economies will increase at a faster rate in future than in the past.

Over the past five years for which volume estimates can be made (1959–64), Pakistan's exports rose at an average rate of about $2\frac{1}{2}$ per

---

[1] The new Revolutionary Government of Burma, which assumed power in March 1962, has so far not published a Development Plan.

[2] *Notes on Perspective of Development, India: 1960–61 to 1975–76.*

cent per annum, so that even the modest target of 3 per cent per annum set in the second Five-Year Plan was apparently not quite attained.[1] An average growth rate of exports exceeding 9 per cent per annum would thus appear unduly optimistic. This conclusion is reinforced by the possibility that the conflict with India could well divert resources into defence industries, and also that the rate of industrialization envisaged in the Plan—on which Pakistan's exports of new manufactures largely depend—is itself related to the successful expansion in foreign exchange earnings from traditional items. Excessive optimism on the latter is likely to make more difficult the purchase abroad of the volume of capital equipment required for the industrialization programme set out in the latest Pakistan Plan, unless the residue can be met from increased foreign aid.

The Tanzanian Plan envisages sharp rates of growth in production of a number of major crops, particularly groundnuts, tea and cotton (10 to 12 per cent per annum) and coffee (6 to 7 per cent per annum), it being assumed, as already discussed, that all the exportable surplus will be sold abroad. In view of Tanzania's relatively low production costs in tea and cotton, this assumption may not be imprudent for these commodities, but groundnuts may be subject to heavy competition from soya, animal fats and marine oils. For sisal, Tanzania's largest single export, the Plan's production target for 1970 implies an annual rate of expansion of rather more than 3 per cent, compared with an average of 2·9 per cent per annum over the 1950s. This appears realistic in itself, even though Tanzania's share of world sisal exports continues to decline. The real difficulty in meeting the Plan target is more likely to come if synthetics successfully invade the baler-twine market, hitherto the mainstay of sisal demand.[2]

Of the countries for which the projected growth rate of exports exceeds the Plan target rate, the excess is more than 1 per cent per annum for Nigeria, Zambia and Jamaica. The Nigerian Plan, published in 1961, was drawn up before the large oilfield discoveries of 1964 and 1965. There is now little doubt that Nigeria will become one of the world's major producers and exporters of petroleum and natural gas by the end of the present decade—a far more rapid expansion than was envisaged in the official Plan. Apart from petroleum, however, little

---

[1] Considerably higher export growth rates for the early 1960s are sometimes quoted (7¼ per cent per annum for 1960/1 to 1964, for example), but these essentially reflect the abnormally low exports of 1961.

[2] This is now very probable. An artificial fibre based on polypropylene went into commercial production in the early part of 1966 and while it is too early to assess its impact, there can be little doubt that it will make inroads on the baler-twine market, particularly as polypropylene will almost certainly become cheaper with the growth of larger and more efficient chemical plant.

indication is given in the Plan about the expected expansion in commodity exports; indeed, it seems probable that, had the petroleum discoveries not taken place, the official export target would have proved too optimistic.

The UN/ECA/FAO study for Zambia argued that world copper consumption was likely to rise by 4 per cent per annum between 1959 and 1970, and assumed that Zambia's share of world copper exports would remain unchanged over this period.[1] The projection in Chapter 5 for copper consumption shows an annual growth rate of some 4 per cent, while between 1960–1 and 1964 the volume of copper shipped from Zambia rose, on average, by over 6 per cent per annum. For Jamaica, the official plan assumes a rather low growth rate for bauxite production, at 3·1 per cent per annum from 1962 to 1968 (from 1960–1 to 1964 bauxite exports rose by $8\frac{1}{2}$ per cent per annum), and no increase in alumina capacity after 1963.[2] If aluminium consumption rises at the rate projected in Chapter 5 (around 7 per cent per annum), then a somewhat more rapid expansion in Jamaican bauxite and alumina exports than is envisaged in the Plan appears probable.[3]

Though the published export targets of some Sterling countries are either manifestly over-optimistic, or excessively cautious, the projections presented in this chapter are not intended to be more accurate forecasts of the probable future trends in their export trade. They are, on the contrary, estimates of the likely growth rates in exports consistent with the underlying assumptions made earlier; and, like all such estimates, they must be taken as expressing only orders of magnitude, each projected rate having a fairly wide margin of error.

4. VOLUME AND VALUE PROJECTIONS

All the country projections for 1975 given earlier were in terms of constant (1960–1) prices. This procedure was necessary since the commodity trade projections—on which the country export projections were based—were derived essentially from projections of the volume of demand for imports in the main industrial areas. It has already been pointed out[4] that consistent projections of commodity prices could be made only if a world supply function (with respect to price, technical progress and other relevant factors) was known, or could reliably be computed, for each commodity. Since our knowledge is still generally

[1] Op. cit. p. 39.

[2] Five-Year Independence Plan 1963–68, Kingston, 1963, p. 64.

[3] In fact, a new alumina plant is to be set up and is expected to start production in 1969, i.e. after the completion of the current planning period. See also p. 175, n. 1.

[4] See pp. 126–8.

vague in this field, it is not possible to project future changes in prices for the majority of commodities with any pretence either of reasonable accuracy or of consistency with the demand projections. The relatively few exceptions are commodities the supply of which is believed to be essentially static, or capable of limited expansion only; commodities the price of which is essentially determined by the price of synthetic or other substitutes; or commodities the price of which was abnormally high (or low) in the base period, 1960–1. In Chapter 5, it was suggested that some increase in the relative prices of certain non-ferrous metals (tin and copper) would be a reasonable assumption to make, while equally, a relative price decline could be assumed for natural rubber, compared with the average price level of 1960–1.

For all other commodities, it was suggested that the period of projection—rather more than a decade—was sufficiently long for the rate of growth in world output to adjust to (or even to over-compensate for) the actual growth in world demand, so that for these commodities no appreciable change in price, in either direction, could be assumed. For some commodities, such as coffee, this conclusion hinged on the further assumption that an effective international agreement between producing and consuming countries, controlling the world price within a fairly narrow range, would continue to remain in force throughout the period up to 1975. As was pointed out earlier,[1] this assumption of constant prices for the great majority of commodities does not imply a belief that their prices are likely, in fact, to remain unchanged; on the contrary, it is virtually certain that they will move in very diverse ways over the next decade or so. Though it is not possible to make any reasonable assumptions about the future course of prices, except for a very few commodities, the likelihood of some significant improvement, or worsening, in a country's export prices needs to be taken into account in assessing its future growth prospects.

Changes in export prices of major commodities in relation to overall export unit values are shown in Tables 6.12 and 6.13 for two recent periods for the more developed and less developed Sterling countries respectively. Any such division into essentially arbitrary periods must be interpreted with some care, since commodity prices are notoriously subject to appreciable random fluctuations, so that comparisons of periods standardized for all commodities could give misleading impressions of the underlying trends. Nonetheless, several generalizations about price changes appear to emerge from the data in Tables 6.12 and 6.13 which are likely to be useful in applying the country export projections to the model of economic growth elaborated earlier.

First, changes in unit values of total exports are the normal pheno-

---

[1] See p. 128.

Table 6.12. *Changes in export prices of major commodities and of total exports from the more developed Sterling countries, 1953–5 to 1964 (percentages)*

	Proportion of total exports in 1960–1	1953–5 to 1960–1		1960–1 to 1964	
		Major commodities	Total exports	Major commodities	Total exports
Australia					
Raw wool	38	−29		+22	
Wheat	13	−17	} −21	+13	} +16
Butter	2	−26		..	
Ireland	..	..	+2	..	+9
Iceland					
Fish	70	+8	+4	+20	+17
New Zealand					
Raw wool	35	−12		+25	
Butter	16	−24	} −10	+28	} +18
Lamb	29	−5		+15	
South Africa					
Raw wool	12	−29	−10	+26	+3

SOURCE: *International Financial Statistics*, I.M.F., Washington.

menon over a period of years. For the period 1953–5 to 1960–1, three out of five more developed Sterling countries experienced changes of 10 per cent or more in export unit values (Table 6.12), while of the fourteen less developed countries (Table 6.13), five experienced changes of 20 per cent or more, three countries fell in the 10 to 20 per cent range, the remaining six having changes from 5 to 9 per cent. Over the shorter period from 1960–1 to 1964, there were also quite substantial shifts in export unit values. This generally confirms the view expressed above that some allowance must be made in any realistic projection for the possibility of a significant change—in either direction—of overall export unit values.

Second, the overall indices of unit values can generally be expected to show an appreciably smaller movement over a period of years than the movements in individual commodity prices. When the prices of major export commodities move in opposite directions, the index for total exports may remain virtually unchanged. The divergent movements in export prices of tea and tobacco from Malawi from 1960–1 to 1964 is an example of this, while partially offsetting price movements for one or other of the two periods can be seen for Malaya (rubber and tin), Kenya (coffee and tea), Tanzania (sisal, cotton and coffee), Uganda (coffee and cotton), and Jamaica (bauxite and sugar). There

13

Table 6.13. *Changes in export prices of major commodities and of total exports from the less developed Sterling countries, 1953–5 to 1964 (percentages)*

	Proportion of total exports in 1960–1	1953–5 to 1960–1 Major	1953–5 to 1960–1 Total	1960–1 to 1964 Major	1960–1 to 1964 Total
Burma					
Rice	67	−35	−28	+21	..
Ceylon					
Tea	64	−12	} −7	−8	} −7
Natural rubber	19	−3		−31	
Malaya					
Natural rubber	58	+16	} +15	−29	} −14
Tin	19	+16		+47	
India					
Jute goods	21	+24	}	..	}
Tea	19	+2	+9	+3	−4
Cotton goods	8	+3	}	0	}
Pakistan					
Raw jute	45	+48	}	−22	}
Jute goods	15	..	+27	..	−18
Raw cotton	8	−8	}	−9	}
Ghana					
Raw cocoa	65	−39	−26	−7	−11
Kenya					
Coffee	29	−28	}	+11	}
Tea	13	+2	−14	−10	..
Sisal	12	+20	}	+38	}
Malawi[a]					
Tea	45	−12	} −7	−19	} 0
Tobacco	37	+9		+17	
Nigeria					
Groundnuts	16	−3	}	−6	}
Palm kernels	14	10		..	
Groundnut oil	3	−2	−6	−10	−5
Palm oil	8	13		3	
Raw cocoa	21	−34		−3	
Natural rubber	8	+38	}	−24	}
Rhodesia[b]					
Tobacco	51	−4	−5	−16	−8
Tanzania					
Sisal	31	+7	}	+44	}
Raw cotton	15	−22	−12	−3	..
Coffee	14	−33	}	+32	}
Uganda					
Coffee	45	−57	} −32	+106	} ..
Raw cotton	33	−11		−5	
Zambia[a]					
Copper	92	−25	−24	+4	+8
Jamaica[b]					
Bauxite	49	+44	} +8	0	} ..
Sugar	23	−6		+45	

SOURCES: *Yearbook of International Trade Statistics*, United Nations, New York; *International Financial Statistics*, I.M.F., Washington; *Commonwealth and Sterling Area Statistical Abstracts*, Board of Trade, London; *Monthly Digest of Statistics*, C.S.O., Salisbury; *Monthly Digest of Statistics*, C.S.O., Lusaka; *Quarterly Digest of Statistics*, Ministry of Finance, Zomba.

[a] 1954–5 to 1960–1.   [b] 1955 to 1960–1.

are, however, a few apparent exceptions to the general rule which arise because prices for the various minor—though collectively important—commodities may be rising (or falling) faster than those of the major commodities shown.

A third feature of the commodity price situation, as shown in Tables 6.12 and 6.13, is that prices of apparently similar commodities exported by different countries have sometimes moved in rather diverse ways. Raw wool exported from Australia, for instance, fell more than twice as fast in price, proportionately, as did New Zealand wool between 1953–5 and 1960–1. Similarly, there were extremely large divergencies between 1960–1 and 1964 in the rise in export prices of coffee from Kenya, Tanzania and Uganda; while prices of tobacco exported by Malawi and Rhodesia moved in opposite directions in both the periods shown. At the same time, there were also examples of export prices of different countries moving closely in step, cocoa exports from Ghana and Nigeria being easily the best example of this. The various divergencies in price movement reflect different supply and demand changes for the different qualities and grades of the same commodity. However difficult it may be to project into the future the price of a given commodity, the task of projecting the price movements of the different qualities and grades—which apply more particularly to the prospects for individual countries—would be infinitely more difficult, and any attempt to do this is likely to involve impossibly large margins of error.

Price assumptions in Economic Development Plans

These various difficulties in attempting to estimate the future trend of commodity prices have also had to be faced by the authors of the various Economic Plans already published by the overseas Sterling countries. In fact, only about one-half of the thirteen countries which have published export targets in their Development Plans make assumptions about changes in their export prices; the rest simply assume that export prices during the plan period will remain unchanged. There are six countries—Iceland, Burma, Ceylon, India, Jamaica and Trinidad—which assume no change in export prices for planning purposes; in some cases (e.g. Iceland) this assumption is made explicitly in the Plan, but in others (e.g. Burma, Ceylon and India) the assumption is implicit and there is no discussion of how changes in export prices would affect the Plan targets.

There are, however, an equal number of Sterling countries—Malaya, Pakistan, Ghana, Kenya, Tanzania and Zambia—which make specific assumptions about the future price levels of their key export products. The Malayan Plan, for example, assumes that by 1970 the average price of natural rubber exports will be only one-half of the 1960 level.[1] In Chapter 5, the assumption made is that natural rubber prices will have fallen by 1975 to 60 to 65 per cent of the 1960–1 average, equivalent to about 55 per cent of the 1960 level. Pakistan has assumed some decline in export prices of raw cotton, cotton goods and jute goods between 1961/2 to 1963/4 and 1969/70; whilst no details of the assumed price declines are given it would appear that they are in the region of 3 to 5 per cent for cotton goods.[2] Ghana, on the other hand, has assumed that the price of raw cocoa in 1969/70 will be no lower than £200 per ton (which was also the 1960–1 average),[3] and this is also the assumption used in the present set of projections.

Kenya and Tanzania make identical assumptions about the price of sisal, namely that it will be £100 per ton by 1970,[4] while Tanzania also assumes a fall to £90 per ton thereafter.[5] The average export price in 1960–1 was £71 for Tanzania and £75 for Kenya, so that the Tanzanian assumption implies a price rise of 25 to 30 per cent between 1960–1 and the early 1970s. This appears to be somewhat optimistic in view of the probable inroads of synthetic materials into traditional end-uses of sisal, and the present projections assume that by 1975 sisal prices will not be significantly different from the 1960–1 average.

For Zambia, the UN/ECA/FAO Mission's report projected copper exports up to 1970 on the basis of £238 per long ton (the average price for 1960–1), but also discussed the implications of alternative prices at higher levels.[6] That report argued that although a rise in copper prices to £280 per long ton would have little effect on export volume, an increase above that price—particularly if £300 were exceeded—would result in a serious fall in export earnings.[7] The efforts made by the international copper companies to stabilize the price since 1964 have been only partially successful. By 1965, the free price on the London Metal Exchange had risen to about £450, and the delivery price quoted by the copper companies had increased to about £285, reaching about £300 by the end of that year; and in 1966, with political crises in Central Africa, the Congo and Chile, the price fluctuated violently between £350 and just under £800. On the basis of the various assumptions made in the detailed discussion of trends in the copper market,[8]

---

[1] The price is assumed to fall from an equivalent of 30d. per lb in 1960 to 17·4d. in 1965 and 15·4d. in 1970 (*Interim Review of Development in Malaya, under the Second Five-Year Plan*, Kuala Lumpur, December 1963, p. 54).

[2] *Outline of the Third Five-Year Plan (1965–70)*, pp. 67–71. The Plan gives the export prices assumed for cotton twist and yarn and for cotton piece goods in 1969/70.

[3] *Seven-year Development Plan, 1963/4–1969/70*, Accra, 1964, p. 233.

[4] *Development Plan, 1964–1970*, Nairobi 1964, p. 50.

[5] *Tanganyika: Five-Year Plan for Economic and Social Development, 1964–1969*, Dar-es-Salaam, 1964, vol. 2, p. 23.

[6] *Op. cit.* p. 31.

[7] *Ibid.* p. 45.

[8] See Appendix B6.

a copper price as low as £238 would be unrealistic for a projection of Zambian exports in 1975; as suggested in Chapter 5, a more consistent assumption would be a price in the region of £300, or about 25 per cent higher than the 1960–1 average, though in view of the current situation in Central Africa this is obviously very uncertain.

Apart from these six countries for which specific price assumptions were mentioned in their Development Plans, one other country— Nigeria—has also adjusted its export targets to allow for probable future changes in prices. According to the Nigerian Plan, projected export prices have been arrived at after careful examination of long-run world market trends,[1] but no details of the assumed price changes are given (though it is stated that price declines were assumed over the plan period). It is thus not possible to determine the realism or otherwise of the Nigerian price assumptions.

The export projections at current prices

The price assumptions made in Chapter 5 thus differ somewhat from the corresponding assumptions in the Development Plans of a number of the main overseas Sterling countries. In the country plans, the assumptions made about the future level of prices appear somewhat optimistic for sisal, whereas for copper and natural rubber the present projections take a more optimistic view. It was argued in Chapter 5 that a rise in tin prices could be assumed somewhat greater than that in copper prices; however, neither of the main Sterling exporters of tin —Malaya and Nigeria—appears to have assumed any change in tin prices over the period covered by its plan. These various differences between the plans and the present projections reflect, to some extent, differences in the periods of time covered; but, in the main, they result from the adoption of different assumptions about the rate of growth in world demand, the rate of substitution by synthetic materials for the natural product and, for cocoa, the effectiveness of an international agreement to control the market.

Only three countries—Ceylon, Malaya and Zambia—are affected by the assumptions (in Chapter 5) that prices of natural rubber, tin and copper will be significantly different in 1975 from what they were in 1960–1. Allowing for the different relative importance of these commodities in the export trade of the three countries, and assuming no change in the prices of other commodities, the price assumptions imply that by 1975 the overall export unit value will be some 15 per cent lower than in 1960–1 for Malaya, about 7 per cent lower for Ceylon, and about 20 to 25 per cent higher for Zambia. No offsetting changes are required in the volume projections for these countries, since the latter had

---

[1] Federation of Nigeria, *National Development Plan, 1962–68*, Lagos, 1961, p. 28.

already taken account of the assumed price changes. The projected growth rates in the volume and value of exports for these three countries are thus as follows:

	Volume		Value at current prices	
	A	B	A	B
	(% per annum, compound)			
Ceylon	1·9	2·2	1·4	1·6
Malaya	3·7	4·2	2·6	3·0
Zambia	4·9	5·6	6·5	7·1

For all the other overseas Sterling countries, the growth rates projected for the volume of exports can be assumed to relate to export values at current prices also.

CHAPTER 7

EXPORTS, CAPITAL FLOWS AND THE CAPACITY TO IMPORT

I. INTRODUCTION

There are two possible ways in which the export projections for the less developed Sterling countries arrived at in the preceding chapter can be used in the context of the *ex post* model of economic growth elaborated earlier. The first is to explore the implications for the rate of growth in GDP of the alternative export projections. Since the underlying hypothesis of the model is that the level of investment has a long-term relationship with the capacity to import, the other elements of the latter must also be projected, or assumed, before the exercise can be undertaken. The procedure adopted here is, briefly, to make alternative assumptions about the net inflow of long-term capital from abroad in 1975 into each country considered, and to project the remaining elements (exports of services and net factor payments abroad) on the basis of these assumptions and of the export projections.

The second way in which the export projections can be used in the model is to treat the net capital inflow as a residual which is determined once an assumption is made about the future growth rate of GDP. Because of the links between GDP, investment and the capacity to import, any given assumption about the growth rate of GDP implies a corresponding level of the capacity to import; given, also, the projection of merchandise exports, and a projection or assumption about exports of services, the net capital inflow (net, also, of factor payments abroad) can then be derived. This approach is particularly relevant for the less developed countries, for which the capital inflow consists essentially of aid in the form of loans or grants, which are the subject of government policies in the developed countries.

The principal emphasis here is placed on the first approach on the ground that the total amount of capital available, either as aid or as private investment, is not in fact in such elastic supply that it can be considered as available to fill a residual gap. At the same time, it is important from the viewpoint of policies affecting both aid and trade to have some fairly detailed assessment of the net capital inflow requirements of the less developed Sterling countries. Some assessment on this basis is also attempted (in Chapter 8) so as to contrast the aid and trade requirements of these countries with the aid and exports they are likely to attain in 1975 on the basis of the present policies of the developed countries.

It seems clear from the analysis of past trends and relationships that such assessments of the future trade and aid position of individual countries are subject to a number of serious limitations. For one thing, even the simple *ex post* model used in Chapter 3 could be applied only to a limited number of Sterling countries; for many countries, the historical data were either largely non-existent in the detail required or were inadequate (for example, they were available only in terms of current prices) or were available for too short a period to allow the structural parameters of the model to be estimated. To some extent, however, these gaps can be remedied by drawing on the relevant data in the Economic Development Plans of the various countries. To the extent that these plans are based on detailed consideration of the investment requirements of individual projects, and of the import content of investment in the different sectors, they should form a reasonable basis for the adoption of the relevant structural parameters of the model.

Even so, there are a number of countries, such as Hong Kong, excluded from the analysis in Chapter 3, for which no Development Plans are available; for such countries, the choice is either to use a set of illustrative parameters, the magnitudes of which are based on those for countries with reasonably comparable economies, or to omit them altogether from the projections of economic growth. The latter approach is adopted here; Hong Kong, for example, is excluded because even illustrative projections for that country seem impracticable in view of the almost total lack of the relevant national accounts statistics.

The present chapter is confined to discussing the projections of the different constituents of the capacity to import (other than merchandise exports) of the various Sterling countries, both more developed and less developed. The implications of these projections for the rate of economic growth of the different less developed countries in the period up to 1975 are examined in Chapter 8.

2. TRENDS IN NET CAPITAL INFLOWS

The first approach to the projection problem mentioned above is to base projections of future growth in GDP on the export projections made earlier, supplemented by specific assumptions about net capital inflows into each Sterling country. It is convenient here to consider the more developed and less developed groups of countries separately, since it is broadly true that the capital inflow into the former consists mainly of private capital, while that into the latter is mainly official aid in one form or another (though several less developed countries, such as Malaya and Hong Kong, do attract substantial amounts of private investment from overseas).[1]

The more developed countries

The trends over the past decade of net long-term capital movements into the more developed overseas Sterling countries show a remarkable diversity. For Australia, there has been a strong upward trend; over the period from 1953 to 1962, the average annual rate of increase in the net total of long-term capital inflow (deflated by import prices so as to indicate a 'volume' change) was almost 9 per cent. For New Zealand, however, there has been no apparent upward trend since 1954–5. For South Africa, by contrast, the official record showed a net capital outflow from 1959 to 1964, though there was a net inflow again in 1965. These figures exclude undistributed profits of foreign firms, branches and subsidiaries retained in South Africa. In view of these quite different trends in the recent past, it would be unrealistic to adopt a uniform assumption for all three countries regarding the future trend of capital imports.

The greater part of foreign investment in Australia in recent years has come from Britain and the United States; both these countries instituted new policies during 1965 to reduce the outflow of capital, in order to alleviate their overall balance of payments deficits. If such policies are continued for any length of time, they are likely to have a substantial impact on the supply of new capital from these two countries for investment in Australia. By the early 1970s, the underlying assumptions of the present projection exercise would, however, imply that the balance of payments was no longer a serious constraint for economic growth in Britain, while in the United States the assumptions would certainly be consistent with the free flow of international capital by that date. Moreover, any reduction in the rate of growth of the capital inflow from Britain and the United States is likely to be offset, in large measure, by an expansion of private investment by countries of continental Western Europe and Japan.[2] On these assumptions implying a continuation of the past rate of growth, the level of net capital inflow into Australia in 1975 would be about double the 1960–1 volume. This seems to be a reasonable estimate consistent with the general assumptions of the projections. However, there is inevitably some degree of uncertainty about the effect of stricter British and United States policies

---

[1] See Table 1.2 for details for 1964–5.

[2] Countries other than Britain and the United States supplied 8½ per cent of the total capital inflow into Australia in the period 1948–55, the proportion rising to 12½ per cent in 1956–64.

regarding overseas investment, so that it is useful also to make an alternative—in this case, a lower—assumption; for this alternative, the 1975 net capital inflow is taken at only one-half greater than the 1960–1 level.

For New Zealand, much will depend on the government's own economic policies. The continuance of past policies to develop manufacturing industries in spite of the narrowness of the domestic market will probably necessitate the raising of further capital issues on the London market. On the other hand, any agreement with Australia on a mutual free-trade area would almost certainly result in Australian manufactures competing successfully in the New Zealand market against a wide range of domestic industries. On balance it seems probable that the further expansion of New Zealand manufacturing and power industries will be secured, even if this means the continuance of tariff protection, and that the level of capital borrowings will rise correspondingly. There were heavy repayments of official long-term capital in 1960 and 1961, so that the 1962–3 position (a net capital inflow, including private capital, of £45 million a year) would appear a more reasonable base for the projections. Two alternative assumptions are made here: first, that the net capital inflow into New Zealand rises by 1975 to one-half greater than in 1962–3, and second, that the 1975 figure remains unchanged compared with that for 1962–3.

Any projection of South Africa's foreign capital position inevitably implies some assumption about the political character of the régime over the next decade, and the reactions of the governments and private industries of other countries to it. The uncertainty surrounding any particular assumption here gives a projection for South Africa a large measure of unreality. It is nonetheless of interest to assess the probable effect on the growth of South Africa's capacity to import of varying the assumptions concerning the overseas capital position. Here quite arbitrary assumptions are made that the net long-term capital inflow is zero in 1975 or, alternatively, that there is a net outflow of the same magnitude as in 1962–3.[1]

The net capital inflow into the Republic of Ireland has shown a marked upward trend since 1955. In 1960, however, the net inflow (£1 million) was abnormally low; in 1962–3, the net long-term capital inflow averaged some £24 million, and a moderate reduction to £16 million (at 1960 prices) is envisaged for 1970 in the current Irish development programme.[2] That programme also envisages, in general terms, a reduction of dependence on external deficits to finance further

---

[1] The net outflow in 1960 (the year of the Sharpeville massacre) was abnormally large. All the figures in the text exclude undistributed profits in South Africa of foreign firms or their branches and subsidiaries (which averaged some £30 million a year in 1962–3).

[2] *Second Programme for Economic Expansion, Part II*, Stationery Office, Dublin, July 1964. This gives external capital borrowing in 1963 as £22 million.

expansion after 1970.[1] The alternative assumptions made here put the net capital inflow in 1975 at either £10 million or £15 million, valued at 1960–1 prices. Capital borrowings by Iceland are normally relatively small; for 1975, they are assumed to be either zero or £5 million, at 1960–1 prices.

The less developed countries

The level of the net capital inflow into the less developed countries in 1975 depends very largely on the aid policies of the donor countries. It is convenient here to consider the effects of these policies at three distinct levels. First, there is the question as to whether the total amount of aid is likely to be increased above the levels achieved in the early 1960s and, if so, by how much. The second consideration is whether the proportion of the total received by the less developed countries of the Overseas Sterling Area is likely to rise, fall or remain substantially unchanged. Finally, within this latter total, can we reasonably expect the country distribution of aid to be very different in 1975 from that of the recent past?

As regards the total flow of aid from donor countries, the outstanding feature of recent years has been that, after a rapid expansion from the mid 1950s to 1961, there has been virtually no further increase in 1962, 1963 or 1964 (see Table 7.1). Whereas the total outflow of official capital[2] from the industrial O.E.C.D. countries rose by some 12 per cent per year from 1958–60 to 1961–2, the corresponding rise from the latter period to 1963–4 was only 1½ per cent per year, as a result of a decline in aid made available through multilateral agencies, a falling off in the rate of growth in bilateral loans, and no further increase in official grants. In this more recent period, aid from the centrally planned countries continued to increase—though also at a reduced rate—and accounted for 6½ per cent of all official aid to less developed countries, as against 3½ per cent in 1958–60.[3]

The future trend of official aid will depend heavily on the willingness and ability of the United States to expand its current levels of foreign aid, in one form or another. To the extent that the United States balance of payments remains in overall deficit, it seems unlikely that

---

[1] *Ibid.* p. 291.

[2] The O.E.C.D. totals for the net outflow of official capital include loans on commercial terms (5 per cent, or higher, rate of interest and twenty years' maturity or less) which would not normally be considered as aid. In 1963, about one-third of total loan commitments by O.E.C.D. countries were on conditions approaching market terms, though the proportion would be considerably smaller (in the region of one-tenth) in relation to the total outflow of official capital. In the text, the term 'aid' is used, for convenience, as indicating the total net outflow of all official capital, whether on commercial or on concessional terms.

[3] The figures in Table 7.1 include aid to less developed O.E.C.D. countries (Greece, Spain and Turkey).

Table 7.1. *Net flow of long-term capital to less developed countries, 1956–64*

	1956–7	1958–60	1961–2	1963–4	Annual rate of growth 1956–7 to 1958–60	1958–60 to 1961–2	1961–2 to 1963–4
	($ *billion*)				(%, *compound*)		
FROM INDUSTRIAL O.E.C.D. COUNTRIES							
Official capital:							
Grants	2·81	3·31	3·97	3·97	6·8	7·5	0
Bilateral loans	0·44	0·78	1·37	1·70	25·7	25·3	11·4
Multilateral contributions	0·32	0·46	0·74	0·60	15·6	21·0	−10·0
Total official	3·57	4·56	6·07	6·27	10·3	12·1	1·6
Private capital	2·90	2·58	2·25	1·93	−4·6	−5·3	−7·4
Total	6·47	7·13	8·32	8·20	4·0	6·4	−0·7
FROM OTHER INDUSTRIAL COUNTRIES	..	0·05	0·07	0·09	..	14·4	13·4
FROM CENTRALLY PLANNED COUNTRIES	..	0·17	0·35	0·45	..	33·5	13·4
Total	..	7·35	8·74	8·74	..	7·2	0

SOURCES: *The Flow of Financial Resources to Less Developed Countries, 1956–63*, O.E.C.D., Paris, 1964; financial press.

any appreciable increase in aid programmes will be authorized;[1] on the other hand, political pressures may well induce the United States to increase substantially its present level of aid to certain areas, such as South-East Asia. No increase in Britain's aid programme can be envisaged while balance of payments difficulties persist,[2] though the underlying assumptions of the present projections imply that by 1975 these difficulties will have disappeared. The other main donor countries are France, West Germany and Japan; the net flows of official aid from all three countries were reduced somewhat between 1961 and 1963, and any substantial expansion seems rather unlikely in the short run.

The flattening out of the aid curve since 1961 is in marked contrast with the continuing growth in the national incomes of the developed countries. In 1960, the General Assembly of the United Nations adopted a resolution urging that 'the flow of international assistance and capital should be increased substantially so as to reach as soon as

[1] The United States Department of Commerce in December 1966 called for a 'more rigorous restraint' on capital outflows in 1967; but presumably the need for general restraint will continue all the while the United States is trying to achieve balance of payments equilibrium in face of the growing exchange burden of the Vietnam war.

[2] In December 1966, the United Kingdom Government announced a cut of £20 million in the aid target for 1967/8.

possible approximately 1 per cent of the combined national incomes of the economically advanced countries'.[1] This resolution, which is widely regarded as an 'aid target', is, in fact, extremely vague. The precise denominator to be used in the calculation of the percentage is left unclear, while the rather general reference to 'financial resources', rather than to the more specific 'aid', allows the inclusion of private capital flows in the numerator. Private capital cannot, of course, be regarded as aid, since the element of real resource sacrifice implied by that term is clearly absent from such flows. Nevertheless, when defending their aid records to international audiences, most donor governments have found it convenient to equate 'financial resources' (including private capital) with 'aid'. However, in the present analysis 'aid' is defined as the net outflow of *official* capital and grants to the less developed countries;[2] and it is this definition which is taken to be the numerator in references to the target of '1 per cent of national income'.[3] In 1962–3, 1 per cent of the combined national incomes of the O.E.C.D. countries (including Japan, but excluding Greece, Spain and Turkey) amounted to $8·3 billion,[4] or some 35 to 40 per cent higher than the total net official capital outflow from these countries in the same period (see also Fig. 7.1). Had the 1 per cent target been achieved by 1961— the year following the United Nations Resolution—the aid total in the period 1961–4 would have been greater by no less than $8½ billion; in other words, the average shortfall over the period was over $2 billion a year.[5]

It could be argued that the failure of the developed countries to increase their allocations for aid since 1961 has been largely due to balance of payments difficulties, and that the underlying assumptions concerning economic growth and the absence of balance of payments difficulties in the present set of projections imply that the previous upward trend in the

---

[1] General Assembly Resolution 1522 (xv). This aid target (1 per cent of the combined national income of the developed countries) was re-affirmed by the United Nations Conference on Trade and Development in 1964 (*Final Act*, Annex A.iv.2).

[2] This definition is still unsatisfactory as a measure of aid since it includes loans at commercial rates of interest; also, the terms on which aid is given—rates of interest, repayment periods, extent of tying, other special conditions, and so on—differ widely among donor countries. Thus the real aid flows—i.e. the real resources sacrificed by the donors—will be much smaller than those implied by the data used here. On the question (and problems) of adjusting for the present value of loans and the market value of tied aid, see John Pincus, *Economic Aid and International Cost Sharing*, Johns Hopkins Press, Baltimore, 1965.

[3] According to O.E.C.D. (*Development Assistance Efforts and Policies, 1966 Review*) the outflow of official capital and grants up to 1965 has only exceeded or reached 1 per cent of national income in two countries, France and Portugal.

[4] At current exchange rates.

[5] This is based on a strict interpretation of the term 'national incomes' in the United Nations Resolution. If a more liberal interpretation is adopted, for example that the General Assembly had in mind the gross national products of the developed countries, the shortfall would be considerably more than $2 billion a year.

total flow of aid is likely to be resumed. Probably the most optimistic assumption that could reasonably be made is that the aid total will increase at the same rate as the total real national incomes of the developed countries

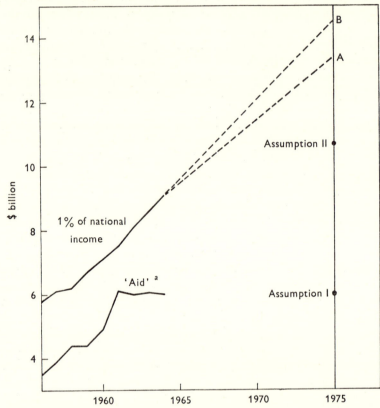

SOURCES: *The Flow of Financial Resources to Less Developed Countries, 1956–1963*, O.E.C.D., Paris, 1964; *Yearbook of National Accounts Statistics, 1964*, United Nations, New York, 1965; *Monthly Bulletin of Statistics*, United Nations, New York.

NOTES: (1) The projections of the aggregate national income of O.E.C.D. countries to 1975 are based on the alternative assumptions A and B made in Chapter 4 (see Table 4.3). (2) The positions designated assumption I and assumption II are the alternative assumptions adopted for the total net capital outflow from O.E.C.D. countries to less developed countries in 1975. For further explanation and assumptions about 'aid' from non-O.E.C.D. countries, see text.

a Actually, total net outflow of official capital, as defined by O.E.C.D. This includes loans at commercial rates which could not normally be regarded as 'aid'.

Fig. 7.1. Net outflow of official long-term capital from O.E.C.D. countries
in relation to their aggregate national incomes, 1956–64.

(as assumed in Chapter 4), that is, the shortfall from the target of ' 1 per cent of national income' will remain more or less constant. On this basis, the total net outflow of official capital would rise from $6·8 billion in 1963–4 to over \$10½ billion in 1975, on assumption A, and to about \$12 billion on assumption B, allowing also for a further increase, to \$0·8 to \$1·0 billion, in aid from centrally planned countries.

At the same time, it would be unwise to ignore the more pessimistic possibility that total aid will, in the event, be little higher in 1975 than in the early 1960s, in spite of the growth in national product in the donor countries in the interim. This could happen either if balance of payments difficulties persist for the main donor countries, or if there is a change in present long-term policies regarding aid programmes. Though this possibility seems distinctly less likely, it is nonetheless of interest to assess the different impact on the economies of the less developed Sterling countries of making this assumption, compared with that arising from the more optimistic one already mentioned. In the present set of projections, then, there are two alternative assumptions regarding total aid to the less developed areas of the world from both O.E.C.D. and other countries: assumption I takes the 1975 total at \$6½ billion, the same as the 1962–3 average, while assumption II takes it at \$12 billion, the upper limit derived by assuming an increase in the same proportion as total real incomes in the developed countries.

The second question raised above was whether the Overseas Sterling Area was likely to receive a very different proportion of the total aid from donor countries in 1975 from that received in the early 1960s. Unfortunately, the aid figures published by O.E.C.D. do not distinguish the recipient countries before 1960. For the years 1960–1, the net flow of official funds from the industrial O.E.C.D. countries to the Overseas Sterling Area averaged 25 per cent of the total, while for 1962–3 the proportion was 26 per cent. No very precise comparison can, however, be made with the mid 1950s, though probably the Sterling share of the total was then appreciably higher; in the meantime, there has been a large expansion in funds flowing to South-East Asia and to Latin America, particularly under various United States aid programmes.

The future course of the Sterling Area's share of total official aid is inevitably uncertain, but there is no particular reason to expect any drastic change, unless major new aid programmes are inaugurated for—to take only the obvious examples—the Mekong River countries or Latin America. In view of the margin of error surrounding the assumptions for total aid to all less developed countries, it would seem reasonably consistent to use the same alternative assumptions for the Sterling Area also. On this basis, the total net inflow of official aid into the less developed Sterling countries in 1975 can be put at either £565 million (as in 1962–3) or £1,000 million (three-quarters greater than in 1962–3).

Finally, what should we expect as regards the country distribution of the assumed aid total? In 1962–3, three-quarters of the total net inflow of about £565 million of official long-term capital into the less developed Sterling countries (but excluding those in the Middle East) went to two countries, India and Pakistan; the various countries of East and West Africa received a good part of the remainder (see Table 7.2). This heavy concentration in a few countries is inevitable, in view of their large size, measured in terms of either total population or total GDP. Indeed, on a *per caput* basis, India received some 25 per cent less, in 1962–3, than the average for all the less developed Sterling countries included in Table 7.2, while Pakistan received 75 per cent more than the average. If the smaller countries are taken into account, the range of variation in aid received per head is very wide indeed, ranging from £10 a year for British Colonies (other than Hong Kong and the Caribbean), which is mainly in the form of grants from the British Government, to under 10 shillings a year for Nigeria.[1]

A similar wide range of variation is found if aid receipts are related to the gross domestic products of the various countries. On this basis, East Africa (Kenya, Uganda and Tanganyika), the remaining British Colonies and Pakistan received the greatest amount of official assistance in relation to their gross products, Jamaica and Trinidad the least.

These variations by recipient country reflect the fact that most aid is made available on a bilateral basis by donor countries, each of which may have different policy objectives.[2] Moreover, most aid so far has been related to individual investment projects, not to the requirements of economic development as a whole; this has inevitably led to many anomalies in the country distribution of the aid total. If all aid were channelled through an appropriate international agency, it would then become necessary for donor governments to agree on common principles of aid distribution. It is not essential here to discuss in any detail what such common principles might be; there are clearly a wide variety of considerations which must be taken into account, including some which are more akin to value judgements than to objective criteria.[3]

One important issue is whether to give more aid to poor countries than to richer (or, rather, less poor) ones, or to concentrate aid on countries which can make the best use of it, or in which aid has a significant indirect beneficial influence on government policies designed to promote economic development. Again, should aid be directed towards stimulating economic growth in countries where the most intractable obstacles to such growth exist; or rather should it be

[1] The low figure for *per caput* aid received by the former Federation of Rhodesia and Nyasaland reflects the winding-up of the Federation in the period covered.
[2] See I. M. D. Little and J. M. Clifford, *International Aid*, Allen & Unwin, London, 1965, for a detailed discussion of the policy objectives of aid.
[3] *Ibid.* ch. 3 ('The Principles of Aid-Giving').

Table 7.2. *Net inflow of official aid into less developed Sterling countries:
actual and possible alternative distributions in 1962–3*

				Possible alternatives		
	Actual			(1) Equal per head	(2) Equal proportion of GDP	(3) Inverse to GDP per head
	Total	Per head	Proportion of GDP			
	(£ million)	(£)	(%)	(£ million)		
Burma	10	0·42	1·8	20	12	23
Ceylon	7	0·70	1·4	9	13	5
India	280	0·62	2·3	371	340	387
Malaya	14	1·81	2·0	6	20	2
Pakistan	140	1·44	4·9	80	80	75
Total, Sterling Asia	451	0·76	2·7	486	465	492
Kenya, Tanzania and Uganda	34	1·33	5·3	21	17	22
Rhodesia/Nyasaland	7½	0·69	1·4	9	15	5
Ghana	18	2·52	3·3	6	14	2
Nigeria	21	0·46	1·9	38	31	43
Total, Sterling Africa	80	0·89	2·9	74	77	72
Jamaica	2½	1·47	1·0	1	7	0
Trinidad and Tobago	− 1	−0·89	−0·4	1	6	0
Other Sterling Caribbean	9	5·63	5·3	1	5	0
Total, Sterling Caribbean	11	2·50	1·7	3	18	0
Other British territories	21	10·00	12·2	2	5	1
TOTAL	563	0·82	2·8	565	565	565

SOURCES: *Balance of Payments Yearbook*, vol. 15, I.M.F., Washington, 1964; *Monthly Bulletin
of Statistics*, United Nations, New York.

concentrated in helping a limited number of (probably wealthier)
countries to the threshold of 'self-sustained'[1] growth? Further relevant
considerations are whether aid should be reduced to the extent to which
private investment capital is available to an under-developed country;
and whether, and to what extent, the loan element in aid should be
limited according to the recipient country's probable future ability for
repaying both interest and principal.

The pursuit of these and other possible criteria for an equitable
distribution of a given aid total would, however, be beyond the scope
of the present chapter. Here, all that is necessary is to evolve some
relatively simple criteria which would appear to provide equitable,
though alternative, bases for aid distribution, and would also allow

[1] In the present context 'self-sustained' growth implies a phase of economic development
financed by exports and capital borrowings from abroad on commercial terms, with no aid.

quantitative results to be readily obtained. Three alternative criteria suggest themselves:

(1) Aid per head of population should be equal for all recipient countries.

(2) Aid should form the same proportion of GDP for all recipient countries.

(3) Aid should be inversely related to the level of GDP per head in the recipient countries.

The first criterion makes no allowances for differences in income and wealth among less developed countries requiring aid; nor does it make any allowance, even implicitly, for differences in the capacity of different countries to utilize aid efficiently. The second criterion would allow more aid to wealthier countries, and this could be justified in broad terms on the ground that such countries would already have a substantial economic infrastructure and adequate supplies of local capital and skills to allow aid to be more profitably utilized than could be done by poorer countries. The third criterion attempts to introduce the principle of progressive redistribution of income, by allowing relatively more aid to poorer countries than to richer ones.

In 1962–3, the less developed Sterling countries received some £565 million in official aid (as defined by the O.E.C.D.). Table 7.2 shows how this total would have been distributed in that period on each of the three alternative criteria suggested here.[1]

On any of these alternative criteria, India would have received substantially more aid in 1962–3 than she actually did; on the 'equal proportion of GDP' basis, her aid receipts would have been higher by some £60 million (about 20 per cent), while on either of the other criteria the increase in her aid would have been some £90–100 million (30 to 40 per cent). Burma and Nigeria would also have received very much more aid, on any of the alternative criteria, than the amounts which they

---

[1] The formulae used were as follows: Ai, Pi, and Qi represent the aid, population and GDP of a given recipient country i, and A, P and Q the corresponding totals for all O.S.A. recipient countries. The three alternative distributions of aid are then:

$$A_{1i} = APi/P, \qquad (7.1)$$

$$A_{2i} = AQi/Q. \qquad (7.2)$$

For the third criterion, it is assumed that if all countries had the same GDP per head, they would receive the same aid per head, while deviations in their GDP per head from the mean GDP per head for all countries would be compensated (in the reverse direction). Thus:

$$A_{3i} = (APi/P)\,(Pi/Qi)\,(Q/P)$$
$$= (A_{1i})^2/A_{2i}. \qquad (7.3)$$

Because of the squared term, the sum of A_{3i} for all countries will not equal A (except fortuitously), so that a correcting factor is required, as follows:

$$A'_{3i} = \frac{[(A_{1i})^2/A_{2i}]\,A}{\Sigma A_{3i}}. \qquad (7.4)$$

actually received in 1962–3. On the other hand, Pakistan would have been a major loser on any one of the alternatives, the loss amounting to £60–65 million or as much as 45 per cent of the average net capital inflow during 1962–3. Ghana and the three East African countries would also have been substantial losers, though on the 'equal proportion of GDP' basis the loss to Ghana would have been relatively small. On any one of the alternative criteria, the British colonial territories would have lost the greater part of the grants made to them by the United Kingdom.

These various gains and losses would, of course, represent much smaller proportions of total foreign exchange availabilities than of the actual aid received. As Table 7.3 shows, the use of the alternative criteria in 1962–3 would have added 7 to 12 per cent to India's total credits, while Pakistan's would have fallen by 17 to 19 per cent, representing a major decline in purchasing power over imports. Apart from Ghana and East Africa, for which total credits would be cut by up to 12 per cent had any of the alternative criteria been in use in 1962–3, the principal sufferers from changing the method of aid distribution would be the British Colonies, but while these territories remain politically dependent on Britain, there is clearly a good case for special aid privileges for them.[1]

It was argued earlier that reasonable alternative assumptions for the total of official capital flows to the less developed overseas Sterling countries in 1975 would be £565 million, the 1962–3 level, or £1,000 million, an increase of about 75 per cent above that level. This total can be assumed to be distributed in much the same proportions among the various countries as in the early 1960s; or one of our three alternative distribution criteria can be used. Of the latter, criterion (3) has been selected as being, in some sense, more desirable than the other two (though some would, no doubt, object to the principle of redistribution in favour of poorer countries). Table 7.4 shows the results of applying this criterion to the assumed aid total, as well as the corresponding capital flows had the actual distribution in 1962–3 been taken as the basis of the calculations.

The differences between the two methods of distributing aid have already been commented upon, but it is of interest to note that these differences are considerably smaller, for many countries, than those arising from the alternative assumptions about the total capital inflow

---

[1] One reason why small British colonies get a high level of aid per head is because 'investment' is 'lumpy' and particularly so with infrastructure. For countries with small populations the provision of necessary infrastructure and public utilities may, in fact, be more expensive than in more populous countries. Apart from any political problems, the distribution of aid on the basis of inversely relating it to GDP per head might therefore run into severe practical difficulties for countries with small populations.

Table 7.3. *Effect of possible alternative distributions of official aid on total credits in the balances of payments of less developed Sterling countries in 1962–3*

	Total credits[a]	Difference between alternative and actual distributions of aid as proportion of total credits		
		(1)	(2)	(3)
	(£ million)	(%)	(%)	(%)
Burma	107	+9	+2	+12
Ceylon	147	+1	+4	−1
India	913	+10	+7	+12
Malaya	309	−3	+2	−4
Pakistan	350	−17	−17	−19
East Africa	176[b]	−7	−10	−7
Rhodesia/Nyasaland	186[b]	+1	+4	−1
Ghana	134	−9	−3	−12
Nigeria	222	+7	+4	+10
Jamaica	90[c]	−2	+5	−3
Trinidad and Tobago	122[c]	+2	+6	+1
Other Sterling Caribbean	120	−7	−3	−7
Other British territories	156	−12	−10	−13

SOURCES: Tables 7.2 and 7.7.

[a] Exports of goods and services, net factor payments abroad and net inflow of long-term capital.

[b] Excluding the intra-trade between the constituent countries.

[c] 1960–1 average.

into the less developed Sterling countries. For India, for example, the change from the 1962–3 basis to criterion (3) implies an increase of about £100 million in net official capital inflow when the Sterling total is £565 million: but an increase of some £300 million, on criterion (3), when the Sterling total is increased from £565 to £1,000 million.

The capital inflow figures yielded by the application of criterion (3) to the assumed Sterling capital inflow totals are those used in the present set of projections. There is, of course, nothing sacrosanct about these figures; different assumptions would yield correspondingly different country totals. It is, however, of some interest to compare the capital inflow figures assumed here with those used in the various Development Plans. For India, the Perspective Plan (published in 1964) envisaged a progressive reduction in dependence on external financial assistance, from £390 million in 1960/1 to £375 million in 1965/6 and £225 million in 1970/1 with a tapering off to zero by the end of the fifth Five-Year Plan in 1975/6.[1] Over the past decade, however, Indian economic plan-

[1] *Op. cit.* pp. 10–11 (cited on p. 188, n. *e*).

Table 7.4. *Alternative assumptions about net official capital flows to the less developed Sterling countries in 1975 (£ million)*

	Based on actual 1962–3 levels		Based on alternative (3)	
	I	II	I	II
Burma	10	18	23	41
Ceylon	7	13	5	9
India	280	497	387	685
Malaya	14	25	2	4
Pakistan	140	248	75	132
East Africa	34	60	22	39
Kenya	..	..	6	11
Tanzania	..	..	9	16
Uganda	..	..	7	12
Rhodesia/Nyasaland	$7\frac{1}{2}$	13	5	9
Malawi	..	..	4	7
Rhodesia	..	..	$\frac{1}{2}$	1
Zambia	..	..	$\frac{1}{2}$	1
Ghana	18	32	2	4
Nigeria	21	37	43	76
Jamaica	$2\frac{1}{2}$	4	0	0
Trinidad and Tobago	..	..	0	0
Other Sterling Caribbean	9	16	0	0
Other British territories	21	37	1	2
TOTAL	565	1,000	565	1,000

SOURCE: Table 6.2.

ners appear to have consistently underestimated the amount of foreign aid required to support their target rates of economic growth,[1] and the assumption made in the Perspective Plan that India will require no further foreign aid after the early 1970s would seem to be extremely optimistic. The lower assumption made in the present projections for net long-term official capital inflow into India in 1975 (£385 million) is roughly the level estimated in the Plan for 1965/6; the higher assumption (£685 million) would still be well within India's capacity to 'absorb' foreign aid by the mid 1970s.

For Pakistan, by contrast, the assumed official capital inflow in 1975 appears to be well below the levels envisaged by the Pakistan planners. In 1960/1, foreign aid amounted to about £90 million, while for 1965 the corresponding total is estimated in the third Five-Year Plan to be some £215 million, rising to about £250 million by 1970, before

[1] See, for example, Little and Clifford, *op. cit.* p. 228.

declining to £220 million in 1975.[1] Thus, the lower of the assumed official capital inflow totals for 1975 (£75 million) is only one-third of the amount for that year envisaged in the Plan, while the higher assumption (£130 million) is two-fifths lower. This considerable discrepancy reflects the operation of criterion (3) in the assumed distribution of aid. If Pakistan's relatively high level of aid per head of population is assumed to continue, then the levels taken in the present projection are that much too low. Since the point could be of major importance to Pakistan, an alternative calculation of her probable growth rate of GDP is also made, taking the Plan figure of 1975 aid as £220 million.

Comparisons of this sort can also be made for a number of other less developed Sterling countries, though there are several which do not state explicitly what assumptions have been made about foreign aid inflows. The Development Plan for Tanzania envisages a net inflow of official capital of £21 million in 1970, compared with the assumption made here of £10 to 15 million in 1975; the Plan for Ceylon takes £11 million for 1968, whereas the present projections assume some £5 to 10 million for 1975; for Nigeria, the Plan gives only totals for the six-year plan period, but for the final year, 1967–8, the figures imply a net official capital inflow of the order of £50 to 60 million, compared with the assumption of £45 to 75 million in the present projections for 1975. Similar comparisons are not possible for other overseas Sterling countries, most of which indicate the size of the external current account deficit envisaged in their Development Plans without specifying the relative importance of the various sources of finance.

Finally, some similar comparisons can be made as regards the assumed level of net private investment from abroad. Of the less developed overseas Sterling countries, private investment represents a substantial proportion of total net capital inflows for Malaya, the Caribbean countries, Ghana and Nigeria. In 1962–3, private capital accounted for about three-quarters of the total inflow into Malaya and Trinidad; for Jamaica, the proportion was about two-thirds, for Nigeria one-half and for Ghana one-third. Both India and Pakistan depend essentially on official capital for foreign financial assistance, the private element representing only 1 per cent of India's, and 11 per cent of Pakistan's, total net capital inflow in 1962–3.

The Malayan Plan does not specify explicitly the assumptions made about the net inflow of foreign private capital. The Interim Review of

---

[1] *Outline of the Third Five-Year Plan*, Government of Pakistan, August 1964, p. 20. The Plan envisaged a progressive decline in foreign aid after 1975, to a figure of £120 million by 1985 (all these aid totals are at 1964/5 prices, except for that for 1960/1, which is at current prices).

the Malayan Five-Year Plan[1] envisages a current account deficit in the balance of payments of some £46 million in 1965, and if about three-quarters of this were financed by private capital from abroad, the latter total for that year would be £35 million.[2] This, however, looks somewhat optimistic (the 1960–1 average was only £12·5 million, while that for 1962–3 was £11·1 million). The projection for 1975 assumes a net private capital inflow at a rate of £15 million a year, the relatively small increase over the levels of the early 1960s reflecting the probability that output of both tin and natural rubber is unlikely to expand appreciably, but that rather more capital will be required to achieve the necessary productivity improvements in these two industries.

The Development Plans for Jamaica, Trinidad, Ghana and Nigeria also do not specify the assumptions made regarding private capital inflows. Little change is projected for Jamaica, but for Trinidad the figure for 1975 is assumed to be either £20 million (as in 1962–3) or £40 million. The Plan for Ghana envisages an import surplus of £36 million by 1969/70; if one-third of this can be taken as financed by foreign private capital (the proportion in 1962–3), the latter would amount to £12 million by 1970; the projection for 1975 assumes an inflow of £15 million. The Nigerian Plan, as already indicated, is by now considerably out of date as regards private capital from abroad, because of the recent petroleum finds. The Plan gives a total for the six-year period (1962–8), which implies a private capital inflow in the final year in the region of £30 to 40 million. There now seem to be two main possibilities, looking ahead to 1975. The first is that investment in the petroleum industry will reach a peak in the late 1960s and then fall off to little more than replacement levels; the second is that such investment will stay at a fairly high plateau during the 1960s (and even result in the attraction of foreign private capital into other industries). Accordingly, two assumptions are made here for 1975; the first is that net private capital inflows amount to £20 million (the 1962–3 figure), the second that they rise to £50 million.

Net private capital inflows into India have been marginal to her total foreign exchange earnings; in 1960–1, they amounted to only £9 million, and fell in 1962–3 to some £3 million. It is assumed here, perhaps optimistically, that by 1975 they will have increased to £20 million a year. This figure is, however, considerably lower than those envisaged in the draft Perspective Plan for 1969/70 (£37 million) or for 1975/6 (£56 million).[3] For Pakistan, the Third Five-Year

---

[1] *Interim Review of Development in Malaya under the Second Five-Year Plan*, Kuala Lumpur, 1963, p. 56.
[2] The actual net inflow of private capital in 1965 for the whole of Malaysia was £39 million.
[3] *Op. cit.* pp. 24, 33.

Plan gives a figure of about £13 million for the net private capital inflow in 1969/70; the projection for 1975 assumes an inflow of £25 million.

3. PROJECTIONS OF THE CAPACITY TO IMPORT

The projections of export earnings made in Chapter 6, together with the assumptions made above regarding net capital inflows, enable projections to be made of the total foreign exchange income of the various overseas Sterling countries in 1975. There are, however, two further component items of the latter to be projected in a manner consistent with the export projections and the capital inflow assumptions: these are exports of services and net factor payments abroad.

The relative importance of exports of services in foreign exchange income varies from country to country. In 1962–3, services accounted for about one-third of the total for Iceland, Ireland, Kenya and Jamaica. The proportion was considerably lower for the other overseas Sterling countries: one-sixth for India, one-eighth for Pakistan and Tanzania, one-tenth for Australia, South Africa, Ceylon, Zambia and Trinidad, and under 5 per cent for Malaya and Ghana. Freight charges for shipping or use of railways for transhipments, together with income for tourism, generally constituted the major items in the services total.

For most countries, the projections to 1975 were based largely on the past relationship between exports of services and exports of merchandise, though account was also taken of the expected change in income from service exports, as expressed in the Development Plans. For several countries, there was a close relationship between earnings from goods and from services over the past decade, and this relationship was assumed to continue in the future, unless some specific change was suggested by planned developments in shipping income (as for India) or in tourism (as for Ireland, Jamaica and several other countries).

It was suggested in Chapter 2 that net factor payments abroad—consisting essentially of interest, profit and dividends on foreign capital investments—could be related in a systematic way to the total foreign debt of each country.[1] The relevant information concerning the total foreign debt is not generally available, but an average rate of interest can be calculated on the incremental changes in the net debt total or, on what comes to the same thing, the cumulative total of net foreign capital inflows over a given period. For Australia, for example, this approach yielded a mean interest rate of 4·2 per cent on the net capital inflow

[1] See pp. 59 and 70.

over the period 1950–61.[1] For the projections, however, it seemed preferable to calculate interest charges separately for private and official capital inflows, especially in view of the probability that the average charge on official loans will be reduced.

Considerable progress has been made in recent years by O.E.C.D. countries in reducing interest rates on official loans to less developed countries, as well as in extending maturity periods. In 1961, the average rate of interest on official loan commitments by all O.E.C.D. countries was 4·7 per cent, but by 1962 this had fallen to 3·6 per cent, with further declines in 1963 and 1964, to 3·4 and 3·0 per cent, respectively;[2] there was, however, a rise in the mean rate of interest to 3·6 per cent, in 1965.[3] The mean rate of interest charged in 1963 varied considerably from one major donor country to another, ranging from about 6 per cent for loans by Canada and Italy to 2·0 per cent for those by the United States. Since 1963, there has been a growing awareness among donor countries of the difficulties to the less developed countries occasioned by growing interest charges, and some donor countries have been issuing loans either free of interest or at a reduced rate of interest. In the present projections, it has been assumed that by 1975 the mean rate of interest on official loans will be 3 per cent. It is of some interest to note that this is also the assumption made in the Indian draft Perspective Plan,[4] which covers the same period as the present projections.

For private capital investments, the mean rate of interest, profit and dividend is likely to be at least 4 per cent (the computed rate for Australia over the past decade) and may be appreciably higher in some countries—such as those in South-East Asia—where the risks appear to be greater. For the more developed Sterling countries, the net interest rate on private capital borrowings is taken at 4 per cent; for India, the rate is assumed to be $5\frac{1}{2}$ per cent,[5] while for all other less developed countries a rate of $7\frac{1}{2}$ per cent has been assumed.

On the basis of these various assumptions, projections of the total

---

[1] A regression equation of the following form was used:

$$N_t = A + i \sum_0^{t-1} F,$$

where N = net factor payments abroad and F = net long-term capital inflow, both deflated by the import price index, A = a constant, and i = the mean interest rate on the annual net capital inflow over the period covered. The regression for Australia covered twelve years, the value for i being 0·042 ($\pm$0·009), with R^2 = 0·706.

[2] *The Flow of Financial Resources to Less Developed Countries, 1956–1963*, O.E.C.D., Paris, 1964, pp. 35–7.

[3] *Development Assistance Efforts and Policies, 1966 Review*, O.E.C.D., Paris, 1967.

[4] *Op. cit.* p. 176.

[5] The interest rate on private capital borrowings from abroad implicit in the figures in the Indian draft Perspective Plan works out at 5·4 per cent.

foreign exchange income of each of nineteen overseas Sterling countries[1] in 1975 can be made, using also the projections of merchandise exports presented in Chapter 6. The results are shown in Tables 7.6 and 7.7 for the more developed and less developed countries, respectively, while a summary of the main totals is given in Table 7.5. For all nineteen countries, which together accounted for about 85 per cent of all merchandise exports from the Overseas Sterling Area in 1960–1, the total projected changes in total foreign exchange income were of the same order of magnitude as those in merchandise exports on assumption A (the lower income-growth assumption), but rather lower on assumption B. This latter difference reflected essentially an appreciably lower rate of growth in the projections of total foreign exchange income than in merchandise exports of the African member countries of the Sterling Area. For the more developed countries, and for the Asian[2] and Caribbean Sterling countries, the more detailed projections for total foreign exchange income were of roughly the same order of magnitude as those for merchandise exports.

Among the more developed countries, the changes projected for total foreign exchange income were rather lower than for exports for both Australia and Ireland, but were significantly higher for New Zealand and South Africa (Table 7.6). A major factor for Australia is the assumption

[1] Uganda and Hong Kong had to be omitted here because of a lack of sufficiently detailed data on their balances of payments.

[2] Excluding, *inter alia*, Hong Kong, Singapore, Sabah and Brunei.

Table 7.5. *Summary of projections of merchandise exports and of total foreign exchange income, 1960–1 to 1975*

(indices for 1975, 1960–1 = 100)

	Exports		Total foreign exchange income			
	A	B	AI	AII	BI	BII
MORE DEVELOPED COUNTRIES	165	180	165	170	185	190
LESS DEVELOPED COUNTRIES						
Asian	150	160	140	160	150	170
African	240	260	200	205	215	220
Caribbean	165	185	160	165	185	190
Total	180	195	160	170	170	190
TOTAL[a]	170	190	165	175	175	190

SOURCES: Tables 7.6 and 7.7.

[a] Nineteen countries, accounting for about 85 per cent of total merchandise exports from the Overseas Sterling Area in 1960–1.

Table 7.6. *Total foreign exchange income of the more developed Sterling countries, 1960–3 and projections for 1975*

	Exports Goods	Ser- vices[a]	Long-term capital inflow[b] I	II	Net factor payments from abroad I	II	Gold[c]	Total I	II	Total, indices I	II
					($£$ million)					(1960–1 = 100)	
Australia											
1960–1	762	104	162[d]		−92		13	949		100	
1962–3	908	128	166[d]		−97		12	1,117		118	
1975: A	1,295	170	240	320	−205	−230	15	1,515	1,570	160	165
B	1,485	185						1,720	1,775	180	185
New Zealand											
1960–1	290	27[d]	11[de]		−11		0	317		100	
1962–3	322	32[d]	45[d]		−14		0	385		121	
1975: A	405	35	45	65	−20	−25	0	465	485	145	155
B	435	40						500	520	160	165
South Africa											
1960–1	453	52	−43		−81		277	658		100	
1962–3	493	70	−51		−76		330	766		116	
1975: A	770	110	−50	0	−40	−60	500	1,290	1,320	195	200
B	840	120						1,370	1,400	210	210
Iceland											
1960–1	25	12	2		−1		—	38		100	
1962–3	32	16	2		−1		—	49		129	
1975: A	50	25	0	5	−2		—	75	80	195	210
B	55	25–30						80	85	210	220
Ireland											
1960–1	158	79	7		13		—	257		100	
1962–3	176	97	22		15		—	310		121	
1975: A	235	120	10	15	5	0	—	370	370	145	145
B	260	130						405	405	155	155

SOURCES: Table 6.6. *Balance of Payments Yearbook*, vol. 15, I.M.F., Washington, 1964.

[a] Including private donations (net).
[b] Official grants and loans, and private capital.
[c] Production less domestic consumption.
[d] Estimated on basis of fiscal year figures.
[e] Including official repayments of $£15$ million.

Table 7.7. *Total foreign exchange income of the less developed Sterling countries, 1960–3 and projections for 1975*

	Exports Goods	Ser- vices[a]	Long-term capital inflow[b] I	II	Net factor payments from abroad I	II	Total I	II	Total, indices I	II
					(£ million)				(1960–1 = 100)	
Burma										
1960–1	83	6	6		− 1		94		100	
1962–3	94	6	7		0		107		114	
1975:A	95 }	5	25	40	−5	−5 {	120	135	130	145
B	105 }					{	130	145	140	155
Ceylon										
1960–1	131	13	5		− 3		146		100	
1962–3	130	13	8		− 4		147		101	
1975[k]:A	160 }	15	5	10	−5	−5 {	175	180	120	125
B	165 }					{	180	185	125	125
India										
1960–1	483	137	260		− 40		840		100	
1962–3	542	151	283		− 63		913		109	
1975:A	755	210 }	405	705	−185	−240 {	1,185	1,430	140	170
B	805	225 }				{	1,250	1,495	150	180
Malaya										
1960–1	324	−6	21		− 30		309		100	
1962–3	310	−3	25		− 23		309		100	
1975[k]:A	470 }	10	20	30	−50	−55 {	450	455	145	145
B	500 }					{	480	485	155	155
Pakistan										
1960–1	140	34	84		− 2		256		100	
1962–3	156	46	158		− 10		350		137	
1975:A	250	50 }	100	155	−35	−40 {	365	415	140	160
B	285	55 }				{	405	455	160	175
Ghana										
1960–1	108	2	46		− 6		161[c]		100	
1962–3	100	2	28		− 7		134[c]		83	
1975:A	230 }	10	20	25	−20	−20 {	255[d]	260[d]	160	160
B	250 }					{	275[d]	280[d]	170	170
Kenya										
1960–1	55[e]	..	..		..		..		..	
1962–3	65[e]	32	21		− 11		107		100	
1975:A	105 }	50	15	25	−20	−25 {	150	155	140	145
B	110 }					{	155	160	145	150
Malawi										
1960–1	10[f]	2	6		− 1		17		100	
1962–3	11[f]	2	4		− 1		16		94	
1975:A }	15	5	5	10	−5	−5	20	25	125	145
B }										

Table 7.7 (cont.)

	Exports		Long-term capital inflow[b]		Net factor payments from abroad		Total		Total, indices	
	Goods	Ser-vices[a]	I	II	I	II	I	II	I	II
	(£ million)								(1960–1 = 100)	
Nigeria										
1960–1	169	8	64		−4		237		100	
1962–3	177	11	40		−6		222		94	
1975:A	515 } 20		65	125	−40	−65	560	595	235	250
B	560						605	640	255	270
Rhodesia										
1960–1	71[g]	5	7		−11		79[h]		100	
1962–3	78[g]	1	−5		−14		67[h]		85	
1975:A	135 } 10		10	10	−20	−20	145[i]	145[i]	185	185
B	150						160[i]	160[i]	200	200
Tanzania										
1960–1	52	8	8		−3		66[j]		100	
1962–3	58	9	..		−3		..		..	
1975:A	100 } 15		15	20	−10	−15	120	120	180	180
B	105						125	125	190	190
Zambia										
1960–1	132	11	1		−24		120		100	
1962–3	131	9	−4		−24		112		93	
1975[k]:A	320 } 20		10	10	−35	−35	315	315	260	
B	355						350	350	290	
Jamaica										
1960–1	62	28	9		−9		90		100	
1962–3	71	..	8		−10		..		..	
1975:A	130	45 } 5		10	−15	−20	165	165	185	185
B	155	50					195	195	215	215
Trinidad and Tobago										
1960–1	117	13	14		−22		122		100	
1962–3	128	..	26		−26		..		..	
1975:A	165	30 } 20		40	−40	−50	175	185	145	150
B	180	35					195	205	160	170

SOURCES: Table 6.7; p. 198 above, and *Balance of Payments Yearbook, loc. cit.*

[a] Including private donations (net).
[b] Official grants and loans, and private capital.
[c] Including £11 million gold production.
[d] Including an assumed £15 million gold production.
[e] Including estimated value of exports to Tanzania and Uganda.
[f] Excluding exports to Rhodesia and Zambia (totalling £1·7 million in 1964).
[g] Excluding exports to Malawi and Zambia (totalling £36·4 million in 1964).
[h] Including £7 million gold production.
[i] Including an assumed £10 million gold production.
[j] Including £1 million gold production.
[k] Exports at current prices (see p. 198).

made earlier of an appreciable rise in private foreign investment; as a result, the burden of interest charges must be taken as increasing also. On the basis of a mean interest rate of 4 per cent, net factor income payments abroad would reach at least £200 million by 1975, representing about one-sixth of Australia's projected export earnings in that year, compared with little more than one-tenth in the early 1960s. For Ireland, the slower growth projected for total earnings than for exports reflects the probability that net investment income from abroad will suffer a substantial decline over the coming decade as a result of rising interest payments on new foreign capital investments in the Republic.

The discrepancy in the projected indices of exports and total foreign income for New Zealand arises because allowance was made earlier for the abnormally low level of net capital inflows in 1960–1; if the comparison is made with 1962–3, the projections for total foreign income are of much the same order as for exports. For South Africa, however, the more optimistic projections for total foreign income than for merchandise exports reflect the expectation that income from exports of services will rise faster than that from merchandise, and the assumption that gold production will rise at a slower rate than in the past.

Among the Asian Sterling countries, for Ceylon and Malaya the projected increases in the growth rates of total foreign exchange income are much the same as those for merchandise exports;[1] for Burma they are greater than, whereas for Pakistan they are appreciably below, the corresponding merchandise export projections. The projections of total foreign exchange for India show a considerable spread according to which assumption is taken about the level of foreign aid (see Table 7.7). For both Ceylon and Malaya, merchandise exports form a very large part of total foreign exchange income, so the agreement between the two projections was to be expected. For Burma the faster growth rate projected for total foreign exchange income than for exports results entirely from the assumption that there would be a substantial increase in official aid to Burma (as a result of the application of the third criterion of aid distribution); some reference is, however, made in Chapter 8 to the probable impact on the Burmese rate of economic growth of the alternative assumption that aid receipts in 1975 would be no higher than the average for 1960–3.

For India, the large difference (£300 million) between the two assumptions about the magnitude of official aid in 1975 results in a substantial spread in the projected indices of total foreign exchange income (from 140 per cent of the 1960–1 average on the AI combination of assumptions, for example, to 170 per cent on the AII combination). On

---

[1] For Ceylon and Malaya the comparison is with the current value projections on p. 198 and not with that in Table 6.7.

either assumption, however, India's net factor payments abroad will rise sharply, on the basis of a mean interest rate of 3 per cent on outstanding debt; by 1975, such interest payments would represent about one-quarter of merchandise export earnings on assumption BI, and nearly one-third on assumption BII. It net interest payments abroad could be limited—by reducing interest rates, introducing periods of grace, and so on—to, say, one-tenth of export earnings (roughly the position in the early 1960s), the indices of total foreign exchange income for 1975 would rise to 155 on combination AI and 195 on BII.

The assumed redistribution of foreign aid on which the projections are based results in lower growth rates for Pakistan's total foreign exchange income than for her exports. Had the Plan figure of £220 million for foreign aid in 1975 been taken instead, the indices for total foreign exchange income would have been substantially higher, especially those based on assumption I. For example, the index for AI would be increased from 140 to 185, while for BII the corresponding increase would be relatively smaller, from 175 to 195.

Among the African countries of the Sterling Area, the projected rates of growth for total foreign exchange income are generally appreciably lower than the corresponding rates for merchandise exports, Zambia being the sole exception. The main reason for this is that the net inflow of long-term capital is assumed either to show a small decline (assumption I), or to rise by a relatively small proportion (assumption II), while on either assumption there would be a large rise in net interest payments on foreign loans and investments. The decline in the assumed net capital inflow on assumption I results wholly from the application of the redistributive principle in foreign aid allocations to official capital inflows into Ghana, this being only partially offset by the assumption of a substantial increase in private foreign capital investment in that country. For Nigeria—the other major capital importer among the African Sterling countries—the reason for the rather wide spread in the assumed figures for net capital inflows was given earlier; in any case, exports of services and net capital inflows are virtually certain to rise, over the coming decade, at a much slower pace than merchandise exports. The somewhat faster growth projected in the total foreign exchange income of Zambia than in her exports reflects the assumption that the recent capital outflow will cease in the near future and will be followed by a relatively substantial net capital inflow. Of the two Caribbean countries, the projected growth rates in total foreign exchange income are appreciably lower than the corresponding export rates for Jamaica, but somewhat higher for Trinidad.

For all the less developed Sterling countries together, even the high assumption about the net long-term capital inflow fails to result in a rate of growth in total foreign exchange income as high as that projected for merchandise exports. The reason is the sharp rise in net factor payments abroad, from about £165 million in 1960–1 to £490 million in 1975 on assumption I, and to £600 million on assumption II. On the latter basis, net factor payments abroad would represent some 14–16 per cent of total projected merchandise exports of the fourteen countries combined, as against only 8½ per cent in 1960–1. If interest, profit and dividends on foreign capital could be limited to 10 per cent of exports, this would go quite a long way towards closing the gap between the projected indices for total foreign exchange income and those for merchandise exports.[1]

The capacity to import

The concept of the 'capacity to import' was defined in an earlier chapter as total foreign exchange income deflated by the movement in import prices.[2] Thus, to transform the projections of total foreign exchange income into projections of the capacity to import, it is necessary to make some assumption about the future course of import prices in the various Sterling countries.

Over the past decade or so, import prices (or, rather, import unit values) of the member countries of the Overseas Sterling Area have generally shown relatively little fluctuation. This is in striking contrast with the sharp movements in export prices which were a feature of the period and which were considered in the previous chapter. Taking changes from the 1953–5 average to 1960–1, for example, only two countries[3] out of the fifteen shown in Table 7.8 experienced changes in import unit values of more than 10 per cent; eight showed changes over the period of 5 per cent or less, the remaining five countries showing changes of 6 to 10 per cent. Over the more recent—though shorter—period, from 1960–1 to 1964, all but one country experienced import unit value changes not exceeding 10 per cent, while nine countries had changes of 5 per cent or less. Moreover, some of these changes were negative, though in both periods the increases predominated.

A major reason why import unit values generally tend to move, in either direction, within a relatively small range is that a substantial

[1] For example, the index of total foreign exchange income would then be 165 on the A I combination (instead of the 160 shown in Table 7.5), and 200 on B II (instead of 190), though both indices would still be below those for merchandise exports.

[2] See p. 87.

[3] The exceptionally large rise in Pakistan's import unit value index appears to reflect in the main the rise in import prices of manufactures, the exclusion of land trade from the index increasing the weighting of manufactures, since most of the overland imports consist of food and materials. The official index is, moreover, weighted by import values in 1948–9, when seaborne imports were largely manufactures.

Table 7.8. *Changes in import unit values, 1953–5 to 1964, and share of primary products in total imports (percentages)*

	Change in import unit values		Share of primary products in total imports in 1964[a]			
	1953–5 to 1960–1	1960–1 to 1964	Food, beverages and tobacco	Crude materials[b]	Fuels	Total
MORE DEVELOPED COUNTRIES						
Australia	+9	+2	5·0	8·7	9·2	22·9
New Zealand	+5	−1	7·9	4·7	7·5	20·1
South Africa	+2	0	4·6	6·8	7·7	19·1
Iceland[c]	−3	−9	11·7	4·9	9·4	26·0
Ireland	+6	+3	17·1	7·8	8·5	33·4
LESS DEVELOPED COUNTRIES						
Ceylon	−3	+5	51·5	1·6	5·4	58·5
India	−1	0	16·2	10·2	6·8	33·2
Malaya	−8	+2	31·1	11·1	7·7	49·9
Pakistan[c]	+34	0	17·2	4·0	7·1	28·3
Ghana	+6	−7	17·0	0·8	5·8	23·6
Kenya	+4[d]	+7	8·8	1·7	12·1	22·6
Nigeria	0	+8	9·2	1·5	7·7	18·4
Tanzania	−1[d]	+2	6·4	1·1	5·2	12·7
Jamaica	+24	+11	22·2	3·4	8·8	34·4
Trinidad	+8[e]	..	12·5	1·5	50·1	64·1

SOURCES: *Yearbook of International Trade Statistics, 1963*, United Nations, New York, 1965; *The Commonwealth and Sterling Area: Statistical Abstract no. 85, 1964*, H.M.S.O., London, 1965.

[a] 1962 for South Africa; 1963 for Pakistan.
[b] Including oils and fats.
[c] In terms of Sterling. The index excludes imports across Pakistan's land frontiers.
[d] 1954–5 to 1960–1.
[e] 1953–5 to 1960.

proportion of the imports of the majority of primary-producing countries consists of food, raw materials and fuels; the prices of which are either reasonably stable (as for petroleum) or else tend to fluctuate appreciably (as for most bulk foodstuffs) or to have a secular downward movement (as for a number of agricultural raw materials). Prices of manufactured goods, on the other hand, have tended to rise at a fairly steady rate over the past decade, apart from a few recession years.[1] Where food, materials or fuels constitute a large proportion of imports, their price movement has often tended to offset the upward secular trend in manufactured goods prices. This offsetting effect has been marked for the overseas

[1] The United Nations index of the export prices of manufactured goods shows an average annual increase of 1.1 per cent between 1955 and 1964.

MEE

Sterling countries, as well as for the majority of non-Sterling primary-producers.

Food forms a large part of Ceylon's imports (one-half the total, by value, in 1964) and is also relatively important for Malaya, Jamaica, Ghana and Trinidad (Table 7.8). Crude materials, including oils and fats, represented about one-tenth of all imports into India and Malaya in 1964, but were negligible for many countries—particularly in Africa —which are still in a very early stage of industrialization. Apart from Trinidad, half of whose imports consist of crude petroleum for refining, fuels generally represent some 5 to 10 per cent of total imports. Though primary products, in aggregate, account for well under half of total imports for most Sterling countries, their prices tend to move generally with their export prices and, to this extent, their movement tends to moderate changes in their terms of trade.

It would, no doubt, be possible in principle to make projections of import unit values for each Sterling country which would be consistent with the various commodity projections and with the underlying assumptions about economic growth in the industrial countries. Import prices of manufactures could be assumed, for example, to continue to rise at much the same rate as in the recent past; while import prices of food, materials and fuels could be assumed to move in ways which were consistent with the relevant projections of world consumption and production. However, as was pointed out at the end of Chapter 6, it would be idle to pretend that consistent calculations of this sort can be done in the present state of knowledge about the workings of the various commodity markets.[1] There is, in any event, some area of doubt as to even the direction of the probable change in import unit values; much will depend on the course of prices of major primary-product imports, as well as on whether the composition of each country's import total shifts towards manufactures or towards food, materials or fuels.

In view of these inevitable uncertainties, it is assumed here that import unit values in 1975 will be generally the same as in the base period, 1960–1. While, however, the main computations of probable future rates of growth in the gross domestic product of the less developed Sterling countries in Chapter 8 are based on this assumption, allowance is also made for the possibility that import unit values will in fact have changed, in one direction or the other, in the course of the period covered by the projections.

For this reason, the projections of total foreign exchange income can now be regarded, in effect, as projections of the capacity to import. These projections are summarized in Table 7.9, in terms of annual growth rates, and are also compared with the corresponding rates of

[1] See pp. 191 ff.

Table 7.9. *Growth rates of the capacity to import: computed, planned and projected (percentage per annum, compound)*

	Computed[a] (1950s)	Plan[b] (1960s)	Projected (1960–1 to 1975)			
			AI	AII	BI	BII
MORE DEVELOPED COUNTRIES						
Australia	3·7	—	3·3	3·5	4·2	4·4
New Zealand	..	—	2·7	3·0	3·3	3·5
South Africa	3·2	—	4·8	4·9	5·2	5·4
Iceland	8·7	2·2	4·8	5·3	5·3	5·7
Ireland	3·9	5·2[c]	2·6	2·6	3·2	3·2
LESS DEVELOPED COUNTRIES						
Burma	2·3	6·9	1·7	2·6	2·3	3·1
Ceylon	2·3	2·8	1·3	1·5	1·5	1·5
India	3·4	5·0[d]	2·3	3·7	2·8	4·1
Malaya	..	3·5	2·7	2·7	3·0	3·0
Pakistan	4·9[e]	5·9	2·4[f]	3·3[f]	3·3[f]	3·9[f]
Ghana	7·6[g]	7·0	3·3	3·3	3·8	3·8
Kenya	..	4·1	2·3	2·6	3·0	3·3
Nigeria	..	5·6	6·1	6·5	6·6	7·0
Rhodesia	..	—	4·3	4·3	5·0	5·0
Tanzania	..	7·9	4·2	4·2	4·6	4·6
Zambia	..	7·3	6·9	6·9	7·7	7·7
Jamaica	8·2	5·1	4·3	4·3	5·5	5·5
Trinidad and Tobago	9·1	2·6	2·5	2·9	3·3	3·6

SOURCES: Tables 3.11, 7.6 and 7.7; national Economic Development Plans.

[a] For precise periods covered, see Tables 3.7 and 3.8.
[b] For precise periods covered, see Table 6.10.
[c] 'Required' growth rate (see also Table 6.11).
[d] 1960/1 to 1970/1.
[e] 1953–5 to 1962–3; for 1953–5 to 1960–1, the rate was 1·5 per cent per annum.
[f] If the Plan assumption of a net capital inflow of £220 million in 1975/6 had been adopted, the growth rate of the capacity to import would have been 4·2 per cent per annum, on assumption A, and 4·7 on assumption B.
[g] 1956–7 to 1960–1.

growth during the 1950s and with the official planned rates for various periods during the 1960s. The principal reasons for the differences between planned rates and projected growth rates have already been discussed; for most countries, the main differences relate to exports or net capital inflows.

Among the less developed countries, the projected growth rates in the capacity to import are substantially below the planned rates for Burma (for which the export target was excessively over-optimistic), India and Tanzania (again, mainly reflecting a less optimistic view of

15-2

future exports), and Pakistan and Ghana (where the shortfalls reflected both more moderate views of the likely future growth in exports and substantially lower assumed levels of aid). Had the Plan assumption for foreign aid in 1975 been used for Pakistan, the rate of growth projected in the capacity to import would have been much closer to the Plan target, ranging from 4·2 to 4·7 per cent per annum, according to the assumption made about the rate of income growth in the industrial countries. Only for Nigeria did each of the alternative projections exceed the Plan, for reasons given earlier.

CHAPTER 8

INVESTMENT AND ECONOMIC GROWTH

I. INVESTMENT IN FIXED CAPITAL

The *ex post* model discussed in Chapters 2 and 3 makes use of the concept of 'investment elasticity', which measures the degree of reaction of investment in fixed capital assets of an economy to changes in its capacity to import. As explained in Chapter 3, this relationship is assumed to work via two sub-relationships: changes in the capacity to import influence the volume of imported capital goods that become available, while changes in the latter influence the level of investment in fixed capital assets. A long-term relationship between investment in fixed capital and the capacity to import was computed in Chapter 3 for each of ten overseas Sterling countries for the 1950s, though only nine of these were judged as significant. Additional evidence of the probable magnitude of the investment elasticity can, however, be derived from the Economic Development Plans of the overseas Sterling countries though, since none use this concept, the 'elasticities' so derived are entirely implicit ones.

These derived investment elasticities all relate to some part, or the whole, of the 1960s. They are shown for twelve of the less developed Sterling countries in Table 8.1, which also shows, for comparison, the computed long-term relationships for the 1950s. The final column of the table shows the investment elasticity which is assumed to operate for each country over the projection period, 1960–1 to 1975.

Of the Asian Sterling countries, comparisons between computed and plan elasticities can be made for Burma, Ceylon and India. For Burma, the Plan appears excessively over-optimistic about the probable expansion in exports,[1] and this depresses the value of the investment elasticity; the assumed value for the projection was therefore taken as the same as that shown by the regression analysis for the 1950s.

The Ten-Year Plan of Ceylon envisaged a trebling in the volume of gross domestic investment (including an allowance for increased stocks) between 1957 and 1968, but an increase in the capacity to import[2] of only one-third over the same period. Since Ceylon is heavily dependent on imports for her supplies of capital equipment,[3] a sharp expansion in investment in fixed capital of the order envisaged in the Plan would

---

[1] See also p. 227.
[2] Calculated before allowance for long-term capital inflows, details of which are not given in the Plan. [3] See Table 3.5.

Table 8.1. *The elasticity of gross investment in fixed capital with respect to the capacity to import*

	Computed[a] 1950s	Plan[b] 1960s	Assumed 1960–1 to 1975
Burma	0·70	0·55	0·7
Ceylon	0·92	6·15	1·3
India	0·74	$\left\{\begin{matrix} 1·83^c \\ 3·93^d \end{matrix}\right.$	2·0
Malaya	—	1·38[e]	2·0
Pakistan	—	$\left\{\begin{matrix} 1·47^f \\ 1·55^g \end{matrix}\right.$	1·5
Ghana	—	1·38	•1·3
Kenya	—	2·70	2·0
Nigeria	—	0·55	1·2
Rhodesia	—	—	2·0
Tanzania	—	2·30	2·0
Zambia	—	2·29[h]	2·0
Jamaica	0·82	1·16	1·0
Trinidad and Tobago	0·34	0·72	0·8

SOURCES: Table 3.9; national Economic Development Plans.

[a] For precise periods covered, see Tables 3.7 and 3.8.

[b] For precise periods covered, see Table 6.10.

[c] 1960/1 to 1965/6.

[d] 1960/1 to 1970/1.

[e] Very approximate; investment total includes stock changes, while capacity to import excludes exports of services, and includes the balance of payments on current account as the nearest total corresponding to the net long-term capital inflow.

[f] 1960/1 to 1964/5, excluding the Indus Basin scheme and the works programme outside the normal budget; if these are included, the investment elasticity is in the region of 1.9.

[g] 1964/5 to 1969/70.

[h] Based on data in UN/ECA/FAO Report, see p. 185, n. 1.

appear to be quite unrealistic without an increase of foreign aid on a massive scale—a contingency clearly not allowed for in the Plan. This conclusion is strengthened by the development of Ceylon's economy since the early years of the Ten-Year Plan. Between 1958 and 1963, for example, the volume of gross investment in fixed assets rose by only 6 per cent, while there was a marginal decline in the capacity to import. In view of this experience, it would seem unwise to assume a much higher investment elasticity for the projections than that computed for the 1950s; a modest increase, from a computed value of 0·9, to 1·3, is assumed here.[1]

[1] The three-year programme introduced in 1962 envisaged a rise of 9 per cent over the period (1961/2 to 1963/4) in gross investment and a rise of about 7 per cent in exports of goods and services and foreign aid, though this would still have left a substantial foreign exchange 'gap' to be covered (see *Short-term Implementation Programme*, Department of National Planning, Colombo, 1962, pp. 39, 46–7).

For India, the investment elasticities implicit in the draft Perspective Plan for the period 1965–75 are also at sharp variance with the computed elasticity (0·7) for the 1950s; they are also very much higher than the implicit Plan elasticity of 1·8 for the third Plan period (1960/1 to 1965/6). For the fourth Five-Year Plan, the implicit elasticity is 7·3, rising to 8·0 for the fifth Plan period.[1] These high elasticities result essentially from two important features of the Indian Plan. First, a rapid development in domestic output of capital goods is envisaged, so that a striking increase in import substitution would occur in this sector if the plan is fulfilled. India's own output of machinery and equipment is planned to be almost quadrupled between 1965 and 1975, implying an annual rate of growth of about 15 per cent. By the latter year, the home industry is expected to meet over 90 per cent of domestic requirements of machinery and equipment, as against only about 65 per cent in 1965.[2] The second major feature is the assumption referred to in Chapter 7: that India's dependence on foreign aid will decline after 1965 and will be terminated by 1975.[3] If it is assumed that the level of foreign aid in 1970 will be the same as in 1965, then the implied investment elasticity for the decade 1960–1 to 1970–1 is reduced from 3·9 (as shown in Table 8.1) to 2·9. Even this latter figure would, however, appear somewhat optimistic, particularly if defence requirements impinge on the rate of growth in output of capital equipment for civilian industries; in the present projections a more modest elasticity of 2·0 has been assumed.

For Malaya, the investment elasticity implied in the second Five-Year Plan (1961–5) cannot be calculated with any precision, since the investment figures shown include stock changes, while the capacity to import excludes exports of services and includes the net balance of payments on current account as a proxy for the net long-term capital inflow.[4] In fact, there was a substantial net outflow of short-term capital in the base year (1960) used in the Plan, and this results in an artificial depression of the investment elasticity as calculated from the Plan estimates. The present projections assume an elasticity of 2·0 for Malaya.

For Pakistan, the investment elasticities implied in both the second and third Five-Year Plans are in the region of 1·5 (excluding investment in the Indus Basin scheme), and this figure has also been adopted in the projections. Similarly for Ghana, the elasticity assumed (1·3) is close to that implied in the Plan period, 1963/4 to 1969/70. A somewhat lower investment elasticity has been used in the projections for Kenya from the one implied in that country's Plan, since gross investment in fixed

---

[1] *Op. cit.* pp. 167–74.   [2] *Ibid.* pp. 12–4.
[3] *Ibid.* p. 24.   [4] *Op. cit.* p. 67.

capital in the Plan's base year (1962) appeared to be abnormally low, and this artificially increased the implied Plan elasticity.

The low investment elasticity (only 0·55) implied in the Nigerian Plan for the period 1962–8 reflects the assumption made by the Plan's authors that the ratio of fixed investment to gross domestic product will remain constant, whereas a rise in the investment ratio would have been more consistent with the assumptions made about the growth in external resources available for financing economic development. The fact that the Nigerian planners also assumed no change in the shares of consumption and of the current external balance in gross expenditure indicates that they envisaged no radical change in the use of resources in the Nigerian economy. Whether the Plan was internally consistent is open to some question but, in any event, the recent developments in the petroleum and natural gas industries imply a considerably larger investment elasticity than that incorporated in the Plan. It is assumed for projection purposes that the elasticity will be 1·2, or almost as high as that for Ghana or for Ceylon.

There is little to go on in deciding on a reasonable assumption for the probable magnitude of the investment elasticity in Rhodesia. The regression for the 1950s appeared to show a high elasticity for the former Federation, but the result was judged to be of dubious value.[1] Here, it is assumed, arbitrarily, that the investment elasticity over the projection period will be 2·0. For Tanzania, the Plan envisages a level of fixed investment in 1970 at nearly three and a half times that of the base year, 1961, whereas the capacity to import (including only merchandise exports and long-term capital inflow) would only double over this period; for the present projections, a ratio of 2·0 has been assumed, implying a more modest rate of growth in investment than that envisaged in the Plan. Similar considerations apply to Zambia, for which the same investment elasticity of 2·0 has been taken.

For Jamaica, the Plan implies a somewhat higher investment elasticity than was derived from the regression for the 1950s, whereas for Trinidad the reverse is the case. The reduction in the investment elasticity implied in the Trinidad Plan is exceptionally sharp, and reflects very largely the Government's view of the probable rapid decline in new investment by the oil companies. Since the present export projections are somewhat more optimistic than those in the Trinidad Plan,[2] it would seem consistent to adopt, also, a somewhat higher investment elasticity than that implied in the Plan. For Jamaica, the projected elasticity is taken at 1·0, or about midway between that implied in the Plan and that calculated from the regression for the 1950s.

[1] See p. 93.
[2] See Table 6.11.

Of the various investment elasticities assumed for the projections, there are clusters at two values: in the range 1·0 to 1·5 (five countries) and at 2·0 (six countries), the elasticity for the other two countries being taken at below unity. These various assumptions appear reasonable in the light of past performance—where this can be measured—or of the structural relationships between investment and the capacity to import as implied in the Development Plans of overseas Sterling countries where these appear to be reasonably realistic. In the event, of course, the *ex post* elasticities may well turn out to be significantly different for a number of countries from those assumed here, either because the pattern and speed of import substitution has evolved differently from that planned, or because the pattern of imports has altered—either towards or away from capital goods and materials for capital goods industries—from that envisaged in the Plans.

The application of the assumed investment elasticities to the projected rates of growth in the capacity to import for each of the countries considered yields projections of the growth rate in each country of gross domestic fixed capital formation. These projected rates are shown in Table 8.2, together with the corresponding rates actually achieved over recent periods and, where applicable, the rates of investment growth envisaged in current Development Plans.

In comparing the projected rates first of all with recent achievements, a very mixed picture emerges. The projections show a dramatic reduction in the investment growth rate for Trinidad compared with the 1950s (when large investments in the petroleum industry sustained the economy), but an equally striking rise in investment in Zambia and Nigeria. For most of the other Sterling countries for which comparisons can be made, modest declines in the investment growth rates are projected, compared with those achieved over the past decade.

The majority of the Development Plans have been designed, *inter alia*, to accelerate the past rates of capital formation. Very sharp increases in investment over recent rates have been planned for by several countries, notably Ceylon and Zambia, and, though reliable data for past periods are not available, almost certainly also by Malaya, Kenya and Tanzania. Consequently, for most of these countries, there is a substantial shortfall between projected and planned rates of growth in fixed capital formation (see Table 8.2). The largest discrepancy is that for Ceylon, reflecting in the main the over-optimism of the Ten-Year Plan concerning the trend of exports and capital inflow from abroad,[1] but for both India and Pakistan the projected rates of investment growth

---

[1] A much more modest target (averaging 3·2 per cent a year) is taken for the growth rate in exports of goods and services in the more recent three-year programme (*Short-term Implementation Programme*, p. 39).

Table 8.2. *Rates of growth in gross domestic fixed capital formation: actual, planned and projected (percentage per annum, compound)*

	Actual		Plan[a]	Projected 1960–1 to 1975			
	1953–60	1960–3	1960s	AI	AII	BI	BII
Burma	2·3	..	3·8	1·2	1·9	1·7	2·3
Ceylon	7·4	1·8	10·3	1·6	1·9	1·9	1·9
India	9·6	..	$\begin{cases}11\cdot6^b\\10\cdot4^c\end{cases}$	4·2	6·2	4·7	6·6
Malaya	..	..	11·5[d]	4·5	4·6	5·2	5·3
Pakistan	..	..	8·6[e]	3·6	4·8	4·6	5·7
Ghana	..	..	6·6	4·0	4·1	4·5	4·6
Kenya	..	..	9·1	4·1	5·3	5·3	5·7
Nigeria	6·8	2·7	3·5	6·8	7·3	7·6	8·1
Rhodesia	3·3[f]	..	—	7·0	7·0	8·0	8·0
Tanzania	..	..	14·3	7·0	7·0	7·3	7·3
Zambia	−2·7[f]	1·7	11·9	10·4	10·4	11·5	11·5
Jamaica	7·1	..	6·4	4·3	4·3	5·5	5·5
Trinidad and Tobago	14·1	..	1·8	2·1	2·4	2·7	3·0

SOURCES: *Yearbook of National Accounts Statistics, 1964,* United Nations, New York, 1965; national Economic Development Plans; national statistics; Tables 7.9 and 8.1.

[a] For precise periods covered, see Table 6.10.
[b] 1960/1 to 1970/1.
[c] 1960/1 to 1975/6.
[d] Including stock changes.
[e] 1964/5 to 1969/70.
[f] 1954 to 60.

are also substantially lower than those provided for in the official Plans. The same is true for Ghana and Kenya. For many of these countries, the export projections and/or the assumptions made here concerning the level of capital inflow are less optimistic than those used by the official planners.

On the other hand, the projected rates of investment growth for Nigeria are double, or nearly double, the planned rate, while there is virtually no difference between projection and Plan for Zambia. For the Caribbean countries, the differences are relatively small, the projections being somewhat lower than the Plan growth rate for Jamaica and somewhat higher for Trinidad.

2. PLANNED AND PROJECTED RATES OF GROWTH IN GROSS DOMESTIC PRODUCT

The *ex post* growth model previously discussed postulated a definite relationship between investment in fixed capital assets and the rate of growth in gross domestic product. The relationship can conveniently be expressed by a gross incremental capital-output ratio (ICOR). It was suggested earlier that it would be unwise to assume that the overall ICOR for any country would be the same in the future as in the past, in view of the many factors which could result in a shift in this ratio.[1]

Some guidance as to the probable direction and magnitude of such shifts during the 1960s compared with the preceding decade can, however, be gained from internal evidence in the various Development Plans. Many of these, indeed, use the ICOR concept as a pivotal relationship in calculating their planned investment requirements;[2] for those which do not use the concept, implied ICORs can readily be calculated. To the extent that future shifts in the ICOR values are determined by changes in the pattern of fixed investment the explicit, or implied, plan ICORs can usefully be taken as a guide. Moreover, the Plans should also take into account, at least in principle, any probable shifts in the ICORs applicable within individual sectors of the economy, though this is inherently a more difficult task than allowing for the effect of a changing sectoral investment pattern on the assumption of constant sectoral ICOR's.

In view of the rapidity with which the sectoral patterns are envisaged as changing in the Development Plans of some Sterling countries, as well as for other reasons, it would not be surprising to find substantial differences between the ICORs found for the 1950s and those built into the Plans for the current decade. A direct comparison of the two periods can be made for only six of the less developed countries in the Overseas Sterling Area (Table 8.3), but nonetheless some tentative conclusions can be drawn. First, for most of these countries, the planned ICORs are not substantially different, one way or the other, from the corresponding calculated ratios for the preceding period. Countries which had relatively low ICORs before will generally continue to have relatively low ICORs, and vice versa, if the various plans are realized (Trinidad being, however, a notable exception to this rule). Second, most countries are planning to reduce their ICORs, compared with their past experiences, Jamaica and Trinidad being the exceptions.

For the present projections, it has been generally assumed that attempts to change the ICOR through economic planning will in the event be only partially successful, and that the actual value of the ICOR for the projection period will be somewhere between the planned value

---

[1] See pp. 79–83.

[2] This is true, for example, of the Burmese and Ceylonese Plans and—to a lesser extent—of the Pakistan Plans. But both Pakistan and India (which also makes use of the ICOR concept for planning purposes) rely mainly on a detailed investment programme based on individual projects.

Table 8.3. *Gross incremental capital–output ratios,*
the 1950s, 1960s and 1960–1 to 1975

	Computed[a] 1950s	Plan[b] 1960s	Assumed 1960–1 to 1975
Burma	3·8	3·2[c]	3·5
Ceylon	3·4	3·0[d]	3·5
India	4·7	3·3[e]	3·5
Malaya	..	3·4	3·5
Pakistan	..	$\begin{cases} 2\cdot8^f \\ 2\cdot9^g \end{cases}$	3·0
Ghana	..	4·3	4·0
Kenya	..	3·2	3·5
Nigeria	..	3·8	3·5
Rhodesia	5·3	—	5·0
Tanzania	..	2·9	3·0
Zambia	4·3	4·0[h]	4·0
Jamaica	3·0	4·0	4·0
Trinidad and Tobago	2·9	5·0	4·5

SOURCES: *Yearbook of National Accounts Statistics, 1964*; national Economic Development Plans.

[a] For precise periods covered, see Table 3·3.
[b] For precise periods covered, see Table 6.10.
[c] Estimated from data in the Plan (corresponds to Plan figure of 2·9 for net incremental capital–output ratio).
[d] *Short-term Implementation Programme, op. cit.*, covering the three years 1961/2 to 1963/4, assumes a capital–output ratio of 3·5.
[e] 1965–70.
[f] 1960–5.
[g] 1965–70 and 1970–5. In the Outline of the third Five-Year Plan, published in 1964, the capital–output ratio for the period 1965–70 was provisionally given as 3·5.
[h] Based on data in UN/ECA/FAO Report, *op. cit.*

and the value calculated for the 1950s. This assumption was made for Burma and India though, strictly speaking, the 'planned' reduction in Burma's ICOR was more an assumption than a result of conscious planning. A similar approach was used for Trinidad, for which the change in the ICOR value assumed in the Plan reflected the government's assessment of the probable results of private investment as much as—if not more than—of planned investment in the public sector. For Ceylon, however, the ICOR taken for the projection was, in effect, that computed for the 1950s rather than the somewhat lower figure in the Ten-Year Plan,[1] while for both Jamaica and Zambia the plan ICORs have been used in the projections.

For Rhodesia the assumed ICOR has been taken as somewhat below

[1] The more recent three-year programme for Ceylon (1961/2 to 1963/4) assumes a capital–output ratio of 3·5, but envisages a reduction by the end of the programme period (*op. cit.* p. 41).

the level computed for the 1950s. There are a further six countries, both Asian and African, for which planned ICORs are available, though comparative data for the 1950s are not available; for each, the assumed ICOR has been taken as fairly close to the planned values.

The various assumptions above about the magnitude of individual country ICORs over the projection period generally appear reasonable, in view of the relative stability over time in the ratios for a number of the countries covered. It would have been possible, in principle, to make alternative assumptions concerning the future ICORs of each country, to allow for the inevitable margin of error in a calculation of this kind. While this procedure would certainly have reduced the apparent—but unreal—precision of taking a single ICOR for the projections, it would also have considerably complicated the presentation of the results. Since the main objective here is to focus attention on the effects of alternative levels of the capacity to import on the growth rate of gross domestic product (GDP), it was decided that the virtues of simplicity of presentation outweighed the disadvantages of spurious precision. In interpreting the results which follow, however, it should be borne in mind that divergencies in the country ICORs from those assumed would also significantly change the growth rates of GDP shown in the projections.

Rates of growth in gross domestic product

None of the overseas Sterling countries considered here are planning for rates of growth in their GDPs of less than 4 per cent per year, compound, while several—Ceylon, India, Pakistan, Tanzania and Zambia —are planning for growth rates of 6 per cent per year or more.[1] The majority of countries are planning to raise their rates of economic growth above those achieved in the early 1960s; for six countries— Burma, Ceylon, India, Ghana, Tanzania and Zambia—the planned increases in growth rates are very substantial. It was pointed out earlier, however, that for Burma comparisons with the Plan are somewhat artificial, since that Plan was in fact never put into operation.[2]

Of the other countries for which comparisons can be made with recent growth rates, Pakistan and Jamaica are both envisaging a modest rise in their growth rates of GDP, while for Malaya and Nigeria the planned rates are below those recently achieved. The recent achievement of Pakistan is remarkable, the sharp rise in the rate of growth since 1959 reflecting, in part, the investments made in the first Five-Year Plan period. The further acceleration in the rate of growth now

---

[1] As mentioned earlier, the current short-term target for Ceylon has been somewhat reduced, to 4·8 per cent per annum.

[2] See p. 189.

envisaged in the Pakistan Plan for the rest of the present decade relies heavily on a sharp expansion in export income and on a rapid development of the industrial sector. In Malaya, on the other hand, the process of industrialization appears to have been developing in recent years at a considerably faster rate than was envisaged in the Plan,[1] while the shortfall in the planned growth rate for Nigeria is largely attributable to the petroleum developments since the Plan was published.

Of the twelve countries for which planned growth rates are shown in Table 8.4, the present projections show rates lower than planned for seven countries, about the same as planned rates for three and higher rates than planned for the remaining two countries. These divergencies reflect, in the main, the differences in the projected export growth rates from those embodied in the Plans, and the different assumptions regarding the future net inflow of long-term capital; these differences have already been discussed in some detail in Chapters 6 and 7 respectively. To some extent, too, the divergencies from the planned rates are due to the adoption of somewhat different incremental capital–output ratios or investment elasticities from those in the Plans, but it is not likely that such differences account in general for more than a relatively small proportion of the discrepancies between the planned and projected growth rates shown.[2]

To take Pakistan as an example, the current Plan envisages a rise in the rate of growth of GDP to the region of 6 per cent per year, whereas the present projections show alternative rates of growth of about 4 to $4\frac{1}{2}$ per cent per year. The investment elasticity assumed in the projections is marginally lower than that in the third Plan (see Table 8.1), while the assumed incremental capital–output ratio is marginally higher (Table 8.3). The major differences, however, are in the much lower export projection than the planned rate of export growth, and in the lower assumed net capital inflow. If the capital inflow taken in the Plan is substituted for the alternative assumed in the projections, the projected growth rate in GDP is increased to 4·5 per cent a year on assumption A and to 4·7 per cent a year on assumption B. The greater part of the remaining 'shortfall', compared with the Plan, results from the differences in the export projections.

To the extent that the differences between the projected and planned

---

[1] The combined output of mining, manufacturing and construction rose, on average, by some 11 per cent per annum between 1960 and 1962 against the planned rate of $7\frac{1}{2}$ per cent per annum between 1960 and 1965. The higher growth rate is due entirely to the construction sector, which had virtually reached the Plan target for 1965 in 1962.

[2] The net effect of assuming different values for the incremental capital–output ratio and the investment elasticity in the projections from those envisaged in the Plans was, in particular, to lower the projected growth rates for Ceylon, India and Kenya and to raise somewhat the growth rate for Nigeria.

Table 8.4. *Rates of growth in GDP: actual, planned
and projected (percentage per annum, compound)*

	Actual		Plan[a] 1960s	Projected 1960-1 to 1975			
	1953-60	1960-4		AI	AII	BI	BII
Burma	5·4	2·1	5·0	4·0	4·2	4·1	4·3
Ceylon	3·8	3·0[b]	6·0[d]	3·8	3·9	3·9	4·0
India	3·5	4·1	{6·4[e] {6·9[f]	4·1	4·6	4·2	4·7
Malaya	4·1[c]	5·7	4·1	4·0	4·1	4·4	4·4
Pakistan	2·5	5·3	{5·9[g] {6·3[h]	3·9[i]	4·2[i]	4·1[i]	4·4[i]
Ghana	··	3·9	5·9	4·9	4·9	5·0	5·1
Kenya	··	··	5·2	3·8	3·9	3·9	4·0
Nigeria	2·7[c]	4·5[j]	4·0	4·8	5·0	5·0	5·2
Rhodesia	6·4[c]	3·6	—	4·1	4·1	4·5	4·5
Tanzania	··	3·4	6·0	5·1	5·1	5·2	5·2
Zambia	8·2[c]	3·6	6·0[k]	6·9	6·9	7·4	7·4
Jamaica	7·4	3·9[b]	5·0	5·0	5·0	5·4	5·4
Trinidad and Tobago	10·0	··	5·1	5·0	5·1	5·2	5·3

SOURCES: *Yearbook of National Accounts Statistics, 1964*; *Monthly Bulletin of Statistics*, United Nations, New York; national Economic Development Plans; Tables 8.2 and 8.3.

[a] For precise periods covered, see Table 6.10.

[b] 1960-3.

[c] 1955-60 (excluding, for Nigeria, the change from 1957 to 1958, because of non-comparability of data).

[d] For the *Short-term Implementation Programme* (1961/2 to 1963/4), the target rate of growth in GDP is put at 4·8 per cent per annum.

[e] 1960/1 to 1970/1.

[f] 1960/1 to 1975/6.

[g] 1959/60 to 1969/70.

[h] 1959/60 to 1974/5.

[i] If the net long-term capital inflow in 1975 had been taken at £220 million, as assumed in the Plan, the projected rates of growth in GDP would have been 4·5 and 4·7 per cent per annum, respectively, for assumptions A and B.

[j] 1960-2.

[k] 1960-70.

rates of growth in GDP of the various Sterling countries reflect differences in the projections of export earnings, it would be reasonable to conclude that the projections are preferable, in so far as they embody a consistent set of assumptions about the rate of economic growth in the industrial countries and about the changing commodity pattern of world trade. This does not necessarily imply that the projections for any particular country are more 'realistic' than the corresponding Plan target, since the achievement of individual countries will depend on a variety of more detailed forces operating within their economies (including changes in their socio-economic structures), as well as on the macro-economic variables of the simple growth model on which the present projections are based. The model used here is, however, of particular use in assessing the order of magnitude of the impact which specific changes in exports or in net capital inflows would have on each country's rate of growth.

As regards the effect of varying the assumption made about the average rate of growth in the industrial countries over the period up to 1975—and, consequently, varying the growth rate of exports—the projections show that, on the various assumptions of the model, a change from the lower to the higher growth assumption for the industrial countries would not raise the growth rate of GDP by as much as 0·5 per cent per annum for any of the overseas Sterling countries. For all thirteen countries covered by the projections, the (unweighted) mean increase in the growth rate of GDP which would result from a change from the lower to the higher income-growth assumption would be 0·25 per cent per annum (Table 8.4).

The countries which would benefit most, in terms of their overall rates of growth, by a move from assumption A to assumption B would be Rhodesia, Zambia and Jamaica, for all of which the increased incomes in the industrial countries would imply a rise of 0·4 per cent a year in GDP growth rates. For Kenya and Tanzania, assumption B implies a GDP growth rate of 0·3 per cent a year higher than on assumption A, while for Malaya and Ghana an increase of 0·3 per cent per annum would be achieved on the basis of one of the alternative net capital inflow assumptions. At the other extreme, only negligible benefits (an increase of only 0·1 per cent per annum in the growth rate of GDP) would result from moving from the conditions implied in assumption A to those of assumption B for Burma, Ceylon and Nigeria (as well as for India, on the less optimistic capital-inflow assumption).

The effect of varying the assumption about the net long-term capital inflow is also much more marked for some countries than for others. Easily the biggest effect is shown for India, where the higher capital inflow assumption results in an increase of 0·5 in the annual percentage growth rate of GDP compared with that based on the lower capital inflow assumption. For Pakistan and Nigeria the corresponding increases are 0·2 per cent per annum, but for all the other Sterling countries included in the calculation the increase is negligible (0·1 per cent or less).

The implication of these results appears to be that, to achieve a substantial increase in their GDP growth rates over the coming decade, most Sterling countries will require a very considerable expansion in their total foreign exchange availabilities over and above those projected here. This could come about either through an expansion in export earnings or through a much larger increase in foreign aid or through some combination of both.[1]

Effect of changes in the terms of trade on the growth rate of GDP

The export projections elaborated in Chapter 6 were based, in general, on the assumption that relative commodity prices in 1975 would not be significantly different from those in the base period, 1960–1; exceptionally, specific changes in prices over the period were assumed for a limited number of primary commodities, these assumptions affecting the projections for only three countries.[2] Equally, when the probable future movement of import prices was discussed, a general assumption had to be made that no change would occur over the projection period taken as a whole.[3]

These rather rigid assumptions were necessary for the projection exercise, since it is not possible to forecast either the direction or the extent of the likely change in import prices of individual countries over a period as long as ten to fifteen years, whilst changes in export prices— other than those assumed—are also not susceptible to any but a much more sophisticated analysis than was possible here. This is not to say, however, that changes in import and export prices are not likely to occur; merely that, with the present state of knowledge, it is not possible to predict such changes with any degree of reliability, nor even to make projections of price changes which are fully consistent with the other projections given earlier.

It is nonetheless of considerable interest to assess the effects on the capacity to import of individual countries, and thus on their projected growth rates of gross domestic product, of possible future changes in the terms of trade. Since there is a wide range of possible combinations of changes in import and export prices, several alternative combinations have been selected for illustrative purposes. As regards import prices, only two possibilities have been allowed for: either import prices in 1975 will be the same as in 1960–1 (the assumption already used in the projections) or they will be 10 per cent higher. To limit the number of alternatives, it has not been assumed that import prices will fall; this seems reasonable in the light of the discussion in Chapter 7 of recent changes in import unit values of the various Sterling countries.

For export prices, the position is somewhat more complicated, since a change in the price assumption implies a corresponding change, in

---

[1] This conclusion assumes that the ICOR and the investment ratio will not be significantly more favourable to growth than those assumed here.

[2] See p. 197.   [3] See p. 226.

the reverse direction, in the volume of exports. The relationship between the initial price change in a country's exports and the consequential change in its export volume depends on the mean price elasticity of world demand for its particular basket of export goods. While approximate magnitudes could be assigned for the mean price elasticities for a few Sterling countries, this could not be attempted generally without a major econometric analysis, which was not possible within the resources of the present study. The effect on a country's export earnings, and hence on its capacity to import and its rate of economic growth, of alternative rates of change in its export prices cannot, therefore, be estimated here. Instead, a 'second best' approach is adopted, namely to assess the effects of alternative assumptions about changes in each country's export *earnings* on its projected rates of growth in GDP. On this approach, the relative contribution of price and volume changes to the assumed changes in export earnings is irrelevant to the calculation.

Three alternative assumptions are made about future changes in export earnings, namely, that in 1975 they are the same as in the projections already made, that they exceed the projections by 10 per cent, and that they fall short of the projections by 10 per cent. For simplicity, the calculations have all been related to a single set of the earlier projections, the BII combination, which represents the most optimistic of the four sets of projections. These three alternatives on the export side have been combined with the two for import prices so that, in principle, there are six alternative combinations; however, one of these (no change in import prices, and export earnings as on assumption B) is identical with the combination underlying the BII projections of GDP. Hence, there are, in effect, five alternative combinations which yield different GDP projections from those already summarized in the last column of Table 8.4.

The results of the calculation are summarized in Table 8.5; the differences in growth rates shown are those which would result from the application of each of the five terms-of-trade assumptions to the BII projections.[1] If import prices are assumed to remain unchanged in 1975, compared with 1960–1, a 10 per cent variation—in either direction—in export earnings from those projected under assumption B would have relatively minor effects on the projected GDP growth rates for the majority of Sterling countries. Only for Rhodesia and Zambia would a 10 per cent shortfall in export earnings in 1975, compared with the levels projected under assumption B, reduce the projected rates of growth in GDP by as much as 0·4 per cent a year; for most countries, the corresponding decline would be only 0·1 or 0·2 per cent a year in

---

[1] The same investment elasticities and ICORs were used for each country as for the BII projections.

Table 8.5. *Effect of alternative assumptions about changes in the terms of trade on the projected growth rates of GDP^a (percentage per annum, compound)*

	No change in Pm		10% rise in Pm		
	10% fall in X	10% rise in X	10% fall in X	No change in X	10% rise in X
Burma	−0·1	+0·1	−0·2	−0·1	0
Ceylon	−0·2	+0·2	−0·4	−0·2	0
India	−0·2	+0·2	−0·5	−0·3	−0·1
Malaya	−0·3	+0·3	−0·6	−0·3	0
Pakistan	−0·2	+0·2	−0·4	−0·2	−0·1
Ghana	−0·2	+0·2	−0·4	−0·2	0
Kenya	−0·2	+0·2	−0·5	−0·3	−0·1
Nigeria	−0·2	+0·3	−0·4	−0·2	0
Rhodesia	−0·4	+0·2	−0·7	−0·4	−0·2
Tanzania	−0·3	+0·3	−0·6	−0·3	−0·1
Zambia	−0·4	+0·4	−0·9	−0·4	0
Jamaica	−0·2	+0·2	−0·4	−0·2	−0·1
Trinidad and Tobago	−0·2	+0·1	−0·3	−0·2	0

SOURCE: Working sheets for Table 8.4.
NOTE: Pm = import prices. X = value of exports.

^{a} The changes shown are the differences compared with the GDP growth rates on assumption BII, as shown in Table 8.4.

GDP growth rates. Similarly, a 10 per cent excess in exports above that projected would result in a rise of only 0·1 or 0·2 per cent a year for the majority of countries. Thus, the export projections could be regarded as having a margin of error of the order of 10 per cent without, in most cases, any very appreciable effect on the projected GDP growth rates.

The position is somewhat different, of course, if import prices are assumed to rise simultaneously with a shortfall in export earnings compared with the projected levels. As can be seen from Table 8.5, a 10 per cent shortfall in export earnings, if combined with a 10 per cent rise in import prices, would have fairly serious adverse effects on the GDP growth rates for a number of countries, assuming no change in the parameters of the model. Thus, on these assumptions, the projected growth rates of GDP would be reduced by nearly 1 per cent a year for Zambia, and by ½ per cent a year or rather more for India, Malaya, Kenya, Rhodesia and Tanzania. This would represent a considerable loss in real income for these countries when cumulated over the whole period up to 1975.[1]

[1] In 1975 alone, this adverse combination of assumptions about export earnings and import prices would imply a shortfall of about 9 to 11 per cent in the gross domestic products of

If a similar rise, 10 per cent, in import prices occured in combination with the achievement of the export projections as under assumption B, the adverse effects on the GDP growth rates would be roughly only one-half of those under the more adverse combination just discussed. If, however, export earnings in 1975 are assumed to exceed the projected levels by 10 per cent, then the adverse impact of a similar percentage rise in import prices on the growth rate of GDP would be fully offset for about half the countries considered, but there would still remain a net adverse effect—though a marginal one—for the other countries.[1]

Rates of growth in gross domestic product per head

The projected GDP growth rates can be shown on a *per caput* basis by adjusting them for probable future trends in total population. For this purpose, the 'medium' projections issued in 1963 by the United Nations have been used. These show widely divergent population growth rates for the various overseas Sterling countries; generally speaking, the less developed countries appear likely to face substantially higher rates of population growth over the coming decade than the more developed. Among the thirteen countries shown in Table 8.6, there are ten whose future population growth is projected at $2\frac{1}{2}$ per cent per annum or higher (including four countries whose population is estimated to grow by at least 3 per cent per annum). The exceptionally low population projection for Jamaica appears to have been made in 1957, and presumably assumes a relatively high level of emigration; this would now appear to be an unlikely assumption unless the recent British restrictions on immigration are lifted or, at least, substantially liberalized.[2]

The projected growth rates in GDP per head vary according to the assumptions made in much the same way as those for total GDP which were discussed above. The *per caput* growth rates are of course considerably lower than those for total GDP for the majority of countries. Comparing the projections with recent achievements, it can be seen from Table 8.6 that for most of the eleven countries for which the comparison can be made, the projected growth rates in GDP per head are higher—in some cases substantially higher—than those achieved in the early 1960s; in the other Sterling countries a retardation, compared with

Rhodesia, Tanzania and Zambia compared with the projected BII levels. For India, Malaya and Kenya the corresponding shortfalls in 1975 would be in the region of 5 to 7 per cent.

[1] The reason why a given increase in import prices has a greater impact on the growth of GDP than an equivalent percentage change in exports is that changes in import prices affect the purchasing power over imports of net capital borrowings as well as of exports.

[2] A substantially higher rate of population growth in Jamaica than that projected by the United Nations, or assumed in the Jamaican Plan (2·0 per cent per annum), would have important implications for the pattern and speed of economic growth in that country. No allowance for such implications could, however, be made in the present projections.

Table 8.6. *Rates of growth in GDP per head: actual and projected (percentage per annum, compound)*

	Actual		Projected 1960–1 to 1975				Estimated population growth rate 1960–1 to 1975[a]
	1953–60	1960–4	AI	AII	BI	BII	
Burma	4·4	−1·9	1·5	1·7	1·6	1·8	2·5
Ceylon	1·2	0·2[b]	0·6	0·7	0·7	0·8	3·1
India	1·4	1·6	1·7	2·3	1·9	2·3	2·3
Malaya	0·9[c]	2·6	1·0	1·1	1·4	1·4	3·0
Pakistan	0·4	3·1	1·2[d]	1·5[d]	1·4[d]	1·7[d]	2·7
Ghana	..	1·3	1·9	1·9	2·0	2·1	3·0
Kenya	..	..	0·9	1·0	1·0	1·1	2·5
Nigeria	0·0	2·5[e]	2·1	2·2	2·3	2·4	2·8
Rhodesia	0·1	0·4	0·7	0·7	1·1	1·1	3·4
Tanzania	..	1·6	2·9	2·9	3·0	3·0	2·1
Zambia	5·3	0·7	3·9	3·9	4·4	4·4	2·9
Jamaica	6·8	3·6[b]	3·5	3·5	3·8	3·8	1·5
Trinidad and Tobago	6·9	..	2·1	2·2	2·2	2·3	2·9

SOURCES: Table 8.4; *Provisional Report on World Population Prospects, as assessed in 1963*, United Nations, New York, 1964.

[a] United Nations estimate, 'medium' variant.
[b] 1960–3.
[c] 1955–60.
[d] If the net long-term capital inflow in 1975 had been taken at £220 million, the projected rates of growth in GDP per head would have been 1·7 and 2·0 per cent per annum, respectively, for assumptions A and B.
[e] 1960–2.

recent rates of growth, is projected. The major increases projected in *per caput* real product, compared with the early 1960s, are for Tanzania and Zambia; for Burma and Ceylon, the increases projected, though modest, would if achieved represent a significant advance from the stagnation of recent years. The major decline in the growth rate of GDP per head is projected for Pakistan; had the Plan figure for net long-term capital inflow been used, the projected rates would be higher by approximately 0·5 per cent per annum, though they would still amount to only one-half the recent rapid achievement. The main reasons for this difference have already been discussed.

Taking the most favourable combination of assumptions (i.e. BII), two-thirds of the countries (ten out of thirteen) are projected as having growth rates in *per caput* GDP of under 2½ per cent a year; only one country—Zambia—is projected to exceed 4 per cent a year. Since the present average level of real product per head in the majority of the less developed overseas Sterling countries is relatively low, the projected rates of growth shown in Table 8.6 are hardly likely to result in a dramatic rise in living standards during the period up to 1975. In 1960–1, the average GDP per head was only £20 to 30 in Burma, India, Pakistan, Kenya, Nigeria and Tanzania, of the countries included in the present calculations. These six countries together had a population of some 610 million, or about 90 per cent of the total population of all less developed Sterling countries. Relatively well-to-do among the latter are Jamaica and Trinidad, with £145 and £225 per head respectively in 1960–1, though both these Caribbean countries are still in the early phases of economic development. Average levels of GDP per head in Malaya, Ghana, Rhodesia and Zambia were in the region of £60–90 in 1960–1; these, though low by the standards of the more developed Sterling countries,[1] are still way above those in the poorest group (see Table 8.7).

If the projected growth rates in GDP per head are applied to the actual levels of *per caput* gross product in 1960–1, estimates of *per caput* levels which would be achieved in 1975, on the various assumptions made, can be obtained. These are also shown in Table 8.7. This calculation shows that, on either the least favourable (AI), or the most favourable (BII), of the assumptions made here, there would not be any dramatic improvement in the average real product (or real income) per head in the majority of these countries over the coming decade. In 1960–1, nine of the thirteen countries had an average GDP per head below £75. By 1975, the corresponding number would have fallen to seven countries, whether the AI or the BII assumption is used; moreover, at that date, six countries are unlikely to have exceeded the £50 per head level.

In order to reach a minimum target level, which is put here at £100 per head, these countries will require a considerable increase in their current rates of economic growth. As can be seen from Table 8.7, both Burma and Tanzania would require growth rates in their *per caput* GDP of 11 per cent or more per annum, whereas their recent performance has been one of relative stagnation. Similarly, sharp increases in performance would be required from Ceylon, India, probably Kenya, and Nigeria and even Pakistan. To achieve this minimum target a decade later, would, of course, allow the required growth rates to be considerably reduced. The round figure of £100 per head is purely an arbitrary objective, taken for illustrative purposes. It is almost certainly too low

---

[1] Average GDP per head in Australia in 1960–1 was about £710, and in New Zealand about £665.

Table 8.7. *Required rates of growth in GDP per head*

	GDP per head			Growth rate required to reach £100 per head by		Date by which GDP would reach £100 per head	
	1960–1	1975		1975	1985	AI	BII
		AI	BII				
	(£)	(£)	(£)	(% per annum, compound)			
Burma	22	25–30	25–30	11·0	6·4	2060	2050
Ceylon	45	50	50	5·7	3·3	2110	2085
India	27	35	35–40	9·5	5·5	2040	2015
Malaya	88	100	105	0·9	0·5	1975	1970
Pakistan	27	30–35	35	9·5	5·5	2080[a]	2045[a]
Ghana	72	95	90–95	2·3	1·4	1980	1980
Kenya	28	30–35	35	9·2	5·3	2150	2080
Nigeria	28[b]	35	35–40	9·2	5·3	2030	2020
Rhodesia	79	85–90	90–95	1·6	1·0	1995	1985
Tanzania	21	30	30–35	11·4	6·6	2020	2015
Zambia	63	110	120	3·2	1·9	1970	1970
Jamaica	145	240	250	..	..	..	..
Trinidad and Tobago	225	300	310	..	..	..	..

SOURCES: *Yearbook of National Accounts Statistics, 1964*; Table 8.6.

[a] If the growth rate of GDP based on the capital inflow assumed in the third Five-Year Plan had been used, the dates by which Pakistan would reach an average GDP per head of £100 would be 2035 on assumption A, 2030 on assumption B.

[b] Value at 1957 prices; population not adjusted to basis of later census total.

as a general indicator of the threshold of self-sustained economic growth; yet even this very minimal figure seems out of reach of many countries if their current or projected growth rates cannot be sharply raised.

If the rates of growth in *per caput* GDP projected for the period up to 1975 are assumed to continue indefinitely thereafter, then the minimum £100 per head target would not be achieved by Burma and Pakistan, for example, until the middle of the next century, while if the least optimistic assumptions remained valid—obviously a purely illustrative hypothesis—then it would take Ceylon and Kenya into the early part of the twenty-second century to reach the minimum target. Of the eleven less developed Sterling countries with present *per caput* GDP below £100, only four—Malaya, Ghana, Rhodesia and Zambia—would reach this target level before the end of the present century if their projected growth were to continue unchanged.

3. *EX ANTE* AND *EX POST* MARGINAL PROPENSITIES TO IMPORT AND TO SAVE

The model used to obtain these statistical results is based on a number of assumptions, a major one being that domestic savings are a residual in the system. It was suggested earlier that, as a check on the internal consistency of the model as applied to particular countries, the residual savings requirement implied in the results of the model for the target year can be compared with an estimate of the savings that would have accrued in that year on the basis of an assumed *ex ante* relationship between the future growth in savings and in income.[1] A further consistency check on the results obtained would be a comparison of the level of imports in the target year as shown by the model with the estimated level that would be achieved given the continuance of an appropriate *ex ante* marginal propensity to import. Both these comparisons are attempted here for as many as possible of the Sterling countries included in the projections.

Marginal propensities to import

The *ex post* growth model used here assumes that imports in the target year are necessarily equal in value to the capacity to import, defined as total credits on current and long-term capital account in the balance of payments at base period (1960–1 average) import prices. The change in the capacity to import thus determines the change in the value of imports of goods and services, and hence the (implied) *ex post* marginal propensity to import. These propensities have been computed for each of the overseas Sterling countries covered by the projections for the period 1960–1 to 1975, distinguishing each of the four projections of the capacity to import (see Table 8.8).

It is not, however, an easy task to determine the corresponding *ex ante* magnitudes of the propensity to import. The first column of Table 8.8 shows the corresponding import propensities for various periods in the 1950s for a number of countries for which the appropriate data are available; but these coefficients, derived from regression equations, are *ex post*, not *ex ante*, values. On the other hand, the propensities derived from intended imports and income levels embodied in Development Plans do come much nearer to the concept of an *ex ante* community propensity (see second column of Table 8.8). These import propensities are sometimes explicit in the Development Plans, but usually they are implicit. Most of the planned propensities—which apply to varying periods during the 1960s—differ significantly from the *ex post* propensities of the preceding decade; for the five less developed countries for

---

[1] See pp. 64–6.

Table 8.8. *The marginal propensity to import:[a]*
computed, planned and projected

	Computed[b] 1950s	Plan[c] 1960s	Assumed ex ante 1960–1 to 1975	Projected ex post 1960–1 to 1975[d]			
				AI	AII	BI	BII
Burma	0·15	0·03	0·10–0·15	0·07	0·09	0·09	0·11
Ceylon	0·46	0·07	0·05–0·10	0·06	0·08	0·08	0·09
India	0·13	0·03[e]	0·03–0·05	0·04	0·05	0·04	0·06
Malaya	..	0·35	0·30–0·40	0·21	0·22	0·26	0·27
Pakistan	..	0·11	0·10	0·05	0·07	0·07	0·08
Ghana	..	0·33[f]	0·20–0·25	0·12	0·13	0·17	0·18
Kenya	..	0·27	0·25–0·30	0·23	0·26	0·31	0·33
Nigeria	..	0·21[g]	0·25	0·35	0·37	0·36	0·39
Rhodesia	..	—	—	0·27	0·27	0·30	0·30
Tanzania	..	0·35	0·35	0·23	0·23	0·26	0·26
Zambia	..	0·52	0·50	0·61	0·61	0·65	0·65
Jamaica	0·39	0·24	0·25	0·30	0·30	0·38	0·38
Trinidad and Tobago	0·67	0·38	0·40	0·26	0·30	0·34	0·38

SOURCES: *Yearbook of National Accounts Statistics, 1964*; national Economic Development Plans; Tables 7.9 and 8.4.

[a] Goods and services.
[b] For precise periods covered, see Table 3.8.
[c] For precise periods covered, see Table 6.10.
[d] Assuming entire increase projected in foreign exchange availabilities between 1960–1 and 1975 is spent on imports of goods and services.
[e] 1960–1 to 1970–1 (the same marginal propensity also applies to the draft Plan for the following quinquennium).
[f] For Plan period 1963/4 to 1969/70. If the Plan figures for 1969/70 are compared with the average of the years 1960–2, however, the marginal propensity to import would be only 0·22 (there was virtually no increase in imports between 1960–2 and 1963–4, though GDP rose by about 10 per cent).
[g] Imports of merchandise only.

which comparison can be made, the plans envisage in each case a substantial reduction in the propensity to import, based essentially on proposed extensions of import substitution by increasing domestic production.

The third column of Table 8.8 shows what are intended to be reasonable assumptions about the magnitude of the *ex ante* marginal import propensities in each of the Sterling countries for the period up to 1975. These assumed values are based essentially on the implicit or explicit import propensities in the current Development Plans, where these exist, except that, where the planned propensities appear to be unusually low as judged by the *ex post* values for the 1950s, it has generally been assumed that the *ex ante* values are somewhere between the official plan figures and the *ex post* calculations.

On this admittedly rather tenuous basis it would appear that, generally speaking, there is a fairly close correspondence between the *ex post* marginal import propensities implied in the model and the assumed *ex ante* propensities (see Fig. 8.1). For the majority of the countries included, the *ex post* marginal import propensities are somewhat below the corresponding assumed *ex ante* values, implying that

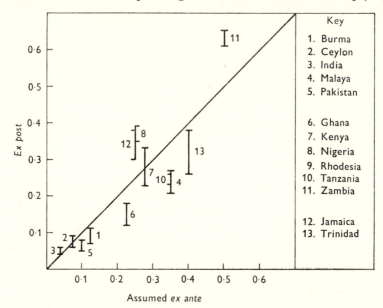

SOURCE: Table 8.8.

NOTE: The mid-point of the *ex ante* values has been plotted against the range of the *ex post* values.

Fig. 8.1. Relation between assumed *ex ante* and residual *ex post* marginal propensities to import.

imports into these countries would need to be restricted by government action if external equilibrium is to be achieved. For three countries, however, namely, Jamaica, Nigeria and Zambia, the reverse position is indicated, the *ex post* marginal import propensity exceeding the corresponding assumed *ex ante* propensities. This could imply that, for these three countries, growth would not be trade-constrained, at the rates of growth projected for them; if so, the model would be inapplicable to these countries. For Nigeria and Zambia, however, economic growth over the projection period may well imply a substantial structural shift in the character of the demand for imports—particularly in favour of plant and equipment for mineral industries—which might result in an upward change in the average import propensity over the projection period. Nonetheless, the possibility of growth in these three countries being effectively constrained by the availability of savings rather than of foreign exchange must be borne in mind.

Marginal propensities to save

Gross domestic savings in 1975, valued at 1960–1 prices, can be derived residually by deducting the assumed totals of long-term net capital inflow in that year from the corresponding estimates of gross domestic capital formation. Since the investment variable in the model relates to fixed capital assets, an assumption had to be made as regards investment in stocks. For all the countries included, the ratio of stock accumulation to fixed investment in 1975 was assumed to be the same as in the early 1960s; since fixed investment represents the preponderant part of total investment, it is unlikely that this (arbitrary) assumption could appreciably distort the results of the calculation.

The treatment of short-term capital movements in the balance of payments is somewhat of a difficulty, especially where such movements were relatively large in the base period. However, the model assumes implicitly that there will be no significant changes in short-term capital (including monetary reserves) in 1975; this follows from the form of relationship used between the capacity to import and the level of investment. Thus, it is logically consistent in the context of this model to assume that gross domestic savings correspond *ex post* to the difference between gross domestic capital formation and the net inflow of long-term capital from abroad.

The *ex post* marginal savings propensities calculated in this way are shown in Table 8.9 for eleven less developed countries for which the calculation could be made. Also shown in this table are computed marginal savings propensities for varying periods during the 1950s, and the marginal savings ratios embodied, usually implicitly, in the current Economic Development Plans. The Plans for most of the Asian and African countries envisage relatively high savings propensities compared with those for the Caribbean countries, and this asymmetry has been generally followed in deciding upon what might be reasonable estimates of the *ex ante* savings propensities.

Among the four Asian countries for which *ex ante* savings propensities could reasonably be assumed,[1] these were all appreciably higher than the

---

[1] No assumption was made for Malaya in view of the apparent negative value of the *ex ante* savings propensity in the Plan. The negative value reflects the abnormal position in the Plan's base period, Malaya having a substantial balance of payments surplus on current account in 1962.

Table 8.9. *The marginal propensity to save:*
computed, planned and projected

	Computed[a] 1950s	Plan[b] 1960s	Assumed ex ante 1960-1 to 1975	Projected ex post, 1960-1 to 1975			
				AI	AII	BI	BII
Burma	0·20	0·26	0·20–0·25	0·00	0·00	0·02	0·00
Ceylon	..	0·28	0·20–0·30	0·07	0·07	0·08	0·07
India	0·32	{0·29[c] 0·25[d]	0·25–0·30	0·13	0·18	0·16	0·20
Malaya	..	−0·08	..	0·09	0·08	0·14	0·12
Pakistan	0·15	0·22[e]	0·17–0·20	0·10[f]	0·10[f]	0·13[f]	0·13[f]
Ghana	..	0·29	0·25–0·30	0·15	0·15	0·18	0·17
Nigeria	..	0·20[g]	0·20	0·21	0·17	0·22	0·18
Rhodesia	0·34	—	0·30–0·35	0·26	0·26	0·30	0·30
Zambia	0·57	0·34[h]	0·35–0·40	0·43	0·43	0·45	0·45
Jamaica	0·15	0·15	0·15	0·19	0·17	0·23	0·22
Trinidad and Tobago	0·22	0·10	0·10–0·15	0·08	0·00	0·11	0·04

SOURCES: Tables 3.10 and 7.7: national Economic Development Plans; *Yearbook of National Accounts Statistics, 1964*; *World Economic Survey, Part I, 1964*, United Nations, New York, 1965.

[a] For precise periods covered, see Table 3.8.
[b] For precise periods covered, see Table 6.10.
[c] 1960/1 to 1970/1.
[d] 1960/1 to 1975/6.
[e] 1965/6 to 1970/1.
[f] If the Plan assumption of foreign aid is used, the *ex post* propensities become 0·13, 0·12, 0·15 and 0·15, respectively.
[g] Approximate (derived as implicit propensity from the Plan figures for gross capital formation and balance of payments deficit).
[h] Based on assumption of higher tax rates than in 1963; on basis of 1963 tax rates, the (implicit) *ex ante* marginal savings propensity would be 0·17.

corresponding *ex post* values. For Burma and Ceylon the discrepancies are due to what now appear to be over-optimistic projections of the rate of growth in GDP, and thus in domestic savings. For India the main element in the difference is probably the lower rate of export growth taken in the present set of projections, compared with the more optimistic Plan figures, while for Pakistan the difference reflects both the more modest export growth projected here (compared with the Plan) and also the appreciably lower level of foreign aid assumed. If foreign aid received by Pakistan is taken at the Plan level, then the *ex post* savings propensity rises to 0·15 on the BII basis.

Of the other countries[1] shown in Table 8.9, the *ex ante* assumptions

[1] Reliable estimates of the *ex post* values of the marginal propensity to save could not be made for Kenya and Tanzania in view of the lack of relevant data for the base period used in the projections.

are very close to the *ex post* residuals for Nigeria and Rhodesia, but for Ghana and Trinidad the *ex post* propensities are appreciably lower than what might have been expected on the basis of no change in tax policies, compared with those envisaged in the current Plans. For Jamaica and Zambia, on the other hand, the *ex post* values are somewhat above the assumed *ex ante* values, thus implying that domestic savings would be the effective constraint on economic growth in these countries. This

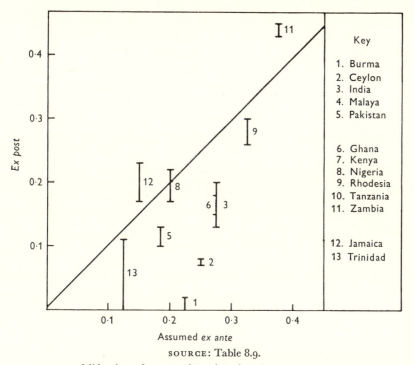

SOURCE: Table 8.9.

NOTE: Mid-points of *ex ante* values plotted against range of *ex post* values.

Fig. 8.2. Relation between assumed *ex ante* and residual
ex post marginal propensities to save.

result for Jamaica and Zambia is consistent with the excess of the residual *ex post* over the assumed *ex ante* import propensity for these two countries which was discussed above. For Nigeria, the savings propensity test was, however, inconsistent with the result of the import propensity test.

For Jamaica and Zambia, possibly also for Nigeria, these results indicate that the *ex ante* savings gap exceeds the *ex ante* trade gap, at the respective projected rates of economic growth. This, in turn, would imply that these growth rates would not, in the event, be achieved unless the shortfall in domestic savings was made good by increased foreign aid above the level assumed.

For the majority of the Sterling countries for which the savings propensity test could be made, however, the *ex ante* and *ex post* values were near enough to imply that no policy changes, in addition to those already embodied in the relevant economic plans, would be required to bring them into equilibrium. For most of these countries the *ex post* savings propensities are considerably below the levels which could reasonably be expected, thus implying that an appreciable proportion of intended saving in these countries would, in the event, be frustrated if the conditions of the *ex post* model are satisfied.[1] There are, of course, other policy options involved, apart from changing tax rates in order to discourage domestic savings. One alternative would be to change the investment programme so as effectively to increase the investment elasticity (with respect to the capacity to import);[2] this would increase the total gross domestic capital formation and, *ceteris paribus*, the *ex post* level of savings. It would not necessarily increase the growth rate of GDP—or, at least, not appreciably—since one would expect, in these circumstances, an offsetting rise in the incremental capital–output ratio, so that the *ex ante* level of savings would not increase.

An alternative approach would be to expand exports above the levels projected here. For most countries the investment elasticities are sufficiently high for an increase in exports to result in a rise in the residual *ex post* savings requirement, though for some countries there might be a certain 'offset' here in the form of higher *ex ante* savings.

4. FOREIGN AID AND EXPORT TARGETS

The implications of the various projections discussed in preceding sections of this chapter are, as already mentioned, that most of the less developed Sterling countries would require a very substantial increase in their total foreign exchange availabilities over and above those already projected, if they are to achieve a reasonable minimum level of real income per head in the not too distant future.[3] An alternative way of posing an economic 'target' would be in terms of the annual rate of growth in GDP or in GDP per head. The United Nations General Assembly resolution of 1960 called for the attainment by the developing countries of a minimum annual growth rate in national income of 5 per cent by the end of the present decade. This objective could be reached

---

[1] See p. 65.

[2] This could be done by intensifying import substitution in the capital goods industries and/or by reducing the 'consumer content' of imports.

[3] See pp. 246–7.

even though many countries fell far below the 5 per cent rate, provided the fall was offset by other developing countries considerably exceeding that rate.

Because the United Nations target was posed for the developing countries taken as a group, it is not strictly applicable to the less developed overseas Sterling countries, either in total or individually. Nonetheless it seems of interest, in connection with the aims of the United Nations resolution, to consider the implications of a conscious decision to bring the slow-growing countries in the Sterling Area up to the minimum of a 5 per cent per annum growth rate in their gross domestic product. This is, in principle, a more ambitious target than that enunciated by the United Nations, for two reasons. First, as already indicated, it implies an *average* growth rate of GDP in excess of 5 per cent per annum for the less developed Sterling countries taken together. Second, the United Nations objective envisaged an acceleration in the rate of growth of the developing countries, reaching the 5 per cent target rate only by 1970. The *ex post* growth model used here is, however, based on the assumption of a constant rate of growth over the projection period up to 1975: a constant, or average, 5 per cent rate of growth over the whole period clearly represents a higher level of economic achievement than one which reaches the same target at the end, or at least in the latter part, of the period. Given the form of the model, however, the adoption of a minimum 5 per cent growth rate is the nearest approach that can be made here to the spirit underlying the United Nations objective.

A further way of posing a general target would be in terms of the rate of growth in GDP per head. As an alternative to the minimum 5 per cent growth rate in GDP, the implications of a minimum $2\frac{1}{2}$ per cent growth rate in GDP per head have also been explored.[1] These two targets are virtually identical for the less developed Sterling countries in aggregate—since the estimated rate of growth in their total population is close to $2\frac{1}{2}$ per cent for the period from 1960 to 1975—but the targets can differ appreciably for countries with relatively high, or relatively low, rates of population increase.

Given these alternative target growth rates, the implications for the capacity to import can be derived from the *ex post* model used earlier, on the basis of the same assumptions as before concerning the investment elasticity and the incremental capital–output ratio in each country. The increase in the capacity to import, over and above the levels projected earlier, that would be required to achieve the target rates of growth in

---

[1] It could, of course, be argued that supporting a minimum growth rate in GDP per head automatically absolves the country concerned from taking positive measures to reduce its rate of population growth.

GDP, or in GDP per head, on the assumptions of the model, can be taken as being met essentially by an increase in the level of foreign aid, or by an increase in merchandise exports, compared with the projected levels, or by some combination of the two. The remainder of this section explores some of the implications of increased aid and increased exports.

Foreign aid requirements

It is convenient, to begin with, to assume that the entire burden of achieving the required increase in foreign exchange availability falls upon foreign aid (taken here to mean 'net official capital inflows'). However, as was seen earlier,[1] a significant proportion of aid takes the form of loans on which interest falls due; and this additional interest must be allowed for in calculating the additional net aid requirement. The problem can be avoided if it is assumed that the additional aid is given solely in the form of grants, but it seems unlikely that this would in fact be so. A reasonable alternative assumption, which is the one used here, would be to divide the additional aid requirement for each country over the projection period into grants and loans in the same proportion as was its total official capital inflow in a recent period (taken here as the average for 1962 and 1963).[2] On this basis, and assuming also that the additional loan requirement bears interest at 3 per cent per annum on average, the required net inflow of official capital into each of the less developed Sterling countries in 1975 can be calculated.

The results (Table 8.10) show that, for the thirteen countries covered by the calculations, the net official capital inflow required to achieve an average rate of growth of 5 per cent per annum in GDP would have to be nearly double the level in 1975 of that assumed in the more optimistic projection (i.e. assumption II). To achieve a minimum growth rate of $2\frac{1}{2}$ per cent per annum in GDP per head, the required capital inflow in 1975 would, in total, amount to almost two and a half times the more optimistic projection level. Compared with actual official capital inflows in recent years, the required levels for 1975 are even more striking: for the 5 per cent GDP growth target, required capital inflows amount to three and a half times the 1962–3 total, while for the $2\frac{1}{2}$ per cent GDP per head target, they are four and a half times that total.[3]

The largest percentage increases, comparing required capital inflows

[1] See p. 203 and Table 7.1.

[2] In fact the proportion of grants in the total flow of official capital to the less developed countries has been falling in recent years but at the same time average interest rates on loans have also fallen.

[3] To the extent that economic growth in certain countries (Jamaica, Zambia and, possibly, Nigeria) is savings-constrained, the calculation of the required level of capital inflow is an underestimate, on the basis of the growth targets used.

Table 8.10. *Net inflow of official capital into less developed Sterling countries, 1960–3 and assumed and required levels in 1975 (£ million)*

| | Actual | | Assumed level in 1975 | | Required levels in 1975[a] | |
	1960–1	1962–3	I	II	For 5 % p.a. growth rate in GDP	For 2½ % p.a. growth rate in GDP per head
Burma	6	10	25	40	145	155
Ceylon	5	7	5	10	155	245
India	260	280	385	685	835	755
Malaya	7	14	2	4	160	295
Pakistan	74	140	75	130	275	325
Sub-total	352	451	492	869	1,570	1,775
Ghana	47	18	2	4	35	100
Kenya	..	17[b]	5	10	75	70
Nigeria	37	21	45	75	110	205
Rhodesia	7	½	½	1	45	125
Tanzania	12[c]	..	10	15	15[d]	15[d]
Zambia	1	1	½	1	1[d]	1[d]
Sub-total	104[e]	58[f]	63	106	280	515
Jamaica	2½	2½	0	0	0[d]	0[d]
Trinidad and Tobago	−1	−1	0	0	0	30
TOTAL	458[e]	510[f]	555	975	1,850	2,320

SOURCES: *Balance of Payments Yearbook*, vol. 15, 1964; Tables 7.4, 8.1, 8.3, 8.4, 8.6 and 8.7.

[a] Assuming exports rise at the higher of the two projected rates (assumption B).
[b] 1963.
[c] 1961.
[d] Assumed to be the same as for assumption II (arithmetically, however, the calculation would yield negative amounts of net official capital inflow for these countries).
[e] Excluding Kenya.
[f] Excluding Tanzania.

with those assumed in the projections, are for those countries (such as Burma and Ceylon) for which exports are projected to grow relatively slowly; or for those countries (such as Malaya and Rhodesia) which have hitherto relied on private, not official, sources for their foreign capital inflow. For India, the required level of aid in 1975 would be £755 or £835 million, according to the growth target selected, or two and a half to three times the 1962–3 average.[1] For Pakistan, the required

---

[1] As mentioned earlier (see p. 212), the Indian draft Perspective Plan assumed a tapering off in foreign aid to zero by 1975–6.

aid level would be two to two and a half times the 1962–3 average. India and Pakistan taken together account for one-half of the increase in foreign aid requirements (about £700 million out of £1,325 million, on the 5 per cent GDP basis) compared with the 1962–3 total of rather more than £500 million; on the 2½ per cent GDP per head basis, India and Pakistan account for under two-fifths of the required increase in aid (£660 million out of about £1,800 million), comparing the 1975 target with actual levels in 1962–3.

The solution of the foreign exchange problems of the less developed countries by relying solely on an appropriate increase in grants and loans from the richer countries would also bring with it a substantial increase in the burden of debt service. Even the more modest levels of foreign capital inflow assumed in the projections given earlier implied very appreciable increases for many countries in the proportion of their net factor payments abroad to their total export earnings.[1] There are several possible approaches that might, in principle, be considered in order to limit this interest burden. One might be to place an upper limit on the proportion which interest and dividend payments represented of total export earnings. Another approach might be to reduce the average rate of interest on foreign official loans below the usual market rate. In either case, the lending governments or financial institutions would bear a loss, and new internationally agreed provisions would need to be made to meet this loss, presumably through the establishment of a new international financial agency.[2]

To illustrate the possible orders of magnitude involved, the two cases mentioned have been quantified, in terms of the previous projections for the less developed Sterling countries, by assuming (1) that net factor payments abroad are limited to 10 per cent of total earnings from exports of goods and services (any additional amount over this limit being provided from a special international fund) and (2) that, as an alternative, the average rate of interest on official loans is reduced to 1½ per cent (the difference between this rate and the market rate being made good by the new international financial agency).

As can be seen from Table 8.11, the more optimistic of the assumptions made earlier about net capital flows in 1975 (i.e. assumption II), implies a very wide range of proportions of net factor payments to total earnings from exports of goods and services in 1975. At one extreme would be India and Trinidad, with estimated proportions of nearly one-quarter, followed by Kenya (one-sixth), and Nigeria and Rhodesia

---

[1] See pp. 223–4.

[2] The second case mentioned here corresponds in principle to the 'Horowitz Proposal', made by Dr D. Horowitz, Governor, Bank of Israel, in his second address before the UNCTAD Committee on Invisibles and Financing Related to Trade, Geneva, December 1965.

(one-eighth); at the other extreme, the proportion for Ceylon would be relatively very small.[1] On the various assumptions made, eight out of the thirteen countries listed in Table 8.11 would have their proportions of net factor payments to total exports at least as high as 10 per cent by 1975. The application of the 10 per cent ceiling would save them some £200 million in that year, of which over £135 million (two-thirds) would accrue to India; Trinidad and Nigeria would also gain appreciable amounts.

On the alternative basis, that the average interest charged on official loans is reduced to 1½ per cent (from the 3 per cent assumed in the projections), the total foreign exchange savings to the countries listed in Table 8.11 would be about £125 million in 1975, of which £90 million (nearly three-quarters) would accrue to India. The remainder would be distributed among seven other countries.

The possible implications of such foreign exchange savings for the rates of economic growth of the various less developed countries can be assessed by using the same *ex post* growth model as before. The reduction in net factor payments abroad resulting from the assumed application of a ceiling of 10 per cent in relation to total export receipts, or of a reduction to 1½ per cent in the interest on official loans, has been assumed to be entirely devoted to increasing the capacity to import (and thus the imports of capital equipment) of each of the countries concerned. The implied increases in the growth rates of GDP can then be computed, using the same investment elasticities and incremental capital–output ratios as before.

The results (Table 8.11) show that the assumed reductions in net factor payments abroad would have significant beneficial effects on the rate of growth of GDP for only a few of the countries concerned. The application of an upper limit of 10 per cent of total exports would increase the annual growth rate of GDP in 1975 by 0·2 or 0·3 per cent for India, Kenya and Trinidad (above the rates implied on assumption B II), but for the other countries the corresponding increases would be between zero and 0·1 per cent. It is of some interest to note that the increase in the growth rate for India resulting from limiting net factor payments to 10 per cent of exports would just offset the loss that would arise should import prices in 1975 be 10 per cent higher than assumed in the projections (see Table 8.5). For Kenya, the gain from the limitation on net factor payments would be of the same order of magnitude as a 10 per cent rise in exports above the projected level for 1975, while for

---

[1] This is because of the earlier assumption that the proportion of grants to loans in 1975 would be similar to that in 1962–3 (when Ceylon did not have much foreign assistance in the form of loans). If, however, any additional capital inflow was mainly in loan form, the interest burden would rise substantially by 1975.

Table 8.11. *Effect on rate of growth of GDP of alternative reductions in net factor payments abroad*

	Net factor payments as proportion of exports[a]			Reduction in net factor payments if limited to		Increase in growth rate of GDP	
	1960–1	1962–3	1975 BII	10% of exports[a]	Interest at 1½%	10% of exports[a]	Interest at 1½%
	(%)	(%)	(%)	(£ million)		(% per annum)	
Burma	1·1	0·0	4·5	—	2	—	0·0
Ceylon	2·1	2·8	2·8	—	1	—	0·0
India	6·5	9·1	23·3	137	90	0·3	0·2
Malaya	9·4	7·5	10·8	6	—	0·0	..
Pakistan	1·1	5·0	11·8	6	10	0·0	0·1
Ghana	5·5	6·9	7·7	—	7	—	0·1
Kenya	..	11·3	15·6	9	2	0·2	0·0
Nigeria	2·3	3·2	11·2	13	9	0·1	0·1
Rhodesia	14·5	17·7	12·5	4	—	0·1	—
Tanzania	5·0	4·5	12·5	2	3	0·0	0·0
Zambia	16·7	17·1	9·4	—	—	—	—
Jamaica	10·0	..	9·8	—	0	—	0·0
Trinidad and Tobago	16·9	..	23·5	28	0	0·3	0·0

SOURCES: As for Table 8.10.

[a] Exports of goods and services.

Trinidad the corresponding gain would be equal in magnitude to the loss which would result if import prices were 10 per cent higher and export earnings 10 per cent lower than projected.

On the alternative assumption, that official loans bear interest at only 1½ per cent a year, India would be the only country whose growth rate would increase, on the various assumptions made, by more than 0·1 per cent a year.

The limitation of interest and dividends on foreign debt could be arranged, in principle, in a number of alternative ways. The illustrative calculations summarized in Table 8.11 indicate that such limitation could well benefit the rate of economic growth of certain countries, provided that the financial savings made were devoted to increasing the capacity to import (and thus the import of development goods) of the countries concerned. However, the resulting increases in growth rates of GDP would be unlikely to be more than marginal, even in countries such as India which are heavily dependent on official borrowing from abroad. The limitation of interest and dividend payments made by less developed countries, whilst easing their external financial difficulties, and to that extent being worthy of support, cannot thus be expected *in itself* to bridge the gap between the projected and the target rates of economic growth for the majority of the less developed Sterling countries.

Export requirements

The alternative approach to financing the foreign exchange gaps projected for individual countries in 1975 is to assume that they will be financed solely by an expansion of exports over and above the levels projected. This 'residual' calculation then gives the level of exports required for external equilibrium at the end of the projection period. The results of the calculation, based on the same parameters as previously used in the *ex post* model, are summarized in Table 8.12; the calculation takes the higher level of net capital inflow in 1975 (assumption II) as the basis.

Total merchandise exports of the thirteen countries included in these calculations amounted to £1·93 thousand million in 1960–1 and to £2·04 thousand million in 1962–3. On the more optimistic projection (assumption B), their total exports would rise to £3·6 thousand million (at 1960–1 prices) by 1975, or by an average rate of 4·5 per cent a year.[1] If, however, each country is to achieve a growth rate of GDP of at least 5 per cent a year, on average, over the period up to 1975, then, if the sole burden of filling the foreign exchange gap is to fall on merchandise exports, these would have to rise to about £4·1 thousand million in 1975, or by an average growth rate of 5·3 per cent a year. The export requirement on this basis would be even higher, some £4·4 thousand million—or a rate of increase of almost 6 per cent a year—if each country is to achieve a minimum target of a 2½ per cent growth rate in GDP per head.[2]

For some countries, notably Burma, Ceylon and Pakistan, the required growth rate of exports, on either target basis, exceeds the corresponding projected rates by such a wide margin that this solution of the foreign exchange problem appears to be unrealistic. For another group of countries, however, among which Nigeria, Tanzania and the Caribbean countries are important examples, increase of the growth rate of exports to the required levels would not seem unduly difficult. Indeed, for both Tanzania and Trinidad the projected growth rates are higher than one of the two required rates of export growth.

Closing the gap between projected and required rates of growth of

---

[1] See Tables 6.7, 8.12.

[2] These calculated export requirements are underestimated in so far as Jamaica, Zambia and possibly Nigeria would be in a phase of savings-constrained growth at the growth rates assumed.

Table 8.12. *Exports from less developed Sterling countries: actual, 1960–3, and required and projected growth rates, 1960–1 to 1975*

	Actual		Required level in 1975[a]		Required growth rate, 1960–1 to 1975[a]		Projected growth rate, 1960–1 to 1975	
	1960–1	1962–3	For 5% p.a. growth rate in GDP	For 2½% p.a. growth rate in GDP per head	For 5% p.a. growth rate in GDP	For 2½% p.a. growth rate in GDP per head	A	B
	(*£ million*)				(*% per annum, compound*)			
Burma	83	94	185	195	5·7	6·1	1·0	1·6
Ceylon	131	130	285	365	5·5	7·3	1·4[e]	1·6[e]
India	483	542	930	865	4·6	4·1	3·1	3·6
Malaya	324	310	605	715	4·4	5·6	2·6[e]	3·0[e]
Pakistan	140	156	400	445	7·5	8·2	3·5	4·4
Ghana	108	100	240	300	5·7	7·3	5·4	6·0
Kenya	55[b]	65[b]	170	165	6·9	7·7	4·6	5·0
Nigeria	169	177	515	590	8·0	8·9	8·0	8·6
Rhodesia	71[c]	78[c]	185	245	6·8	8·9	4·5	5·2
Tanzania	52	58	100	85	4·5	3·6	4·5	5·1
Zambia	132	131	195	220	2·7	3·6	6·5[e]	7·1[e]
Jamaica	62	71	125	55	5·1	..[d]	5·4	6·5
Trinidad and Tobago	117	128	150	200	1·8	3·8	2·4	3·1
TOTAL	1,927	2,040	4,085	4,445	5·3	5·9	3·8	4·5

SOURCES: Tables 6.11, 7.7, 7.9, 8.1, 8.3, 8.4, 8.6 and 8.7.

[a] Assuming net inflow of official capital on more optimistic basis (assumption II in Table 8.10).
[b] Including estimated value of exports to Tanzania and Uganda.
[c] Excluding exports to Malawi and Zambia.
[d] Negative.
[e] At current prices.

exports, or at least closing part of the gap, would no doubt require changes in economic policy on the part of both the less developed countries concerned and the industrial countries which form their major export markets. Some of the policy implications of the various illustrative calculations discussed here are explored further in the next chapter. A general conclusion which can reasonably be drawn from the calculations is that no single line of policy—whether it be reliance on increased foreign aid, or on increased access to the markets of the industrial countries, or limitation of interest on foreign debt—can be expected *by itself* to carry the full burden of supporting a reasonable minimum rate of economic growth in a number, possibly the majority, of the less developed Sterling countries. What is required is a series of interrelated policy changes which would result in increased foreign exchange availabilities to these countries both on merchandise exports and on invisible and capital accounts.

CHAPTER 9

POLICY ISSUES

I. THE PRINCIPAL FINDINGS OF THE STUDY

The main analysis in previous chapters of the past and probable future rates of growth of selected countries in the Overseas Sterling Area has been based on the hypothesis that there is a definite relationship between exports and foreign capital inflows, on the one hand, and the rate of growth in the real product, on the other. This relationship is, however, a changing one and the change can be very substantial in any country over a period of ten to fifteen years, which is the projection period used, whilst differences between countries in the degree to which the gross product is affected by given changes in export income can also vary greatly. Though it is not possible to predict with any accuracy the future growth of national product from any given level of exports or foreign aid, the procedure used in the last chapter (of making alternative assumptions concerning the magnitudes of the key parameters involved in this relationship) does seem to provide some quantitative orders of magnitude, and some general qualitative conclusions, which it is essential to bear in mind when considering possible policy changes. Of these, the following have been selected as among the most important as regards their implications for governmental policies.

First, the narrow commodity specialization of the various countries covered by this study has been of major importance as an influence on their export performance. The majority of the less developed Sterling countries are still heavily dependent on one or two principal primary commodities in their export trade, and relatively few countries have yet achieved any substantial progress in the diversification of their export structures. The greater diversity of export lines in the more developed countries and the spread of exports of certain of the less developed countries into industrial products imply that for such countries the relative stagnation of world demand for some exports can be balanced, or outweighed, by the more dynamic demand for others. But less developed countries traditionally dependent on a narrow product specialization, for which the world market is sluggish, are likely to be caught in a vicious circle of stagnation, unless appropriate remedial policy changes can be made. There seems little doubt that a considerable number of the less developed Sterling countries require substantial, even drastic, shifts in the commodity pattern of their export sectors away from commodities with relatively poor growth prospects if they are to achieve a higher, and sustained, rate of economic growth in the future.

Second, the efforts of the majority of the less developed Sterling countries to expand their export earnings by positive measures of development planning have so far met with limited and uneven success. For a number of important primary commodities—cocoa and sugar are outstanding examples—for which demand in the main importing countries is relatively inelastic with respect to both price and income, or where imports are subject to some form of restriction, the expansion in exportable supplies has led in certain years to sharp price declines to the detriment of the export earnings of the producing countries. For other commodities, the efforts to expand exports have been largely frustrated by the growing encroachment of synthetic materials on the traditional uses of the natural products. Only for metals and minerals, among the major groups of primary commodities, have the efforts of the overseas Sterling countries to expand their export earnings met with general success. Among manufactured goods, again, the growth in exportable supplies has been limited to a substantial extent by quantitative and other restrictions on imports by the main industrial countries.

Third, all the less developed Sterling countries, and some of the more developed ones, have now adopted economic planning as an essential tool in the urgent task of economic development. Although there is great variety as regards the institutional forms through which development planning is carried out,[1] the majority of Sterling countries are consciously planning for appreciable rates of increase in their export earnings. These export plans are, however, subject to a number of limitations. One limitation, for perhaps the majority of Sterling countries, is that current plans are inevitably based on a continuation of their traditional specialization in a narrow range of export products. The advantages of diversification, particularly into semi-processed and fully manufactured goods for which export markets are relatively more expansive, are now generally realized by planners, but progress is likely to be slow for many countries, at least in the coming ten years.

A second limitation, evident from the analytical discussion in earlier chapters, is that in a number of Sterling countries the statistical basis of effective economic planning is inadequate, or even largely non-existent. The current Development Plans of such countries appear to be based, to a substantial extent, on informed guesses about the magnitude of

---

[1] The institutional forms vary from virtually complete State control of the economy (Burma), through a mixture of State and private enterprise (notably in India and Pakistan), to general guidelines of development leaving the initiative essentially in the private sector (as in the Caribbean countries).

important sectors of the economy, or about various key parameters, particularly the marginal propensity to save and the marginal propensity to import. A major effort seems urgently required to improve the statistical basis of economic planning as an essential pre-requisite for more effective action in the future.[1]

A third limitation on the effectiveness of current export planning arises from the fact that many export targets set are unrealistic. This can happen either because of an unrealistic—usually optimistic—assessment of the probable future trend in world import demand for the commodities concerned, or because the assumption made about the country's future share of world trade is inconsistent with the corresponding assumptions made by other countries. The Burmese plan is, perhaps, the obvious case of an over-optimistic assessment of the future trend of export demand, but the export targets of several other Sterling countries also appear to be based on optimistic assumptions about the growth in world demand for their main export products.[2] The mutual inconsistency of the plans of different countries is, however, probably the main reason for export targets being unrealistic. The plans of Ceylon, India and the countries of East Africa to increase their shares of the world tea market cannot all be successful; their implementation could, moreover, lead to a continued downward pressure on tea prices to the disadvantage of all the exporting countries. Similar considerations would apply to the plans of both India and Pakistan to increase their shares of world trade in jute manufactures. Some form of international co-ordination of export plans to avoid excessive pressure on the world market resulting from 'unconsciously planned' over-supply might well be considered here.

All these conclusions, arising from the main body of the analysis, relate entirely to the expansion of export earnings. In addition, several conclusions emerge regarding capital flows—the other major element in the capacity to import of the overseas Sterling countries. First in this group is the failure of the net capital inflow into the less developed Sterling countries to show any significant tendency to rise since 1961. In the initial years of the present decade, the net inflow of private and official capital into the less developed Sterling countries accounted for about one-fifth of their total foreign exchange income,[3] though for some countries—notably India and Pakistan—the corresponding proportions were considerably higher. If the total net capital inflow into this group of countries in 1975 is no higher than it was in 1962–3, then the rate of

---

[1] What is suggested is the establishment, not of over-elaborate statistical services, but of a system for the regular provision of reliable key statistics.

[2] In some cases (as for Tanzanian sisal) this is due to the spread in the use of synthetic substitutes at a faster rate than was apparently envisaged when the Plan was drawn up.

[3] See Table 1.2 and Table 7.7, which covers fourteen countries.

growth in the capacity to import would probably be insufficient to support an average growth rate in GDP of as much as 5 per cent a year for the majority of these countries. With a stagnant level of foreign aid, and with no significant relaxation of protectionism by the industrial countries, it would take an appreciable number—perhaps the majority —of the less developed Sterling countries well into the next century before they would be likely to achieve even a modest target of an average real product per head of £100 (at 1960–1 prices).

Doubling the 1962–3 level of aid by 1975 is likely to result in only marginal improvements in the rate of growth in GDP for most Sterling countries, though the growth rate for India would rise by about ½ per cent per annum (compared with the situation where aid was kept at the 1962–3 level), on the various detailed assumptions made in Chapter 8. In order to achieve a minimum average rate of growth in GDP of 5 per cent a year, the level of foreign aid received by the less developed Sterling countries as a group would need to have risen by 1975 to the region of two and a half times the 1962–3 level (or to treble that level if the minimum target is an average growth rate of 2½ per cent a year in GDP per head). These calculations assume no substantial change in the protectionist policies of the industrial countries, on the one hand, and no major improvement in the relationship between capital investment and the increment of output in the less developed Sterling countries, on the other.

Appreciable changes in the terms of trade would significantly alter the order of magnitude of the results. The illustrative calculations presented in Chapter 8 were based on the arbitrary assumptions that export earnings and import prices would differ by as much as 10 per cent from the more optimistic of the alternative projections for 1975. Even on these somewhat moderate assumptions, it was seen that the adverse combination of a 10 per cent shortfall in exports and a 10 per cent excess in import prices, compared with the projected values, would have quite serious adverse effects on the growth of GDP in a number of the less developed Sterling countries.[1] Any more drastic adverse change in the terms of trade would have correspondingly greater effect on the growth rates which could be achieved by the countries concerned. Conversely, unexpected increases in export prices (or declines in import prices), if sustained for any period, could well have a considerable favourable impact on their rates of economic growth.

A second feature of the earlier discussion of capital inflows was their asymmetrical distribution as between the various Sterling countries. The greater portion of private capital flows to the more developed countries, particularly Australia, while official capital flows almost

---

[1] See pp. 208–10.

entirely to the less developed countries. Moreover, within the total for the latter group, the distribution of official aid by individual countries follows no consistent pattern; rather, it appears to be mainly a reflection of the fact that most aid is made available by donor countries, each of which may be pursuing different policy objectives. Moreover, the greater part of aid has so far been related to individual investment projects, not to the requirements of economic development as a whole. A more integrated international approach to the principles of aid-giving and aid-receiving seems now urgently needed; some suggestions in this regard were made in Chapter 7[1] and are further discussed below.

A third conclusion in the general field of capital flows is that the burden of interest and dividend payments on foreign investment has already become relatively heavy for many overseas Sterling countries, whether judged in relation to earnings from merchandise exports or in relation to total foreign exchange income. Net factor payments abroad in 1962–3, for example, exceeded 10 per cent of merchandise export earnings for seven out of fourteen major less developed Sterling countries,[2] while the projections show—on the more favourable, BII, assumptions—that this percentage would probably be exceeded by ten of the same fourteen countries by 1975. Limiting this burden in some appropriate way would help the growth prospects of most of the overseas Sterling countries, but any relaxations in lending terms and conditions which at present appear practicable are unlikely to improve the general growth prospects of most of these countries to any marked extent.

These general conclusions, emerging from the various calculations presented in earlier chapters, are all dependent on the validity of the numerous assumptions made. Some assessment of the implications of possible changes in these assumptions (for example, as to changes in the terms of trade, the levels of capital inflow, the mean rate of interest on official loans, the rate of economic growth in the industrial countries, and the competitive position in export markets of the main Sterling countries) have been introduced, as appropriate, throughout the earlier discussion. Variations such as these, as well as in the parameters of the model used in the calculations, could well have appreciable effects on the probable growth rate of individual Sterling countries. However, the gap between desirable 'target' rates of economic growth, on the one side, and the alternative rates that appear likely to be achieved on present economic policies, on the other, remains wide enough, for most of the less developed countries, for some further consideration to be given to desirable changes in policy. The following sections consider in

---

[1] See pp. 209–10.
[2] See Table 7.7.

more detail the implications for trade and capital flow policies of the analytical results of the present study, before a final review of the more general implications of the results for economic growth policies as such.

2. IMPLICATIONS FOR TRADE POLICIES

Policies influencing the rate of growth in exports from the overseas Sterling countries can conveniently be considered in two separate—though related—categories, namely, policies within those countries themselves designed to expand their export earnings, and those in the countries which form the main markets for the Overseas Sterling Area's exports.

Trade policies of the overseas Sterling countries

Four main policy issues appear to emerge from the results of the projections analysis: the need to increase competitiveness in world export markets of the traditional exports of overseas Sterling countries; the need to diversify the export structure away from a 'stagnant' to a 'dynamic' commodity pattern; the need for co-operation among the less developed countries in order to expand the volume of their intra-trade; and the need to expand their markets in the centrally planned group of countries.

As regards the need to increase export competitiveness, a distinction should be made between (a) commodities—such as tropical beverages—in which competition in the world market is essentially among the less developed countries only (whether Sterling or non-Sterling), and (b) commodities—such as natural rubber and vegetable oils and oil-seeds—in which the less developed countries compete on a substantial scale with producers (either of similar natural products or of synthetic materials) in the main importing countries. In the former case, reductions in cost in any one producing country would, if reflected in export selling prices, increase that country's competitive position, but at the expense of a corresponding export loss by another less developed country. To the extent that both these countries were in the Sterling Area, the change in competitive positions would probably have no significant effect, on balance, on the Area's overall growth prospects. In the latter case, however, an increase in competitiveness in traditional export products would increase the market share of the overseas Sterling country concerned at the expense of producers in importing (mainly industrial) countries, so that the overall growth prospects of the Overseas Sterling Area could, to that extent, be improved.

Achieving an improvement in the competitive position for the major 'traditional' primary commodities would normally involve reductions in unit cost resulting from increased yields in the case of agricultural crops, or improved technology in the case of minerals and metals. However, the concept of 'competitive power' is wider than price competition alone, since it embraces quality, packaging, standardization and other non-price aspects of competition. Increased investment in quality improvements and the introduction of standard grades, where appropriate, would considerably improve the competitive position of a number of primary commodity exports of overseas Sterling countries.[1]

The second policy issue for the less developed countries mentioned above—the problem of export diversification—is the most important from the long-term viewpoint. Development planning in these countries needs to allow for the expansion and structural change of the export sector as an integral part of general economic growth. The process assumes that the planners make careful and objective assessments of the probable future trends in world demand for both present and potential export commodities, so that a rationally based programme of diversification into relatively expanding export lines can be drawn up, taking into account the country's available resources. To the extent that the more 'dynamic' commodities would normally consist of manufactured goods (including semi-manufactures), export diversification in the sense used here also implies industrialization. Though the early stages of industrialization would normally consist essentially of the development of import-saving industries, thought also needs to be given to the possibilities of inaugurating new industries specifically oriented to export markets. To the extent that import-saving industries can be expanded in scale at diminishing unit costs, the possibility of these becoming viable exporting industries also needs careful exploration.[2]

Although industrialization, and a consequent diversification of the export sector away from primary products, may constitute one way out of the 'vicious circle' of the export lag leading to too slow a rate of economic growth, this way out is open only to a certain range of countries. Small 'one-crop' countries, in particular, and even relatively large though economically backward countries with poor natural resources, may find the costs of industrialization virtually prohibitive, though even here it might well be possible to introduce viable industries for the processing of local produce for export markets. Moreover, the possibilities of diversification *within* the primary-producing sectors of the overseas Sterling countries should also not be overlooked. The wide variation in export prospects for different primary commodities implies

---

[1] The recent introduction of a standard specification for natural rubber sheets, for example, has led to a significant rise in demand for this type of natural rubber.

[2] This approach assumes the avoidance of general monetary and fiscal policies which raise the general level of costs and so undermine specific policies designed to improve the competitive position of exports of manufactures on the world market.

an obligation on the planning authorities to consider the opportunity costs of switching resources into different kinds of primary production. At the same time, international co-operation designed to control the growth of world production of particular commodities—such as those in persistent surplus—might give preferential treatment to those countries for which the costs of switching resources into alternative uses are relatively high.

Diversification programmes, especially if they involve the transfer of resources into manufacturing, inevitably require a considerable amount of finance, part of which would be used to purchase equipment or materials from abroad. The need for such diversification is greatest for countries heavily dependent on one, or a few, commodities for which world supply has been—or is likely to become—in excess of world demand at prices which would be reasonably remunerative to the majority of producers.[1] At the same time, however, the pressure of excess supply on the world market tends to result in export prices and producers' incomes which are at too low a level to allow the governments of the countries concerned to accumulate either the tax revenue or the foreign exchange reserves that would be required to finance adequate schemes of diversification. The solution of this problem therefore requires some form of foreign aid and/or some programme of international co-operative action in the field of commercial policy; this is discussed further below, since it involves changes in policies on the part of the industrial countries also.

The third issue distinguished above regarding the trade policies of the overseas Sterling countries was the problem of expanding the volume of their intra-trade. There seems little doubt that the intra-trade between the overseas Sterling countries is small in relation to their population and national income. This reflects very largely the economic backwardness of many of the less developed countries of the Area, in which the available export surplus takes the form of specialized crops traditionally in demand in Britain and other industrial countries. The development of an intra-trade in foods among the overseas Sterling countries (as well as between them and other less developed countries) would help the nutritional balance in the food-deficit countries like India while assisting the export trade of food-surplus countries. The promotion of the intra-trade in semi-processed and manufactured goods would assist the economic viability of manufacturing industries in the less developed Sterling countries by extending their market, and thus allowing them to benefit from economies of large-scale production. Whatever the commodity in which the intra-trade is expanded, the

---

[1] Coffee, sugar and natural rubber, for example, would all fall into this category, at least as regards the first half of the 1960s.

less developed countries stand to gain, not only by the fuller utilization of their indigenous resources, but also by saving in foreign exchange on imports of such foods and manufactures from the industrial areas as they can now replace by domestic production; the foreign exchange so saved could then be made available for the purchase of development goods from the industrial areas.

The promotion of the intra-trade of the less-developed countries of the Sterling Area should not, however, be conceived as an exclusively 'Sterling' project. To do so would be to deprive both Sterling and non-Sterling countries of the less developed world of some of the economic advantages of increased specialization in international trade. Although each Sterling country is linked to the same reserve currency, each has to balance its external accounts *vis-à-vis* the rest of the world taken as a whole. Moreover, the degree of complementarity between the economies of different countries, whether or not they are classified as 'more developed' or 'less developed', has no rational relationship to the particular reserve currencies to which their monetary systems are linked. Accordingly, a more general approach to the problem is required, involving some form of economic collaboration between all the less developed countries, Sterling as well as non-Sterling, to stimulate their mutual trade as one means of promoting their rate of economic growth.

Finally, expanding markets for many of the products of overseas Sterling countries might be found in the centrally planned group of countries. The latter's consumption of tropical beverages, for example, is relatively low in relation to population and national income per head, and the same is true for several other primary commodities. Prospects for expanding exports of industrial materials and manufactures to the centrally planned countries have been taken into account in the projections in earlier chapters, but if the existing bilateral pattern of this trade could be made more flexible, or moved to a multilateral basis, and if these countries would consciously plan to increase their imports of manufactures from the less developed countries, this flow of trade could undoubtedly continue to expand at a relatively rapid rate.

Trade policies of the industrial countries

There are several important areas in which the policies of the industrial countries appreciably influence the rate of growth in exports from the overseas Sterling countries. These are, more especially, their protectionist policies which discriminate against imports in favour of domestic producers; preferences favouring imports from some groups of less developed countries at the expense of others; and policies with regard to international commodity arrangements. In addition, it is useful to consider the development of the synthetic materials industries under this heading, though there are at present no specific 'policies' affecting their growth.

Protection of domestic agriculture is widespread in all the industrial countries, but assumes a variety of forms, from simple tariffs through quantitative restrictions on imports to support prices for domestic production and direct subsidies to farmers. Over a wide range of agricultural produce, this protectionism does not directly affect the exports of the less developed Sterling (or non-Sterling) countries, since the latter's main products consist of tropical and sub-tropical commodities while the industrial countries' output is very largely in temperate-zone products. However, for certain products direct competition does exist, most importantly for sugar and vegetable oils and oilseeds. The export projections shown in earlier chapters were based, as already explained, on the assumption that there will be no substantial change in the degree of protection currently afforded by the industrial countries to their domestic producers. Any appreciable relaxation of this protection would benefit overseas Sterling (as well as non-Sterling) producers of such products, and the amounts involved could be relatively large for certain specialist producing countries.[1]

The Commonwealth preference system, established at the Ottawa Conference of 1932, has been a major supporting factor in the exports of the overseas Sterling countries to the United Kingdom. This is not merely because of the degree or coverage of the tariff preferences,[2] but also because they have been in existence long enough for intra-Commonwealth channels of trade to become firmly enough established

---

[1] For sugar, the net monetary benefit to Sterling countries would depend also on whether the present system of preferential prices obtainable under the Commonwealth Sugar Agreement was maintained if protection of British (as well as other industrial countries') sugar beet production were reduced or eliminated. Professor H. G. Johnson has calculated, on the basis of carefully specified assumptions, that free trade in the world sugar market would have raised the 1959 export earnings of the less developed sugar-producers by at least £268 million. In addition, the substitution of imports for beet production in the protectionist countries could have given rise to real resource savings in those countries of about £180 million which could have been made available to the less developed countries at no cost to the donors. Professor Johnson shows that the gains to the less developed countries from free trade would outweigh those from a more efficient system of protection (such as deficiency payments), and also tentatively concludes that the increase in resources available to the less developed countries as a result of free trade would be greater than that produced by a policy of 'internationalizing' sugar protection (Harry G. Johnson, *Economic Policies towards Less-developed Countries*, Allen & Unwin, London, 1967, Appendix D).

[2] An examination of the preferences extended by the United Kingdom on imports from the Commonwealth Preference Area showed that, in 1962, 61 per cent by value of Britain's imports from the Area enjoyed tariff preference, the average preferential margin on such imports being 11·8 per cent (see R. W. Green, 'Commonwealth Preference: United Kingdom Customs Duties and Tariff Preferences on Imports from the Preference Area', *Board of Trade Journal*, 31 December 1965).

to remain in existence even when they would not now appear justified solely by the tariff preference. On the other hand, discriminatory preferential systems operated by other industrial countries[1] have had adverse effects on exports from the Overseas Sterling Area.

The abolition of the Commonwealth preferential system would undoubtedly have adverse effects on the Overseas Sterling Area's exports of certain products at present enjoying appreciable preferential margins, as well as appreciable, even severe, adverse effects on exports from particular countries.[2] There would also be offsetting gains to such countries, in so far as they are currently importing manufactures from Britain under preference which they could otherwise obtain at lower cost from other industrial countries. The net potential loss or gain which is likely to accrue to each of the overseas Sterling countries from the abolition of the Commonwealth preferences could therefore be assessed only by a detailed analysis of the trading pattern and competitiveness of each country. The net balance of loss or gain would also depend on whether the discriminatory preferences operated by industrial countries outside the Commonwealth were being abolished. A general movement towards the abolition, or at least the gradual phasing out, of discriminatory preferences is likely to have very different effects on the export prospects of the various overseas Sterling countries. It may therefore be necessary to institute some form of intergovernmental financial compensation to those countries which would suffer appreciable net losses during the phasing-out period or in the years immediately following the abolition of discriminatory preferences.

Protection of domestic manufacturing industries is also general practice in the industrial countries. In all these countries, the rates of import duty tend to be generally higher, the greater the degree of fabrication of the product, the crude material often being imported free of duty. Under such conditions the effective rate of protection for domestic industries—measured with regard to value added in production—is usually considerably higher than the nominal tariff rate on imports of the finished product.[3] For textile fabrics, non-ferrous metals, leather

[1] The import controls operated by France in favour of products emanating from the franc zone have been particularly discriminatory in character. The French preferential system is now in process of incorporation in the wider E.E.C. Convention of Association with the Associated Overseas Territories. This Convention, signed at Yaoundé in July 1963, entered into force on 1st June 1964.

[2] In 1962, for example, the average margin of preference enjoyed in the British market (over competing imports) exceeded 20 per cent for Barbados, Mauritius, Guyana, Fiji and the former Federation of Rhodesia and Nyasaland (R. W. Green, *loc. cit.*).

[3] The effective import tariff on the value added in manufacture is higher than the nominal tariff so long as the nominal tariff on the crude material is lower than that on the manufacture in question (see Bela Balassa, 'Tariff Protection in Industrial Countries: an Evaluation', *Journal of Political Economy*, vol. 73, no. 6, December 1965, for a theoretical analysis and practical application of the concept of effective tariffs).

and other semi-finished manufactures—all actual or potential exports of less developed (including Sterling) countries—the effective tariffs of the main industrial countries are more than double the nominal rates.[1] A change in the tariff structure of the industrial countries so as to reduce the effective tariffs on such manufactures or, alternatively, the introduction of a general system of tariff preferences on imports from all less developed countries, whether Sterling or not, would be likely to stimulate the expansion of manufactured exports from such countries.[2]

The case for a drastic relaxation in the network of import restrictions and of the protectionist systems now prevalent in the main industrial countries rests not simply on the beneficial impact of such relaxation on the export prospects of the less developed countries; more generally, by promoting a new and expanded level of specialization in both economically advanced and less developed countries, it would allow both groups of countries to achieve a more efficient allocation of economic resources, and thus a higher level of real income than they would otherwise enjoy. In addition, any increase in foreign exchange earnings by the less developed countries which would accrue from the relaxation of protectionism would very largely be spent on purchases of capital equipment and other manufactures required for development purposes from the industrial countries. This 'feed-back', which is essentially dynamic in character, as opposed to the static gains from the more rational allocation of resources already mentioned, would support the trend within the latter countries towards a relative concentration of activity on capital goods and other technically more sophisticated products while at the same time providing a useful balance of payments offset to the increased cost of imports from the less developed countries.

The other area in which the trade policies of the industrial countries impinge heavily on the export prospects of the overseas Sterling countries is that of international commodity arrangements. An examination of possible alternative institutional arrangements designed to promote the export earnings of the less developed countries from primary products obviously falls outside the scope of the present study. Nonetheless, it is worth making the point that any interference with the workings of the market mechanism must take into account the two major functions of market prices: the function of rational allocation of resources, and that of the distribution of real income between the different trading countries.

[1] *Ibid.* pp. 579–80.

[2] Professor Balassa has estimated, for example, that if tariffs on imports of manufactures from developing countries into industrial countries were eliminated, the volume of such imports would rise by 38 per cent for the United States, 30 per cent for the United Kingdom and 28 per cent for the E.E.C. (*ibid.*).

The free market system in primary commodities has, in general, operated to influence resource allocation in the direction indicated by the underlying changes in demand conditions. Even here, however, there have been many cases of maladjustment, particularly of over-investment in capacity where the commodity is subject to a long gestation period (coffee being the obvious example). Moreover, where governmental interference has created a relatively narrow residual market, as for sugar, by the creation of preferential channels of trade, prices on the free (or residual) market become subject to excessive fluctuations, which thereby largely vitiate the allocative function they are supposed to serve.

Although commodity prices have had an important allocative function working—though haltingly in many cases—in the direction of economic rationality, they have also had undesirable results for many producing countries as regards their other function, the distribution of real income. To the extent that prices of particular commodities are depressed, as a result either of excess production or of intensified competition from synthetics, the exporting countries concerned are thereby deprived of the export income which they need to enable them to finance programmes of diversifing into export products whose prospects are more favourable. From a world point of view, this is also a limitation on the optimum employment of factors of production and, as a consequence, the real income of the industrial countries is necessarily adversely affected.

For this reason, it seems important that the traditional view of inter-governmental commodity arrangements, including formal commodity agreements, should be revised. Instead of being looked upon as devices to restrict supply in order to stabilize the world price at a level above the long-term 'equilibrium' price, they would be more appropriately regarded as a means of phasing out excess capacity (and of preventing the emergence of excess capacity in the future) by providing producing countries with resources adequate for financing appropriate diversification programmes. To the extent that international commodity arrangements are not able, in practice, to achieve this objective, there is a case for appropriate financial transfers to the producing countries in need of such diversification.

The adverse impact of the development of the synthetic materials industries on the exports of overseas Sterling countries was shown in earlier chapters to be quantitatively very severe.[1] In so far as this development is intimately connected with the process of industrial growth in the economically advanced countries, it would be foolish to attempt to retard its progress by government intervention. Indeed, the benefits

[1] See Chapters 1 and 5.

of the technological progress involved in the development of synthetics must eventually be expected to spread on an increasing scale to the less developed countries. In the short and medium term, however, many of the latter are faced with relatively stagnant export prospects as a result of the increasing displacement by synthetics of their traditional exports of natural products. The general lines of policy that the developing countries might follow to combat this—increasing the competitiveness of traditional exports and diversifying their export structures—have already been discussed. As regards policy in the industrial countries, consideration could be given to the removal of any subsidy or tax preference currently applied to synthetic materials competing to a significant extent with natural products of importance in the export trade of the less developed countries. In particular, government grants to scientific research institutes working on the development of synthetic substitutes for natural materials or for tropical beverages might be reconstituted so as to spread such research over a longer period. Fundamental research to develop synthetic foods, however, could be of vital importance in the world's fight against hunger and malnutrition, and should, if anything, be intensified.

3. IMPLICATIONS FOR CAPITAL-FLOW POLICIES

Several major conclusions as regards policies affecting capital flows to overseas Sterling countries are indicated by the projection results presented in previous chapters. These relate to the total net flow of long-term capital; to the country distribution of the total; to the burden of interest and dividend payments for the debtor countries; and to the need for compensatory or supplementary finance to offset unexpected changes in export earnings and in the terms of trade.

It would seem from the various alternative projections made in Chapter 8 that, while relaxations of restrictions on the free flow of commodity trade (together, possibly, with the introduction of trade preferences for the products of less developed countries) would considerably assist the growth prospects of many of the less developed Sterling countries, trade policy changes need to be supported by policies designed to increase the net flow of long-term capital to the Overseas Sterling Area as a whole. As regards official aid—which is directed almost entirely to the less developed countries—the achievement of a target aid level by the O.E.C.D. countries of 1 per cent of their total national incomes would imply a rise in aid from these countries from about $6½ billion in 1962–3 to $13–14 billion (at constant prices) in 1975. If the Overseas Sterling Area continued to receive about one-quarter of the total, their aid receipts would accordingly increase from $1·6 billion (almost

£570 million) in 1962-3 to some $3·5 to 3·7 billion (or £1,250 to £1,340 million) by 1975, allowing for some additional aid from the centrally planned countries.

Even the achievement of this, the United Nations', target of 1 per cent of national incomes would, however, fall far short of the aid requirements of the less developed Sterling countries necessary to achieve a minimum growth rate of 5 per cent in their individual national products.[1] If no policy changes favouring the exports of these countries are assumed, the level of their foreign aid requirements would be in the region of £1,850 million in 1975 if they are to achieve this minimum growth target, or some £2,300 million if the target is the attainment of a growth rate of 2½ per cent a year in GDP per head. In other words, to achieve these growth targets, the net capital inflow requirements of the less developed Sterling countries in 1975 would be in the region of three and a half to four and a half times the level of aid these countries received during the early1960s. Assuming again, for illustrative purposes, that the overseas Sterling countries would still account for one-quarter of all aid from O.E.C.D. countries, these higher levels implied in the alternative growth targets would represent between 1½ and 2 per cent of the aggregate real national incomes of O.E.C.D. countries in 1975. This purely illustrative calculation is worth bearing in mind in view of the apparent difficulties which the majority of O.E.C.D. countries are experiencing in achieving the 1 per cent aid target.

There is no reason to believe that the less developed countries of the Sterling Area are essentially different, in their need for a higher level of foreign aid to assist their economic development, from other developing countries.[2] What seems to be wanted urgently is a concerted change in aid policies which would not only lift the level of total aid flows by at least the order of magnitude indicated in the illustrative calculations for the less developed Sterling countries, but also establish this aid programme on the basis of a long-term commitment by the donor countries. This would allow the less developed countries to make their development plans with a much greater degree of confidence than has hitherto been possible.

The present rather haphazard distribution of the total available aid to individual recipient countries has no rational economic basis. To achieve a rational method of distribution, it is necessary for donor countries to reach agreement on some general principles of aid-giving. A detailed consideration of what such principles might be falls outside the scope of the present book. Essentially, however, a choice has to be made

---

[1] See Table 8.10.

[2] See, for example, the foreign aid requirements calculations by Chenery and Strout, 'Foreign Assistance and Economic Development', cited on p. 6.

between giving aid where it can most effectively be used (though the criteria to judge the 'effectiveness' of aid would be difficult to formulate and even more difficult to apply), and giving aid to those most in need (i.e. to the poorer countries or, alternatively, to poorer areas within countries). It might also be possible to devise formulae which would combine these two possible objectives in different proportions.

The third issue, that of limiting the burden on the less developed countries of interest and dividend payments on foreign official debt, has already been discussed in Chapter 8. It was there suggested that possible alternatives might be to limit such interest payments to a given proportion of export earnings and to limit the rate of interest on new official loans to a nominal figure (taken in that chapter at $1\frac{1}{2}$ per cent for illustrative purposes). For either alternative to be workable, a new international financial agency would be needed, supported by grants from the economically advanced countries.[1]

Though private long-term capital is of only minor importance in the total capital inflow into the less developed Sterling countries taken as a whole, private capital has played a major role in investment in several countries, notably Malaya, Nigeria and the Caribbean countries. Private capital has tended to be concentrated, however, in a fairly limited range of industries, particularly metal-mining and petroleum. It would probably be unrealistic to expect a substantial rise in foreign private investment in estate agriculture, or in manufacturing industry in countries which insist on retaining company control in the hands of their nationals, or which restrict the repatriation of dividends. Countries of this type will have to rely very largely on official aid (including government loans) for their capital inflow from abroad.

It is not possible to make any precise assessment of the part that Britain is likely to play by 1975 in meeting the capital requirements of the present overseas Sterling countries. A recent detailed consideration by the National Institute of Economic and Social Research of the possible configuration of Britain's overseas accounts in 1975 was based on the assumption that official aid (net of repayments) to developing countries would rise from about £150 million a year in 1962–3 to £350 million in 1975, while private investment in developing countries would be no higher (at £100 million) in 1975 than in the early 1960s.[2] Most of this assumed capital outflow would presumably be directed to countries of the Sterling Commonwealth. The figures imply that a

---

[1] As suggested in the 'Horowitz Proposal' (see p. 258).

[2] R. L. Major, 'Capital and Invisible Transactions in Britain's Balance of Payments' (in *The British Economy in 1975*, by W. Beckerman and Associates, Cambridge, 1965). The figures quoted include both grants and loans.

slightly higher proportion of national income would be devoted to aid in 1975 than in the early 1960s though, as the author points out, a much larger amount of aid could be made available if 'aid were to become very much more important than it is now in the hierarchy of objectives of economic policy'.[1]

The official aid requirements of the less developed Sterling countries for the alternative growth targets assumed in this study[2] would probably be in the range £2,000 to 2,500 million, allowing for the various smaller countries not included in the detailed calculations. It should be borne in mind that these aid requirements assume no policy changes significantly favourable to the export earnings of the Sterling countries. If, now, it is assumed that Britain would supply about 40 per cent of the official net capital inflow, as in the early 1960s, the United Kingdom commitment would be £800 to 1,000 million for such aid in 1975. This represents roughly two and a quarter to three times the level considered to be a reasonable hypothesis in the National Institute study mentioned above, though that study did not rule out a major increase in the level of aid provision.

Thus, if economic growth targets of the orders of magnitude assumed here are to be achieved, the relative contribution of the United Kingdom to the total aid requirements of the less developed countries of the Overseas Sterling Area is likely to decline, unless Britain appreciably increases the proportion of national income devoted to aid and/or appropriate changes are made in economic policies which would result in a much larger total of export earnings by the less developed Sterling countries than the more optimistic of the projections shown here.

Finally, there appears to be a need for some form of international compensatory or supplementary financing designed to offset unexpected changes in export earnings and in the terms of trade of the less developed Sterling (and also non-Sterling) countries. The compensatory financing facility of the International Monetary Fund, as extended in 1966, provides for short-term financing (up to 50 per cent of a country's quota with the I.M.F.) to offset adverse changes in export earnings from one year to another. As regards longer-term supplementary financing, the International Bank for Reconstruction and Development has reported favourably on the feasibility of a scheme designed to help 'developing countries overcome the problem of unexpected shortfalls in their export earnings that result in disruption of sound development programs'.[3]

---

[1] Major, p. 109.

[2] I.e. a growth rate of 5 per cent a year in GDP, or 2½ per cent a year in GDP per head.

[3] *Supplementary Financial Measures: a Study requested by the United Nations Conference on Trade and Development—1964*, International Bank for Reconstruction and Development, Washington, December 1965.

Some similar provision would seem to be required to allow for un-expected adverse movements in import prices.

4. ECONOMIC GROWTH POLICIES

The various alternative projections of the growth rates of gross domestic product of the different Sterling countries presented in Chapter 8, and on which the discussion of desirable policy changes has been based, were derived from a relatively simple macro-economic model of the relationship between the external sector and the economy's general rate of growth. In reality, this relationship is a complex and changing one, the changes expressing themselves—using the terminology of the model—in different values of the overall incremental capital–output ratio and of the investment elasticity.

It is open to governments, as a conscious act of policy, to plan to increase the investment elasticity and/or reduce the incremental capital–output ratio. They can achieve the former by a programme of import substitution in the supply of capital equipment; or by utilizing domestic resources more fully in the capital goods sector; or by increasing the proportion of capital goods in their total imports. The latter objective could be achieved principally by re-arranging the investment programme so as to concentrate on projects with relatively short gestation periods (though this procedure might slow down the growth rate in subsequent plan periods). To the extent that such policy changes are embodied in current Development Plans, they have already been largely taken into account in the projections presented in Chapter 8. Where, however, rather sharp increases in the investment elasticity, or rather sharp declines in the incremental capital–output ratio, have been planned, the projections generally assume more modest changes, though always in the direction indicated by the relevant Plan. Thus, the growth rates projected here may be somewhat on the low side for such countries if they do, in the event, achieve their policy targets in these two respects. The same would hold for any country which managed to increase its investment elasticity, or reduce its incremental capital–output ratio, to a greater degree than was envisaged in its Development Plan. It would in any case seem essential for the poorer Sterling countries to try to find less capital-intensive ways of promoting economic growth than they have done in the past.

The alternative methods open to governments to achieve such changes in the key 'growth parameters' fall within the field of development economics proper, and are therefore outside the scope of this study. Similarly, policies designed to increase the education and skills of the population cannot be considered here in the detail they merit, though they may well be vitally important in increasing the 'absorptive capacity' of less developed countries as regards the quantum of imported capital equipment that can be economically installed and operated within a given period, as well as allowing generally for more flexibility in the allocation of resources. These and related development policies internal to the economies of the overseas Sterling countries, need to be pursued with realism and vigour: for them to be fully effective—in terms of increasing the growth rate of these economies—they would, however, need to be pursued in conjunction with more liberal trade and aid policies such as those suggested above.

THE DETAILED COMMODITY PROJECTIONS

APPENDIX A I

TROPICAL BEVERAGES

The present pattern of trade

Exports of the three tropical beverage crops—cocoa, coffee and tea—from overseas Sterling countries amounted in 1964 to some £400 million, or about 7 per cent of their total merchandise exports in that year. The dependence on one or other of these beverage crops is, however, very great for some countries. Ghana, Ceylon and Uganda, for example, rely on such crops for about 60 per cent of their export earnings, and for Kenya the proportion in 1964 was one-half (see Table A I). A similar high dependence on beverage crops exists in a number of non-Sterling countries, particularly in some of the smaller Latin American coffee-producing countries.

Table A I. *Exports of tropical beverages, 1964*

	Value of exports				Total as proportion of all exports
	Cocoa*a*	Coffee	Tea	Total	
	(£ million)				(%)
OVERSEAS STERLING AREA					
India	—	10	94	104	17
Ceylon	1	—	86	86	62
Ghana	68	1	—	69	66
Nigeria	40	1	—	41	19
Uganda	—	35	2	38	58
Kenya	—	15	8	23	49
Tanzania	—	11	2	13	18
Other countries	5	8	6	18	..
Total O.S.A.	113	81	197	392	7
NON-STERLING COUNTRIES	71	729	29	829	2
TOTAL	184	810	226	1,221	2
O.S.A. as percentage of TOTAL	*61*	*10*	*87*	*32*	..

SOURCES: *Trade Yearbook, 1965*, F.A.O., Rome, 1966; *Yearbook of International Trade Statistics, 1964*, United Nations, New York, 1966.

a Beans only.

The relative importance of the Overseas Sterling Area in the world market varies substantially as between the different beverage crops. Sterling countries account for almost nine-tenths of the value of world tea exports, three-fifths of world cocoa exports, but only one-tenth of world coffee exports. Thus, while the prospects for future growth in Sterling exports of tea depend essentially on the movement in world demand for that beverage, the prospects for Sterling cocoa and, especially, for Sterling coffee depend on the relative shares of Sterling producing countries in the world market as much as on the movement in world demand.

Tea is unlike cocoa and coffee in that a substantial proportion of world consumption takes place in the primary-producing countries. Britain is easily the most important market for tea, accounting in 1964–5 for some two-thirds of total net imports into the industrial countries. For coffee, the United States is the dominant market, taking about half the total imports into the industrial areas. In recent years, the main impetus to the growth in coffee consumption has come from the E.E.C. countries, whose net imports rose by some 70 per cent between 1953–7 and 1964–5; about half this increase represented the growth in West German coffee consumption. For cocoa, the E.E.C. and the United States together account for the bulk of imports into the industrial countries.

Prospects for demand

Projections of demand for the three beverage crops have been made by applying estimated or assumed income elasticities for the main consuming areas to the standard assumptions about income and population growth.[1] World *cocoa* consumption (outside the producing countries) rose in the first half of the 1960s at over twice the rate achieved in the previous quinquennium (Table A2). This reflected the sharp expansion in production in West Africa, from the 1960/1 season, and the consequent substantial reduction in cocoa prices. World production in the mid 1960s, however, has tended to level off while consumption has maintained its upward trend and, if this pattern continues, prices are not likely to repeat the decline experienced in the early 1960s.

The prospects for production are, however, somewhat uncertain, partly because of lack of data about the numbers and age distribution of cocoa trees, and partly because the yield per tree can be significantly affected by farm practices, such as protection against pests and disease, as well as by age. However, even if the rate of growth in output declines from 1965 to 1975 from the unusually rapid expansion in the preceding quinquennium, it seems probable that production will, on average, at least keep pace with, and could well exceed, the probable growth in world demand at prices equivalent to the 1960–1 average level. In the present projections, it is assumed that cocoa prices in 1975 will be equal

[1] See Tables 4·1 and 4.2.

to the average of the years 1960–1, that is, equivalent to 25 cents a lb., or some 25 per cent above 1964–5 average. It should be stressed that this is purely an assumption, not an estimate of what is the most likely price in the mid 1970s.

Table A2. *Cocoa bean grindings, 1953-65 and projections for 1975*

	Rates of growth				Grindings			
	1953–7 to 1960–1	1960–1 to 1964–5	1960–1 to 1975		1960–1	1964–5	1975	
			A	B			A	B
	(% *per annum*)				(*Million metric tons*)			
United Kingdom	−4·6	5·0	2·3	2·7	0·08	0·10	0·11	·012
E.E.C.	5·6	5·5	2·1	2·6	0·31	0·38	0·42	0·44
Other Western Europe	5·0	7·5	3·8	4·4	0·08	0·10	0·13	·014
United States	1·2	4·4	2·5	2·7	0·23	0·28	0·33	0·34
Other industrial countries	6·6	13·2	6·0	6·6	0·03	0·04	0·06	0·06
Total	2·4	5·6	2·6	3·0	0·72	0·89	1·04	1·10
Primary-producing countries[a]	2·7	6·6	4·0–5·0		0·03	0·04	0·05–0·06	
Centrally planned countries	15·2	15·9	8·0–10·0		0·08	0·14	0·24–0·32	
TOTAL	3·3	6·8	3·3–3·7	3·5–4·0	0·83	1·08	1·33–1·42	1·38–1·47

SOURCE: *Cocoa Statistics*, F.A.O., Rome.

[a] Other than cocoa-producing countries.

The income elasticities given in the F.A.O. study[1] could not, for various reasons, be used here mechanically to project cocoa grindings in 1975. The 1960–1 *per caput* figures for grindings were still much depressed by the exceptionally high cocoa prices between 1957 and 1960, and—partly as a consequence of this—in the first half of the 1960s consumption was rising at a much faster rate than those elasticities would have indicated, even when allowing for the effect of very low cocoa prices in, for example, 1962 and 1965. For all industrial areas, higher income elasticities than those estimated by the F.A.O. were used, based on the more recent trends; from this basis, the projections indicated a rise of some 25 to 30 per cent in *per caput* cocoa grindings between 1960–1 and 1975. After allowing for estimated population growth, total cocoa

[1] *Agricultural Commodities—Projections for 1970*, F.A.O., Rome, 1962. The income elasticities used were 0·1 for Britain, the United States and Canada, 0·3 for the E.E.C., 0·6 for other Western Europe, and 0·7 for Japan.

grindings in the industrial areas in 1975 may be put at approximately 1·04 million tons on the low income-growth basis, and 1·10 million tons on the higher income basis. Compared with the position in 1960–1, this would represent an average rate of growth of 2·6 and 3·0 per cent a year respectively—a significant decline on the relatively rapid growth achieved in the early 1960s (see Table A2). The projected 1975 consumption is in fact only about 10 per cent above the actual grindings reported for 1966 in the industrial countries.

Cocoa consumption in primary-producing countries is also assumed to grow at a somewhat reduced rate compared with that for the early 1960s, while a similar assumption has also been made for the centrally planned countries, though in the latter case the assumed range in the growth of consumption (8 to 10 per cent a year) continues to be considerably higher than the corresponding growth rates projected or assumed for other areas. In total, world demand for cocoa (outside the producing countries) is projected to rise, on average, by roughly $3\frac{1}{2}$ per cent a year on the low income-growth assumption, and by about $3\frac{3}{4}$ per cent a year on the higher income basis.

As already indicated, considerable doubt must remain about the future course of cocoa prices. Had the assumption been made that, in the mid 1970s, cocoa prices would be much the same as the average for 1964–5, for instance, then (on the basis of the same income elasticities) world demand would rise about a half per cent point a year more than the rate projected in Table A2; and total demand in 1975 would be some 50 to 100,000 tons higher than that projected.

For *coffee*, the projections indicate little change from the rate of growth in world consumption achieved during the first half of the 1960s (2·6 per cent a year) on the lower income-growth assumption, and a slightly higher rate (some 3·0 per cent a year) on the higher income-growth basis. There are, however, a number of major uncertainties to be considered.

First, there was a notable decline in United States net imports of coffee in 1964–5, and while this was evidently mainly a reflection of reductions in United States stocks,[1] it also resulted from some decline in consumption. In terms of green coffee, consumption per head of the population aged ten years and over has fallen from 20·4 lb. in 1961 to 19·5 lb. in 1964 and 18·8 lb. in 1965. This decline appears to be due mainly to a change in drinking habits in the United States, particularly among the younger generation.[2]

[1] United States coffee stocks declined by 17 thousand tons, on average, during 1960–1, rose by 58 thousand tons in 1962–3, and declined again, by 45 thousand tons, in 1964–5 (see *Annual Coffee Statistics, 1965*, Pan-American Coffee Bureau, New York, 1966).

[2] The average number of cups of coffee drunk per day fell between the winters of 1961 and 1966 by 28 per cent for the 10 to 14 age group, by 11 per cent for those aged 15 to 19, and by

Whether this recent decline in coffee drinking among the younger age groups is a forerunner of further shifts in demand away from coffee is impossible to tell. It is assumed here that, over the projection period 1960–1 to 1975, the average income elasticity of demand for coffee in the United States is zero; this, in effect, assumes some small positive income elasticity over the decade 1965–75. For the other industrial areas, the income elasticities used in the F.A.O. study have been used here.[1]

Table A3. *Net imports of coffee, 1953–65 and projections for 1975*

	Rates of growth				Net imports			
	1953–7 to 1960–1	1960–1 to 1964–5	1960–1 to 1975		1960–1	1964–5	1975	
			A	B			A	B
	(% per annum)				(Million metric tons)			
United Kingdom	9·6	3·9	2·8	3·5	0·06	0·07	0·09	0·10
E.E.C.	6·3	5·2	2·3	3·0	0·62	0·76	0·96	1·06
United States	1·8	−0·4	1·4	1·4	1·30	1·28	1·59	1·59
Other industrial countries	7·6	5·8	4·5	5·0	0·36	0·45	0·68	0·72
Total	3·9	2·3	2·5	2·8	2·34	2·56	3·32	3·47
Primary-producing countries[a]	5·3	2·6	2·5–3·0		0·17	0·19	0·24–0·26	
Centrally planned countries	..	13·6	6·5–9·0		0·06	0·10	0·15–0·20	
TOTAL	4·3	2·6	2·6–2·7	2·9–3·0	2·57	2·85	3·7–3·8	3·9–4·0

SOURCES: *Trade Yearbooks*, F.A.O., Rome.

[a] Other than coffee-producing countries.

A second uncertainty concerning the projection for world coffee demand relates to the import requirements of the centrally planned countries. Their coffee imports rose substantially during the first half of the 1960s, mainly as a result of trade agreements with individual producing countries. There would appear to be ample scope for further expansion, except perhaps in the Soviet Union, which is traditionally a tea-drinking country. The net import requirements of this group of countries in 1975 are arbitrarily put at some 50 to 100 per cent above the level reached in 1964–5.

25 per cent for the 20 to 24 age group. For those aged 30 and over, however, the decline was relatively small (5 to 10 per cent). (See *Annual Coffee Statistics*, for 1962 and 1965.)
[1] These were 1·0 for the United Kingdom and 'Mediterranean Europe', 0·6 for the E.E.C., 0·4 for the rest of Western Europe, 0·6 for Canada, and 1·5 for Japan.

A third uncertainty concerns the future course of coffee prices. However, moderate changes in world coffee prices are not likely to have substantial effects on demand. One reason is that changes in retail coffee prices are generally proportionately much smaller than those in import prices. Another is that demand in the main consuming countries is relatively inelastic (Italy, however, being an exception). For example, a decline of 10 per cent in the import price of coffee in the E.E.C. countries would, on average, result in a rise in consumption of the order of only 1½ to 2 per cent. Though the world coffee market is likely to continue to be influenced by the existence of surplus stocks for the greater part of the 1960s, the operation of export quotas under the International Coffee Agreement is likely to confine any price decline to moderate proportions.

Table A4. *Net imports of tea, 1953–65 and projections for 1975*

	Rates of growth				Net imports			
	1953–7 to 1960–1	1960–1 to 1964–5	1960–1 to 1975 A	B	1960–1	1964–5	1975 A	B
	(% *per annum*)				(*Million metric tons*)			
United Kingdom	0·8	—	0·7	0·7	0·23	0·23	0·26	0·26
United States	0·7	4·7	2·0	2·5	0·05	0·06	0·07	0·07
Other industrial countries	4·2	4·7	2·0	2·2	0·05	0·06	0·07	0·07
Total	1·3	1·5	1·4	1·4	0·33	0·35	0·40	0·40
Primary-producing countries[a]	3·9	1·3	1·5–2·0		0·18	0·19	0·22–0·24	
TOTAL	2·1	1·4	1·4–1·6	1·4–1·6	0·51	0·54	0·62–0·64	0·62–0·64

SOURCES: *Trade Yearbooks*, F.A.O., Rome; *Annual Bulletin of Statistics*, International Tea Committee, London.

[a] Excluding tea-producing countries.

For *tea*, consumption per head in Britain—by far the largest single import market—appears already to have reached a saturation level, and the projections assume that consumption will rise in proportion to total population. Tea has been losing ground to coffee, though future prospects might be influenced by the relative strengths of sales promotion measures in favour of one or the other beverage; another uncertainty relates to the effect of competition from soft drinks, particularly among the younger age groups. In the United States, by contrast, tea in recent years appears to have gained relatively to other drinks, and this change in tastes has been assumed to continue, though with diminished force, over the coming decade. The growth in consumption in other industrial countries is also projected at lower rates than in the recent past.

The demand for tea is appreciably more income-elastic in developing countries than in the high-income industrial areas. Net imports into non-tea-growing primary-producing countries rose at a relatively slow rate over the first half of the 1960s compared with the preceding period from the mid 1950s (see Table A 4). This slowing down was due in part to import substitution (for example in Iran[1],) but mainly it appears to reflect the foreign exchange scarcity of the majority of tea-importing developing countries over the more recent period. In so far as this scarcity can be assumed to continue, it would seem reasonable to expect a continuation of the relatively low rate of growth of tea imports into developing countries. The projections in Table A4 take an arbitrary range of $1\frac{1}{2}$ to 2 per cent a year increase, only marginally higher than the rate achieved in the first half of the 1960s.

The results of these various projections indicate that world import demand for tea is likely to rise at an average rate in the region of $1\frac{1}{2}$ per cent a year over the period 1960–1 to 1975. In the event, consumption could rise faster than this, perhaps by 2 per cent a year, given a faster rate of growth in production than over the past decade so that a lower level of prices could engender a more substantial expansion in demand in the primary-producing countries. If the growth in production was raised appreciably above the recent trend rate, the effective constraint on world trade might then become, as already indicated, the foreign exchange positions of the tea-importing countries.

Exports from the Overseas Sterling Area

The share of the overseas Sterling countries in world exports of all three tropical beverage crops has risen somewhat over the first half of the 1960s. This is also true if Sterling exports are related to world net imports, or to consumption outside the producing countries, as in Table A5. For *cocoa*, the rise in the Sterling share reflects the substantial expansion in production in Ghana and Nigeria to which reference was made earlier. The preferential tariffs enjoyed by the former French territories in Africa in the E.E.C. countries[2] have not adversely affected

---

[1] Tea production in Iran rose from an average of 13 million lb. in 1957–9 to 26 million lb. in 1962–4; over the same period imports fell from 24 to 13 million lb.

[2] The common external tariff of the E.E.C. countries on imports of raw cocoa, which was originally set at 9 per cent *ad valorem*, was reduced to 5·4 per cent under the Yaoundé Convention between the Community and the eighteen associated African states (which entered into force in 1964). The new rate is only marginally higher than the weighted average of the tariff rates of the E.E.C. member countries in 1961–2 (5·0 per cent). The Sterling share of

the Sterling share of the latter's cocoa imports, nor would they appear to be a major factor for the future. The prospects for the Sterling share of world trade in cocoa would thus seem to depend essentially on the long-term potential of Ghana and Nigeria to expand their output on a competitive basis. Though productivity in these two countries is likely to increase further in the period up to 1970, some allowance must be made for the probability that by the mid 1970s yields from the older plantings will have begun to fall. By that time, the average age of cocoa stock in other producing countries might well be appreciably lower than in these two West African countries. For this reason, no further increase has been assumed in the Sterling share of world cocoa grindings in the net importing countries from the level reached in 1964–5, though there is inevitably a fair margin of error involved here. On this assumption, Sterling exports in 1975 would reach some 0·9 to 1·0 million tons,[1] equivalent to an annual rate of growth of 3·4 to 3·8 per cent a year between 1960–1 and 1975 on the low income-growth basis, and 3·6 to 4·1 per cent a year on the high one. These projections include the effect of increasing demand from centrally planned countries, where, despite the sharp rise in their cocoa imports during the past decade, there is still room for a further significant expansion in cocoa consumption.

Table A5. *Exports of tropical beverage crops from the Overseas Sterling Area, 1953–65 and projections for 1975*

	O.S.A. exports			As proportion of world net imports		
	Cocoa	Coffee	Tea	Cocoa[a]	Coffee	Tea
	(*Thousand metric tons*)			(*Percentages*)		
1953–7	365	112	394	53	6	86
1960–1	557	207	421	67	8	83
1962–3	642	239	461	67	9	85
1964–5	728	279	465	68	10	86
1975: A	900–960	450–530	530–550	} 68	12–14	86
B	940–1,000	470–560	530–550			

SOURCES: *The Commonwealth and the Sterling Area: Statistical Abstract*, Board of Trade, London; and as for Tables A2–A4.

[a] Proportion of grindings outside the cocoa-producing countries.

For *coffee*, the rise in the Sterling share of world net imports from 6 per cent in 1953–7 to 10 per cent in 1964–5 was mainly the result of a shift in consumer preferences towards *robusta* varieties, a substantial

raw cocoa imports into E.E.C. countries was 46 per cent in 1957–8, before entry into force of the Treaty of Rome; by 1964–5 the proportion was marginally higher at 48 per cent.
[1] The argument here assumes no supply limitation on growth of Sterling exports.

proportion of which comes from Sterling countries in Africa. This shift has been most pronounced in the United States, where the proportion of *robusta* in total coffee imports rose from 7 per cent in 1955 to 12 per cent in 1960 and to 25 per cent in 1965.[1] For the present projections, this shift in preference has been assumed to continue over the coming decade, the Sterling share of world net coffee imports being taken within a range of 12 to 14 per cent in 1975 against only 8 per cent in 1960–1. On this assumption, Sterling exports in 1975 would reach some 450 to 550 thousand tons, representing an average annual growth rate of about $5\frac{1}{2}$ to $6\frac{1}{2}$ per cent on the low income-growth assumption, and about 6 to 7 per cent on the high income basis. Had no further shift to Sterling coffee from the 1964–5 position been assumed, the average rate of growth in Sterling coffee exports between 1960–1 and 1975 would be reduced to 4 and $4\frac{1}{2}$ per cent a year on the low and high income-growth assumptions respectively.

For *tea*, the share of Sterling countries in world net imports declined somewhat from 1953–7 to 1960–1 and then recovered (Table A5). The major uncertainties concerning future prospects are, first, the extent to which Indonesia—where production in 1964–5 was still well below the pre-war level—can expand her exportable production and, second, whether China will enter the world export market on any substantial scale. In the longer run, either possibility, should it occur, could result in a marked decline in the Sterling share of the world export market as well as in a fall in tea prices. It is assumed here that neither of these possibilities will occur in the period up to 1975, and that the Sterling share will be much the same as in the mid 1960s. On this basis, Sterling tea exports would rise from some 420 thousand tons in 1960–1 to 530 to 550 thousand tons in 1975, representing an annual growth rate of 1·6 to 1·9 per cent over the period.

[1] See *Annual Coffee Statistics, 1965.*

APPENDIX A 2

SUGAR

The present pattern of trade

Sugar constitutes one of the major primary commodity exports of the Overseas Sterling Area, accounting in 1964 for some 3½ per cent of total exports from these countries. Exports are, however, fairly highly concentrated in a relatively small number of countries. In 1964, for example, four countries—Australia, Mauritius, Jamaica and South Africa—accounted for two-thirds of the area's total sugar exports; while eight countries—Fiji, Guyana, Trinidad and Tobago, Barbados and the four largest exporters already mentioned—accounted for over nine-tenths of the total.

The importance of sugar varies widely among the different exporting countries. At one extreme are small countries depending mainly on sugar for their export earnings. Over nine-tenths of exports from Mauritius, by value, consists of sugar; for Fiji, the proportion is four-fifths, for Barbados, three-quarters (Table A 6).[1] At the other extreme, for Australia—the largest Sterling sugar-exporting country—and for South Africa, sugar accounts for less than one-tenth of their total export earnings.

Although some Sterling countries are heavily dependent on sugar exports, they are to a large extent shielded from fluctuations in the world price of sugar by the Commonwealth Sugar Agreement, which provides for exports from Commonwealth producing countries to the United Kingdom of 'negotiated price quotas'; these are quantities the exporters are obliged to make available and the United Kingdom is obliged to purchase, such quantities being purchased at agreed preferential prices.[2] The purchase price for 'negotiated price quota' raw sugar imported by the United Kingdom was about 5½ United States cents per lb. from 1958 to 1965. Over this period, the free market price has undergone some violent fluctuations but, apart from a short period in 1963, has remained well below the preferential price.

The Commonwealth Sugar Agreement is not the only preferential arrangement affecting world trade in this commodity. All sugar imports into the United States are subject to quota allocation under the United States Sugar Act of 1948[3] (and as subsequently amended) and

[1] The proportions relate to 1964. The corresponding proportion for Cuban dependence on sugar in that year was 78 per cent.

[2] Canada and New Zealand also purchase sugar at preferential prices under the Agreement.

[3] Quotas are allocated to divide the home market between domestic production and imports, as well as between different foreign sources of supply.

Table A6. *Exports of sugar, 1964*

	Value of exports			As proportion of total exports
	Raw	Refined	Total	
	(£ million)			(%)
STERLING COUNTRIES				
Australia	62	1	63	6
Mauritius	25	—	25	94
Jamaica	20	—	20	26
South Africa	17	0	17	4
Fiji	16	—	16	82
Guyana	11	—	11	34
Trinidad and Tobago	9	—	9	7
Barbados	7	—	7	74
Other overseas Sterling countries	17	16	33	..
Total, Overseas Sterling Area	185	17	201	4
United Kingdom	—	31	31	1
Total, Sterling	185	47	232	2
NON-STERLING COUNTRIES				
Developed	18	52	70	0·2
Developing	459	37	496	7
of which: Cuba	*199*	—	*199*	*78*
Centrally planned	10	77	87	1
Total, non-Sterling	487	166	653	1
TOTAL	672	214	885	1
O.S.A. as percentage of TOTAL	27	8	23	..

SOURCE: *Trade Yearbook, 1964*, F.A.O., Rome, 1966.

these too receive preferential prices, at about the same level as those under the United Kingdom scheme. The other main preferential channels are the Cuban sales to the Soviet Union (at 6 U.S. cents per lb.) and the trade between France and the French Overseas Departments (also at about 6 U.S. cents per lb.). In all, trade within these preferential channels represented about one-half of world raw sugar exports in 1965. The 'residual' or free market is thus a narrow one, particularly in relation to world production, so that relatively small changes in supply tend to have a disproportionately large effect on the free market price. Between 1963 and 1965, for example, the free price was abnormally depressed;[1] since the preferential price arrangements of the Commonwealth Sugar Agreement cover only two-thirds of all raw sugar exports from the Overseas Sterling Area, the prolonged depression

[1] Sugar prices on the free market fell from the abnormally high average of 8·3 cents per lb. in 1963 to 2·0 cents in 1965 and 1·76 cents in 1966.

in the free market price had an adverse effect in this period on the value of sugar exports from certain Sterling countries, even though the free market was expanding.[1]

The prospects for export earnings from sugar thus depend on the future configuration of any international agreement to stabilize the residual sugar market and to raise the free market price to levels remunerative to the producers,[2] as well as on the likely future trend in consumption.

Prospects for consumption

Sugar consumption levels differ widely between countries, per head of population, the influence of dietary habits and other special factors accounting for a good part of these differences. Dietary habits tend to change relatively slowly, and changes in consumption levels over a decade or so are generally much more a reflection of economic influences, that is, changes in real income (and its distribution) and changes in sugar prices relative to those of other goods.

There is a definite relationship between changes in *per caput* sugar consumption and changes in income and in relative sugar prices. In poorer countries, both the income and price elasticities of demand for sugar tend to be high—the reverse being true for wealthy countries. Detailed regression equations covering a large number of countries published by the Food and Agriculture Organization indicate average income elasticities ranging from 1·2 for 'low-income' countries to 0·7 for 'medium-income' and 0·4 for 'high-income' countries; the corresponding price elasticities were −1·1, −0·9 and −0·4.[3] Similar results were obtained in the present study by regressions of *per caput* consumption on *per caput* real income for thirty-five developed and less developed countries. These regressions[4] indicated a fairly sharp decline in income elasticity as consumption rises from low to medium levels, and a more gradual decline from medium to high levels, with income elasticity in effect at zero in some countries at the higher income levels. Among the latter, where sugar consumption per head is virtually at saturation level, are the United States, United Kingdom, Canada and West Germany.

On the basis of the computed income elasticities[5] the projections of sugar consumption, summarized in Table A 7, were arrived at. For

---

[1] Total exports on the free market rose from about 9 million to 10 million tons between 1963 and 1965.

[2] It would seem that average production costs of raw sugar between 1963 and 1966 were in the region of 4 U.S. cents per lb.

[3] A. Viton and F. Pignalosa, *Trends and Forces of World Sugar Consumption*, F.A.O., Rome, 1961 (especially Table 19).

[4] Semi-logarithmic equations were used on annual series for the period 1950–9.

[5] In general some allowance was made for the probability that income elasticities of demand for sugar will decline somewhat over the coming decade.

this purpose sugar prices in 1975 were assumed to be the same as in the base period 1960–1; in other words, the free market price was assumed to rise by some two-thirds between 1966 (when prices fell to the abnormally low level of 1·76 cents a lb.) and 1975.

Table A 7. *Sugar consumption in industrial and primary-producing countries, 1953–65 and projections for 1975*

	Rates of growth				Consumption[a]			
	1953–7 to 1960–1	1960–1 to 1964–5	1960–1 to 1975				1975	
			A	B	1960–1	1964–5	A	B
	(% per annum)				(*Million metric tons*)			
INDUSTRIAL COUNTRIES								
United Kingdom	1·4	−0·4	0·7	0·7	2·9	2·9	3·2	3·2
E.E.C.	3·8	3·4	2·3	2·7	5·4	6·2	7·4	7·9
Other Western Europe	4·6	2·7	2·0	2·3	2·9	3·3	3·8	4·0
United States	2·0	1·1	1·0	1·0	8·8	9·2	10·2	10·2
Canada	1·7	2·2	1·5	1·8	0·8	0·9	1·1	1·2
Japan	5·6	5·3	4·1	4·8	1·5	1·8	2·7	2·9
Total, industrial	2·8	2·1	1·7	2·0	22·3	24·2	28·4	29·4
PRIMARY-PRODUCING COUNTRIES[b]								
Sterling	5·3	4·7	4·0	4·5	1·5	1·8	2·6	2·8
Non-Sterling	4·0	4·3	3·5	4·0	5·0	5·9	8·2	8·8
Total, primary-producers	4·2	4·4	3·6	4·1	6·5	7·7	10·8	11·6
TOTAL	3·2	2·7	2·2	2·5	28·8	31·9	39·2	41·0

SOURCES: *Statistical Bulletins* and *Sugar Year Books,* International Sugar Council, London.
   [a] Actual consumption.   [b] Other than net sugar-exporting countries.

The results of the projections indicate that, for the industrial countries as a whole, sugar consumption is likely to rise by about 1·7 per cent a year on average between 1960–1 and 1975 on the low income-growth assumption, and by 2·0 per cent a year on the high one. These rates are marginally lower than the 2·1 per cent a year recorded over the first half of the 1960s, when the growth of consumption was probably somewhat inflated in certain countries purchasing mainly or partly in the free market (Japan and Canada, for instance) during 1964–5. For both Britain and the United States the projected rise in consumption reflects solely the anticipated increase in total population, but for most of the other industrial countries a further (small) increase in *per caput* consumption must be anticipated. Table A 7 also shows the corresponding projections for primary-producing countries other than sugar exporters;[1] for these, the growth rate of consumption is likely to continue to exceed that of the industrial countries as a result of higher income elasticities.

Taking the industrial countries and the non sugar-exporting primary-producing countries together, total sugar consumption is projected to rise from about 29 million tons in 1960–1 to 39 million tons in 1975 on the low income-growth assumption, and to 41 million tons on the high basis.

These projections also assume that no significant changes are made in the incidence of taxation on retail sugar prices in the consuming countries. The wide variation in the price elasticity of demand for sugar has already been mentioned. In particular, in so far as the less developed countries impose high taxes on sugar, the potential market is probably substantially greater than is indicated in the projections in Table A 7. As illustrative of the order of magnitude of the possible effect on consumption, an estimate made by R. H. Snape for 1959 indicates that world demand for sugar (outside the centrally planned countries) would have been higher by 3·9 million metric tons, representing over 70 per cent of world net trade in the free market if (a) all excise taxes had been eliminated and (b) tariff and non-tariff barriers to imports had been replaced by protection in the form of deficiency payments.[2] Allowing for the additional resources required to produce the 3·9 million tons, Professor H. G. Johnson estimates that the net benefit accruing to the sugar-exporting countries resulting from such policy changes would have been in the range $79 to $112 million for 1959.[3]

Imports in relation to consumption

In all the industrial countries, domestic production of sugar is encouraged by one form of protectionism or another. The operation of the United States Sugar Act, already referred to, is only one example of the restriction on imported sugar. Britain, the E.E.C. and other European countries also subsidize, or otherwise protect, their domestic sugar-beet industries. Moreover, technological improvements since the war have made great headway in sugar-beet farming, so that yields have risen appreciably, thus adding to profitability. As a consequence, domestic sugar production in the industrial countries rose by some 2½ million tons between 1953–7 and 1960–1 (equivalent to an annual

---

[1] Projections of sugar consumption for the net sugar-exporting countries are not included here because these markets are not directly relevant to the estimation of future exports of sugar from Sterling countries.

[2] R. H. Snape, 'Some Effects of Protection in the World Sugar Industry', *Economica*, vol. 30, February 1963.

[3] H. G. Johnson, *Economic Policies towards Less-developed Countries*, Allen & Unwin, London, 1967, Appendix D. For the benefit ensuing from free trade in sugar, see p. 273, n. 1.

growth rate of 4 per cent a year) and by a further 2 million tons (3·3 per cent a year) from 1960–1 to 1964–5. Net sugar imports into these countries, by contrast, rose by only ¾ million tons in the first period (to 8·8 million tons in 1960–1) and not at all in the second.

Table A8. *Net imports of sugar into industrial and primary-producing countries, 1953–65 and projections for 1975*

| | Net imports as proportion of consumption | | | | Net imports | | | |
| | | | | | | | 1975 | |
	1953–7	1960–1	1964–5	1975	1960–1	1964–5	A	B
	(Percentages)				*(Million metric tons)*			
INDUSTRIAL COUNTRIES								
United Kingdom	70	67	67	65–70	1·97	1·92	2·1–2·2	2·1–2·2
E.E.C.	3	—	5	0–5	—	0·31	0·0–0·4	0·0–0·4
Other Western Europe	37	20	27	25–30	0·60	0·88	1·0–1·1	1·0–1·2
United States	46	49	38	35–40	4·31	3·47	3·6–4·1	3·6–4·1
Canada	86	80	86	80–85	0·65	0·78	0·9	1·0
Japan	100	86	78	70–75	1·28	1·40	1·9–2·0	2·0–2·2
Total	44	39	36	33–38	8·81	8·76	9·5–10·7	9·7–11·1
PRIMARY-PRODUCING COUNTRIES[a]								
Sterling	86	77	61	50–55	1·17	1·09	1·3–1·4	1·4–1·5
Non-Sterling	41	41	44	40–45	1·87	2·56	3·3–3·7	3·5–3·9
Total	51	50	48	42–47	3·04	3·65	4·6–5·1	4·9–5·4

SOURCE: As for Table A7.

[a] Other than net sugar-exporting countries.

The displacement of imports by domestic production has been particularly large, since 1960–1, in the United States, where the gap in supplies created by the break with Cuba was filled partly by an expansion in the domestic sugar quota, as well as by a re-allocation of the Cuban quota among other exporting countries. By 1964–5, imports met only 38 per cent of United States consumption compared with 49 per cent in 1960–1, the import volume falling by some 800 thousand tons over this period (see Table A8). The projections assume no change in current United States import policy; if net imports in 1975 are assumed to represent 35 to 40 per cent of consumption, they would amount to some 3½ to 4 million tons compared with 4·3 million tons in 1960–1.

Sugar imports accounted for 10 per cent of consumption in the present E.E.C. area before the war, but by the mid 1950s the proportion had declined below 5 per cent, largely as a result of a substantial expansion in French output. The E.E.C. common agricultural policy for sugar, which came into force in the middle of 1967, is based on an internal target price, with an associated variable import levy. The levy operates so that imported sugar cannot be purchased within the E.E.C. area at a price lower than the target price. In order, however, to avoid the accumulation of surplus stocks, it is envisaged that the price guarantee should be limited to a certain quantity of production. If necessary, the E.E.C. regulations allow for the imposition of a basic quota (equal to the average crop for the years 1961/2 to 1963/4) which would be purchased at the intervention price. Output up to a maximum of 35 per cent above the quota would be purchased at a lower price, while any output above the 35 per cent extra limit would have to be exported without subsidy.[1] The withdrawal of the earlier proposal to subsidize the export of surplus domestic production would imply that the E.E.C. is likely to remain a net importer of sugar, albeit on a relatively small scale. In the present projections, a range of 0 to 5 per cent has been assumed for the proportion of net imports to consumption in 1975 (Table A 8).

For the other industrial areas, the proportion of consumption to be met by imports in 1975 has been taken at much the same levels as those of 1964–5. For the Sterling primary-producers (other than sugar-exporting countries) a further decline in the import proportion has been assumed, thus continuing the secular fall; for non-Sterling primary-producers, however, the import proportion has been taken at much the same level as during the early 1960s.

These various assumptions imply that net imports of sugar into the industrial countries will rise from 8·8 million tons in 1960–1 to about $9\frac{1}{2}$ to $10\frac{1}{2}$ million tons in 1975, on the low income-growth assumption, and to some $9\frac{1}{2}$ to 11 million tons on the higher growth basis. The projected rise in Japanese net import requirements accounts for a large proportion of the total increase. The other main areas for which the projected increases are appreciable are 'other Western Europe' and Canada. As already indicated, however, it would seem likely that imports into the United States—the largest single import market for sugar among the Western industrial countries—will be lower in 1975 than they were in 1960–1 if present protectionist policies are continued.

It is therefore worthwhile considering the extent to which possible changes in present policies might affect the balance between production and imports. One possible policy would be an agreement among the industrial countries to limit their domestic sugar production to the level

---

[1] For a fuller description of the E.E.C. system of regulating its internal sugar market, see M. G. W. Hallmans and A. S. Ivanov, *A Review of Recent Developments in the World Sugar Market, 1960–65*, International Sugar Council, London, 1966.

reached in a recent period and thus allow any further increase in domestic consumption to be met from increased imports. Since domestic beet-sugar production in the industrial countries is mostly high-cost in relation to cane sugar produced in developing countries, such a limitation of beet production would seem to be a minimum step towards a more rational allocation of the world's resources in sugar production. If production in the industrial countries was restricted[1] to the average level reached in the years 1964 and 1965—to take a purely illustrative example—then by 1975 net imports of sugar into these countries would be some 12 million tons on the low income-growth assumption, and 12½ million tons on the higher. In other words, even this minimum approach would result in a substantial additional volume of imports by 1975 to meet the projected rise in consumption. The increase over the figure in Table A8 would be some 1½ to 2½ million tons (about 15 to 25 per cent) on either income-growth assumption.

Another possible alternative would be for the industrial countries to take appropriate measures that would allow the import proportion to rise to an agreed higher level. If, to take another purely illustrative example, the import proportions of the various industrial countries were allowed to rise by 1975 to reach the average for the period 1953–7, then net imports of sugar in 1975 would total 13 and 14 million tons respectively on the two income-growth assumptions. This would represent an additional net import of some 30 to 35 per cent[2] above the projections in Table A8. These calculations indicate that a significant reduction in the present degree of protection afforded to domestic sugar production in the industrial countries would result in a substantially higher level of exports from the primary-producing sugar-exporting countries.[3]

Exports from the Overseas Sterling Area

Because of the existence of preferential arrangements over a large proportion of world trade in sugar, the projections of probable net sugar imports do not necessarily indicate the prospects for expanding exports from Sterling countries. If the various preferential arrangements continue substantially unchanged, preferential access to the United Kingdom market will be assured for Sterling sugar-exporting countries, but because the potential expansion in Britain's consumption is small, any substantial growth in Sterling exports would have to come elsewhere.

Two major changes occurred in the first half of the 1960s which

---

[1] The administrative difficulties of enforcing such a scheme are abstracted from here.

[2] Comparing with the means of the projections, for simplicity of presentation.

[3] For a discussion of the economic effects of complete abolition of sugar protection, see H. G. Johnson, *op. cit.*

would, if continued, appreciably benefit sales of Sterling sugar outside Britain. First, the United States break with Cuba was followed by a re-allocation of import quotas, including new quotas for certain Sterling countries;[1] as a result the share of sugar from Sterling countries in total United States imports rose from zero in 1960 to one-sixth in 1965 (Table A 9). The second was a shift in sources of Japanese imports from Latin American sugar to Australian and South African; whereas the Sterling share of Japan's sugar imports was only about one-tenth until 1961, the percentage rose to one-quarter in 1962 and to two-fifths during 1963–5. The rapid expansion in Sterling exports of sugar to Japan seems to result essentially from the competitive character of sugar production in Australia and South Africa, reflecting their relatively high yields. In the present projections it has been assumed that the Sterling proportion of Japanese sugar imports in 1975 will be almost one-half, much the same as in 1965.

Table A 9. *Exports of sugar from the Overseas Sterling Area, 1957–65 and projections for 1975*

							O.S.A. exports		
	O.S.A. share of world exports							1975	
	1957–9	1961	1965	1975	1961	1965	A	B
	(Percentages)					*(Million metric tons)*			
INDUSTRIAL COUNTRIES									
United Kingdom	64	69	86	80–85	1·69	1·94	1·7–1·9	1·7–1·9
United States	—	12	16	15–18	0·48	0·58	0·5–0·7	0·5–0·7
Canada	72	95	89	90	0·68	0·74	0·8	0·9
Japan	11	10	43	40–50	0·13	0·61	0·8–1·0	0·8–1·1
Total, industrial	22	30	36	..	2·98	3·87	3·8–4·4	3·9–4·6
PRIMARY-PRODUCING COUNTRIES[a]									
Sterling	21	26	21	20–30	0·31	0·26	0·3–0·4	0·3–0·4
Non-Sterling	2	1	0	0–2	0·03	0·01	..	..
Total, primary-producers	8	10	5	..	0·34	0·27	0·3–0·4	0·3–0·4
TOTAL	24	25	26	..	3·32	4·14	4·1–4·8	4·2–5·0

SOURCE: As for Table A 7.

[a] Other than net sugar-exporting countries.

Among primary-producing countries which are net sugar-importers, the Sterling share of the import market is substantial for member

[1] United States quotas for Sterling exporting countries in 1965 were mainly for Australia, the West Indies, India and South Africa.

countries of the Sterling Area but negligible for non-Sterling countries, as can be seen from Table A9. In the present projections the Sterling shares of these import markets in 1975 have been taken as corresponding approximately with the range experienced in the first half of the 1960s.

On the basis of all these assumptions, exports of sugar from overseas Sterling countries to the industrial areas are projected to rise from some 3·0 million tons in 1961 and 3·9 million tons in 1965 to 3·8 to 4·4 million tons in 1975 on the low income-growth assumption, and to 3·9 to 4·6 million tons on the higher basis. Thus, even on the more optimistic assumption, any increase envisaged above the 1965 level would be a very marginal one; on the lower income-growth assumption, Sterling sugar exports in 1975 could be much the same as in 1965. A very similar conclusion emerges for the projection of Sterling sugar exports to primary-producing countries. As mentioned earlier, all these projections assume the continuance of current protectionist policies in the industrial countries. The projections for sugar exports would show a substantial increase over the decade 1965–75 if protection of beet-sugar production in the industrial countries was appreciably reduced during the period. Whether and to what extent this increase in volume sold would result in an increase in export value would largely depend on whether the preferential prices paid by Britain for Commonwealth sugar remained intact; and on the effect on the free market price of sugar of the assumed reduction in protection in the industrial countries.

APPENDIX A 3

MEAT

The present pattern of trade

The world's livestock industries are largely concentrated in temperate-zone countries covered by North America, Europe and the U.S.S.R., Oceania, Argentina and Uruguay. The overseas Sterling countries accounted for over one-quarter by value of all meat exports in 1964, but for mutton and lamb the proportion was as high as nine-tenths. For beef and veal the Sterling share of world exports (one-third) was also appreciable, but for other fresh meat (mainly pork and offal) and for canned and preserved meat the Sterling share was only one-tenth (see Table A 10). Fresh pork and offal are exported mainly by the United States and Western Europe; by far the largest exporter of canned and preserved meat is Denmark. The particular specializations of the overseas Sterling countries in certain types of meat are important in assessing the probable future trend in their export trade.

Table A 10. *Exports of meat, 1964*

	Value of exports					Meat as pro-portion of total exports
	Beef and veal	Mutton and lamb	Other fresh meat	Canned and preserved meat	Total	
	(*£ million*)					(%)
STERLING COUNTRIES						
Australia	71	13	6	6	95	9
New Zealand	29	53	7	2	91	25
Ireland	14	4	4	12	34	16
United Kingdom	3	1	4	4	11	0·3
Other countries	6	1	2	11	19	..
Total, Sterling	122	72	23	33	250	3
NON-STERLING COUNTRIES						
Industrial	96	4	162	205	466	1
Developing	138	5	30	35	209	3
Centrally planned	9	0	38	46	94	1
Total, non-Sterling	243	9	230	287	769	2
TOTAL	366	81	253	320	1,019	2
Sterling countries as percentage of TOTAL	*33*	*89*	*9*	*10*	*25*	..

SOURCE: *Trade Yearbook, 1965*, F.A.O., Rome, 1966.

Of the Sterling countries, New Zealand is most dependent on meat for her export income (it provided one-quarter of her total exports in 1964). Ireland is also heavily dependent—to an appreciable but declining extent—on meat (one-sixth of total exports), almost all of which is shipped to the United Kingdom. In addition she exports live animals for slaughter in Britain and on the Continent; in 1964 exports of meat and live animals together (£96·2 million) represented about 45 per cent of total Irish exports. Less than one-tenth of Australia's export income in 1964 came from meat (largely beef and veal). Among non-Sterling countries, only Argentina, Uruguay and Denmark are heavily dependent on meat exports.

The major proportion of the post-war rise in meat production has been in the United States and in continental Western Europe. In both areas livestock-breeding has been encouraged by farm support policies, including the fixing of minimum prices for the main varieties of bovine meat. Moreover, the general rise in costs in the developed countries over the past decade has differed sharply from that of other agricultural produce entering world trade; from 1953–5 to 1963–5, for example, meat export unit values rose by 22 per cent whereas unit values of all agricultural produce in world trade fell by 8 per cent over the same period.

The prospects for meat exports from the countries of the Overseas Sterling Area depend on several factors. The first is the rate at which consumption is likely to go on rising in the main importing areas. The second is whether any significant change can be expected in the degree to which the importing areas are dependent on imports for their supplies of meat; this depends on the prospects for further improvements in productivity in their livestock-breeding industries as well as on their policies of protection against competing imports. Finally, much will depend on the rate at which Sterling countries can expand their exportable meat surpluses at competitive prices.

Prospects for consumption

Nearly three-quarters of all the meat consumed in the world (outside centrally planned countries) is consumed in North America and Western Europe. About half the rest is consumed in the six major meat-exporting countries of the Southern Hemisphere. Of the total consumption in the industrial countries, almost half is in the United States alone (Table A11).

Estimates for the United States suggest that consumption of beef is more responsive to rising income than to price changes. A recent study by R. F. Daly of the U.S. Department of Agriculture puts the income elasticity of demand for beef and veal at 0·67; the price elasticity is put at only 0·20.[1] For Britain, the position appears to be different, in that the price elasticities for the main varieties of fresh meat exceed the corresponding income elasticities. Poultry is an exception, since the income elasticity considerably exceeds unity (unlike the income elasticities for the other varieties) and is much the same—if signs are ignored—as the price elasticity. In the E.E.C. area the pattern of income elasticity is not very different from the British, except that beef and veal have a much higher elasticity and poultry a rather lower one.[2]

Table A 11. *Meat consumption in the industrial countries, 1953–63 and projections for 1975*

	Consumption per head					Total consumption			
		Rates of growth						1975	
		1953–1 to 1960–1	1953–7 to 1962–3	1960–1 to 1975					
	1960–1			A	B	1960–1	1962–3	A	B
	(*Kg.*)	(*% per annum*)				(*Million metric tons*)			
U.K.	69·4	1·9	2·3	1·0	1·4	3·49	3·80	4·3	4·5
E.E.C.	55·5	3·7	4·9	2·1	2·7	9·58	10·48	14·3	15·5
Other Western Europe	34·8	3·0	4·7	2·7	3·6	2·74	3·04	5·2	5·9
U.S.A.	84·5	0·9	0·9	0·7	0·8	15·11	15·68	20·7	21·1
Canada	77·3	0·1	0·5	0·9	1·1	1·41	1·50	2·1	2·2
Japan	4·0	7·9	11·9	7·8	9·2	0·41	0·59	1·2	1·4
TOTAL	52·3	1·8	2·5	1·6	1·9	32·74	35·09	47·8	50·6

SOURCES: *Food Consumption in O.E.C.D. Countries*, O.E.C.D., Paris; *Meat*, Commonwealth, Economic Committee, London.

Projections of the probable level of meat consumption in 1975 can be made on the basis of these calculated income elasticities together with ones for other countries estimated by the Food and Agriculture Organization (F.A.O.) for total meat consumption.[3] The F.A.O. estimates show a wide range in income elasticities, from 1·5 in Asia and the Far East (excluding Japan) and 1·3 in Africa (excluding South Africa) and the Near East, in both of which areas meat consumption per head is still relatively very small, at one extreme, to elasticities of 0·1 or 0·2 for

[1] R. F. Daly, *Agriculture in the Years Ahead*, Southern Agricultural Workers Conference, Atlanta, Georgia, 3 February 1963.

[2] *Le Marché commun des Produits agricoles: Perspectives '1970'*, Série Agriculture 10, E.E.C., Bruxelles, 1963.

[3] *Agricultural Commodities—Projections for 1970*, Special Supplement to *F.A.O. Commodity Review, 1962*, F.A.O., Rome, 1962.

Australia and New Zealand, which have the highest meat consumption per head.

By applying these elasticities to the alternative assumptions about the rate of growth in real income per head in the various countries and assuming no change in meat prices in relation to other prices, meat consumption per head in the industrial countries is estimated to rise from 52 kg. per annum in 1960–1 to 65 kg. (25 per cent) on assumption A and to 68 kg. (31 per cent) on assumption B. On the higher income-growth assumption, meat consumption per head would rise over the period by nearly 70 per cent in 'other Western Europe', by almost 50 per cent in the E.E.C., by some 20 to 25 per cent in Britain, but by only 12 per cent in the United States, which would still, however, continue to have the greatest consumption level per head.

The sharpest increases are likely to continue to be in beef, veal and poultry, with a modest rise in pork but little in mutton and lamb.

On a tonnage basis, consumption in the industrial areas is projected to rise from 33 million tons to 48 million tons by 1970 on assumption A (a rise of some 45 per cent) and to 51 million tons on assumption B (55 per cent). On the higher growth assumption, the largest contributions to the total increase in consumption of almost 20 million tons would be made by the United States and the E.E.C. (6 million tons each). Almost one-half the total increase projected would be in beef and veal.

Outside the industrial areas, total consumption in the major meat-producing countries is projected to rise by 65 to 70 per cent over the period; in other primary-producing countries the rise would be even larger (85 to 100 per cent). Nonetheless, meat consumption per head in the latter group would still be extremely low by 1975—only about one-eighth of the comparable level projected for the industrial areas, including Japan.

Prospects for production and net imports

Because the greater part of meat consumption in the industrial countries is met by their own livestock industries, the effect of the projected growth in consumption on meat imports from primary-producing countries will depend on the rate at which meat production can be increased in industrial countries. This, in turn, will depend heavily on farm support policies, particularly in Western Europe, as well as on the secular improvement of productivity in the livestock industries.

By far the largest increase in meat production over the past decade has taken place in the United States. Between 1953–7 and 1962–3 production there rose by 3·2 million metric tons (2·5 per cent a year), accounting for nearly two-fifths of the total increase in meat production in the industrial countries (8·4 million tons) during this period. Meat production in E.E.C. countries rose by 2·6 million tons, the rate of growth (4 per cent a year) exceeding that in the United States. Both the United States and the E.E.C. are virtually self-sufficient in meat, though imports into the United States have sizeably increased since 1960 as a result of a rising demand for beef. 'Other Western Europe' is a large meat-exporting region; Denmark and Yugoslavia, in particular, export both fresh and canned meat in substantial quantities to other industrial countries.

The United Kingdom is an exception, but the proportion of consumption met from home production has been rising: from 58 per cent in 1953–7 to 61 and 63 per cent in 1960–1 and 1962–3 respectively. Britain is now virtually self-sufficient in pork and poultry; for beef and veal, the proportion of consumption met from home supply had risen from one-half before the war to almost three-quarters by 1962–3, but for mutton and lamb the 1962–3 proportion (two-fifths) was the same as pre-war.

Over the coming decade, the prospects are for a further considerable expansion in meat production in the industrial countries. This would result partly from increases in the animal population, but mainly because the probable steady improvement in livestock-breeding, animal husbandry and feeding practices would raise the average weight of animals slaughtered. Moreover, government policies in the main producing countries are generally directed towards encouraging the further expansion of home meat output, but the precise effect of any given policy on the future level of output remains uncertain.

Apart from the secular improvement in productivity per livestock unit, the output of meat depends to a large extent on the relation between the prices of meat and of feedingstuffs as well as that between milk and meat prices. In the United States the elasticity of supply of livestock products in recent years in response to changes in product/feed price relationships has been in the region of 0·2 (for instance, a 10 per cent rise in livestock product prices over feed prices would result in a 2 per cent rise in output), but a recent authoritative projection assumes a long-run elasticity of 0·4 for the projection to 1970 and 0·6 for that to 1980.[1]

For the United Kingdom, the elasticity of production with respect to changes in own prices has been estimated at 0·5 for cows, 0·77 for calves reared, 1·29 for ewes, 4·09 for sows and 2·00 for adult fowls[2]. While a rise in feed prices would tend to restrict the growth in beef output, it

[1] R. F. Daly, op. cit.

[2] Colin Clark and others, *United Kingdom: Projected Level of Demand, Supply and Imports of Farm Products in 1965 and 1975*, U.S. Department of Agriculture, Washington, 1962.

would at the same time encourage mutton production, as sheep compete with cows in livestock-rearing.

Feed prices seem likely to fall relatively to meat prices over the next decade. The American study quoted above assumes that prices of feed grains and hay will decline by 22 per cent between 1962–3 and 1970, with no further change from 1970 to 1980, whereas meat prices are assumed to rise by 2 per cent until 1970, with an additional 6 per cent rise in the next decade. On this basis, the output of cattle and calves in the United States is projected to increase by one-third by 1970 and by more than two-thirds by 1980, compared with 1962–3; poultry, one-fifth by 1970 and more than one-half by 1980; and hog production, nearly one-third by 1980.[1]

Estimates of United Kingdom meat production in 1975 were made in a recent Oxford study on varying assumptions about the rate of income growth and product/feed price relationships.[2] On the highest income-growth assumption (which closely approximates to assumption A in the present study) and on the 'low feed prices' assumption, home beef and veal output is projected to go up 21 to 22 per cent from 1955–9 to 1975; the corresponding increases for other items are: mutton and lamb, 31 to 32 per cent; pork, 19 to 21 per cent; offal, 22 per cent; bacon and ham, 19 per cent.[3] For all meat, home production is projected to increase by 38 to 39 per cent (in tonnage) over this period, whereas total supplies including imports would increase by almost the same percentage, so that there would be no overall change in the import proportion.

In the E.E.C., the common agricultural policy is designed to encourage meat production among the Six, stabilize the internal market and provide a fair standard of living to producers. For pig meat and poultry the policy is effected by a variable import levy system, while beef and veal imports are to be regulated by the common external tariff. A recent study, by the E.E.C. Secretariat, of the trends in agricultural production estimates the 1970 level of beef and veal output in the E.E.C. area at 4·7 to 5·2 million metric tons, according to the assumptions made.[4] This represents an increase of some 30 to 45 per cent above the 1960–1 average of 3·6 million tons, and would imply a net import of 55 to 340 thousand tons in 1970, compared with 260 thousand tons in 1958 (the base year of the E.E.C. study) and 90 thousand tons in 1960–1. French beef and veal production is projected to rise to 2·1 to 2·4 million tons by 1970.

The prospects for net imports into the E.E.C. countries by 1975

[1] Daly, *op. cit.* p. 9.
[2] Clark and others, *op. cit.*   [3] *Ibid.* table 50.
[4] *Le Marché commun des Produits agricoles: Perspectives '1970'*, E.E.C., Brussels.

depend very largely on the rate of growth in French meat output.[1] If this develops in accordance with the official plans and projections, the E.E.C. area would cease to be a net importing region, and might well become a net exporter, albeit on a relatively small scale.

'Other Western Europe' is a net exporting area for meat, the bulk of the exports coming from Denmark. In 1960–1, about 70 per cent (by weight) of Danish meat exports consisted of canned meat, bacon and ham, and these can be expected to rise to meet the projected increases in net imports in Britain, the United States and, to a smaller extent, other Western European countries. Japanese meat imports are likely to expand, but the absolute quantity is likely to remain relatively small.

These are general considerations about the probable direction and extent of the expansion in meat production in industrial countries; they can be combined with corresponding projections of meat consumption to yield estimates of net imports in 1975 on the various assumptions made (Table A 12).

Table A 12. *Net imports of meat into the industrial countries,*
1960–3 and projections for 1975

	Net imports as proportion of consumption			Net imports			
						1975	
	1960–1	1962–3	1975	1960–1	1962–3	A	B
	(Percentages)			*(Million metric tons)*			
United Kingdom	40	34	33–36	1·39	1·31	1·4–1·6	1·5–1·6
E.E.C.	5	7	5–7	0·45	0·76	0·7–1·0	0·8–1·1
Other Western Europe	−33	−30	−20 to −25	−0·90	−0·91	−1·0 to −1·3	−1·2 to −1·5
United States	0·7	2	1–1½	0·10	0·24	0·2–0·3	0·2–0·3
Canada	1	1	1–2	0·01	0·02	} 0·1	0·1
Japan	7	7	7–10	0·03	0·04		
TOTAL	3	4	2½–4	1·08	1·46	1·1–2·0	1·1–2·0
TOTAL *less* other Western Europe	7	7	5½–7	1·98	2·37	2·4–3·0	2·6–3·2

SOURCES: *Food consumption in the O.E.C.D. countries,* O.E.C.D., Paris; *Meat,* Commonwealth Economic Committee, London; *Trade Yearbooks,* F.A.O., Rome.

For the United States, a marginal increase is assumed in the proportion of consumption met by net imports in 1975 compared with 1960–1. There was a sharp rise in American imports in the late 1950s and early 1960s, mainly of lower-grade beef for manufacturing purposes (to fill a

---

[1] Under the fourth Plan, beef and veal production was expected to rise to 1·75 million tons by 1965. Actual production in 1965 was about 1·62 million tons.

gap from a switch in home production to prime beef). Beef and veal imports into the United States averaged only about 12 thousand tons a year during 1953–6, but had jumped to over 220 thousand tons in 1960–1, to some 400 thousand tons in 1962, and to almost 800 thousand tons in 1963. These high rates of import are unlikely to continue for any length of time, partly because of protectionist pressures—negotiations with the main exporting countries in 1963 resulted in the operation of a voluntary quota on beef shipments to the United States—and partly because in the longer run the balance of home supplies is likely to be redressed, at least to some extent, in favour of the manufacturing grades.

For the United Kingdom, however, it seems unlikely—judged on present trends and policies—that the net import proportion will change significantly, over the longer term, from the 1962–3 position. For the E.E.C. a range of 5 to 7 per cent is assumed for the net import proportion, the underlying assumption being that there will be some shortfall in production compared with current plans and projections. Net exports from 'other Western Europe' are assumed to decline somewhat as a proportion of consumption, to allow for the probable relatively rapid increase in meat consumption per head in this area. For Japan, the net import proportion for 1975 has been taken as much the same as in 1960–3.

On the basis of these assumptions, net imports of meat into the industrial countries would rise to 1 to $1\frac{1}{2}$ million metric tons in 1975, compared with 1·0 million tons in 1960–1 and 1·5 million tons in 1962–3. The expansion in 1962–3 was due partly to the higher United States imports, already mentioned, and partly to a sharp rise in Italian meat consumption, which was met by increased imports. The projections indicate little change, in total, from the position in 1962–3, except that a decline is projected in net imports into the E.E.C. area, offset by higher imports by the United States and, to a lesser degree, by Britain. A large proportion of any increase in these two countries would probably be in beef and veal; but Britain's imports of mutton and lamb are also likely to increase compared with the early 1960s and a further expansion in the trade in canned meat seems likely.

Exports from the Overseas Sterling Area

The Sterling producing countries are generally more export-oriented than the non-Sterling countries; in the early 1960s one-sixth of carcass meat output in the former was shipped abroad, as against only 5 per cent for the latter. The longer-term prospects for exportable supplies depend on the trends in production and in home consumption in the major producing countries. Meat production in Australia and New Zealand is likely to expand as a result of increasing productivity in their livestock industries. Production levels in Argentina, however, seem unlikely to rise substantially over at least the next decade, because of the legacy of neglect of pastures, farm buildings and equipment. Production in other Latin American countries may well expand, but it seems doubtful whether, in total, meat production for export from Latin America will show any substantial increase in the period up to 1975.

Consumption per head of carcass meat is higher in Australia and New Zealand than in any other of the main producing countries, consumption being almost at saturation level. In Argentina and Uruguay meat consumption, both in total and in relation to population, declined between the mid 1950s and the early 1960s, reflecting the falling off in production mentioned earlier. It thus seems probable that Sterling producing countries will increase their share of total meat exports from the primary-producing countries in the coming decade, especially if meat consumption in Latin America increases to any appreciable extent.

The Overseas Sterling Area countries are, in any case, the traditional sources of supply of Britain's imports of meat. Over 90 per cent of Britain's mutton and lamb imports come from Sterling sources, particularly New Zealand, but only about one-third of her beef and veal imports are of Sterling origin. The Sterling share of other industrial countries' imports has so far been negligible, except for the United States, where imports of beef from Australia and New Zealand rose from a negligible amount in the mid 1950s to an average of some 175 thousand metric tons in 1960–1, and there were further sharp increases in 1962 and 1963. The greater part of the increase in American demand for imported manufacturing grades of beef was thus met from Sterling sources.

The Sterling Area's market shares in 1975 depend on a number of factors difficult to foresee, and any projection must inevitably be subject to considerable error. For the British market, it would seem that a decline in the Sterling share of canned meat and, possibly, beef imports might be offset by the effect on imports of the probable change in consumption pattern. Beef consumption—with a relatively low Sterling share—is likely to rise less, for example, than consumption of mutton and lamb, where the Sterling share is high. Other factors, for example a possible export surplus of beef in the United States or the E.E.C., could also powerfully affect the outcome. By and large, it does not seem unreasonable to assume, from present trends and policies, that the Sterling share of Britain's meat imports will not substantially differ from recent proportions.

For imports to the United States, similar considerations apply. It is thus implicit that recent gains by Australia and New Zealand will largely be held and that the Sterling Area's share of meat imports will continue to be higher for the United States than for Britain. For the other industrial meat-importing countries, the Sterling share from 1960 to 1963 was only 5 or 6 per cent by value. The production trends indicate that by 1975 this share may well show a significant increase. It is also assumed that the Sterling share of meat imports by primary-producing countries will remain in the region of one-third.

These assumptions are set out in Table A 13, where they are combined with the earlier projections of net imports into each major market in 1975.[1] It is also assumed that the projected trend in *net* imports reflects a similar trend in *gross* imports of meat in terms of value at 1960–1 prices. By applying the market share percentages to the gross import figures, Sterling Area meat exports in 1975 can then be projected on the basis of assumptions made earlier.

Table A 13. *Imports of meat into the industrial countries from the Overseas Sterling Area, 1960–4 and projections for 1975*

| | O.S.A. share of meat imports | | | | Imports from O.S.A. | | | |
| | | | | | | | 1975 | |
	1953–4	1960–1	1963–4	1975	1960–1	1963–4[a]	A	B
	(*Percentages*)				(*£ million at 1960–1 prices*)			
United Kingdom	39	30	29	28–30	100	100	93–107	100–114
United States	4	37	48	40–45	46	79	71–96	71–100
Other industrial countries	6	5	6	5–10	11	21	21–36	21–36
Total	27	24	23	18–24	157	200	185–239	192–250

SOURCES: *Commodity Trade Statistics*, United Nations, New York; *Foreign Trade Statistics, Series C*, O.E.C.D., Paris.

[a] Actual value.

The projections show an increase in total meat exports from the Overseas Sterling Area, between 1960–1 and 1975, of some 20 to 50 per cent on the lower income-growth assumption and of 25 to 60 per cent on the more optimistic one. These ranges are inevitably wide, since Sterling exports represent a changing fraction of net imports, which themselves are only marginal to total consumption. Of the many explicit assumptions on which these projections rest, perhaps the most important are the continuance of present agricultural and import policies in Britain and the E.E.C. area; the continuance of substantial import demand for manufacturing beef by the United States; the ability of Australia and New

[1] It should be noted that the projections of exports from the Overseas Sterling Area are in values at constant prices, not in tonnage.

Zealand to achieve a substantial increase in their production at higher levels of productivity; and no appreciable change in the relative prices of different varieties of meat, compared with the position in 1960–1. Any substantial departure from these assumptions would invalidate the projections shown.

Another assumption has been that newly developed methods of production in the broiler industry for chickens are not applied on a large scale to the chief varieties of carcass meat. If they are, this would no doubt have a major effect on supplies and prices in the industrial countries, and could well have a serious adverse effect on meat exports from the Overseas Sterling Area. These prospects are uncertain and in any case lie outside the control of overseas Sterling countries.

What would lie within their control would be an effort to increase their share of world trade in canned meat. As indicated, their present share is relatively small and, indeed, there has been some substitution in the British market over the last ten years from Australian and New Zealand canned meat to supplies from Western Europe, particularly from Denmark, Holland, Yugoslavia and Poland. Although, in Sterling Area exports, canned meat is unlikely to rival carcass meat, an increase in exportable supplies of Sterling canned meat at competitive prices would improve the Area's prospects for meat exports in general.

APPENDIX A 4

DAIRY PRODUCE

The present pattern of trade

Production of butter, cheese, eggs and other dairy products is mainly concentrated in temperate zone areas, and exports come almost exclusively from the higher-income countries of these areas. New Zealand and Australia are the chief Sterling exporters; butter accounts for between 60 and 70 per cent (by value) of their total exports of dairy products (see Table A 14). The overseas Sterling countries accounted in total for two-fifths of world butter exports in 1964; the proportion for cheese was one-sixth, for milk and milk products one-seventh; while for eggs it was rather marginal at about one-twentieth.

Table A 14. *Exports of dairy products, 1964*

		Value of exports				As pro-portion of total exports
	Butter	Cheese	Milk and milk products	Eggs and egg products	Total	
		(£ million)				(%)
STERLING COUNTRIES						
New Zealand	54	17	6	0	78	22
Australia	23	5	7	2	37	3
Ireland	7	2	4	0	13	6
Other countries	2	1	8	3	14	..
Total, Sterling	86	26	26	4	142	1
NON-STERLING COUNTRIES						
Industrial	100	117	157[a]	47	421	1
Developing	6	2	1	5	13	0·2
Centrally planned	16	6	4	21	48	1
Total, non-Sterling	122	126	161	73	481	1
TOTAL	208	152	187	77	623	1
O.S.A. as percentage of TOTAL	*41*	*17*	*14*	*6*	*23*	..

SOURCE: *Trade Yearbook, 1965*, F.A.O., Rome, 1966.

[a] Includes milk powder shipped under United States aid programmes.

New Zealand is the only Sterling country dependent to any appreciable extent on dairy products for her export earnings; in 1964, for example, dairy products represented over one-fifth of the total value of exports. In this respect, New Zealand resembles Denmark rather than any other Sterling country.

Almost all butter and cheese exports from New Zealand and Australia are sold in the United Kingdom, where, however, they are in competition with supplies from continental European countries, particularly Denmark and Holland. Imports of butter into the United Kingdom are free of import duty but have been subject to import quota control since 1962. Cheese is admitted under Open General Licence;[1] Commonwealth supplies of cheese, however, are protected by preferential import duties.[2]

In a recent period (1964–5), the United Kingdom took over four-fifths of Australian butter exports and over nine-tenths of New Zealand shipments. For cheese, the Australian proportion is considerably lower, Britain taking only three-fifths of the total, other export markets for Australian cheese including Japan, West Germany and the United States. New Zealand, however, is essentially dependent on the United Kingdom market for her exports of cheese, almost nine-tenths of her cheese exports being shipped to Britain in 1964–5.

Future prospects for Sterling exports of butter and cheese therefore depend overwhelmingly on the evolution of demand in Britain, and on the probable growth in Britain's own production of these commodities. In the discussion below, a continuance of the Commonwealth Preference Area is necessarily assumed.[3]

Butter

Butter consumption per head in the United Kingdom has risen at a relatively slow rate over the first half of the 1960s (0·6 per cent a year); the sharp rise compared with 1953–7 reflects the relative scarcities of food rationing in the early 1950s (see Table A 15). The income elasticity of demand for butter in the United Kingdom was officially calculated at 0·27 from family expenditure data for 1962,[4] while the same source gave a price elasticity of −0·38. The experience of the past decade also suggests that butter consumption is sensitive to changes in the ratio of prices of butter and margarine.[5]

In making the projections, it has been assumed that the relative prices of butter and margarine in 1975 will be much the same as in the

---

[1] Except for cheese from Eastern Europe, which is subject to restriction under bilateral quota arrangements.

[2] The United Kingdom imposes an *ad valorem* tariff of 15 per cent on imports of non-Commonwealth cheese, other than blue-veined, on which the tariff is 10 per cent (blue-veined cheese from E.F.T.A. countries being duty-free).

[3] The possibility of Britain and other E.F.T.A. countries joining the Common Market has not been taken into account, partly because the outlook for such proposals was still uncertain at the time of the present study, and partly because the effects of Britain's entry into the E.E.C. area on exports of dairy produce from Sterling countries—especially New Zealand—cannot be determined before the precise terms of such entry are negotiated.

[4] See *Domestic Food Consumption and Expenditure, 1962*, H.M.S.O., London, 1964.

[5] See J. A. C. Brown, *Income and Price Elasticity of Demand for Milk and Milk Products*, O.E.C.D., Paris, 1962.

base period, 1960–1; and that the trend away from fatty foods for health reasons—apparent in the United States—will not spread to Britain, at least during the period of the present projections. Using the income elasticity mentioned in conjunction with the standard assumptions about the growth of population and real income per head,[1] total butter consumption in the United Kingdom in 1975 is projected to rise to 570 and 600 thousand tons on the low and high income-growth assumptions respectively (Table A 15).

There is inevitably some doubt about the assumption of a constant ratio of butter and margarine prices. Butter prices in Britain have been considerably lower than those in continental Western Europe,[2] but it is possible that the British prices may rise (over margarine) if imports of butter continue to be restricted. A rise in butter prices of, say, 10 per cent would imply a total consumption in 1975 some 20 to 25 thousand tons lower than the projections shown in Table A 15.

This method of projecting also assumes, as indicated, that the recent trend in the United States away from the consumption of fatty foods, including butter, will not appear in Britain. Over the past ten years, butter consumption per head in the United States has fallen by about 2 per cent a year purely as a result of changes in consumer preferences and other trends.[3] A reduction of this order would evidently make a substantial difference to the projection for British consumption of butter.

The proportion of domestic consumption met by imports has remained at about 90 per cent ever since the early 1950s. Though a guaranteed price for milk produced is paid only for a fixed quota, deliveries above quota being paid for at actual market prices, this system has not prevented milk—and butter—production from increasing as domestic consumption expanded. It is assumed here that domestic butter production will continue to rise at much the same rate as consumption, or at only a slightly lower rate, so that import requirements would rise to some 500 to 550 thousand tons in 1975. This would represent average rates of growth in butter imports of 1·3 to 1·7 per cent a year from 1960–1 to 1975 on the lower income-growth assumption, and 1·5 to 1·9 per cent a year on the higher income-growth basis.

The share of Britain's butter imports supplied by overseas Sterling countries has remained static, at 55 to 60 per cent, over the past decade. If import quotas continue in force, they appear likely to be used to perpetuate the existing shares of the British import market held by the

---

[1] See Tables 4·1 and 4·2.

[2] In 1965, for example, the wholesale price of Danish butter in Britain averaged $1·02 per kg., compared with average prices of $1·69 per kg. in Western Germany and $1·82 per kg. in France (Paris).

[3] See R. F. Daly, *op. cit.*

traditional butter-exporting countries. Assuming that the 1975 Sterling share remains within the range 55 to 60 per cent of total imports, total butter shipments from the Overseas Sterling Area to Britain in 1975 would be 280–330 thousand tons, the projections being virtually the same for both the income-growth assumptions. Had the Sterling share been taken at 56 per cent, as in 1964–5, the 1975 figures would have been 285–295 thousand tons and 290–310 thousand tons on the two income-growth assumptions, representing average growth rates of 1·5 to 1·7 and 1·6 to 2·1 per cent a year respectively over the period from 1960–1. This compares with a growth rate in Britain's imports of butter from Sterling sources of 2·7 per cent a year from 1960–1 to 1964–5.

Table A 15. *Consumption and imports of butter and cheese in the United Kingdom, 1953–65 and projections for 1975*

	Consumption per head	Total consumption		Imports	Import from O.S.A.	Import proportion of consumption	O.S.A. share of imports
		Actual	Apparent				
	(*Kg.*)	(*Thousand metric tons*)				(%)	(%)
BUTTER							
1953–7	6·7	343	351	321	191	91	60
1960–1	8·6	454	470	421	230	90	55
1962–3	8·8	474	470	418	235	89	56
1964–5	8·8	465	494	460	256	93	56
1975: A	9·7	570	560[a]	505–530	280–320	90–95	55–60
B	10·2	600	580[a]	520–550	285–330		
CHEESE							
1953–7	4·2	220	224	135	106	60	79
1960–1	4·5	238	246	135	99	55	73
1962–3	4·7	252	250	140	99	56	70
1964–5	4·8	258	263	152	105	58	69
1975: A	5·2	310	310[a]	180–185	125–130	58–60	70
B	5·5	325	325[a]	190–195	133–137		

SOURCE: *Dairy Produce* (various issues), Commonwealth Economic Committee, London.

[a] No stock change has been assumed for 1975.

Exports of butter from overseas Sterling countries to destinations other than Britain are likely to remain negligible as long as the dairy industries of Western Europe and North America (the other major consuming areas) continue to be protected, to a greater or lesser degree, by import tariffs or quotas, or by price guarantees or other forms of income support.

Cheese

Cheese consumption per head in Britain rose by 1·3 per cent a year from 1953–7 to 1960–1, and by 1·6 per cent a year from 1960–1 to 1964–5. The lower rate of growth in the later 1950s is explained by the fact that cheese prices were rising relatively to other food prices (by some 10 per cent) over this period. The income elasticity of demand for cheese, calculated from family expenditure data for 1962, was 0·25, slightly less than the corresponding elasticity for butter.[1] This calculated elasticity was assumed to hold over the projection period, though an allowance was also made for a moderate trend in consumer preferences in favour of cheese.

Assuming that cheese prices in 1975 are much the same, in relation to food prices generally, as they were in 1964–5, the projections (Table A15) indicate that cheese consumption in Britain would rise to some 310 to 325 thousand tons in 1975. The proportion of consumption met from imports has varied within a fairly narrow range. In 1964–5, for example, the import proportion (58 per cent) was almost the same as in 1953–7 (60 per cent). Domestic cheese production is also likely to expand in line with consumption if current government policies affecting the use of liquid milk continue, so that it would seem reasonable to assume no appreciable change in the proportion of imports to consumption over the projection period. On this assumption, Britain's cheese imports in 1975 will be in the range of 180 to 195 thousand tons, depending, in part, on the income-growth assumption made.

The Sterling share of Britain's cheese imports has also been very stable, in the region of 70 per cent, over the first half of the 1960s. Unless consumer preferences show a marked change away from cheddar —which comes mainly from Australia and New Zealand—to continental European special varieties, it does not seem likely that the Sterling share will fall appreciably in the future. If the 1975 Sterling share is also taken at 70 per cent of total imports, Britain's imports of Sterling Area cheese in that year would amount to 125 to 135 thousand tons. This would represent an average annual growth rate of 1·6 to 1·8 per cent a year between 1960–1 and 1975 on the low income-growth assumption and 2·0 to 2·2 per cent a year on the higher. It is not likely that changes in Sterling cheese exports to markets outside Britain would have any significant effect on these projections.[2]

[1] *Domestic Food Consumption and Expenditure, 1962.*
[2] Assuming, as already indicated, that Britain does not join the E.E.C.

APPENDIX A5

FRUIT

The present pattern of trade

Exports from the Overseas Sterling Area in 1964 accounted for one-fifth by value of total world trade in fruit, including dried and canned fruit and fruit juice, as well as fresh fruit.[1] As can be seen from Table A 16, the Sterling share was highest for canned fruit and fruit juice (one-quarter of world exports) and lowest for citrus fruit (one-tenth) and bananas (well under one-tenth).

Table A 16. *Exports of fruit, 1964*

	Value of exports						As proportion of total exports
	Apples and pears	Citrus fruit	Bananas	Total fresh fruit*a*	Canned fruit, juices, etc.	Total	
	(*£ million*)						(%)
STERLING COUNTRIES							
Australia	12	1	—	35	12	47	4
South Africa	8	16	—	28	19	46	10
Jamaica	—	0	6	6	2	9	11
Malaya	0	0	—	0	4	4	1
Other countries	3	4	3	11	8	19	..
Total, Sterling	23	21	9	81	44	125	1
NON-STERLING COUNTRIES							
Industrial	56	103	4	191	75	266	1
Developing	12	62	112	189	33	222	3
Centrally planned	15	3	0	26	18	43	1
Total, non-Sterling	83	168	117	405	126	533	1
TOTAL	106	190	126	486	171	657	1
O.S.A. as percentage of TOTAL	22	11	7	16	26	19	..

SOURCES: *Trade Yearbook, 1964*, F.A.O., Rome, 1966; *Yearbook of International Trade Statistics, 1964*, United Nations, New York, 1966.

a Including 'other' fresh fruit.

The fruit exports of the Sterling Area are largely concentrated in four countries, Australia, South Africa, Jamaica and Malaya, of which the first two countries are by far the largest exporters. The specializations of the different exporting countries vary a good deal; Jamaican fruit

[1] This discussion excludes consideration of edible nuts, sometimes classified with fruit.

exports, for example, consist mainly of bananas, while Malaya exports are largely canned pineapples. Australia exports apples and pears as well as canned fruit, while South African shipments consist mainly of citrus and canned fruit.

Britain is easily the dominant market for Sterling fruit exports; this reflects the tariff preferences accorded to Commonwealth producers in the United Kingdom market. For example, in 1962–3 Britain took three-fifths of all exports of apples from Sterling countries, two-thirds of the exports of pears and fruit juices, some three-quarters of grapefruit and canned fruit, and virtually all the exports of bananas. Exceptionally, Britain provided a market for only two-fifths of Sterling oranges, the E.E.C. area being a rather larger market than Britain in this case. Thus, if the Commonwealth preference system remains in being in substantially its present form, it would seem that the prospects for overseas Sterling fruit exports—apart from oranges—hinge essentially on the growth in demand in the United Kingdom. If Britain entered the Common Market, the elimination of the tariff preference would undoubtedly result in a smaller share of Sterling fruit in British imports; on the other hand, most or all of this potential loss could be offset by corresponding gains in sales to E.E.C. countries.

Apples and pears

These are discussed together, for convenience; to some extent, they are substitutes, and the major Sterling exporting countries—Australia and South Africa—export both. In the United Kingdom, *per caput* consumption rose fairly sharply during the first half of the 1960s (by over 5 per cent a year), after a sluggish growth in the preceding decade. The rapid growth in recent years was, however, the result of unusually good harvests during 1964–5, and this rate of growth cannot be expected to continue. The projections for *per caput* consumption were based on an income elasticity of 0·7,[1] which, when combined with the standard assumptions on population and income growth, yielded growth rates of total consumption of 2·6 and 3·4 per cent a year, on the low and high income-growth assumptions respectively (Table A 17).

The proportion of imports to consumption has tended to decline marginally over the period since 1960–1; for 1975, the import proportion is assumed to lie either slightly above, or slightly below, the 1964–5 average. The Sterling share of Britain's apple and pear imports has, however, been rising since 1960–1, mainly because Italian apples have tended to be displaced by Australian and South African supplies. The projections assume a further small increase in the Sterling share of Britain's imports in the decade up to 1975; imports from Sterling

---

[1] See *Domestic Food Consumption and Expenditure, 1962*, H.M.S.O., London, 1964.

M E E

countries in 1975 would then be some 40 to 55 per cent higher than in 1960–1 on the lower income-growth assumption, and 60 to 70 per cent higher on the more optimistic one.

Table A 17. *Consumption and imports of apples and pears in the United Kingdom, 1953–65 and projections for 1975*

	Con-sumption per head	Total con-sumption	Net imports	Imports from O.S.A.	Imports as proportion of con-sumption	O.S.A. share of imports
	(*Kg.*)	(*Million metric tons*)			(%)	(%)
1953–7	15·8	0·81	0·22	0·12	27	55
1960–1	16·5	0·87	0·27	0·15	31	55
1962–3	17·3	0·93	0·28	0·18	30	62
1964–5	20·4	1·11	0·30	0·19	27	63
1975: A	22	1·26	0·33–0·35	0·21–0·23	} 26–28	65
B	24	1·40	0·36–0·39	0·24–0·25		

SOURCE: *Fruit* (various issues), Commonwealth Economic Committee, London.

Citrus fruit

Britain and the E.E.C. are the principal markets for exports of citrus from Sterling countries. In 1964–5, for example, Britain took rather more than one-third of South African shipments of oranges, the E.E.C. countries taking over two-fifths; in the same period, two-thirds of South African exports of grapefruit went to Britain. *Per caput* consumption of citrus fruit in Britain (including the fruit equivalent of juices) rose on average by 2·3 per cent a year from 1953–7 to 1960–1, but fell off somewhat in the early 1960s, though the total quantity consumed in 1964–5 was the same as in 1960–1 (see Table A 18). The projection of *per caput* consumption in 1975 was based on an assumed income elasticity of 0·8, which assumes some fall in the elasticity compared with the position in the early 1960s.[1] On this basis, *per caput* consumption would rise on average by 2·0 and 2·9 per cent a year, respectively, on the low and high income-growth assumptions. Allowing for the esti-mated rise in population, total citrus fruit consumption in Britain is projected to rise by 2·8 and 3·7 per cent a year, respectively, on the alternative income-growth assumptions.[2]

The Sterling share of Britain's imports (and consumption) of citrus fruit (including citrus fruit juice) has remained virtually unchanged, at

[1] According to official estimates, the income elasticity of demand for oranges in 1962 was 0·78, while that for other citrus fruit was 1·28 and for fruit juice 1·23 (p. 321, n. 1).

[2] Over the decade 1964–5 to 1975, the projected growth rates in consumption would be higher (3·9 and 5·1 per cent a year respectively).

just under 40 per cent over the first half of the 1960s. About half the imports from Sterling sources (in fruit equivalent) consist of juice, compared with about a third from non-Sterling sources. Since the demand for juice is more income-elastic than that for fresh citrus as such, the greater proportion of fruit juice in the trade with Sterling countries could result in a moderate rise in the Sterling share in total imports. However, much will depend on the relative rates of expansion in citrus production in the major growing areas and on the development of processing facilities. The present projections, which take the 1975 Sterling share at about the same proportion as in 1964–5, indicate that Britain's demand for citrus imports from Sterling countries might rise by 2·6 to 3·0 per cent a year from 1960–1 to 1975 on the low income-growth assumption, and by 3·5 to 3·9 per cent a year on the higher income basis.

Table A 18. *Consumption and imports of citrus fruit[a] in the United Kingdom and E.E.C., 1953–65 and projections for 1975*

	Con-sumption per head	Total con-sumption	Net imports	Imports from O.S.A.	Imports as proportion of con-sumption[b]	O.S.A. share of imports
	(Kg.)	(Million metric tons)			(%)	(%)
UNITED KINGDOM						
1953–7	13·5	0·69	0·69	0·25	100	36
1960–1	15·2	0·80	0·80	0·31	100	39
1962–3	14·2	0·76	0·76	0·30	100	37
1964–5	14·7	0·80	0·80	0·32	100	39
1975: A	20·4	1·19	1·19	0·45–0·48 }	} 100	} 38–40
B	23·0	1·35	1·35	0·51–0·54 }		
E.E.C.						
1953–7	14·1	2·32	1·20	..	52	..
1960–1	18·5	3·19	1·64	0·08	51	5
1962–3	19·3	3·41	1·86	0·11	55	6
1964–5	21·5	3·88	2·13	0·17	55	8
1975: A	27·0	5·15	2·85–3·10	0·29–0·31 }	} 55–60	} 10
B	30·0	5·75	3·15–3·45	0·32–0·35 }		

SOURCE: As for Table A 17.

[a] Including the fruit equivalent of fruit juices.
[b] For the E.E.C., the percentages relate to net imports.

Citrus consumption has risen substantially faster in the E.E.C. area over the last ten years than in the United Kingdom. On a *per caput* basis, E.E.C. consumption increased by 5·0 per cent a year from 1953–7 to 1960–1, but from then until 1964–5 the growth rate fell off to 3·8 per cent a year. Assuming an average income elasticity of 0·7, the assumptions about population and income growth imply that total demand for citrus fruit, including the fruit equivalent of citrus juice, would rise from 1960–1 to 1975 by 3·4 and 4·1 per cent a year, respectively, on the two income-growth assumptions. The projections assume, further, no significant change in the import proportion of consumption, and a continuation of the past trend in favour of a rising share of Sterling citrus fruit (and juice) in total imports. On these assumptions, the E.E.C. imports from Sterling countries would rise from 80 thousand tons in 1960–1 to some 300 to 350 thousand tons in 1975.

Taking the United Kingdom and E.E.C. markets together, imports from Sterling countries are projected to rise, on the assumptions made, from 1960–1 to 1975 by 4·5 to 5·0 per cent a year on the low income basis, and by 5·4 to 5·8 per cent a year on the higher income basis.

Bananas

Bananas account for a relatively small proportion, by value, of fruit exports from the Overseas Sterling Area (only 7 per cent in 1964), though for certain Caribbean countries—Jamaica and the Windward Islands, in particular—bananas are an important source of export earnings. Virtually all the banana exports from these countries find a market in the United Kingdom, where they benefit from quantitative restrictions and import duties on lower-cost supplies from Ecuador and other Central American countries.

Consumption per head in Britain was essentially static over the first half of the 1960s. Imports in both 1963 and 1964 were, however, adversely affected by hurricane damage to West Indies production, while imports from West Cameroun, formerly a large source of supply, were substantially reduced in 1964 on the withdrawal of Commonwealth preference for that country in September 1963. Allowing for these special factors, the figures in Table A 19 indicate an underlying upward trend in banana consumption per head. Taking an assumed income elasticity of demand of 0·5,[1] the income-growth and population assumptions imply that total demand for bananas in Britain would rise from rather less than 400 thousand tons a year in the first half of the 1960s to somewhere in the range 500 to 550 thousand tons by 1975. By comparison with the base period, 1960–1, the projections imply an annual growth rate in demand of 2·1 per cent on the low income-growth assumption and 2·7 per cent on the higher income basis.

The Sterling share of British imports, which had been in the region of about 70 to 80 per cent over the previous decade, rose to 90 per cent in 1964–5. The projection for 1975 also assumes a Sterling share for

_____
[1] See reference on p. 321, n. 1.

that year of 90 per cent, implicitly assuming the continuance of Commonwealth preference and of quantitative restrictions on imports from the 'dollar countries' of Central America. On this basis, Britain's imports of bananas from Sterling sources would rise by 3·9 and 4·6 per cent a year, respectively, on the alternative income-growth assumptions. There would seem not to be any constraint on the supply side likely to prevent such rates of growth in trade volume from being achieved.

Canned fruit

Australia, South Africa and Malaya are the principal Sterling exporters of canned fruit, about three-quarters by value of their combined exports being shipped to the United Kingdom. While *per caput* consumption grew at a relatively rapid rate in the late 1950s (by nearly 6 per cent a year from 1953–7 to 1960–1), the growth rate subsequently fell to only 2·3 per cent a year from 1960–1 to 1964–5 (see Table A19). There are, however, considerable year-to-year fluctuations in supplies, reflecting largely the crop out-turn in each season. The income elasticity of demand was estimated at 0·55 for 1962[1] and, assuming a similar elasticity to hold over the projection period, with no change in relative prices, total demand would rise on average by 2·3 and 2·8 per cent year on the two income-growth assumptions, respectively, between 1960–1 and 1975. The projection on the low income-growth basis indicates a continuation of the recent rate of increase in United Kingdom consumption; on the higher income assumption, the indicated growth in demand would seem well within the probable growth in available supplies, especially in view of past rates of growth in supply.

The proportion of imports in total United Kingdom canned fruit consumption rose from an average of 75 per cent during the period 1953–7 to about 80 per cent in the first half of the 1960s, reflecting, in part, relaxations of import restrictions on canned fruit produced in the United States and Japan. Quota restrictions on imports of certain canned fruits from these countries, however, remain in force mainly as a form of protection for Commonwealth and South African produce. Assuming the continuance of these restrictions, it would seem reasonable to envisage little change in the import proportion of consumption in the coming decade, unless consumer preferences shift in favour of, or away from, the types of canned fruit produced domestically. The Sterling share of imports into the United Kingdom has remained in the region of 60 per cent over the past quinquennium; variations in the proportions reflect good or bad seasons for fruit crops in the major producing countries. Assuming a Sterling share in 1975 of 60 per cent, total United

[1] *Ibid.*

Table A19. *Consumption and imports of bananas and canned fruit in the United Kingdom, 1953–65 and projections for 1975*

	Con-sumption per head	Total con-sumption	Net imports	Imports from O.S.A.	Imports as pro-portion of con-sumption	O.S.A. share of imports
	(*Kg.*)	(*Million metric tons*)			(%)	(%)
BANANAS						
1953–7	5·9	0·30	0·30	0·23	100	77
1960–1	6·8	0·36	0·36	0·25	100	68
1962–3	6·9	0·37	0·37	0·27	100	73
1964–5	6·8	0·37	0·37	0·33	100	90
1975: A	8·3	0·49	0·49	0·44	} 100	90
B	9·0	0·53	0·53	0·48		
CANNED FRUIT						
1953–7	6·2	0·32	0·24	0·16	75	67
1960–1	8·4	0·44	0·36	0·21	82	58
1962–3	9·5	0·51	0·40	0·23	78	58
1964–5	9·2	0·50	0·40	0·25	80	63
1975: A	10·4	0·61	0·49	0·29	} 80	60
B	11·3	0·66	0·53	0·32		

SOURCE: As for Table A17.

Kingdom imports of canned fruit from Sterling sources in that year would be in the region of 300 thousand tons—rather more on the higher income-growth assumption and rather less on the lower. This would imply annual growth rates from 1960–1 of 2·4 and 2·9 per cent respectively.

APPENDIX B I

COTTON AND WOOL

The present pattern of trade

With the development of the synthetic fibre industries in the industrial countries, the pattern of world demand for the various competing fibres has undergone a dramatic change over the past two decades. This change has also been reflected, though to a lesser degree, in the pattern of world trade. In 1964—the latest year at the time of writing for which complete statistics were available—exports of man-made fibres (cellulosic and synthetic) from the industrial countries accounted for one-eighth of the total value of world trade in the major apparel fibres; raw cotton and raw wool, which had dominated the scene in earlier decades, each accounted for some two-fifths of the total.[1]

The export interest of the Overseas Sterling Area is predominantly in the raw wool market. Here, Australia, New Zealand and South Africa together provided as much as three-quarters of total world exports, by value, in 1964. Moreover, their exports, particularly Australia's, consist of the better qualities, most suitable for apparel uses. Minor Sterling exporters include India and Pakistan, whose exports consist of coarser wools particularly suitable for carpet manufacture.

The United States is by far the largest single exporter of raw cotton, acting in effect as a price leader in the world cotton market, as well as being a residual supplier by virtue of its large surplus stocks. The overseas Sterling countries in aggregate supply under one-tenth of the world export market, the largest exporters in 1964 being Pakistan, Uganda and Tanzania.

There is also a marked contrast between the Sterling exporters of cotton and wool as regards their main markets. The predominant proportion of wool is shipped to the industrial countries of Western Europe, North America and Japan; in 1964–5, for example, these countries took rather more than 90 per cent of all raw wool exports from Australia, New Zealand and South Africa. The main markets for Pakistani wool are Britain and the United States, but for wool exports from India the Soviet Union has been the major purchaser since 1962. The distribution of cotton exports from the overseas Sterling countries by area of destination is quite different from that of wool, particularly inasmuch as Sterling exports of cotton to developing countries generally

---

[1] Excluding exports from the centrally planned countries (see Table B I).

account for a substantial proportion (one-third in 1964–5) of total cotton exports.

Export prospects for cotton and wool are extremely important for most of the overseas Sterling exporting countries concerned. Raw wool, for example, accounted for about a third of the total export earnings both of Australia and New Zealand (though only an eighth of South African earnings) in 1964. Raw cotton brought in one-quarter of Uganda's export receipts in the same year, one-sixth of Pakistan's, and one-eighth of Tanzania's (Table B 1).

Table B 1. *Exports of cotton, wool and man-made fibres, 1964*

	Value of exports				Total as proportion of total exports
	Raw cotton[a]	Raw wool	Man-made fibres	Total	
	(£ million)				(%)
STERLING COUNTRIES					
Australia	—	371	1	372	34
New Zealand	—	135	—	135	35
South Africa	—	56	0	56	12
Pakistan	26	5	—	31	17
Uganda	16	—	—	16	24
India	9	6	0	15	2
Tanzania	10	—	—	10	13
Nigeria	6	—	—	6	3
Other countries	7	6	0	13	..
Total, O.S.A.	73	579	1	653	12
United Kingdom	—	17	19	37	1
Total, Sterling	73	596	21	690	7
NON-STERLING COUNTRIES					
Industrial	244	40	156	440	1
Developing	395	75	9	480	6
Centrally planned	106	26	..	..	..
Total, non-Sterling	745	141	..	..	..
TOTAL	819	737	..	..	..
O.S.A. as percentage of TOTAL	9	78	..	..	..

SOURCES: *Trade Yearbook, 1965*, F.A.O., Rome, 1966; *Yearbook of International Trade Statistics, 1964*, United Nations, New York, 1966; *Commodity Trade*, Series B, O.E.C.D., Paris.

[a] Excluding cotton linters.

Consumption of fibres in the industrial countries

The demand for an individual fibre such as cotton or wool depends on a number of factors, the most important being the demand for the end-products—particular items of apparel, household or industrial textiles—and the relative proportions of the different fibres consumed in each end-use. Demand for end-products can reasonably be related to changes in total population (or, if necessary, in population by age group or other relevant characteristics) and in real income per head. Changes in the relative proportions of different fibres consumed are, however, more complex; they reflect not only changes in relative fibre prices, but also the differing technological characteristics of competing fibres and, in particular, the different suitability of each in the manufacture of specific end-products. Since technology is continually developing, the relative balance of technological advantage of the different fibres is also subject to change and is accordingly more uncertain to project into the future.

In view of the close interchangeability of cotton, wool, rayon and synthetic fibres over almost the entire range of end-uses, it seems essential, to begin with, to consider the demand for them as a single entity. The present set of projections accordingly sets out the probable level of demand in 1975 for all textile products embodying these fibres, and then considers the likely share of each fibre in total consumption in that year. This approach also has the virtue of maintaining an overall consistency between the projections of demand for the individual fibres.

Apart from the demand for end-products for consumption in the industrial countries, the latter's usage of raw cotton and raw wool is also dependent on the export of cotton and wool yarns and manufactured textiles to other areas. These factors are separately considered below.

The usual way of aggregating the domestic consumption of textile products is on a weight basis. This approach, however, ignores the big differences between the 'utility poundages' of different fibres, i.e. the differences between them in usage per unit of weight for the same end-use. Synthetic fibre fabrics, for example, have a far larger superficial area per unit of weight than have any fabrics made of natural fibres, and it is the superficial area which is the relevant unit for a wide range of end-products. One way of allowing for this would be to aggregate the consumption figures in terms of approximate superficial area equivalents. However, it would be very difficult to arrive at the appropriate equivalence conversion factors, which would no doubt differ from country to country. Another approach, used here, is to aggregate the consumption of the different textile products in terms of their value at constant prices; this allows for differences in 'utility poundages' to the extent that these are reflected in the price differential between the various fibres. The unit values used represent the average wholesale prices of the different fibres in the years 1960 and 1961, so that the values of domestic consumption thus computed represent the values of the fibre content, not the values of the finished end-products.[1]

The value of consumption at 1960–1 prices of textiles made from cotton, wool and man-made fibres has been computed for each industrial area, and converted to a *per caput* basis. The results, summarized in Table B2, show that *per caput* consumption rose on average by some 4½ per cent a year from 1953–7 to 1962–3, taking the industrial countries as a whole. Countries where *per caput* consumption rose less rapidly than the average tended to be those, for example Britain and the United States, where *per caput* textile consumption was already relatively high. Easily the fastest growth rate in textile consumption occurred in Japan, reflecting the rapid rise there in *per caput* real income since the early and middle 1950s, also the great expansion in Japanese textile supplies.

Total domestic fibre consumption per head, valued at constant prices, was found to bear a close relationship with real income per head in each industrial country. A semi-logarithmic function was found to give a good fit to the data in all cases;[2] this function implies a declining elasticity of demand for textile products as real income per head rises. Using these results, the corresponding values of consumption per head for 1975 were derived on the basis of the standard assumptions about the growth in real income per head in each industrial area.[3]

The projections indicate a slowing down in the rate of growth of domestic textile consumption per head in the industrial areas from nearly 4 per cent a year (from 1953–7 to 1960–1) to 2½ or 3 per cent a year respectively, on the low or high income-growth assumptions, for the projection period 1960–1 to 1975. The reduction in growth rate would apply to all the industrial areas, the most dramatic being for Japan, where the volume of textile consumption per head was increasing on average by some 15 per cent a year in the latter part of the 1950s. However, by the early 1960s, the growth rate had already declined sharply to about 5 per cent a year, and is likely to fall further as incomes rise and consumer demand becomes more varied in pattern. For the United States, but not for any of the other industrial countries, it has been assumed that by 1975 a saturation level in textile consumption will have been reached; for the United States, therefore, the projection is the same on both the income-growth assumptions.

---

[1] The calculation of the value of finished textile products consumed in the different industrial countries would have to make allowance for differences in fabrication costs of the various products, as well as for the differences in costs of fibres used. In general, however, a greater value is added in processing of higher-cost fibres.

[2] Using the form $C/N = a + b \log (Y/N)$, where C denotes the value of consumption of textile products at constant prices, Y real income per head, and N total population. The regressions covered annual figures for the years 1953–63 inclusive, the value of R^2 exceeding 0·85 in all cases.　　　　　　　　　　　　　　　　　[3] See Table 4.2.

Table B2. *Apparel*[a] *fibre consumption in the industrial countries,
1953–63 and projections for 1975*

	Rates of growth				Values[b]			
	1953–7 to 1960–1	1960–1 to 1962–3	1960–1 to 1975		1960–1	1962–3	1975	
			A	B			A	B
	(% *per annum*)				(£ *at 1960–1 prices*)			
CONSUMPTION PER HEAD								
United Kingdom	4·1	1·7	1·3	2·0	5·93	6·15	7·15	7·85
E.E.C.	5·4	5·5	2·6	3·3	4·46	4·96	6·45	7·15
Other Western Europe	3·7	6·4	2·6	2·9	2·71	3·07	3·95	4·10
United States	1·4	8·7	2·3	2·3	6·46	7·64	8·95	8·95
Canada	0·9	8·8	2·3	3·3	4·89	5·79	6·80	7·85
Japan	15·2	5·1	2·7	3·3	5·14	5·68	7·50	8·20
TOTAL	3·8	6·8	2·5	2·9	4·82	5·50	6·90	7·30
					(£ *million at 1960–1 prices*)			
TOTAL CONSUMPTION								
United Kingdom	3·9	2·6	2·1	2·8	310	326	420	460
E.E.C.	6·1	7·4	3·4	4·2	758	875	1,230	1,370
Other Western Europe	4·8	8·4	3·8	4·2	351	413	605	635
United States	2·5	10·2	3·7	3·7	1,178	1,430	1,990	1,990
Canada	3·1	9·7	4·3	5·3	88	106	160	185
Japan	13·6	5·2	3·5	4·2	482	534	795	870
TOTAL	5·0	7·9	3·5	3·9	3,166	3,684	5,205	5,510

SOURCES: *Per Caput Fiber Consumption Levels—1948–58*, Commodity Bulletin no. 31, F.A.O., Rome, 1960; *Monthly Bulletin of Agricultural Economics and Statistics*, January 1962, F.A.O. Rome; *World Apparel Fiber Consumption*, F.A.O., Rome, 1965.

[a] It is estimated that about three-fifths of the cotton, wool and man-made fibre tonnage processed in industrial countries is absorbed in apparel, the remainder in household and industrial goods.

[b] The calculations were based on the following average unit values for 1960 and 1961 (in £ per metric ton): cotton, 257; wool, 757; cellulosic fibres, 357; non-cellulosic man-made fibres, 1,270.

Table B2 also shows the projections for total textile consumption in the various industrial countries derived by multiplying the *per caput* projections by the estimated populations in 1975.[1] For the industrial areas as a whole, total textile consumption is projected to rise on average by 3½ per cent a year from 1960–1 to 1975 on the low income-growth assumption, and by some 4 per cent a year on the more optimistic basis.

[1] See Table 4.1.

Shares of cotton and wool

The next step in the projection is to consider the likely change over the coming decade in the shares held by cotton and wool in total textile consumption in the industrial countries. The trends in these shares over the period since 1953–7 are summarized in Table B3. Cotton's share has been sharply reduced as a result of inroads by rayon in the earlier years, and increasingly by the newer synthetics since the end of the 1950s, in a wide range of end-uses.[1] The displacement of cotton has been particularly severe in the United States, where the newer synthetic fibres have been displacing rayon and wool as well as cotton, in clothing and in many household and industrial applications.

The decline in the share of wool in the total has generally been much less than for cotton over the past decade. There has been a trend towards the use of lighter-weight clothing, particularly in the United States, where blends of wool and synthetic fibres have been successfully introduced, the existence of a sizeable duty on the import of apparel wool being an encouragement. However, in many countries there is a distinct consumer preference for wool apparel.

The future trend in the relative shares of the various fibres in total textile consumption is somewhat uncertain and any estimates necessarily contain a considerable margin of error. For one thing, it seems probable that relative prices will change over the coming ten years, and this could well influence the shares of cotton and wool to a significant extent. A major factor here could be the new cotton price policy of the United States. Not only was the price of cotton to domestic manufacturers reduced in 1964 to accord more with the lower price already being paid by foreign manufacturers but, following the Food and Agriculture Act, 1965, the export price of American cotton has been further reduced and will therefore remain more competitive in the world market, so reducing the burden of unsold stocks. This price reduction, if maintained, is likely to result in some improvement in the relative competitive position of cotton as against rayon in a number of important end-uses. Another factor, of increasing importance in recent years, has been the improvement to the technical properties of cotton fabrics by treating them with synthetic finishes; this has substantially improved the competitive position of cotton. A third element is the possibility of influencing consumer preference by promotional campaigns; a new body—the International Institute for Cotton—established in 1966 to

---

[1] The method of measurement, in terms of values, considerably magnifies the decline in the share of cotton, compared with the usual method of measuring in tonnage terms. In either case, the decline is exaggerated to the extent that the expansion in the share of man-made fibres reflects their substitution for materials other than cotton.

promote the use of cotton could also have some impact on the pattern of consumer demand over a period of years.

On balance, the relative competitive position of cotton seems likely to improve over the coming decade, compared with the past one, barring any new major technological breakthrough in the development of man-made fibres. In the present projections, therefore, it has been assumed that the rate of displacement of cotton by competing fibres will be appreciably less in future than it has been over the past decade. The assumptions made (see Table B3) imply that, for the industrial areas as a whole, the share held by cotton will decline from one-third of total textile consumption in value terms in 1960–1 to little more than one-fifth by 1975.

Table B3. *Shares of cotton and wool in total apparel fibre consumption in the industrial countries, 1953–63 and projections for 1975* (*per cent of total fibre consumption*)[a]

	Cotton				Wool			
	1953–7	1960–1	1962–3	1975	1953–7	1960–1	1962–3	1975
United Kingdom	31	25	21	15–17	38	31	30	25–27
E.E.C.	36	30	25	19–21	34	28	24	20–22
Other Western Europe	40	37	33	28–30	37	33	31	23–24
United States	47	40	34	24–26	15	14	12	8–10
Canada	38	33	30	27–28	26	20	18	15–17
Japan	38	29	23	16–17	20	19	17	15–17
TOTAL	41	34	29	20–24	25	22	19	15–17

SOURCES: As for Table B2.

[a] In terms of values at constant (1960–1) prices.

The relatively gentle decline apparent in the share held by wool over the period since 1953–7 has generally been assumed to continue. During the early 1960s, it declined only marginally (though the E.E.C. is an exception), but some further declines seem probable over the next decade. The assumptions made for the various industrial areas imply that, for them all, the share held by wool will decline from one-fifth of the total value in 1960–1 to about one-sixth in 1975.

Consumption and net exports of cotton and wool textiles

The assumed percentage shares, when applied to the total projections of the value of domestic consumption of textiles (Table B2), yield separate projections for the quantity of cotton and wool textile demand.[1] These indicate a decline in the annual rate of growth of consumption of both cotton and wool textiles over the period of projection, compared with the later 1950s. Compared with the early 1960s, however, the projections indicate some modest recovery in cotton textile consumption from the low levels reached in 1962–3; for wool textiles, the growth rate achieved in the early 1960s ($1\frac{1}{2}$ per cent a year) is intermediate between the high and low projections for the period up to 1975 (Table B4).

Table B4. *Consumption of cotton and wool textiles in the industrial countries, 1953–63 and projections for 1975*

	Rates of growth				Quantities			
	1953–7 to 1960–1	1960–1 to 1962–3	1960–1 to 1975 A	B	1960–1	1962–3	1975[a] A	B
	(% per annum)				(Million metric tons)			
COTTON TEXTILES								
United Kingdom	—	−6·3	−1·0	−0·4	0·31	0·27	0·26	0·29
E.E.C.	2·7	−1·7	0·5	1·3	0·89	0·86	0·96	1·07
Other Western Europe	3·5	1·9	2·0	2·4	0·51	0·53	0·68	0·72
United States	−0·3	0·5	0·5	0·5	1·85	1·87	1·97	1·97
Canada	0·3	4·4	3·1	4·2	0·11	0·12	0·17	0·20
Japan	7·8	−5·4	−0·3	0·2	0·54	0·48	0·51	0·56
TOTAL	1·7	−0·9	0·6	0·9	4·21	4·13	4·55	4·81
WOOL TEXTILES								
United Kingdom	−0·1	0·4	0·8	1·4	0·13	0·13	0·14	0·16
E.E.C.	1·7	0·5	1·4	2·2	0·28	0·28	0·34	0·38
Other Western Europe	2·8	4·5	1·4	1·7	0·15	0·17	0·19	0·20
United States	1·2	1·1	0·6	0·6	0·22	0·22	0·24	0·24
Canada	−1·0	4·3	2·5	3·8	0·02	0·03	0·03	0·04
Japan	12·7	0·4	2·2	3·1	0·12	0·12	0·17	0·19
TOTAL	2·5	1·4	1·3	1·9	0·92	0·94	1·10	1·20

SOURCES: Tables B2 and B3.

[a] Means of ranges.

On either income assumption, wool textile consumption is projected to grow at a faster rate than that for cotton goods; but even for wool the projected growth rate (1·3 or 1·9 per cent a year, according to which income assumption is used) is well below that for textiles as a whole (3·5 or 3·9 per cent a year).

To these projections for domestic consumption must be added an allowance for net exports of cotton and wool textiles from the

[1] The values of cotton and wool textiles (at 1960–1 prices) projected for 1975 were converted back to a tonnage basis by use of the unit values given in Table B2, footnote *b*.

industrial countries. Net exports of cotton textiles amounted to 350 thousand metric tons on average during 1953–7, fell to 260 thousand tons in 1960–1, and declined again, to 187 thousand tons, in 1962–3. This decline was a reflection of several distinct factors. First, there has been an increase in imports of cheap cotton goods into the industrial countries (mainly into Britain from the Sterling Asian countries); second, the growth of import-substituting textile industries in many developing countries has appreciably reduced the export outlets of the traditional cotton textile centres of Western Europe; and, third, the latter have also lost ground to the low-wage industries in India, Pakistan and other developing exporter countries in markets in Africa, Asia and Latin America. All these tendencies are likely to continue in the future. It has been assumed here that net exports of cotton textiles from the industrial countries will continue to decline, though at a some-what reduced rate, compared with the recent past (see Table B5). Total demand for raw cotton in the industrial countries, on the various assumptions made, would be only marginally higher in 1975 than in 1960–1 on the low income-growth basis and only about 7 per cent greater on the high one.

Supply and demand for raw cotton and wool

In considering future trends in raw cotton supplies, the United States must be taken separately as the main producer and net cotton exporter. Production of cotton in the United States remained substantially un-changed over the past decade, a reduction in the planted area being off-set by a sharp increase in average yields. The new American cotton policy, involving (among other disincentives to cotton-growing) a much reduced support price to farmers, seems likely to result in a substantial reduction in cotton acreage, though this may well be partly offset by a further rise in yields. Production in 1975 is assumed to have fallen to 2·9 to 3·0 million tons from 3·1 million tons in 1960–1, 3·2 million tons in 1962–3, and 3·3 million tons in 1964–5. Production in other industrial countries (Greece and Turkey) has risen relatively sharply in the period 1960–5 as a result of increased yields; a further increase has been assumed over the following decade.

The projections of net trade in raw cotton, shown in Table B5, have been derived as residuals from the projections of demand and of pro-duction already discussed, assuming no significant changes in stocks of raw cotton in 1975. They indicate that net imports of raw cotton into the industrial countries other than the United States may be somewhat less in 1975 than they were in 1960–1, on the low income-growth assumption, while on the more optimistic basis they might be higher by only 5 to 6 per cent.

However, United States exports of raw cotton were unusually high in the 1959/60 and 1960/1 seasons, when they averaged 1·5 million tons a year; they fell off considerably in the following two seasons, and recovered somewhat, to 1·1 million tons on average, in the 1963/4 and 1964/5 seasons. The decline projected in American cotton production is not likely, however, to be associated with any appreciable decline in United States exports from the 1964–5 level; the 1975 projections indicate exports at much the same level as the 1964–5 average on the high income-growth basis and somewhat less on the low basis.

Table B 5. *Cotton and wool demand and supply in the industrial countries, 1960–5 and projections for 1975*

	1960–1	1962–3	1964–5	1975[a] A	1975[a] B	Rates of growth 1960–1 to 1975[a] A	Rates of growth 1960–1 to 1975[a] B
	(Million metric tons)					(% per annum)	
COTTON							
Cotton textiles:							
Domestic consumption	4·21	4·13	..	4·55	4·81	0·6	0·9
Net exports	0·26	0·19	..	0·16	0·17	−2·3	−2·1
TOTAL DEMAND	4·47	4·32	..	4·71	4·98	0·4	0·8
Raw cotton:							
Domestic production:							
United States	3·14	3·18	3·33	2·90	3·00	−0·5	−0·3
Other industrial countries	0·33	0·43	0·46	0·53	0·58	3·3	4·0
Net imports:							
United States	−1·52	−0·89	−1·07	−0·93	−1·03	−2·3	−1·9
Other industrial countries	2·34	1·99	2·08	2·21	2·43	−0·3	0·4
TOTAL SUPPLY	4·29	4·71	4·80	4·71	4·98	0·7	1·0
WOOL							
Wool textiles:							
Domestic consumption	0·92	0·94	..	1·10	1·20	1·3	1·9
Net exports	0·05	0·04	..	0·04	0·04	−1·5	−1·5
TOTAL DEMAND	0·97	0·98	..	1·14	1·24	1·1	1·7
Raw wool:							
Domestic production	0·20	0·19	0·18	0·20	0·22	—	0·7
Net imports[b]	0·73	0·73	0·72	0·94	1·02	1·8	2·3
TOTAL SUPPLY	0·93	0·92	0·90	1·14	1·24	1·4	2·0

SOURCES: As for Table B2; *Cotton Statistics*, International Cotton Advisory Committee, Washington; *World Trade in Wool and Wool Textiles* and *Wool Intelligence*, Commonwealth Economic Committee, London.

[a] Means of ranges.   [b] Estimated clean equivalent.

In any event, it would appear probable that United States raw cotton exports in 1975 will be substantially lower than in 1960–1, when about three-quarters of the total went to other industrial countries. If it is assumed also that in 1975 some three-quarters of United States exports will be sold to other industrial countries and some allowance is made for re-exports of cotton from countries in Western Europe, gross imports from the primary-producing areas into industrial countries other than the United States would rise from 1·33 million metric tons in 1960–1 to about 1·7 and 1·8 million tons in 1975 on the low and high income-growth assumptions respectively, or at annual rates of growth of 1·7 and 2·1 per cent.

Net exports of wool textiles from the industrial countries almost doubled between 1953–7 and 1960–1, but fell off in 1962–3 as a result of reduced exports from the United Kingdom. However, it would seem consistent with the general assumptions of economic growth underlying the projections to assume that the demand for imports of wool textiles by the primary-producing countries will not decline appreciably in the long term. It is assumed here that the 1975 level will be the same as in 1962–3. On this basis, total demand for wool textiles in the industrial countries is projected to increase by 1·1 and 1·7 per cent a year between 1960–1 and 1975 on the low and high income-growth assumptions respectively (Table B5).

The major producers of raw wool in the industrial areas are Britain, 'other Western Europe' and the United States. The maintenance of guaranteed prices for domestic wool in Britain, with increased demand for lamb, would indicate the probability of a stable sheep population; fleece weights might be marginally higher in 1975 than in the early 1960s. For 'other Western Europe', it has been assumed that there will be little variation in either sheep numbers or fleece yields. Some decline in United States wool production has, however, been assumed; output fell by some 20 per cent between 1960–1 and 1964–5, and as the decline continued in the following year, the incentive price to wool-growers established under the National Wool Act was raised. The average for the 1964–5 period has been taken as the basis for the 1975 projection. In all, wool production in the industrial countries in 1975 is taken at the same level as in 1960–1 on the low growth assumption, and one-tenth higher on the more optimistic one.

Net imports of raw wool into the industrial countries—derived as a residual, as in Table B5—would accordingly rise to about 1 million metric tons in 1975, from about ¾ million tons a year in the early 1960s.

Exports from the Overseas Sterling Area

Since the overseas Sterling countries supply only a relatively small proportion of the raw cotton imports of the developed countries, the latter's raw cotton imports from Sterling sources will depend very much on the relative competitive position of Sterling cotton as well as on the growth in demand projected earlier. Over the first half of the 1960s the Sterling Area's raw cotton production rose by about 6 per cent a year, while exports from Sterling countries rose by nearly 14 per cent a year (partly reflecting substantial purchases in 1964–5 by the centrally planned countries from Pakistan, Tanzania and Uganda). The future Sterling share of raw cotton imports into the industrial countries is necessarily uncertain because of the unpredictability of United States production and export policies. But some rise in this share over the coming decade seems likely because of the growth potential in output for export by the main Sterling producing countries, compared with others—particularly in view of a possible reduction in exports from the United States.

Exports to other developing countries accounted for about one-third of total raw cotton shipments from overseas Sterling countries in 1960–1, as against one-half going to the developed countries. Exports to developing countries rose rapidly in the first half of the 1960s (by an average rate of about 9 per cent a year), reflecting in the main the growing requirements of cotton textile industries such as Hong Kong's,[1] which depend on imported cotton. Future prospects depend, to a large extent, on the export potential for Hong Kong's cotton textiles, particularly in Western Europe and North America. On the assumption that cotton textile and clothing exports from Hong Kong rise by about 6 per cent a year[2] on average, Sterling exports of raw cotton to developing countries in 1975 would be in the region of 160 thousand tons, compared with about 70 thousand tons in 1960–1. Exports of raw cotton to centrally planned countries are likely to remain small.

On the basis of these various projections, the total raw cotton exports of the overseas Sterling countries in 1975 might be in the region of 300 thousand metric tons on the low income-growth assumption and 350 thousand tons on the higher basis, representing annual growth rates of 2·7 and 3·6 per cent a year respectively.

For raw wool, it can be assumed that exports from the Overseas Sterling Area to the industrial countries rise in proportion to the projection for the

---

[1] In the 1965/6 season for example, Hong Kong alone took one-quarter of the total raw cotton exports of Pakistan, Tanzania and Uganda.

[2] See Appendix C for further discussion of the prospects for exports of cotton manufactures from Hong Kong.

latter's net imports, as shown in Table B5. Exports to developing countries in 1960–5 averaged some 10 thousand tons a year, and this trade could well increase in the future. Exports to the centrally planned countries (nearly 40 thousand tons, on average, during 1960–5), however, might fall off somewhat as the synthetic fibre industries become developed in these countries. In all, the evidence would indicate an average growth rate in raw wool exports from Sterling countries of about the same as that for import demand of the industrial countries (i.e. 1·7 or 2·3 per cent a year), though it could well be less than this.

APPENDIX B 2

JUTE AND JUTE GOODS

The present pattern of trade

Raw jute is exported in quantity only by Pakistan, but is grown for use in domestic textile industries in a number of countries, notably India, China, Brazil and Thailand. In addition, these and other countries produce jute-like fibres (mesta, kenaf, etc.) in substantial amounts—Thailand being normally a major exporter of kenaf. Jute goods, on the other hand, are exported mainly by India, though Pakistan has gained an increasing share of the world market over the past decade. Together, India and Pakistan account for the bulk of world exports of jute goods, Western European countries for almost all the remainder.

Table B6. *Exports of jute and jute goods, 1964*

	Value of exports			As proportion of total exports
	Raw jute	Jute goods	Total	
	(£ million)			(%)
India	3	135	138	23
Pakistan	62	23	85	48
Thailand	9	—	9	4
Total	74	158	232	23

SOURCE: *Yearbook of International Trade Statistics, 1965*, United Nations, New York, 1967.

Jute and jute goods together contribute an important proportion of total export earnings for both India and Pakistan. In a recent year (1964), they accounted for about a quarter of total exports from India, and almost one-half of those from Pakistan (Table B6). Apart from exports to India, which took 13 per cent of Pakistan's jute exports in 1964/5, the greater part of raw jute exports go to Western Europe. In 1964/5, for example, Britain took 15 per cent of Pakistan's exports, the E.E.C. accounted for one-quarter and other countries of Western Europe for a further 7 per cent. Exports to centrally planned countries represented about one-seventh of the total in that period.

World output of jute and allied fibres has risen substantially since the mid 1950s. From 1953–7 to 1960–1, the output of true jute rose by almost 3 per cent a year, on average, while that of allied fibres rose by nearly 10 per cent a year. For both jute and allied fibres, the rate of growth in output increased during the first half of the 1960s, as did also the growth in mill consumption in the chief producing countries. Exports of raw jute, however, have risen relatively little over the past decade, a decline in the late 1950s being followed by a rise in the early 1960s. Exports of jute goods, on the other hand, have risen throughout the period, by only 1 per cent a year on average in the later 1950s, and by 3 per cent a year in the first half of the 1960s (see Table B 7).

Table B 7. *World^a 'balance sheet' for jute and allied fibres, pre-war and 1953-65*

	pre-war	1953–7	1960–1	1962–3	1964–5	Rates of growth 1953–7 to 1960–1	1960–1 to 1964–5
		(Million metric tons)				*(% per annum)*	
Production:							
Raw jute	1·52	1·60	1·87	2·26	2·15	2·9	3·6
Allied fibres^b	..	0·23	0·38	0·56	0·63	9·5	13·5
Total	..	1·83	2·25	2·82	2·78	3·8	5·4
Mill consumption in producing countries	1·31	1·35	1·56	1·71	1·83	2·7	4·1
Stock change^c	..	..	+0·24	+0·35	−0·24	..	..
Exports:							
Raw jute	0·78	0·94	0·78	0·95	1·03	−3·4	7·2
Jute goods	1·21	1·05	1.11	1.13	1.25	1·0	3·0

SOURCES: *Statistical Supplement: Jute Goods available for Home Use*, F.A.O., Rome, 1962 (CCP/Jute, Ad hoc 62/4/Add.1); *Demand for Jute Goods—Post-war Trends and Prospects for the Sixties*, F.A.O., Rome, 1964; *Commodity Review, 1965 and 1966*, F.A.O., Rome.

^{a} Excluding Sino-Soviet countries.
^{b} Kenaf, mesta, etc.
^{c} India and Pakistan only.

Prospects for demand

The relatively slow growth in jute consumption over the post-war period conceals very different trends in the demand for jute goods in the main consuming countries and in the main end-uses of jute. First, there has been a marked contrast between expanding demand for jute in the United States and relatively static demand in Western Europe. Between 1953–5 and 1964–5, the consumption of jute goods in the United States rose on average by nearly 4½ per cent a year; by contrast, the corresponding increase in the E.E.C. countries was only about 1 per cent a year, while in Britain there was an absolute decline, also averaging about 1 per cent a year. Second, in all the main industrial countries, there has been a marked rise over the past decade in the relative importance of floor coverings as an outlet for jute, and a corresponding decline in the relative importance of packaging uses (Table B8). Packaging remains, however, the major use of jute in the industrial areas, accounting for about two–fifths of total jute consumption in 1964–5; whilst in the primary-producing areas of the world, packaging uses constitute by far the predominant outlet for jute.

Table B8. *Estimated end-uses of jute in the main industrial countries, 1953–5, 1960–1 and 1964–5*

		Packaging	Floor coverings	Other	Total (= 100%)
		(%)	(%)	(%)	(*Thousand metric tons*)
United Kingdom	1953–5	41	22	37	191
	1960–1	34	27	39	176
	1964–5	37	38	25	168
E.E.C.	1953–5	..	..	..	243
	1960–1	55	29	16	265
	1964–5	47	36	17	264
United States	1953–5	53	11	36	303
	1960–1	40	15	45	386
	1964–5	31	26	43	469
Total[a]	1953–5	..	..	..	870
	1960–1	47	21	32	1,020
	1964–5	41	30	29	1,150

SOURCES: *Statistical Yearbook of the European Jute Industry, 1966*, Association of European Jute Industries, Paris; T. S. Robertson, *Jute Utilisation in the United Kingdom and the E.E.C.*, CCP: JU 66/6, F.A.O., Rome; *Demand for Jute Goods*, CCP/Jute 64/6, F.A.O., Rome.

[a] Including estimates for other industrial countries.

(a) Packaging

Jute sacks and bags are used mainly to package bulky agricultural produce and chemical fertilizers. World output of the major bulk commodities suitable for such packaging has expanded considerably over the past decade or two, and is now at a substantially higher level than before the war. Total consumption of jute in packaging uses, however, has shown only a marginal increase over the pre-war level. In the principal industrial countries, there has been substitution against jute on a substantial scale, particularly by the use of multiwall paper sacks instead of jute sacks. For the United States, an analysis for the decade up to 1958 showed a strong trend away from burlap (i.e. hessian) sacks, which could be attributed largely to technological factors.[1] A

[1] A. Maizels, C. Freeman and J. A. Rowlatt, 'Trends in World Demand for Jute Manufactures', *Monthly Bulletin of Agricultural Economics and Statistics*, January 1961, F.A.O., Rome.

similar analysis, based on figures up to 1963, however, indicates only a small trend away from jute.[1] These results seem to indicate that the widespread substitution of paper sacks for jute which was such a notable feature of the 1950s had largely come to an end by the early 1960s, by which time the consumption of jute for packaging would appear to have become more closely related to the output of bulk packageable commodities.

The main commodities for which jute packaging is used in the United States are raw cotton, animal feed, potatoes, rice and fertilizers. A recent study by Mr R. F. Daly, of the United States Department of Agriculture,[2] contains projections of production and consumption of the main crops in the United States in 1970 and 1980 on the basis of assumptions about the rate of income growth, probable changes in relative prices and trends in consumer preferences for particular foods. Using Daly's projections, but adjusting them to conform with the alternative income-growth assumptions used here, and weighting the projection for each of the five main commodities by jute consumption for packaging each in 1960–1, an estimate of jute packaging requirements can be arrived at for 1975. This calculation shows an increase of the order of $1\frac{1}{2}$ per cent a year on the lower income-growth basis (assumption A), and one of about 2 per cent a year on the higher (assumption B), from the 1960–1 level (see Table B9).

For the other industrial countries, and for primary-producing countries, the projections of output of packageable commodities (taken as rice, potatoes, cotton, wool, sugar, coffee, cocoa and fertilizers) were based largely on the projections, or assumptions, made for these commodities elsewhere in this study, supplemented where necessary by projections published by F.A.O.[3] The calculation indicates that the rate of growth of output of bulk packageable commodities is likely—on the various assumptions made—to be of the order of $1\frac{1}{4}$ to 2 per cent a year

---

[1] Using the double logarithmic form:

$$\log J = \log a + b_1 \log P_1 + b_2 \log P_2 + ct,$$

where J represents the proportion of jute (in specified packaging uses) in total consumption of packaging materials, P_1 the relative price of jute and paper, P_2 the relative price of jute and cotton, and t a time trend, the regression results were as follows:

	b_1	b_2	c	R^2
1948–58	0·73	−0·16	−0·033	0·885
	(0·32)	(0·39)	(0·005)	
1948–63	−0·01	−0·36	−0·005	0·432
	(0·41)	(0·64)	(0·002)	

[2] R. F. Daly, *Agriculture in the Years Ahead* (paper presented at the Southern Agricultural Workers Conference, Atlanta, Georgia, U.S.A., 1963).

[3] *Agricultural Commodities—Projections for 1975 and 1985*, F.A.O., Rome, 1967.

for the industrial countries (virtually the same as for the United States), and some $2\frac{1}{2}$ to $3\frac{1}{2}$ per cent a year for the primary-producing countries.

In view of the past trend of displacement of jute sacks by other packaging, particularly paper sacks and polythene bags, and by the development of bulk-handling techniques, it cannot be expected that the consumption of jute per unit of output (the 'jute consumption ratio') will not continue to decline in the future also. It is assumed here that the jute consumption ratio in packaging uses will decline by 10 to 15 per cent between 1960–1 and 1975 in the United States, and by 10 to 20 per cent in other industrial countries. In the primary-producing countries, substitution against jute has so far not been a major factor, though mechanical handling of agricultural commodities has been making inroads in the traditional uses of jute sacks in Australia, New Zealand, and South Africa. For the primary-producing countries as a whole, the decline in the jute consumption ratio is taken to be the same as for the United States.

Table B9. *Jute consumption in packaging, 1960–5 and projections for 1975*

| | Output of packageable commodities[a] | | | Jute consumption ratio[b] | | Jute consumption in packaging | | | |
| | | 1975 | | | | | | 1975 | |
	1964–5	Low	High	1964–5	1975	1960–1	1964–5	A	B
	(Indices, 1960–1 = 100)					*(Million metric tons)*			
United States	110	125	135	98	85–90	0·15	0·15	0·16–0·17	0·17–0·18
Other industrial countries	108	120	130	94	80–90	0·32	0·33	0·32–0·36	0·33–0·37
Total	108	121	131	..	..	0·47	0·48	0·48–0·53	0·50–0·55
Primary-producing countries[c]	110	140	160	100	85–90	0·73	0·80	0·90–0·95	1·00–1·05
TOTAL	109	129	143	..	..	1·20	1·28	1·38–1·48	1·50–1·60

SOURCES: As for Table B8 and *Production Yearbooks*, F.A.O., Rome.

[a] Rice, potatoes, sugar, cotton, wool, coffee, cocoa and fertilizers.
[b] Ratio of jute used in packaging to the output of packageable commodities.
[c] Excluding the main jute-producing countries (India, Pakistan, Thailand and Brazil).

For all areas together (outside the main jute-producing countries), the projections indicate that world demand for jute in packaging uses is likely to continue to grow at a relatively slow rate. Over the first half of the 1960s, the total rose by some $1\frac{1}{2}$ per cent a year, whereas the projections indicate a rise of 1 to $1\frac{1}{2}$ per cent a year on the lower income-growth assumption, and $1\frac{1}{2}$ to 2 per cent a year on the more optimistic basis, over the period up to 1975.

(b) Floor coverings

The demand for jute for use in floor coverings depends on three main factors: the final demand for the floor coverings themselves; the proportion of the different types of floor coverings in the total (since the amount of jute used per unit of area produced varies considerably from one type to another); and the degree to which substitution between jute and other materials is taking place. These three aspects are discussed below, this discussion being confined to the main industrial countries, which probably account for the bulk of world output of floor coverings other than hand-made carpets.

Production of floor coverings is highly concentrated in four countries —the United States, Britain, Belgium and West Germany—which together produce over four-fifths of the total for the industrial countries. There has been an upward trend in production (and consumption) in all these countries over the post-war period, but the major expansion has been in the United States. An analysis of the movement in carpet consumption can be made for both the United States and Britain in terms of price and income changes. For the United States, a regression of *per caput* carpet consumption on the deflated average price of carpets and real personal disposable income per head yielded an income elasticity of 2·3 at the 1963 level of consumption, with a corresponding price elasticity of −0·2;[1] though the price elasticity was not significantly different from zero, it was a plausible result.[2]

For the United Kingdom, a similar regression covering the period 1952–63 yielded an income elasticity of 1·2 and a price elasticity of −1·4 at the 1963 consumption level.[3] The income elasticity as calculated is under one-half of the corresponding elasticity in the United States. On the other hand, the demand for carpets appears to be considerably more price-elastic in Britain than in the United States. Corresponding data for other countries are not readily available, but the income elasticities operating in most Western European countries may well be nearer the American than the British level.

---

[1] The elasticities were 2·34 ($\pm$0·73) for the income elasticity and −0·18 ($\pm$0·23) for the price elasticity, using a semi-logarithmic function based on annual series for the period 1951–63 inclusive ($R^2 = 0.940$). For a comparable regression for 1951–8, the income and price elasticities at the 1958 consumption level were 2·37 ($\pm$0·67) and −0·38 ($\pm$0·16) respectively, with $R^2 = 0.965$.

[2] The large standard error of the price coefficient is probably due partly to the effect of changes in consumer credit conditions on the volume of domestic sales.

[3] The elasticities were 1·16 (+0·45) and −1·40 (+0·54), with $R^2 = 0.800$.

For the projections, it has been assumed that production of floor coverings will rise at the same rate as consumption. For the United States and Britain, the projections have been based on the regressions mentioned above. These indicate that production would rise by 120 or 150 per cent in the United States from 1960–1 to 1975, according to the income-growth assumption used, and by 70 and 95 per cent respectively in Britain. For the other industrial countries, it has been assumed that the average income elasticity is 1·5. On these (rather arbitrary) assumptions the total output of floor coverings in the industrial countries would rise by 5½ and 6½ per cent a year, over the projection period, on the alternative income-growth bases.

The demand for jute in floor coverings will also be influenced to some extent by changes in the pattern of output. The amount of jute backing used in the manufacture of tufted carpets has increased appreciably over the past decade, from 0·25 kg. per square metre of tufted carpet in 1954 to 0·35 kg. in 1960 and 0·47 kg. in 1963, mainly as a result of using double thickness of jute cloth for backing purposes. In 1963, according to the United States Census of Manufactures, woven wool carpets used, on average, between 0·5 and 0·55 kg. of jute per square metre. Thus, a continuation of the trend in favour of tufted products is likely to reduce the average jute requirements somewhat in terms of the total production of carpets. An offsetting factor, at least in Britain and some continental European countries, is that, as real incomes rise, consumers are likely to shift the pattern of their purchases of floor coverings in favour of carpets and away from linoleum, which uses on average less jute per unit of area than do carpets.[1]

A more important influence on the demand for jute in floor coverings is likely to be the trend in substitution between jute and alternative backing materials. In the United States, kraftcord was displacing jute on a substantial scale in the early 1950s in the production of woven carpets, and further substitution would seem to have occurred later in the decade.[2] Moreover, as from 1963, carpet backing of synthetic material was introduced in the United States carpet industry for the first time,[3] and substitution on a large scale for jute by synthetics (particularly by polypropylene, which is a relatively cheap synthetic material) cannot be ruled out in the future. In linoleum, too, jute has

---

[1] Linoleum produced in the United Kingdom used about 0·25 kg. of jute per square metre in 1959.

[2] In 1954, the United States wool carpets and rugs industry used 64 million lb. of jute yarn and 19 million lb. of paper yarn. In 1958, the woven carpet and rug industry used 43 million lb. of jute yarn and 15 million lb. of paper yarn; by 1963, the usage of jute yarn had declined to 32 million lb., whereas consumption of paper yarn was virtually unchanged at 14 million lb. (see *1963 Census of Manufactures*, United States Department of Commerce, Washington, 1966).

[3] *Basic Facts about the Carpet and Rug Industry, 1964*, American Carpet Institute, New York.

been losing ground to other materials, particularly paper and paper-board.

The future movement of the jute consumption ratio will depend heavily on the degree of success of the new types of synthetic carpet backing being developed in the mid 1960s. The present projections are based on the optimistic assumption that there will be no dramatic synthetic 'breakthrough' in this respect, and that jute will remain the major backing material in the manufacture of floor coverings throughout the projection period. On this assumption, it would seem likely that the jute consumption ratio will move differently in the United States and in Western Europe. In the United States, there is little room for a further shift into tufted carpets (which in 1964 accounted for 84 per cent of all shipments of broadloom carpets), which—as indicated earlier—are also using more jute than in 1960–1 as a result of 'double-backing' practice. It is assumed here that, for the United States, the jute consumption ratio in 1975 will be 10 to 20 per cent higher than in 1960–1. In Western Europe, however, there is ample room for a further substantial shift in carpet production into the tufted variety and, mainly for this reason, the jute consumption ratio in Britain and the E.E.C. is assumed to decline to 85 to 95 per cent of the 1960–1 level (Table B 10).

Table B 10. *Jute consumption in floor coverings in certain industrial countries, 1960–5 and projections for 1975*

	Production of floor coverings, indices			Jute con-sumption ratio in 1975	Jute consumption in floor coverings			
	1964–5	1975 A	1975 B		1960–1	1964–5	1975 A	1975 B
	(*1960–1 = 100*)				(*Thousand metric tons*)			
United Kingdom	140	170	195	85–95	48	64	70–80	80–90
E.E.C.	..	200	230	85–95	76	94	130–145	150–165
United States	170	255	290	95–105	60	121	145–160	165–180
TOTAL[a]	..	..	..	..	220	340	450–500	500–550

SOURCES: As for Table B 8.

[a] Including estimates for other industrial countries.

On the basis of these various assumptions, jute requirements for floor coverings in the three industrial areas covered by our estimates would rise by 5 to 5½ per cent a year on the low income-growth assumption, and by 6 to 6½ per cent a year on the higher income basis. It should be emphasized that these projections take an optimistic view of the probable future rate of substitution of synthetic materials for jute in this end-use.

(c) *Other uses*

Apart from floor coverings and packaging, jute has a variety of minor uses. The most important are in rope and twine, electrical cable cores and sheaths and fuse yarns, and upholstery and soft furnishings. Jute is also used in automotive felts, roofing felt, webbing and sandbags, but there is little systematic information available about the magnitude of consumption in these end-uses.

There appears, however, to have been a tendency for some substitution against jute in a number of these minor uses. In rope and twine, jute utilization in the United States fell by over 40 per cent between 1947 and 1954, and by a further 50 per cent from 1954 to 1958. Though jute rope and twine production rose between 1958 and 1963 from 13 to 20 million lb., they declined in relative importance in total output of this industry, mainly as a result of a sharp growth in output of synthetic rope and twine to 23 million lb. in 1963. In roofing felts, however, jute is unlikely to be displaced by alternative materials such as asbestos or glass fibre, which are considerably more expensive.

No reliable estimates of the relevant commodity output can be made for these miscellaneous uses of jute. It seems likely that some end-uses, such as rope and twine, may not increase appreciably in the future, but other uses might well grow with the expansion in commodity output. Over the first half of the 1960s, jute consumption in these miscellaneous uses grew, on average, by rather less than 1 per cent a year. It is assumed here that, over the period up to 1975, jute consumption in 'other uses' will be virtually static (on the low income-growth basis), or will rise by roughly $\frac{1}{2}$ to 1 per cent a year (on the higher income assumption).

These various assumptions and projections are set out in summary form in Table B 11. The projected rates of growth, by main consuming area and main end-use, are intended as indications of major tendencies rather than precise quantitative projections. The summary results show that certain broad changes are probable on the assumptions made. First, world demand for jute (outside the centrally planned countries and the jute-producing countries) is likely to grow at a lower rate, over the decade up to 1975, than in the preceding decade or during the first half of the 1960s. Second, the projected increase in world demand for jute would be shared in roughly equal proportions by the industrial and the primary-producing countries. In the industrial countries, the increase would be predominantly in floor coverings; in the primary-producing countries, packaging would account for the major part of the projected rise in jute consumption. If new synthetic materials achieve a technological 'breakthrough' in the floor covering industry during the coming decade, however, this would have a drastic adverse impact on jute requirements in the industrial countries, which could well offset, or more than offset, the projected increase in demand in the primary-producing areas.

Table B 11. *Jute consumption in 1960–5 and projections for 1975*

| | Jute consumption | | | | Rates of growth from 1960–1 | | |
| | | | 1975 | | | | 1975 |
	1960–1	1964–5	A	B	1964–5	A	B
	(Million metric tons)				*(% per annum)*		
United Kingdom	0·18	0·17	0·18–0·21	0·20–0·25	−1·3	0·0–1·2	0·9–2·5
E.E.C.	0·26	0·26	0·27–0·31	0·29–0·32	0·0	0·3–1·2	0·8–1·4
United States	0·39	0·47	0·51–0·55	0·55–0·59	5·0	1·9–2·4	2·4–2·9
Other industrial countries	0·19	0·25	0·27–0·30	0·30–0·32	7·2	2·5–3·2	3·2–3·6
Total	1·02	1·15	1·23–1·37	1·34–1·48	3·1	1·3–2·1	1·9–2·6
Primary-producing countries	0·73	0·80	0·90–0·95	1·00–1·05	2·3	1·5–1·8	2·2–2·5
TOTAL	1·75	1·95	2·13–2·32	2·34–2·53	2·7	1·4–2·0	2·0–2·6
of which:							
Packaging	1·21	1·28	1·38–1·48	1·50–1·60	1·4	0·9–1·4	1·5–2·0
Floor coverings	0·22	0·34	0·45–0·50	0·50–0·55	11·5	5·1–5·8	5·8–6·5
Other uses	0·32	0·33	0·30–0·34	0·34–0·38	0·8	−0·4 to +0·4	0·4–1·2

SOURCES: As for Table B 8.

Some allowance also needs to be made for jute imports by the centrally planned countries. In 1960–1, they imported some 75 thousand tons of raw jute, the figure rising to over 100 thousand tons in 1963 and about 130 thousand tons in 1964. In addition, India exported a further 130 thousand tons of jute manufactures to the Soviet Union in 1964/5. The outlook for this flow of trade is uncertain, but there would appear to be ample scope for a further considerable expansion. By 1975, the total imports of jute and jute goods into the centrally planned countries are arbitrally assumed to lie within the range of 350 to 500 thousand tons.

The prospects for Sterling exports

The projections of jute consumption given above were made on the basis of a number of assumptions about probable future trends in consumer preferences and in technological developments; they also implicitly assumed that jute prices would not be appreciably different, in relation to prices of substitute materials, in 1975 from the position in the early 1960s. The implications of this price assumption for world jute production are difficult to quantify, but some general review of likely trends in jute production over the coming decade is necessary in order to assess whether the assumption appears to be a reasonable one.

The other major problem in projecting Sterling Area exports in 1975 lies in making an assessment of the ratio of raw jute exports to those of jute manufactures. The higher the proportion of jute manufactures, the higher will be the value of exports from the Sterling jute-producing countries, for any given level of jute consumption in the rest of the world.

Over the period from 1956–8 to 1962–3, world jute production (outside China and the Soviet Union) rose by 3·8 per cent per annum on average, from 1·82 million tons in 1956–8 to 2·28 million tons in 1962–3; by far the greater part of the increase was accounted for by an expansion in Indian production, reflecting an increase in average yields as well as an extension in the planted area. In Pakistan, too, the area planted to jute has tended to rise (though, as in India, there have been large variations from one season to another), but average yields in 1961/2 and 1962/3 were unusually low.

Both India and Pakistan are aiming at substantial increases in raw jute production in the period up to 1970 (see Table B 12). In both countries, government measures are being directed towards increases in yields, by the introduction of improved varieties, irrigation schemes, and so on. However, the 1970 targets imply a considerably faster improvement in average yields in the late 1960s than appears to be feasible on the basis of past trends, and actual output in 1970 may well be below these targets, unless there is a significant rise in the ratio of jute prices to rice prices (in which case farmers would tend to switch from rice to jute cultivation[1]) and/or unless large-scale technical assistance designed to achieve greater productivity is provided to the jute farmers.

It might therefore be more reasonable to assume that the 1970 targets were reached by 1975 rather than by 1970; even this more moderate assumption implies either a marked success in efforts to increase average yields, particularly in Pakistan, or an appreciable rise in the relative profitability of planting jute rather than rice. If these targets were, in fact, reached by 1975, world output of jute and allied fibres (outside the centrally planned countries) in that year would be about 3·7 million tons, or some 850 thousand tons (30 per cent) above the average for the seasons 1961/2 to 1963/4.

[1] S. M. Hussain ('A Note on Farmer Response to Price in East Pakistan', *Pakistan Development Review*, vol. 4, no. 1, 1964) found that over the period 1948–63 the area planted to jute varied by 4 per cent, on average, for a 10 per cent variation in the ratio of jute prices to rice prices in the previous season. This result compares closely with that reached in other studies (see, for example, Ralph Clark, 'The Economic Determinants of Jute Production', *Monthly Bulletin of Agricultural Economics and Statistics*, September 1957, F.A.O., Rome).

Table B 12. *Trends in production of jute and allied fibres, 1956–65 and plans for 1970 and 1975 (million metric tons)*

	Actual				Plan	
	1956–8[a]	1959–61[a]	1962–3	1964–5	1970	1975
JUTE						
Pakistan	1·02	1·04	1·10	1·07	1·40[b]	..
India	0·75	0·83	1·05	0·95	1·35[c]	1·69[d]
Other countries[e]	0·06	0·08	0·13	0·15	..	..
Total	1·82	1·95	2·28	2·17	..	..
ALLIED FIBRES						
India	0·24	0·23	0·32	0·26	0·36[c]	..
Thailand	0·02	0·09	0·17	0·34	..	..
Other countries[e]	0·14	0·05	0·08	..	..	..
Total	0·30	0·37	0·57	..	..	..
TOTAL	2·12	2·32	2·85	..	..	..

SOURCES: D. Hamilton-Russell, *Post-war Trends in the Production of Jute, Kenaf and Allied Fibers*, CCP/Jute/64/8, F.A.O., Rome, July, 1964; *Production Yearbook, 1966*, F.A.O., Rome, 1967; Economic Development Plans.

[a] Years ending mid-year of period stated.
[b] 1969/70.
[c] 1970/1.   [d] 1975/6.
[e] Excluding China and the Soviet Union.

Domestic consumption of jute goods in India and Pakistan rose by 200 thousand tons (70 per cent) between 1953–5 and 1962–3. A recent F.A.O. estimate for 1975 put the total at 700 to 880 thousand tons for that year,[1] implying annual average growth rates of 3·3 to 5·1 per cent from 1961–3, compared with the 6·6 per cent over the period from 1953–5 to 1961–3. Taking an average growth rate of 5 per cent for purely illustrative purposes, domestic consumption in India and Pakistan would rise by some 400 thousand tons between 1964–5 and 1975. Allowing for increased requirements in other producing countries, the total increase in domestic consumption in the Far East producing countries might perhaps lie within the range of 400 to 450 thousand tons. If so, the exportable surplus of jute (including allied fibres) and jute goods in 1975 would be some 400 to 500 thousand tons above the 1964–5 level. This is lower than the projection made earlier of the increase in import requirements by the rest of the world on the higher income-growth assumption (B) of some 500–800 thousand tons; but would be within the range of the projected increase in import requirements (300–600 thousand tons) on the lower growth assumption (A).

[1] *Agricultural Commodities—Projections for 1975 and 1985.*

From these various calculations, it would seem that current production prospects are not substantially out of line with the prospects for consumption, assuming no change in relative jute prices, and that there are no additional adverse effects from technological developments. In view of the inevitably high margin of error in all these projections, the apparent excess of demand for jute over the projected supply in 1975, on the higher income-growth assumption, cannot be taken as implying the likelihood of any upward pressure on prices in such circumstances. Indeed, pressure in the reverse direction could well result if there is a major 'breakthrough' by synthetics in the main traditional uses of jute.

Exports of jute manufactures

Since jute manufactures have a considerably higher unit value than raw jute, the greater the proportion of manufactures in the exports of India and Pakistan, the greater will be their export earnings for a given combined tonnage of exports of jute and jute goods. In 1965, for example, the unit value of Pakistan's exports of raw jute was 1,120 rupees per metric ton, compared with Indian exports of 1,630 rupees for new jute sacking bags, 2,170 rupees for new jute hessian bags and 2,320 rupees for hessian cloth.

Over the past decade, there has been a sharp change in the geographical pattern of jute manufacturing, the whole of the expansion in world output of jute goods taking place outside Western Europe. In 1954, Western Europe accounted for one-third of all world output (outside the centrally planned countries), whereas by 1963 the proportion had been reduced to one-fifth, mainly as a result of the rapid development of the industry in Pakistan and its further growth in India.[1] The jute-processing industry in Western Europe is generally protected by import tariffs and quota restrictions against competition from the lower-cost products of India and Pakistan. In Britain, this protection takes the form of a mark-up on import prices of jute goods from India and Pakistan. In recent years, the mark-up on the principal bag-making cloths has been reduced, thus allowing the cheaper imported cloths to take a larger share of the domestic market, while the home industry has tended to concentrate on better quality cloths, particularly carpet backing.[2]

This trend is likely to spread further in the coming decade, as the industry in Western Europe becomes increasingly concentrated on supplies for the carpet industry. However, since the European industry

[1] In 1963, Western Europe produced about 500 thousand metric tons of jute goods, compared with 1,260 thousand tons in India and nearly 320 thousand tons in Pakistan.

[2] See A. Maizels and J. A. Rowlatt, 'The Competitive Position of Jute Manufactures in Western Europe and the Far East', *Monthly Bulletin of Agricultural Economics and Statistics*, March 1962, F.A.O., Rome.

seems unlikely to expand its total output to any substantial extent, the increase in consumption projected earlier would, if attained, allow for some increase in imports from India and Pakistan. The potential expansion here is, however, likely to be relatively much smaller than in the United States, in which market Indian and Pakistani goods compete, as far as the tariff is concerned, on equal terms with the Western European product. The problem of increasing exports from the two Sterling countries lies essentially in expanding their output of the higher quality products. To the extent that this can be achieved, the value of their exports would rise at a somewhat faster rate than is indicated by the projections in tonnage terms in Table B11.

NATURAL RUBBER

The present pattern of trade

Natural rubber is extremely important to the export trade of a number of countries in South-East Asia, both Sterling and non-Sterling. Over 60 per cent of Malaysia's exports by value in 1964, for example, consisted of natural rubber,[1] a similar proportion being exported by South Vietnam. Indonesian statistics have to be partially estimated, but it would seem that natural rubber accounted for about two-fifths of Indonesia's export earnings in 1964. In the Sterling Area, only Ceylon and Nigeria—other than Malaysia—are substantial exporters of natural rubber, which constituted 16 and 6 per cent respectively of their export earnings in 1964.

Table B13. *Exports of natural and synthetic rubber, 1964*

	Value of exports			Rubber as proportion of total exports
	Natural rubber	Synthetic rubber	Total	
	(£ million)			(%)
STERLING COUNTRIES				
Malaysia	187	—	187	61
Ceylon	22	—	22	16
Nigeria	12	—	12	6
Other overseas Sterling countries	4	—	4	..
United Kingdom	—	8	8	0·2
Total, Sterling	224	8	232	2
NON-STERLING COUNTRIES				
Industrial	—	134	134	0·4
Developing	188[a]	1	189	3
Total, non-Sterling	188	135	323	1
TOTAL	412	143	555	1
O.S.A. as percentage of TOTAL	54	—	40	..

SOURCES: *Trade Yearbook, 1965*, F.A.O., Rome, 1966; *Yearbook of International Trade Statistics, 1964*, United Nations, New York, 1966; *Foreign Trade, Series C*, O.E.C.D., Paris.

[a] Including estimates for Indonesia.

[1] See Table B13.

While natural rubber is produced entirely outside the industrial countries, these have developed their output of synthetic rubber at a rapid rate since the end of the war. Up to the late 1950s, synthetic rubber was produced almost exclusively in the United States, but since then there has been a rapid expansion in capacity in Western Europe and Japan and in Eastern Europe and the U.S.S.R. Even so, the United States still accounted for the major share of total production of this commodity in the Western industrial countries in the mid 1960s.[1] Its share of synthetic rubber exports has been appreciably reduced since 1960 as a result of rapid expansion in exports from E.E.C. countries.

Exports of natural rubber from Sterling countries in 1964 accounted for about one-half of all natural rubber exports from developing countries in that year; the greater part of non-Sterling supplies came from Indonesia. As a proportion of world exports of *all* rubber, however, exports from Sterling countries represent only two-fifths of the total. Although the greater part of Sterling natural rubber exports are sold in the markets of the chief Western industrial countries, appreciable, though varying, proportions are exported to the Soviet Union and other centrally planned countries. In 1965, for example, the Western industrial markets took three-fifths of natural rubber exports from Malaysia, but only one-third of the (much smaller) exports from Ceylon. Ceylon's main export market in that year was the centrally planned countries (especially China): they took three-fifths of her total shipments. The primary-producing countries took one-sixth of Malaysia's exports in 1965, but only 6 per cent of Ceylon's (Argentina, India and Mexico being the biggest purchasers).

The present projections of Sterling exports in 1975 are based mainly on estimated levels of demand for natural rubber in the Western industrial countries. The future trend of demand in the centrally planned countries is uncertain, and alternative assumptions have had to be made. For the primary-producing countries, demand for imports of natural rubber has been assumed to grow roughly at the same rate as in the recent past.

Rubber consumption in the industrial countries

The major outlet for rubber is the manufacture of vehicle tyres and tubes, which accounted for about three-fifths of total rubber consumption in 1965 in the United States, Britain, France and Western Germany. In Canada, tyres composed about 70 per cent of the total; in Japan, nearly 50 per cent. Apart from tyres and tubes, including tyre retreads and tyre repairs, rubber is consumed in a wide range of industrial uses,

[1] The United States' share fell from 89 per cent in 1955 to 76 per cent in 1960 and to 62 per cent in 1965.

mainly rubber floor coverings, rubber adhesives, footwear, cables and tubes. Total demand for rubber thus depends in part on the output growth pattern of all these products. Even within the tyre industry, a change in the relative importance of tyre production for cars, commercial road vehicles and other vehicles (including bicycles) can have an appreciable influence on total rubber consumption.

Table B 14. *Rubber consumption in the main industrial countries, 1953–65 and projections for 1975*

	Rates of growth				Consumption			
	1953–7 to 1960–1	1960–1 to 1964–5	1960–1 to 1975		1960–1	1964–5	1975	
			A	B			A	B
	(% *per annum*)				(*Million metric tons*)			
United Kingdom	3·0	5·3	5·1	6·2	0·29	0·36	0·60	0·70
E.E.C.	8·9	6·3	6·7	8·0	0·69	0·89	1·77	2·10
Other Western Europe	8·3	12·4	10·1	10·7	0·16	0·26	0·65	0·70
United States	1·7	6·6	3·6	4·0	1·57	2·03	2·60	2·80
Canada	2·3	9·9	4·0	4·5	0·09	0·14	0·16	0·17
Japan	16·2	10·6	9·1	10·3	0·24	0·37	0·85	1·00
Total	4·4	7·4	5·5	6·4	3·04	4·05	6·63	7·47

SOURCE: *Rubber Statistical Bulletin,* International Rubber Study Group, London.

One way of projecting future demand for rubber would be to make estimates of the probable level of demand, in each industrial country, for each of the various end-products mentioned, based on the assumptions about the growth of population and real income made earlier. Such a detailed and complex analysis would fall outside the scope of the present study. Instead, total rubber consumption in each country has been related to the volume of manufacturing production. For all the industrial countries, there is a very close relationship between the two. Regressions of rubber consumption on the relevant indices of manufacturing production, based on annual data for the period 1953–65, showed an extremely good fit to the original data for all the industrial areas.[1] The regression results were used as a basis for projecting total consumption of rubber in 1975 in each industrial area (see Table B 14).

The projections indicate that, if the past relationship computed between rubber consumption and manufacturing production holds for

---

[1] For the United Kingdom and Japan, linear equations of the form $C_t = a + bP_t$ were used, where C denotes total rubber consumption and P the index of manufacturing production. For the other countries, the form used was $\log C_t = a + b_1 P_t + b_2 P_t^2$. In all cases, R^2 exceeded 0·95.

the future as well, total rubber demand in the industrial countries in 1975 will be in the region of 6½ million metric tons on the low income-growth assumption, and 7½ million metric tons on the more optimistic income assumption. These results imply that the average growth rate of rubber consumption over the period from 1960–1 to 1975 will decline somewhat (to some 5½ or 6½ per cent a year, according to the income-growth assumption used), compared with the relatively high rate (7½ per cent a year) achieved in the early 1960s; this arose essentially from the sharp industrial boom in those years and the associated rapid expansion in automobile production.

Of the industrial countries, the highest growth rates in demand are projected for 'other Western Europe' and Japan. In both areas, rubber consumption rose by more than 10 per cent a year during the first half of the 1960s, and similar rates of growth are projected, on the basis of the income-growth assumptions, for the remainder of the projection period. A considerable slowing down in the rate of increase in United States consumption is projected, but for the E.E.C. area the projections indicate an increase on the growth rate of the early 1960s, though not on that for the late 1950s. By 1975, if the country pattern of consumption develops as indicated by the projections, the United States will account for rather less than 40 per cent of total rubber consumption in the industrial countries, as against rather more than 50 per cent in 1960–1. By contrast, the E.E.C. share of the total will have risen to 27 or 28 per cent from 23 per cent over the same period.

In all the industrial countries, the share of natural rubber in total rubber consumption has been falling over the past two decades, and this process is likely to continue in the future. The decline has gone furthest in North America; by 1964–5, only 25 per cent of rubber used in the United States consisted of the natural product, the corresponding proportion for Canada being 31 per cent. In Western Europe, synthetic rubber consumption began to make a major impact on the demand for natural rubber only towards the end of the 1950s, and the process of substitution has not yet caught up with that in North America: by 1964–5, the share of natural rubber was still in the region of 50 per cent. In Japan, the share of natural has been sharply reduced, though it still exceeded 50 per cent in 1964–5 (see Table B 15).

Future trends in the share of natural rubber in total consumption cannot be determined with any precision. It would seem that the past decline in the share has resulted from a number of different factors, both price and non-price. Synthetic rubber has had the great advantage of more stable prices; natural rubber has been subject to substantial fluctuations in price, making it for some periods relatively unattractive to manufacturers of rubber products. In addition, continuous technical developments in synthetic rubbers have widened the area of potential substitution, to the detriment of the natural product.

However, there are two reasons for believing that the rate of substitution may slow down in the future. First, natural rubber prices have in recent years become much more heavily influenced by the stability of synthetic prices; and it seems likely that price fluctuations in the natural product will become appreciably smaller and closely aligned with the prices of synthetic substitutes. The second reason is that, though technological developments—especially the new stereo rubbers—are likely to continue to displace natural with synthetic rubber, such displacement can no longer be a major factor in a number of end-uses for which the substitution of natural by synthetic rubber is by now almost complete.

Table B 15. *Consumption of natural rubber in the main industrial countries, 1960–5 and projections for 1975*

	Natural as proportion of total rubber consumption			Natural rubber consumption				Rates of growth 1960–1 to 1975	
						1975			
			Assumed			A	B	A	B
	1960–1	1964–5	1975	1960–1	1964–5				
	(%)	(%)	(%)	(*Million metric tons*)				(*% p.a.*)	
United Kingdom	59	51	35	0·18	0·19	0·21	0·24	1·1	2·5
E.E.C.	57	46	32	0·40	0·41	0·57	0·67	2·5	3·6
Other Western Europe	65	55	35	0·11	0·14	0·23	0·25	5·2	5·8
United States	29	25	20	0·46	0·51	0·52	0·56	0·9	1·4
Canada	36	31	25	0·03	0·04	0·04	0·04	2·0	2·0
Japan	70	55	35	0·17	0·20	0·30	0·35	4·0	5·1
TOTAL	44	36	28	1·35	1·49	1·87	2·11	2·3	3·1

SOURCE: As for Table B 14.

Estimates of the probable share of the natural product in total rubber consumption by 1975 (see Table B 15) are, nonetheless, subject to a fair margin of error. However, demand for natural rubber in the industrial countries is projected on this basis to increase by 2·3 and 3·1 per cent a year on the low and high income-growth assumptions respectively. In absolute terms, this implies an increase from 1·4 million metric tons in 1960–1 to between 1·9 and 2·1 million metric tons in 1975. Virtually the entire increase in consumption would be in continental Western Europe and Japan: consumption in Britain and the United States would rise by only a marginal amount, while no change from the level attained by 1964–5 is projected for Canada.

Rubber consumption in other areas

In addition to demand in the industrial countries, allowance has to be made for probable, or assumed, changes in demand for natural rubber elsewhere. Consumption of both natural and synthetic rubber in the primary-producing countries has risen fairly rapidly over the past decade. From 1953–7 to 1960–1, the annual rate of growth in consumption was as high as 17 per cent, consumption in the latter period averaging 430 thousand metric tons a year. From then until 1964–5 (when consumption rose to 620 thousand tons a year), the growth rate declined to an average of $8\frac{1}{2}$ per cent a year—even so, it was more than double the corresponding growth rate in the industrial countries. Future prospects are somewhat uncertain, since much will depend on the degree of success in implementing plans for industrial development in a number of developing countries—particularly India, Argentina, Mexico and Brazil—as well as on the rate of expansion in automobile production, particularly in Australia. It is assumed here that from 1964–5 up to 1975, the growth rate in rubber consumption in the primary-producing countries as a whole will decline somewhat from the rate achieved during the early 1960s, and will lie within the range 5 to 6 per cent a year. On this assumption, rubber consumption in these countries will increase to 1·0 to 1·1 million metric tons by 1975.

A remarkable development in these countries in recent years has been the sharp rise in their synthetic rubber consumption. This is, in part, a result of the development of new synthetic rubber industries: Australia began synthetic rubber production in 1961, Brazil in 1962, India in 1963, South Africa in 1964 and Argentina in 1965. Together, their total output of synthetic rubber in 1965 was 90 thousand metric tons—rather more than half their combined synthetic rubber consumption for that year (158 thousand tons).

For the primary-producing countries in total, the proportion of natural rubber in their total rubber consumption has substantially fallen over the past decade. In 1953–7, it had fallen to 65 per cent, while by 1964–5 it was down to 56 per cent. If recent rates of displacement continue, the share of the natural product in 1975 could hardly exceed 30 per cent of total rubber consumption. However, it would seem likely that the rate of displacement will be less than in the recent past (for much the same reasons as those suggested about consumption in the industrial countries) and it is assumed here that the 1975 share of natural rubber will be in the range of 35–45 per cent. On this argument, the demand for natural rubber in the primary-producing countries will have risen from 350 thousand tons in 1964–5 to somewhere between 350 and 500 thousand tons in 1975.

Table B 16. *Production of natural and synthetic rubber,*
1953–65 and projections for 1975

	Rates of growth			Production			
	1953–7 to 1960–1	1960–1 to 1964–5	1960–1 to 1975	1960–1	1962–3	1964–5	1975
	(% per annum)			(Million metric tons)			
NATURAL RUBBER							
Malaysia:							
Estates	3·4	3·2	2·4–3·1	0·43	0·45	0·49	0·60–0·67
Smallholdings[a]	3·2	3·6	5·6–6·0	0·38	0·40	0·44	0·83–0·88
India and Ceylon	0·5	6·7	4·3–5·2	0·12	0·13	0·16	0·22–0·25
Total, Sterling countries	2·9	3·9	4·1–4·7	0·93	0·99	1·08	1·65–1·80
Non-Sterling countries	0·9	2·0	1·9–2·8	1·14	1·12	1·23	1·50–1·70
TOTAL	1·8	2·9	3·0–3·7	2·07	2·13	2·32	3·15–3·50
SYNTHETIC RUBBER							
United States	8·1	6·0	..	1·44	1·62	1·82	..
Other industrial countries	30·5	19·0	..	0·51	0·71	1·02	..
TOTAL	11·8	9·9	..	1·95	2·33	2·84	..

SOURCE: As for Table B 14.

[a] Including production in Sabah and Sarawak.

Imports of natural rubber by the centrally planned countries have
been relatively stable, at some 500 thousand tons, in each year from
1961 to 1965. In 1965, about half this total went to the Soviet Union;
China too was a major market. Prospects over the coming decade are
exceedingly uncertain. The current Soviet Five-Year Plan, for instance,
envisages self-sufficiency in rubber supplies by 1970, so that Russia's
demand for natural rubber will depend essentially on how far her plan
for synthetic rubber production is fulfilled. Nor can future demand by
China be projected on the basis of past trends, though it seems likely
that Chinese requirements will be much larger by 1975 than in the
mid 1960s. An arbitrary assumption must therefore be made; total
natural rubber demand of the centrally planned countries in 1975 is
taken here as somewhere between a lower limit of ½ million tons (as in
the mid 1960s) and 1 million tons. The margin of error is clearly very
substantial.

On the basis of all these assumptions, world demand for natural rubber would rise from 2·1 and 2·3 million metric tons in 1960–1 and 1964–5 respectively to 2·7 to 3·3 million tons on the low income-growth basis and 3·0 to 3·6 million tons on the high one in 1975.

Rubber production

An upper limit to natural rubber production in 1975 is set by the life cycle of the rubber tree. As it takes seven years for a tree to come into bearing, no stock planted after 1968 can contribute to production in 1975. The rate of replanting after 1968 does, admittedly, have some bearing on the availability of old stock which, if it were not replaced, would continue to be tapped when prices justified it. However, in view of the potential increases in yields and the upward pressures on operating costs in the production of natural rubber, replanting can be expected to proceed on a substantial scale.

Reasonably good estimates can be made for 1975 of potential output in Malaysia and Ceylon, for both of which detailed statistics of new plantings and replantings are available. Taking these into account, also the probable increase in yields,[1] production on Malaysian estates is estimated to rise from 1960–1 to 1975 at a rate somewhat less than that of the last ten years, whilst for smallholdings in Malaysia the projected rate of increase is appreciably higher than the past rate. Thus, total natural rubber output in the whole of Malaysia is put at about 1·45 to 1·55 million tons in 1975, compared with 800 to 900 thousand tons a year in the early 1960s.[2] Production in India and Ceylon[3] is projected to double between 1960–1 and 1975 (see Table B16). For the Sterling producing countries as a group, natural rubber production is projected to reach 1·65 to 1·80 million metric tons by 1975, equivalent to an annual rate of increase of 4 to 5 per cent from 1964–5 to 1975.

Among the non-Sterling producers, projections for Indonesia inevitably contain a substantial margin of error. Production on estates remained virtually static, at some 225 thousand metric tons, from 1960 to 1965, while smallholders' output fluctuated between 370 and 470 thousand tons a year. It is assumed for Indonesia that between 1965 and 1975 some increase in annual output—taken arbitrarily at 20 to 40 per cent over the decade—will be achieved, as a result of policies to encourage replantings and raise productive efficiency. A substantial

---

[1] Newly planted clones in Malaysia are estimated to yield about 1,400 kg. per hectare on estates and about 1,100 kg. per hectare on smallholdings, compared with average yields in planted areas of 624 and 400 kg. respectively.

[2] For West Malaysia only, the 1975 projection is 1·35 to 1·45 million metric tons. This compares with an estimate of 1·1 to 1·2 million (long) tons for 1970 made by the Malayan Rubber Research Institute (quoted in *Interim Review of Development in Malaya under the Second Five-Year Plan*, Kuala Lumpur, December 1963).

[3] Ceylon's production is likely to be favourably affected by a subsidy scheme to encourage replanting with high-yielding stock.

increase in output seems probable in Thailand, due partly to financial assistance for replanting. Moderate increases are projected in other producing countries.

In total, world natural rubber production is estimated to rise from 2·1 and 2·3 million metric tons in 1960–1 and 1964–5 respectively to between 3·15 and 3·50 million tons by 1975. This is extremely close to the projection of 3·0 to 3·6 million tons for world demand for natural rubber on the high income-growth assumption; but on the low income-growth basis, with demand projected at 2·7 to 3·3 million tons, a natural rubber surplus of up to 750 thousand tons is indicated. It should be emphasized that the demand projection assumes that natural rubber prices will be determined by prices of competing synthetic rubbers, so that the 1975 level of natural rubber prices is likely to be appreciably lower than the 1960–1 average. Otherwise, the projected share of natural in total rubber consumption would have to be taken much lower than that estimated here, so that, even on the high income-growth basis, an excess of production would probably be indicated for 1975.

Synthetic rubber production continued its rapid expansion in the first half of the 1960s (see Table B16), though considerable excess capacity has emerged, partly as a result of technical obsolescence. Nonetheless, forward plans exist for a further big increase in capacity. Between the end of 1966 and the end of 1969, world synthetic rubber capacity (outside the centrally planned countries) is planned to rise by some 800 thousand metric tons (6 per cent a year).[1] On the basis of the demand projections given above, world demand for synthetic rubber outside the centrally planned countries would rise between 1964–5 and 1975 by 6·2 to 6·4 per cent a year on the low-income growth basis, and by 7·4 to 7·6 per cent a year on the more optimistic. These growth rates are well below the rate of expansion over the past decade, and would seem within the capability of the synthetic rubber industry. With synthetic capacity projected to expand by at least 6 per cent a year over the coming decade, it seems almost certain that synthetic prices will not rise appreciably, taking into account the probability of further economies of scale and new technological developments. The implication for the natural rubber producers is that they will have to effect a substantial improvement in productivity if they are to market the indicated increase in output at prices competitive with the synthetic product.

---

[1] Clayton F. Ruebensaal, 'World Synthetic Rubber—its Manufacture and Markets', *Rubber and Plastics Age*, October 1966.

VEGETABLE OILS AND OILSEEDS

The present pattern of trade

Vegetable oils and oilseeds are, in aggregate, one of the major primary commodity exports of the Overseas Sterling Area. In 1964 they were valued at some £150 million, accounting for nearly 3 per cent of total exports from the Area. Nigeria is by far the largest single exporter, followed by Ceylon, Malaya, and India (Table B 17); other Sterling exporters include South Africa, Gambia and the Pacific Islands.

Table B 17. *Exports of vegetable oils and oilseeds, 1964*

	Value of exports			As proportion of total exports
	Oilseeds	Oils	Total	
	(*£ million*)			(%)
STERLING COUNTRIES				
Nigeria	59	19	78	36
Ceylon	4	12	16	11
Malaya	3	12	15	4
India	3	9	12	2
South Africa	5	1	6	1
Other countries	19	9	28	..
Total, Sterling	93	61	154	2
NON-STERLING COUNTRIES				
Industrial	251	139	390	1
Developing	147	111	259	3
Centrally planned	27	11	38	1
Total, non-Sterling	425	261	686	1
TOTAL	518	322	840	1
O.S.A. as percentage of TOTAL	*18*	*19*	*18*	..

SOURCES: *Yearbook of International Trade Statistics*, United Nations, New York; *Trade Yearbook, 1963*, F.A.O., Rome.

The importance of trade to the economy of each exporting country varies greatly. Gambia, New Guinea and Nigeria are heavily dependent on oilseeds as a major source of foreign exchange, deriving from them between 40 and 100 per cent of total earnings. By contrast, oils and oilseeds accounted for one-tenth or less of total exports of the other main Sterling exporters.

The 'Sterling' oils

The oils and oilseeds exported from the Overseas Sterling Area consist almost entirely of four groups: coconut oil (including copra), groundnut oil (including groundnuts), palm oil, and palm kernels.[1] These groups account for over 90 per cent by value of the total oils and oilseeds exported by the Area. Within the four, the Sterling countries account for an appreciable proportion of world exports: over half for palm kernels, two-fifths for groundnuts (including oil) and palm oil, and one-third for copra (including coconut oil). Outside the four groups, the Overseas Sterling Area's share in world exports is very small indeed.

Principal end-uses

While each vegetable oil has its own special characteristics, improvements in processing methods have made the different oils increasingly interchangeable and therefore more competitive with one another. Moreover, vegetable oils or their products have always been in competition with animal fats and marine oils. Therefore, to examine the demand prospects for 'Sterling' oils, the prospects for consumption of oils and fats as a whole must first be examined. Food-type oils and fats[2] fall into two broad categories. First, there are those used wholly or mainly for edible purposes: this group includes lard, whale oil and the 'soft' vegetable oils (of which only groundnut is a 'Sterling' oil). The second group, used in substantial quantities in food-processing, is also used in the manufacture of soap and other specialized industrial products. The vegetable oils in this second category are described as 'hard' oils and they are all 'Sterling' oils: coconut, palm-kernel and palm. Coconut and palm-kernel oil have a high lauric acid content which is necessary for quick and abundant lather in soap. Palm oil is also used in soap, but all three are applied extensively in margarine manufacture and, following a decline in their use in soap, have been finding additional outlets in other food-processing. Fish oil and tallow are the main competitors of these 'Sterling' oils, particularly in the making of soap.

The proportion of 'Sterling' oils in each main end-use varies a good deal from one country to another and over time. This reflects, partly, the different availabilities of substitute oils, animal fats and marine oils in the different consuming countries and, partly, the existence of special trading ties with particular producing countries and of government restrictions on imports or usage of particular oils.

---

[1] Termed for convenience in this appendix the 'Sterling' oils.

[2] Industrial oils—linseed, tung and castor—are exported largely by non-Sterling countries, and do not compete with the food-type oils; consequently, they are not considered in the present analysis.

Thus, the prospects of Overseas Sterling Area exports of vegetable oils and oilseeds depend on three broad factors: first, the likely future trend in demand for the main products using 'Sterling' oils; second, the process of substitution between 'Sterling' oils and other vegetable oils, marine oils and animal fats in these end-products; third, the probable share of the world market in 'Sterling' oils which the overseas Sterling countries themselves can reasonably be confident of supplying.

Consumption of vegetable oils in the industrial countries

In the industrial countries as a whole, the most important individual end-uses for vegetable oils and animal fats are the manufacture of margarine, soap, and compound cooking fat. In 1962–3, margarine accounted for about one-fifth of consumption in the industrial countries of all food-type oils and fats (other than butter), compound cooking fat for about one-seventh, and soap for about one-tenth. These end-uses are considered in turn below.

(a) Margarine

Margarine tends to be substituted for butter when butter prices rise; the reverse takes place when butter prices fall. Total consumption of both is not very income-elastic at the high income levels in Western Europe; probably a saturation level in *per caput* consumption has been reached in Britain and some other European countries, particularly in Scandinavia, where consumption of butter and margarine *per head* is higher than in any other area in the world.

In the early fifties there was a rapid rise in the proportion of margarine in total consumption, but this fell considerably in Britain as supplies of butter improved and, later, as butter prices fell; but in the rest of Western Europe the proportion has remained substantially unchanged at the levels of the mid 1950s. In North America, the margarine proportion has risen steadily throughout the post-war period. This is partly a consequence of relaxation of restriction on margarine production and distribution, improvements in the quality of margarine and, more recently, publicity on the relationship between animal-fat consumption and heart disease.

The demand projections below have been based on estimates of income and price elasticities in each of the main industrial areas. The projections in Table B18 exclude North America and Japan, because the consumption of 'Sterling' oils in the manufacture of margarine in these countries is negligible; several countries of Western Europe have been excluded owing to inadequacies in the data. For the latter, it was assumed that the basic elasticities and the proportion of 'Sterling' oils used in margarine manufacture would be broadly similar to those of the countries covered, and an estimate for consumption of 'Sterling' oils in these countries is provided in Table B 20 below.

For the United Kingdom an income elasticity of demand for margarine with respect to the price of butter has been assumed at 0·3 for the projection period (based on the annual estimates of the National Food Survey Committee).[1] For the other main margarine-consuming countries, income and price[2] elasticities were estimated from annual data over the period 1951–1961, and a wide range of both elasticities was shown. For France and Belgium the calculated income elasticities at the 1960 levels of *per caput* consumption exceeded unity, while the elasticity for West Germany was, in effect, zero.[3] To reduce the considerable margin of error implicit in these regression results, average income and price elasticities were computed for two country groups— the E.E.C. (excluding Italy) and Scandinavia (i.e. Denmark, Norway and Sweden)—by weighting the country elasticities[4] by their respective margarine consumption in 1960–1. The average income elasticities so obtained (0·4 for the E.E.C. and 0·5 for Scandinavia) were used to project the level of margarine consumption in 1975.

For the movement in the ratio of margarine to butter prices[5] the range of probability is considerable, much depending on the price and marketing policies pursued by the governments of the consuming countries, in particular on those pursued in the E.E.C. It would seem reasonable to allow for a fall in butter prices in this area[6] and it has been assumed that the butter/margarine price ratio will fall by some 10 to 25 per cent between 1960–1 and 1975. For Britain, the probable trend of future prices is uncertain. Butter prices were in fact rather low in 1960–1 and had risen by some 18 per cent by 1963. They might continue to rise if imports remain restricted, but a long-term rise in butter prices may be checked by rising milk output associated with higher meat production. Given the absence of any clear alternative, the projections for Britain and Scandinavia assume no change in the price ratio.

Allowing for population increase, total consumption of margarine in Britain, E.E.C. (excluding Italy) and Scandinavia in 1975 is projected at some 20 per cent above the level in 1960–1. This increase would of course be altered if, say, the butter price rose in Britain or fell further than assumed in the E.E.C.

---

[1] *Domestic Food Consumption and Expenditure, 1962*, H.M.S.O., London, 1964.

[2] The 'price' here refers to the ratio of margarine to butter prices at the retail stage.

[3] The computed elasticities were: France, 1·30 ($\pm$0·18); Belgium, 1·68 ($\pm$0·18); Germany, 0·01 ($\pm$0·31).

[4] These elasticities were taken at zero when they did not exceed their standard errors.

[5] Margarine prices are assumed constant; manufacturers prefer to maintain fairly stable selling prices and vary output in response to changes in demand.

[6] See Appendix A 4.

Usage of 'Sterling' oils.[1] As already mentioned, the United States uses almost no 'Sterling' oils at all in margarine; the predominant ingredient is soyabean oil, which is relatively cheap as a result of government price support and tariff policies. In Western Europe a wider variety of oils is used, in proportions more responsive to relative price changes.

Table B 18. *Consumption of 'Sterling' oils in margarine in Western Europe,[a]*
1954–63 and projections for 1975

| | Actual | | 1975 | | Rates of growth | | | |
| | | | | | 1954–7 to 1960–1 | 1954–7 to 1962–3 | 1960–1 to 1975 | |
	1960–1	1962–3	A	B			A	B
	(Kg.)					*(% per annum)*		
Margarine consumption per head	8.9	8.6	9·9	10·1	−0·4	−0·8	0·8	0·9
	(Million metric tons)							
Total margarine consumption	1·71	1·68	2·00	2·10	0·5	0·1	1·2	1·2
Total oils and fats consumption	1·49	1·42	1·80	1·80	−0·3	−0·5	1·3	1·3
	(%)							
'Sterling' oils as proportion of total	45	42	35	35	—	—	—	—
	(Million metric tons)							
Consumption of 'Sterling' oils in margarine	0·67	0·60	0·60	0·60	−5·9	−5·8	−0·7	−0·7

SOURCES: *Vegetable Oils and Oilseeds*, C.E.C. London; *Coconut Situation*, F.A.O., Rome; *Dairy Produce*, C.E.C., London.

[a] United Kingdom, E.E.C. (excluding Italy), Denmark, Norway and Sweden.

In Britain and the other European countries there has been a substantial shift away from the 'Sterling' oils to soyabean and fish oils and to lard. This has been based, on the whole, on grounds of price and could go much further, depending to a large extent on future United States support policies for soyabean production. The expansion in fish oil supplies is likely to continue and its use in margarine production will rise. The share of 'Sterling' oils in margarine production may well fall to one-quarter or less; while for the E.E.C., the 'Sterling' share is assumed to fall from an estimated 50 per cent in 1960–1 to about 40 per

[1] International trade in margarine is very small, in relation to both total production and the amount of fats and oils used in its manufacture. The projection for consumption has therefore been assumed to be a satisfactory proxy for the production figure in estimating 'Sterling' oil usage.

cent in 1975. The 'Sterling' share has been falling steadily over the past decade in Scandinavia where it is assumed to reach about 20 per cent by 1975.

The assumptions are brought together in Table B 18, which projects consumption of 'Sterling' oils in margarine production to fall by about 10 per cent between 1960–1 and 1975. As already noted, much depends on United States support policies for soyabeans and on available supplies of lard and fish oils, all of which seem likely to be substituted further for the more expensive 'Sterling' oils. The loss to the latter by such substitution may, in the event, be less than is assumed (particularly should there be a major expansion in 'Sterling' oil production), but, given present trends and policies, it does not seem likely to be much less, and it could be more.

(b) Soap

The relative decline in usage of fats and oils in soap manufacture derives in the main from an absolute contraction in soap production in the industrial countries resulting from the development of synthetic detergents. By 1960–1, soap production had declined, compared with 1951, by nearly 50 per cent in the United States and by over 20 per cent in Britain and Western Europe.

Inter-country differences in *per caput* soap and detergent output reflect, in part, 'structural' differences such as temperature variations, degree of hardness in water supplies, degree of urbanization and air pollution, and so forth. However, they also reflect differences in exports. The United States, for example, exports approximately 11 per cent of its soap output and 16 per cent of its synthetic detergents. Apart from France, exports of soap from continental Western Europe are very small, as also are exports of synthetic detergents.

(i) *Substitution against soap.* In the early post-war period the soap shortage encouraged the development of synthetic detergents for retail sale,[1] and their technical advantages have resulted in what appears to be a permanent substitution for soap in many household uses. In the United States, where the process of substitution has gone furthest, soap accounted for just one-quarter of total soap and detergent production in 1960–1, compared with just over one-half for Western Europe. Japan was a relatively late starter in detergent production but since 1958 the substitution against soap has been extremely fast: in 1960–1 the proportion of soap was 73 per cent, compared with 86 per cent in 1951; but by 1964 it had fallen to 40 per cent. This process is likely to continue in future, and the proportion of soap in the Japanese total is unlikely to be more than 15 per cent by 1975. In North America it is also likely to be

---

[1] They were used, before the war, mainly by the textile industry.

about 15 per cent by then. In continental Western Europe, the area of substitution should widen, if the experience of the United States is a guide (for example, by the introduction of synthetic toilet soaps), and by 1975 the soap proportion may well have fallen to about one-third. The rate of substitution against soap in the United Kingdom has been distinctly slower over the recent past than in the other industrial areas; it is assumed that the rate will increase slightly and that in 1975 the proportion of soap will be in the region of 35 per cent, compared with 55 to 60 per cent over the period 1960–3.

(*ii*) *The trend in production.* Per *caput* production of soap and detergents together has generally risen in the industrial areas over the past decade, though, with the exception of Japan, the rise has been a modest one. In Britain and continental Western Europe *per caput* consumption increased at about half the rate of increase in *per caput* income.

For Britain, a semi-logarithmic regression of *per caput* consumption[1] on *per caput* real income for the period since 1954 yielded an income elasticity of 0·79 (±0·15) at the 1960–1 level of *per caput* consumption. This elasticity is assumed to fall to about 0·6 over the projection period and, coupled with the further assumption that exports will approach 120–175 thousand metric tons, a rise of some 18 to 35 per cent in *per caput* production of soap and detergents is projected between 1960–1 and 1975. For the United States, a similar time-series regression gave an income elasticity of 0·4 (±0·16). This same elasticity is assumed to hold over the projection period for North America as a whole, implying an increase in *per caput* consumption of soap and detergents of some 11 to 14 per cent. For Japan, where *per caput* consumption of soap and detergents is still relatively small, the income elasticity is much higher than in Britain or the United States. A semi-logarithmic regression for the period 1953–60 gave an income elasticity of 0·98 (±0·10) at the 1960 level of consumption. The projection of *per caput* consumption assumes a lower elasticity of 0·6 over the projection period.

Comparable elasticity estimates based on time series are not possible for continental Western Europe because of the lack of sufficient data on synthetic detergents. The projections assume a fairly steady increase in *per caput* production in both the E.E.C. and 'other Western Europe', the decline in soap being more than offset by the rise in detergents. An increase of over 30 per cent in *per caput* production is projected in the E.E.C.: this is based on an assumed income elasticity of 0·6 and an increase in exportable production from about 50 thousand tons to between 75 and 95 thousand in 1975. For 'other Western Europe' an income elasticity of 0·5 is assumed, arbitrarily.

---

[1] Production *less* net exports.

Table B 19 combines the assumptions for *per caput* production levels with those for the probable share of soap in the totals to arrive at estimates for total soap production in 1975. These show an absolute decline in the industrial countries of up to 20 per cent between 1960–1 and 1975. The largest falls would be in Japan, North America and Britain.

Table B 19. *Consumption of 'Sterling' oils in soap in the industrial countries, 1954–63 and projections for 1975*

| | Actual | | 1975 | | Rates of growth | | | |
| | | | | | 1954–7 to 1960–1 | 1954–7 to 1962–3 | 1960–1 to 1975 | |
	1960–1	1962–3	A	B			A	B
	(*Kg.*)				(% *per annum*)			
Soap and detergent production per head[a]	9·7	10·3	12·0	13·0	1·4	1·6	1·5	2·0
	(%)							
Soap as proportion of total[b]	42	37	23	23	—	—	—	—
	(*Million metric tons*)							
Soap production	2·29	2·12	1·80	1·90	−2·0	−2·4	−1·6	−1·2
Total oils and fats consumption	1·44	1·38	1·13	1·20	−2·4[c]	−2·7[c]	−1·7	−1·3
	(%)							
'Sterling' oils as proportion of total	24	23	21	21	—	—	—	—
	(*Million metric tons*)							
Consumption of 'Sterling' oils in soap	0·34	0·32	0·24	0·26	—	—	−2·4	−1·9

SOURCES: *Coconut Situation*, F.A.O., Rome; *Vegetable Oils and Oilseeds*, C.E.C., London; *The Chemical Industry*, O.E.C.D., Paris.

[a] Includes estimates for synthetic detergents for several countries, particularly for 1954–7.
[b] 53 per cent in 1954–7.
[c] Estimated.

(*iii*) *Usage of 'Sterling' oils.* The main vegetable oils used in soap-making are 'Sterling' oils—palm oil and the lauric oils, coconut and palm-kernel. The United States uses predominantly coconut oil because of the preferential treatment given to Philippine copra and coconut oil; Britain uses mainly palm-kernel and palm oil.

Since the war the trend in all the industrial countries has been to substitute animal fats (tallow and greases) for vegetable oils in soap. Animal fats are considerably cheaper than the competing vegetable oils and supply has expanded with the increase in livestock in the industrial countries. Meat consumption will continue to advance rapidly in the future,[1] so this process of replacement can be expected to go on, albeit at a slower rate. In North America, animal fats now account for 80 per cent of all oils and fats used in soap production, but this share is unlikely to increase much more owing to the importance of coconut oil for its lathering properties. In Britain, the major trend has been the substitution of animal fats for palm oil. The process was apparently accelerated in the early 1960s by a series of successive shortfalls in West African palm-oil production. Although a recovery in West African output could slow down the rate of substitution, the 'Sterling' oils proportion in Britain in 1975 may well be under 20 per cent.

For the E.E.C., the data for fats and oils consumption in soap are far from complete; the evidence suggests a similar pattern of substitution. However, this has not always been against the 'Sterling' oils—in Germany and the Netherlands substitution has been more against acid oils, though it has been quite marked against the 'Sterling' oils in France. The scope for further replacement of the 'Sterling' oils appears to be quite large (except in France) and the 'Sterling' proportion is assumed to fall to one-quarter by 1975. In view of the general lack of data, the 'Sterling' proportion in 'other Western Europe' has been taken as being the same as that for the E.E.C.

For the industrial countries as a whole, the 'Sterling' proportion is likely to fall from about one-quarter of total fats and oils consumption to about one-fifth in 1975, a decline in total usage of some 25 to 30 per cent over the projection period. This is clearly a very adverse element in the prospects for 'Sterling' oils. Of course, the extent of the decline depends on the assumptions made; while the inadequacy of basic data for many of the consuming countries involves a fairly high margin of error. Nevertheless, the 'Sterling' soap-making oils have been subject to two markedly adverse trends: the substitution of synthetic detergents for soap and of animal fats for vegetable oils. Both trends must be expected to continue.

There is one offsetting tendency, however, to be borne in mind. This is the increasing use of vegetable oils in the manufacture of synthetic detergents. It is due to the growing demand for low-lathering detergents, for which two main factors are responsible. The first derives from the concern at the pollution of inland waterways and the consequent demand for detergents that are more quickly decomposed by the micro-organisms in water. The second is the growing popularity of the lather-intolerant drum-type washing-machine in Europe and North America. Both the primary alkylsulphates and certain types of nonionics which are needed to meet these requirements are based on vegetable oils.

---

[1] See Appendix A 3.

However, favourable though this trend may be, it is most unlikely to offset the overall decline in demand.[1]

(c) Compound cooking fat

The United States is by far the largest producer of compound cooking fat, but only about one per cent of the total oils and fats used in its manufacture are 'Sterling' oils. This proportion is unlikely to change. The proportion is higher for Canada but the trend there is not likely to have any significant impact on world consumption of 'Sterling' oils.

In the United Kingdom the 'Sterling' oils in 1960–1 accounted for 34 per cent of total oils and fats used for cooking-fat production. In 1954–7 the proportion was 43 per cent, the decline being due to increased usage of lard, supplies of which were increased by imports from the United States. However, these imports will probably decline—yields are falling in America—while the downward trend of United Kingdom cooking-fat production appears to have been arrested. The consumption of 'Sterling' oils in this end-use in 1975 is therefore likely to be higher than the 1960–1 level; it is assumed, somewhat arbitrarily, to be about 60 thousand tons. For Western Europe (other than the United Kingdom) and Japan, production of compound cooking fat has been included in 'other' end-uses.

(d) Other uses

The remaining end-uses consist very largely of table and salad oils and various industrial applications. In the United States, table and salad oils consist mainly of soyabean, cottonseed and corn oils; most of the 'Sterling' oil consumed consists of coconut oil, of which about one-third is for edible uses (mostly in the flour, confectionery and other food trades). The remainder goes into inedible fatty acids, synthetic detergents and other non-food products. *Per caput* consumption of 'Sterling' oils in these end-uses has been rising over approximately the last ten years. This rise, due in part to increased usage in synthetic detergents, is expected to continue. It is assumed that *per caput* consumption of 'Sterling' oils in North America in 1975 will be about 1·8 to 1·9 kg. per head, as against 1·6 kg. in 1960–1.

Consumption of 'Sterling' oils in miscellaneous uses in Britain has also been rising over the past decade. Groundnut oil has been responsible for about half the increase, probably because of growing demand for it in culinary uses. Factors contributing to this demand for groundnut oil are the spreading habit of buying quick-frozen foods and a possible rise

---

[1] Indeed, synthetics could never replace soap as an equally important end-use, for the detergent value of fats and oils converted to synthetics is about 3½ times as great as the equivalent quantity converted to soap.

in consumption of salad oil and dressing: but little is known about the trends in consumption of these items. It is assumed here that *per caput* consumption of 'Sterling' oils will rise from just under 4 kg. to between 5 and 6 kg. in 1975.

In the E.E.C. the greater proportion of 'Sterling' oils consumed in 'other' uses consists of groundnut oil used for culinary purposes in France. This commodity is favoured by strong consumer preferences and by import restrictions on competing soft oils. For the E.E.C. as a whole, a moderate rise in *per caput* consumption of 'Sterling' oils from 3 kg. to between $3\frac{1}{2}$ and 4 kg. has been assumed over the projection period. For 'other Western Europe' it is assumed, fairly arbitrarily, that *per caput* consumption will rise from about 3 kg. to between 4 and 5 kg.; and for Japan, consumption of 'Sterling' oils for miscellaneous purposes is projected to rise roughly in proportion to the rise in total real income.

Summary of the projections for consumption of 'Sterling' oils in 1975

The projections, summarized in Table B20, show that consumption of 'Sterling' oils for use in soap and margarine is likely to decline over the projection period, but that this decline will be more than offset by increased consumption in 'other' end-uses. Because of the different relative importance of each end-use for the individual 'Sterling' oils, the projections indicate slightly different prospects for each oil. Thus, groundnut oil, which is not used at all in soap manufacture, and coconut oil, of which only a very small amount is used for soap, would appear to have somewhat better prospects than palm and palm-kernel oils, where soap is a major end-use. However, the tendency for the soap oils to find increasing alternative outlets makes it impossible to draw any firm conclusions about the separate prospects for each oil.

On balance, it appears likely that consumption of 'Sterling' oils in the industrial countries will rise by some 15 to 25 per cent (on the low and high income assumptions) between 1960–1 and 1975. However, it is important to bear in mind that this conclusion depends very largely on estimates of future consumption of these oils in 'other' uses. These estimates are inevitably uncertain, and considerably more detailed information by end-use than is now available (particularly in Western Europe) would be needed before more reliable estimates could be made.

Exports from the Overseas Sterling Area

Throughout the 1950s and early 1960s, the share of the Overseas Sterling Area in world production of the 'Sterling' oils has not changed greatly. Copra and groundnut production have risen but the increase has gone more to domestic consumption than to exports. Compared with some non-Sterling vegetable oils (notably soyabean) and with animal fats, the growth rate of O.S.A. output and exports has not been very impressive.

However, replanting and rehabilitation programmes are currently under way in many of the main Sterling producing countries and the Development Plans of most countries indicate that their governments are anxious to expand production. Indeed, the prospects for the O.S.A. increasing its share of world production of groundnuts and palm products would appear to be good; the prospects for copra and coconut oil are more doubtful because of the probable rate of expansion in the Philippines.

Table B 20. *Consumption of 'Sterling' oils in the industrial countries, 1954–63 and projections for 1975*

| | Actual | | 1975 | | Rates of growth | | | |
| | | | | | 1954–7 to 1960–1 | 1954–7 to 1962–3 | 1960–1 to 1975 | |
	1960–1	1962–3	A	B			A	B
	(*Million metric tons*)				(*% per annum*)			
Margarine[a]	0·71	0·65	0·66	0·67	−5·9[b]	−5·8[b]	−0·5	−0·5
Soap	0·34	0·32	0·24	0·26	−5·8	−4·4	−2·4	−1·9
Compound cooking fat[c]	0·06	0·06	0·08	0·09	−9·6	−6·9	2·0	2·9
Other uses[de]	1·27	1·37	1·74	1·98	4·5	4·0	2·2	3·1
Total	2·38	2·40	2·72	3·00	−1·3	−0·6	0·9	1·6
of which:								
United Kingdom	0·44	0·37	0·45	0·52	−4·8	−5·6	0·3	1·3
E.E.C.	1·15	1·14	1·23	1·31	1·1	0·8	0·5	1·0
Other Western Europe	0·27	0·31	0·32	0·37	0·5	2·5	1·3	2·3
North America	0·45	0·49	0·53	0·58	3·4	3·5	1·1	1·7
Japan	0·08	0·09	0·18	0·21	3·3	4·1	5·8	6·8

SOURCES: As for Tables B 18 and B 19.

[a] Including estimates for consumption in margarine production for those European countries not included in Table B 18.

[b] As for Table B 18.

[c] North America and United Kingdom only; remaining countries included in 'other uses'.

[d] Includes Italian consumption in margarine production.

[e] Excludes groundnuts consumed as nuts or as peanut butter in the U.S.A. and Japan, and groundnuts used for seed and feed in the U.S.A.

In developing countries, a feature of economic growth is the tendency for domestic consumption of agricultural produce to rise as real income rises. This has applied to consumption of vegetable oils in some of the main producing countries over the past decade.[1] As a general process it is likely to continue in the future and to be a restraint on the potential

[1] For example, between 1948–52 and 1962–3, Indian consumption of groundnuts rose, in total, by about 60 per cent; or about 35 per cent on a *per caput* basis.

exportable surplus of vegetable oils. It is also possible that this process will be more important in the peasant economies of Asia than in Africa; if so, the restraint is more likely to apply to copra and coconut oil than to palm products and groundnuts.[1]

Preferential arrangements by importing countries

Very definite patterns of world trade in vegetable oils and oilseeds have been established in the past, primarily reflecting political and currency ties and investments in the plantations of the producing countries by seed-crushing industries in the industrial areas. Britain and France, for example, have traditionally bought their supplies from their former dependent territories, while the United States buys copra and coconut oil almost exclusively from the Philippines.

Two major changes have taken place in the pattern since 1952. One is the declining share of the O.S.A. in British imports, which has been offset by an increasing share of the import market in continental Western Europe. The other is the growth in exports from North America, essentially soyabean shipments to the E.E.C. and to Japan. These trends can reasonably be expected to continue. The tariff and tax arrangements in the E.E.C. (also the changes envisaged in these arrangements) are likely, on balance, to be favourable to the exports of the O.S.A. Moreover, the admission of Nigeria—the largest single exporter in the Sterling Area—to associate status should have a favourable effect on her exports to the E.E.C.

However, trade diversion is unlikely to have a very significant net effect on O.S.A. exports. The predominant influence will continue to be the total level of demand for fats and oils, and the degree of substitution of animal fats and other vegetable oils for the four 'Sterling' oils. If the setbacks which have affected output in some of the 'Sterling' oils in the recent past can be avoided, then, at best, it can be hoped that the Overseas Sterling Area will maintain its share of total 'Sterling' oil consumption in the industrial countries.

There is the further possibility that the O.S.A. might expand its exports to other primary-producing countries. Consumption of vegetable oils and oilseeds is expected to grow rapidly in these countries over the projection period. However, recent experience indicates that these countries tend to meet a growing domestic consumption by increased production rather than by increased imports, so that opportunities for developing trade in oilseeds between the primary-producing countries may be limited. The outlook for exports in 1975 from Sterling Area producers is, at best, a moderate expansion of some 15 to 25 per cent above the level for 1960–1.

[1] With the exception of Indian groundnuts.

APPENDIX B 5

HIDES AND SKINS

The present pattern of trade

Hides and skins are by-products of the livestock industry. Meat, dairy products and wool are produced chiefly by the developed countries, which therefore contribute the greater part of world production of hides and skins. The Western industrial countries accounted, in 1964, for not far short of half the total value of world exports of hides and skins; the Overseas Sterling Area accounted for a further third but, if fur skins are excluded, the Sterling share was over two-fifths (Table B21).

Table B21. *Exports of hides and skins, 1964*

	Value of exports			All hides and skins as proportion of total exports
	Hides and skins	Fur skins	Total	
	(£ million)			(%)
STERLING COUNTRIES				
Australia	35	2	37	3
India*a*	27	—	27	4
New Zealand	15	—	15	4
South Africa	9	6	15	3
Nigeria	5	0	5	2
Pakistan	3	0	3	2
Other overseas Sterling countries	10	0	10	..
United Kingdom	4	1	5	0·1
Total, Sterling	108	9	117	1
NON-STERLING COUNTRIES				
Industrial	98	64	162	0·5
Developing	47	1	48	1
Centrally planned	7	21	28	0·4
Total, non-Sterling	152	86	238	0·5
TOTAL	260	95	355	1
O.S.A. as per cent of TOTAL	*42*	*9*	*33*	..

SOURCES: *Yearbook of International Trade Statistics, 1964,* United Nations, New York; *Foreign Trade*, Series B, O.E.C.D., Paris.

a Including exports of rough-tanned hides and skins.

The majority of Sterling exports of hides and skins are sold in the Western industrial countries; the same is true for exports from the industrial countries themselves, their mutual trade in 1964 representing over 80 per cent of the total. The principal Sterling exports consist of sheep skins from Australia, New Zealand and South Africa, goat skins and rough-tanned leather from India, and cattle hides and calf skins from Australia and New Zealand. Hides and skins generally represent, however, only a small proportion of total exports from the main producing countries. Exports of fur skins from Sterling countries are extremely small, and are not considered here.

Prospects for demand

Leather footwear is the predominant end-use of hides and skins, though other manufactures, including bags, belting, gloves and upholstery are also of some importance. Footwear consumption per head increased rapidly in Western Europe and Japan over the past decade, but in North America there was a marginal decline (see Table B22). The figures relate to all types of leather footwear, including men's, women's and children's, without allowing for relative changes between these three categories, so that, to some extent, the trends reflect changes in age and sex distribution as well as in real income per head. By the mid 1960s, nearly three pairs of footwear a head were purchased annually in the United States, and just over two pairs a head in Canada; no change in these levels has been assumed in the projections for 1975.

For the other industrial countries, the projections of footwear consumption per head have been based on assumed income elasticities,[1] combined with the standard assumptions about real income growth. For continental Western Europe, the rate of growth in footwear consumption per head over the period up to 1975 is projected at somewhat lower than rates achieved over the first half of the 1960s. For Japan, for which no income-elasticity estimates are available, the future growth rates in consumption have also been taken at levels a little below recent rates. For Britain, the projected growth rate, on the lower income hypothesis, is the same as the recent rate of growth; on the higher income basis, it is appreciably higher. By 1975, on the assumptions made, leather footwear consumption per head in Britain and in the E.E.C. area, at about 2·9 pairs per annum, would have reached the level attained in the United States by the early 1950s.

In most industrial countries, foreign trade in footwear is relatively small,[2] so that the projections for consumption can reasonably be taken

[1] Semi-logarithmic regressions of footwear consumption per head on real income per head over the period 1954 to 1961 yielded an income elasticity of 0·90 ($\pm$0·06) at the 1961 level of consumption, for the E.E.C. countries ($R^2 = 0.973$); for EFTA countries, other than the United Kingdom, the corresponding elasticity was 1·29 ($\pm$0·05), with $R^2 = 0.990$.

[2] In 1965, for example, net imports accounted for 5 per cent of apparent consumption in the United States, and 3 per cent in the United Kingdom; for the E.E.C., net exports represented 10 per cent of domestic production in that year.

Table B 22. *Footwear^a consumption per head in the industrial countries, 1960–5 and projections for 1975*

	Rates of growth				Consumption per head			
	1953–5 to 1960–1	1960–1 to 1964–5	1960– to 1975		1960–1	1964–5	1975	
			A	B			A	B
	(% *per annum*)				(*Pairs*)			
United Kingdom	3·2	1·4	1·4	2·0	2·3	2·4	2·7	2·9
E.E.C.	5·4	5·8	3·2	4·1	1·6	2·0	2·6	2·9
Other Western Europe	..	5·5	3·5	4·0	1·0^b	1·2^b	1·7	1·8
United States	−0·2	0·0	0·0	0·0	2·9	2·9	2·9	2·9
Canada	0·0	−0·7	0·0	0·0	2·2	2·1	2·2	2·2
Japan	..	7·1	6·0	7·0	0·5^c	0·6^c	1·1	1·3
TOTAL	..	2·5	1·9	2·3	1·7	1·9	2·3	2·4

SOURCE: *The Hides, Skins and Footwear Industry*, O.E.C.D., Paris.

^{a} Footwear with leather uppers. ^{b} Including some estimates. ^{c} Estimated.

as close approximations to the corresponding rates of growth in domestic production. The latter will also indicate the probable growth rate in demand for hides and skins for footwear uses, though allowance must be made at this stage for the substitution of other materials (especially rubber and plastics) for leather. Over the past decade, there was a substantial degree of substitution away from the use of leather for footwear soling. By 1965, only one-quarter of footwear with leather uppers produced in the United States also had leather soles, compared with some two-fifths a decade earlier. The rate of substitution against leather soling was even faster in the United Kingdom, the proportion of footwear with leather soles having fallen to only one-sixth in 1965, as against three-fifths a decade earlier. This substitution affected the usage of cattle hides and calf skins, rather than that of sheep and goat skins (which are used for shoe linings, as well as in non-footwear uses such as gloves and upholstery). During the later 1950s, the consumption of cattle hides and calf skins per unit of leather footwear produced declined by 5 or 6 per cent a year in the United Kingdom and the E.E.C. countries, and by about 2½ per cent a year in the United States (where a major part of substitution had taken place earlier). In the first half of the 1960s, the rates of substitution were generally lower in Western Europe, while substitution had actually ceased, on balance, in North America. The projections assume, however, that there will be some further, though slower, substitution in North America over the decade up to 1975, while a continuation of the previous trend against the usage of all forms of leather is assumed for other industrial countries, though generally at a more modest rate than in the past (Table B 23). Even so, these assumptions may well be on the optimistic side, since they take no account of the possibility of large-scale substitution of new synthetic leathers for natural leather in footwear uppers.

Table B23. *Consumption of hides and skins per footwear unit in the industrial countries, 1953–65 and assumptions for 1975 (kg. per pair of footwear produced)*

	Cattle hides and calf skins				Sheep and goat skins			
	1953–5	1960–1	1964–5	1975	1953–5	1960–1	1964–5	1975
United Kingdom	2·05	1·31	1·20	0·9–1·1	0·34	0·28	0·28^a	0·22–0·25
E.E.C.	2·33	1·67	1·37	1·1–1·3	0·28	0·22	0·22	0·18–0·20
Other Western Europe	..	1·71	1·78^a	1·2–1·4	..	0·37	0·38^a	0·28–0·32
United States	1·12	0·95	0·96	0·75–0·85	..	0·19	0·13	0·10–0·12
Canada	1·45	1·08	1·12	0·8–1·0	0·06	0·06	0·08	0·05–0·06
Japan	..	..	3·12	1·8–2·2	..	..	0·06	0·04–0·05

SOURCES: *The Hides, Skins and Footwear Industry*, O.E.C.D., Paris; *Facts and Figures on Footwear, 1961*, National Shoe Manufacturers' Association Inc., New York; *Census of Manufactures, Shoe Factories and Boot and Shoe Finding Manufacturers*, Dominion Bureau of Statistics, Ottawa; *Hides and Skins*, quarterly, C.E.C., London.

^{a} 1962–3.

Consumption and net imports

On the basis of these various assumptions,[1] the total demand for hides and skins in the industrial countries can be projected (see Table B24). For cattle hides and calf skins, demand—represented by the consumption series—is projected to remain virtually unchanged in North America, comparing 1975 with the position in 1964–5, but in Western Europe an average increase of 2½ per cent a year is projected on the lower income-growth assumption, and 3½ per cent a year on the higher. For sheep and goat skins, a similar asymmetrical pattern of growth is projected, with consumption in Western Europe rising by 1·8 and 2·6 per cent a year on the two income-growth assumptions.

Production of hides and skins in the industrial countries must be expected to continue to increase over the coming decade. The projections generally imply some decline in the rates of growth in animal populations achieved since the mid 1950s, while slaughtering rates in

[1] The comparison of total hides and skins consumption with footwear production implies that, in the projections, there is a definite relationship between the future growth of footwear production and that of the production of other leather goods.

1975 have been assumed to be the same as in 1960–1 for each of the industrial countries. In so far as feeding practices improve and the average carcass weight of livestock increases, the projected increase in hides and skins production will be proportionately somewhat smaller than the corresponding increase in meat production. On this basis, the projections indicate that, by 1975, production of both classes of hides and skins in the industrial countries is likely to be about one-sixth above the 1964–5 levels on the lower growth basis, and about one-quarter higher on the more rapid growth assumption. Net imports in the industrial countries as a group are projected to rise by about $2\frac{1}{2}$ to 4 per cent a year from 1964–5 to 1975 in the case of cattle hides and calf skins, and by some $1\frac{1}{2}$ to 2 per cent a year for sheep and goat skins.

Table B24. *Consumption, production and net trade of the industrial countries in hides and skins, 1960–5 and projections for 1975 (thousand metric tons)*

	Cattle hides and calf skins[a]			Sheep and goat skins[b]		
	Con-sumption	Pro-duction	Net trade	Con-sumption	Pro-duction	Net trade
NORTH AMERICA						
1960–1	529	731	−202	98	46	+52
1964–5	553	880	−327	72	37	+35
1975: A	550	925	−375	75	30	+45
B	550	985	−435			
WESTERN EUROPE AND JAPAN						
1960–1	950	572	+378	150	76	+74
1964–5	1,081	603	+478	188	84	+104
1975: A	1,400	825	+575	225	110	+115
B	1,550	885	+665	245	120	+125
TOTAL:						
1960–1	1,479	1,303	+176	248	102	+126
1964–5	1,634	1,483	+151	260	121	+139
1975:A	1,950	1,750	+200	300	140	+160
B	2,100	1,870	+230	320	150	+170

SOURCES: *The Hides, Skins and Footwear Industry*, O.E.C.D., Paris; *Hides and Skins*, quarterly, C.E.C., London.

[a] Wet salted weight.   [b] Dry weight.

The projected increase for cattle hides and calf skins contrasts sharply with a decline in net imports of almost 4 per cent a year, on average, over the decade up to 1964–5. The latter, however, reflected not only a sharp substitution against sole leather, already mentioned, but a substantial expansion in United States hides and skins shipments to Western

Europe. The projections assume a further rise in such shipments, but at a rate modest enough not to offset the further rise projected in the net import requirements of Western Europe.

Prospects for Sterling Area exports

The Overseas Sterling Area supplied about 40 per cent of all cattle hides and calf skins imported by the industrial countries from other areas in the years 1960–3; the proportion rose to over 45 per cent in 1964–5, mainly as a result of reduced shipments from Argentina. It has been assumed that the Sterling share in 1975 will remain within the range 40 to 45 per cent of the total; then Sterling exports of cattle hides and calf skins would either fall over the decade up to 1975 by up to about $\frac{1}{2}$ per cent a year on the lower income-growth assumption or would rise by 0 to $1\frac{1}{2}$ per cent a year on the higher income-growth basis (Table B25). These projected rates would be substantially lower than the rate achieved over the preceding decade (5·3 per cent a year), for reasons indicated earlier. For sheep and goat skins, the corresponding projected rates are 1·4 to 2·1 per cent a year and 1·9 to 2·7 per cent a year (on the two alternative income-growth assumptions) over the period from 1964–5 to 1975, compared with the 4·0 per cent a year growth rate achieved over the preceding decade.

Table B 25. *Exports of hides and skins from the Overseas Sterling Area, 1960–5 and projections for 1975*

| | Imports into industrial countries from O.S.A. as proportion of total imports[a] | | Exports from O.S.A. | |
	Cattle hides and calf skins	Sheep and goat skins	Cattle hides and calf skins	Sheep and goat skins
	(Percentages)		*(Thousand metric tons)*	
1960–1	41	69	112	161
1962–3	40	68	131	170
1964–5	46	67	141	167
1975: A	40–45	65–70	{ 125–140	195–210
B			145–160	205–220

SOURCES: As for Table B24.

[a] From non-industrial countries only.

A number of uncertainties in the future outlook for hides and skins exports must, however, be borne in mind. A major uncertainty relates to the possible substitution of synthetic material for footwear uppers. Should this occur on any substantial scale, the consequent displacement of natural leather could well offset the greater part of the growth projected in demand for cattle hides and calf skins. At the same time, substitution against hides and skins on any large scale would probably result in a serious price decline, especially for cattle hides. Another unknown, though one which would work in the opposite direction, is the extent to which Sterling producers can raise the quality of locally tanned hides and skins, so as to export leather on a competitive basis. A considerable addition to export earnings could be achieved in this way,[1] though to do so would involve additional capital investments (which, in some cases, might have more profitable alternative uses).

[1] Some indication of the increase in export value that might be achieved by exporting leather rather than hides and skins is provided by data for the leather industry in the United Kingdom, the value added in that industry in 1958 being about 45 per cent of the cost of hides and skins tanned.

APPENDIX B 6

NON-FERROUS METALS

The pattern of trade

Exports from the Overseas Sterling Area of the five major non-ferrous ores and metals—aluminium, copper, lead, tin and zinc—accounted for one-fifth, by value, of total world exports of these commodities in 1964. For tin, the Sterling proportion was as high as one-half; for aluminium (including bauxite and alumina) and for zinc, only one-tenth (Table B 26). For ores alone, the Sterling share of world trade would be higher in all these metals, since the industrial countries' exports of metals include those processed from imported ores.

Of the various Sterling countries with major export interests in non-ferrous metals, Zambia is exceptional in being almost completely dependent on one metal—copper—for her earnings from merchandise exports. In 1964, two-fifths of Jamaica's exports came from bauxite and alumina, while in the same year bauxite contributed one-eighth of Guyana's export total, and tin one-fifth of Malaya's. For the other main Sterling exporters of non-ferrous metals—Australia, South Africa and Nigeria—metals constituted relatively small proportions (5 or 6 per cent) of their total exports.

About nine-tenths, by value, of overseas Sterling exports of non-ferrous ores and metals are sold to the industrial countries of Western Europe, North America and Japan. The projections of future trends in these exports therefore depend essentially on the probable growth rate of consumption of non-ferrous metals in these industrial countries, and on the proportion of that consumption met by home production and by imports.

Consumption in the industrial countries[1]

The rate of growth in consumption of the various non-ferrous metals depends on three main factors. There is, first, the rate of growth in industrial production—more especially, in the output of the major metal-using industries—in the different industrial countries. As will be seen later, there is a high degree of association between the movement in industrial production and that in total non-ferrous metal consumption. Second, non-ferrous metal consumption is influenced by the pattern of

---

[1] 'Consumption' is measured here at the unfabricated metal stage. The figures therefore do not allow for international trade in semi-fabricated, or fully manufactured, non-ferrous metal products.

industrial growth, both as between the different industrial countries and as between the main end-products concerned. Third, within each end-use of the various metals, consumption depends also on the rate of substitution between alternative materials, whether metal, plastic, wood or other substitute. The area of substitution can be widened by new technical developments in production and in fabrication methods, while the rate of substitution is also influenced by actual and expected changes in relative prices.

Table B26. *Exports of non-ferrous metals,[a] 1964*

	Value of exports						Non-ferrous metals as proportion of total exports
	Aluminium[b]	Copper	Lead	Tin	Zinc	Total	
	($£$ million)						(%)
STERLING COUNTRIES							
Zambia	—	149	1	—	5	155	92
Malaya	2	—	—	85	—	87	22
Australia	5	9	30	0	14	59	5
Jamaica	34	—	—	—	—	34	43
South Africa	0	19	4	1	2	26	5
Nigeria	—	—	—	13	—	13	6
Guyana	12	—	—	—	—	12	12
Other countries	2	11	1	1	0	15	1
Total, Overseas Sterling Area	55	188	36	100	21	399	7
United Kingdom	18	40	5	11	2	75	2
Total, Sterling	73	228	41	110	23	475	5
NON-STERLING COUNTRIES							
Industrial	360	386	37	30	91	904	3
Developing	30	263	36	47	42	418	5
Centrally planned	60	22	15	15	35	148	2
Total, non-Sterling	451	670	88	92	169	1,470	3
TOTAL	523	898	129	202	192	1,944	3
O.S.A. as percentage of TOTAL	*11*	*21*	*28*	*49*	*11*	*21*	..

SOURCES: *Yearbook of International Trade Statistics*, United Nations, New York; national trade statistics.

[a] Including ores and concentrates.   [b] Including bauxite and alumina.

The demand by the industrial countries for imports of ores and metals depends not only on their rate of consumption, but also on their rate of stock accumulation or decumulation, and on their domestic production of ores and of secondary metal. The relative importance of secondary metal and of stock movements in total consumption over the past decade is indicated in Table B 27. The production of secondary metal in 1962–3 accounted for as much as two-fifths of total copper consumption, while the proportions were also appreciable for the other metals: one-third for lead, one-quarter for tin and one-fifth for aluminium and zinc. Except for a decline in the relative importance of secondary metal in lead consumption, the proportions for 1962–3 showed little change compared with the mid 1950s.

There was general stock accumulation of metals in the period 1953–7, during which metal prices were rising, but stocks of lead and tin declined in the later period, 1962–3. The decline for lead resulted largely from reducing the unnecessarily large stocks accumulated during 1960–1, when world production was in excess of consumption. In 1962–3 there was an increase in consumption accompanied by voluntary cuts in output by producers. For tin, lagging mine production and a substantial rise in demand had resulted in a shortage of supply, the gap being filled by releases from the United States strategic stockpile.[1] Non-metallic uses of bauxite and alumina—such as for abrasives, refractories and chemicals—probably account for not far short of 10 per cent of total consumption, though these uses appear to have increased over the past decade at a lower rate than has consumption of aluminium metal.

The dependence of the industrial countries on imports for their supplies of primary non-ferrous metal varies widely, from almost complete dependence, in the case of tin, to only one-third for zinc. The import content of primary metal consumption was about two-thirds for aluminium in both the periods shown in Table B 27, and about one-half for copper and lead.

For the projections of net imports into the industrial countries, the approach adopted here is to project, first of all, the total consumption of each metal; then, by allowing for probable levels of future secondary production, domestic ore production and stock change, to derive net imports as a residual demand. The most refined method of projecting consumption would be to consider the main end-uses of each metal separately in the various industrial countries, and to assess the probable future rate of growth in demand in each end-use. This would automatically allow for shifts in the area—and commodity—patterns of metal-using output, but would also involve considerable complications owing to the complex pattern of materials substitution in the various uses of the different metals.

---

[1] The United States announced in March 1962 that there were 166 thousand metric tons of tin surplus to requirements in its strategic stockpile, and in September 1962 it began to release some 200 tons of tin a week for sale.

Table B27. *Relative importance of primary and secondary metals in total non-ferrous metal consumption in the industrial countries, 1953–7 and 1962–3*

		Aluminium[a]	Copper[b]	Lead[c]	Tin	Zinc	Total[d]
		(% of total consumption)					
APPARENT CONSUMPTION							
Primary metal:							
Production of ore[e]	1953–7	33	32	37	3	63	33
	1962–3	26	32	31	2	56	31
Net imports of ore[e] and metal	1953–7	54	27	32	84	29	40
	1962–3	61	27	31	62	24	39
Secondary metal[f]	1953–7	21	45	40	27	19	35
	1962–3	20	41	32	27	20	31
STOCK CHANGES AND NON-METALLIC USES[g]	1953–7	−8	−4	−9	−14	−11	−8
	1962–3	−7	0	6	9	0	−1
		(Million metric tons)					*(£ thousand million)[h]*
TOTAL CONSUMPTION (= 100%)	1953–7	2·86	4·33	2·35	0·18	2·36	2·14
	1962–3	4·78	5·58	2·64	0·19	3·04	2·90

SOURCES: *Metal Statistics*, Metallgesellschaft A.G., Frankfurt-am-Main; *Statistical Summary of the Mineral Industry*, Overseas Geological Surveys, H.M.S.O., London; *Statistics of Non-Ferrous Metals*, and *The Non-Ferrous Metals Industry*, O.E.C.D., Paris; *Lead and Zinc Statistics*, International Lead and Zinc Study Group, New York; *Statistical Yearbook*, International Tin Council, London.

[a] Bauxite, alumina and aluminium, including alloys.
[b] Excluding alloys.
[c] Including hard or antimonial lead.
[d] Based on values at 1962–3 prices.
[e] Estimated metal content of domestic production and net imports of ores and concentrates. Where data for the metal content of ores and concentrates were not available, the following percentages of metal content to gross weight were used: bauxite, 19; alumina, 50; burnt cupreous pyrites, 2; copper concentrates, 25; copper matte, 50; lead concentrates, 75; zinc concentrates, 50.
[f] Scrap used in refineries, scrap used directly and in alloys.
[g] Residual, including changes in strategic stockpiles and the tin buffer stock, as well as consumption in chemical processes and in other non-metallic uses. Negative figures indicate stock accumulations plus non-metallic uses.
[h] Values at 1962–3 prices.

Instead, a more general approach has been adopted which entails two stages of projections. The first is a projection of the total volume of non-ferrous metals consumption, taking all five metals as a group. The second stage entails a subdivision of this total into the constituent metals.

Projections of total non-ferrous metals consumption

Since non-ferrous metals are used almost entirely by manufacturing industries, one would expect there to be a close relationship between the movement of industrial production and that of non-ferrous metals consumption. Regressions of annual series of total non-ferrous metals consumption on the index of manufacturing production were computed for the period 1953–63 for each of the main industrial areas,[1] and these were used to project, for 1975, total non-ferrous metals consumption in each of these areas, using the assumed level of manufacturing production in 1975 as a basis.[2] Total consumption was arrived at by aggregating the value of consumption of each of the five main non-ferrous metals at constant (1962–3) prices. The resulting series represents the *quantum* of non-ferrous metals consumption and is directly comparable with the usual indices of volume of manufacturing production.

The results of this projection, summarized in Table B28, imply that over the period up to 1975 the 'output elasticity' of demand[3] for non-ferrous metals in the industrial countries as a group will be in the region of 0·9. For the United Kingdom and 'other Western Europe', the output elasticity is unity, while for Japan it just exceeds 0·9. For the E.E.C., however, the output elasticity is only 0·75, and it is as low as 0·67 for the United States. By contrast, the output elasticity for Canada (1·15) is the only one to exceed unity. This reflects, to a large extent, the fact that an appreciable proportion of Canadian non-ferrous metals 'consumption', as here defined, consists of semi-manufactures which are exported (mainly to the United States). If consumption were defined net of foreign trade in 'semis', the output elasticity of demand would probably be below unity for Canada too.

For the industrial countries as a group, the projections indicate that total non-ferrous metals consumption will rise by about 4½ per cent a year, on average, from 1960–1 to 1975 on the lower income growth-rate assumption, and by over 5 per cent a year on the higher. These

---

[1] The linear form $Y = a + bX$ was used, where Y denotes the total value of non-ferrous metals consumption at constant prices, X the index of manufacturing production, and a and b are constants. For all areas, the goodness of fit of the equations was high (R^2 exceeding 0·9 in all regressions).

[2] As shown in Table 4.4.

[3] I.e. the percentage change projected in demand for non-ferrous metals in total as a ratio of the assumed percentage change in manufacturing production.

rates are both higher than that achieved over the period from 1953–7 to 1960–1 (about 3¾ per cent a year), though they represent a slowing down compared with the unusually fast rate of growth in non-ferrous metals consumption during the early 1960s.

Table B 28. *Consumption[a] of non-ferrous metals in the industrial countries, 1953–65 and projections for 1975*

	Rates of growth				Consumption				
	1953–7 to 1960–1	1960–1 to 1964–5	1960–1 to 1975 A	B	1960–1	1962–3	1964–5	1975 A	B
	(% per annum)				(£ million at 1962–3 prices)				
United Kingdom	3·1	2·6	3·0	3·9	347	336	384	535	605
E.E.C.	7·6	3·8	4·1	5·1	702	717	816	1,250	1,430
Other Western Europe	8·0	4·4	5·4	5·9	194	204	230	415	445
United States	−0·1	9·2	3·5	4·0	1,073	1,288	1,523	1,785	1,895
Canada	2·0	9·3	4·9	5·2	74	88	105	145	155
Japan	16·4	10·4	8·8	9·6	232	263	344	780	875
TOTAL	3·7	6·7	4·4	5·2	2,622	2,896	3,402	4,910	5,405

SOURCE: *Metal Statistics*, Metallgesellschaft A.G., Frankfurt-am-Main.

[a] As defined in Table B 27; not taking international trade of metals in manufactured or semi-manufactured products into account.

Within the total, the projections indicate some significant shifts in the relative importance of the different industrial areas as consumers of non-ferrous metals. In 1960–1, for example, the United States accounted for 41 per cent of the total consumption of the industrial countries, in terms of value, the proportion rising to 44 per cent in 1962–3; by 1975, however, the United States' share is projected to fall to some 35 to 36 per cent of the total. Virtually the whole of this decline in the relative importance of the United States as a consumer is accounted for by a corresponding relative increase in projected non-ferrous metals consumption in Japan (from 9 per cent of the total in the period 1960–3 to 16 per cent in 1975). The projections also indicate a marginal decline in Britain's share of the total (from 12 to 13 per cent in the early 1960s to 11 per cent in 1975), but no significant change in the comparative importance of the E.E.C. area (projected to remain at about 25 per cent of the total).

The share of individual metals in total non-ferrous metals consumption

Once the total volume of non-ferrous metals consumption has been projected for a given future period, the consumption of the constituent metals can be determined by estimating the relative share of each in the total. Changes in such shares can conveniently be considered as a resultant of two factors: first, the relative rates of growth in output of the principal end-products of each metal and, second, the rate of substitution between each metal and alternative materials in each end-use. The rate of substitution, in turn, is dependent on two broad competitive factors, namely, relative prices of actual and potential substitutes, and the relative technical advantages and disadvantages of each.

Some assessment of the relative magnitudes involved in changes in relative shares over the past decade is indicated in Table B29, which compares the share of each of the main non-ferrous metals in each industrial area in a recent period (1964–5) with that about a decade earlier. Looking first at the aggregates for all the industrial countries, the outstanding change has been the rapid advance of aluminium, from about 25 per cent of total consumption in 1953–7 to over 30 per cent by 1964–5. About two-fifths of that gain was at the expense of copper (consumption of which declined from about 49 to 46½ per cent in the same period), most of the remaining gain in aluminium's relative share being associated with relative declines for lead and tin. The share of zinc, however, remained virtually unchanged, at about 10 per cent of the total.

The country patterns of change showed some striking divergencies, though there were also certain similarities. The outstanding similarity has been the relative growth in aluminium consumption in each area. However, while in Canada and 'other Western Europe' the shift to aluminium was largely associated with a relative decline in copper consumption, in all other areas the relative decline in copper was outweighed by the fall in the combined share of lead, tin and zinc.

These country patterns are important in so far as they show differences in the structure of production and the pattern of end-uses of the different metals. Such differences may be expected to continue in the future, to a greater or lesser extent, and allowance for them must be made, so far as possible, in the projections of demand for individual metals.

At the same time, there are some important general features, indicated in Table B29, particularly the fact that in every industrial area distinguished the relative share of aluminium has appreciably risen over the decade covered, while among the other metals the relative share of copper has generally fallen most (though there are some exceptions to this). To what extent these general features can reasonably be expected to continue depends, in the first place, on an objective analysis of the relative importance of price and non-price competitive factors in the market for each metal; and, in the second place, on the assumptions made about future changes in relative prices and in technological factors.

Table B 29. *Shares of main metals in total non-ferrous metals consumption in the industrial countries, 1964–5 and changes from 1953–7 (percentages of total value^a)*

	United Kingdom	E.E.C.	Other Western Europe	United States	Canada	Japan	Total
Aluminium: 1964–5	25·3	26·5	28·5	38·8	27·5	23·2	31·7
Change from 1953–7	*+3·7*	*+7·8*	*+7·8*	*+9·3*	*+5·1*	*+10·9*	*+7·2*
Copper: 1964–5	49·9	49·2	47·6	41·4	53·9	55·1	46·4
Change from 1953–7	*+0·4*	*−1·9*	*−6·6*	*−4·4*	*−7·5*	*−2·3*	*−2·4*
Lead: 1964–5	9·2	7·5	9·5	5·9	6·1	5·2	6·8
Change from 1953–7	*−0·5*	*−2·6*	*−0·6*	*−2·4*	*−2·3*	*−3·3*	*−2·2*
Tin: 1964–5	6·6	5·8	5·9	5·0	4·4	5·3	5·4
Change from 1953–7	*−2·4*	*−1·7*	*−1·4*	*−2·2*	*−1·2*	*−2·8*	*−2·1*
Zinc: 1964–5	9·0	11·0	8·5	8·9	8·1	11·2	9·7
Change from 1953–7	*−1·2*	*−1·6*	*+0·7*	*−0·5*	*+0·8*	*−2·5*	*−0·5*

SOURCE: *Metal Statistics*, Metallgesellschaft A.G., Frankfurt-am-Main.

^{a} At constant (1962–3) prices.

To assist the analysis at this point, some experimental regressions were computed for Britain and the United States, taking the share of each metal in total non-ferrous metals consumption as the dependent variable, and the relative prices of the various metals, together with a trend factor, as independent variables. A linear form of equation[1] was used for annual data covering the period 1950–63 for the United Kingdom, and 1948–63 for the United States. The results are summarized in Tables B 30 (aluminium and copper), B 31 (lead and zinc) and B 32 (tin). The general procedure was to include, in the initial equation for each metal, price relatives for all the other four non-ferrous metals; and, where any coefficient proved to be statistically non-significant, to recalculate the regression equation omitting the

[1] The equation used was of the following form:

$$S_1 = a + b_1(P_1/P_2) + b_2(P_1/P_3) + b_3(P_1/P_4) + b_4(P_1/P_5) + b_5 t,$$

where S_1 represents the share of metal 1 in total non-ferrous metals consumption, P_1 to P_5 represent the wholesale prices of the five metals, respectively, and t represents time. Similar equations were used for the other metals.

corresponding variable.[1] In one case (United States aluminium consumption), this procedure led to three equations being computed, since a significant coefficient (for the relative price of aluminium and tin) on the first regression became non-significant on the second.

For *aluminium*, all the regressions provided good 'explanations' of the variance in the dependent variable. The final regressions accounted for 97 per cent of the variance in the share of aluminium in the United States, and 86 per cent of the variance in the United Kingdom. They indicated that, in both countries, the share of aluminium in the total depended on the relative price of aluminium and copper, together with a trend factor, while, for the United Kingdom only, the relative price of aluminium and zinc was also a significant factor. It is of interest to note that the trend coefficient remained relatively stable as the price variables included in the equations changed, and also that, in the final regressions, the trend coefficients for the two countries were virtually identical.[2] They demonstrate that, after eliminating the effect of changes in the relative prices of the five metals, the (percentage) share of aluminium in total consumption, valued at constant prices, has tended to rise over the period since 1950 at an average rate of two-thirds of a percentage point a year. In Britain, for example, the share of aluminium in 1962–3 would have been 26·8 per cent (instead of the 24·7 per cent actually recorded) had there been no change in relative prices of aluminium, copper and zinc over the period since 1953–7. The smaller rise in aluminium's actual share was due in the main to a fall in the copper/aluminium price ratio between 1953–7 and 1962–3.

The fact that the ratio of aluminium to copper prices was the only one of the four price relatives to be statistically significant for both countries indicates that *copper* is the principal non-ferrous competitor with aluminium in the latter's main end-uses. It is of considerable interest, therefore, to note that none of the various regressions indicated any significant relationship between changes in the aluminium/copper price ratio and copper's share of total non-ferrous metals consumption. This may be a reflection of the fact that only a comparatively small proportion of aluminium is used in electrical equipment (including transmission lines), which constitutes the principal use of copper. It is possible, however, that a more detailed analysis would reveal stronger relationships in specific end-uses between the aluminium/copper price ratio and copper's share of total non-ferrous metal consumption.

For the United States, for example, one-quarter of total domestic

---

[1] This procedure was not, however, followed in every case.

[2] The price-substitution elasticity of demand for aluminium with respect to the aluminium/copper price ratio was also very similar in the two countries. Taking means of the various series, the price-substitution elasticity was −0·28 (±0·09) for the United Kingdom and −0·21(±0·08) for the United States.

consumption of aluminium in 1964 was accounted for by building and construction and a similar proportion went into the manufacture of transportation equipment; for copper, the corresponding proportions were only one-sixth and one-tenth. Almost half the total copper used in the United States in that year went into electrical engineering products, including electric transmission lines, whereas electrical uses took only one-tenth of total aluminium consumption. The competition between the two metals also extends over a wide range of minor uses. Comparable statistical data by industrial uses are not generally available for other industrial countries, though the available information indicates that competition between the two metals has been growing, particularly in electrical uses.[1]

Table B 30. *Effect of price changes on the shares of aluminium and copper in total consumption of non-ferrous metals: United Kingdom and United States*

Share of		Coefficient of ratio of own price to price of					Coefficient of t	R^2
		Aluminium	Copper	Lead	Tin	Zinc		
Aluminium								
United Kingdom	(1)		−7·54 (2·94)	1·40 (1·81)	1·51 (13·96)	−2·11 (1·61)	0·51 (0·24)	0·875
	(2)		−6·68 (2·56)			−1·63 (0·72)	0·69 (0·10)	0·864
United States	(1)		−13·30 (2·55)	−1·07 (1·68)	−38·49 (14·09)	7·02 (1·73)	0·57 (0·08)	0·990
	(2)		−10·74 (3·10)		12·10 (9·94)		0·64 (0·04)	0·972
	(3)		−10·39 (3·14)				0·67 (0·03)	0·969
Copper								
United Kingdom	(1)	−2·31 (3·05)		−3·44 (2·02)	15·28 (15·58)	0·33 (1·87)	0·53 (0·36)	0·496
	(2)	−0·52 (2·62)		−1·78 (1·59)			0·34 (0·38)	0·217
United States	(1)	1·46 (0·95)		−0·47 (0·43)	5·89 (5·47)	−2·97 (0·66)	−0·22 (0·03)	0·991
	(2)					−1·92 (0·26)	−0·28 (0·02)	0·986

SOURCE: Basic data from *Metal Statistics*, Metallgesellschaft A.G., Frankfurt-am-Main.

[1] During the period of high copper prices, in 1966, there appeared to be a definite substitution of aluminium for copper in some uses, but it is not clear to what extent this was a temporary phenomenon.

The regressions for *lead* and *zinc* suggest that there may be a price substitution element in some end-uses between these metals and aluminium—one would expect to find this in the building industry, for example—though in only one of the regressions for lead in the United States was the coefficient for the relevant price ratio significantly different from zero. The share of lead in total non-ferrous metals consumption has a strong downward trend in both Britain and the United States, while for zinc the downward trend is much more marked in the former country than in the latter. These trend coefficients sum up a number of separate factors, including changes in the output-pattern of end-products as well as technological developments in the various competing materials.

Table B31. *Effect of price changes on the shares of lead and zinc in total consumption of non-ferrous metals: United Kingdom and United States*

		Coefficient of ratio of own price to price of					Coeffi-cient of t	R^2
		Alu-minium	Copper	Lead	Tin	Zinc		
Lead								
United Kingdom	(1)	2·36 (1·79)	−2·23 (2·72)		−33·05 (13·40)	2·93 (1·46)	−0·18 (0·09)	0·626
	(2)				−12·43 (9·88)		−0·17 (0·08)	0·403
United States	(1)	−3·87 (1·32)	3·93 (1·60)		11·21 (11·26)	−0·65 (1·13)	−0·12 (0·03)	0·945
	(2)	−1·70 (1·06)					−0·15 (0·03)	0·912
Zinc								
United Kingdom	(1)	−2·46 (2·37)	−0·65 (3·87)	3·84 (1·97)	−14·92 (17·36)		−0·42 (0·13)	0·643
	(2)	−1·41 (0·85)					−0·18 (0·06)	0·444
United States	(1)	−3·35 (2·08)	4·36 (2·39)	−0·79 (1·67)	16·25 (14·15)		−0·05 (0·04)	0·769
	(2)	−0·16 (1·00)					−0·07 (0·02)	0·677

SOURCE: Basic data from *Metal Statistics*, Metallgesellschaft A.G., Frankfurt-am-Main.

For *tin*, the regression for the United Kingdom also showed a strong downward trend; for the United States the down trend, though less marked, was associated with negative coefficients for the price ratios of tin with aluminium and zinc. Though neither coefficient was significantly different from zero, recent developments in the United States (especially the use of aluminium in canning) indicate that there may well be an appreciable substitution against tin in that country in the future. In a sense, this is a technological rather than a purely (short-term) price substitution, but for projection purposes it is more convenient to assume that it represents a long-term price-substitution effect. Consequently, the coefficient for the tin/aluminium price ratio was also assumed to be significant for this purpose.[1]

Table B32. *Effect of price changes on the share of tin in total consumption of non-ferrous metals: United Kingdom and United States*

		Coefficient of ratio of own price to price of				Coefficient of t	R^2
		Aluminium	Copper	Lead	Zinc		
United Kingdom	(1)	−0·01 (0·15)	0·13 (0·21)	0·11 (0·10)	0·11 (0·11)	−0·34 (0·06)	0·947
	(2)					−0·22 (0·03)	0·855
United States	(1)	−0·81 (0·25)	0·53 (0·27)	0·27 (0·18)	−0·53 (0·19)	−0·15 (0·04)	0·916
	(2)	−0·13 (0·17)			−0·30 (0·22)	−0·09 (0·03)	0·833

SOURCE: Basic data from *Metal Statistics*, Metallgesellschaft A.G., Frankfurt-am-Main.

The various regression results above were used as the basis of projections of the probable share of each metal in total non-ferrous metals consumption in Britain and the United States in 1975. They were also used as a guide in estimating the 1975 percentages for each metal in the other industrial areas. For all areas, it was assumed that the underlying technological trends would operate over the period up to 1975 in much the same degree as in the past.[2]

As regards the price factor, the most important assumption relates to the aluminium/copper price ratio. Here, it has been assumed that copper prices will rise by 25 per cent over the projection period in relation to aluminium prices. This is essentially an arbitrary assumption, based largely on the fact that the main element of cost in aluminium production consists of electric energy, the real cost of which has fallen substantially over the past decade, and might well decline still more

[1] An alternative approach would be to assume that the down trend in the share of tin in American non-ferrous metals consumption would be appreciably greater than that shown in the regression equation.

[2] To the extent that the trend coefficients in Tables B30–B32 reflect changes in prices of materials other than non-ferrous metals (e.g. steel or plastics), this assumption also implies that such relative price changes will continue in the future.

over the next. In view of the increasing cost of expanding tin production, it has also been assumed—again arbitrarily—that the ratio of tin to aluminium prices will rise by 35 per cent from 1960–1 to 1975.

For lead and zinc, it does not seem practicable to make any particular assumption about future price changes which would have a reasonably valid basis. One difficulty is that these two metals are in joint supply, so that prices of one or the other are likely to change if world demand is rising at different rates in the two markets. As will be seen later, the projections indicate a rather faster growth in demand for zinc than for lead in the industrial countries and, to this extent, zinc prices might rise in relation to the price of lead. However, since the regressions showed that neither zinc nor lead consumption, at least in Britain and the United States, is sensitive to changes in the lead/zinc price ratio, while changes in the ratio of zinc or lead prices to prices of other metals appeared generally to have had no significant effect on metals consumption, it has been assumed that lead and zinc prices in 1975 will be much the same as in the early 1960s.

On the basis of these various assumptions, the share of each metal in total non-ferrous metals consumption was projected for 1975, for each of the industrial areas separately.[1] These projected shares were then applied to the 1975 value totals (see Table B 28) to arrive at estimated values of consumption of each metal in each area. Finally, these values were converted back to metal equivalents by the use of the relevant 1962–3 unit values, the results being aggregated for the industrial countries as a whole. The aggregates (shown in Table B 33) indicate that, broadly, the past pattern of growth is likely to continue in the future. Aluminium is projected to remain the metal with the fastest growth rate in consumption, though the projected growth—6·8 or 7·5 per cent a year, according to the income-growth assumption used— is appreciably slower than that achieved in the first half of the 1960s.[2] Copper consumption is projected to rise at an annual rate of 3·7 or 4·4 per cent, again lower than the rate achieved in the first half of the 1960s, but slightly higher than for the longer period from 1953–7 to 1962–3. The projection for lead consumption (3·0 or 3·8 per cent a year) is of the same order of magnitude as for the first half of the 1960s, while that for zinc is lower. For tin, the projection (1·1 or 1·8 per cent a year) would indicate a reversal of the slight down trend in consumption recorded in recent years.

[1] For the industrial areas in total, the projected 1975 shares averaged as follows: aluminium, 37; copper, 43½; lead, 6½; tin, 4½; zinc, 8½ (figures refer to percentage of total value of non-ferrous metals consumption at 1962–3 prices).

[2] The growth rate of metal consumption for the period 1960–1 to 1964–5 is inflated as a result of the United States recession in 1960. This affected aluminium particularly.

Table B33. *Consumption of non-ferrous metals in the industrial countries, 1953–65 and projections for 1975*

	Aluminium	Copper	Lead	Tin	Zinc
Rates of growth (% *per annum*)					
1953–7 to 1960–1	5·8	3·5	0·8	2·9	3·2
1953–7 to 1962–3	7·1	3·4	1·6	1·3	3·4
1960–1 to 1964–5	10·8	5·9	3·7	−0·4	5·8
1960-1 to 1975: A	6·8	3·7	3·0	1·1	3·8
B	7·5	4·4	3·8	1·8	4·4
Consumption (*million metric tons*)					
1953–7	2·86	4·33	2·35	0·18	2·36
1960–1	3·90	5·22	2·46	0·21	2·80
1962–3	4·78	5·58	2·64	0·19	3·04
1964–5	5·88	6·56	2·85	0·20	3·51
1975: A	10·00	9·00	3·80	0·24	4·70
B	11·00	10·00	4·20	0·27	5·20

SOURCE: *Metal Statistics*, Metallgesellschaft A.G., Frankfurt-am-Main.

Net imports into the industrial countries

Since net imports into the industrial countries consist of ores, concentrates and primary metals, the demand for the latter can be derived as a residual from the projections of metal consumption, after allowing for the probable future level of production in the industrial countries of non-ferrous ores and secondary metal, and of their direct use of non-ferrous scrap.

Production of ore in the industrial countries was generally assumed to increase in the period up to 1975 at the same average rate as over the past decade. Secondary production and the volume of direct usage of scrap depends on the availability and cost of scrap metal, as well as on the technical factors governing the use of scrap. The availability of scrap metal, in turn, depends on several factors, the most important being the total stock and age distribution of metal products, and the relative price movements of the various primary metals. The projection of secondary production should properly be approached by the use of an econometric analysis of the scrap metal market, but this would have put the research involved beyond the scope of the present study. Instead, the simple assumption was made that secondary production and direct use of scrap would increase in the same proportion as consumption. However, for the sake of consistency, a slight upward adjustment was made in the projection for secondary copper production and the direct use of tin scrap, in view of the assumptions about the rise in copper and tin prices in relation to the aluminium price; a similar downward adjustment was made for secondary aluminium production.

The projections for net imports of ores and metals by the industrial countries, derived as described above, are summarized in Table B34. Net imports of bauxite, alumina and aluminium metal, in terms of metal content, are projected to rise by about $6\frac{1}{2}$ and 7 per cent a year on the low and high income-growth assumptions respectively, representing a continuation of the previous decline in their rate of growth. Net imports of copper are projected to increase by about $4\frac{1}{2}$ and $5\frac{1}{2}$ per cent a year, somewhat above the rate for the first half of the present decade. Considerable increases in the net import growth rate are projected, however, for both lead and zinc ores and metal; while for tin, net imports are projected to rise, thus reversing the decline from 1960–1 to 1964–5. Against this it should be noted that for lead and zinc in particular the projections for net imports are fairly sensitive to changes in assumptions about future trends in output of ores in the industrial countries. If the rate of growth of ore production in the United States were to rise, for example, over the coming decade, the growth rate of net imports of these metals would be appreciably less than those shown in Table B34.

Table B34. *Net imports of non-ferrous metals into the industrial countries, 1953–63 and projections for 1975*[a]

	Aluminium	Copper	Lead	Tin	Zinc
Rates of growth (% *per annum*)					
1953–7 to 1960–1	9·8	5·6	−0·3	−1·6	−1·7
1953–7 to 1962–3	8·7	3·8	1·0	−2·3	−0·8
1960–1 to 1964–5	7·6	3·3	0·3	−3·4	1·7
1960–1 to 1975: A	6·3	4·5	3·9	1·7	4·2
B	6·8	5·3	4·4	2·4	5·0
Net imports[b] (*million metric tons*)					
1953–7	1·55	1·15	0·75	0·15	0·81
1960–1	2·60	1·52	0·74	0·14	0·74
1962–3	2·91	1·48	0·81	0·12	0·75
1964–5	3·49	1·73	0·75	0·12	0·79
1975: A	6·30	2·90	1·30	0·17	1·40
B	6·80	3·20	1·40	0·19	1·50

SOURCES: *Metal Statistics*, Metallgesellschaft A.G., Frankfurt-am-Main; *Statistical Summary of the Mineral Industry*, Overseas Geological Surveys, H.M.S.O., London; *Statistics of Non-Ferrous Metals*, and *The Non-Ferrous Metals Industry*, O.E.C.D., Paris; *Lead and Zinc Statistics*, International Lead and Zinc Study Group, New York; *Statistical Yearbook*, International Tin Council, London.

[a] In terms of metal content.   [b] Ores and metals.

An allowance must now be made for the likelihood that, over the next decade, the proportion of net imports (into the industrial countries) consisting of metal will rise, at the expense of imports of ores and concentrates. The reason for this is that many ore-producing countries in the developing areas are planning to instal new metal refining plants or to extend existing refining capacity. In addition, any further expansion of ore production in the developed areas is likely to displace imports of ore, rather than of metal. Taking into account the published Development Plans of the various producing countries, some assessment can be made of the probable distribution in 1975 of net metal imports into the industrial countries (see Table B35). The principal change envisaged is an appreciable rise in the proportion of aluminium imported in the form of alumina (with a consequent fall in the relative importance of net imports of bauxite), mainly as a result of planned expansions in alumina capacity in Australia, Jamaica and Guyana.

Table B35. *Volume of net imports into the industrial countries, and of exports from the Overseas Sterling Area, of the principal non-ferrous metals, 1960–1 and projections for 1975*

	Net imports into industrial countries			Exports from the Overseas Sterling Area				
		Growth rates, 1960–1 to 1975			Growth rates, 1960–1 to 1975		1975	
	1960–1	A	B	1960–1	A	B	A	B
	(£ million)	(% per annum)		(£ million)	(% per annum)		(£ million at 1960–1 prices)	
Aluminium	43	10·9	11·5	48	10·4	11·0	200	215
Copper	325	4·6	5·5	154	4·3	5·0	280	315
Lead	46	3·9	4·5	24	4·3	4·9	44	48
Tin	107	1·7	2·4	70	3·0	3·7	106	118
Zinc	32	5·0	5·8	10	4·2	5·0	18	20
TOTAL	554	4·9	5·6	306	5·3	6·1	648	716

SOURCES: As for Table B34 and *The Commonwealth and the Sterling Area: Statistical Abstracts*, Board of Trade, London; *Yearbook of International Trade Statistics*, United Nations, New York.

Since metal is more valuable, per ton of metal content, than ores and concentrates, this projected shift in the composition of net imports towards metal will result in higher rates of growth in net imports when measured in terms of value at constant prices than when measured in terms of metal content. For all five metals, the volume[1] of net imports is projected to rise by some 5 to 6 per cent a year, on average, from 1960–1 to 1975; had no shift from ores to metals been assumed, the growth

[1] Defined as value at constant prices.

rate in net import volume would have been only some 4 to 5 per cent a year. The fastest growth rate, in volume terms, is projected for bauxite, alumina and aluminium (11 to $11\frac{1}{2}$ per cent a year), the lowest for tin concentrates and metal ($1\frac{3}{4}$ to $2\frac{1}{2}$ per cent a year).[1]

Exports from the Overseas Sterling Area

By far the greater proportion of Overseas Sterling Area exports of non-ferrous ores and metals goes to the Western industrial countries. In 1962–3, for example, these countries took 99 per cent of Sterling exports of bauxite, alumina and aluminium and about 90 per cent of copper and lead. For tin and zinc, the proportions were somewhat lower—85 and 71 per cent, respectively—though the industrial markets still predominated.

Projections of non-ferrous metals exports from the Overseas Sterling Area were therefore based essentially on the estimates for net imports into the industrial countries. Exports to other markets—mainly primary-producing countries—were assumed to grow at much the same rate as in recent years. The projections (summarized in Table B35) show growth rates for the various metals which closely resemble those for net imports into the industrial countries; differences between the two are almost wholly due to assumptions about probable changes in the share of industrial countries' imports held by Sterling suppliers.

For tin, Sterling exports are projected to grow appreciably faster than industrial countries' net imports. It was assumed that the prospect of an increase in tin production is more favourable in the Sterling countries than in the producing countries outside the Sterling Area. Production in Malaya will probably stay at a high level, despite the partial exhaustion of the known high-grade deposits in that country. Although Nigeria —the other large Sterling tin producer—is also facing the problems of working low-grade ores, it has been assumed that its present production of tin would be maintained. Australia, with its recent discoveries of tin deposits, is beginning to emerge from a minor status in tin-mining to take an important place in world exports of tin. Australian tin production is expected to exceed domestic demand by 1969 and some export contracts have already been concluded. On the other hand, tin production in Indonesia has shown an almost continuous fall since the mid 1950s. There are attempts to improve efficiency and increase production, but in view of the large investments needed to renew the mostly

---

[1] It should also be mentioned that by 1975 some developing countries (Chile and Zambia for example, in the case of copper) might have increased domestic fabrication of their metal production; this could result in a moderate shift towards exports of manufactures, thus influencing the projections here, which take no account of metal trade in the form of manufactures or semi-manufactures.

deteriorated mining equipment, a recovery on a substantial scale is not envisaged by 1975. The increase in tin production both in Bolivia and in Thailand is hampered by the numerous difficulties in tin mining and the more costly methods needed for working new, mostly marginal deposits.

Sterling exports of lead are projected to grow at a somewhat faster rate than net imports into industrial countries—the result of a probable faster growth in exportable production in Australia than elsewhere. For zinc, however, Sterling exports are assumed to continue to grow marginally less fast than net imports into the industrial countries.

MANUFACTURES

By ANN MORGAN

Manufactured goods[1] already play a major role in the exports of the Overseas Sterling Area. In 1964 they exceeded £700 million in value, equivalent to 13 per cent of domestic exports from the countries concerned. But trade is concentrated in a handful of countries—Hong Kong, India, Australia, South Africa, Ireland and Pakistan—which together provide 90 per cent of the total, Hong Kong alone supplying more than one-third of O.S.A. exports of manufactures.

A similar concentration is apparent in the commodity composition of trade. In the major Asian countries, abundance of cheap labour has promoted the development of an export trade in textiles and clothing; in countries rich in resources, with well developed mining industries—Australia and South Africa—exports are concentrated in steel (including pig iron and ferro-alloys), machinery and metal manufactures. Moreover, within these groups the bulk of exports is frequently supplied by two or three specific products, entailing an even higher degree of concentration than is indicated by figures for broad classes of manufactures. Hong Kong and Ireland show a more diversified pattern, but, in both, light-industry products of a labour-intensive character predominate. Elsewhere, a great part of trade derives from one or two products —casein and paper in New Zealand, iron and steel in Rhodesia, plywood and veneers in Ghana and Nigeria—which are based on certain natural resources or are the by-product of a major primary industry.

In relation to world trade in manufactures, the O.S.A. countries' role is negligible outside the textiles and clothing group, where in 1964 it supplied 8 per cent of world exports. The relative importance of exports from Sterling developing countries is considerably greater, however, in relation to those of other developing countries; for example, more than half of all manufactured exports and over two-thirds of textile and clothing exports from developing countries in 1964 came from Sterling sources (see Table C1). There are various reasons why this should be so; one major reason is the existence of the Commonwealth trading system, more especially Commonwealth preference and free entry to the United Kingdom market.

[1] Manufactures are here defined as all non-food manufactured goods (including handicraft products) except jute goods, leather and non-ferrous metals, which have been discussed in Appendix B, and diamonds. This definition corresponds approximately to SITC sections 5–8, less 653.1, 656.1, 611, 667 and 68.

Table C1. *Exports of manufactures, 1964*

	Value of exports					Manufactures as proportion of total domestic exports
	Textiles and clothing	Steel machinery and metal manufactures	Chemicals	Other manufactures	Total	
	(£ million)					(%)
STERLING COUNTRIES						
Hong Kong	145	31	3	74	253	91
India	82	18	7	16	123	20
Australia[a]	6	69	17	16	108	10
South Africa	4	38	17	12	71	15
Ireland	15	16	2	16	49	23
Pakistan[a,b]	18	2	3	8	31	18
New Zealand[b]	1	1	6	7	15	4
Rhodesia[c]	2	8	1	2	13	16
Malaya	1	1	4	4	10	3
Trinidad	1	—	6	1	8	5
Jamaica	4	—	1	1	6	8
All other	2	1	5	12	20	1
Total O.S.A.[d]	281	185	72	169	707	13
United Kingdom	315	2,188	412	458	3,373	79
Total, Sterling	596	2,373	484	627	4,080	41
NON-STERLING COUNTRIES						
Industrial	2,398	13,630	2,923	4,420	23,371	66
Developing	118	71	90	168	447	6
Centrally planned	335	2,690	340	945	4,310	59
Total, non-Sterling	2,851	16,391	3,353	5,533	28,128	56
TOTAL	3,447	18,764	3,837	6,160	32,208	54
O.S.A. as percentage of total	8	1	2	3	2	..
Developing O.S.A.[e] as percentage of developing total	68	46	18	43	51	..

NOTE. SITC definition of titles: *Textiles and clothing* 65 + 84 (less jute goods); *steel, machinery and metal manufactures* 67 + 7 + 69 (also includes 81 for Hong Kong); *chemicals* 5; *other manufactures* 6 + 8 less (611 + 65 + 667 + 67 + 68 + 69 + 84). Figures have been adjusted to these classifications so far as the data permit, and known re-exports have been eliminated. The trade of certain minor countries is not included.

SOURCES: *Yearbook of International Trade Statistics 1964, Monthly Bulletin of Statistics*, United Nations, New York; *Foreign Trade Statistical Bulletins*, O.E.C.D., Paris; country trade statistics; N.I.E.S.R. estimates.

[a] Including re-exports.
[b] July–June trade year 1963–4.
[c] Excluding exports to Zambia and Malawi.
[d] Excluding exports from Aden and Singapore.
[e] O.S.A. less Australia, South Africa, Ireland, New Zealand and Iceland.

With few exceptions, of which rayon and synthetic textiles and motor vehicles are perhaps the most important, manufactures from the preference area, that is, Canada and the O.S.A. less Jordan, Iceland and Libya, enter Britain duty-free. The margin of preference on semi-manufactures and on labour-intensive finished goods of the kind commonly exported by developing countries is usually high. According to a P.E.P. study,[1] the average preference margin on all manufactures (here defined to include leather and jute goods) imported into the United Kingdom from the preference area was 12 per cent in 1957; 79 per cent of these goods actually benefited from a tariff preference, the average margin on preferred goods being 16 per cent. If Canada were excluded, these figures would be rather higher, owing to the greater proportion of finished goods enjoying preference margins in excess of 20 per cent in non-Canadian trade. Tariff preferences are also given to a wide range of manufactures originating in the preference area by most of the high-income Commonwealth countries and a number of others, though this concession is frequently not extended to Asian O.S.A. exporters, more particularly India and Pakistan.

The influence of tariff preferences and the Commonwealth trading system is discernible in the direction of trade. The available statistics do not permit the delineation of an exact picture of trade flows, but the broad pattern is clear: O.S.A. exports of manufactures have tended to be directed to the United Kingdom market or to neighbouring, often preferential, Commonwealth markets. Thus India exports chiefly to Britain or to Sterling Area countries bordering the Indian Ocean, and Australia to Britain, New Zealand and Malaya; this pattern holds good for most other countries. Exports to the United States, which is becoming an increasingly important market for O.S.A. manufactures, are gradually diversifying the direction of trade, as are exports to continental Western Europe though so far rarely to any significant degree. It appears, however, that only where a relatively large volume of trade has been achieved have countries departed much from the traditional pattern.

O.S.A. exports of manufactures have grown very rapidly during the past decade. The six main exporters raised sales from an average of £348 million in 1957–9 to £451 million in 1960–1 and £635 million in 1964.[2] The annual average rate of growth for this group of countries was remarkably well sustained, falling only from 11 per cent in the first part of the period to 10 per cent in the second; but the variations

[1] *Commonwealth Preference in the United Kingdom*, Political and Economic Planning, London, August 1960.

[2] All value figures in this chapter are in terms of current prices, with the exception of the trade projections for 1975, which are expressed in 1960–1 prices.

between countries were very great. Ireland and Pakistan consistently maintained rates close to or in excess of 20 per cent per annum; Hong Kong achieved rates of 18 and 14 per cent, Australia 10 per cent or above; India, after a poor start, pushed the rate up to 8 per cent in the period 1960–1 to 1964; South Africa, however, was exporting slightly less by the end of the period than it had been in 1957–9. Performance in respect of the main commodity groups was equally diverse, as the figures in Table C2 show.

Table C2. *Annual rates of change in exports of main groups of manufactures from selected Sterling countries (percentage per annum)*
I, 1957–9 to 1960–1; II, 1960–1 to 1964

		Textiles and clothing	Steel, machinery and metal manufactures	Chemicals	Other finished goods	Other semi-manufactures	Tota
Hong Kong	I	+19	+10	+7	+24	+18	+18
	II	+18	+15	−1	+18	+9	+14
India	I	−1	+67	+18	+4	+2	+4
	II	+6	+14	+8	+10	+2	+8
Australia	I	+17	+10	+11	+26	+9	+12
	II	+29	+9	+18	+2	+17	+10
South Africa	I	−4	+9	−1	−5	−3	+3
	II	−9	−2	+2	−10	−2	−3
Ireland	I	+23	+13	+34	+29	+11	+19
	II	+15	+27	+28	+18	+13	+19
Pakistan	I	+11	..	..			+20
	II	+25	+10		+42		+28
TOTALS	I	+9	+13[a]	+6[a]	+18[a]	+5[a]	+11
	II	+11	+8[a]	+8[a]	+13[a]	+6[a]	+10

SOURCES: As Table C1.

[a] Excluding Pakistan.

Differences in the commodity composition and direction of trade do little to explain differences between the performance of the main O.S.A. exporters in overseas markets. India's poor showing could be partly attributed to its concentration on cotton textiles; yet Pakistan, even more concentrated, achieved the highest rates of total export growth. Of the two countries which are principally exporters of metals and machinery, Australia did well in almost all commodity groups, South Africa badly. There are no factors common to all the countries concerned which provide even a partial explanation of past performance.

This diversity of experience makes any attempt to project O.S.A. exports of manufactures a hazardous business. It would be inappropriate to relate the expansion of trade to the growth of income or some similar variable in the industrial countries. The assumption that O.S.A. exports are sold principally in high-income countries does not hold for much of the Area's trade in manufactures, while for certain commodities the level of exports to industrial areas is determined to a considerable degree by the trade policies of the importing countries. Moreover, in many lines exports have barely been initiated and it is probable that ten years hence a high proportion of O.S.A. exports of manufactures will consist of goods not yet exported by primary-producing countries and currently produced only on a small scale. At the same time, if plans for industrialization are successfully implemented, there are likely to be major changes in costs as between developed and developing countries, and between the developing countries themselves.

In these circumstances, it seems appropriate to concentrate on the most important established flows of trade, dealing only very briefly with other goods: that is, on Asian Sterling textiles and clothing, where the basis for projection is a little firmer than in respect of other manufactures; and on steel, machinery and metal manufactures, not only because of their present importance but because it is here that the major exporters of manufactures in the O.S.A. hope to achieve their biggest gains. The projections are presented in the form of a range from low to high, centred on what is judged in the light of available evidence to be the most probable level of trade. But it should be stressed that because so much depends on the creation of new capacity in the exporting countries and the policies of importing countries, these projections are very speculative.

Asian Sterling textiles and clothing

Approximately two-fifths of Asian Sterling countries' exports of textiles and clothing are normally supplied by cotton yarn and cloth, mostly of low quality and correspondingly low unit value. Sterling Asia's combined share in the value of world[1] exports has risen consistently over the past decade, principally because of the growth of exports from Hong Kong and Pakistan, but it remains about one-third smaller than their share in the volume of trade, which has in most years been close to 20 per cent for both yarn and cloth. Low quality has, moreover, limited the market in which they can sell. The types and qualities of yarn and finished cloth required in the industrial countries are produced only to a limited extent. Hence sales of these goods are

[1] World exports are here defined as exports from O.E.C.D. member countries plus India, Pakistan and Hong Kong.

directed on the whole to other developing countries, and the bulk of cotton textile exports to industrial areas consists of grey cloth.

In practice, then, the Asian Sterling countries are selling to two clearly differentiated markets, the industrial areas and the rest of the world. The penetration of markets in the industrial areas began in the first half of the 1950s with the development of large-scale exports to Britain under the aegis of the Commonwealth preference system. The Asian Sterling countries rapidly secured two-thirds of the United Kingdom market for grey cloth, though they made relatively little headway in selling finished cloth. The introduction of 'voluntary' quotas on exports from Commonwealth Asia to Britain checked the rate of expansion and, in so doing, prompted the development of sales to other industrial areas, first the United States and latterly the E.E.C. Trade followed the same pattern as in Britain: a surge in exports of cheap grey cloth brought retaliatory restrictions on the volume of trade, which have been formalized within the framework of the G.A.T.T. Long-Term Textile Arrangement; and this in turn encouraged the exporting countries to diversify into better quality and more highly finished cloth. Asian Sterling exports of grey cloth to the industrial areas have been growing much less rapidly since 1960–1 than they did previously, while exports of other cloth have tended to rise more rapidly. Even so, the Asian Sterling share in grey cloth imports into the industrial areas is still three times or more as large as the share in imports of finished cloth.

The rise in Asian Sterling exports to the rest of the world has been limited both by import substitution and by general import restrictions on account of balance of payments difficulties in a number of major African, Middle Eastern and South-East Asian import markets. Asian Sterling textile exporters are particularly vulnerable to the effects of import substitution in the developing areas since the cheap, technically simple cloths which predominate in their exports are precisely those that are the first to be produced by any country establishing a textile industry. They are also, and for the same reason, particularly susceptible to competition from other new producers, such as China and Taiwan.

The volume of exports from individual Sterling Asian countries, and their share in world trade, has fluctuated widely from year to year since the mid 1950s, in response to the growth of output in Pakistan and Hong Kong, export incentives and import controls, and the movement of export prices. The accompanying chart indicates that the latter has been a major influence. The unit value indices used as a measure of prices reflect, of course, changes in the composition and quality as well as in the price of exports. None the less, it would seem that, in face of a highly elastic demand for their products, Pakistan and Hong Kong

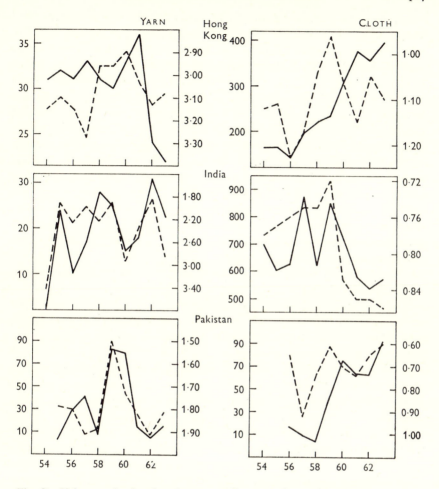

Fig. C1. Volume and unit value of cotton textile exports from Asian Sterling countries, 1954–63.

———— volume (left-hand scale), – – – – unit value (right-hand scale inverted).
Volume: yarn mn lb; cloth mn yds, except Hong Kong mn sq yds.
Unit values: yarn Rs/HK $ per lb; cloth Rs per yd/HK $ per sq yd.

increased their shares in world cloth markets, while higher yarn prices have been associated with a decline in yarn exports. In India, rising prices have since 1960 depressed exports of both yarn and cloth.

The origins of the rise in Indian export prices are to be found in a complex of factors, many of them relevant not only to exports of cotton textiles but to the export prospects of all Indian manufactures. Pressure was exerted from two sides. Costs increased steadily: the price of raw cotton rose owing to a shortfall in domestic output that could not, because of the foreign exchange shortage, be made good by imports; wages rose still more under the combined influence of the rise in 'dearness allowance' payments linked to the cost-of-living index and strong trade union pressure. Between 1959 and 1963 the price of Jarilla cotton in Bombay rose by 47 per cent and the average annual earnings of mill workers by 18 per cent. Since the increase in output per man-hour was insignificant, labour costs per unit of output rose almost in parallel with earnings. The second factor was the inflation in the economy at large, engendered by deficit financing and the surge in investment in the late 1950s, which inflated home demand with effects on exports perhaps even more serious than that of the rise in costs. Strong home demand has generally been associated with a fall in the ratio of exports to production, most notably during 1960 to 1962—the years in which India's share in world cloth exports contracted sharply. The comparatively minor export promotion measures introduced in the late 1950s, of which the most important was an import entitlement system related to the value of exports, were wholly inadequate to counter the pull of the home market.

The switch might have been less drastic and the rise in costs less pronounced had the mill sector of the cotton textile industry, which provides the bulk of exports, been allowed to develop capacity and output to the maximum possible within the limits set by the shortage of raw cotton. Government policy, however, has promoted the growth of the decentralized sector—handlooms and powerlooms—at the expense of the mills. In 1965 a ceiling was imposed on mill output and heavy excise duties were introduced on certain grades of mill cloth; the results can be seen in the stagnation of mill cloth production since 1957—it averaged 4,910 million yards in 1962–3 against 5,140 million in 1954–6 —and the rise in the decentralized sector's output from an estimated 1,790 million yards in 1956 to 3,140 million yards in 1963. The Government also discouraged the growth of mill weaving capacity through the industrial licensing system, under which all new capacity and substantial expansion of capacity require official sanction. Moreover, it prevented cost-saving investment by restrictions on the installation of automatic looms, which have only recently been relaxed, and on the redeployment of labour. These controls, together with the high cost and difficulty of obtaining machinery (machinery imports also required a licence from the government) led to a gradual decline in the number of looms installed between 1956 and 1962 (since when loomage has regained and surpassed the 1956 level), while there was only a modest rise in the number of spindles installed. An increase in shift working did little to raise effective capacity, since it appears to have been accompanied by a fall in output per machine-hour.

Pakistan has experienced some of the same difficulties as India, but in three important respects it has either avoided or neutralized them: since the late 1950s, raw cotton supplies have in most years been more nearly adequate to meet industry's requirements and raw cotton prices have remained close to or below the level prevailing in 1956, when the country first began to export cotton textiles on a large scale; capacity has been steadily increased, permitting a rise in yarn output from 301 million lb. in 1956 to an average of 452 million lb. in 1962–3 and in mill cloth output from 500 million yards to 728 million yards;[1] and the pull of higher home market prices following decontrol in 1959 has been counteracted by the export bonus scheme. This scheme exerted so strong an effect on yarn exports in 1959 and 1960 that a serious internal shortage developed and the bonus was removed from yarn in early 1961; it was reintroduced some eighteen months later, since when yarn exports have recovered from the very low level of 1962–3, though a ceiling has been imposed on the volume of exports. In the early years of its operation the bonus was less effective in stimulating cloth sales. Among the reasons for this failure, according to a study of the scheme by Bruton and Bose,[2] 'domestic demand for cloth was such that shifting sales from the domestic market to the export market resulted in rising domestic prices that effectively limited the extent of the shift'. Cloth exports fell in 1961 and 1962 but, with a big rise in output and a fall in the domestic price, they rose sharply again in 1963.

In both India and Pakistan, then, the experience of the past decade shows that export availabilities are liable to be curtailed by the pressure of home demand. It seems unlikely that measures such as devaluation can permanently alter this situation, which is essentially a supply problem; only if there is a real surplus of capacity over domestic demand, or in the unlikely event that imported supplies are freely available, will the threat of a disproportionate rise in home prices disappear. Because of the high income elasticity of demand for cloth[3] and the rate of population growth, the problem is likely to persist. In the open economy of Hong Kong, however, there is no such difficulty. The domestic consumer (almost exclusively the clothing industry) can purchase imported textiles as readily as locally manufactured yarn and cloth; while the manufacturer can obtain unlimited supplies of raw

[1] Handloom output increased at a similar rate. Assuming a constant conversion rate of 4·5 yards of cloth per lb. yarn, and allowing for the absorption of some surplus yarn by the hosiery industry and others, handloom cloth production rose from about 535 million yards in 1956 to 780 million yards in 1962–3.

[2] H. J. Bruton and S. R. Bose, *The Pakistan Export Bonus Scheme*, Institute of Development Economics, Karachi, 1963.

[3] According to a study by the Central Statistical Office, the income elasticity of demand for cloth in India is 1·4; cf. Manmohan Singh, *op. cit.* on p. 165, n. 1.

materials and machinery at world market prices free of duty, and is not subject to any form of government control on investment or the re-deployment of labour. In these circumstances, Hong Kong has been able to adapt to world market conditions more swiftly and effectively than either India or Pakistan, despite the restraints imposed by short-ages of land and water. Even so, Hong Kong has not adapted as fully as it might, witness its excessive concentration on grey cloth exports.

The export performance of the Asian Sterling countries is likely to be increasingly influenced in future by their ability, or otherwise, to adapt the composition and quality of output and correspondingly to adjust their methods of production. In respect of textiles sold to the developing areas, the need for change arises principally from two causes already briefly mentioned—the effect of import substitution on sales of low-quality products and the growth of low-cost, low-quality competition from other new suppliers. In Western Europe, and possibly in North America, the Asian Sterling exporters are faced with a situation different in origin but likely to be similar in effect.

The measures now being taken to reorganize European, and especially the British, cotton textile industries are expected to result in substantial cost reductions. Indeed, it is claimed that the most modern mills have production costs no higher than those in Asia and are fully competitive over the whole range of yarn and cloth output.[1] While it is permissible to doubt that there will be a wholesale levelling down of costs, it does seem that Asian exporters stand to lose some of their cost advantage in selling to Europe and in competing with European producers in third markets; though how far the change in relative costs will go cannot be judged. More serious impediments to the growth of Asian Sterling exports may arise from changes in the products and in the organization of a reinvigorated European industry. The trend towards mixing other fibres with cotton and the development of a more vertically integrated industry, integrated in marketing as well as production, threaten to curtail the extent of the market in which Asian Sterling producers can compete, given the present state of their industry. Again one cannot judge how far the process will go but it seems possible that develop-ments in importing countries will discourage any long-run rise in grey cloth imports. Even where a large rise in total imports of cloth from the developing countries is permitted, categorization can be used to ensure that it is not concentrated in one particular type or quality.

From developments during the past decade, it would appear that the future level of O.S.A. exports of cotton textiles will depend on a great number of influences, more especially: the relationship between supply

---

[1] See, for example, A. M. Alfred, *U.K. Textiles—a Growth Industry*, Manchester Statistical Society, November 1965.

and demand in the exporting countries; the movement of costs; the level of world demand and government policies in respect of imports; and the extent to which producers can adapt their output to changes in effective demand without pricing themselves out of world markets. The trade projections given here for 1975, however, relate solely to the potential volume of imports into the industrial and the developing countries. The more fundamental questions of supply, costs and prices have perforce been left out of account; it has been assumed that the policies necessary to secure a sufficient export surplus to maintain the Asian Sterling countries' share in world imports will be adopted.

Both India and Pakistan have, in fact, shown themselves ready to adjust their rates of exchange, whether by a partial or total devaluation, in order to keep their export prices in line with world prices; both, particularly India, are initiating measures which should increase the availability of export supplies (in 1963 the Government of India, for the first time since 1956, sanctioned a significant increase in mill capacity); and both have written into their Development Plans a rise in exports over the 1960–1 level.[1] Nevertheless, there is a risk, ignored in the projections, that the Asian Sterling countries as a group will fail to maintain their share of world cotton textile exports; unfortunately there seems little likelihood, short of a dismantling of all quota restrictions and tariffs on cotton textile imports from developing into developed countries, that they will increase their share in world trade.

The growth of imports into industrialized areas from the 'low-cost producers' in the developing countries is currently governed by the G.A.T.T. Long-Term Arrangement on Cotton Textiles and the quota restrictions enforced by the importing countries. In Britain, the quotas restrict imports until 1970 to the average obtaining in 1962–5. India and Hong Kong have accepted fixed quotas; Pakistan could in theory take a bigger share of the general quota, but this possibility has been ignored in projecting sales to Britain. Exports from Sterling Asia have therefore been projected to 1970 at the 1962–5 average and a small increase has been assumed thereafter in line with the projected rate of increase in United Kingdom cotton consumption.[2] It has further been assumed that, as a consequence of structural changes in the British cotton industry and the diminishing role of the merchant converter, the absolute level of grey cloth imports will decline, allowing Asian Sterling countries to supply a higher proportion of other cloths of greater unit value (see Table C3).

---

[1] The Indian Plan provides for a rise in exports of cotton yarn and cloth, valued at constant prices, of 45 per cent over the 1962–3 level by 1970–1; Pakistan's third Five-Year Plan provides for a 30 per cent rise between 1962–3 and 1969–70.

[2] See Appendix B1.

In North America, with more liberal import policies, imports from the developing countries may rise at or close to a rate of 5 per cent per annum. As there was a sharp but temporary cut-back in imports in 1960–1 (the normal base year for the projections), the assumed rates of growth—4·5 and 5 per cent—have been applied to imports in 1962–3 in order to derive the projection for 1975. Further, since United States import restrictions in effect bear most heavily on grey cloth, it has been assumed that imports of the latter will not rise much above the level of the early 1960s, and that any sizeable increase in the volume of Asian Sterling exports to North America must derive from a rapid rise in sales of other cloth.

Table C3. *Exports of cotton cloth from Asian Sterling countries to industrial areas, 1954–6, 1960–4 and projections for 1975*

	United Kingdom		North America		E.E.C.		Total	
	Grey cloth	Other	Grey cloth	Other	Grey cloth	Other	Grey cloth	Other
Value[a] (£ million)								
1954–6	9·6	0·6	0·5	0·5	0·2	—	10·2	1·0
1960–1	20·2	3·2	6·1	1·7	0·9	—	27·2	4·9
1962–3	17·8	3·9	8·7	3·6	0·8	0·1	27·3	7·5
1964	22·2	4·5	8·5	5·0	1·9	0·3	32·6	9·8
Imports from Sterling Asia (*percentage of total imports*)								
1964	58·9	17·1	41·4	11·9	7·4	0·2	38·9	8·2
Volume of exports (*thousand metric tons*)								
1960–1 estimates[b]	30·8	3·8	12·9	2·1	1·7	0·2	45·4	6·1
Adjusted base figures	30·8	5·4	18·4	4·1	3·7	1·8	52·9	11·3
1975: low	25·0	12·5	21·0	18·0	3·5	3·0	50·0	34·0
high	25·0	14·0	21·0	20·0	7·0	9·0	53·0	43·0

SOURCES: *Foreign Trade Statistical Bulletins*, O.E.E.C. and O.E.C.D.; *Hong Kong Trade Statistics*; *Monthly Trade Statistics of India*; *Foreign Trade Statistics of Pakistan*; N.I.E.S.R. estimates.

[a] Based on import data.
[b] Based on incomplete data from reporting countries.

In the E.E.C., quota restrictions cover only certain products from the developing countries and even here a high rate of increase is allowed for, while 'free' imports could rise very fast, judging by the surge in imports from Sterling Asia in the early 1960s. On the other hand, imports of grey cloth hardly could or would be permitted to rise at the same rate as in recent years, especially as by 1964 Sterling Asian cloth formed a significant percentage of total E.E.C. imports. At the worst, grey cloth imports should maintain the current level: this view underlies the low projection for 1975; at best they might be permitted to double. For other cloth a minimum rate of increase of 5 per cent per annum has been assumed, for the same reasons as in North America; but for the high projection the rate of increase achieved in 1960–4 was assumed to continue: there is still a very large market for the Sterling Asian countries to exploit, and internal cost trends in the E.E.C. are likely to work in their favour.

On these assumptions, the volume of cloth imports from Asian Sterling countries into their main markets in the industrial areas would by 1975 exceed the base level by about 30 per cent on the low projection and by 50 per cent on the high (the rise over 1960–1 is, of course, greater). Exports of yarn to industrial areas are insignificant outside the United Kingdom, whose imports from Sterling Asia have been assumed to remain constant.

Because of import substitution, the growth of import demand for yarn and cloth in the primary-producing countries may be much slower than in the industrial areas. The projections in Table C4 distinguish four areas among those countries that are currently net importers of cotton textiles: raw cotton producers in Asia and Africa, other Asia and Africa, Latin America, and the high-income primary-producers (Oceania and South Africa). The division of Asia and Africa into two has been made to allow for the fact that import substitution has generally proceeded more rapidly in countries that are raw-cotton producers than in other countries. For these two areas, and in the high-income group, the assumed rates of import substitution to 1975 are based on those observed since the war, modified in the light of recent experience. A similar assumption for Latin America implies, however, the emergence of a large export surplus during the 1970s, which, in view of the very big increase in supply required to meet domestic demand, appears unlikely. It seemed wiser to assume that a rough balance would be achieved between imports and exports.[1]

The ratios of net imports to consumption thus derived were applied to estimates of total consumption based on population forecasts and assumed consumption per head. F.A.O. data show a fairly steady rise in the latter of about one per cent per annum compound in the high-income group and one-half per cent in Latin America, implying a low income elasticity of demand. The income elasticity of demand in African and Asian countries is probably much higher, possibly close to

---

[1] It is, of course, possible that Latin America as a group will achieve a net export surplus. However, the Latin American countries would find it hard to establish themselves in overseas markets in competition with the low-labour-cost Asian suppliers; and their past performance suggests that they will not in fact be able to do so.

or more than unity in expenditure terms. In default of reliable data on population and income for these countries, this hypothesis cannot be tested. F.A.O. data, which by understating the rate of population growth may overestimate the rise in fibre consumption per head, show annual rates of increase close to 3 per cent for both cotton producers and others in Africa and Asia. This rate has therefore been taken as a likely maximum and one per cent annually as a likely minimum. High and low projections were not made for the other areas.

Table C4. *Net imports of cotton textiles into primary-producing countries, 1960–3 and projections for 1975*

	Africa and Asia[a]		Latin America	Oceania and South Africa	Total
	Raw-cotton producers	Other			
Cotton textile consumption (*kg. per head*)[b]					
1960–1	1·13	1·27	3·12	3·76	1·87
1962–3	1·21	1·22	2·99	3·58	1·83
1975: low	1·30	1·47	3·39	4·34	2·12
high	1·73	1·95	3·39	4·34	2·43
Net imports (*percentage of consumption*)					
1954–6	69·9	89·7	9·1	72·0	46·2
1960–1	54·9	80·0	5·7	66·5	40·7
1962–3	52·7	82·6	5·5	58·7	39·8
1975	18·5	65·5	—	45·0	27–30
Net imports of cotton textiles (*thousand metric tons*)[b]					
1960–1	102·5	354·5	38·3	84·3	579·6
1962–3	109·6	346·1	37·0	73·4	566·1
1975: low	56	485	—	92	633
high	75	644	—	92	811

SOURCES: As Table C1; *Per Caput Fiber Consumption Levels, 1948–1958*; *Monthly Bulletin of Agricultural Economics and Statistics*; *Per Caput Fiber Consumption 1962–1964*, F.A.O., Rome.

[a] Excluding countries that were net exporters of cotton textiles in 1960–1.

[b] Raw cotton equivalent.

The results of these calculations are, on the low projection, a rise of just under 10 per cent in total import demand expressed in raw cotton equivalent, and on the high a rise of 40 per cent. On the assumption that Sterling Asian countries maintain their share in the import market, this implies equivalent increases in the volume of total yarn and cloth sales to the developing countries. As in the case of exports to industrial areas, it appears that there is little scope for increasing sales of grey cloth (in this instance because of import substitution); any sizeable increase in the volume of trade implies a rise in the proportion of finished cloth in total exports and hence a rise in the average unit value of exports.

Applying the projections for industrial and other countries to data for 1960–1,[1] and making an allowance for differences in rates of growth for grey and other cloth, the rise in the value of Sterling Asia's exports is shown to be some 10 per cent greater than the projected increase in volume:

		Exports to		
		Industrial countries	Other countries	Total
Volume (*thousand metric tons*)	1960–1	55·4	105·6	161·0
(index, 1960–1 = 100)	1975: low	157	109	126
	high	181	140	154
Value (*£ million*)	1960–1	31·4	52·9	84·3
(index, 1960–1 = 100)	1975: low	177	110	135
	high	207	143	167

These projections imply that whereas finished cloth contributed just under 40 per cent of total cloth exports by volume in 1960–1, it must contribute between 50 and 60 per cent in 1975. Should the producing countries fail to adapt supply to the changing pattern of demand, not merely the value but also the volume of cloth exports might well be lower. On a more optimistic view, however, the projections may understate the rise in earnings, since no allowance is made for any general improvement in quality that is likely to be associated with a change in the composition of exports.

A further two-fifths of Sterling Asia's exports in this group (i.e. textiles and clothing) consists of clothing, almost entirely from Hong Kong. Here the prospects are still more uncertain because the trade is so poorly documented, and because during the past decade it has been going through a period of wholly exceptional growth that could well come to an end before 1975. Between 1954–6 and 1964, the value of world clothing exports[2] more than trebled; the increase in the volume of trade was nearly of the same order, judging by the movement of domestic clothing prices in the main producing countries. Over the same period, Hong Kong's exports rose more than fivefold, so that its share in world exports increased from 9 to 14 per cent.

Low wages, an abundant supply of readily trained labour, ease of

---

[1] The distribution of 1960–1 exports between industrial (United Kingdom, North America and E.E.C.) and other countries has been partially estimated. Published trade statistics for Sterling Asian countries show the direction of 70 to 90 per cent of exports only.

[2] Excluding exports from centrally planned and from primary-producing countries.

entry into the industry and concentration on relatively few standardized items promoted a massive increase in Hong Kong's output, probably more than 95 per cent of it for export, at extremely low prices. The Colony's cost advantage in this labour-intensive industry can be expected to persist. The growth of the labour force should be sufficient both to allow for still more very large increases in capacity and to prevent any rise in wages getting seriously out of line with wage movements in competing countries. Nor, outside certain sections of the knitting industry, are there as yet signs that the industrialized countries can, as they are attempting to do in cotton textiles, offset their labour-cost disadvantage by substituting capital. Hong Kong's cost advantage does not, however, operate effectively over the whole of trade in clothing. The organization of the industry, Hong Kong's distance from its main markets and from suppliers of some materials, and problems of quality and fashion cancel it out in certain lines. On the other hand, in respect of some types of clothing (cotton shirts, for example, and knitted gloves) Hong Kong may have saturated the potential market for its products. To sustain a rate of growth of trade at anything like the pace of the last ten years would depend on the development of new mass-consumption articles as well as the maintenance of low prices.

Demand for imported clothing originates chiefly in the industrial countries. Total clothing expenditure in these areas will, if the pattern of the last ten years persists, grow almost as fast in real terms as income.[1] Since the mid 1950s, however, imports have been rising several times as fast as expenditure in all the main importing areas save Canada. The most plausible interpretation of the import boom is that this represents a delayed reaction to postwar changes in costs and in the organization of production and marketing. (Inside Europe, the reduction of import duties has given added impetus to the growth of trade, but clearly this is no more than part of the story.) It seems reasonable to assume, therefore, that once the adjustment is completed, the rate of import growth will fall off rapidly, though it will not necessarily drop to the rate at which total clothing expenditure grows. A crude projection made in the light of this assumption suggests that the import market for clothing in industrial areas will by 1975 be about twice as large as in 1964.

Hong Kong's share of imports into some of the main importing areas is already very large. It would be straining credulity to assume it can raise its shares in the British, American and West German markets much beyond their present level, the more so as sales of cotton clothing

[1] Published estimates of the income elasticity of demand for clothing in industrial countries range from 0·7 to 1·2 (see A. Maizels, *Industrial Growth and World Trade*). National accounts data for the main industrial areas for the years 1955 to 1964 indicate that it is 0·9 or higher in the United States, Britain and the E.E.C.

are restricted by quota under the Geneva Textile Arrangements. Its share in Canadian and Scandinavian imports is also showing signs of stabilizing. In other European countries—the rest of E.E.C. in particular —there may be considerable scope for Hong Kong to supply a growing proportion of the market. Thus it can probably raise its exports to the industrial countries as a group rather faster than their total imports rise. In the developing areas, however, though Hong Kong may equally be able to increase its share of the import market, expansion is being held in check by import substitution. Exports to the rest of the world have been and are likely to continue growing much *less* rapidly than sales to industrial areas.

Table C5. *Hong Kong's exports of clothing, 1954–6 to 1964*

						Rates of growth	
						1954–6 to 1960–1	1960–1 to 1964
	1954–6	1957–9	1960–1	1962–3	1964		
			(£ million)			(% per annum)	
Exports from:							
world[a]	219	312	451	569	714	14	14
Hong Kong	19[b]	36[b]	59	79	101	23	17
Hong Kong as percentage of world exports	*8·6*	*11·5*	*13·0*	*13·9*	*14·2*	··	··
Imports from Hong Kong to							
United Kingdom	4·0	7·8	14·9	25·5	33·4	27	26
North America	0·8	10·7	21·9	24·6	32·5	83	12
E.E.C. and Scandinavia[c]	0·5	3·8	9·9	18·0	28·0	70	35
			(% of total imports)				
United Kingdom	34·1	36·3	35·1	44·2	47·5	··	··
North America	1·4	11·7	17·4	15·8	17·4	··	··
E.E.C. and Scandinavia[c]	0·9[b]	4·3[b]	6·6	7·8	8·9	··	··

SOURCES: *Foreign Trade Statistical Bulletins*, O.E.E.C. and O.E.C.D.; *Yearbook of International Trade Statistics*, United Nations, New York; *Hong Kong Trade Statistics*; N.I.E.S.R. estimates.

[a] North America, O.E.C.D. member countries in Western Europe except Spain, Japan and Hong Kong.

[b] Partly estimated.   [c] Scandinavia: Denmark, Norway and Sweden.

In total, the growth of world import demand should be such that Hong Kong can about double the 1964 level of sales by 1975. This projection is consistent with what little is known of the Colony's ability to raise output. In terms of 1960–1 prices, therefore, Hong Kong's 1975 clothing exports are projected at about £195 million on the low assumption and £230 million on the high. The annual average rate of increase is put at 6·2 to 7·8 per cent from 1964 to 1975.

Exports of clothing from India and Pakistan were very small until 1962, less than £1 million annually in all. In the following two years, both raised their exports sharply, to about £3·2 million and £0·7 million respectively. The bulk of India's trade still goes to neighbouring countries in the developing areas, but it is now beginning to exploit the market potential of the industrial countries. Clothing imports from India into industrial areas rose from under £0·3 million in 1962 to nearly £1 million in 1964; imports from Pakistan rose from about £100,000 to £450,000.

These changes could mark the first stages in the development of an export trade in clothing similar to Hong Kong's. India and Pakistan may be presumed to have a significant labour-cost advantage in exporting to industrial areas, even though it is probably less than Hong Kong's because labour is less adaptable; but they appear to lack the entrepreneurial talent that is one of the reasons for Hong Kong's success. Moreover, with a large home market to exploit and a much wider range of choice in industrial development, capital and talent seem likely to prefer other industries; while their preference will, unless there are fundamental changes in policy, be reinforced by government measures to promote import substitution and the development of heavy industries. While, therefore, the rate of growth of clothing exports may be very high indeed—they might well be ten times as large in 1975 as in 1960–1 —the absolute value of export earnings is likely to remain relatively small.

These considerations hold for a number of other textile industries newly established in India and Pakistan. In some instances (synthetics are the outstanding case) there is the additional problem of finding large capital sums. The traditional textile industries—coir manufactures and handmade carpets in India, carpets in Pakistan—are, on the other hand, unlikely to achieve a high rate of export growth because demand is rising slowly in the industrial areas, which are the main markets for these items.

Steel, machinery and metal manufactures

Trade in the second major class of O.S.A. exports of manufactures (steel, machinery and vehicles, and miscellaneous metal manufactures) is a good deal more diversified in origin and composition than the Area's trade in textiles and clothing. Five out of the six main O.S.A. exporters have developed relatively large sales. Australia and South Africa are principally exporters of iron and steel and machinery; Hong Kong concentrates on light metal and electrical goods; Ireland is primarily an exporter of household equipment and light electrical goods. India has barely initiated exports in this group, from which it hopes to gain so much: steel is already an important though variable item; light machinery provides about two-thirds of the balance. These differences in the composition and character of trade, and in the stage and type of industrial development they reflect, will be the main determinants of future export growth. It may reasonably be assumed that world demand for all the products concerned will expand sufficiently fast to permit the O.S.A. countries to sell abroad everything they can produce at competitive prices.

The argument that future exports will be governed more by domestic developments than by external demand holds good even of those two countries, Australia and South Africa, with a fairly sophisticated industrial base and a correspondingly diversified trade. This point can be established by comparing their experience during the past decade. Both find their most important export outlet for machinery, vehicles and metal manufactures in a neighbouring country, Australia in New Zealand and South Africa in Rhodesia, where, in addition to the natural advantage conferred by geography, each enjoys preferential tariff treatment. But whereas New Zealand's imports from all sources have risen swiftly, Rhodesia's have stagnated. Thus South African exports to Rhodesia were £16 million in 1954–6 and £17·5 million in 1960–1 but fell to £12·5 million in 1962–3; while Australian sales to New Zealand in the corresponding trade years were £23 million, £22·5 million and £40 million. Australia benefited, moreover, from the exceptionally high rate of growth of import demand in a number of South-East Asian markets, particularly since 1960; the corresponding markets for South African goods in central and east Africa were far less buoyant.

Clearly, had Rhodesian import demand continued to rise in the early 1960s, South Africa would have stood a much better chance. Even so, it might have been unable to raise sales. The 1960–1 peak in exports of machinery, vehicles and metal manufactures coincided with a period of slack domestic demand. When the level of internal activity rose, goods were diverted to the home market despite the big simultaneous rise in output. In short, South African exports are to a considerable degree the result of a temporary surplus of domestic supply over demand, rather than an established trade. Australia, on the other hand, has sufficient capacity in many lines to raise export and home sales simultaneously. Moreover, and this demonstrates its ability to compete overseas, it has been able to develop a much bigger volume of sales to distant markets in which it has no special position, witness the far slighter concentration on its neighbouring market. By 1962–3 Australia was sending 37 per cent of exports to New Zealand (as against 57 per cent in 1954–6), 16 per cent to industrial areas, principally Britain and the United States of America, and 47 per cent to the rest of the world. South African exports to Rhodesia were 60 per cent of a much smaller total in 1962–3, exports to industrial areas barely 4 per cent and exports elsewhere 35 per cent.

Table C6. *Exports of steel, machinery and metal manufactures[a]*
from selected overseas Sterling countries, 1957–9 to 1964
and projections for 1975

	Value of exports				Main items in 1964	Projected growth rates 1960–1 to 1975[b]	
	1957–9	1960–1	1962–3	1964		Low	High
	(£ million)				(% of total value)	(% per annum)	
Australia	41	52	59	69	Machinery (36); iron and steel (27); motor vehicles (19)	6	7·5
South Africa	33	41	39	38	Iron and steel (53); machinery (31); motor vehicles (4)	4·5	5·5
Hong Kong	15	19	26	31	Metal manufactures[c] (48); transistor radios (20)	10	12
India	3	12	9	18	Iron and steel (46)	13	15
Ireland	5	7	9	16	Machinery (51); transport equipment (28)	12	14
TOTAL	97	131	142	172	—	8	9

SOURCES: *Yearbook of International Trade Statistics,* United Nations, New York; *Hong Kong Trade Statistics.*

[a] SITC 67, 69, 71, 72, 73 and, for Hong Kong only, 81.
[b] In volume terms.   [c] Including SITC 81.

In iron and steel the situation is apparently reversed, with South Africa showing a much more diversified trade pattern and being able in consequence to offset the effects of a decline in African demand by selling to Europe and the United States. In 1962–3, 64 per cent of exports went to industrial areas compared with 19 per cent to Rhodesia and 16 per cent elsewhere; 1954–6 sales were in the proportion of 24 per cent, 60 per cent and 16 per cent. In the trade years 1962–3, Australia sent 46 per cent of iron and steel to New Zealand (as compared with 33 to 36 per cent in earlier years) and 19 per cent to industrial countries where in 1960–1 it had sent 38 per cent and in 1954–6 31 per cent. In this instance, it was Australia that was caught by excessive dependence on one market—Japan—when a temporary reduction in pig iron imports sharply reduced Australian sales in 1962–3. However, if this special factor is left out of account, Australian steel exports have grown steadily and the direction of trade has been increasingly diversified-South Africa's success stems from the development of a highly special. ized trade in pig iron and ferro-alloys, which comprise the bulk of its non-African exports. In general, it tends to export goods at a lower stage of processing than does the Australian steel industry.

Australia's proven ability to compete in world markets, if only on a small scale as yet, supports the generally accepted view that exports of steel and engineering products will rise swiftly over the coming decade. The basis of this expansion is Australia's comparative advantage in steel production. It is true that even now capacity is barely adequate to meet domestic demand and that, because of the length of time required to create new capacity, domestic demand may still from time to time cut into export supplies. This was one of the points made by the Vernon Committee in their review of Australian export prospects.[1] Given the necessary increase in capacity, however, there is no impediment to the expansion of steel exports at highly competitive prices.[2]

The future of machinery and vehicle exports is more problematical. As is well known, the small scale of much Australian production keeps costs high. (The level of import duties is indicative of the inability of many Australian engineering firms to compete with overseas suppliers; domestic steel supplies, on the other hand, hold their own against imports without benefit of tariff protection.) Australian subsidiaries of international companies often have a limited export franchise. Shortages of skilled labour have been and still are a problem. However, there is nothing in all this to prevent a big rise in exports; and Australia is exceptionally well placed to supply developing countries in South-East Asia with the capital goods they must import, whilst the Australia–New Zealand Free Trade Agreement will give it a still firmer grip on its most important market.

No official export projections have been made for steel and machinery alone, but since they form so high a proportion of Australia's exports of manufactures, the rate at which they grow must be close to the average. The Vernon Committee quoted a target growth rate for all Australian exports of manufactures of 7·5 per cent per annum compound; an earlier report by the Committee for Economic Development of Australia (C.E.D.A.)[3] concluded that a rate of at least 6 per cent would be feasible;

[1] *Report of the Committee of Economic Enquiry*, Canberra, May 1965.

[2] Some idea of Australia's cost advantage as a steel producer may be gained by reference to the steel price data quoted in Appendix F of the Vernon Committee Report. The price of structural steel per ton in domestic markets in 1964 was: Australia—£A42.8.3; United Kingdom—£A49.6.5; United States—£A55.15.0; Japan—£A50.14.10.

[3] *Australia's Export Potential*, Committee for Economic Development of Australia, Melbourne, 1964.

others have assumed still higher rates because these figures are so much lower than the rates recently achieved. This latter view fails, however, to allow for the almost inevitable slackening in the rate of export growth after the first entry into export markets, and for the boost given to sales by the introduction of export incentives in recent years. A straightforward projection of past trends, making allowance for a declining rate of growth and for the erratic behaviour of steel exports to Japan, suggests that the best estimate is close to the Vernon Committee and the C.E.D.A. figures; rates approximating to these have accordingly been adopted in the projections. Machinery and motor vehicle exports can be expected to grow rather more swiftly, but steel (assuming no recovery in sales to Japan) and other products at rates below the average for the group as a whole.

South Africa is hoping to achieve rates of export growth in this class as good as or better than Australia's, according to the export projections in its Economic Development Programme,[1] and optimism has been encouraged by the recovery of export sales in 1965; but a number of factors suggest that these will do less well. The limited extent of existing export markets for engineering products implies that costs are less competitive than Australia's, except in certain specialized lines; and the greater South African emphasis on import substitution will not help, even if it does not hinder, cost reduction. South African motor vehicle producers reckon that domestically manufactured components are on average 45 per cent more expensive than comparable imported items;[2] the effect of this in combination with government pressure to increase the South African content of locally produced cars is sufficiently obvious. South African industry has the same problems as Australian in regard to scale of production, it has the same difficulty in securing skilled labour, and it is likely to find other problems more intractable. (Foreign capital may be presumed to be less readily available to South African industry than to Australian.) Until South Africa has achieved both a real surplus of capacity over domestic demand and a more competitive level of costs, it is unlikely to match up to the rate of export growth foreseen in Australia.

In projecting South African exports in this class, other than steel exports, an average annual increase of 4 to 5 per cent has been assumed outside the Rhodesian market. Sales to Rhodesia seem likely to grow quite a lot more slowly, bringing the average down to about 3 per cent against the mean rate of 6 per cent assumed in the Development Programme. Exports of iron and steel can reasonably be expected to do

[1] *Economic Development Programme for the Republic of South Africa, 1964–1969.*
[2] S. G. Orpen, 'Local Content Scheme for Motor Industry', *Financial Times*, Supplement on South Africa, 26th April 1966.

better than was envisaged in the Programme; by 1964 they were already close to its low projection for 1969. Since so high a proportion of the total consists of ferro-alloys supplied to steel industries in advanced countries, they have been projected at rates close to those calculated by Professor Balassa for iron ore exports from developing countries.[1] For the group as a whole, therefore, exports in 1975 are put at a little under and over twice the 1960-1 figure, on the low and high projections respectively.

Hong Kong's success as an exporter of metal and electrical products derives, as might be expected, from its low labour costs: with few exceptions, its exports in this group are highly labour-intensive. Among metal goods, the most important single products—torches and enamel-ware—are exports of comparatively long standing, which do not have much potential for growth (apart from the secular increase in sales associated with rising world import demand) because markets have been more or less saturated. With increasing diversification, however, exports in this group have risen steadily, as have sales of light machinery, electric consumer goods, steel and ships. Unusually for Hong Kong, this latter group of industries was initially developed to serve the home market and a high proportion of exports goes to developing countries. Thus it is interesting that their export performance has been no less good than that of many export-oriented industries.

Finally we come to the exports of Hong Kong's leading growth industry—transistor radios—which shows the pattern of very rapid development normally expected from the Colony, based initially on sales to the preferential British market and the United States, and now expanding to embrace markets in Western Europe, South-East Asia and Africa. If trade continues to follow the normal pattern for Hong Kong, the rate of export growth will decrease sharply within the next few years, but there is nothing to indicate when the turning point will come. Exports of transistors have been projected on the assumption that the growth rate will begin to decline in the second half of the 1960s and fall steeply away after 1970. Exports of all other items have been projected in line with recent trends. This gives a total for the group in 1975 some four to five times as large as in 1960-1, and between two and three times as large as for 1964.

Of all the O.S.A. exporters of steel and engineering goods, India has the most ambitious plans for the future, and its prospects are the most difficult to assess. Its exports of steel have fluctuated widely in recent years in response to changes in the supply–demand balance in the Indian market and provide no guidance to future performance. Exports of engineering products have risen regularly and steeply, but they are

[1] Bela Balassa, *Trade Prospects for Developing Countries.*

at present so tiny in relation to domestic output that here again the past is a poor guide to the future.

India, like Australia and South Africa, should have a comparative advantage as an exporter of steel and steel-based products, deriving from its raw material resources. It is also under strong compulsion to exploit this advantage to the full, since so many of its traditional exports are faced with inelastic demand overseas. But the problems of achieving a volume of sales commensurate with its natural export potential are formidable; here, even more than in the textile industry, the growth of Indian exports is likely to be retarded by the pressure of home demand on scarce supplies, by the high cost of investment, and by low labour productivity.

Manmohan Singh in his analysis of prospects for Indian exports of engineering products has attributed Indian industry's poor performance during the 1950s to the lack of any incentive to export 'when there is a large and growing demand for all types of engineering goods in the country'.[1] Add to this that imports are severely restricted and domestic prices are above world levels, and it becomes plain that producers can normally secure a higher rate of profit by selling exclusively to the home market. Export incentives and devaluation have done something to change the situation by increasing the profitability of exports since the late 1950s, but the twin problems of high costs and prices and inadequate capacity to generate a surplus for export remain essentially unaltered. Even where export targets have been specifically related to estimates of future capacity and home demand, which is by no means always the case, it is open to question whether the desired level of capacity can be achieved and whether the growth of domestic demand has been underrated as so often in the past.

The Indian Perspective Planning Division has set up targets for steel exports of 500,000 tons in 1970/1 and 1·5 million tons in 1975/6.[2] These figures were related to estimates of capacity of 20 million and 31 million ingot tons respectively. The *Memorandum on the Fourth Plan* allows only for capacity of 16·5 million tons in 1970/1 and it is doubtful if even this level can be reached. Thus by 1975 capacity seems unlikely to exceed 20 million to 25 million tons. Assuming that the Perspective Planning Division have in this instance overestimated the growth of demand because they are relating it to a rate of economic growth unlikely to be achieved, India might be able to produce some 500,000 tons for export in 1975, though in the light of past experience this should probably be taken as the maximum possible. The Perspective Plan is even more sanguine with respect to exports of machinery and metal products,

---

[1] Manmohan Singh, *op. cit.*

[2] *Notes on Perspective of Development, India: 1960–61 to 1975–76.*

proposing a figure for 1975 about thirteen times as large as exports in 1964. To achieve even half as much would require the rate of increase in exports recorded from 1958 to 1964 to be sustained year in, year out, whereas a decline in the rate of growth appears far more likely. So, in line with expectations about steel exports, exports of machinery, vehicle and metal manufactures have been assumed at best to reach a figure that is about one-third of the Perspective Planning target. Even so, the projections for the group as a whole appear to be on the optimistic side, for they imply exports four to four and a half times as large in 1975 as in 1964.

Ireland, too, has ambitious targets written into its development pro-gramme but here the potential may have been underestimated. The *Second Programme for Economic Expansion*[1] proposed an annual average rate of increase in industrial exports over the years 1960 to 1970 of 9·3 per cent. Industrial exports are defined as including processed food-stuffs, so that the rate implied for engineering products is presumably rather higher. Certainly engineering exports have far exceeded the rate set for all industrial goods, very nearly reaching the 1970 target by 1964. It is true that the 1964 figure was somewhat exceptional, including abnormally large deliveries of ships, but the growth of machinery and metal manufactures exports has been little if at all lower. Generous incentives to foreign investors have promoted rapid development of new capacity and almost as generous export incentives have provided strong inducements to export, while tariff reductions have discouraged the creation of purely import-substituting industries. Export efforts so far have been mostly concentrated on the United Kingdom market, but a start has been made on exploiting openings in continental Europe and North America. A combination of factors—rising output utilizing Irish labour and foreign capital, the strong official emphasis on raising produc-tivity and cutting costs, Ireland's geographical closeness to markets in the industrial areas, and the possibility that it will join an enlarged European Community before 1975—all together argue in favour of a continuation of high rates of export growth. Past exports have accord-ingly been projected to 1975, with allowance for a slackening in the rate of growth after the first burst of export expansion, to give a figure for metals and engineering exports in 1975 two to three times as large as the 1964 figure, and five to six times as large as for 1960–1.

Summary of projections

The remaining classes of O.S.A. exports of manufactures may be dealt with briefly. Exports of chemicals, apart from traditional items such as essential oils, are likely to grow very rapidly. Much new capacity

[1] *Second Programme for Economic Expansion*, Stationery Office, Dublin, July 1964.

is being developed, based in a number of cases on cheap raw material supplies, for instance natural gas in Pakistan; and world import demand is probably growing faster in this than in any other class of manufactures. For the main O.S.A. exporters, chemical exports proper have been projected to 1975 in line with the past trend of growth, which has been fairly regular. Exports of essential oils and of dyeing and tanning materials have been separately projected. Both are sold principally to the industrial countries. For the former, which are chiefly used in the manufacture of perfume and other luxuries, an income elasticity of 1·25 has been assumed. Vegetable-based dyeing or tanning extracts are likely to suffer increasing substitution by synthetics, and no increase in trade over the 1960–1 level has been allowed for.

Similar projections in line with recent trends have been made for exports of miscellaneous finished goods, though in this class such a method of estimation is more open to question. It covers a very wide range of products, mostly of a fairly labour-intensive character but varying greatly in the degree of skill required in production. It is particularly hard to assess future potential in Hong Kong, whose most important exports in this group are rubber footwear, toys and plastic flowers, the rest ranging from cameras to cottage-industry products. In general, it seemed best to assume that the rate of export growth will fall steeply from the high levels recorded in recent years. For toys, however, a more gradual decline has been assumed. Toy manufacture is particularly well suited to local conditions, overseas demand is buoyant and the Colony has a relatively small share in world markets; so this might well become another major industry for Hong Kong.

The pace and pattern of industrial development and the trend of past exports suggest that Ireland and Australia, like Hong Kong, will be able to raise exports rapidly in this class. But the two Asian countries that might be expected to emulate Hong Kong's performance—India and Pakistan—are apparently held back in this sector, as in the clothing trade, by lack of entrepreneurial skill to exploit a possible labour-cost advantage. Exports are small and have grown comparatively slowly. There is no reason to suppose that they will do very much better in future.

Of the remaining exports of manufactures from the O.S.A., paper and wood products have been separately projected. In the former case, it appears likely that sales will be directed chiefly to nearby primary-producing countries where the income elasticity of demand is high— about 1·5 according to F.A.O. projections of paper demand in developing areas. The problem for the O.S.A. countries will be not so much to find markets as to expand supplies, since their own requirements are growing fast. Wood products, chiefly veneers and plywoods, are exported principally to industrial countries. Consumption in these countries is rising sharply, and it is expected that, despite tariff discrimination against processed and in favour of unprocessed timber, imports will rise faster still. The growth of exports of other miscellaneous manufactures has been estimated in the light of recent performance.

Table C 7. *Exports of manufactures from Overseas Sterling Area countries, 1960–4 and projections for 1975*

	Rates of growth			Value of exports			
	1960–1 to 1964	1960–1 to 1975		1960–1	1964	1975	
		Low	High			Low	High
Main exporters	(% *per annum*)			(£ *million*)			
Textiles and clothing:							
Asian countries	10·2	5·4	6·9	175	245	380	460
Others	9·7	7·3	8·6	18	25	50	60
Steel, machinery and metal manufactures	8·2	7·8	9.4	131	174	380	465
Chemicals	9·7	8·3	9·8	35	49	115	140
Other finished goods	13·4	7·4	8·2	68	106	190	215
Other	8·5	5·5	7·7	28	36	60	80
Total, main exporters[a]	10·0	6·7	8·1	455	635	1,170	1,410
Other countries	16·1	7·1	8·6	37	62	100	120
TOTAL, O.S.A.[b]	10·5	6·8	8·1	492	697	1,265	1,530

SOURCES: As for Table C 1.

[a] Hong Kong, India, Australia, South Africa, Ireland, Pakistan.
[b] As in Table C 1 but excluding Malaya, for which data prior to 1964 are not available.

Exports from minor suppliers, other than of steel, machinery and chemical products, have been assumed to grow at similar rates to those projected for exports from the six main countries as a group, adjusted upwards for some commodities in the light of large increases secured in exports from 1960–1 to 1964. Apart from Rhodesia, no minor exporter appears well placed to develop trade in steel or engineering products, and whereas Rhodesian steel exports have been assumed to rise in line with world import demand, a small increase only has been allowed for other countries. The growth of chemical sales by these countries is likely to be inhibited by the character of their existing exports and by the low stage of development of the chemical industry. In this class too, therefore, a small increase only has been allowed.

Taking the O.S.A. as a whole, the future for exports of manufactures looks extremely promising, with total sales by 1975 projected at rather more than two and a half to three times the 1960–1 level. The gains will, however, be unevenly distributed, tending to be least in those countries where they are most needed. India, for example, appears likely to do less well than any other country save South Africa in terms of the rate of increase in exports from 1960–1 to 1975; and if it fails to develop its sales of steel and engineering products it will do poorly indeed in raising foreign exchange revenue.

These various projections of exports of manufactures from the overseas Sterling countries have necessarily been based on extrapolations of current trends, development plans and, where possible, on estimates of the probable future growth in world demand. A thorough analysis of the export potential of these countries, and particularly of the developing Sterling countries, would necessitate also a realistic assessment of the growth of their physical production capacity. Indeed, the most cursory inspection of the Development Plan of any country that hopes to raise its exports of manufactures to a significant level makes it clear how much the future volume of exports depends on the construction of new industrial plant.

LIST OF WORKS CITED

I. OFFICIAL PUBLICATIONS

(1) INTERNATIONAL

COMMUNAUTÉ ECONOMIQUE EUROPÉENNE

Le Marché commun des produits agricoles: Perspectives '1970', Serié Agriculture 10 (Bruxelles, 1963).

FOOD AND AGRICULTURE ORGANIZATION OF THE UNITED NATIONS

Agricultural Commodities—Projections for 1970, Special Supplement to *F.A.O. Commodity Review, 1962* (Rome, 1962).
Agricultural Commodities—Projections for 1975 and 1985 (Rome, 1967).
Cocoa Statistics (Rome, quarterly).
Coconut Situation (Rome, twice yearly).
Commodity Review (Rome, annual).
Demand for Jute Goods—Post-war Trends and Prospects for the Sixties, CCP: Jute 64/6 (Rome, 1964).
Jute Utilisation in the United Kingdom and the E.E.C., by T. S. Robertson, CCP: Jute 66/6 (Rome, 1966).
Monthly Bulletin of Agricultural Economics and Statistics (Rome).
Per Caput Fiber Consumption Levels, 1948–1958, Commodity Bulletin no. 31 (Rome, 1960).
Per Caput Fiber Consumption Levels, 1962–1964, COa/66 (Rome, 1966).
Post-war Trends in the Production of Jute, Kenaf and allied Fibers, by D. Hamilton-Russell, CCP: Jute/64/8 (Rome, July 1964).
Production Yearbook (Rome).
Statistical Supplement: Jute Goods available for Home Use, CCP/Jute, Ad hoc 62/4/Add. 1 (Rome, 1962).
Synthetics and their Effects on Agricultural Trade, Commodity Bulletin no. 38 (Rome, 1964).
Trade Yearbook (Rome).
Trends and Forces of World Sugar Consumption, by A. Viton and F. Pignalosa, (Rome, 1961).
World Apparel Fiber Consumption (Rome, 1965).

INTERNATIONAL BANK FOR RECONSTRUCTION AND DEVELOPMENT

Supplementary Financial Measures: a Study requested by the United Nations Conference on Trade and Development—1964 (Washington, December 1965).

INTERNATIONAL MONETARY FUND

Balance of Payments Yearbook (Washington).
International Financial Statistics (Washington, monthly).

ORGANIZATION FOR ECONOMIC CO-OPERATION AND DEVELOPMENT

The Chemical Industry (Paris, annual).
Development Assistance Efforts and Policies, 1966 Review (Paris, 1967).
The Flow of Financial Resources to Less-developed Countries, 1956–1963 (Paris, 1964).
Food Consumption in the O.E.C.D. Countries (Paris, November 1963).
The Hides, Skins and Footwear Industry (Paris, annual).
Income and Price Elasticity of Demand for Milk and Milk Products, by J. A. C. Brown (Paris, 1962).

Industrial Statistics, 1900–1962 (Paris, 1964).
The Non-ferrous Metals Industry (Paris, annual since 1962).
Statistical Bulletins: Commodity Trade, Series B (Paris, quarterly).
Statistical Bulletins: Foreign Trade, Series C (Paris, quarterly).
Statistics of Non-ferrous Metals (Paris, annual up to 1961).

UNITED NATIONS
Conference on Trade and Development
Final Act, Annex A. IV. 2 (New York, 1964).
Department of Economic and Social Affairs
Provisional Report on World Population Prospects, as assessed in 1963 (New York, 1964).
Studies in Long-term Economic Projections for the World Economy: Aggregative Models (New York, 1964).
A Study of Industrial Growth (New York, 1963).
World Economic Survey (New York, annual).
Economic Commission for Africa *and* Food and Agriculture Organization of the United Nations
Report of the UN/ECA/FAO Economic Survey Mission on the Economic Development of Zambia (Ndola, 1964).
Economic Commission for Asia and the Far East
Economic Survey of Asia and the Far East (Bangkok, annual).
General Assembly
Resolution 1522 (XV) (New York, 1960).
Statistical Office
Commodity Trade Statistics, Statistical Papers, D (New York, quarterly).
Monthly Bulletin of Statistics (New York).
Yearbook of International Trade Statistics (New York).
Yearbook of National Accounts Statistics (New York).

(2) NATIONAL

AUSTRALIA

Committee of Economic Enquiry
Report of the Committee of Economic Enquiry, 2 vols. (Canberra, May 1965). The 'Vernon Report'.
Commonwealth Bureau of Census and Statistics
Monthly Review of Business Statistics (Canberra).
Commonwealth Treasury
The Meaning and Measurement of Economic Growth, Supplement to *Treasury Information Bulletin*, November 1964 (Canberra).

BURMA

Ministry of National Planning
Second Four-Year Plan, 1961/2–1964/5 (Rangoon, 1961).

CANADA

Dominion Bureau of Statistics
Census of Manufactures, Shoe Factories and Boot and Shoe Finding Manufacturers (Ottawa, annual.)

CEYLON

Department of National Planning
Ten-Year Plan, 1959–68 (Colombo, 1959).
Short-term Implementation Programme (Colombo, 1962).
Ministry of Planning and Economic Affairs
The Development Programme, 1966–7 (Colombo, 1966).

GHANA

Office of the Planning Commission
Seven Year Development Plan, 1963/4–1969/70 (Accra, 1964).

HONG KONG

Department of Commerce and Industry
Hong Kong Trade Statistics (monthly).

ICELAND

Government of Iceland
Economic Programme, 1963–66 (Reykjavik, 1963).

INDIA

Department of Commercial Intelligence and Statistics
Monthly Statistics of Foreign Trade (Calcutta).
Planning Commission.
The Third Five-Year Plan, 1960–61 to 1965–66 (New Delhi, 1961).
Notes on Perspective of Development, India: 1960–61 to 1975–76 (New Delhi, 1964).

IRELAND, REPUBLIC OF

Department of Finance
Second Programme for Economic Expansion, Part II (Dublin, Stationery Office, July 1964).

JAMAICA

Ministry of Development and Welfare
Five Year Independence Plan 1963–68 (Kingston, 1963).

KENYA

Government of Kenya
Development Plan, 1964–1970 (Nairobi, 1964).
Ministry of Finance and Economic Planning
The Growth of the Economy, 1954–1962 (Nairobi, 1963).

MALAWI

Ministry of Finance
Quarterly Digest of Statistics (Zomba).

MALAYA

Economic Planning Unit of the Prime Minister's Department
Second Five-Year Plan, 1961–65 (Kuala Lumpur, 1961).
Interim Review of Development in Malaya under the Second Five-Year Plan (Kuala Lumpur, 1963).

NIGERIA

Federation of Nigeria
National Development Plan, 1962–68 (Lagos, 1961).

PAKISTAN

Central Statistical Office
Foreign Trade Statistics of Pakistan (Karachi, monthly).
Government of Pakistan
The Second Five-Year Plan (1960 to 1965) (Karachi, 1960).
Outline of the Third Five-Year Plan (1965–70) (Karachi, 1964).

RHODESIA

Central Statistical Office
Monthly Digest of Statistics (Salisbury).

SOUTH AFRICA

Department of Planning
Economic Development Programme for the Republic of South Africa, 1964–1969 (Capetown, 1964).

Tanzania

Ministry of Economic Affairs
Tanganyika: Five Year Plan for Economic and Social Development, 1964–1969 (Dar-es-Salaam, 1964).

Trinidad and Tobago

National Planning Commission
Second Five-Year Plan, 1964–68 (Port of Spain, 1965).

Uganda

Planning Commission
Work for Progress—the Second Five-Year Plan, 1966–71 (Entebbe, 1966).

United Kingdom

Board of Trade
The Commonwealth and the Sterling Area: Statistical Abstract (London, H.M. Stationery Office, annual).
Central Statistical Office
Annual Abstract of Statistics, (London, H.M. Stationery Office).
United Kingdom Balance of Payments 1966 (London, H.M. Stationery Office, 1966).
Commonwealth Economic Committee (now Commodities Division of the Commonwealth Secretariat)
Dairy Produce (London, H.M. Stationery Office, annual).
Fruit (London, H.M. Stationery Office, annual).
Grain Crops (London, H.M. Stationery Office, annual).
Hides and Skins (London, H.M. Stationery Office, quarterly).
Industrial Fibres (London, H.M. Stationery Office, annual).
Meat (London, H.M. Stationery Office, annual).
Plantation Crops (London, H.M. Stationery Office, annual).
Tropical Products Quarterly (London, H.M. Stationery Office).
Vegetable Oils and Oilseeds (London, H.M. Stationery Office, annual).
Wool Intelligence (London, H.M. Stationery Office, monthly).
World Trade in Wool and Wool Textiles, 1952–1963 (London, H.M. Stationery Office, 1965).
Department of Economic Affairs
The National Plan, Cmnd. 2764 (London, H.M. Stationery Office, 1965).
Ministry of Agriculture, Fisheries and Food
Domestic Food Consumption and Expenditure, 1962 (London, H.M. Stationery Office, 1964).
Overseas Geological Surveys
Statistical Summary of the Mineral Industry (London, H.M. Stationery Office, annual).

United States

Department of Agriculture
United Kingdom: Projected Level of Demand, Supply and Imports of Farm Products in 1965 and 1975 (Washington, 1962).
Department of Commerce
1958 Census of Manufactures (Washington, Government Printing Office, 1961).
1963 Census of Manufactures (Washington, Government Printing Office, 1966).

Zambia

Central Statistical Office
Monthly Digest of Statistics (Lusaka).
Office of National Development and Planning
First National Development Plan (Lusaka, July 1966).

II. BOOKS, ARTICLES AND SERIAL PUBLICATIONS

ALFRED, A. M. *U.K. Textiles—a Growth Industry* (Manchester Statistical Society, November 1965).

AMERICAN CARPET INSTITUTE. *Basic Facts about the Carpet and Rug Industry, 1964* (New York, 1964).

ASSOCIATION OF EUROPEAN JUTE INDUSTRIES. *Statistical Yearbook of the European Jute Industry* (Paris).

BALASSA, B. *Trade Prospects for Developing Countries* (Homewood, Illinois, Richard D. Irwin, 1964).
  'Tariff Protection in Industrial Countries: an Evaluation', *Journal of Political Economy*, vol. 73, no. 6, December 1965.

BRUTON, H. J. and BOSE, S. R. *The Pakistan Export Bonus Scheme* (Karachi, Institute of Development Economics, 1963).

CHENERY, H. B. 'Patterns of Industrial Growth', *American Economic Review*, vol. 50, no. 4, September 1960.

CHENERY, H. B. and BRUNO, M. 'Development Alternatives in an Open Economy: the Case of Israel', *Economic Journal*, vol. 72, no. 285, March 1962.

CHENERY, H. B. and MacEWEN, A. 'Optimal Patterns of Growth and Aid: the Case of Pakistan', *Pakistan Development Review*, Summer 1966.

CHENERY, H. B. and STROUT, A. M. 'Foreign Assistance and Economic Development', *American Economic Review*, vol. 56, no. 4, September 1966.

CLARK, R. 'The Economic Determinants of Jute Production', F.A.O. *Monthly Bulletin of Agricultural Economics and Statistics*, September 1957.

COMMITTEE FOR ECONOMIC DEVELOPMENT OF AUSTRALIA. *Australia's Export Potential* (Melbourne, 1964).

DALY, R. F. *Agriculture in the Years Ahead*, Southern Agricultural Workers' Conference (Atlanta, Georgia, February 1963).

DUPREZ, C., KESTENS, P. and POPOVIC, Z. 'Les importations de biens en provenance des pays sous-développés et la capacité d'importer que ces pays en tirent—Essai de prévision pour 1970', *Cahiers Economiques de Bruxelles*, no. 28, 4ᵉ trimestre, 1965.

GREEN, R. W. 'Commonwealth Preference: United Kingdom Customs Duties and Tariff Preference on Imports from the Preference Area', *Board of Trade Journal*, 31st December 1965.

HAIG, B. D. 'The Treasury on the Measurement of Economic Growth', *Australian Economic Papers*, vol. 4, June–December 1965.

HALLMANS, M. G. W. and IVANOV, A. S. *A Review of Recent Developments in the World Sugar Market, 1960–65* (London, International Sugar Council, 1966).

HOROWITZ, D. Second address before the UNCTAD Committee on Invisibles and Financing Related to Trade (Geneva, December 1965). The 'Horowitz Proposal'.

HUPKES, G. J. and BERG, M. VAN DEN. *A Survey of Contemporary Economic Conditions and Prospects for 1962* (University of Stellenbosch, Bureau for Economic Research, 1961).

HUSSAIN, S. M. 'A Note on Farmer Response to Price in East Pakistan', *Pakistan Development Review*, vol. 4, no. 1, 1964.

INTERNATIONAL COTTON ADVISORY COMMITTEE. *Cotton: Part 1, Monthly Review of the World Situation* (Washington).
  Cotton: Part 2, World Statistics (Washington, quarterly).

INTERNATIONAL LEAD AND ZINC STUDY GROUP. *Lead and Zinc Statistics* (New York, monthly).

INTERNATIONAL RUBBER STUDY GROUP. *Rubber Statistical Bulletin* (London, monthly).

INTERNATIONAL SUGAR COUNCIL. *Statistical Bulletin* (London, monthly).
  Sugar Year Book (London).

INTERNATIONAL TEA COMMITTEE. *Annual Bulletin of Statistics* (London).

INTERNATIONAL TIN COUNCIL. *Statistical Year Book* (London).

JOHNSON, H. G. *Economic Policies towards Less-developed Countries* (London, Allen & Unwin, 1967).
  International Trade and Economic Growth (London, Allen & Unwin, 1958).

JONES, K., MAIZELS, A. and WHITTAKER, J. 'The Demand for Food in Industrial Countries, 1948–60', *National Institute Economic Review*, no. 20, May 1962.

KUNDU, A. 'The Economy of British Guiana, 1960–1975', *Social and Economic Studies*, vol. 12, no. 3, September 1963.

LITTLE, I. M. D. and CLIFFORD, J. M. *International Aid* (London, Allen & Unwin, 1965).

LOVASY, G. 'Inflation and Exports in Primary Producing Countries', I.M.F. *Staff Papers*, vol. 9, no. 1, March 1962.

McKINNON, R. 'Foreign Exchange Constraints in Economic Development and Efficient Aid Allocation', *Economic Journal*, vol. 74, no. 294, June 1964.

MAIZELS, A. *Industrial Growth and World Trade*, National Institute of Economic and Social Research, Economic and Social Studies, 21 (Cambridge, University Press, 1963).

MAIZELS, A., CAMPBELL-BOROSS, L. F. and RAYMENT, P. B. W. 'Trade and Development Problems of the Under-developed Countries: the Background to the United Nations Conference', *National Institute Economic Review*, no. 28, May 1964.

'Exports and Economic Growth in the Overseas Sterling Area: 1960/61 to 1975', *National Institute Economic Review*, no. 38, November 1966.

MAIZELS, A., FREEMAN, C. and ROWLATT, J. A. 'Trends in World Demand for Jute Manufactures', F.A.O. *Monthly Bulletin of Agricultural Economics and Statistics*, January 1961.

MAIZELS, A. and ROWLATT, J. A. 'The Competitive Position of Jute Manufactures in Western Europe and the Far East', F.A.O. *Monthly Bulletin of Agricultural Economics and Statistics*, March 1962.

MAJOR, R. L. 'Capital and Invisible Transactions in Britain's Balance of Payments', *The British Economy in 1975*, by W. Beckerman and Associates, National Institute of Economic and Social Research, Economic and Social Studies, 23 (Cambridge, University Press, 1965).

METALLGESELLSCHAFT A. G. *Metal Statistics* (Frankfurt am Main, annual).

MORGENSTERN, O. *On the Accuracy of Economic Observations* (Princeton, University Press, 1963).

National Institute Economic Review, no. 39, February 1967, p. 23.

NATIONAL SHOE MANUFACTURERS' ASSOCIATION INC. *Facts and Figures on Footwear, 1961* (New York, 1961).

NEISSER, H. and MODIGLIANI, F. *National Incomes and International Trade: a Quantitative Analysis* (Urbana, University of Illinois Press, 1953).

ORPEN, S. G. *Local Content Scheme for Motor Industry* (*Financial Times* Supplement on South Africa, 26 April 1966).

PAN-AMERICAN COFFEE BUREAU. *Annual Coffee Statistics* (New York).

PINCUS, J. *Economic Aid and International Cost Sharing* (Baltimore, Johns Hopkins Press, 1965).

POLITICAL AND ECONOMIC PLANNING. *Commonwealth Preference in the United Kingdom* (London, August 1960).

RAMPERSAD, F. *Growth and Structural Change in the Economy of Trinidad and Tobago, 1951–1961* (University of the West Indies, Jamaica, 1964).

ROSENSTEIN-RODAN, P. N. 'International Aid for Underdeveloped Countries', *Review of Economics and Statistics*, vol. 43, no. 2, May 1961.

RUEBENSAAL, C. F. 'World Synthetic Rubber—its Manufacture and Markets', *Rubber and Plastics Age*, October 1966.

SINGH, M. *India's Export Trends and the Prospects for Self-sustained Growth* (Oxford, Clarendon Press, 1964).

SNAPE, R. H. 'Some Effects of Protection in the World Sugar Industry', *Economica*, vol. 30, no. 117, February 1963.

TACQUENIER, C. 'Les importations de biens des pays développés capitalistes en provenance des pays sous-développés—Répartition par zones d'origine en 1970', *Cahiers Economiques de Bruxelles*, no. 33, 1er trimestre, 1967.

VRIES, B. A. DE. *The Export Experience of Developing Countries* (Baltimore, Johns Hopkins Press, 1967).

INDEX

PUBLICATIONS OF THE
NATIONAL INSTITUTE OF ECONOMIC
AND SOCIAL RESEARCH

published by

THE CAMBRIDGE UNIVERSITY PRESS

Books published for the Institute by the Cambridge University Press are available through ordinary booksellers. They appear in the three series below.

ECONOMIC & SOCIAL STUDIES

* At present out of print.

OCCASIONAL PAPERS

* At present out of print.

STUDIES IN THE NATIONAL INCOME AND EXPENDITURE OF THE UNITED KINGDOM

Published under the joint auspices of the National Institute and the Department of Applied Economics, Cambridge.

THE NATIONAL INSTITUTE OF ECONOMIC AND SOCIAL RESEARCH
publishes regularly
THE NATIONAL INSTITUTE ECONOMIC REVIEW
A quarterly Review of the economic situation and prospects.
Annual subscription £2. 10s.; single issues 15s. each.
The Review is available directly from N.I.E.S.R.
2 Dean Trench St., Smith Square, London, S.W. 1

The Institute has also published
FACTORY LOCATION AND INDUSTRIAL MOVEMENT: *a Study of Recent Experience in Britain*, volumes I and II
By W. F. Luttrell
N.I.E.S.R. 1962. pp. 1080. £5. 5s. net the set.

TRANSLATED MONOGRAPHS: *a new series on current economic problems and policies.*

No. I   *The IVth French Plan* by FRANCOIS PERROUX, with the original foreword by Pierre Massé, Commissaire Général au Plan, and a new foreword to the English edition by Vera Lutz. Translated by Bruno Leblanc.
pp. 72. 10s. net.

These also are available directly from the Institute.